RELIGIOUS HUMAN RIGHTS IN GLOBAL PERSPECTIVE

RELIGIOUS HUMAN RIGHTS IN GLOBAL PERSPECTIVE
Religious Perspectives

Edited by

John Witte, Jr.
Director, Law and Religion Program
Jonas Robitscher Professor of Law
Emory University

and

Johan D. van der Vyver
I.T. Cohen Professor of International Law and Human Rights
Fellow, The Carter Center
Emory University

MARTINUS NIJHOFF PUBLISHERS
THE HAGUE / BOSTON / LONDON

A C.I.P. Catalogue record for this book is available from the Library of Congress.

ISBN 90-411-0176-4 (Hb, Vol. 1)
ISBN 90-411-0177-2 (Hb, Vol. 2)
ISBN 90-411-0178-0 (Hb, Set of 2 volumes)
ISBN 90-411-0179-9 (Pb, Vol. 1)
ISBN 90-411-0180-2 (Pb, Vol. 2)
ISBN 90-411-0181-0 (Pb, Set of 2 volumes)

Published by Kluwer Law International,
P.O. Box 85889, 2508 CN The Hague, The Netherlands.

Sold and distributed in the U.S.A. and Canada
by Kluwer Law International,
675 Massachusetts Avenue, Cambridge, MA 02139, U.S.A.

In all other countries, sold and distributed
by Kluwer Law International,
P.O. Box 85889, 2508 CN The Hague, The Netherlands.

cover photograph: Corky Gallo, *Emory University*
© Law and Religion Program, *Emory University*

Printed on acid-free paper

Contents

Acknowledgements

———————————— ⤫ ⤪ ————————————

This volume and its companion, *Religious Human Rights in Global Perspective: Legal Perspectives*, are products of an ongoing project on religion, democracy, and human rights undertaken by the Law and Religion Program at Emory University. We wish to express our deepest gratitude to our colleagues on the Emory University Committee on Law and Religion for their enthusiastic support of this project—Dean Howard O. Hunter and Professors Frank S. Alexander, Harold J. Berman, and the late Donald W. Fyr of Emory Law School; Dean David F. Bright and Professors David R. Blumenthal and Paul B. Courtright of Emory College; and Dean R. Kevin LaGree, Dean Rebecca S. Chopp, and Professor Jon P. Gunnemann of the Candler School of Theology. We also wish to offer our warmest thanks to President William M. Chace and Provost Billy E. Frye of Emory University for their continued solicitude for the Law and Religion Program.

A number of colleagues at Emory Law School have contributed generously to the completion of this volume and its companion. Ms. Eliza Ellison served as principal administrator of this project and its publications. Mr. Daniel G. Ashburn served as research coordinator, with the assistance of Ms. M. Christian Green and Ms. Holliday Osborne. Ms. Anita Mann provided administrative support. Mr. Corky Gallo furnished technical support. Ms. Louise Jackson, Ms. Glennis O'Neal, Ms. Radine Robinson, and Ms. Marie Warren provided secretarial services. We are enormously indebted to each of these colleagues for their invaluable contributions to this project and volume.

We would like to express our appreciation to our friends at Martinus Nijhoff Publishers in The Hague, particularlyMs. Lindy Melman and Mr. Alan Stephens, for the privilege of publishing with them.

This project and its publications have been made possible by a generous grant from The Pew Charitable Trusts, Inc. in Philadelphia, Pennsylvania. On behalf of the Law and Religion Program, we wish to thank the Trusts, particularly President Rebecca M. Rimel and program directors,

Dr. Joel Carpenter and Dr. Kevin Quigley, for their gracious and unstinting support of our efforts.

John Witte, Jr.
Johan D. van der Vyver

Preface

DESMOND M. TUTU
Anglican Archbishop of Cape Town

I am pleased to be able to offer a preface to this volume on religious rights. I will want to speak really from the perspective of the Christian faith, which is the one that I know best, and hope that my comments would apply *mutatis mutandis* to other religious faiths as well. This will also serve to protect me from arrogance and triumphalism as I rehearse the pathological aspects of Christianity. I hope I will then be able to speak with a salutary modesty.

There is a story, which is fairly well known, about when the missionaries came to Africa. They had the Bible and we, the natives, had the land. They said "Let us pray," and we dutifully shut our eyes. When we opened them, why, they now had the land and we had the Bible. It would, on the surface, appear as if we had struck a bad bargain, but the fact of the matter is that we came out of that transaction a great deal better off than when we started. The point is that we were given a priceless gift in the word of God: the gospel of salvation, the good news of God's love for us that is given so utterly unconditionally. But even more wonderful is the fact that we were given the most subversive, most revolutionary thing around. Those who may have wanted to exploit us and to subject us to injustice and oppression should really not have given us the Bible, because that placed dynamite under their nefarious schemes.

The Bible makes some quite staggering assertions about human beings which came to be the foundations of the culture of basic human rights that have become so commonplace in our day and age. Both creation narratives in Genesis 1-3 assert quite categorically that human beings are the pinnacle, the climax, of the divine creative activity; if not climactic, then central or crucial to the creative activity. In the first narrative the whole creative process moves impressively to its climax which is the creation of human beings. The author signals that something quite out of the ordinary is about to happen by a change in the formula relating to a creative divine action. Up to this point God has merely had to speak "Let there be. . . ." and by divine fiat something comes into being *ex nihilo*. At this climactic point God first invites his heavenly court to participate with him, "Let us create man in our image"—something special has come into being.

Remarkably this piece is in fact in part intended to be a jingoistic propaganda piece designed to lift the sagging spirits of a people in exile whose fortunes are at a low ebb, surrounded as they are by the impressive monuments to Babylonian hegemony. Where one would have expected the author to claim that it was only Jews who were created in the image of God, this passage asserts that it is all human beings who have been created in the divine image.

That this attribute is a universal phenomenon was not necessarily self evident. Someone as smart as Aristotle taught that human personality was not universally possessed by all human beings, because slaves in his view were not persons. The biblical teaching is marvelously exhilarating in a situation of oppression and injustice, because in that situation it has often been claimed that certain groups were inferior or superior because of possessing or not possessing a particular attribute (physical or cultural). The Bible claims for all human beings this exalted status that we are all, each one of us, created in the divine image, that it has nothing to do with this or that extraneous attribute which by the nature of the case, can be possessed by only some people.

The consequences that flow from these biblical assertions are quite staggering. First, human life (as all life) is a gift from the gracious and ever generous Creator of all. It is therefore inviolable. We must therefore have a deep reverence for the sanctity of human life. That is why homicide is universally condemned. "Thou shalt not kill" would be an undisputed part of a global ethic accepted by the adherents of all faiths and of none. For many it would include as an obvious corollary the prohibition of capital punishment. It has seemed an oddity that we should want to demonstrate our outrage that, for example, someone had shown scant reverence for human life by committing murder, by ourselves then proceeding to take another life. In some ways it is an irrational obscenity.

The life of every human person is inviolable as a gift from God. And since this person is created in the image of God and is a God carrier a second consequence would be that we should not just respect such a person but that we should have a deep reverence for that person. The New Testament claims that the Christian person becomes a sanctuary, a temple of the Holy Spirit, someone who is indwelt by the most holy and blessed Trinity. We would want to assert this of all human beings. We should not just greet one another. We should strictly genuflect before such an august and precious creature. The Buddhist is correct in bowing profoundly before another human as the God in me acknowledges and greets the God in you. This preciousness, this infinite worth is intrinsic to who we all are and is inalienable as a gift from God to be acknowledged as an inalienable right of all human persons.

The Babylonian creation narrative makes human beings have a low destiny and purpose—as those intended to be the scavengers of the gods. Not so the biblical *Weltanschauung* which declares that the human being created in the image of God is meant to be God's viceroy, God's representative in having rule over the rest of creation on behalf of God. To have dominion, not in an authoritarian and destructive manner, but to hold sway as God would hold sway—compassionately, gently, caringly, enabling each part of creation to come fully into its own and to realize its potential for the good of the whole, contributing to the harmony and unity which was God's intention for the whole of creation. And even more wonderfully this human person is destined to know and so to love God and to dwell with the divine forever and ever, enjoying unspeakable celestial delights. Nearly all major religions envisage a *post mortem* existence for humankind that far surpasses anything we can conceive.

All this makes human beings unique. It imbues each one of us with profound dignity and worth. As a result to treat such persons as if they were less than this, to oppress them, to trample their dignity underfoot, is not just evil as it surely must be; it is not just painful as it frequently must be for the victims of injustice and oppression. It is positively blasphemous, for it is tantamount to spitting in the face of God. That is why we have been so passionate in our opposition to the evil of apartheid. We have not, as some might mischievously have supposed, been driven by political or ideological considerations. No, we have been constrained by the imperatives of our biblical faith.

Any person of faith has no real option. In the face of injustice and oppression it is to disobey God not to stand up in opposition to that injustice and that oppression. Any violation of the rights of God's stand-in cries out to be condemned and to be redressed, and all people of good will must willy-nilly be engaged in upholding and preserving those rights as a religious duty. Such a discussion as this one should therefore not be merely an academic exercise in the most pejorative sense. It must be able to galvanize participants with a zeal to be active protectors of the rights of persons.

The Bible points to the fact that human persons are endowed with freedom to choose. This freedom is constitutive of what it means to be a person—one who has the freedom to choose between alternative options, and to choose freely (apart from the influences of heredity and nurture). To be a person is to be able to choose to love or not to love, to be able to reject or to accept the offer of the divine love, to be free to obey or to disobey. That is what constitutes being a moral agent.

We cannot properly praise or blame someone who does what he or she cannot help doing, or refrains from doing what he or she cannot help not doing. Moral approbation and disapproval have no meaning where there is no freedom to choose between various options on offer. That is what enables us to have moral responsibility. An automaton cannot be a moral agent, and therein lies our glory and our damnation. We may choose aright and therein is bliss, or we may choose wrongly and therein lies perdition. God may not intervene to nullify this incredible gift in order to stop us from making wrong choices. I have said on other occasions that God, who alone has the perfect right to be a totalitarian, has such a profound reverence for our freedom that He had much rather we went freely to hell than compel us to go to heaven.

An unfree human being is a contradiction in terms. To be human is to be free. God gives us space to be free and so to be human. Human beings have an autonomy, an integrity which should not be violated, which should not be subverted. St. Paul exults as he speaks of what he calls the "glorious liberty of the children of God" and elsewhere declares that Christ has set us free for freedom. It is a freedom to hold any view or none—freedom of expression. It is freedom of association because we are created for family, for togetherness, for community, because the solitary human being is an aberration.

We are created to exist in a delicate network of interdependence with fellow human beings and the rest of God's creation. All sorts of things go horribly wrong when we break this fundamental law of our being. Then we are no longer appalled as we should be that vast sums are spent on budgets of death and destruction, when a tiny fraction of those sums would ensure that God's children everywhere would have a clean supply of water, adequate health care, proper housing and education, enough to eat and to wear. A totally self sufficient human being would be subhuman.

Perhaps because of their own experience of slavery, the Israelites depicted God as the great liberator, and they seemed to be almost obsessed with being set free. And so they had the principle of Jubilee enshrined in the heart of the biblical tradition. It was unnatural for anyone to be enthralled to another and so every fifty years they celebrated Jubilee, when those who had become slaves were set at liberty. Those who had mortgaged their land received it back unencumbered by the burden of debt, reminding everyone that all they were and all they had was a gift, that absolute ownership belonged to God, that all were really equal before God, who was the real and true Sovereign.

That is the basis of the egalitarianism of the Bible—that all belongs to God and that all are of equal worth in His sight. That is heady stuff. No political ideology could better that for radicalness. And that is what fired our own struggle against apartheid—this incredible sense of the infinite worth of each person created in the image of God, being God's viceroy, God's representative, God's stand-in, being a God carrier, a sanctuary, a temple of the Holy Spirit, inviolate, possessing a dignity that was intrinsic with an autonomy and freedom to choose that were constitutive of human personality.

This person was meant to be creative, to resemble God in His creativity. And so wholesome work is something humans need to be truly human. The biblical understanding of being human includes freedom from fear and insecurity, freedom from penury and want, freedom of association and movement, because we would live ideally in the kind of society that is characterized by these attributes. It would be a caring and compassionate, a sharing and gentle society in which, like God, the strongest would be concerned about the welfare of the weakest, represented in ancient society by the widow, the alien, and the orphan. It would be a society in which you reflected the holiness of God not by ritual purity and cultic correctness but by the fact that when you gleaned your harvest, you left something behind for the poor, the unemployed, the marginalized ones—all a declaration of the unique worth of persons that does not hinge on their economic, social, or political status but simply on the fact that they are persons created in God's image. That is what invests them with their preciousness and from this stem all kinds of rights.

All the above is the positive impact that religion can have as well as the consequences that flow from these fundamental assertions. Sadly, and often tragically, religion is not often in and of itself necessarily a good thing. Already in the Bible there is ample evidence that religion can be a baneful thing with horrendous consequences often for its adherents or those who may be designated its unfortunate targets. There are frequent strictures levelled at religious observance which is just a matter of external form when the obsession is with cultic minutiae and correctness. Such religion is considered to be an abomination, however elaborate the ritual performed. Its worth is tested by whether it has any significant impact on how its adherents treat especially the widow, the orphan and the alien in their midst. How one deals with those who have no real clout and who can make no claim on being given equitable and compassionate treatment, becomes a vital clue to the quality of religiosity.

This certainly says many things, one of which is surely that God recognizes a particular worth in those who, humanly speaking, are nonentities. It is a paradox that God should show His graciousness, mercy, and love through His concern for those whom the world considers to be so utterly lacking in social, political, or economic significance, and it must be that they do have a worth that does not depend on these extrinsic attributes.

There have been some glorious moments inspired by the religious faiths in which people believe. Frequently in our struggle against the evil that was apartheid, we stood arm-in-arm as Christians with Jews, Muslims, and Hindus. And what a glorious vindication happened with the inauguration of Nelson Mandela as the first democratically elected President of a liberated, a new South Africa. Many acknowledge the crucial role that religious leaders played to bring to birth the new and free South Africa.

We must hang our heads in shame, however, when we survey the gory and shameful history of the Church of Christ. There have been numerous wars of religion instigated by those who claimed to be followers of the One described as the Prince of Peace. The Crusades, using the Cross as a distinctive emblem, were waged in order to commend the Good News of this Prince of Peace amongst the infidel Muslims, seeking to ram down people's throats a faith that somewhere thought it prided itself on the autonomy of the individual person freely to choose to believe or not to believe. Religious zealots have seemed blind to the incongruity and indeed contradiction of using constraint of whatever sort to proclaim a religion that sets high store by individual freedom of choice. Several bloody conflicts characterize the history of Christianity, and war is without doubt the most comprehensive violation of human rights. It ignores reverence for life in its wanton destruction of people. It subverts social and family life and justifies the abrogation of fundamental rights.

Christians have waged wars against fellow Christians. St. Paul was flabbergasted that Christians could bring charges against fellow Christians in a court of law. It is not difficult to imagine what he would have felt and what he would have said at the spectacle of Christians liquidating fellow Christians as in war. Christians have been grossly intolerant of one another as when Christians persecuted fellow Christians for holding different views about religious dogma and practice. The Inquisition with all associated with it is a considerable blot on our copybook. The Church has had fewer more inglorious occasions than those when the Inquisition was active. Christians have gone on an orgy of excommunicating one another just because of disagreements about doctrine and liturgy, not to mention the downright obscurantism displayed in the persecution of the likes of Galileo and Copernicus for propounding intellectual views that were anathema to the Church at the time.

Slavery is an abominable affront to the dignity of those who would be treated as if they were mere chattels. The trade in fellow human beings should have been recognized as completely contrary to the central tenets of Christianity about the unspeakable worth and preciousness of each human person. And yet Christians were some of the most zealous slave owners who opposed the efforts of emancipators such as William Wilberforce. The Civil War in the United States of America in part happened because of differences of opinion on the vexed question of slavery. Devout Christians saw no inconsistency between singing Christian hymns lustily and engaging in this demeaning trade in fellow humans. Indeed one of the leading hymn writers of the day was also an enthusiastic slave owner.

Christians have been foremost supporters of anti-semitism, blaming Jews for committing deicide in crucifying Jesus Christ. A devastating chapter in human history happened with Hitler's final solution culminating in the Holocaust. Hitler purported to be a Christian and saw no contradiction between his Christianity and perpetrating one of history's most dastardly campaigns. What is even more disturbing is that he was supported in this massive crime against humanity by a significant group called German Christians. Mercifully there were those like Dietrich Bonhoeffer and others who opposed this madness, often at great cost to themselves as members of the confessing church. Christianity has often been perversely used in other instances to justify the iniquity of racism. In the United States the rabid haters of blacks, the Ku Klux Klan, have not balked at using a flaming cross as their much feared symbol. One would have to travel far to find a more despicable example of blasphemy. Apartheid in South Africa was perpetrated not by pagans but by those who regarded themselves as devout Christians. Their opponents, even though known to be Christians, were usually vilified as Communists and worse. Many conflicts in the world have been started and certainly been made worse by religious and sectarian differences—so the conflict in Northern Ireland, in the Sudan, many of the conflicts in the Indian subcontinent and in the Middle East. Religious differences have exacerbated the horrendous bloodletting in Bosnia euphemistically described as ethnic cleansing.

Religion should produce peace, reconciliation, tolerance, and respect for human rights but it has often promoted the opposite conditions. And yet the potential for great good in the impact and influence of religion remains and was recognized by the Parliament of the World's Religions meeting last year in Chicago. The Parliament concluded that there would be no new global order unless there was first a global ethic which would be "a fundamental consensus concerning binding values, irrevocable standards and personal attitudes."

I can testify that our own struggle for justice, peace, and equity would have floundered badly had we not been inspired by our Christian faith and assured of the ultimate victory of goodness and truth, compassion and love against their ghastly counterparts. We want to promote freedom of religion as an indispensable part of any genuinely free society.

Introduction

JOHN WITTE, JR.
Emory University

At the close of the second millennium, the world is torn by crisis and tumult—by a moral Armageddon, if not a military one. With the memories of world wars, gulags, and the Holocaust still fresh in our minds, we see the bloody slaughter of Rwanda and the Sudan, the tragic genocide of the Balkans, the massive unrest of the Middle East, Western Africa, Latin America, and the former Soviet bloc. On every continent, we see clashes between movements of incremental political unification and radical balkanization, gentle religious ecumenism and radical fundamentalism, sensitive cultural integration and rabid diversification, sensible moral pluralization and shocking moral relativism. Even in the ostensibly peaceful societies of the West, bitter culture wars have aligned defenders of various old orders against an array of social, legal, and cultural deconstructionists. "Cultural conflicts are increasing and are more dangerous today than at any other time in history," Czech President Vaclav Havel declared in 1994. "The end of the era of rationalism has been catastrophic, [for now] the members of various tribal cults are at war with one another. . . . The abyss between the rational and the internal, the objective and the subjective, the technical and the moral, the universal and the unique constantly grows deeper."[1]

---

[1] Vaclav Havel, "Speech on July 4, 1994 in Philadelphia, on Receipt of the Liberty Medal," reported and excerpted in *Philadelphia Inquirer* (July 5, 1994): A08; *Buffalo News* (July 10, 1994): F8; *Newsweek* (July 18, 1994): 66. See also chapters by Martin Marty, Max L. Stackhouse and Stephen B. Healey, and Charles Villa-Vicencio herein. For a sampling of the vast literature on this theme, see Donald Horowitz, "The Challenge of Ethnic Conflict: Democracy in Divided Societies," *Journal of Democracy* 4(4) (1993): 18; Samuel P. Huntington, "The Clash of Civilizations?" *Foreign Affairs* (Summer, 1993): 22; Mark Juergensmeyer, *The New Cold War: Religious Nationalism Confronts the Secular State* (Berkeley, CA, 1993); Martin E. Marty and R. Scott Appelby, eds., *Fundamentalisms and the State* (Chicago, 1993); id., *Fundmamentalisms Comprehended* (Chicago, 1995).

Religious beliefs and believers have suffered miserably in these "culture wars."[2] 1995, the United Nations Year of Tolerance, is becoming just another dark year in a dark decade of religious intolerance. Religious nationalism and fundamentalism have conspired to bring violent death and dislocation to hundreds of religious believers around the world each year. Political secularism and cynicism have combined to bring civil denial and deprivation to religious believers of all faiths. Temples and mosques are denied entrance to neighborhoods. Churches and charities are denied autonomy of governance. Clerics and charities are denied licenses to minister. Pilgrims and missionaries are denied visas and charters. Natives and refugees are denied totems and homelands. Parents and children are denied liberties of education. Employers and employees are denied opportunities to exercise their faiths. To be sure, the collapse of many authoritarian regimes in the past decade has begun to open new venues and avenues for religion to flourish. International and local laws have begun to embrace more generous religious rights provisions. Religious communities have begun to apply their theological learning and moral suasion to the cause of religious rights. But today, by common estimates, more than two billion people still enjoy only partial freedom of thought, conscience, and belief.

It is time for us to take religious rights seriously[3]—to shake off our political indifference and parochial self-interest and to address the plight and protection of people of all faiths. It is time to "exorcise the demons of religious intolerance"[4] that have beset both religious and non-religious peoples around the world and to exercise the "golden rules" of religious rights—doing unto other religious believers and beliefs what we would have done to us and ours.[5]

Human rights norms provide no panacea to the world crisis, but they are a critical part of any solution. Religions are not easy allies to engage, but the struggle for human rights cannot be won without them. For human rights norms are inherently abstract ideals—universal statements of the good life and the good society. They depend upon the visions of human communities and institutions to give them content and coherence, to provide *"the scale of values governing the[ir] exercise and concrete mani-*

---

[2] James Davidson Hunter, *Culture Wars* (New York, 1991).

[3] Cf. Ronald Dworkin, *Taking Rights Seriously* (New York, 1977).

[4] The phrase is from Luke Timothy Johnson's chapter herein.

[5] For Christian formulations, see Matthew 7:12 ("Do unto others as you would have them do unto you."). For Judaic formulations, see Hillel, B. Shabbat, 31a ("what is hateful to you do not do to your fellow"), quoted in the chapter by David Novak herein at note 66. For Muslim formulations, see the chapter by Riffat Hassan herein and the sources and discussion in Abdullahi Ahmed An-Na'im, *Toward an Islamic Reformation: Civil Liberties, Human Rights, and International Law* (Syracuse, NY, 1990), 162-163.

festation."[6] Religion is an ineradicable condition of human lives and communities; religions invariably provide universal sources and "scales of values" by which many persons and communities govern themselves. Religions must thus be seen as indispensable allies in the modern struggle for human rights. To exclude them from the struggle is impossible, and indeed catastrophic.[7] To include them—to enlist their unique resources and to protect their unique rights—is vital to enhancing and advancing the regime of human rights.

"[T]he only real hope of people today is probably a renewal of our certainty that we are rooted in the Earth and, at the same time, the cosmos," Havel declared last year after receiving the Liberty Medal. "This awareness endows us with the capacity for self-transcendence. Politicians at international forums may reiterate a thousand times that the basis of the new world order must be universal respect for human rights, but it will mean nothing as long as this imperative does not derive from the respect of the miracle of being, the miracle of the universe, the miracle of nature, the miracle of our own existence. Only someone who submits in the authority of the universal order and of creation, who values the right to be a part of it, and a participant in it, can genuinely value himself and his neighbors, and thus honor their rights as well."[8] These primordial religious ideas, together with religious doctrines and institutions in all their denominational variety and vigor,[9] provide a vital resource for the realization of religious and other rights.

This volume and its companion take the measure and test the meaning of religious human rights, using the methods and insights of religion and law, theology and jurisprudence. This volume takes up the *religious* sources and dimensions of religious rights; the companion volume takes up their *legal* sources and dimensions. Comprehensive analysis of this topic, of course, properly requires a score of volumes thicker than this one. Selection, truncation, and distillation are necessary evils. We have restricted our analysis to the three religions of the Book and the four corners of the Atlantic. In this volume, we focus our religious discussions of

---

[6] Jacques Maritain, "Introduction," to UNESCO, *Human Rights: Comments and Interpretations* (New York, 1949), 15-16, quoted and discussed in David Hollenbach, "Human Rights and Religious Faith in the Middle East: Reflections of a Christian Theologian," *Human Rights Quarterly* 4 (1982): 94, 96. See also the chapters by Villa-Vicencio herein and by John S. Pobee in the companion volume, Johan D. van der Vyver and John Witte, Jr., eds., *Religious Human Rights in Global Perspective: Legal Perspectives* (The Hague, 1995), and John S. Pobee, "An African Christian in Search of Democracy," in John Witte, Jr., ed., *Chrisianity and Democracy in Global Context* (Boulder/San Francisco, 1993), 267, 277ff.

[7] See chapters by Marty, Huber, Novak, Hassan, Stackhouse & Healey, Michael Broyde, and Abdullahi Ahmed An-Na'im herein.

[8] Havel, "Speech on July 4."

[9] See chapters by Marty, An-Na'im, and Stackhouse & Healey herein.

rights on Judaism, Christianity, and Islam, making only comparative asides about other religious and cultural traditions. In the companion volume, we focus our legal discussion on Europe, the Middle East, Africa, Latin America, and North America, with opening and closing discussions of religious rights developments by the United Nations and regional organizations. The discussion throughout both volumes is deliberately intercultural, interreligious, and interdisciplinary in character. The writings of high churchmen and statesmen stand alongside those of liberationists and freedom fighters. The perspectives of Jews, Christians, and Muslims, jurists, theologians, and ethicists, Africans, Europeans, and Americans all find a place.

The "rights talk"[10] of Christianity, Judaism, and Islam, which is the focus of this volume, lends itself readily to comparative analysis. Each of these religious traditions is a religion of revelation, founded on the eternal command to love one God, oneself, and all neighbors. Each tradition recognizes a canonical text as its highest authority—the Bible, the Torah, and the Qur'an. Each tradition designates a class of officials to preserve and propagate its faith, and embraces an expanding body of authoritative interpretations and applications of its canon. Each tradition has a refined legal structure—the canon law, Halakha, and Shari'a—that has translated its enduring principles of faith into evolving precepts of works. Each tradition has sought to imbue its religious, ethical, and legal norms into the daily lives of individuals and communities. These texts and traditions, ideas and institutions, norms and narratives of Christianity, Judaism, and Islam have much to offer to current discussions of human rights in general. They are the best source and resource for a discussion of religious human rights. For, as Martin Marty stresses, any solution to the problem of religious human rights "requires a religious address."[11]

To be sure, none of these religious traditions speaks unequivocally about human rights, and none has amassed an exemplary human rights record over the centuries. Their sacred texts and canons say much more about commandments and obligations than about liberties and rights.[12] Their theologians and jurists have resisted the importation of human rights as much as they have helped in their cultivation. Their internal policies and external advocacy have helped to perpetuate bigotry, chauvinism, and violence as much they have served to propagate equality, liberty, and fraternity. "The blood of thousands"[13] is at the doors of

---

[10] Mary Ann Glendon, *Rights Talk: The Impoverishment of Political Discourse* (New York, 1991).

[11] See chapter by Marty herein.

[12] See chapters by Johnson, Novak, and An-Na'im herein.

[13] See chapter by John T. Noonan, Jr. in the companion volume.

churches, synagogues, and mosques, John Noonan reminds us—that of dissidents, women, children, and sojourners, most prominently. The bludgeons of religious pogroms, crusades, jihads, inquisitions, and ostracisms have been used to devastating effect, both within and among these three great faiths.[14] No religion of the Book can begin to address the problem of religious human rights without what Luke Johnson calls "metanoia"—frank confrontation with and confession of its dark side.[15] No "religious address" can begin without what Abdullahi An-Na'im calls a "hermeneutic of human rights"—a method of interpreting sacred texts and traditions that is designed to recover and transplant those religious teachings and activities conducive to human rights.[16]

The ancient teachings and practices of Christianity, Judaism, and Islam have much to commend themselves, as the following chapters amply demonstrate. Each tradition has produced a number of the basic building blocks of a comprehensive theory and law of religious human rights—conscience, dignity, reason, liberty, equality, tolerance, love, openness, responsibility, justice, mercy, righteousness, accountability, covenant, community, among other cardinal concepts.[17] Each tradition has developed its own internal system of legal procedures and structures for the

---

[14] See chapters by Johnson, Broyde, Hassan, Jean Bethke Elshtain, Michael S. Berger & Deborah Lipstadt, and Donna Arzt herein.

[15] See chapters by Johnson and Villa-Vicencio herein and by Pobee and Makua wa Mutua in the companion volume.

[16] See Abdullahi Ahmed An-Na'im, "Toward an Islamic Hermeneutics for Human Rights," in id., et al., eds., *Human Rights and Religious Values: An Uneasy Relationship* (Grand Rapids, 1995), 229; Max L. Stackhouse, *Creeds, Societies, and Human Rights* (Grand Rapids, 1986). See also chapters by Marty, Johnson, Novak, Berger & Lipstadt, An-Na'im, Hassan, and Stackhouse & Healey herein. In the vast new literature calling for such a "human rights hermeneutic" see, e.g., David Sidorsky, ed., *Essays on Human Rights: Contemporary Issues and Jewish Perspectives* (New York, 1979); Aaron Kirschenbaum, "Human Rights Revisited," *Israel Yearbook on Human Rights* 6 (1975): 228; Eckehart Lorenz, ed., *How Christian are Human Rights?* (Geneva, 1981); International Commission of Jurists, et al., *Human Rights in Islam: Report of a Seminar Held in Kuwait, December, 1990* (Geneva, 1982); Wolfgang Huber & Heinz Eduard Tödt, *Menschenrechte: Perspektiven einer menschlichen Welt* (Stuttgart, 1977); Charles Villa-Vicencio, *A Theology of Reconstruction: Nation-Building and Human Rights:* (Cambridge, 1992). For a popular introduction, see the special issue of *Breakthrough* (Winter/Spring, 1989).

[17] See chapters herein by Huber, Novak, Hassan, Stackhouse & Healey, Wood, Desmond M. Tutu and J. Bryan Hehir. For other recent surveys, see, e.g., Walter Kasper, "The Theological Foundations of Human Rights," *The Jurist* 50 (1990): 148; Ann Elizabeth Mayer, "Current Muslim Thinking on Human Rights," in Abdullahi Ahmed An-Na'im and Francis Deng, eds., *Human Rights in Africa* (Philadelphia, 1992), 113; id., *Islam and Human Rights: Tradition and Politics* (Boulder/San Francisco, 1991); David Novak, "Is There a Concept of Individual Rights in Jewish Law?" *Jewish Law Association Studies* (1994): 129; Michael J. Perry, "Is the Idea of Human Rights Ineliminably Religious?" *University of Richmond Law Review* 27 (1993): 1023; Martin Shupak, "The Churches and Human Rights: Catholic and Protestant Human Rights Views as Reflected in Church Statements," *Harvard Human Rights Journal* 6 (1993): 127; Robert Traer, *Faith in Human Rights: Support in Religious Traditions for a Global Struggle* (Washington, 1991).

protection of rights, which historically have and still can serve as both prototypes and complements to secular legal systems.[18] Each tradition has, for centuries, defined and adjudicated the rights of women, children, minorities, and dissidents in a manner deserving of consideration—if not always emulation.[19] Each tradition has its own advocates and prophets, ancient and modern, who have worked to achieve a closer approximation of religious rights ideals for themselves and others.[20]

The Province of Religious Human Rights

The phrase "religious human rights" does not admit of easy definition, or even delimitation. Each component term—"religious," "human," and "rights"—is inherently ambiguous. The combination of these terms only compounds the ambiguity. It is part of the burden of these volumes to explore their meaning in various religious, cultural, and legal contexts. No consensus of opinion or common definition emerges from these ef-

---

[18] See chapters by Tierney, Broyde, and William Johnson Everett herein. The most important prototype for Western style (religious) human rights was the medieval canon law of the Catholic Church. This law defined the rights of the clergy to their liturgical offices, their exemptions from civil taxes and duties, and their immunities from prosecution and compulsory testimony. It defined the rights of ecclesiastical organizations like benefices, monasteries, and charities to form and dissolve, to accept and reject members, to establish order and organization, to acquire, use, and alienate property. It defined the rights of religious conformists to worship, proselytize, maintain religious symbols, travel on religious pilgrimages, and educate their children. This elaborate system of religious rights—though devised for the governance of the established church alone—was, after the Protestant Reformation, incorporated into the heart of Western laws governing religion and the church. The gradual expansion of religious toleration after the sixteenth century did not destroy the Roman law and canon law systems of religious rights. Rather, it extended its protections and privileges to an ever greater variety of religious groups and individuals—and today forms many of the basic guarantees of a religious rights regime. See Harold J. Berman, *Law and Revolution: The Formation of the Western Legal Tradition* (Cambridge, 1993); Brian Tierney, *Religion, Law, and the Growth of Constitutional Thought, 1150-1650* (Cambridge, 1982); R.H. Helmholz, ed., *Canon Law in Protestant Lands* (Berlin, 1993); id., *Roman Canon Law in Reformation England* (Cambridge, 1990); Udo Wolter, *Ius canonicum in iure civile* (Köln, 1975).

There are modern analogues to this early example of "legal transplantation" of religious law into secular law. Today a good deal of Jewish halakhic law has been transplanted into the civil and constitutional law of Israel, and Muslim Shar'ia law is being transplanted into the laws of several nations in South Asia, the Middle East, and Africa. (See chapters by Broyde, Berger & Lipstadt, and Arzt herein and by Asher Maoz and Said Arjomand in the companion volume.) Champions of the universality of Western-style human rights might be discomfited to learn of the distinct canon law and Christian theological lineage of these rights. Critics of the contemporary experiments of legal transplantation in Judaic and Islamic regimes might be comforted to learn of the past success of such an experiment.

[19] See chapters by Marty, Tierney, Everett, Broyde, Berger & Lipstadt, Hassan, Arzt, and John E. Coons herein.

[20] See chapters by Tutu, Hehir, Cotler, and Wood herein.

forts, but a broad outline of essential terms and concerns can be discerned.

First, it is well understood among the authors of these volumes that the term "religious" must be assigned some boundaries to be useful for a theory and law of religious rights. If religion is to be assigned a special place in the human rights pantheon—if religion is in need of special protections and privileges not afforded by other rights provisions—some means of distinguishing religious rights and claims from all others must be offered. Fairness commands as broad a definition as possible, so that no legitimate religious claim is excluded. Prudence counsels a narrower definition, so that not every claim becomes religious (and thus no claim becomes deserving of special religious rights protection). To define "religion" too closely is to place too much trust in the capacity of the lexicon or the legislature. To leave the term undefined is to place too much faith in the self-declarations of the claimant or the discernment of local judges and administrators.

It is equally well understood that "defining 'religion' is probably the most difficult exercise" in crafting a theory and drafting a law on religious rights.[21] No universal definition can readily embrace today's religiously heterogeneous world. No bright line tests can readily resolve all penumbral cases. It is not always easy to distinguish between legal and non-legal norms, genuine and spurious religious claims. "Charlatanism is a necessary price of religious freedom."[22] Grand generalizations and hairsplitting distinctions, a sense of proportion, moderation, and equity on the part of believers and officials alike, are essential features of any successful religious rights regime.[23]

International legal instruments provide very broad definitions of "religion," which several authors herein endorse.[24] Article 18 of the 1948 Universal Declaration of Human Rights makes a sweeping guarantee: "Everyone has the right to freedom of thought, conscience, and religion; this right includes freedom to change his religion or belief, and freedom, either alone or in community with others and in public or private, to manifest his religion or belief in teaching, practice, worship, and obser-

---

[21] See chapter by Dinah Shelton & Alexandre Kiss in the companion volume at note 19 and accompanying text.

[22] See chapter by Peter Cumper in the companion volume, quoting an Australian case, *Church of the New Faith v. Pay Roll Tax Commissioners* (1983), 57 AJLR 785, at 791.

[23] See chapter by Noonan in the companion volume.

[24] See chapters by Cotler, Arzt, and Wood herein and by David Little and Michael Roan in the companion volume. The most ambitious attempt at definition, beyond prevailing international laws, is in the chapter by Shelton & Kiss.

vance."[25] The Declaration's conflation of the terms "religion," "thought," "conscience," and "belief" continues in subsequent international instruments—most notably the compulsory 1966 Covenant on Civil and Political Rights,[26] and the 1981 Declaration on the Elimination of All Forms of Intolerance and of Discrimination Based on Religion or Belief, the fullest international statement on religious rights.[27] The Declaration's recognition of religion as individual and communal, internal and external, private and public, permanent and transient likewise persists.[28] An important 1993 General Comment by the UN Human Rights Committee emphasizes that "[t]he terms belief and religion are to be broadly construed" and "not limited . . . to traditional religions or to religions and beliefs with institutional characteristics or practices analogous to those of traditional religions."[29] By general consensus today, international human rights law recognizes as religious numerous theistic, non-theistic, and atheistic faiths.[30]

This capacious definition of religion in international law has left it largely to individual states and individual claimants to define the boundaries of the regime of religious rights. As the following chapters reveal, no common definition or uniform method has been forthcoming. Indeed, the statutes, cases, and regulations of many countries embrace a bewildering array of definitions of "religion," which neither local officials nor commentators have been able to integrate. Some courts and legislatures make a simple "common sense" inquiry as to the existence of religion. Others defer to the good faith self-declarations of religion by the claimant. Others seek to find sufficient analogies between existing religions and new religious claimants. Others insist on evidence of a god or something transcendent that stands in the same position as a god. Others analyze the motives for formation of the religious organization or adoption of a religious belief, the presence and sophistication of a set of doctrines explicating the beliefs, the practice and celebration of religious rites and liturgies, the degree of formal training required for the religious leaders, the strictures on the ability of members to practice other relig-

---

[25] The full text is provided in Ian Brownlie, ed., *Basic Documents on Human Rights*, 3d ed. (Oxford, 1992), 21.

[26] Ibid., 125.

[27] Ibid., 109.

[28] See chapters by Wood and Cotler herein, and by Little, Roan, Natan Lerner, and W. Cole Durham, Jr. in the companion volume.

[29] Human Rights Committee, General Comment No. 22(48) concerning Article 18 (CCPR/C/21/Rev.1/Add. 4, 27 September 1993).

[30] See chapters by Lerner, Roan, and Shelton & Kiss in the companion volume. See also Natan Lerner, *Group Rights and Discrimination in International Law* (Dordrecht/Boston/London, 1991), 75ff.

ions, the presence and internal enforcement of a set of ethical rules of conduct, and other factors.[31]

In my view, the functional and institutional dimensions of religion deserve the strongest emphasis in defining the province of religious human rights. Of course, religion viewed in its broadest terms embraces all beliefs and actions that concern the ultimate origin, meaning, and purpose of life, of existence. It involves the responses of the human heart, soul, mind, conscience, intuition, and reason to revelation, to transcendent values, to, what Rudolf Otto once called, the "idea of the holy."[32] But such a definition applied at law would render everything (and thus nothing) deserving of religious rights protection. Viewed in a narrower institutional sense, religion embraces, what Leonard Swidler calls, a creed, a cult, a code of conduct, and a confessional community.[33] A creed defines the accepted cadre of beliefs and values concerning the ultimate origin, meaning, and purpose of life. A cult defines the appropriate rituals, liturgies, and patterns of worship and devotion that give expression to those beliefs. A code of conduct defines the appropriate individual and social habits of those who profess the creed and practice the cult. A confessional community defines the group of individuals who embrace and live out this creed, cult, and code of conduct, both on their own and with fellow believers. By this definition, a religion can be traditional or very new, closely confining or loosely structured, world-avertive or world-affirmative, atheistic, nontheistic, polytheistic, or monotheistic. Religious claims and claimants that meet this definition, in my view, deserve the closest religious rights consideration.

---

[31] See the chapters by Marty, Everett, Broyde, and Wood herein, and by Pobee, Shelton & Kiss, Noonan, Tamas Földesi, T. Jeremy Gunn, and Asher Maoz in the companion volume. See also sources and discussion in European Consortium for Church-State Research, *The Legal Status of Religious Minorities in the Countries of the European Union* (Thessalonica/Milan, 1994); Kent Greenawalt, "Religion as a Concept in Constitutional Law," *California Law Review* 72 (1984): 753; Ninan Koshy, *Religious Freedom in a Changing World* (Geneva, 1992); Donna J. Sullivan, "Advancing the Freedom of Religion or Belief Through the UN Declaration on the Elimination of Religious Intolerance and Discrimination," *American Journal of International Law* 82 (1988): 487; John Witte, Jr., "Whether Piety or Charity: Classification Issues in the Exemption of Churches and Charities From Property Taxation," in Conrad Cherry and Rowland A. Sherill, eds., *Religion, The Independent Sector and American Culture* (Atlanta, 1992), 135.

[32] Rudolf Otto, *The Idea of the Holy: An Inquiry into the Non-Rational Factor of the Idea of the Divine and Its Relation to the Rational*, 2d ed. (New York, 1950).

[33] See Leonard Swidler, ed., *Religious Liberty and Human Rights in Nations and Religions* (Philadelphia, PA, 1986), vii. The Special Rapporteur on religious liberty, Elizabeth Odio-Benito, has written similarly that religion is "an explanation of the meaning of life and how to live accordingly. Every religion has at least a creed, a code of action, and a cult." U.N. Doc. E/CN.4/Sub.2/1987/26, at 4 (quoted and discussed in the chapter by Shelton & Kiss in the companion volume, note 20 and accompanying text).

Second, it is well understood among the authors of these volumes that religious *human* rights are both individual and associational in character. The individualist orientation of human rights norms grounded in Enlightenment and post-Enlightenment reasoning[34] must be balanced by the communal definitions of human rights recognized by all three religions of the Book.[35] Individuals certainly have the right to formulate, deny, or change their religious beliefs, and to act, speak, write, and associate with others in accordance with them. But religious associations, too, have rights to function in expression of their founding religious beliefs and values. Thus churches, temples, and mosques have rights to organize, assemble, worship, and enforce certain religious laws.[36] Parents and families have rights to rear, educate, and discipline children in expression of their religious convictions.[37] Religious publishers and suppliers have rights to produce the particular products needed for their religious cultus. Religious schools have rights to educate and discipline children in accordance with the basic norms and habits of their religious traditions. Again, no easy lines can be drawn between religious and non-religious associations. No easy calculus is at hand to resolve disputes between individual and corporate religious rights. Each tradition has offered a considerable—and controversial—body of theological and legal learning to parse these issues.[38]

Third, it is understood that religious human rights can be asserted against both state officials and other individuals or associations. Under most contemporary legal systems, rights assertions against state officials are governed by *public* law, which includes national and provincial constitutions as well as international conventions and treaties that have been ratified. Rights assertions against other individuals or voluntary associations are governed by *private* law, which includes laws of contract, tort, property, inheritance, and other subjects. When such rights are asserted against other individuals within the same religious community, both the private law of the state and the internal law of the religious community may govern. Distinguishing the respective jurisdictions of secular law

---

[34] See chapters by Marty, Novak, Berger & Lipstadt, Arzt, and Stackhouse & Healey herein.

[35] See chapters by An-Na'im, Hassan, and Villa-Vicencio herein, together with those of Durham, Lerner, Pobee, Mutua, and Martin Heckel in the companion volume.

[36] See chapters by Everett and Broyde herein.

[37] See chapters by Broyde and Coons herein.

[38] See chapters by Elshtain, Broyde, and Arzt herein.

and religious law in these disputes has been the subject of perennial legal and theological controversy, yielding a variety of constitutional models.[39]

Fourth, it is well understood that religious human rights are both protective and affirmative in character—as immunities and entitlements, protections and empowerments.[40] Religious rights provide religious individuals and institutions with both (1) *freedom from* improper intrusions and prohibitions by government officials or other citizens and groups on their religious beliefs and actions; and (2) *freedom to* engage in religious conduct, and to procure the means for such engagement. These might be called the "liberty dimensions" and "entitlement dimensions" of religious human rights.

At its core, the liberty dimension of religious rights entails freedom of conscience for the individual and freedom of association for religious groups—or, more simply, religious toleration. Even if one form of religion is established or favored by civil law or social custom, religious rights require that all individual subjects be able to adopt religious beliefs, and that all peaceable religious institutions be able to organize and perpetuate themselves without coercion or undue burdens by the state or other individuals. Even in the proverbial "age of Constantine," where one form of Christianity was established in the West, this minimal form of religious toleration was afforded to certain religious outsiders.[41] Likewise, in established Islamic regimes today, some religious outsiders are granted this minimal modicum of religious liberty.[42]

More fully conceived, the liberty dimension of religious rights requires that the state accommodate the religious beliefs and practices of individuals and associations and exempt them from generally applicable laws and policies which compel them to act, or to forgo action, in violation of their religious convictions. This fuller understanding of religious liberty embraces a variety of state policies that have become widely recognized in state constitutions. Religious believers are granted conscientious objection from participation in war and the military or immunities from oath-swearing, from work on holy days, from payment of religious

---

[39] See chapters by Everett, Broyde, and Arzt herein. See also Johan van der Vyver, *The Juridical Functions of State and Church* (Durban, 1972); Stephen D. Smith, *Foreordained Failure: The Quest for a Constitutional Principles of Religious Freedom* (Oxford, 1994).

[40] See chapters by Hehir, Elshtain, Everett, Coons, and Novak, and Wood herein and by Földesi and Harold J. Berman in the companion volume.

[41] See chapter by Tierney herein. For the phrase "age of Constantine," see the chapter by Heckel in the companion volume and Martin E. Marty, "The Virginia Statute Two Hundred Years Later," in Merrill D. Peterson and Robert C. Vaughn, eds., *The Virginia for Religious Freedom* (Cambridge, 1988), 1-3.

[42] See chapters by An-Na'im and Arzt herein and by Said Arjomand in the companion volume.

taxes, or from participation in civic ceremonies and activities that they find religiously odious. Religious organizations are exempted from property and income taxation, from zoning and landmark regulations, or from state prohibitions on religious, gender, cultural, or other discrimination. These special forms of "religious accommodation" for individuals and groups are among the most generous expressions of religious liberty.[43]

At its core, the entitlement dimension of religious rights requires that individuals be allowed to exercise their religious beliefs privately and groups be allowed to engage in private collective worship. More fully conceived, religious entitlements embrace an individual's ability and means to engage in religious assembly, speech, and worship, to observe religious laws and rituals, to pay religious taxes, to participate in religious pilgrimages, to gain access to religious totems, and the like. They also embrace a religious group's power to promulgate and enforce internal religious laws of order, organization, and orthodoxy, to train, select, and discipline religious officials, to establish and maintain institutions of worship, charity, and education, to acquire, use, and dispose of property and literature used in worship and rituals, to communicate with co-believers and proselytes, and many other affirmative acts in manifestation of the beliefs of the institution.[44]

Though these "liberty" and "entitlement" dimensions of religious rights are complementary and often overlapping, they do not always yield identical prescriptions. These differences are nowhere more evident than in conflicts over the so-called relations of church and state. American writers, armed with the disestablishment clause of the First Amendment, often emphasize that religious *liberty* requires the separation of church and state, and the cessation of state support for religion. Only the secular or neutral state can guarantee religious liberty, it is argued, and only separation can guarantee neutrality.[45] Europeans, Africans, and Latin Americans, for whom a disestablishment clause is largely foreign, often emphasize that religious *entitlements* require the material and moral cooperation of church and state.[46] Indeed, a number of religious groups

---

[43] For American developments of the "accommodation" doctrine, see chapter by John Witte, Jr. and M. Christian Green in the companion volume.

[44] A rather thorough list is provided in the 1981 UN Declaration on the Elimination of All Forms of Intolerance and of Discrimination Based on Religion or Belief, reprinted in Brownlie, ed., *Basic Documents on Human Rights*, 109 and in Principles 16 and 17 of the 1989 Vienna Concluding Document, in 28 I.L.M. 527, discussed in the chapters by Lerner and Durham in the companion volume.

[45] See discussion in chapters by Hehir, Cotler, and Wood herein and by Cumper, Földesi, and Witte & Green in the companion volume.

[46] See discussion in chapters by An-Na'im, Arzt, and Villa-Vicencio herein and by Heckel, Földesi, Pobee, Arjomand, Paul Sigmund, Stanley Muschett Ibarra, and Paul Mojzes in the companion volume.

in the former Soviet bloc and sub-Saharan Africa today regard restitution and affirmative state action towards religion as a necessary feature of any religious rights regime—if nothing else, to undo and overcome past confiscation and repression.[47] Similarly, some Catholic groups in Latin America urge cooperation of religious and political bodies to preserve the "Catholicization" of public life and culture,[48] Islamic revivalists in various countries urge similar arrangements to enhance the "Islamicization" of the community,[49] and Jewish groups argue similarly to protect the Jewish character of the State of Israel. To cooperate or to separate, to aid or to avoid one another, is a fundamental question confronting religions and states around the world. Answers to this question have yielded a wide spectrum of theoretical perspectives and constitutional solutions.[50]

These cultural differences on so basic a question as the relation of church and state, illustrates a fifth point, emphasized by Harold Berman: Religious human rights, like all human rights, must find their source and sanction simultaneously in morality, history, and politics.[51] Religious human rights cannot be reduced simply to moral preferences or to customary privileges or to political provisions alone. (For all their value, even international standards should not, in my view, be idealized or idolized.) Religious human rights must be understood in more holistic terms, always open to emendation and amendment, and constantly weighed from different perspectives.[52] From a moral perspective, religious human rights are rooted in the natural qualities of the person and community, in external sources of morality like the creation order, the natural law, and the divine covenant, or in sacred statements of morality, like the Bible, the Talmud, or the Qur'an. Such rights derive their ultimate sanction from the moral condemnation of violators. From an historical perspective, religious human rights are rooted in the customs and traditions of a people and invariably shaped by the historical experiences that they have witnessed. They derive their sanction from communal condemnation and social stigmatizing of violators. From a political per-

---

[47] See chapters by Heckel, Földesi, Mojzes, and Mutua in the companion volume.

[48] See chapters by Sigmund and Muschett in the companion volume.

[49] See chapters by An-Na'im and Arzt herein and by Arjomand in the companion volume.

[50] See typologies in the chapters by Hehir and Cotler herein, and by Johan van der Vyver, Durham, Mojzes, and Shelton & Kiss in the companion volume.

[51] See chapter by Harold J. Berman in the companion volume. See also id., *Faith and Order: The Reconciliation of Law and Religion* (Atlanta, 1993), 289-312 and Howard O. Hunter, ed., *The Integrative Jurisprudence of Harold J. Berman* (Boulder/San Francisco, 1995).

[52] See chapters by Tierney, Huber, An-Na'im, and Stackhouse & Healey herein. Berger & Lipstadt, in fact, argue that "reifying" or "codifying" one or two interpretations of rights (in their case of women) can be very harmful.

spective, religious human rights are rooted in the constitutional and statutory laws of the national and transnational state, and derive their sanction from the legal punishment inflicted on violators. Any claim to religious human rights, and any formulation of a doctrine of religious human rights, has to be assessed from at least these three perspectives. Different combinations of these perspectives invariably yield different formulations of religious human rights.

Finally, it is wise to remember that religious prejudice works openly and in secret, and must be met with both blunt and delicate instruments. In this "Dickensian era of human rights," as Irwin Cotler calls it—with the best of international religious rights provisions but the worst of local religious rights abuses—this counsel is all the more pressing. We need to parse the false dialectics of universalist versus relativist, Western versus non-Western theories of human rights to address the pressing problem of religious rights abuses.[53] This problem needs to be addressed both locally and globally, legally and theologically. On the one hand, the many local forms of religious conflict and abuse must be assayed through local study and assuaged through locally-tailored human rights norms. No global norms on religious rights can be sufficiently precise to do justice to the needs of local religious rivals. Legal solutions to the problem of religious abuse will require detailed local understanding and intense cultivation of a local rights culture. On the other hand, any such local initiatives must be consistent with general principles of both law and theology. Prevailing international and constitutional norms on religious rights must be respected and extended to address the specific problems of religious rights abuse in various parts of the world. Prevailing Christian, Judaic, and Muslim perspectives must be extended to balance their divine commandments to preserve and perpetuate their faiths with the human counsels to tolerate religious pluralism and to respect the rule of law and rights.

The State of Religious Human Rights

The theories and laws of religious human rights in vogue today were not formed out of whole cloth. They were "slowly learned, through centuries of cruel experience" and growing enlightenment, Brian Tierney tells us.[54] This religious rights tradition, though largely lost in current

---

[53] See chapters by Cotler, An-Na'im, and Arzt herein and by Lerner in the companion volume. See also Abdullahi Ahmed An-Na'im, Ann Elizabeth Mayer, Sumner B. Twiss, and William Wipfler, "Universality vs. Relativism in Human Rights," in John Kelsay and Sumner B. Twiss, eds., *Religion and Human Rights* (New York, 1994), 31-60.

[54] See the chapter by Tierney herein.

discussions of human rights, remains an important source of instruction and inspiration today—and a number of chapters herein provide windows on that history.[55]

In this century, the subject of religious human rights and their violation first came to popular prominence in the aftermath of World War II. Several factors contributed to the sudden new interest in the subject—the horrors suffered by Jews and Christians in Nazi Germany, Stalinist Russia, and Maoist China, the repression of religious missionaries and emigrés to Africa and Asia, the sudden proliferation of new (or newly prominent) religions demanding protection and treatment equal with that of older religions, among other factors. In response, jurists and theologians produced elaborate theories of religious and other human rights. Religious communities issued bold confessional statements and manifestoes on the subject.[56] The United Nations, regional international organizations, and individual states began to outlaw religious discrimination. Non-governmental and inter-governmental organizations were established to monitor the plight of religious minorities, to litigate and lobby on their behalf, and to educate their constituents.[57]

This sudden new interest in religious rights was part of the broader "rights revolution" that erupted in America, Europe, and elsewhere in the 1950s and thereafter. In America, this rights revolution yielded a powerful new grassroots civil rights movement, a welter of landmark civil rights cases, an array of new rights legislation punctuated by the Civil Rights Act in 1964, and an unprecedented outpouring of literature on human rights. In Europe this rights revolution produced a welter of post-war constitutional reforms and an array of landmark constitutional

---

[55] See chapters by Tierney, Huber, Novak, Arzt, and Wood herein, and by Durham, Lerner, Heckel, Cumper, Berman, Arjomand, and Noonan in the companion volume. For other overviews, see Sidney Z. Ehler and John B. Morrall, eds., *Church and State Through the Centuries* (Newman, MD, 1954); Joseph LeCler & Marius-Francois Valkhoff, *Les premiers défenseurs de la liberté religieuse* (Paris, 1969), 2 vols.; Heinrich Lutz (hrsg.), *Zur Geschichte der Toleranz und Religionsfreiheit* (Darmstadt, 1977); Henry Kamen, *The Rise of Toleration* (New York, 1967); A.J. Carlyle, *The Christian Church and Liberty*, repr. ed. (New York, 1968); Noel B. Reynolds and W. Cole Durham, Jr., eds., *Religious Liberty in Western Thought* (Atlanta, 1995); David Daube, "The Rabbis and Philo on Human Rights," in Sidorsky, ed., *Essays on Human Rights: Contemporary Issues and Jewish Perspectives*, 234; S.D. Gotein, "Human Rights in Jewish Thought and Life in the Middle Ages," in ibid., 247; James Parkes, *The Jew in the Medieval Community: A Study of His Political and Economic Situation*, 2d ed. (New York, 1976); Solomon Grayzel, *The Church and the Jews in the XIIIth Century* (Philadelphia, 1933).

[56] See chapters by Hehir, Novak, and Cotler herein. See summaries in Jörg Bauer, et al., *Zum Thema Menschenrechte* (Stuttgart, 1977); Huber & Tödt, *Menschenrechte*; Reformed Ecumenical Synod, *RES Testimony on Human Rights* (Grand Rapids, 1983); Traer, *Faith in Human Rights*.

[57] See chapters by Hehir and Cotler herein, and by Lerner and Roan in the companion volume.

cases.[58] At the international level, the Universal Declaration of Rights of 1948 offered a grand statement of human rights, which brought forth numerous declarations, covenants, and conventions on more discrete rights. The United Nations established a Human Rights Committee and a number of subcommissions and special rapporteurs on topics such as racial and religious discrimination. Academies and institutes throughout the world produced a prodigious new literature on human rights.

After expressing some initial interest, however, intellectual and political leaders of this rights revolution consigned religious rights to the bottom of what Henry Abraham once called "The Honor Roll of Superior Rights." Freedom of speech and press, parity of race and gender, provision of work and welfare, and similar causes captured much of the energy and emoluments of the rights revolution. After the 1950s, academic inquiries and activist interventions into religious rights and their abuses became increasingly intermittent and isolated, inspired as much by parochial self-interest as by universal golden rules. The rights revolution seemed to be passing religion by.

This deprecation of religious rights was not simply the product of calculated agnosticism or callous apathy—though there was ample evidence of both. Rights leaders were often forced, by reason of political pressure or limited resources, to address the most glaring rights violations and abuses. Physical abuses—torture, rape, war crimes, false imprisonment, forced poverty—are easier to track and treat than spiritual abuses, and often demand more immediate attention. In desperate circumstances, it is sometimes better to be a Good Samaritan than a good preacher, to give food and comfort before gospels and doctrines. The relative silence of religious communities until recently seemed to lend credence to this prioritization of effort.[59] With the exception of the Roman Catholic Church after the Second Vatican Council (1962-1965) and certain Jewish and ecumenical organizations,[60] most religious groups made only modest contributions to the theory, law, and activism on religious rights. The general theological principles set out in their post-War manifestoes on rights were not converted to specific precepts or programs. Their general endorsement of religious rights provisions in early international and constitutional texts were not followed by specific lobbying and litigation efforts. Whether mainline religious communities were content with their own condition, or intent to turn the other cheek or look the other way in the face of religious rights abuses, their relative silence did considerable harm to the cause of religious rights and liberties.

---

[58] See chapters by Heckel, Cumper, and T. Jeremy Gunn in the companion volume.

[59] See chapter by James Finn in the companion volume.

[60] See chapters by Huber, Hehir, Cotler, and Wood herein.

The deprecation of religious rights over the past three decades has had several deleterious effects on the rights revolution, and on religious rights themselves.

First, this deprecation has "impoverished" the general theory of human rights embraced by the rights revolution.[61] On the one hand, it has cut many rights from their roots. The right to religion, Georg Jellinek wrote exactly one century ago, is "the mother of many other rights."[62] For the religious individual, the right to believe leads ineluctably to the rights to assemble, speak, worship, proselytize, educate, parent, travel, or to abstain from the same on the basis of one's beliefs. For the religious association, the right to exist invariably involves rights to corporate property, collective worship, organized charity, parochial education, freedom of press, and autonomy of governance. To ignore religious rights is to overlook the conceptual, if not historical,[63] source of many other individual and associational rights. On the other hand, this deprecation of religious rights has abstracted rights from duties. The classic faiths of the Book adopt and advocate religious rights in order to protect religious duties. A religious individual or association has rights to exist and act not in the abstract but in order to discharge discrete religious duties. Religious rights provide the best example of the organic linkage between rights and responsibilities.[64] Without the example of religious rights readily at hand, leaders of the rights revolution have tended to lose sight of these organic connections and to treat rights in the abstract.

Second, this deprecation of religious rights has sharpened the divide between Western and non-Western theories of rights. Many non-Western traditions, particularly those of Islamic, Hindu, Buddhist, Taoist, and indigenous stock, cannot conceive of, nor accept, a system of rights that excludes religion. Religion is for these traditions inextricably integrated into every facet of life. Religious rights are thus an inherent part of rights of

---

[61] Using Glendon's term in *Rights Talk: The Impoverishment of Political Discourse.*

[62] Georg Jellinek, *Die Erklärung der Menschen- und Bürgerrechte: Ein Beitrag zur modernen Verfassungsgeschichte* (Leipzig, 1895), 42.

[63] Several authors herein argue that, historically, religious rights were among the first rights to be recognized, and are among the "first freedoms" of any constitutional order. See chapters by Cotler, Hassan, Wood, and Stackhouse & Healey herein and by Durham and Lerner in the companion volume. Other authors, while not denying the centrality of religious rights today, argue that religious rights were among the last rights to be widely accepted at law. See chapters by Tierney and Huber herein and by Noonan in the companion volume. The differences between these views might turn in part on how full and systematic a form of religious rights prevails; certainly, several basic guarantees for religion were already on the books of ancient Roman and Judaic law, if not always honored in practice. This difference notwithstanding, no one denies that recognition of religious rights is indispensable today, or that it was only when religious rights were fully recognized that other human rights could be adequately recognized and protected.

[64] See chapters by Novak, Berger & Lipstadt, An-Na'im, and Arzt herein.

speech, press, assembly, and other individual rights as well as ethnic, cultural, linguistic, and similar associational rights. No system of rights that ignores or deprecates this cardinal place of religion can be respected or adopted.[65] Since Western notions of rights dominate international law, many non-Western societies have neither accepted nor adopted the basic international declarations and covenants on human rights.

Third, this deprecation of religion has exaggerated the role of the state as the guarantor of human rights. The simple state vs. individual dialectic of modern human rights theories leaves it to the state to protect rights of all sorts—"first generation" civil and political rights, "second generation" social, cultural, and economic rights, and "third generation" environmental and developmental rights. In reality, the state is not, and cannot be, so omnicompetent—as the recently failed experiments in socialism have vividly shown.[66] A vast plurality of "voluntary associations" or "mediating structures" stands between the state and the individual, religious institutions prominently among them. Religious institutions, among others, play a vital role in the cultivation and realization of all rights, including religious rights.[67] They create the conditions (if not the prototypes) for the realization of first generation civil and political rights. They provide a critical (and sometimes the principal) means to meet second generation rights of education, health care, child care, labor organizations, employment, artistic opportunities, among others. They offer some of the deepest insights into norms of creation, stewardship, and servanthood that lie at the heart of third generation rights.[68]

Religion and religious human rights must be reintegrated into the contemporary field of human rights. Human rights leaders need to close the gaps between academic and activist, legal and theological, religious and secular, governmental and voluntary groups. Arcane academic inquiries into religious rights of themselves do little to help victims of religious oppression; continued ad hoc intervention on behalf of religious dissidents only perpetuates the listless activism that has plagued this field. Legal scholars cannot continue to discuss religious rights statutes

---

[65] See chapters by Huber, Novak, An-Na'im, Arzt, Villa-Vicencio, and Stackhouse & Healey herein, and by Arjomand and Pobee in the companion volume.

[66] See chapters by Finn and Földesi in the companion volume.

[67] See chapters by Marty and Coons herein and by Witte & Green in the companion volume. See also, in the burgeoning literature on social pluralism, Peter Berger and Richard John Neuhaus, *To Empower People: The Role of Mediating Structures in Public Policy* (Washington, 1977); Jacques Maritain, *Man and the State* (Chicago, 1954); James W. Skillen and Rockne M. McCarthy, eds., *Political Order and the Plural Structure of Society* (Atlanta, 1991); Michael Walzer, *Spheres of Justice: An Argument for Pluralism and Equality* (New York, 1983).

[68] See chapter by Wolfgang Huber herein and id., "Rights of Nature or Dignity of Nature?" *The Annual of the Society of Christian Ethics* (1991): 43.

and cases in isolation from the profound theological implications of their inquiries; theologians cannot continue to propound abstract theological statements and confessions on rights without attention to their practical implementation and effect. Religiously-based theorists and activists on religious rights cannot isolate themselves from other believing and non-believing theorists and activists.

This volume and its companion are offered in the spirit of reconciliation and integration that the field of human rights so desperately needs. "Of the writing of books, there is no end," the ancient Prophet reminds us, "and much study is a weariness of the flesh." (Ecclesiastes 12:12). But until the Final Word is written—until we all put on what the Prophet calls "the whole duty of man" to fear God and keep his command-ments"—the writing of books cannot end.

Religious Dimensions of Human Rights

MARTIN E. MARTY
University of Chicago

From Enlightenment Dreams to Religious Realism

A ny thoughtful person who surveys the human rights scene around the globe today cannot help but notice how central is the religious dimension. Scholars in the Western world and, no doubt, many of their colleagues elsewhere, have good reason to rub their eyes in wonder over this central position of religious concerns. At least since the eighteenth-century Enlightenment in Europe and the Americas, through the course of the modern experience, the situation was different. It became almost a matter of reflex for observers from the academic, literary, and diplomatic worlds to expect religion to diminish in significance, if not disappear altogether from many public spheres.

A visit to the mental attic of historical impressions that most of us carry around would reinforce a single impression. It was consistently assumed that as Enlightenment reason and science spread, something else must decline. That something included the sense of the sacred and the transcendent and the institutions of "superstition and priestcraft." Religion, in most of its forms, would lose significance and power. If religion had ever represented interests involving the case for human rights, or if it had ever motivated people to seek such rights—and the case for most religions having done so was frail—no longer would this be the circumstance. Philosophy, anthropology, and politics would provide the new language for rights.

Furthermore, it was assumed in most academic circles that whatever of religion survived would be of a genial, tolerant, philosophically-enlightened sort. This meant that faith would not be a motor for dissent against establishment, a bond between people who suffered deprivation of rights, or an element in the assurance of rights.

1

J. Witte, Jr. and J.D. van der Vyver (eds.), Religious Human Rights in Global Perspective, 1-16.
© 1996 *Kluwer Law International. Printed in the Netherlands.*

All those dreams of the Enlightenment, not easy to isolate in documentation because of their protean reach but pervasive in the West in any case, have been replaced by realistic scenes of a very different character. The monstrous totalitarian systems of the twentieth century, be they Fascist, Nazi, Communist, Maoist, or whatever, set out to suppress rights, beginning with those of religious people. Yet the systems and structures of Fascism, Nazism, Communism, and in many ideological respects Maoism, have imploded and are shattered. Their progenitors have been exposed and repudiated, their strategies have been seen to have failed, and their repressions to have been finally found ineffective.

What has outlasted these inventions have been the voices of religions. Often these appeared in the form of small and despised sects, whose adherents kept insisting on their own rights through all the years of oppression until at last they prevailed. Also outlasting the anti-spiritual ideologies have been some religious voices that present rationales for assuring rights not only of adherents of a single group in question but also, beyond it, of other-believers, non-believers, and victims of repression in general.

Three Ways in Which Authors in This Book Address the Change

Such a surprising change in ethos and turn in world affairs demands and deserves examination, an examination that thematically unifies the chapters in this collection. The logic of their three-part sequence is clear and manifest.

First, a set of scholars has laid a ground work by engaging in *historical and theological inquiries* that will help provide a different accounting of rights than that which was part of reflexive thought and scholarly instinct for so long. None of the authors in this section writes in an uncritical or triumphalist tone about the past contribution of religious thought and action to the talk about rights or to the acts of helping assure human rights. These scholars are all aware of the sorry record of religion when it was legally established, as was characteristically the case. They know that religious leaders were often those who repressed rights, and that believers were often apathetic about making the case for these, and were frequently submissive to oppressive authorities.

On the other hand, these scholars help disinter long obscured facts and understandings. They demonstrate that many religious expressions have been supportive of human rights. Quite naturally, many of these were expressly religious rights. One expects this to be the case, as much as one expects lawyers to examine legal rights, journalists and academics to defend the liberty of the press and academic freedom, or philosophers to explore freedom to propagate in public what they had been thinking. Yet to those who study these cases it becomes clear that just as religious freedom is in many ways the first freedom, so religious rights are the primary rights, and that they imply and produce corollaries from far beyond religious realms. Protect religious beliefs, exercises, and organizations, they observe with some consistency, and you are likely to be extending other rights further.

A second group of essayists looks at the *"rights structure" of religious communities and traditions.* If it is rather difficult to relocate ideas that generate religious support for religious and other rights, as the first group of scholars has done, it is very simple to examine the record, especially the record of "unfinished business."

However well-intended the religious may be, and however bold their talk of concern for rights, their leaders have often been quite selective in choices of their ways to put their language of defense to work. Ancient texts, long traditions, and perduring interests of the powerful to retain power has led and often leads leadership to fail to provide this "rights structure" in ways that will assure rights to the whole community. Historically three groups have apparently suffered most, or at least their sufferings are most vivid in the consciousness of our contemporaries. These include women, who have often been overlooked or even trampled on in many traditions marked by male religious authority. Second are children, who may be victims of parental and other adult deprivations or rights. Then come dissenters and dissidents, who trouble religious and other authorities. A study of the records in all three cases may be a contribution to the enlargement of human rights concern on the part of the religious.

A third group of scholars deals with *inconsistency, anomaly, or shortsightedness on the part of religious leadership.* Urgent as these leaders may be in their expressions of the religious rights of their own group, and insistent as they can be about the validity of these and the hearing that they deserve, they are not always consistent. They want their own rights, but they are not always on the front lines in conflicts whose outcome is to be the assurance of rights for others. Even more problematic is the record of people who hold power in religions and often go out of their way to restrict the rights of many in their own believing communities and traditions. One must ask whether there is something distinctive about religion that leads to such contradictory behavior or shortsightedness. Is failure to assure rights on this front typical of behavior in other spheres of life as well, or is it especially obvious when religious agents speak in favor of rights but often act like their secular counterparts in simply trying to hold power and limit the rights of others?

Needed: A Religious Approach to Religious Rights

An introductory thesis might serve readers well as they follow the logic of the sequence of essays here. I shall argue that among all the other ways to explore the situation of rights, one has been neglected but, if recovered, it should contribute to understanding and action. This is what we might call a religious approach to discussion of religious human rights. However we may define "religion" or "religious"—issues of definition cannot be fully addressed on these pages—one can argue a case for such an approach at the outset and, I hope, sustain the argument to the end. This argument centers on the notion that there are *religious* dimensions to struggles over *religious* human rights, and that religious studies in their many forms can illumine the inquiry.

Such a proposal and understanding does not require every religious phenomenon to be the subject of reductionism, as currently is often the case. When reductionism is privileged, religious issues simply and quickly get translated to psychological, anthropological, sociological, or economic and political factors. The quest for religious human rights in such cases is reduced to "nothing but." This reduction would lead to a situation in which when one hears the voice of the religious there is a temptation to say, "this concern for religious rights is nothing but a power move by dissenters who want to be victorious insiders." Or "this talk about rights by the religious amounts to nothing but their psychological impulses to find identity." Or "they want a better economic deal for their class, and make their way by invoking religious claims."

Religious approaches would find scholars and diplomats suspending disbelief in the presence of *homo religiosus*. They would take seriously the claims of individuals and groups to be grounded in "ultimate concern," and to see their individual and group identity issuing from response to myths and symbols, rites and ceremonies, metaphysical claims and behavioral correlates of that concern.

When Religions Oppress the Religious

A different version of the thesis instead leads one to contend that a religious problem needs a religious address. For examples of where this subject comes up, here is a catalog:

A Catholic theologian complains that the freedom that is claimed to be a possession or quality of Catholicism is not extended to someone like that theologian herself when and insofar as she calls into question any aspect of churchly authority. Her freedoms to engage in such inquiry are denied, and she is ostracized if not actually driven from employment by any institution connected with the church.

A religious organization does not respect the rights of its employees to bargain collectively and form unions, even while its leaders are occupied with advocacy for such unionizing and bargaining rights in other spheres of employment. Where, one asks, is the consistency?

A teacher in a church-related college is threatened with loss of tenure, shunned, and virtually or actually driven out because academic rights are always secondary to religious claims as these are being guarded and professed by the momentarily-in-power leaders of that religion who support and represent the authority but never freedom in such a college.

The child of Christian Scientists, Jehovah's Witnesses, or one or another of the small "healing sects" is deprived of the rights to life and health, thanks to the parental obedience to churchly teaching that is disrespectful of such rights—and the child needlessly dies.

A woman in a strict Jewish or Muslim group is victimized by her husband, by male authority, or the executors of rites and ceremonies of passage. She has nowhere to escape and no way to find an advocate who will help her enjoy rights of protest against such ceremonies and deprivations. Where are her rights?

A couple in Israel refuses to recognize the religious authority of the Orthodox rabbis who are established in power in an otherwise secular state, and has to leave Israel for the marriage to be performed.

A novelist who writes experimentally and takes imaginative risks to the point that his or her work is perceived as heresy or blasphemy is the victim of a *fatwa*, becomes a marked person, and has to hide in exile in order to enjoy the primal human right of "life," of getting to stay alive when religious authority would do the killing.

A Pakistani woman is raped by her employer. When her father would prosecute her case, she learns with him that while the rapist, if found guilty, might suffer some penalty, that she would be put to death for adultery according to the legal prescriptions of her religion in her culture—and she has nowhere else to go to enjoy the right to stay alive. Here, as elsewhere, it is the religion itself that produces the need for defenders of religious freedom.

Members of religious groups in numbers of nations are virtually bound by authority so that they cannot challenge their own communities' prohibitions against birth control at United Nations conferences on the subject.

Native Americans get reservated, and few non-Indians pay attention to their needs, including their need to defend rights to practice tribal rites of a sacred character and to do this apart from the superimposition of the will of their conquerors and reservators.

In all these frequent and typical kinds of cases, religious rights are the issue within traditions where many claim that a language and a polity exist to help assure rights.

The Challenges that Accompany a Religious Address

A special challenge presents itself in all such cases when religious problems suggest religious addresses, if not always solutions. An array of these present themselves at once.

For beginnings, one asks: What business does one religion or set of religious leaders have intruding on the religious practices of another group? When is such intrusion appropriate and when is it not? What rights do religionists have to protect themselves from efforts to convert them, especially when this is done by the use of instruments of power or deception? What rights do people have to impose their views on those who practice rites that are offensive to others? A vivid example is female circumcision. Many cultural relativists who fight for the right of other religions simply to be themselves find that there are boundaries beyond which such defense will not go. Thus they find religiously legitimated practices like female circumcision offensive and, on grounds alien to the practitioners of such a rite, want it stopped. Closer to home: it must be asked: Were the rights of religious groups unprotected and misunderstood when the United States government moved against the Branch Davidians in Waco, Texas?

Such questions do not permit easy answers. They do show that understandings of what religion is or what religions are about are important for addressing issues of law or even of preference and taste. An old saying has it that "it takes a thief to catch a thief." It may take a religious scholar or jurist of religious sensibilities to throw special light on the issue of what is at stake in the sensibilities of other religionists. Such a person may not produce satisfying or sufficient addresses to the problem of rights, but he or she may throw welcome light on the subjects when they are at issue.

A second, counterpart question introduces a cautionary note: Might it not be that a religious inquiry or understanding could actually complicate rights talk? Maybe the secularist, tone deaf to or opposed to the claims of any and all religion, can be a safeguard. Not without reason did the partisans of Enlightenment toleration argue that there was a special calling for those who sought universal patterns of reasoning to defend rights across cultural and sectarian boundaries. So the question is in place: Might not religious impulses only make matters worse when rights are being suppressed?

Third, one is prompted to ask, what is it about religion that leads partisans to adduce it with such passion and self-assurance on all sides in discussions of rights, including religious rights? Certainly some answers to that question would include the fact that most religions regard themselves as rooted in the transcendent, the supramundane, the extraordinary realms of existence. Since that is the case, when they speak up, in gambling terms, they "raise the stakes" over talk about rights in the mundane and ordinary spheres. Thus, a person or community claims an experience of the sacred, one that induces awe. Consequently, a communal or social expression takes form, in order to help fortify those who experience a hierophany and to help inspire them to share knowledge of it. Such an experience is always empowering; it authorizes action toward various outcomes, some of them murderous against those who are not moved by the originating vision, or who oppose its propagation.

These experiences of the sacred, these responses to revelation or enlightenment, do not always match each other across the boundaries in other religions. Thus in interfaith dialogue on human rights, one might hear the monotheist make a case. Only when the one God does the revealing and when this God speaks, insisting that the human is made in the divine image and has consequent rights, can there be a realization of rights. Well and good for fellow monotheists who worship the same God. But their witness is quickly countered by the Buddhist who believes that it is precisely the presence of *theos*, of God, that limits rights. The question from the dialogue partner then comes: What must the Jew or Muslim or Christian "give up" to advance dialogue about rights and rights themselves? For a beginning sample, says the Buddhist, dogma and monotheism must go. Clearly, when sincere but opposing voices like these are heard, a new realism is manifest in discussions. The interests "thicken" and grow more complex. They will not be reduced or casually removed from the table.

Fourth, the introduction of specifically religious voices into religious and other rights talk makes the speakers and what they say both less comprehensible to outsiders and more vivid and satisfying to insiders in the particular traditions and communities. People of various faith communities live in and develop what phenomenologist Alfred Schutz calls different "universes of discourse." These might include universes related to race, ethnicity, tribe, gender, class, culture, aesthetics, or national experience. Religious experience connected with any of these raises everything to a new plane of complication or to a new depth of understanding. In either case, faith and practices associated with it cannot be ignored.

One further must deal with the disparity of understandings within each religious community, or with the conflict resulting from the disparities. Thus family quarrels within religions often lead to suppression of rights. Islamic fundamentalist groups, by insisting on literal application of Shari'a, religious law, often embarrass, inconvenience, and thwart more moderate Muslim leaders and citizens, for example, in the matter of the rights of women. The winners and losers in the Southern Baptist Convention or Missouri Synod Lutheran fights make appeals to the same primal texts and long elaborative traditions. But their interpretations vary, and the winners find the losers *de trop* and expel them from responsible positions or respectability within the denomination. Both Pope John Paul II and dissenting theologians appeal to biblical texts, but the Pope holds the power to take away license to teach priests if he disagrees with the theologians, whose resort to arguments for academic freedom and the accuracy of their interpretations of the Catholic tradition go unheeded and are ineffectual in the power situation.

A sixth creative complication when one introduces religious concerns to rights talk comes when a mediator seeks some sort of common ground. This is done so that there can be meaningful conversation across the boundaries of these separate universes of discourse or family conflicts. The cultural absolutist has it easy: *my* religion is the only right one, the only one that assures and deserves rights; *others* are all wrong. They have no rights, or at least can make no compelling case for expressing and defending them.

The cultural relativist seems to have an equal advantage, though probably at the expense of any satisfactory outcome when there is conflict. Such a relativist says that anthropologists can always find somewhere, in some tribe or communion, a religiously-certified practice that violates any conception of common grounding, natural law, or whatever. This is the case with human rights as with everything else.

In this context, a basic dispute surfaces in every kind of cross-cultural conclave. This has to do with whether rights belong to the individual or to the community. In many inquiries, the pro-community voices often speak up in terms that are disturbing to advocates of individual rights. Thus one hears: "Human rights are a product of modern, post-Enlightenment, liberal, secular humanism. This is a religiously alienating humanism because it elevates the individual to the point that the group is forgotten"—yet it is precisely the group that makes the strongest religious claims. Conversation across the boundaries of debate over "rights of individuals over groups" versus "rights of groups" is always more difficult. This is especially the case when either side is or both sides are eager to ground their positions and claims in religious revelation or tradition.

Given the Difficulties: Why Adduce Religious Approaches?

Given complications like these and the many more that one can easily imagine, there is good reason to ask a basic question about the thesis that a religious problem needs a religious address. If religion is so complicating, so difficult, why deal with it? Why not be content with casual recourse or willful reversion to non- or anti-religious arguments derived from Enlightenment era understandings of secular reasoning? If religion brings as much heat as light, why not extinguish it, or at least bracket it in polite discourse? At least, the practice of using such language in 1945 and 1948 helped the United Nations come to sufficient consensus or sufficient assertion of persuasive power that there could even be a UN Charter. Such an approach made it possible for the nations to speak of "faith in fundamental human rights" and to produce a Universal Declaration of Human Rights. On its grounds, the UN could produce contentions like these: "Everyone has the right to education," and education should promote "understanding, tolerance and friendship among all nations, racial or religious groups. . . ."

It is often asked, on credible grounds, whether in today's religiously-expressive world such lines could be written and forwarded with any hope of approval. Would Islamic, Jewish, Christian, Sikh, Hindu, and other fundamentalists and their spiritual kin be able to argue their cases on such grounds of shared "faith" and "understanding?" Hardly. Then, the question reoccurs: Why introduce language that reflects an awareness that there are millions of such voices today, voices of people who would not accept the Declaration language? Why not leave well enough from 1945 and 1948 alone? Why not hope that no one who notices the shifts in presuppositions within the international community, since then will not acquire power to upset the UN? Again, why bring up religion?

The realist has answers ready: The world community deals with religion because it is there and will not go away. If some forms of faith and institutions have dwindled, cooled, or even disappeared in the northern spiritual ice belt, there are temperate and tropical zones of spirituality where religion prospers. There it is the main motivator in the discussion of rights or their limits. The scholar or the adjudicator deals with religion because its professor claims that its impulses have derived from the vertical dimensions of experience. They issue from God or the heavens before respondents connect them with the horizontal elements. On that secondary plane, humans interact with each other both within and beyond the boundaries of religious communities. Because of their transcendent and absolute source, these are seen as nonnegotiable.

Some Assets of Religion in the Field of Human Rights

To write as we have here is to deal one-sidedly with religion, and it is reassuring to note that many authors in this book and its sequel have much to say compensatorily, on the assets, not the liabilities, of religious advocacies. It is easy to portray the complications and neglect to mention the solaces and aids that religion can and does bring. Thus it is tempting for one to be passive in the face of the manifest differences among and the intractable oppositions of many religions to each other and of some or all citizens against the non-religious. Yet in practice, the boundaries between faith communities or those who differ within them are not always so impermeable as here suggested. Potential alliances of elements from differing communities are not always simply so out of range and reach as militants and dogmatists often suggest. Especially in free and thus pluralist republics, there are boundary-crossings of many sorts on diverse occasions. One might here speak of a criss-crossing of interests, goals, and alliances.

To illustrate from North America: When colonial America was turning into the national United States, the issue of religious rights was prime. Political and philosophical leaders like George Washington and Patrick Henry, inspired by the God of Reason and Nature in the courts of the American Enlightenment, squared off against other Enlightenment advocates like Thomas Jefferson and James Madison. They debated whether any trace of religious establishment should survive and asked whether there would be ample religious human rights if it did. Both sets of founders used arguments grounded in witness to the God of Reason or Reason itself.

On the other hand and at the same time, the Protestant religious community was also divided among advocates of vestigial religious establishment and the voice of protest. Thus a dissenter like Elder John Leland, who believed in all the orthodox Protestant stories of salvation effected through Jesus, made profound practical as well as emotional common cause with Thomas Jefferson, who emphatically did not share that basis of belief. Both Enlightened and dissenting Christian advocates were strengthened in their pro-human rights stance by their religious outlook. Both used the depth of their own commitments to what they believed as an instrument for comprehending why the other found so much to be at stake and fought so vigorously for these rights.

Continuing the Concerns into the Future

If a religious problem needs a religious address and if religion does not seem to be disappearing globally or nationally, it is understandable that citizens and believers among them, would want to peer into the future in order to prepare themselves for debate, action, and further comprehension. Here as elsewhere, no single profile presents itself under the simple category "religion," but a new range of problems comes into view to demand attention.

Thus, the observer reckons with the fact that historically the issue of human rights in religion has not been perceived as being clearly anticipated or enjoined in ancient sacred texts. The writers of these texts, in response to revelation or transcendent experience, had what to them were wider, deeper, and longer interests. For example, they would have described themselves as having been busy saving souls and not setting up government or argument. When supporting such interests they may often have obscured or neglected human rights or even worked against realizing them, to the glory of the God of authority.

Second, religious cultures evolve. Just as the ancient texts are rarely rich in the use of explicit rights language, so they do not freeze traditions, even those that claim to be frozen in literalist interpretations. They all belong to history, and they experience inevitable cultural change. An example that courses along in the background as a figurative stream in this essay has been the rationalist but not irreligious Enlightenment as experienced and expressed in the European and American contexts and followed agents of both, their cultural offspring. On the soil of Christendom at a particular moment there developed what Crane Brinton called a new religion, an invention called the Enlightenment, with a big "E." Its advocates spoke of human rights in new terms. Most religious groups, whether they immediately supported the new talk or were dragged screaming into the sphere that it defined and illuminated, soon found it congenial and began to make claims that promoting such rights was their impulse all along. Hannah Arendt, among many others, noted how almost all the religions liked to claim that they were present at the creation of such rights-frameworks. She politely suggested, in effect, that such religious spokespersons might at least send a card of thanks to modernity, to the Enlightenment, for having led them to the delayed—fifteen century late!—discovery of the latent pro-human rights, pro-religious rights, elements in their treasury.

In *On Revolution*, Arendt deals almost ironically with this subject:

> A few words need still be said about the not infrequent claims that all modern revolutions are essentially Christian in origin, and this even when their professed faith is atheism.... Secularization, the separation of religion from politics and the rise of a secular realm with a dignity of its own, is certainly a crucial factor in the phenomenon of [democratic] revolution.... The fact is

that no revolution was ever made in the name of Christianity prior to the modern age, so that the best one can say in favor of this theory is that it needed modernity to liberate the revolutionary germs of the Christian faith, which obviously is begging the question.[1]

Thus some have discovered what Glen Tinder has spoken of as a stress on "the exalted individual" within a faith like Christianity, because there exist a prime belief in human creation "in the image of God" and the sharing of a human nature with Jesus Christ, who is God "incarnate" in human form. Certainly, that exalted individual, who was often obscured when the human was described only in "total depravity" terms, possessed rights that Christian faith had to assure, it was subsequently and effectively argued in many circles. The exalted individual might indeed belong to the believing community, but his or her individual rights in the West were regarded as being prior to the collective or communal rights that were more appropriately understood as prime with religious tribal communities.

Religious revelation, community, and expression, as these "thickened" discourse about rights, could not solve arguments about them. Religion, it has been argued in the twentieth century as it was by people like James Madison and Baptist elder and rights advocate John Leland in the eighteenth century, can help assure the rights of others. This assurance, say some advocates, need not result because of the obscuring or muting of religious concerns. It is not necessary to reduce them to only highly non-committal, low-conviction, "tolerant" forms of faith in order to make them ready to be brought to bear on the issue.

Indeed, properly understood and cultivated, it might well yet turn out to be the case that it is now often the religions of deep commitment and high conviction that are of greatest aid. In that case, it is not the corrupted heir of eighteenth-century Enlightenment philosophy that best promotes tolerance by arguing that all beliefs have the same claims and quality as all others.

To rephrase the question: How might one best defend the rights of those who serve as the "other" within a religious community? Or, stated more mildly, on what grounds should one urge the "toleration" of those people, with their rights, across the boundaries of community? Make it sound personal: How can I assure you that I will defend your rights and tolerate you despite our differences?

My thesis relates to an understanding or proposal made by Gabriel Marcel—though I do not think it is dependent upon a Marcelian Western

---

[1] Hannah Arendt, *On Revolution* (New York, 1963), 18-19.

existentialist Catholic philosophical framework. The case includes many psychological dimensions, but psychology does not exhaust it. There are valuable intellectual aspects and pragmatic elements. At the very least, what is here adduced is an attempt to use one's *own* religion and religious outlook to help move beyond mere toleration to the defense and assurance of the rights of those in *another* religion who have other outlooks.

Marcel made this proposal in the essay on "The Phenomenology and Dialectic of Tolerance," published in the English translation of his book *Creative Fidelity*.[2] Marcel has uncharacteristically been unable to come up with elegant terminology for his proposal. He calls it "counter-intolerance," for example. This phrase is not easily reduced to bumper-sticker memorability; despite years of reflection I have not come up with much of anything that serves well either. But Marcel's concept strikes me as being valid despite the fact that it is not easy to express positively. Rather than clutter this discussion with many references, I shall concentrate on this one for illustrative purposes, as already made clear.

Marcel argues that "toleration" (translated here to include the concept of defending the rights of someone "within" and "between" religious communities) is not or is not only a psychological reality, but must be approached phenomenologically. One is always tolerant, he argues, *with respect to something*. Tolerance is not mere "non-prevention, non-prohibition," which in our case would mean not merely an attempt to prevent deprivation of the rights of another or to prevent a religion from ruling in prohibitive ways. The truly tolerant one is concerned to do more than "support" your human rights. Thus:

> Tolerance is ultimately the negation of a negation, a counter-intolerance; it seems difficult for tolerance to be manifested before intolerance; tolerance is not primitive; it is to action what reflection is to thought. In any case, it is inconceivable without a certain power which sustains it and to which it is, as it were, attached; the more it is tied to a state of weakness, the less it is itself, the less it is tolerance. It has at least "a vestige of a mandate" connected with it. One is a steward, one has a trust to be responsible about rights of others; one is not merely psychologically moved to be empathic about one whose rights have been taken away. The accent falls less on the sincerity of the "tolerant" one than on the way she acts upon something conceived as a mandate. Tolerance, like intolerance, "is also manifested in the name of . . . in the higher interest of . . ." (which is where religion comes in).

---

[2] Gabriel Marcel, *Creative Fidelity*, trans. Robert Rosthal (New York, 1964).

Thus in the matter of opinion, in our case "opinion" that lies behind the need for rights on the part of women, children, dissidents, and others:

> To the extent that I hold to my opinion, am aware of sticking to it, it may be—provided that I clearly envisage the *other* together with the tie relating him to his opinion—that I put myself in the other's place such that I can conceive his opinion to be worthy just because of the intense conviction with which he holds it; it may be that my awareness of my own conviction is somehow my guarantee of the worth of his, instead of it being the case, that I cannot as a skeptic take seriously any conviction whatever (and if there is tolerance from this point of view, it will be of a degenerate form, to the extent that it is indifferent and nothing more).

Marcel restates this:

> I recognize within myself that the validity of a belief consists in the fact that it expresses my actual being; my subjective reality; hence a belief which is alien to my own will seem to me to be the expression—although different—of another personal reality which must also be safeguarded. [He here discusses rights and proselytism in an informative way—but we leave that for another day.]

> The fundamental question is to determine the principle on which we can base a tolerance which is really a counter-intolerance, but which is not, at the same time, the expression or mark of a complete skepticism, but rather the living incarnation of a faith.

Here it is relevant to revisit the saying that in the world of criminals, it is said of the thief that "it takes one to catch one." In the world of the religiously intense, also, "it takes one to know one." We often see evidence of some admiration on the part of the profoundly committed (for example, to dogma, law, God) across religious boundaries. Marcel introduces us to a world where the intensely religious can "know" another one in the form of the woman, the child, the dissident, who is also full of conviction.

An aside: speaking within a theistic framework that would not satisfy all religions but has some bearing on the three faiths represented in these chapters, Marcel adds—let me paraphrase—in our translation and context: if I act aggressively there will be consequences. It will be discerned that I am "acting out of self-interest and in order to satisfy my desire to proselytize; or, what is still more serious, that I am a servant of a God of prey whose goal it is to annex and enslave. And it is precisely here that we find the frightful betrayal I alluded to earlier: I impose on the person I claim to convert, a loathsome image of the God whose interpreter I say I am."

Marcel would have us move "beyond tolerance," toward the zone of "an absolute religion"; not, "below tolerance," which would be a mere legal-political assurance that minimal rights be allowed the other.

The last thing I would picture is that the spread of ideas of "counter-intolerance" would mean that tomorrow ayatollahs would recall all fat-was, modern popes would agree with modern Catholic feminists, or that Israel's orthodox rabbis would consort with humanistic Jews. Yet the twentieth century *has* on occasion produced people and groups that might be associated with adjectives such as pioneer, frontier, horizontal, experimental, and exemplary. They have attempted to understand and work to assure the rights of others not on the basis of an easy universalism or a tolerance that verges on belieflessness or indifference. Instead, their advocacy is grounded precisely in deep religious commitments that, while particular (or perceived to be such), aspire to the universal.

Rather than name names, I would point to the popes, civil rights workers, Islamic agents of peace, Jews who work for the rights of other Jews and for peace with non-Jews, and spiritually profound discerners who speak and work for "amnesty" and for "political prisoners," at risk to themselves. They do not impose their absolutes or universals on others. They do not even aspire to serve a "God of prey," whether or not they ever make efforts to convert others. But they move beyond empathy and psychology to *understand* the complex of another religion or culture and to work for rights within it. At its best, the modern international rights movements have been based on such approaches. Advocacy of such an approach here is also not to be seen as absolute or exclusive, though one might hope that it would somehow become universal in availability in the various traditions. This elaboration of one approach is only illustrative. It is a bid and beckoning for others to come forth with rationales for defending and assuring rights to dissidents within and beyond one's own religious community and civil culture.

To believe that one can deal with issues of rights while neglecting religion is to lose power to deal with most human beings. To believe that one can deal with them from some supposed neutral point above the religious fray, for example in the name of secular Enlightened republicanism, is to show unawareness that the religions of the world regard Enlightenment reasoners to be one more set of competitors on the religious scene. Therefore, it is my consistent point, one has no choice but to look for the kind of religious assets that Hannah Arendt found Western religionists claiming, after the secular revolution forced or inspired them to do so. They might follow that up with a search for the kind of counter-intolerance that leads the religiously convinced to find a warrant to assure the rights for others, as Marcel urged.

It may be that rights will be most assured when between religious communities, there will emerge symbioses, some common experiences, dialogues that promote understanding, diplomatic relations, anything that causes "criss-crossing" of loyalties. As communities form alliances, they also pick up insights about "the others" and help assure their rights. As members of religious communities engage in conversation they can be surprised into new comprehensions. Then, when the conversation partners take a break, they might see their own faith commitments in new lights.

In every case, one pictures that *when* rights get argued and defended on religious grounds, they can be at least as secure as when the rationale is restricted to the bases proposed by secular rationalism since the Enlightenment. Not indifference to religion or the incomprehensibility of the other, but reflective difference, based on the always ambiguous and problematic but resource-rich religious traditions, can become an instrument for enlarging and assuring human rights. To neglect such a possibility in our religiously crowding and jostling world would seem to be a misreading of the signs of the times and a neglect of potentially positive resources.

Religious Rights:
An Historical Perspective

─────────── ❧ ❧ ───────────

BRIAN TIERNEY[1]
Cornell University

In the years since World War II religious liberty has been proclaimed as a human right in several United Nations documents, and all the major Christian churches have affirmed their commitment to the same ideal. It was not always so. A leading scholar in this field observed recently that "[f]or several thousand years the history of religion was marked by religious intolerance and persecution." After mentioning specifically the persecutions of one another by Christians of various persuasions, he added: "Clearly religion and freedom have not been natural allies."[2] This is the situation we have to bear in mind when we reflect on the historical background to the modern idea of religious rights.

The Western experience that I want particularly to consider is in some ways paradigmatic, since a doctrine of natural rights—or human rights as we say nowadays—first grew up in the Christian West. Of course, all the great religious cultures of the world have given expression to ideals of justice and right order in human affairs, but they have not normally expressed those ideals in terms of subjective natural rights. (It would be hard, for instance, to imagine a Confucian Hobbes or Locke.) Even in the West, a doctrine of religious rights emerged only painfully and belatedly, out of a tradition that had earlier found it much easier to acknowledge other kinds of rights. Nowadays it has become commonplace to maintain, as Pope John Paul II recently asserted, that religious rights are the "cornerstone" of all other rights. But, viewed in historical

---

[1] This chapter includes some paragraphs that I originally published in R. Davis, ed., *The Making of Modern Freedom* (Stanford, 1994). I am grateful for permission from Stanford University Press to use the material here.

[2] James E. Wood, Jr., "Editorial: Religion and Religious Liberty," *Journal of Church and State* 33 (1991): 226.

J. Witte, Jr. and J.D. van der Vyver (eds.), Religious Human Rights in Global Perspective, 17-45.
© *1996 Kluwer Law International. Printed in the Netherlands.*

perspective, religious rights came last; these rights were the most difficult to conceive of, let alone put into practice.

The Roman Catholic Church was the last of the great Christian denominations to embrace wholeheartedly the principle of religious freedom. This at least had the advantage that its leaders could form a mature and well-considered version of the doctrine. Hence the *Declaration on Religious Liberty* of Vatican Council II, promulgated in 1965, provides an appropriate starting point for our discussion:

> This Vatican Council declares that the human person has a right to religious freedom. This freedom means that all men are to be immune from coercion on the part of individuals or of social groups and of any human power . . . the right to religious freedom has its foundation in the very dignity of the human person as this dignity is known through the revealed word of God and by reason itself.[3]

This passage of the *Declaration* referred, in all-embracing fashion, not only to coercion by the state but by "any human power." It defined religious freedom specifically as a "right" and a right inherent in the human person, a natural or human right therefore. This natural right, discernible by human reason, was also said to be rooted in divine revelation and so intrinsic to the Christian faith. The *Declaration* contained only a bland and innocuous hint that these affirmations represented a radical reversal of a policy of religious repression that the Catholic church (and the mainstream Protestant churches too) had maintained for centuries. The hint came in an observation that the demands of human dignity "have come to be more fully known to human reason through centuries of experience." How true these words are can be gathered from a decree of another general council, promulgated in 1215, just 750 years before the *Declaration* of Vatican Council II. This is from the Fourth Lateran Council:

> We excommunicate and anathematize every heresy that raises itself against the holy, orthodox, and Catholic faith. . . . Secular authorities, as they wish to be esteemed and numbered among the faithful, ought to take an oath that they will strive in good faith and to the best of their ability to exterminate all heretics pointed out by the church.[4]

My task as a historian is to try to explain how we got from there to here, from the repression of heretics to a declaration on religious liberty. A skeptic, faced by the two conciliar texts, might observe that the Chris-

---

[3] W.H. Abbot, trans., *The Documents of Vatican II* (New York, 1966), 678-680.

[4] H.J. Schroeder, trans., *The Disciplinary Decrees of the General Councils* (St. Louis, 1937), 242.

tian religion evidently meant one thing in 1215 and something quite different in 1965. A more sympathetic observer might acknowledge that the church has indeed modified its teachings in the course of time but that this is only because the "centuries of experience" that Vatican II mentioned have led on to deeper insights into the truths that were originally proclaimed by the church's founder. As Jacques Maritain observed in discussing human rights, our understanding has increased "as man's moral conscience has developed."[5]

This idea of a growth of understanding in time is not a novel concept, based on modern historicism. In the thirteenth century the Franciscan theologian Peter Olivi wrote of the need for "new explication in the holy church of God—more and more through the course of time—of the sublime truths of faith." Olivi's master, St. Bonaventure, wrote of "seeds" of truth in scripture that slowly ripened in the minds of men, and he added that "Scripture and its mysteries cannot be understood unless the course of history is known."[6] Such writers were not arguing that divine revelation changes, but that human understanding of scripture deepens in the course of the centuries. We might add that some kinds of understanding, it seems, can be achieved only by undergoing specific historical experiences, sometimes harsh and bitter ones. This is especially true when we consider the theme of religious rights.

In the following discussion I want first to consider some aspects of early Christian teaching and then explain how, even in the medieval church, there were some developments of Christian thought that might seem favorable to a growth of religious liberty. (We shall find in the medieval period, for instance, vigorous assertions of the church's freedom from control by secular governments, strong affirmations of the value of individual conscience, and a newly emerging doctrine of natural rights.) Next I will try to explain why, for many centuries, such ideas were outweighed by an apparently insuperable body of counterargument favoring coercion of religious dissidents. Finally, we shall need to consider how a new—or renewed—ideal of religious freedom took root in the early modern era, with a glance at the relevance of all this historical experience for the global problems of our modern age.

The Early Church

From the beginning of the Christian era there were elements in Christian tradition that could lead on either to a doctrine of religious lib-

---

[5] Jacques Maritain, *The Rights of Man and Natural Law* (New York, 1943), 65.

[6] On the views of Olivi and Bonaventure see Brian Tierney, *Origins of Papal Infallibility*, 2d ed. (Leiden, 1988), 72-76, 109-114.

erty or to a practice of persecution. Jesus himself taught a doctrine of universal love. "I say to you, love your enemies, do good to those who hate you" (Matthew 5:44). Jesus disclaimed the role of a political Messiah, relying on coercive force, when he said: "My kingdom is not of this world" (John 18:36). And he offered a new kind of freedom to his followers: "You shall know the truth and the truth shall make you free" (John 5:32). Paul, too, wrote eloquently of "the freedom wherewith Christ has made us free" (Galatians 4:31). And perhaps an ideal of spiritual liberty was always implicit in the Judeo-Christian understanding of the human person as a morally autonomous individual, endowed with conscience and reason and free will. But if an ideal of religious freedom was always implicit in Christian thought, it was certainly not always explicitly asserted. There was always a potentiality for intolerance in the early Christians' disregard for all other religions, their conviction that they alone knew the one true God, that they alone were on the one true path to salvation, that all those outside the church were lost in a world of darkness and sin and error.

Still, a belief in the righteousness of one's own cause does not necessarily imply that one should coerce others into joining it. During the early days of the church Christians generally favored religious toleration, if only because they were so often the victims of persecution; but of course the situation changed dramatically after the emperors themselves became Christians. When Constantine issued the "Edict of Milan" in 313 he granted toleration to the Christian church and to all other religions "so that every man may worship according to his own wish." Later, the emperors adopted a more repressive attitude toward non-Christian religions; but, in the fourth century, Christian apologists like Hilary of Poitiers and Lactantius still defended the principle of religious freedom. And toward the end of the century, St. Martin of Tours bitterly condemned a group of bishops who persuaded the emperor to execute a supposed heretic, Priscillian. Perhaps the case for religious liberty was expressed most eloquently in the words of Lactantius.

> Liberty has chosen to dwell in religion. For nothing is so much a matter of free will as religion, and no one can be required to worship what he does not will to worship.[7]

A decisive turning point in patristic thought came in the teaching of Augustine (354-430). In 395, when Augustine became bishop of Hippo in north Africa, he found the church in that region divided by a bitter schism between orthodox Catholics and a dissident group known as Do-

---

[7] Lactantius, *De divinis institutionibus*, in *Patrologia Latina* (Paris, 1844), 6: col. 1061.

natists. Religious animosities gave rise to frequent civil disturbances, with riots and street fighting in the cities between the two factions. For years Augustine argued that only peaceful persuasion should be used to end the schism. Finally, however, he accepted the view of his fellow-bishops that the civil power should be called in to repress the dissidents. The works he wrote in defense of this policy seem to contradict his earlier writings where he had emphasized freedom in religious matters. But Augustine always maintained that he was seeking only the salvation of the heretics. "It is better to love with severity than to deceive with indulgence," he wrote. Augustine justified the use of coercion against heretics by citing the parable of Jesus about a rich man who prepared a great feast. When none of the intended guests would accept the invitations he sent out, the master dispatched his servants to bring in alternative guests. But the servants told him that there was still room at the table:

> Then the Lord said to the servant "Go out into the highways and hedges and compel them to come in" (Luke 14:23).

The key words for Augustine were the last ones (*compelle intrare*). In his interpretation, the guests who refused their invitations were the Jewish people; those who accepted voluntarily were the Gentiles who became Christians; and those who were "compelled to enter" were heretics who had left the church and could licitly be coerced into returning.[8] Modern historians who have studied Augustine sympathetically point out that he always preferred discussion and persuasion in religious controversies; that he did not favor the harshest penalties against heretics—he did not advocate the death penalty, for instance; that for him the purpose of coercion was not to punish but to win back the heretic to the true faith and so to ensure his ultimate salvation. Less sympathetic historians have designated Augustine as "the prince and patriarch of persecutors" and as "the first theorist of the Inquisition." Certainly his views remained enormously influential throughout the Middle Ages. For a thousand years the church pursued a policy of suppressing religious dissent. Before turning to that theme, however, we need to consider some aspects of medieval religion that could—and eventually did, though only after centuries of struggles and vicissitudes—contribute to a growth of religious freedom.

---

[8] *Writings on the Donatist Controversy. Library of the Nicene and Post-Nicene Fathers*, J. R. King, trans. (New York, 1887), 4:642.

Church and State

The most obvious way in which the leaders of the medieval church contributed (unintentionally of course) to the emergence of modern religious liberty was by their insistence on the freedom of the church from control by temporal rulers. In the Middle Ages there was never just one hierarchy of government exercising absolute authority, but always two—church and state as we say nowadays—often contending with one another, each limiting the other's power. This duality of government was a rather unusual development in human history. In societies larger than a tribal unit or a city-state the most common form of rulership has been some form of theocratic absolutism. The Pharaohs of Egypt, the Incas of Peru, the emperors of Japan were all revered as divine figures. The order of society was seen as a part of the divine order of the cosmos; the ruler provided a necessary link between heaven and earth. Typically, in such societies, religious liberty was neither conceived of nor desired.

Christianity was different from the beginning. It grew up in an alien culture, the sophisticated classical civilization of Greece and Rome. To become a Christian or to persist in the religion was a matter of free personal choice, often involving considerable self-sacrifice. For early Christians, the emperor was not a divine ruler but a persecutor of the true faith. The tension between Roman state and Christian church was expressed classically in the words of Jesus himself: "Render to Caesar the things that are Caesar's and to God the things that are God's" (Mark 12:17). In all ages Christians have remembered, too, the words of Peter: "We ought to obey God rather than man" (Acts 5:29). After the conversion of Constantine and the establishment of a Christian empire there was indeed a possibility for a time that the church might become merely a sort of department of religious affairs in an imperial theocratic church-state. But, as the imperial power crumbled in the West, the independent role of the church was vigorously reasserted by Pope Gelasius (492-496):

> Two there are, august emperor, by which this world is chiefly ruled, the sacred authority of the priesthood and the royal power . . . in the order of religion, in matters concerning the reception and right administration of the heavenly sacraments, you ought to submit yourself rather than rule.[9]

There were *two* authorities in the world; whole areas of religious thought and practice were excluded from the control of the temporal ruler. The text of Gelasius was assimilated into the medieval corpus of canon law and endlessly quoted and discussed in later disputes.

---

[9] Brian Tierney, *The Crisis of Church and State, 1050-1300* (New York, 1964), 13.

The whole issue of empire and papacy arose again when Charle-magne sought to establish a new theocratic empire (c. 800), and his claims were reiterated by his successors of the Ottoman and Salian dynasties of Germany. Claiming to be vicars of God on earth, the kings assumed the right to control their churches; they regularly appointed bishops in the lands they ruled and invested them with the ring and staff that were the symbols of spiritual office. When, from time to time, a German emperor invaded Italy and occupied Rome, he chose and appointed popes, just as he appointed other bishops.

The church seemed to be drifting into another form of theocratic mo-nism. But a dramatic change came in the pontificate of Gregory VII (1073-1085). Gregory condemned the whole existing order of society as radi-cally contrary to divine justice. He declared himself willing to fight to the death for the "freedom of the church," a phrase he used like a kind of battle-cry. To implement his policy, he forbade the prevailing practice of lay investiture (the appointment of bishops by kings) and so inaugurated a struggle that historians used to call the Investiture Contest but that is now often referred to simply as the Papal Revolution. Henry IV, king of Germany and later emperor, denounced Gregory as a pseudo-pope and a heretic; Gregory responded by deposing Henry from his kingship. The fight that ensued between pope and emperor was both a war of propa-ganda and a real civil war in Germany and Italy. At one point Henry had to humiliate himself before the pope at Canossa and humbly beg his for-giveness; but later his armies occupied Rome and drove Gregory into ex-ile. In the end neither side could prevail and, after both of the original protagonists had died, a compromise peace was patched up in the Con-cordat of Worms (1122).[10]

The struggle between popes and kings was reenacted over and over again in the following centuries. After denouncing the theocratic preten-sions of kings, the popes were often tempted to assert a theocratic role for themselves. Sometimes they put forward extreme claims to a kind of overlordship of Christian society in both spiritual and temporal affairs. The point is, however, that such claims were always resisted and never generally accepted by medieval kings or their peoples. The theocratic claims of the papacy reached a high-water mark in Boniface VIII's Bull, *Unam sanctam* (1302), with its uncompromising declaration: "It is alto-gether necessary for every human creature to be subject to the Roman pontiff."[11] But Boniface was defeated and humiliated in the struggle with the king of France that had been the occasion of his pronouncement.

---

[10] Ibid., 53-73.
[11] Ibid., 188.

Because neither side could make good its more extreme claims, a dualism of church and state persisted in medieval society and eventually it was rationalized and justified in many works of political theory. The French theologian, John of Paris, for instance, writing in 1302 (the year of *Unam Sanctam*) wrote a treatise *On Royal and Papal Power* which presented a carefully balanced dualism, assigning to each power its proper function. "The priest is greater than the prince in spiritual affairs," John wrote, "and, on the other hand, the prince is greater in temporal affairs."[12]

The persistent dualism in medieval society that we have described was far removed from a modern "wall of separation." In the Middle Ages, the powers of church and state constantly overlapped and interacted and impinged on one another; but the church remained committed to a radical limitation of state power in the sphere of religion. By the end of the Middle Ages, the Catholic kings had again acquired a large measure of control over church appointments; but, in the Reformation era, the revived theory of royal divine right was challenged by new forms of protest that led to new ways of asserting religious rights.

Freedom of the church from control by the state is one important part of modern religious liberty. But it is only a part. The *libertas ecclesiae* that medieval popes demanded was not freedom of religion for each individual person but the freedom of the church as an institution to direct its own affairs. It left open the possibility, all too fully realized from the twelfth century onward, that the church might organize the persecution of its own dissident members. And, when the interests of church and state happened to coincide, as they often did in dealing with heresy, there was room for a savage suppression of religious dissent. But, even during the centuries of persecution, there were some aspects of medieval thought and practice that could have been conducive to an alternative tradition of religious toleration.

For one thing, medieval canonists and moral theologians often upheld the overriding value of the individual conscience as a guide to right conduct. When Paul wrote: "Everything that is not from faith is sin" (Romans 14:23), the Ordinary Gloss to the Bible (the standard medieval commentary on the text) explained that the words "not from faith" meant "all that is contrary to conscience." In the twelfth century, Peter Abelard expanded the argument. He taught that to act against one's conscience was always sinful, even if the conscience erred in discerning what was right.[13] A century after Abelard, Thomas Aquinas addressed this same

---

[12] Ibid., 209.

[13] *Peter Abelard's Ethics*, D. E. Luscombe, ed. and trans. (Oxford, 1971), 55-57, 67, 97.

question. It might seem that we are not obliged to follow an erring conscience, he wrote, because we are not obliged to obey the command of a lower authority when it conflicts with that of a higher one; but conscience might favor our acting contrary to the law of God, who was the supreme authority. In reply, Thomas quoted the Ordinary Gloss to Romans 14:23 and explained that we are only obliged to follow the command of the higher authority when we *know* that it conflicts with our present judgment. An erring conscience could be formed in good faith if one were ignorant of the higher law. A person was always obliged to do what his conscience discerned as good, even though the conscience might be mistaken.[14]

The same doctrine was taught by the canonists. It was expressed in two judgments of Pope Innocent III (1198-1216) that were incorporated into the corpus of medieval canon law. The Ordinary Gloss to the Decretals, a work studied in law schools throughout Europe, explained their implication. "One ought to endure excommunication rather than sin . . . no one ought to act against his own conscience and he should follow his conscience rather than the judgment of the church when he is certain . . . one ought to suffer any evil rather than sin against conscience."[15]

We are not dealing here with a right to religious liberty but with a duty to obey one's conscience. Still, an emphasis on the primacy of the individual conscience was an important element in later theories of religious rights. The medieval position was that a person was right to follow his conscience but that he might suffer at the hands of the authorities if his conscience led him to illicit behavior. Similarly, in the modern world, individuals may be led by a sincere conscience to violate the law—as in some forms of civil rights or anti-war protest—but the law will hold them responsible for their actions. There is one further point: medieval moralists did not hold that people should act on mere subjective whims. Everyone was required to use the utmost diligence and every resource of knowledge and understanding to form a correct conscience. Failure to do this was sinful. In practice, it was assumed that most cases where an erring conscience led to illicit behavior involved culpable ignorance or culpable negligence.

In one sphere, the emphasis on individual conscience did lead to a degree of religious toleration. Medieval doctrine always taught that non-Christians could not be forcibly converted to Christianity. God's grace was a free gift, and it had to be freely accepted. In practice the only substantial populations of non-Christian people scattered throughout the

---

[14] Thomas Aquinas, *Summa theologiae*, 1.2ae.19.5.

[15] *Decretales Gregorii Papae IX cum glossis* (Lyons, 1624), gloss ad 5.39.44.

Western church were Jewish communities, and the principle of toleration
was explicitly applied to them. The attitude of the medieval church toward the Jews, as toward heretics, was shaped by the teaching of
Augustine, though in this case it had a more benign effect. Augustine
held that, although the Jewish people had erred at the time of Christ, still
it was God's will that they should always survive. They existed to give
permanent independent witness to the divine law revealed in the Old
Testament. They could also attest to the words of the prophets which
Christians understood as foretelling the coming of Christ. (Infidels could
not maintain that the Christians had just made up the prophecies about a
coming Messiah when the Jews also affirmed their reality.) And accordingly, to fulfill this role, some of the Jewish people would exist until the
end of time. The acceptance of this theology shaped the official attitude
of the medieval church toward the Jews. They were indeed discriminated
against—made to wear a distinctive dress, excluded from positions of
authority in government—but they were allowed to have their own
synagogues and to practice their own religion. The attitude of the papacy
was one of toleration, grudging toleration no doubt, but still a recognition that Jews had a right to exist in a Christian society. The policy was
defined by Gregory I (590-604) in a letter that became a part of the permanent canon law of the church.[16] "Just as the Jews ought not to be allowed more than the law concedes," he wrote, "so too they ought not to
suffer harm in those things that the law does concede to them." From the
beginning of the twelfth century onward it became customary for the
Jewish community of Rome to obtain a restatement of Jewish rights from
each new pope at the beginning of his reign. In the real-life world of the
Middle Ages, needless to say, savage outrages against Jewish communities occurred all too often; but they were due to outbursts of mob violence or actions of secular rulers. They were contrary to the law and
teaching of the church.

The Idea of Natural Rights

There was one further area in which medieval thinkers began to develop a doctrine that would be important for later theories of religious
liberty—the idea that all persons possess natural rights.

No consensus exists among modern scholars about the origin of this
doctrine or how it is related to the tradition of Christian thought. Jacques
Maritain simply assumed that the idea of human rights was always implicit in the Judeo-Christian teaching on the dignity and value of each

---

[16] *Decretales*, 5.6.9.

human person.[17] At the opposite extreme, Leo Strauss focused on the supposedly atheistic philosophy of Thomas Hobbes, whom he regarded as the founder of modern rights theories, and concluded that the idea of natural rights was alien to the whole preceding classical and Christian tradition.[18] Disciples of Strauss will still maintain that "[t]he very idea of natural rights is incompatible with Christian doctrine."[19] But this view seems untenable if only because there certainly were Christian natural rights theorists before Hobbes—Suarez and Grotius for instance. An intermediate point of view, that has come to be widely accepted, was put forward by Michel Villey. He held that the idea of natural rights was indeed derived from Christianity but from a distorted and aberrant form of Christian thought, specifically from the fourteenth-century, nominalist and voluntarist philosophy of William of Ockham. Villey argued that Ockham inaugurated a "semantic revolution" when he interpreted the Latin word *ius* (right) as meaning a subjective power (*potestas*).[20] But subsequent research has shown that the association of "right" and "power" was quite common in earlier medieval jurisprudence. Before 1200, for instance, the canonist Huguccio wrote, concerning a bishop-elect: "He has the power (*potestas*) of administering, that is the right (*ius*) of administering."[21]

According to the most recent work, the origin of the later natural rights theories is to be found in the Christian jurisprudence of the late twelfth century, especially in the works of the canonists of that era.[22] The twelfth century was an age of renewal in many spheres of life and thought. New networks of commerce grew up. There was new art, new architecture, a new literature of courtly romance. Religious thought placed a new emphasis on the individual human person—on individual intention in assessing guilt, on individual consent in marriage, on individual scrutiny of conscience.[23] And in the secular sphere, at every level of society we find an intense concern for individual rights and liberties.

---

[17] Maritain, *The Rights of Man*, 64-66.

[18] Leo Strauss, *Natural Right and History* (Chicago, 1950), 166-202.

[19] "Walter Berns Comments," *This World* 6 (Fall, 1983): 98.

[20] Michael Villey, *La formation de la pensée juridique moderne*, 4th ed. (Paris, 1975), 252, 261.

[21] R.L. Benson, *The Bishop-Elect: A Study in Medieval Ecclesiastical Office* (Princeton, 1968), 118, n.5.

[22] Brian Tierney, "Origins of Natural Rights Language: Texts and Contexts, 1150-1250," *History of Political Thought* 10 (1989): 615-646; Charles J. Reid, "The Canonistic Contribution to the Western Rights Tradition: An Historical Inquiry," *Boston College Law Review* 33 (1991): 37-92.

[23] On the juristic implications of these attitudes see especially Harold J. Berman, *Law and Revolution: The Formation of the Western Legal Tradition* (Cambridge, MA, 1983).

Above all, the twelfth century was an age of legal renaissance marked by the recovery of the whole corpus of classical Roman law, and by the first adequate codification of the accumulated canon law of the church in Gratian's *Concord of Discordant Canons*, completed circa 1140. In the following decades a succession of great jurists, inspired by the old texts, found ways to express all the new impulses of their own age in juridical language. For us the crucial development was that the new personalism in religious life, and the everyday concern with rights in secular society, infected the language of the canonists when they came to discuss the concept of *ius naturale*, natural right. Earlier the phrase *ius naturale* had been understood in an objective sense to mean natural law or "what is naturally right." But the canonists who wrote around 1200, reading the old texts in the context of their more humanist, more individualist culture, added another definition. In their writings, *ius naturale* was now sometimes defined in a subjective sense as a faculty, power, force, ability inhering in individual persons. From this initial subjective definition, the canonists went on to develop a considerable array of natural rights. Around 1250 Pope Innocent IV wrote that ownership of property was a right derived from natural law and that even infidels enjoyed this right, along with a right to form their own governments.[24] Other natural rights that were asserted in the thirteenth century included a right to liberty, a right of self-defense, a right of the poor to support from the surplus wealth of the rich.[25] What was still notably lacking was a developed concept of religious rights.

By around 1300 a sophisticated legal language had grown up in which a doctrine of natural rights could be expressed. The next step was the assimilation of the juristic idea of rights into works of political philosophy. William of Ockham was indeed important here. He drew on the earlier canonistic tradition but went beyond it. One of his major contributions was to reshape the scriptural idea of evangelical liberty into a doctrine of natural rights. When Paul wrote about Christian freedom he meant freedom from the law of the Old Testament or freedom from sin, but Ockham used Paul's texts to argue for freedom from any tyrannical government, especially within the church. Not even the pope, he wrote, could injure "the rights and liberties conceded to the faithful by God and nature."[26] Ockham also developed a concept of "suppositional" or contingent natural rights, related to basic human needs, but applied in dif-

---

[24] *Commentaria Innocentii ... super quinque libros decretalium* (Frankfurt, 1570), ad 1.2.7, fol. 3v, and 3.34.8, fol. 429v.

[25] Tierney, "Origins," 638-44.

[26] "An princeps," in *Guillelmi de Ockham opera politica*, H. S. Offler, ed., 3 vols. (Manchester, 1956-74), 1:251.

ferent ways in different circumstances.[27] The idea could perhaps have some relevance for modern problems concerning the applicability of general norms in a world of cultural diversity.

Ockham's ideas were developed further by Jean Gerson, an eminent theologian who wrote around 1400. Gerson gave a very influential definition of *ius* as "a power or faculty belonging to each one in accordance with the dictate of right reason" and argued that, even in man's fallen state, humans retained many such rights.[28] Also, Gerson took up and developed further the idea that Christ's law was a law of liberty. In the existing church this was no longer the case, Gerson complained. On the contrary, Christians were oppressed by an intolerable burden of laws and regulations and obligations imposed by human authority, that is by the church hierarchy. Such enactments were like snares and nets to trap the soul, he wrote.[29] By fusing Paul's doctrine of Christian liberty with his own idea of natural rights, Gerson went on to argue that the essential obligation of a Christian was to accept freely the divinely revealed law of scripture and the natural law that his reason and conscience could discern. In the last resort one could exercise an inherent natural right of self-defense that no human law could take away against any oppressive authority, even an oppressive pope. Gerson's words sometimes have an almost modern sound, and his ideas were indeed very important in the growth of later natural rights theories. They were transmitted to the early modern world mainly by the Spanish scholastics of the sixteenth century, especially in the course of their debates about the rights of American Indians. Bartolomée de las Casas in particular tried to defend the Indians against subjugation and forced conversion by appealing to a doctrine of natural rights based on medieval legal and theological sources.[30]

Given all these aspects of medieval thought—an insistence on the primacy of the individual conscience, a rejection of forced conversion, a nascent theory of natural rights—one might reasonably hope that at least some medieval thinkers would have moved on from these premises to assert a full-fledged doctrine of religious liberty. Nothing of the sort happened. Every medieval writer who discussed this question saw heresy as a sin and a crime that was properly judged by the church and properly

---

[27] H.S. Offler, "The Three Modes of Natural Law in Ockham: A Revision of the Text," *Franciscan Studies* 37 (1977): 207-18.

[28] "De vita spirituali animae," in *Jean Gerson Oeuvres complètes*, P. Glorieux, ed., 10 vols. (Paris, 1960-73), 3: 141-42.

[29] Ibid., 129. On these views of Gerson see Brian Tierney, "Conciliarism, Corporatism, and Individualism: The Doctrine of Individual Rights in Gerson," *Cristianesimo nella storia* 9 (1988): 81-111.

[30] Brian Tierney, "Aristotle and the American Indians—Again," *Cristianesimo nella storia* 12 (1991): 295-322.

punished by the secular power. Even Gerson had no conception of religious freedom as we understand it; indeed, he participated in the trial and burning of John Hus. Gerson could defend the rights of Christians within the church, but it never occurred to him to assert that heretics had rights against the church. Before we can understand how real religious rights emerged in the early modern world, we need to consider why they were so persistently denied in the preceding centuries.

Heresy and Persecution

In his classic little book, *The Whig Interpretation of History*, Herbert Butterfield warned historians against "present-mindedness." We should not impose our own ideas on the past, he urged, but rather seek to understand each historical era "in its own terms." The sort of question we ought to ask, Butterfield suggested, is not: How did we get our religious liberty? But rather: Why were people in former ages so given to persecution?[31] It seems to me that both questions are legitimate ones for a historian, but obviously we cannot begin to address the first question until we have considered the second one. And it is not an easy question to answer.

In the late Roman empire, laws against heresy, sometimes imposing the death penalty on offenders, were enacted by imperial authority. But in the centuries after the fall of the empire there was little organized persecution, though heretics or people suspected of heresy were sometimes lynched by fanatic mobs. When cases came before church courts, the usual penalty was excommunication. A more systematic repression began from the twelfth century onward, even as new doctrines of natural rights were growing into existence. This was partly because of the spread of new heresies and partly because of the growing institutionalization of the church. As the church became more aware of itself as an ordered society with its own system of law and organs of government, it became less tolerant of those who rejected its authority. In 1199, Pope Innocent III declared, in the decretal *Vergentis*, that heresy was equivalent to treason.[32] Heretics were traitors to God, he wrote, just as others guilty of treason were traitors to the emperor. The most threatening heresy of the time was that of the Cathars or Albigensians who had come to dominate substantial areas of southern France. In 1208 Innocent counterattacked by unleashing the Albigensian Crusade, an invasion of southern France by Catholic forces from the north which perpetrated savage massacres in cities that were strongholds of the heretics and effectively destroyed the

---

[31] Herbert Butterfield, *The Whig Interpretation of History* (London, 1931), 18.
[32] *Decretales Gregorii* IX, 5.7.10.

Cathar civilization in Provence. Then, in 1215, Innocent's Fourth Lateran Council issued the general condemnation of heretics that I have already quoted. Secular governments also enacted harsh penalties against heresy. In 1231, Emperor Frederick II decreed that the appropriate punishment was death by burning; the words of his statute indicate the common attitude to heretics:

> Heretics try to tear the seamless robe of our God. They are violent wolves. . . . They are sons of depravity. . . . Therefore we draw the sword of vengeance against them. . . . Committed to the judgment of the flames, they should be burned alive in the sight of the people.[33]

Other rulers enacted similar legislation, and burning at the stake became the common punishment for heresy. About this same time, Pope Gregory IX (1227-1241) first began to commission groups of inquisitors, usually Dominican and Franciscan friars, to seek out and punish heretics. By the mid-thirteenth century, such inquisitors were at work in all parts of the church.

In some areas of political thought, medieval ideas were not so different from our own. Medieval people had quite well-developed concepts of representation and consent and government under law. But, when we turn to the idea of individual religious rights, their whole mindset was so alien to ours that it takes a considerable effort of historical imagination to enter into their world of thought. Perhaps we can find a starting point in a remark of the great legal historian, Frederic Maitland: "In the Middle Ages the church was a state." The church, he pointed out, had its own institutions of government, its own bureaucracy, its own laws and law courts. In the Middle Ages, secular political power was fragmented. The old Roman empire had passed away, and the attempt to found a medieval Christian empire had failed—partly indeed because of the struggle between popes and emperors that we have considered. National monarchies in France and England were only just beginning to grow into existence. The only bond of unity that held Western Christian society together was the bond of a common religion. Nowadays the focus of our loyalty is the state; we look to the state to protect our security and our liberty; to be a "stateless person" in the twentieth century is a most unhappy fate. The other side of the coin is that we do not tolerate people who are perceived of as traitors to the state. We charge them with treason; we inflict punishment on them, sometimes capital punishment in extreme cases. A plea of personal sincerity, that the traitor has acted from good motives, in accordance with his own conscience, is not a sufficient

---

[33] *The Constitutions of Melfi*, J. Powell, trans. (Syracuse, 1971), 7.

defense. Medieval people regarded heretics in much the same way; they held them guilty of treason to the church, and they treated them as traitors. When a common religion defined the whole way of life of a society, to reject it was to cut oneself off from the community, to become a sort of outlaw—and a dangerous outlaw from a medieval point of view.

When Thomas Aquinas first discussed the issue of heresy he began by presenting a series of apparently cogent arguments in favor of toleration.[34] In the first place, there was the parable of the wheat and the tares from Matthew 13. In this story the good grain and the weeds were allowed to grow together until the time of harvest lest, in destroying the weeds, some of the wheat was destroyed too. In commenting on this, Aquinas quoted John Chrysostom, an early church father, who had explicitly interpreted the text as meaning that heretics were not to be killed because, if this were permitted, some of the innocent would probably suffer along with the guilty. Again, Aquinas noted, canon law taught that Jews were not to be forcibly converted. Moreover, faith required the free assent of the will; and God himself had said, through the prophet Ezekiel: "I do not will the death of a sinner." Against all this, Aquinas quoted one text of Scripture, the one Augustine had already used: "Compel them to enter." And Aquinas understood it in the same sense as Augustine. The texts in favor of toleration applied to Jews and infidels; it was true that they could not be converted by force. But those who had already accepted the faith could be compelled to return to it if they fell into heresy. To explain this, Aquinas used the analogy of a vow or promise. A man could not be compelled to take a vow, but if he chose to do so he was obliged to fulfill it. In a later discussion, Aquinas compared heretics to counterfeiters of false money.[35] It was a more serious offense to corrupt the faith than to corrupt the currency, he argued. Hence, just as counterfeiters were executed, so too heretics could be put to death. Sometimes the health of the whole body required that a diseased limb be cut away.

John Noonan, discussing these texts from the standpoint of a lawyer rather than a theologian, has pointed out that they are based on a series of legal fictions and unpersuasive analogies. It was a fiction that persons baptized in infancy had freely vowed to accept the faith; the comparison between counterfeiters and heretics confused the material realm of property with the spiritual realm of truth; and the use of the phrase *compelle intrare* transferred the words from the context of a parable about the kingdom of God to a context of law and earthly jurisdiction.[36] However

---

[34] Aquinas, *Summa theologiae*, 2.2ae.10.8.

[35] Ibid., 2.2ae.11.3.

[36] John T. Noonan, Jr., "Principled or Pragmatic Foundations for the Freedom of Conscience," *Journal of Law and Religion* 5 (1987): 205.

cogent such objections may appear to us, one has to add that the arguments of Aquinas seemed entirely convincing to the medieval audience he was addressing.

Medieval people were so convinced of the truth of their religion that they could never see dissent from the accepted faith as arising simply from intellectual error, from a mistake in judgment. They thought that heresy must somehow stem from malice, from a perverted will that deliberately chose evil rather than good, Satan rather than God. Aquinas wrote: "Unfaithfulness is an act of the intellect, but moved by the will."[37] This was the root cause of the medieval hatred of heresy. The heretics were seen, not only as traitors to the church but as traitors to God. To medieval people it seemed that they had rejected God's truth and God's love out of pride and self-love, the love of their own self-contrived errors. They had set themselves on a path that could lead only to eternal damnation and, unless they were restrained, they would lure countless others to the same terrible fate. Elementary justice and charity, it seemed, required that they be rooted out. The Inquisition that pursued this task with increasingly harsh and cruel measures, including the use of torture to extort confessions, was accepted as a necessary safeguard of Christian society.

Thinking about the Inquisition may remind us of two aphorisms that Lord Acton quoted.[38] The first is the well-known saying of Mme de Staël: "To understand all is to forgive all." The other, less indulgent, is from the Duke de Broglie: "We should beware of too much explaining lest we end up with too much forgiving." Neither aphorism is altogether satisfying for a historian. Our task is surely to understand and explain as fully as possible; but we do not have to condone everything that we have tried to understand; and, when everything possible has been said in mitigation, the medieval theory and practice of religious persecution will seem abhorrent to most modern people. Over a period of centuries, thousands of persons were hunted down, tortured, and killed for a crime that, to us, might seem a mere eccentricity of personal belief.

A critical observer, looking back over the history of the West for the past thousand years and at the policies pursued in many parts of the world during the present century, might suppose that persecution is a normal pattern of human conduct. He might think that Butterfield had got his question upside down after all. Perhaps the real question a historian has to answer is not: Why were they so given to persecution? But

---

[37] Aquinas, *Summa theologiae*, 2.2ae.10.2.

[38] Lord Acton, "Inaugural Lecture," in id., *Lectures on Modern History*, J.N. Figgis and R. V. Laurence, eds. (London, 1906), 27.

rather: Why are we so committed to an ideal of religious liberty? This is the final topic that we have to consider.

The Emergence of Religious Rights

In the context of medieval life, religious persecution seemed both right and necessary. No one could see that "freedom of the church" could mean freedom of conscience for each individual Christian or that the duty to obey one's conscience might imply a right to act in accordance with it, or that a natural right to liberty was radically incomplete if it did not include a right to freedom of religion. The Reformation of the sixteenth century created a new historical context in which all these matters were reevaluated in the light of new understandings of Christian teaching shaped by new historical experiences in the centuries after Martin Luther's first protests.

The changes that came about were not due to any intangible "spirit of Protestantism" or to the specific teachings of the first great reformers. It would indeed be hard to discern any seeds of religious liberty in Luther's rantings against Catholics and Jews, or in Calvin's grim-lipped defense of persecution after the execution of Servetus. Luther, Calvin, Beza, Bullinger, Melanchthon all accepted the entirely conventional view of their time that heretics should be suppressed, just as their Catholic contemporaries did. Moreover, Lutheranism gave Europe the doctrine of the "godly Prince" whose duties included the suppression of idolatry and error; and Calvin introduced a new kind of clerical theocracy that could be as intolerant as the medieval church hierarchy. Religious liberty arose out of a play of contingent events that no one had planned and no one had foreseen.

Thomas Carlyle observed that new historical events do not spring from one single cause but from a whole web of causation, from "all other events, prior or contemporaneous."[39] Then, he noted, the new event combines with all the other ones to give birth to further change. This is the sort of situation we have to deal with in considering religious liberty. Between 1500 and 1700, a new web of causation was created. Europe experienced a series of savagely destructive wars of religion that ended in stalemates and a splintering of religious unity into innumerable competing sects. Eventually, this led on to a growth of national states that could command the loyalty of subjects who professed a variety of religious beliefs. But before that final outcome was achieved, religious groups who rejected an established faith found themselves persecuted in many coun-

---

[39] Thomas Carlyle, "On History," in *Critical and Miscellaneous Essays: Collected and Republished*, 7 vols. (London, 1872), 2:257.

tries—Huguenots in France, Roman Catholics and Puritan separatists in England, Lutherans in the Catholic principalities of Germany, and every kind of dissenter from Catholic orthodoxy in Spain.

In each country, the groups that were being persecuted sought toleration for their own beliefs; but these demands were not at first based on any devotion to religious liberty as such. The right and duty of the ruler to punish religious error was taken for granted; it was just that each group was convinced that it alone held fast to the truth. In England, an anonymous pamphlet of 1615 urged King James I to relax the laws against Puritans but to inflict the death penalty on Catholics.[40] At the other end of the religious spectrum, the Jesuit Robert Parsons protested against an oath of allegiance demanded of Catholics with an eloquent plea against coercion: "For he that should force a Jew or a Turke to sweare, that there were a blessed Trinity . . . against their conscience should synne grievously."[41] But Parsons was defending a church that persecuted religious dissidents wherever it had the power to do so. Each religious group believed that it should be tolerated because it was right and, usually, that its adversaries should be persecuted because they were wrong. Oliver Cromwell said, in a moment of exasperation: "Everyone desires to have liberty, but none will give it."[42] Looking back rather disdainfully on the whole situation, J.N. Figgis wrote of the competing sects: "It was . . . the inability of any single one to destroy the others, which finally secured liberty."[43]

There is truth in this, but it is not quite the whole truth. From the middle of the sixteenth century onward a few voices were raised in defense of a genuine religious freedom. Among Protestant groups, the Anabaptists and Baptists always condemned coercion in matters of religion. And the execution of Servetus for heresy in Calvin's Geneva (1553) evoked a response from Sebastian Castellio, *On Heretics, Whether they Should be Persecuted* that provided the first full-scale argument for freedom of conscience.

A century later, a volatile and complex situation that arose during the English Civil War made England for a time the principal forcing ground for the ideal of religious freedom. The Parliament that defeated Charles I was controlled by Presbyterians who wanted to impose, by force if necessary, a rigorous Presbyterian discipline on the English church. Their po-

---

[40] W.K. Jordan, *The Development of Religious Toleration in England*, 4 vols. (Cambridge, MA, 1932-40), 2:209.

[41] Ibid., 500.

[42] W. Abbott, ed., *The Writings and Speeches of Oliver Cromwell*, 4 vols. (Cambridge, MA, 1937-47), 3: 547.

[43] J.N. Figgis, *Churches in the Modern State* (London, 1913), 101.

sition was summed up in a statement of Thomas Edwards: "A toleration is against the nature of reformation, a reformation and a toleration are diametrically opposite; the commands of God given in his word for reformation do not admit of toleration."[44] But the armies that had won Parliament's victories were filled with members of dissenting sects— Congregationalists, Baptists, Unitarians, Fifth Monarchy Men, Muggletonians, and many others. They all demanded and, under Cromwell, enjoyed for a time a measure of toleration. Moreover, in the vast pamphlet literature that grew up, some spokesmen went further and began to argue for a real religious liberty for all, not just toleration for one group. The Presbyterian Richard Baxter, when serving as a chaplain to one of Cromwell's regiments, noted disapprovingly that, among the soldiers, "their most frequent and vehement disputes were for liberty of conscience as they called it; that . . . every man might not only hold, but preach and do in matters of religion what he pleased."[45] Perhaps the most impassioned plea came from Roger Williams, who had known persecution both in old England and New England. In *The Bloudy Tenent of Persecution*, Williams wrote:

> It is the will and command of God that (since the coming of his Sonne the Lord Jesus) a permission of the most Paganish, Jewish, Turkish, or Antichristian consciences and worships be granted to all men in all Nations and Countries.[46]

It was not unusual for seventeenth-century Protestants to urge toleration for "Jews and Turks." This was just a way of reaffirming the old medieval doctrine against forced conversion. But Williams was exceptional in his willingness to tolerate even Roman Catholics. He wrote that even Catholics had consciences "more or less," and that their consciences were to be respected. A man who converted to Catholicism in good faith might still be a "loving and peaceable" person, according to Williams.[47]

In the early modern world, the practice of persecution was attacked by three main lines of argument which we might characterize as based on skepticism, or on expediency, or on an appeal to the underlying principles of the Christian faith itself. The arguments were not all of equal value. The first two could lead on only to a plea for some limited degree of toleration; only the third could provide a basis for a principled commitment to an ideal of religious freedom.

---

[44] Thomas Edwards, *Antapologia* (London, 1641), 285.

[45] A.S.P. Woodhouse, ed., *Puritanism and Liberty: Being the Army Debates (1647-9) from the Clarke Manuscripts* (Chicago, 1951), 388.

[46] *The Complete Writings of Roger Williams*, 7 vols. (New York, 1963), 3:3.

[47] Ibid., 4:317, 508.

The skeptical approach was rooted in Renaissance humanism. The humanists began by dismissing all the finespun arguments of scholastic philosophy as dreary nonsense; then some of them carried over the same attitude in considering the arcane theological disputes that divided the Christian churches of their own day. This was the underlying attitude of Castellio. (Before writing his treatise on toleration he had composed another work on *The Art of Doubting*.) The skepticism of the humanists was not (at least not at first) a skepticism about the fundamental truths of Christian faith. Castellio wrote: "No one doubts that there is a God, whether He is good and just, whether He should be loved and worshipped. . . ."[48] On the other hand, the things that Christians did not agree about—doctrines concerning predestination, free will, baptism, the eucharist, the Trinity—were matters of controversy precisely because they were not clearly revealed in scripture. The truth about such things could not be known with certainty, Castellio thought. So it was futile and cruel for Christians to persecute one another over these matters. This line of argument was continued by the Italian, Acontius, and then, in mid-seventeenth-century England, by writers like William Walwyn and Francis Osborne.

The Huguenot exile, Pierre Bayle, presented a more radically skeptical attack on religious persecution. His work provides a link between the questioning of the Christian humanists and the more thoroughgoing skepticism of the Enlightenment, when a defense of toleration was often associated with indifference or hostility to all religious teaching. We should not underestimate our debt to the Enlightenment. No doubt, the skeptical mockery of a Voltaire was needed to expose the lingering cruelties and superstitions of established religion. But perhaps in the end skepticism is not enough. Humans are religious animals, and if their old faiths are worn away by too much doubt they are likely to invent new and more savage substitutes. The Enlightenment did not lead on to a new era of peace and harmony; it led to a reign of terror in revolutionary France and a new round of religious persecution.

The second line of argument in favor of toleration was simple expediency. This attitude was typified in Henry IV of France who changed his religion from Protestant to Catholic in order to gain the French crown but then, as a Catholic king, issued the Edict of Nantes (1598) that granted substantial liberties to Protestants. Henry's contemporary, Queen Elizabeth of England, also pursued a religious policy guided mainly by reason of state. Reasons of economic policy were cited too. The Spanish regent in the Netherlands, Don Juan of Austria, wrote in 1577: "The Prince of Or-

---

[48] Sebastian Castellio, *On Heretics*, Roland H. Bainton, trans. (New York, 1935), 294.

ange has always insisted . . . that freedom of conscience is essential to commercial prosperity."[49] The greatest theoretical exponent of the argument from expediency was the political philosopher Jean Bodin. He acknowledged that religious uniformity was desirable, and he did not doubt that the state could lawfully suppress religious dissent; but he argued that, when a new religion had become so entrenched that it could not be suppressed without a danger of civil strife, the most reasonable policy was to tolerate it.[50] A king's duty to maintain the public welfare took precedence over his obligation to uphold religious truth. A problem with the argument from expediency is that, in many circumstances, toleration is not the most obviously expedient course of action. Often it seems that the most effective way to maintain order and unity is to crush dissent. It was a rather unusual set of circumstances in the seventeenth century that made persecution so often ineffective. The argument from expediency left open the likelihood of renewed persecution when circumstances changed again.

The third argument for toleration was ultimately the most important one. Over and over again the idea was asserted—though not indeed generally accepted, for these are still dissident voices—that the practice of persecution was radically contrary to the teaching of Jesus himself. This argument was included in the works of many different thinkers. Castellio wrote of persecution that "Satan could not devise anything more repugnant to the nature and will of Christ." Pierre Bayle argued in a similar fashion. He framed his case for toleration as a commentary on the text, "Compell them to enter," the text that Augustine and Aquinas had used to justify persecution; but Bayle argued in a different spirit that to understand the words of Christ in this way was "contrary to the essential spirit of the Gospel itself."[51] Bayle was a man of skeptical temperament, but the same kind of argument was put forward by writers of fervent religious faith. Roger Williams presented various considerations in favor of religious freedom, but the fundamental one was that persecution was "directly contradicting the spirit and mind and practice of the Prince of Peace."[52]

The awareness that religious liberty needed to be grounded on Christian principles as well as on pragmatic considerations of expediency was well expressed in an English pamphlet of 1614. The author wrote: "A

---

[49] Quoted in H. Kamen, *The Rise of Toleration* (London, 1967), 149.

[50] Jean Bodin, *Six Books of the Commonwealth*, M. J. Tooley, trans. (Oxford, 1955), 4.7, 140-142.

[51] Castellio, *On Heretics*, 123; *Pierre Bayle's Philosophical Commentary*, A.G. Tannenbaum, trans. (New York, 1987), 1.3, 42.

[52] Williams, "Bloudy Tenent," in id., *Complete Writings*, 3:219.

man would think we had been schooled and whipt long enough to it by our calamities." That is to say, recent practical experience had shown the ill-effects of persecution. But the author added at once that "liberty of conscience is no new doctrine." Rather, he declared, it was "as old certainly as the blessed word of God."[53] The new exigencies of the time led discerning Christians to understand more deeply the implications of their old faith. The more learned authors quoted the early patristic texts in favor of religious freedom. Often the parable of the wheat and tares was cited as an argument for toleration. A Baptist pamphlet of 1661 declared that liberty of conscience was "a part of the Christian religion."[54] In the Netherlands, Dirck Coornhert, arguing against the skeptical views of Justus Lipsius, defended religious freedom as a part of the authentic teachings of Christ, and insisted that the truth of those teachings could be known with certainty.[55] Among the English writers, John Milton took up St. Paul's texts about Christian liberty, the texts that Ockham and Gerson had appealed to earlier, and derived from them an argument that the use of force in matters of faith was contrary to "the very weightiest and inmost reasons of Christian religion."[56]

In this new climate of opinion, when persecution was increasingly condemned as contrary to the teachings of Jesus, all the old medieval strands of argument about the freedom of the church from secular control, the overriding authority of conscience, and the existence of natural rights were taken up again and woven into new patterns. These arguments, I suggested earlier, could all have been conducive to a doctrine of religious liberty, but in the context of medieval life they never led on to that result. In the post-medieval world, in a new historical context, the arguments were carried further to conclusions that perhaps had always been implicit in them but that had never been explicitly affirmed.

The old claim that the church ought not to be controlled by secular rulers was now taken to mean that the civil magistrate had no right to interfere with any person's choice of religion. Protestant dissenters often

---

[53] "Religion's Peace," in E.B. Underhill, ed., *Tracts on Liberty of Conscience and Persecution (1614-1661)* (London, 1846), 10-11. The anonymous author continued, "War and its miseries have overspread all lands. Love, meekness, gentleness, mercy, the truest badges of Christianity, have been damned and banished; and, in their room, cruelty, hard-heartedness, respect of persons, prisons, tortures, etc., things that our blessed Lord and Master, and his apostles never (ap)proved . . . have had great sway for these many hundred years."

[54] "Sion's Groan," in Underhill, ed., *Tracts*, 379.

[55] Justus Lipsius argued that, since the truth concerning the matters that divided the Christian sects could not be known anyway, the civil magistrate was justified in punishing dissenters from an established church. Skepticism did not always lead to toleration! On the views of Lipsius and Coornhert see R. Tuck, *Philosophy and Government, 1572-1651* (Cambridge, 1993), 58.

[56] Woodhouse, *Puritanism and Liberty*, 227.

pointed out that the magistrate was no more infallible than the pope or
the bishops. It followed that, as William Walwyn observed, "he who is in
an error may be the constrainer of him who is in the truth."[57] Another argument against government coercion of religion pointed out that progress in the understanding of divine revelation could be achieved only
through free and reasoned discourse. When Milton wrote of "the reforming of the Reformation itself" in a coming new age, he was arguing
specifically for freedom of the press.[58] Medieval theologians had sometimes envisaged a gradual progress in the understanding of scripture
through the course of the centuries. The new insight was that such progress required freedom of thought and expression.[59]

The view that any meaningful freedom of the church required that
the civil magistrates refrain from interfering in matters of religion was
widespread among members of the separatist groups in England. During
the army debates held at Whitehall in 1648, one of them declared: "No
man or magistrate on the earth hath power to meddle in these cases."[60] A
Leveller pamphlet written in the following year set out the same doctrine
that the First Amendment would eventually proclaim for Americans:

> [W]e do not impower or entrust our said representatives to . . .
> compell by penalties or otherwise any person to any thing in or
> about matters of faith, Religion or Gods worship or to restrain
> any person from the profession of his faith, or exercise of his Re-
> ligion according to his conscience. . . .[61]

Roger Williams, arguing against any sort of unified church-state, introduced the phrase "wall of separation" when he wrote of a "wall of separation between the Garden of the church and the Wilderness of the
world."[62]

Another strand of medieval argumentation that underwent radical
development in the early modern era concerned the authority of the individual conscience. In the middle of the seventeenth century, the prevailing view was still that religious disagreements sprang "from malice,

---

[57] W.B. Haller, *Tracts on Liberty in the Puritan Revolution, 1638-1647*, 3 vols. (New York,
1934), 3:70.

[58] John Milton, *Milton: Areopagitica*, J.W. Hales, ed. (Oxford, 1904), 45.

[59] Milton's contemporary, John Goodwin, also developed the idea of a progressive understanding of scripture. For him, "Revelation was an unfinished but progressive process of
indefinite duration." See W.B. Haller, *Liberty and Reformation in the Puritan Revolution* (New
York, 1955), 252.

[60] Woodhouse, *Puritanism and Liberty*, 141.

[61] "An Agreement of Free People," in W.B. Haller and G. Davies, eds., *The Leveller
Tracts, 1647-1653* (New York, 1944), 323.

[62] Williams, *Writings*, 1:392.

rooted in sin."[63] But by then alternative opinions were also being expressed. The Latitudinarian Anglican, Chillingworth, declared in 1638:
"An honest man . . . a true lover of God, and of his truth . . . may embrace
errour for truth."[64] In the subsequent years of civil war it became increasingly difficult for men of good will and good sense to believe that
their neighbors, sometimes men they had fought with side by side in a
common cause, were really inspired by active malice to do the work of
the devil because of a disagreement about some obscure point of theology. Yet this belief in the malice of the dissenter had been the essential
basis of the medieval abhorrence of heresy. When differences of religious
opinion could be seen as effects of intellectual error rather than of perverted will, the way was open to reconsider the proper attitude to a mistaken conscience. William Walwyn took up the text "Whatever is not of
faith is sin," the same text that medieval authors had used to defend the
primacy of conscience, but arrived at a conclusion that no medieval
theologian had reached: "[E]very man ought to have Liberty of Conscience of what Opinion soever."[65] Walwyn argued that a person's conscience could be directed only by his own individual reason. A person
could not be compelled to believe as true something that reason and conscience told him was false. If, under compulsion, he acted against his
conscience, he sinned; but, and this was the new twist to the argument,
the one who compelled him was a party to the sin and was acting like a
tyrant.[66] This became a common argument among those who defended
freedom of conscience. Even an extreme royalist like Michael Hudson argued that a magistrate who compelled a man to act against his conscience
forced him to commit the sin of hypocrisy, and that the magistrate himself was guilty of "sacrilegious intrusion upon those sacred prerogatives
which God hath preserved unto himself."[67] The Anglican divine Jeremy
Taylor argued at length that a person who followed an erring conscience
did not sin in doing so and, again, concluded with a plea for religious
freedom: "If God will not be angry at men for being invincibly deceived,
why should men be angry one at another?"[68] Sometimes the forcing of a
person's conscience was compared to physical rape; in the pungent language of Roger Williams it was "spirituall and soule rape."[69]

---

[63] Haller, *Liberty and Reformation*, 251. This was the opinion that John Cotton still maintained in his dispute with Roger Williams. See Williams, *Writings*, 3:42.

[64] W. Chillingworth, *The Religion of Protestants* (Oxford, 1638), 21.

[65] Haller, *Tracts on Liberty*, 3:67.

[66] Ibid., 3:71, 86.

[67] Hudson's views are discussed in Tuck, *Philosophy and Government*, 270.

[68] Jordan, *Toleration*, 4:405.

[69] Williams, "Bloudy Tenent," 3:219.

The final outcome of all the new argument about conscience was a fusion of the new ideal of religious liberty with the older doctrine of natural rights. Freedom of conscience came to be seen as one of the natural rights of man, guaranteed by natural law and discernable by the "light of reason" or "light of nature." The parliamentary leader, Henry Vane, for instance, asserted that freedom of religion could be claimed "upon the grounds of natural right."[70] Roger Williams has also been called an extreme exponent of natural rights because of his all-embracing argument for freedom of conscience,[71] but this seems to be a misunderstanding of his position. I do not think Williams ever used the language of natural rights.[72] William Penn, however, did so, and with "classic clarity," according to Searle Bates. Penn wrote: "I ever understood an impartial liberty of conscience to be the natural right of all men. . . ."[73] He argued that the people did not and could not give up this natural right to any government formed by the original contract that first established a political society. Hence, subsequently, government could have no lawful power to invade this right of the individual. As one might expect, the constitution of Pennsylvania in due course echoed the words of the founder and proclaimed "a natural and unalienable right" to freedom of worship. As a Quaker, Penn stood outside the mainstream of the religious thought of his age, but his eminently respectable contemporary, Bishop Burnet, expressed a similar view: "I have long looked on liberty of conscience as one of the rights of human nature, antecedent to society, which no man could give up. . . ."[74] Going back to the roots of Christian tradition Burnet also undertook a translation of Lactantius and, in his preface to it, again argued for toleration. John Locke, too, in his influential *Letter Concerning Toleration*, wrote that "liberty of conscience is every man's natural right."[75] Outside England, Pierre Bayle defended the rights of conscience,[76] and Spinoza drew on his own idiosyncratic doctrine of natural rights in asserting an inalienable right to freedom of religion.[77]

---

[70] Henry Vane, *A Healing Question Propounded* (London, 1656), 5.

[71] Haller, *Tracts on Liberty*, 1:60.

[72] Williams relied on his own idiosyncratic understanding of scripture rather than on any appeal to natural rights in defending religious freedom. He inveighed against the "light of nature" in "The Examiner Defended," in Williams, *Writings*, 7: 242, "Come to the light of nature—and then I ask, if it be not a downright Doctrine of Free-will, in depraved nature?"

[73] M. Searle Bates, *Religious Liberty: An Inquiry* (New York, 1945), 297, quoting William Penn, *England's Present Interest Discovered* (London, 1679).

[74] Gilbert Burnet, *History of My Own Times*, 6 vols. (Oxford, 1823), 5:107.

[75] John Locke, *A Letter Concerning Toleration*, M. Montuori, ed. (The Hague, 1963), 95.

[76] Bayle, *Philosophical Commentary*, 161, 173, 193.

[77] "A Theologico-Political Treatise," in R.H.M. Elwes, ed., *The Chief Works of Benedict de Spinoza*, 2 vols. (London, 1883), 1:257.

By the end of the seventeenth century, reasonably adequate theories of religious rights had been formulated. Implementing them took much longer. Persecution became more sporadic in the eighteenth century, but it was not until the liberal revolutions of the nineteenth century that freedom of religion became widely established in the constitutions of Western states and not until the twentieth century that the major Christian churches proclaimed religious rights as an essential feature of the Christian faith itself.

Conclusion

The peoples of Western Europe slowly learned, through centuries of cruel experience, to acknowledge at least the practical necessity of tolerating religious differences among Christians; and, at best, they came to see religious freedom as an ideal inherent in their traditional faith. We need to ask in conclusion what relevance this distinctively Western Christian experience can have for a world of many religions and diverse cultures.

Some critics have suggested that all the brave new pronouncements about human rights, including religious rights, simply inflate Western concepts into universal values and then assume without question that such values are valid for all other societies, regardless of their histories and cultures. Perhaps, it is suggested, this is just another kind of Western chauvinism. On the other hand, it is evident that the whole world has willingly accepted some aspects of Western culture, notably Western technology. And Wolfgang Huber has argued that it would be merely arrogant for the West to export its material culture on a worldwide scale while assuming that other societies are incapable of appreciating Western ideals or learning from Western experience.[78] Technology itself, we may note, is a product of several centuries of distinctively Western cultural evolution; but the fruits of technology—a computer or an internal combustion engine—can easily be replicated in societies with quite different cultural traditions. The situation is evidently more complex when we consider the fruits of Western religious experience; it is easier to export an artefact than to implant an ideal. And certainly, in this sphere, communication could not be along a one-way highway. The West had to learn—or relearn—the practice of nonviolence from India, through Mahatma Ghandi. Modern Western ideas, including religious ideas, on respect for the environment and for all species of life, have been shaped in part by currents of Buddhist thought. Moreover, we should not expect to

---

[78] Wolfgang Huber, "Christianity and Democracy in Europe," *Emory International Law Review* 6 (1992): 35-53.

find Western ways of institutionalizing religious rights duplicated exactly in any African or Asian society (and, indeed, the institutional arrangements vary a great deal in the West from country to country).

Yet, for all this, the actual state of the world suggests that the lessons
the West learned so painfully may indeed have a universal relevance.
Evidently, the global utopia envisaged in the various United Nations
pronouncements has not yet arrived. In some countries religious minorities are openly persecuted or at best denied full civic rights. New forms
of religious fundamentalism inspire hatred and fear of all those outside
the chosen group. In many regions, from Northern Ireland to Sri Lanka—
in the republics of the former Soviet Union, in what was once Yugoslavia,
in parts of the Islamic world—ancient religious animosities have fused
with ethnic rivalries to produce new and explosive socio-religious compounds. The resulting violence ranges from individual assassinations to
large-scale massacres to outright civil war. Religious conflict is a major
cause of global disorder in the modern world. The recognition of religious rights is a necessity if a more peaceful world-order is ever to be
achieved.

Obviously, all societies cannot reenact the specific experiences of
early modern Europe that shaped the modern idea of religious rights;
and indeed that would be a dismal prospect. But during the present
century, people in all parts of the world have experienced for themselves
the grievous effects of religious conflict and religious persecution. It
would certainly be expedient to end such savageries. One might think
that we too should have been "schooled and whipt by our calamities"
into recognizing this. And perhaps a certain skepticism might be an appropriate response to the claims of the more fanatical fundamentalists.
But modern pragmatism and modern skepticism seem insufficient to as-
suage the existing conflicts within religions and between religions. Perhaps the only answer for all peoples is the one that Christians discovered
so painfully when they compared the words of Jesus with all the hatreds
and cruelties of their contemporary world; that is, the need for a return to
the original sources of religious tradition and a reconsideration of their
implications in the light of our accumulated centuries of experience.
Modern Christian pronouncements on religious rights base those rights
on the dignity of human beings as children of God. But Mohammed, too,
said: "Verily we have honored every human being." Jesus told us to love
those who hate us, but Gautama Buddha also declared: "Hatred does not
cease with hatred; hatred ceases only with love." Among all the founders
of the great world religions we can find an attitude of respect and compassion for the human person that is the best argument—the only ultimately compelling one—for religious liberty. Often contingent historical

circumstances have distorted human understanding of the original revelations and intuitions that lie at the root of our religious traditions. Perhaps the best antidote for all the false fundamentalisms of our age might be a true fundamentalism, a return to the words and spirit and example of the great founders.

Human Rights and Biblical Legal Thought

WOLFGANG HUBER

Lutheran Bishop of Berlin-Brandenburg

I t is astonishing how long it took Christian theologians both to give a proper and substantive interpretation of modern human rights and to inquire in what sense modern human rights are influenced by a Biblical understanding of law. Only in the 1970s did such research begin in earnest, motivated by two interests. First, there was an interest to clarify the motives for Christians and churches to promote human rights and to practice solidarity with the victims of oppression and alienation. Second, there was a great debate whether modern human rights truly can be called "universal," when such rights are obviously related to the specific cultural and religious traditions of Judaism, Christianity, and the Western Enlightenment. Both questions were of great importance, both theoretical and practical, for a consistent understanding of the universality of human rights was necessary to motivate individuals and associations to work for human rights.

In recent years, a third perspective has added further weight to the question of the religious roots of modern human rights. This is the debate on a "global ethic" or—as I prefer to call it—a "planetary ethos."[1] The manifold crises of our times demand common ethical convictions for present humanity. Religions are being asked to contribute to the cultivation of this planetary ethos based on their specific traditions. In this context, the question is to what extent human rights can be understood as basic elements of such a planetary ethos. This debate has given new urgency and implications to the question of the relationship between "universal" human rights and different religious and cultural traditions.[2]

---

[1] See Hans Küng, *Das Projekt Weltethos* (München, 1991); Wolfgang Huber, *Die tägliche Gewalt. Gegen den Ausverkauf der Menschenwürde* (Freiburg im Breisgau, 1993).

[2] For a general overview, see Ronald Traer, *Faith in Human Rights: Support in Religious Traditions for a Global Struggle* (Washington, 1991).

J. Witte, Jr. and J.D. van der Vyver (eds.), Religious Human Rights in Global Perspective, 47-63.

In this chapter, I shall try to clarify the relationship between modern human rights and the Biblical ethos.[3] The influence of the Biblical Torah on Christian legal thought and on contemporary human rights theory certainly needs to be clarified. Some scholars have adopted a rather simplistic view, stating that modern human rights are simply Old Testament legal traditions in a new guise.[4] In reality, the connections between the Bible and modern human rights are much more subtle. The way to evaluate the impact of Biblical traditions on our understanding of law is a complicated task—though the effort has been facilitated by new investigations on the development of concepts of law in the Biblical traditions themselves. The research done, for example, by Frank Crüsemann on the historical process by which the body of Biblical law steadily incorporated new fields and subjects of interpretation, culminating in the Torah, demonstrates the insufficiency of a concept which declares simply that the Decalogue, as the timeless summation of the Torah, can be applied regardless of consequences to questions of our time.[5] We must be consistent in our historical understanding not only of the Torah but also of how Biblical legal thought affected the development of law in Europe and later in America.

I have divided this chapter into three parts. First, I shall describe the path by which the Biblical impulse came to affect legal thought in the European and American West. Second, and related, I shall address the question as to what connects human rights theory with the Torah and what distinguishes them from one another. Finally, I shall turn to the current debate over what religion can contribute to further development of human rights theory and beyond that to a planetary ethos.

The Biblical Motif and Western Legal Thought

The path by which the Biblical motif affected Western legal development can be roughly divided into five stages.[6] The *first stage* commenced with the Christianization of the Roman Empire, a process that ap-

---

[3] For the framework of my theological approach to a human rights theory see W. Huber and H.E. Tödt, *Menschenrechte: Perspektiven einer menschlichen Welt*, 3d. ed. (München, 1988).

[4] See, e.g., F. Crüesemann, "Tora und christliche Ethik," in R. Rendtorff and E. Stegeman (hrsg.), *Auschwitz, Krise der christlichen Theologie: Eine Vortragsreihe* (München, 1980), 159, 171ff.

[5] Frank Cruesemann, *Die Tora: Theologie und Sozialgeschichte des alttestamentlichen Gesetzes* (München, 1992), esp. 409ff., 423ff.

[6] For an example where the history of Western marriage and family law is divided into these five stages of development, see John Witte, Jr., "The Reformation of Marriage Law in Martin Luther's Germany, Its Significance Then and Now," *Journal of Law and Religion* 4 (1986): 293 and id., "A New Concordance of Discordant Canons, Harold J. Berman on Law and Religion," *Emory Law Journal* 42 (1993): 523, 548ff.

proached its zenith with the conversion of Constantine. Legal institutions, often closely connected with the Roman state religion, were transformed to reflect Jewish and Christian ideas of morality. This transformation is most clearly shown in the institution of marriage, which was now conceived as a heterosexual, monogamous, and lifelong union. The extent to which such legal changes reflected the Old Testament and Judaism or the New Testament and Christianity was not at the time considered a significant question. Events of this type were perceived as part of the Christianization of the Roman Empire against a background of the disinheritance of Judaism. In terms of dialectics, this Christianization of the Roman empire effected simultaneously the secularization of Christianity and the definitive emancipation of Christianity from its Jewish roots. The radical nature of the Christian mission was thereby weakened. Even the ideas it incorporated of a right created from the perspective of the weak were adapted to the prevailing power structure.

The *second stage* of the influence of the Biblical motif on Western legal development came with the events that Harold J. Berman has called "the Papal Revolution" of circa 1050 to 1200.[7] The Papal Revolution brought a comprehensive systematization of legal rules—a concordance of discordant canons in various legal fields. In the *Decretum Gratiani* of 1140, this process was first applied to canon law and eventually carried over into other legal fields. The medieval adoption of Roman legal ideas ensued in accordance with such ideas on the inner coherence of legal rules. By grounding this newly systematized law in principles of natural law, medieval writers simultaneously stated the authority that guaranteed the inner consistency of the law. As the principles of natural law could be discovered by revelation but could also be recognized through the use of reason, this step itself implied an epochal emancipation from the Biblical roots of Western legal thought. The secularization of Western legal thought thus began definitely not in the modern period, but with the transformations born of Constantine as well as the Papal Revolution.

Particularly momentous was the image of the human person that guided Western legal thought from the Papal Revolution onwards. The person was conceived as an individual—more precisely as a Christian individual, for personhood was established through the act of baptism.[8]

---

[7] Harold J. Berman, *Recht und Revolution: Die Bildung der westlichen Rechtradition* (Frankfurt am Main, 1991), 144ff.

[8] This opinion was summarized and stressed in a canon of the Codex Iuris Canonici of 1917, to which Hans Dombois has repeatedly drawn attention: "Baptismate homo constituitur in Ecclesia Christi persona" (CIC 1917 c. 87). See Hans Dombois, *Das Recht der Gnade* (Witten, 1969), 1:309ff.

This definition of a person had implications not only for the ecclesiastical field but for political community as well. Baptism signified the commencement of civil rights (in many areas as late as the nineteenth century). Moreover, according to the decisions of the Fourth Lateran Council of 1215, civil rights could be claimed only by those who, after baptism, participated in confession and holy communion at least once a year, namely at Easter. With excommunication, consequently, one lost association not only with the ecclesiastical community but also with the political community and its civil rights.

This new concept of the person introduced into Western legal thought also allowed for a new classification between various groups of persons. On the one hand, a distinction was drawn between Christians and the unbaptized or excommunicated, that is, the Jew, the heathen, and the heretic. A further distinction was drawn between holders of the power of jurisdiction in ecclesiastical and lay arenas. In this context, the *Decretum Gratiani* spoke conclusively of two species of Christians (*genera Christianorum*). The clerical *genus* was comprised of priests and monks. The lay *genus* was comprised (in a negative sense) of those who held no power of jurisdiction and (in a positive sense) of those who had permission to engage in secular activities.[9] Finally, distinctions with respect to both *genera Christianorum* were drawn between men and women, who within the framework of a patriarchal structure of church and society were accorded very different rights and obligations.

Although the Papal Revolution substantially shifted the concept of the individual human person to the center of the legal system, it was still far removed from the idea of universal human rights. The division of the church into two species, the corporate classification of society, and the exclusion of the unbaptized and excommunicated from both ecclesiastical and civil rights foreclosed any idea that there was one set of rights equally applicable to all men. Thus even the English Magna Carta of 1215, so frequently taken as the harbinger of the modern catalogue of human rights,[10] was not a universal but rather a corporate declaration of rights. It codified those rights that the English barons had wrung from King John.

The *third stage* of the influence of the Biblical motif on Western legal development came with the Protestant Reformation. The secularization which the Reformation effected for the perception of reality applied

---

[9] See Wolfgang Huber, "Kirche in der Welt: Zum Verhältnis von Laien und Theologen in der Kirche," in G. Grohs and G. Czell (hrsg.), *Kirche in der Welt: Kirche der Laien?* (Frankfurt am Main, 1990), 11-26.

[10] Thus, for example, its text is reproduced in W. Heidelmeyer (hrsg.), *Die Menschenrechte: Erklärungen, Verfassungsartikel, Internationale Abkommen* (Paderborn, 1972), 471ff.

equally to law. The Reformers recognized the autonomy of legal relationships against ecclesiastical claims of authority. They also deprived the celibate status of priests of any superiority over the life of married laymen. At least in the initial stages of the Reformation, the estates changed from hierarchical principles of social classification to groupings at an equal level of fields of responsibility in Christian life. Freedom of conscience and of religion were recognized as those frontiers at which claims of authority by the political power should find their limit. In the sectarian conflicts that followed the Reformation the view persisted, in the face of constantly renewed resistance, that the rights of the human person would win respect only where freedom of conscience was acknowledged. Together with the impetus of Renaissance humanism and late scholasticism, the Reformation paved the way for a turning point in the human image that urged recognition of the equal dignity of all men.[11] Now the idea emerged that all men possess equal rights before the state, namely those of life, liberty, and property, which cannot be taken from them either by social contract or by state power. The self-determination of every human person that should thereby be ensured had particular impact in the religious field.[12] To this extent religious freedom from the outset stood at the center of modern human rights theory.

The sectarian conflicts that followed the Reformation certainly had a further effect, which takes us to the *fourth stage* of this path. Since the struggle over the truth of the faith led not simply to disputes but also to bloody war, Western writers came to the conviction that the state legal system must be constructed on some other basis than that of religion. This turning point became evident in the design of the state prescribed by Thomas Hobbes' *Leviathan*, equally so in the famous thesis of Hugo Grotius that a legal system must continue even if we assume that God does not exist (*etsi Deus non daretur*).[13] The state itself should be the source of the law. The era of positivism was at hand. This stage can be characterized as a time of nationalization of the law. It provoked a demand for counterpoises to state authority. Such counterpoises were seen in the human and civil rights that were first formally codified following the American and French revolutions.

The influence of Judaic and Christian heritages on these developments varied. The American declarations of rights arose from a spirit of

---

[11] For further consideration of the following developments, see Wolfgang Huber, "Menschenrechte/Menschenwürde, " *Theologische Realenzyklopädie* (Berlin, 1992), 22: 577-602, esp. 578ff.

[12] See especially John Locke's *Two Treatises of Civil Government*, published in 1690.

[13] For further discussion of Grotius and Hobbes, see W. Huber and H.-R. Reuter, *Friedenethik* (Stuttgart, 1990), 79ff.

Christian Enlightenment, which in particular converted the thought that all men are created equally in the image of God to the conviction that all men are by nature born free and equal. The French declarations of human and civil rights were, on the one hand, influenced by developments in America but, on the other hand, marked by an anticlerical enmity against Christianity—and hence also against Christianity's Jewish roots. This heightened the impression that Christian legal thought and modern awareness of human rights are worlds apart. Through this prejudice Christian theology in Europe for more than a century and a half locked itself out from access to constructive adoption and interpretation of human rights.

The Age of Enlightenment, to which we owe the first modern catalogue of human rights, also saw the creation of the preconditions for the *fifth stage* of Biblical influence on the Western legal consciousness. These preconditions lay principally in the rediscovery of human subjective responsibility and autonomy. The independence of human self-determination from all claims of authority—godly as well as worldly—was the decisive postulate of the Enlightenment. The decisive conclusion was that all claims to validity must be created anew in the rationality of the human subject. Ambivalent though its preconditions and its effects might be, this idea provided a definitive contribution to recognition of the human person in its legal subjectivity as the decisive reference point for legal thought. Yet in the constitutional systems of many states this idea made a very gradual appearance, and it was more than a century and a half before it became a decisive component of international law with the Universal Declaration of Human Rights of 1948. The horror towards both the unfathomable violence of Nazism and the terror of Stalinism contributed decisively to the acceptance of the idea of the legal subjectivity of the individual in the international community of nations. The breakthrough achieved in the Universal Declaration of Human Rights of 1948 subsequently acquired concrete form through regional human rights treaties and international conventions, particularly the United Nations covenants of 1966.

The development of human rights is not bound exclusively to these five stages, but human rights cannot be understood without consideration of the ideas set out in each of these stages. The relationship of human rights to the motif of the Torah and its elaboration by Christians is much more involved than can be perceived in a simple secularization scheme. Secularization theories generally argue that, up to the threshold of modern times, Christianity retained its religious character, then underwent a process of secularization through the power of autonomous reason, thereby losing contact with its origins. At least as to Christianity's influence on the development of law, however, the story is much more complicated. On the one hand, Biblical legal thought had already undergone a number of transformations in developments during the pre-modern era, each with its own secularizing impulse. On the other hand, even in the modern era, legal development was marked not merely by *one* process of secularization but by two overlapping developments, which I characterize as *nationalization* and *subjectivization*.

In all five of these periods, reference to the Biblical tradition did indeed occur. The Biblical tradition was frequently cited—if nothing else to legitimate the legal status quo. This suggests a caveat: modern law, including modern human rights theory, can be coupled with Biblical legal thought only from afar and at the level of principle. On the one hand, Biblical legal thought should not be used simply to define and legitimate the structure and content of modern legal systems. On the other hand, it is incorrect to separate the legal system from the question of the theological basis for its validity and to leave it to its "self-legality." Contemporary legal systems and Biblical legal thought cannot be isolated from each other in a model of separation.

An adequate understanding of the proper relationship of modern legal systems to Biblical legal thought today requires critical reflection—a critical view of contemporary relationships from the perspective of Biblical thought and a critical view of the offerings of Biblical thought from the perspective of contemporary experiences and opinions. Hermeneutical honesty demands that we theologians concern ourselves with such processes of mutual criticism. No other passable way is in sight for the development of a theological ethic of law. For both the confluence and the separation of modern legal systems and Biblical legal thought will lead in equal measure to an impassable thicket.

Two developments suggest that we find ourselves today on the threshold of a *sixth stage* in the encounter between Biblical legal thought and Western legal systems. First, there are many signs that the process of modern subjectivization and individualization is bringing self-destructive consequences. It now seems unavoidable that we must take a new direction, to venture once again to think about the common good, the community, the environment, and a viable future.[14] We need to think anew about the common bond between individuality and social consciousness in human understanding, to acknowledge a human subjectivity that includes the acceptance of obligations to the community. Such thought requires a concept of human self-unfolding that includes maintaining the conditions of communal life in nature and society. Such

---

[14] See, e.g., H.E. Daly and J.B. Cobb, Jr., *For the Common Good: Redirecting the Economy toward Community, the Environment, and a Sustainable Future* (Boston, 1989).

thought requires a concept of human freedom that recognizes that responsibility for others is an expression of precisely this freedom. It requires a new coupling of liberal and communitarian traditions, rooted especially in the Biblical impetus in Western legal thought, especially in the Biblical concept of justice.[15] Biblical justice aims not simply to enable each person to receive *his* or *her* lawful rights, but rather to ensure rights for the *other* also and to enable the community to survive under conditions of *equal* freedom for all. In this further development of legal thought, through the coupling of liberal and communitarian traditions, Biblical legal ideas can achieve significant meaning.

Second, we face the task of developing a planetary legal consciousness, whose validity rests upon the principles of a planetary ethos.[16] The task of maintaining the viability of Planet Earth and ensuring dignified living conditions for humanity demands cooperation beyond the borders of cultural tradition and religious conviction. Western legal thought has lost sight of this task precisely because of its blindness to the religious dimensions of law. On account of this blindness, Western legal thought frequently stands uncomprehendingly opposed to the coupling of law and religion in other traditions. This explains why in the West itself a new discussion has erupted over the Eurocentric character of human rights, which are said to be incapable of taking root in regions of the world where other cultures and religions prevail.[17] The claim that human rights are exclusively bound up with European and American ways of understanding is found chiefly among authors who view these ways of understanding only in highly mutilated form. They fail to consider the significance of Judaism and Christianity, indeed of all religions, for law and human rights. Omitting the religious dimensions of law, however, further deepens the gulf between Western and non-Western legal conceptions. For believers in Islam, Buddhism, Hinduism, or Confucianism assume the inner unity of law and religion. Those in the West who aspire to ask how human rights theory can take root in these cultures must also look again at the collapsed connection between law and religion in his own culture.

---

[15] See Harold J. Berman: *Faith and Order, The Reconciliation of Law and Religion* (Atlanta 1993), 251ff.

[16] This discussion was primarily inspired by Hans Küng, *Projekt Weltethos* (München, 1990). For my proposals, deviating from those of Küng, see Wolfgang Huber, *Die tägliche Gewalt. Gegen den Ausverkauf der Menschenwürde* (Freiburg, 1993), 150ff.

[17] See, among many others, H.M. Enzensberger, *Aussichten auf den Bürgerkrieg* (Frankfurt am Main, 1993).

Human Rights Theory and the Torah

In our time, human rights are understood as much more than protections against the abuse of state power. This protective function of human rights remains critical and indispensable. Equally significant, however, is the role of human rights in setting the direction for social development and ethical decisions. This is all the more valid in that these developments and decisions are currently marked by a basic conflict between, what I shall call, an "ethic of dignity" and an "ethic of interest."[18]

An *ethic of interest* argues that there are no higher principles which help to achieve consensus in ethical conflicts with public significance. Such principles are always in dispute within a pluralistic society. Insofar as they refer to religious roots, they are regarded, according to this reasoning, as publicly incommunicable.[19] Ethical judgments, therefore, have to be directed exclusively towards the interests of the persons involved. Priority has to be granted to that which considers the greatest number of preferences of the greatest number of participants. The decisive implication of this approach is that, within the ethical assessment, consideration may be given only to those persons who themselves are capable of developing preferences. According to this approach, the capacity of having and articulating interests is the decisive, defining characteristic of the person. Only persons in this sense have their own place in ethical assessments.

Ethicists who argue along these lines make the implicit claim that they have the right to determine what makes humans human. They subject humans to disposition by other humans. An *ethic of dignity* responds with quite the contrary claim. Its modern development is rooted in a basic rediscovery of the Protestant Reformation. It states that the human person is not created by his or her own performance and cannot achieve final recognition through his or her own works. Not human perfection but Godly grace constitutes the human person. Human dignity is not dependent on the disposition of other humans, nor on the powers of society or the state. The human person in his or her limited time is granted an unending dignity that is no product of human efforts but rather a pure, unearned gift of God.[20]

---

[18] This basic conflict is evident in the most different fields; it has lately become especially noticeable in discussions regarding the right to life of the handicapped and the terminally ill. For other fields, see Huber, *Die tägliche Gewalt*, 44ff; id., "Grenzen des medizinischen Fortschritts aus ethischer Sicht," *Zeitschrift für Evangelische Ethik* 38 (1994): 41-53.

[19] In the German discussion this opinion is most extremely advocated, following the suggestion of Peter Singer, by N. Hoerster, *Abtreibung im säkularen Staat: Argumente gegen den §218* (Frankfurt am Main, 1991).

[20] That is the unreduced, actual meaning of Luther's basic anthropological decision, to contrast the philosophical definition of a human, according to which man is endowed with

After the Protestant Reformation, this ethic of dignity also assumed secular forms. The philosophy of Immanuel Kant cast this ethic in purest form. Kant posed the categorical imperative in a way that requires one to acknowledge humanity in the person of another as in oneself—not simply as a means, but equally as an end in itself.[21] This formula repeats the thought that no human person can lay complete claim to dispose of, or to define, another person. The oft-criticized lack of definition in the concept of human dignity[22] — for instance in connection with medical ethics—reflects this dimension in which the human person is seen as free from all human claims of power and authority. The concept of dignity would lose that function at just the moment we attempt to encompass it by definition; for definitions are in themselves forms of human authority.

The ethic of dignity is currently under strong attack. Its strongest support rests in the thought of human rights and their codification. Human rights, therefore, have not only a legal purpose but also an ethical significance. They form the most important example of a connection, anchored in the definition of human dignity, between ethics and law, which for the sake of the humanity of society cannot be surrendered. They also find their parallel structure in Biblical legal thought. For these social precepts are, as can already be seen in The Book of the Covenant (Exodus 20, 22-23, 33), specially characterized in that they connect law and ethics—rights and duties—to each other.[23]

How is this coupling constructed in the case of human rights? Following the idea of human rights to its core, we find that it resides indubitably in the conviction of the untouchable dignity of all persons, the recognition of which is to be found in the guaranteeing of freedom, equality, and participation for all.[24] Each formulation of human rights presupposes that the legal position of the human person with respect to society and the state is determined by something not initially guaranteed

---

reason, with the theological definition, according to which man is justified by faith alone ("hominem iustificari fide"). See Martin Luther, *Disputatio de homine* (1536), Thesis 32, in WA, 39/1: 176-177, with a modern German translation in Martin Luther, *Ausgewählte Schriften*, K. Bornkamm und G. Ebeling, hrsg. (Frankfurt am Main, 1983), 2:294-297.

[21] Immanuel Kant, *Grundlegung zur Metaphysik der Sitten*, BA 66ff., in Immanuel Kant, *Werke*, W. Weischedel, hrsg. (Wiesbaden, 1956), 4:61.

[22] See "Die Begriffe 'Menschenwurde' und 'Sanctity of Life' und ihre Tragweite für ethische Konfliktlagen in der modernen Medizin," in *Ethik in der Medizin* 6 (Heidelberg, 1993): 53-58.

[23] See Cruesemann, *Die Tora*, 224ff. in debating E. Otto's thesis on the differentiation of ethics from law in social precepts, which, as Cruesemann correctly states, have just misjudged their point. See E. Otto, "Sozial- und rechtshistorische Aspekte in der Ausdifferenzierung eines altisraelischen Ethos aus dem Recht," *Osnabrücker Hochschulschriften, Schriftenreihe des FB 3/9* (Osnabrück, 1987): 135-161.

[24] See Huber and Tödt, *Menschenrechte*, 75ff.

by society and the state, but something that they can simply recognize as given and respect as inalienable. The Virginia Bill of Rights of 1776 captured this view as follows: "All men are by nature free and independent and possess certain native rights."[25] The Universal Declaration of Human Rights of 1948 declared: "Recognition of the dignity within all members of the human family and of their equal and inalienable rights [forms] the foundation of freedom, justice and peace in the world."[26] The Basic Law of Bonn describes this as the untouchable dignity of the human person.

Kant's attempt to give the concept of dignity its own basis in the self-purpose of man as a rational being does not deny that this concept has its origin in the Biblical thought of man as the image of God. The search for a root of the parallelism between human rights and Biblical legal thought finds it primarily in the great significance which was attributed to the doctrine of the human person as the image of God in the history of Christian thought.

For, in fact, even if Biblical law had not expressly referred to the human person as the image of God, even if it lacked correspondence to the concept of human dignity, there can still be no doubt that precisely its distinct and unmistakable accents have to be explained by their origin in the respect for the integrity of the human person who is called and incorporated by God in his Covenant. This community with God is all that matters. The commandments to give honor to God alone set the scope and the preconditions for Israel's social legislation. The same basis leads Jewish law to give special attention to those whose integrity is endangered by life's external circumstances—slaves, strangers, widows, and orphans, who are deprived of their husbands' or fathers' protection.

This necessarily simplified characterization of the social legislation in the Book of the Covenant also reveals how certain components of Biblical legal thought go beyond the catalogues of modern human rights. One of these components is found in the direct coupling of the legal status of the human person in society with giving honor to one God alone. Modern catalogues of human rights, on the contrary, are based upon the recognition of a plurality of religious orientations to which an equal law is to be applied. Another component is revealed in the clear partisanship with which Biblical law sides with the weaker, those at risk in their legal standing. Human rights catalogues, on the other hand, are characterized by non-partisanship; they deny any special priority to individual groups, be they privileged or marginalized. Thus, for example, there is no subjective right of asylum in the international catalogues of human rights; in-

---

[25] Heidelmeyer (hrsg.), *Die Menschenrechte*, 54.
[26] Ibid., 239.

stead, modern human rights tend to require states to guarantee asylum within the scope of what is possible for those states. Thus the claim to asylum by those seeking it receives no priority over any other claims. Clear partisanship on behalf of those whose rights are particularly threatened forms no obvious component in modern catalogues of human rights, but it remains a sharp-edged tool that can be utilized for their improvement and for further-reaching steps in their translation.

I have detailed the difference between Biblical legal thought and modern catalogues of human rights by posing the question of how Biblical legal thought goes beyond contemporary formulations of human rights. Certainly, we must also ask the converse question of how contemporary human rights norms go beyond Biblical legal thought? Here, too, there are two components with basic significance, namely freedom of religion and equal recognition of all men and women as holders of human rights.

In 1895, the German jurist Georg Jellinek argued that the declarations of human rights of his time had, historically, been centered on the demand for freedom of religion and conscience, that is, upon a demand heralded through the Protestant Reformation and claimed by religious minorities in England and America.[27] History does not entirely bear out Jellinek's thesis. For example, the Virginia Declaration of Rights of 1776 initially treated religious freedom briefly only in Article 16, which article had no recognizable or even necessary connection to the other fifteen articles in the Virginia Declaration of Rights.[28] This and other early American bills of rights were inspired more by the struggle for economic and political emancipation of the colonies from England, and less by the religious self-determination of Christian groups. It is nonetheless correct to state that the discovery of Christian freedom in the Protestant Reformation and the understanding, won through bitter historical experience, of the need for religious toleration prepared the ground for the modern development of human rights. Without the early modern movements for religious toleration and freedom, the growth of human rights would be unimaginable. To this extent, a central element of all human rights is indeed the universal guarantee of freedom of conscience, belief, and religion. The inalienability of the human person, and the untouchability of human dignity, can be guaranteed only if religious beliefs and their individual and corporate expression remain free from all external constraint. This idea must be foreign to Biblical legal thought; for here the coupling between giving honor to only one God and the legal form of community

---

[27] Georg Jellinek, *Die Erklärung der Menschen- und Bürgerrechte* (1895), reprinted in R. Schnur (hrsg.), *Zur Geschichte der Erklärung der Menschenrecht* (Darmstadt, 1974), 1-77.

[28] Cf. Huber and Tödt, *Menschenrechte*, 124ff.

life is so narrowly conceived that the recognition of an equal right for those professing another faith does not arise.

A similar contrast between Biblical legal thought and modern human rights theory is evident in the view that all persons possess human rights. The twentieth century experience of totalitarian regimes subjected human rights theory to a radicalism that must appear foreign to earlier centuries and certainly so to Biblical legal thought. Hannah Arendt reflects this radicalism, in the context of the horrors of the Nazi regime, in a way which can be summarized as follows: One must seek to uncover that absolutely fundamental right, without which a human person is incapable of living a life compatible with human dignity. This right resides in the "right to have rights." Every person must be a member of a community that recognizes and accepts him or her. As a "pure person"—beyond the multiplicity of citizen rights—he or she has only a single right, namely to be a subject with a legal status. Where a person is denied this fundamental right to be the holder of rights within the confines of a community under the law, human dignity is no longer respected. Wherever the right to hold rights is taken away, all other rights would also lapse. Whoever is without legal subjectivity is considered by others simply as a means, as consumable labor, as a dispensable refugee, and so on.[29]

This reasoning shows—well beyond the present state of the codification of human rights—the perspective by which, in particular, the assignment of rights (including the rights of asylum) to refugees is a touchstone of the extent to which a society or the international community of nations adopts the essence of human rights and gives them legal form. If one poses the question with respect to the millions of people presently registered as stateless refugees with the United Nations High Commissioner for Refugees, it seems that further development of the consciousness of human rights as well as of the tools for protecting those rights is urgently required. Affording universality to the idea of human rights and thus asserting that all men and women have equal claim to fundamental human rights still lies beyond Biblical legal thought.

Religious Contributions to Human Rights Theory

It is now time for religions to interpret and develop the idea of human rights in an inter-religious and inter-cultural dialogue that seeks to identify the basic components of an emerging planetary ethos. Such dialogue will succeed, however, only if it is essentially open, and its partici-

---

[29] Hanna Arendt, "Es gibt nur eine einziges Menschenrecht," *Die Wandlung* 4 (1954): 754-770.

pants abandon all claims to exclusivity. Whosoever wishes to afford to
human rights worldwide legal force and to achieve ethical agreement as
to a planetary ethos must observe specific restraint with respect to the
ethical foundations of human rights.[30]

What is meant here can be clearly seen in Article 1 of the Universal
Declaration of Human Rights: "All men are born free and equal in rights
and dignity. They are endowed with reason and conscience and should
meet each other in a spirit of brotherliness." This formulation connects
three ethical traditions. The claim that all persons are born free and equal
in rights and dignity establishes a link to the Jewish and Christian belief
that all persons are created in the image of God. The statement that all
persons are endowed with reason and conscience adopts the belief in reason of the Enlightenment. The advice concerning fraternity recalls the
traditions of the French Revolution and the labor movement.

Today the appeal to these three traditions alone seems far too narrow. Human rights norms today must be based upon a broader foundation. To be essentially open, human rights discourse must incorporate the
global multiplicity of religions and cultures. The formulation of human
rights should not exclude, but should accommodate, this multiplicity. We
should demand a high degree of ideological and religious restraint in our
formulations of law as well as of human rights. That is the only way in
which the law can ensure its essential openness and thus respect the relationship between law and ethics.

Although they are essentially different, law and ethics should not be
entirely juxtaposed in this process. Human rights law reflects one of the
organic connections between law and ethics. Just as in the modern era
various ethical considerations with equal claims to validity have appeared alongside one another, so, too, various understandings of human
rights have made equal claims to validity. It is true that recognition of
certain human rights does not necessarily depend on the fulfillment of
specific duties. One such example is the recognition of the freedom and
equality of all persons whose integrity is guaranteed by the state and
who are entitled to participate in political decisions and social benefits.
Nevertheless, human rights provide the basis for a series of moral—and
thus legally unassailable—duties for individuals. A person has the right
to lead a life of responsible freedom, to recognize others as equals, to defend those whose basic rights are threatened, to overcome all forms of
victimization or discrimination, to guarantee actively everyone's opportunity for political participation.

---

[30] The following section draws on Huber, *Die tägliche Gewalt*, 172ff.

Human rights, however, do not depend for their legal and ethical contents simply on agreements among various cultural and religious traditions. Human rights also challenge these traditions, with their unmistakable differences of basic ethical beliefs, to establish the foundations of a common ethos. Human rights discourse is developing in this direction today, for human rights provide points of convergence among various ethical beliefs of mankind, and these points of convergence point the way toward a planetary ethos. In the acknowledgement of the inalienable dignity of the human person as well as of the freedom, equality, and participatory rights of all persons, certain basic components of a planetary ethos can already be seen.

In certain important areas, changes in ethical attitudes have also brought new evaluations of human rights. Thus important changes in the perceptions of relationships between men and women have affected the interpretation of human rights. Declarations of human rights have asserted from the outset that all human persons are by nature entitled to the same rights. For centuries, however, women have been treated unequally. In the international legal community, the opinion has gradually emerged that talk of human rights can be valid only if the rights of women are not merely proclaimed but also accorded equal respect in practice to those of men.

To be sure, the demands of a planetary ethos cannot be placed on the same footing as human rights, nor can the principles of a planetary ethics all be found in or adopted by catalogues of human rights. The current debate over a "third generation" of human rights reveals clearly this disjuncture.[31] The category of "third generation rights" is said to include the rights to development, peace, and protection of the environment as well the right to participate in "the common inheritance of mankind"— the resources of the deep ocean floor and the utilization of space, and the natural and cultural products of the earth. Similar extensions will be proposed if "rights of nature" are separated from human rights.[32] While all such matters are of fundamental concern to a planetary ethos, posing them in human rights terms jeopardizes their precise meaning and even their ultimate legal character.

The principles of a planetary ethos cannot simply be equated with current human rights norms. It is time to formulate independent, far-reaching principles through which understanding can be sought among

---

[31] For more detail, see Huber and Reuter, *Friedensethik*, 331ff.

[32] For more detail, see Wolfgang Huber, "Rights of Nature or Dignity of Nature?" *The Annual of the Society of Christian Ethics* (1991): 43-60.

cultures and religions.[33] Current discourse about human rights provides an important impetus for this. It makes clear that these principles must include mutual recognition of the equal dignity of all human persons and mutual demands for their freedom, their equality, and their active participation in community life. It further shows that with these principles special weight is to be attached to the same dignity for women, the demand for social justice, and the preservation of nature.

The diverse religious communities of the world are challenged to interpret and develop not only the legal character of human rights but also the ethical content of a planetary ethos. Such a planetary ethos cannot be established through abstract study. It will only gain stature if it is alive in the community in which people compose and transmit their moral convictions. Only if the story-telling communities in which people develop and gain their identities are open to the common tasks of humankind will duties towards humankind and non-human nature penetrate moral consciousness. It is important, therefore, to anchor the further development of ethical orientation on the basis of religious communities but also of secular, humanistic communities. The planetary ethos should not simply be formulated by a representative elite. It should be anchored in a broad process of clarification in which the multiplicity of faiths could find expression. We should hope and strive for a responsible declaration of a world ethos, not from a small group of people, but from broad discussion on the responsibility with which humanity is faced. On this long path,

---

[33] Hans Küng directed his interest not so much towards ethical principles—that is, rules for testing rules—but rather towards ethical rules themselves, which, he claimed, found acceptance among all major religions. Ethical rules, however, that are developed in the various political, cultural or religious communities as answers to the question of the good and succeeding life, are characterized by a broad spectrum of variations. What is required is not their similarity but their capacity for being compatible with universalist principles. Küng's proposals for rules that all major religions could accept—do not kill, do not lie, do not steal, do not commit indecent acts, respect one's parents—are in most respects adopted from the Christian version of the Decalogue and for the rest are in urgent need of interpretation in view of all the ethical conflict questions that currently exist. In view of the decisive questions for the future of mankind—violence against man and nature, hunger and overpopulation, apathy and lack of active participation—they provide no clear direction. See Hans Küng, "Eine Welt—eine Menschheit—ein Ethos: Zehn Thesen," *Evangelische Kommentare* 26 (1993): 488. The "World Parliament of Religions" that met in Chicago from August 28 to September 4, 1993, relied in its "Declaration of a Global Ethic" on the Golden Rule; it further varied this in the demand that every person be treated as a person. The Golden Rule, however, seems to offer no evidence for the relationship between present and future generations, particularly for the majorities in the industrialized nations. It also fails to consider the necessary changes in the relationship between man and nature. Both proposals fail to develop the principles of a planetary ethos much beyond the ethical core of human rights but rather stay behind it. See H. Küng and K.J. Kuschel, eds., *A Global Ethic. The Declaration of the Parliament of the World Religions* (London and New York, 1993).

consideration of the relationship between modern human rights and Biblical legal ideas is a small but necessary step.

All interpretations of human rights have to be open to a plurality of possible foundations. Otherwise the concept of human rights would not be compatible with a modern understanding of religious freedom, as stated by the 1981 U.N. Declaration on the Elimination of All Forms of Intolerance and of Discrimination Based on Religion or Belief. The necessity of an open interpretation of contemporary human rights was captured by the Final Document of the United Nations Conference on Human Rights held in Vienna in June 1993. After controversial discussions, the Vienna Conference arrived at a common understanding of the basis for a future international order. Democracy, development, and human rights are for this final document the common denominators for the future social and political order on an international scale. All three denominators, however, need an interpretation which is open for the different traditions and experiences in different parts of the world. Such an openness implies the task of giving a "thick interpretation" (as Clifford Geertz calls it) to the impact of every tradition for a better understanding and for a better practice of human rights. The task of the foregoing analysis was to clarify some of the conditions for such a "thick interpretation"—at least as far as the biblical traditions are concerned.

Religious Rights and Christian Texts

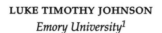

LUKE TIMOTHY JOHNSON
Emory University[1]

A nyone turning to Christian sources for help in supporting religious rights as human rights should be prepared for some conster-
nation. Both the normative Christian texts and the larger part of
the Christian tradition offer as much reason for confusion and concern as
for celebration.

Confusion is created by the realization that the normative texts of the
Christian tradition do not speak in any obvious way to the question of
religious rights or human rights. The Bible does not employ the sort of
philosophical or legal discourse in which the language of "rights" finds a
natural home.[2] As thoroughly religious literature of antiquity, furthermore, it takes for granted that all people are in some sense "religious."[3]
The Bible does not need to argue for a right it assumes.

These texts also fail to address our questions directly because of different assumptions about the nature of religion itself. The ancient Mediterranean world did not consider religion as one aspect of life among
others. It was at once public and pervasive and enmeshed with the fundamental structures of society.[4]

---

[1] Significant assistance in preparing this chapter was provided by Mary F. Foskett,
Ph.D. Candidate, Graduate Division of Religion, Emory University.

[2] See, e.g., M. Villey, "Les origines de la notion de droit subjectif," *Revue historique de
droit français et etranger* ser. 4, 24 (1946): 201-227; B. Tierney, "Villey, Ockham and the Origin
of Individual Rights," in J. Witte, Jr. and F.S. Alexander, eds., *The Weightier Matters of the Law:
Essays on Law and Religion* (Atlanta, 1988), 1-31; G. Samuel, "Epistemology, Propaganda and
Roman Law: Some Reflections on the History of the Subjective Right," *The Journal of Legal
History* 10 (1989): 161-179.

[3] The Epicureans' rejection of the standard forms of religion earned them particular
enmity (see Plutarch, *Reply to Colotes* 22 [Mor. 1119F] and 27 [Mor. 1123A]), even though the
Epicureans' response to their founder had obvious religious dimensions (*Reply to Colotes* 17
[Mor. 1117 A-B]).

[4] Among many examples, see only Libanius, *Oration XXX*, 34; Cicero, *Pro Flacco* 28;
Plutarch, *Reply to Colotes* 31-34 [Mor. 1125C-1127E]. See also T. M. Parker, *Christianity and the
State in the Light of History* (New York, 1955), 1-21.

J. Witte, Jr. and J.D. van der Vyver (eds.), Religious Human Rights in Global Perspective, 65-95.
© 1996 *Kluwer Law International. Printed in the Netherlands.*

Nor is the contemporary tendency to think of religion in terms of the personal rather than the social, in terms of private belief rather than public liturgy, shared by the writings of the Hebrew Bible which were taken over by the Christians by way of the Greek translation called the Septuagint and eventually designated the Old Testament, with deference to the collection of specifically Christian writings that were eventually canonized as the New Testament.

The Christian scriptures, in short, do not in any direct or obvious way provide support for the contemporary proposition that "it is a human right to be religious." Another way of framing the issue of "religious rights," of course, is in terms of the freedom to be religious differently. But if by religious rights we are speaking of tolerance for religious diversity both in thought and in expression, then an assessment of the Christian tradition should also create concern, for it has been for much of its history an agent for the suppression of religious liberty.

Anyone speaking from within the Christian tradition on this issue, as I am in this chapter, must begin with such a frank admission. Christians have been, and continue to be, the least credible of witnesses to the blessings of tolerance and the human right to religious liberty.

Christianity's Record of Religious Intolerance

There is probably no need to review the evidence demanding such a confession. Christianity's record is impressive if not admirable. Beginning as a sect of Judaism, it engaged from the start in debates with both Jewish and Gentile competitors. Its fight with other forms of Judaism involved the claim to represent the authentic form of that tradition. Its fight with all other forms of worship continued Judaism's own insistence that only one confession could be true and all others false. Early Christian apologists who claimed a share in Rome's tolerance of religious diversity[5] did not seem to appreciate that Rome's unusual intolerance in its case was a response to its own intolerance of diversity: Christians did not merely want a place in the sun, they claimed that theirs was the only legitimate place.[6]

When Constantine granted Christianity first toleration and then privilege, it did not take long for this same intolerance to be manifested against an increasingly weakened paganism, and above all against diver-

---

[5] See the classic argument for "equal justice" in Athenagoras, *Embassy* 1-2 and Tertullian, *Apology* II, 1-20.

[6] The point is made brilliantly by J. Simon, *La liberté de conscience*, 2d ed. (Paris, 1857), 66-67.

sity of belief and practice within the Christian empire.[7] Christianity willingly accepted the help of the state to establish its own claims to unique and absolute legitimacy.[8]

It is painful but necessary to remember Christianity's intolerance of the religious rights of Judaism through centuries of anti-semitism, and its use of political force to effect controlling laws, inquisitions, expulsions, and the suppression of the sacred texts by which that community lived.[9] It is equally important to recall Christianity's intolerance of Islam, and its centuries-long effort, under the deeply ambiguous rubric of crusades, to eliminate this powerful and more tolerant rival.[10] Nor was Christianity any kinder to diversity within: orthodoxy was indeed the imperial religion, and the only safe place to practice an unapproved form of Christianity was outside the boundaries of empire.[11]

Both the Roman Catholic and the Orthodox forms of Christianity have in their central traditions celebrated and defended intolerance under the simple conviction that error has no rights, and it is the prerogative of the Christian state to defend the truth by eliminating error.[12] The

---

[7] For a sympathetic analysis of Constantine's own attempts to continue a tradition of toleration, see H. Doerries, *Constantine and Religious Liberty*, trans. R.H. Bainton (New Haven, 1960).

[8] As early as the 340s, Firmicus Maternus addressed a treatise to Constantine's sons, *De Errore Profanorum Religionum*, calling for the emperor to destroy paganism by force. It was Theodosius I (379-395) who was the decisive figure in the establishment of the "Christian Empire." But even under him, the rhetorician Libanius could make appeal for continued toleration of the pagan cultus. See *Oration* XX and XXX). For the progression, see R.L. Fox, *Pagans and Christians* (New York, 1989), 648-81; J. Pelikan, *The Excellent Empire: The Fall of Rome and the Triumph of the Church* (San Francisco, 1987), 93-115; Parker, *Christianity and the State*, 43-64; and R. MacMullen, *Christianizing the Roman Empire, A.D. 100-400* (New Haven, 1984), 86-101.

[9] For a rapid survey of events, see S. Grayzel, *A History of the Jews*, rev. ed. (New York, 1968), 303-473; for the literature concerning the roots of Christian anti-semitism, see J.G. Gager, *The Origins of Anti-Semitism* (New York, 1985), 3-34; for documentary evidence, see J.R. Marcus, *The Jew in the Medieval World: A Source Book: 315-1791* (New York, 1969), 3-181.

[10] The classic study of the crusades is S. Runciman, *A History of the Crusades*, 3 vols (Cambridge, 1951-54); for the temporal as well as spiritual benefits accruing to participants in the crusades, see J.A. Brundage, *Medieval Canon Law and the Crusader* (Madison, WI, 1969).

[11] This truism of ecclesiastical history can be supported by any standard work, such as K. Bihlmeyer, *Church History*, rev. ed., H. Tuechle, ed., V.E. Mills, trans. (Westminster, 1968).

[12] See J. LeCler, "Religious Freedom: A Historical Survey," *Concilium* 18 (1966): 3-20. The most notorious instrument of coercion was the inquisition, especially in Spain. See H.C. Lea, *A History of the Inquisition in Spain*, 4 vols (New York, 1922); H. Kamen, *Inquisition and Society in Spain in the Sixteenth and Seventeenth Centuries* (Bloomington, 1985). That this attitude was not simply a medieval one is shown by the 1964 article by the Spanish theologian P.G. Lopez. Arguing for the absolutist imposition of Catholicism in Spain, he says, "Moreover, Spaniards discontented for religious reasons have no right to enjoy more ample religious freedom than they do enjoy. For one reason, they are non-Catholics, and therefore in error; and error, even when in good faith, has strictly speaking no right to show itself or be professed." "La Democracia como regimen politico Christiano, III," *Razon y Fe* 134 (1946): 166,

same deadly equation was carried over into Protestantism. With very few exceptions the reformers were as intolerant and sanguinary as their Catholic opponents.[13] The ideological and political battles that characterized the Reformation and post-Reformation period are a monument to Christian intolerance. The religious wars that ravaged Europe throughout the sixteenth and seventeenth centuries, the missionary competition between Catholic and Protestant that went hand-in-hand with colonialism in Asia, Africa, and the Americas, the spirit of hostility that until very recently enabled Catholics and Protestants each to refer to the other as heretical, are all manifestations of the same deep intolerance of religious difference.[14]

Christianity has also, it is true, had voices that have spoken out, often passionately, often at the cost of great personal suffering, for the recognition of the religious rights of others. Any such honor roll must include the names of Thomas More and Desiderius Erasmus, Balthazar Hubmaier, Caspar Schwenkfeld, Martin Bucer, Menno Simons, David Joris, Sebastian Castellio, Faustus Socinus, Jan Komensky, Hugo Grotius, Michel de l'Hospital, William Penn, John Owen, and Samuel Pufendorf.[15] And these voices could cite support for their position from the New Testament: Paul's statement "there must be factions among you in order that those who are genuine among you may be recognized" (1 Corinthians 11:19), and Jesus' parable of the wheat and the tares (Matthew 13:24-30). Both passages served to support the inevitability of diversity within Christianity, and the necessity of waiting for God to sort it out.[16]

---

cited in J.C. Murray, "Current Theology on Religious Freedom," *Theological Studies* 10 (1949): 409-432.

[13] See Parker, *Christianity and the State*, 143-72, and H. Kamen, *The Rise of Toleration* (New York, 1967), 22-55.

[14] A lively and literate exposition of this period is found in P. Johnson, *A History of Christianity* (New York, 1979), 267-457; for the effect of mutual Christian intolerance on thinkers seeking a more universalist understanding of religion, see the chapters on Jean Bodin (1530-1596) and Herbert of Cherburg (1583-1648) in J.S. Preus, *Explaining Religion: Criticism and Theory from Bodin to Freud* (New Haven, 1987), 3-39.

[15] See Kamen, *The Rise of Toleration*, passim. For a useful collection of primary sources from the Reformation period, see M. Hoffmann, *Toleranz und Reformation* (Gütersloh, 1979).

[16] For the text from Paul, see Cyprian of Carthage, *On the Unity of the Church*, 10. The parable of the wheat and the tares, with its command, "Let both grow together until the harvest," was a favorite text. See R.H. Bainton, "The Parable of the Wheat and the Tares as the Proof Text for Religious Liberty to the End of the 16th Century," *Church History* 1 (1932): 67-89. Manfred Hoffmann uses Martin Luther's successive interpretations of this parable as a way of charting the reformer's growing intolerance in the face of diversity. See M. Hoffmann, "Reformation and Toleration," in M. Hoffmann, ed., *Martin Luther and the Modern Mind: Freedom, Conscience, Toleration, Rights* (New York, 1985), 85-124; see also M. Brecht, "Divine Right and Human Rights in Luther," in ibid., 61-84.

A far more powerful antecedent was supplied, however, by Augustine's interpretation—forged out of frustration at the height of the Donatist controversy—of Luke 14:23, "compel the people to enter" (in the Vulgate, *compelle entrare*) as a warrant for religious coercion.[17] And here is a strange fact: Christian pleas for toleration came most frequently from those who were among the minority and persecuted groups rather than the established traditions. It was Calvin who in 1553 had Michael Servetus put to death in Geneva, defending the principle that "kings are commanded to protect the doctrine of piety by their support," and it was Sebastian Castellio who rebuked him with the devastating observation, "To kill a man is not to defend a doctrine, but to kill a man. When the Genevans killed Servetus, they did not defend a doctrine, they killed a man."[18]

It is also true that Christianity has over the past three centuries slowly worked itself to a principled position of religious toleration and freedom.[19] It happened more quickly in the Protestant camp,[20] but eventually and more systematically in Roman Catholicism, first with Pope John XXIII's *Pacem in Terris* (1963), with its unequivocal statement, "Every human being has the right to honor God according to the dictates of an upright conscience, and the right to profess his religion privately and publicly," and then with the Declaration on Religious Freedom issued by the Second Vatican Council (1965).[21]

There is, however, a second odd fact attached to this progression, which is that movement toward toleration tended to come more from the

---

[17] See esp. Augustine, *Letter*, 185. A review of the texts and a sympathetic contextualization is provided by F. Van der Meer, *Augustine the Bishop* (London, 1961), 78-128.

[18] Sebastian Castellio, *Contra Libellum Calvini* (1612), cited in Kamen, *The Rise of Toleration*, 80.

[19] For a crisp summary of Christianity's increasingly positive appropriation of democratic ideals (equality and freedom, pluralism and toleration), see J. Witte, Jr., "Christianity and Democracy: Past Contributions and Future Challenges," *Emory International Law Review* 6 (1992): 55-69.

[20] See L. Vischer, "Religious Freedom and the World Council of Churches," *Concilium* 18 (1966): 53-63 for a review of the important stages, including the World Council declarations in Amsterdam (1948) and New Delhi (1961). An important preparation was laid by the sponsorship of research into religious liberty world-wide by M.S. Bates, *Religious Liberty: An Inquiry* (New York, 1945). Despite some inadequacies (enumerated in the reviews by E.A. Ryan and J.C. Murray, *Theological Studies* 7 [1946]:146-163), the study provided a comprehensive framework for future work.

[21] For the Roman Catholic progression, see L. Janssens, *Freedom of Conscience and Religious Freedom*, B. Lorenzo, C.F.X., trans. (Staten Island, 1965); P. Pavan, "The Right to Religious Freedom in the Conciliar Declaration," *Concilium* 18 (1966): 37-52; W. Kaspar, "The Theological Foundations of Human Rights," *The Jurist* 50 (1990): 148-166. For a review of Protestant and Roman Catholic statements, see M. Shupack, "The Churches and Human Rights: Catholic and Protestant Human Rights Views and Reflected in Church Statements," *Harvard Human Rights Journal* 6 (1993): 127-157.

critics of traditional or biblical Christianity than its adherents. It was Enlightenment critics such as Baruch Spinoza and John Locke who gave the clearest and most formal statement of the principle that religious liberty is rooted in the rights of individual persons.[22] And it was the philosopher Pierre Bayle who in 1686 finally and definitively challenged the exegetical accuracy and moral propriety of Augustine's interpretation of *compelle entrare*.[23] Finally, it was the hard lessons learned from the disenfranchisement of religion after the age of revolution that enabled even Roman Catholicism finally to recognize that the Constantinian Era was over, and that, however grudgingly, the right to religious liberty must be recognized as a fundamental human right.[24]

The Lessons of History

Two lessons emerge from this historical review. The first is that the establishment of Christianity as a state religion is bad both for others and for Christianity itself: the strain of intolerance and absolutism within this tradition that is buffered when Christians are in the minority seems inevitably to reappear whenever Christianity exercises effective political control. The second is that such intolerance is rooted not only in human sinfulness but in the normative texts of Christianity: the Old Testament and New Testament alike give more than ample support for intolerance.

These are, we know, not only historical lessons; they are illustrated by the daily headlines. The contemporary Christians who are most fervent in their labor for the realization of the kingdom of God in America, spelled out in terms of a Christian cultural hegemony, are also the Christians who are most emphatically "biblical" in their ideology, and who find it most plausible to suggest that everything not explicitly Christian is

---

[22] See Baruch Spinoza's *Tractatus Theologico-Politicus* (1670) and John Locke's *Letter Concerning Toleration* (1689), with two further letters in 1690 and 1693.

[23] See Pierre Bayle (1647-1706): "To refute this absolutely [Augustine's interpretation] I rely on this principle of natural light, that any literal meaning which includes an obligation to commit crimes, is false." Pierre Bayle, *Commentaire philosophique sur ces paroles de Jesus-Christ: Contrains-les d'entrer*, cited in Kamen, *Rise of Toleration*, 237.

[24] It is noteworthy that John Courtney Murray, the most influential Roman Catholic theorist concerning the human right to freedom, argued not from scripture but from the moral lessons derived from the American experiment in democracy. Among his many writings, see "Current Theology: Religious Freedom," and "Freedom of Religion I: The Ethical Problem," in *Theological Studies* 6 (1945): 85-113, 229-286; "Current Theology on Religious Freedom," *Theological Studies* 10 (1949): 409-432; "The Problem of Religious Freedom," *Theological Studies* 25 (1964): 503-575; "Religious Freedom" in J.C. Murray, ed., *Freedom and Man* (New York, 1965), 131-140; "Arguments for the Human Right to Religious Freedom," in J.L. Hooper, ed., *Religious Liberty* (Louisville, 1993), 229-244.

thereby implicitly in the service of Satan: "We know that we are of God, and the whole world is in the power of the evil one" (1 John 5:19).

The point to which I have been moving, then, is this: for Christians to join the effort to ensure the religious rights of all as specifically human rights, they need to make more than a moral commitment; they need also to engage in a difficult intellectual struggle. It is not enough for Christians to forswear the sins of the past, or even embrace the collapse of the Constantinian era, for the virus that created the fevers of fanatic intolerance and that welcomed the coercive power of the state remains dormant and potentially dangerous within the texts of the Christian tradition.[25]

Christians are caught, I suggest, in a specifically *hermeneutical* problem from which the only relief is a specifically hermeneutical therapy. Lacking a vigorous and throughgoing re-reading of their normative traditions, the Christian commitment to religious tolerance cannot but be superficial and ephemeral. Given another political context or another moral climate, and the virus that has been merely suppressed rather than eliminated will again infect Christian consciousness. Indeed, as already noted, it continues to do so even now among groups whose proud badge of identification is their "biblical" character. In order for Christians to make a decisive turn in another direction, they must undergo a *metanoia* that is not only a change of heart, but above all a change of mind.

The scope of such a project is clearly larger than this chapter or any number of essays, conferences, and councils. A start can be made, however, (1) by recognizing the necessity of a hermeneutical engagement; (2) by indicating the ways in which the biblical writings are host to the virus of intolerance; and (3) by pointing to a way of reading the tradition in a way that its toxic elements can be neutralized if not eliminated.

The Necessity of Hermeneutics

I propose that the writings of the New Testament inherited an already significant trace of intolerance with its appropriation of Torah, and intensified it by the absoluteness of its claims and the sharpness of its rhetoric against rival claimants to the inheritance of Torah, but that its language took on a whole new dimension and power when the writings of a sect fighting for its existence became, in turn, the canonical scripture of a world-religion, and then the charter for a Christian empire. If this is the case, then it is not enough to eschew the claim to *imperium*; it is necessary as well to engage the claims of the *canon*.

---

[25] A. Roy Eckhardt has noted concerning anti-semitism: "The Christian world may change, or seek to change. The New Testament does not change, and there is no way to change it." See id., *Jews and Christians: The Contemporary Meeting* (Bloomington, 1986), 66.

But if such is the case, if the writings of the New Testament are so fatally infected with intolerance, why not abandon them altogether? The option seems attractive, particularly, as we have observed, the most tolerant Christians have tended also to be the most latitudinarian, while the most intolerant have been the most rigidly scriptural. But it is an option that is short-sighted and ultimately doomed to failure. As in the case of other elements in the Christian writings that subsequent experience has forced us to view from a more critical perspective, the solutions offered by abandoning the texts or expurgating them simply do not work.[26]

There are three interrelated reasons. The first is that Christianity is in essence a historical and social phenomenon whose identity is secured and renegotiated in every generation by means of this same set of texts that has remained stable since the second century. Just as for medieval Jews the burning of Torah was equivalent to destroying the community, so the abandonment of the New Testament writings would mean the end of historical Christianity. The resulting religion might be worth considering, but it could not be considered as Christian.

The second reason is that the New Testament, despite its many critics, is not *only* about sexism and anti-semitism and the suppression of sexual and religious diversity. Indeed, as millions of Christians through the ages have testified not only by their words but also by their lives, these texts are not even mostly about such things. They are, rather, witnesses and interpretations of the power of God to transform human life from fear into freedom and from patterns of destructive enmity into patterns of generous love and service. To abandon the texts means as well to abandon a form of existence shaped by what Paul called the *nous Christou*, "the mind of Christ" (1 Corinthians 2:16), that distinctive pattern of the Jesus Messiah whose faithful obedience to God was spelled out in the most extravagant accessibility and service to humans.

The third reason is intensely practical. If liberal Christians committed to sexual equality and religious tolerance abandon these texts as useless, they also abandon the field of Christian hermeneutics to those whose fearful and—it must be said—sometimes hate-filled apprehension of Christianity will lead them to exploit and emphasize just those elements of the tradition that have proven harmful to humans. If what Phyllis Trible has perceptively termed "texts of terror"[27] within the Bible are not en-

---

[26] See my discussion of the hermeneutical options with regard to anti-semitic language in "The New Testament's Anti-Jewish Slander and the Conventions of Ancient Polemic," *Journal of Biblical Literature* 108 (1989): 419-423.

[27] She used the term with reference to passages that have been used to support the suppression of women. See Phyllis Trible, *Texts of Terror: Literary-Feminist Readings of Biblical Narratives* (Philadelphia, 1984).

countered publicly and engaged intellectually by a hermeneutics that is at once faithful and critical, then they will continue to exercise their potential for harm among those who, without challenge, can claim scriptural authority for their own dark impulses.[28]

I have used the terms "faithful" and "critical" to describe this hermeneutical engagement. It is critical insofar as it is willing to question biblical texts vigorously for their religious coherence and moral appropriateness, without special pleading. While recognizing these texts as the gift of God to the Christian community and as bearing normative authority for shaping Christian life, it also declares that God's bestowal of the Holy Spirit is an even greater gift that calls the community to discern both its own experience and the words of the Scripture in a continuing conversation. This hermeneutics is therefore also faithful because it chooses to continue rather than to close the conversation, because it does the texts the honor of taking them seriously in what they say, and because it has faith that this process of discernment will enable the texts to speak more authentically "according to the mind of Christ."[29]

The Sources of Intolerance in Christianity

In this part of the chapter I am unable to consider those social and psychological factors leading to intolerance of every sort among Christians as among other humans, although they are of obvious importance.[30] Instead, I deal only with the specifically religious roots of religious intolerance within Christianity as such. I see two main causes. One is rooted in the Christian experience of monotheism, the other in the polemical rhetoric forged to defend that experience. In both we can see a progression in the use of language, from its function as an expression of the truth of religious experience and conviction, to the making of absolute claims about reality as such, claims that explicitly exclude the legitimacy of other kinds of religious experience.

The Exclusive Tendencies of Monotheism. The dominant religious system of the ancient world was polytheism, which was itself funda-

---

[28] I discuss the analogous hermeneutical problem with regard to patriarchal structures and sexist language in the New Testament, in L.T. Johnson, *1 Timothy, 2 Timothy, Titus* (Atlanta, 1987), 62-74.

[29] A fuller discussion of this approach to what I call an "ecclesial hermeneutics" can be found in L.T. Johnson, *Decision-Making in the Church: A Biblical Model* (Philadelphia, 1983), and id., "The Authority of the New Testament in the Church: A Theological Reflection," in C.R. Blaisdell, ed., *Conservative, Moderate, Liberal: The Biblical Theology Debate* (St. Louis, 1990), 87-99.

[30] On these fuller dimensions of the issue, see J. Newman, *On Religious Freedom* (Ottawa, 1991).

mentally pluralistic and was capable of incorporating into itself a variety of local and particular devotions. When the world of the divine is imaged as an extended family, there is always room for new members. It was the practice of the Hellenistic and Roman empires, furthermore, to encourage the syncretic accommodation of specific religions within this larger system. An important part of Roman propaganda was its invitation to the gods of conquered territories to enjoy the benefits of worship within the *imperium*.[31]

Within this world, the monotheism found among the Jews was distinctive. It was not like the philosophical monotheism of the philosophers who discerned behind diverse gods and goddesses a single divine power.[32] It was rather the refinement of an ancient tribal henotheism, in which a personal deity established his power by means of warfare against other gods.[33] Greek philosophical monotheism developed by extrapolating the logic of religious diversity. Jewish monotheism developed on the basis of the suppression of other religions. Only by reducing all other gods to false claimants —idols—could Yahweh alone be acclaimed as God. That Israel's Yahweh was a "jealous" God was axiomatic, for he could have "no other gods before him."[34] Yahwistic monotheism, however, had to fight a long battle within Israel against the more inclusive tendencies of the dominant polytheistic systems of Canaan,[35] and its weapons were those of intolerance. The exclusive allegiance demanded by Yahweh meant the destruction of all the "high places" dedicated to other gods[36]—or even, when monotheism combined with cultic centralization, the high places dedicated to Yahweh outside of Jerusalem.[37] Purveyors of false religion and false prophets were to be eliminated by death.[38]

---

[31] According to Pliny the Elder, *Natural History* 28:4, it was the practice of Roman priests to invoke the titular gods of a city under attack by Roman forces, inviting them to leave it and come over to Rome, where they would receive worship as good or better. See also Minucius Felix, *Octavius* 6:1-7:6.

[32] For a classic expression of this tendency, see Dio Chrysostom, *Oration* 12 ("The Olympic Discourse").

[33] See F.M. Cross, *Canaanite Myth and Hebrew Epic: Essays in the History of Israel* (Cambridge, 1973).

[34] See Exodus 20:3; Deuteronomy 5:7-8; 6:14.

[35] See Deuteronomy 4:15-19; 7:25-26; 12:30-31; 29:16; 32:16-18; Judges 2:19. See also M. Smith, *The Early History of God: Yahweh and the Other Deities in Ancient Israel* (San Francisco, 1990).

[36] For passages against various religious practices of the nations, see Deuteronomy 18:9-12; 23:17; 2 Kings 17:17-18. For passages against the "high places" where unapproved worship occurred, see Leviticus 26:1; 1 Kings 14:23-24; 22:53; 2 Kings 14:4; 15:35; 17:10-12.

[37] See Deuteronomy 12:1-14; 2 Kings 23:4-20.

[38] See Numbers 16:31-35; Leviticus 20:2; 20:27; Deuteronomy 18:20.

It was this militant monotheism, hardened and purified by the experience of the exile, that was inherited by Christianity, along with the polemic against idolatry developed not only in the prophetic literature,[39] but especially in the Jewish apologetic literature that responded to Gentile charges of superstition and misanthropy levelled against this odd "second race" that was an increasingly visible presence in Greco-Roman culture.[40] Writings such as the *Wisdom of Solomon* responded to Hellenistic anti-semitism with the most scathing attacks on pagan religion, reduced to an "idolatry" responsible for every sort of private and public vice.[41] And it was the Septuagint translators of the Psalms who first made the equation exploited by early Christian apologetic: "all the gods of the nations are demons."[42]

The full dimensions of monotheism's attack on religious diversity was less apparent in Judaism than it was to be in Christianity. Despite its many converts, it remained in essence the religion of a numerically insignificant nation, and was properly regarded as the cult of a specific people.[43] The public face of Judaism encountered by Gentiles in representatives such as Philo Judaeus, furthermore, emphasized the universalist, philosophical, and moral aspects of monotheism, rather than its exclusiveness.[44] Only when that form of Judaism called Christianity carried the same exclusive claims into a world-wide and astonishingly successful mission among the Gentiles, did the Graeco-Roman world find it necessary to combat religious intolerance with civil intolerance and persecution.[45]

---

[39] See Isaiah 40:18-20; 41:7, 29; 44:9-20; 45:20; Jeremiah 10:1-16; Hosea 4:11-19; 13:1-3; Micah 5:10-15; Habbakuk 2:18-19.

[40] In the broadest sense of the term, virtually all Hellenistic Jewish literature was "apologetic," but in the narrower sense, the category includes Josephus' *Antiquities of the Jews* and *Against Apion*, and Philo's *Embassy to Gaius* and *Against Flaccus*. These writings anticipated many of the elements of Christian Apologetic.

[41] Wisdom 13:1-14:28. For other examples, see Johnson, "The New Testament's Anti-Jewish Slander," 434-36.

[42] LXX Psalm 95:5. This Psalm is quoted as a proof-text for the Christian demonization of pagan cults by Origen, *Against Celsus* VII, 69. See also the statements that pagans worship demons rather than gods in Deuteronomy 32:17, Baruch 4:7, and Psalm 105:37 (LXX).

[43] For a sketch of the Jewish situation in the diaspora, see L.T. Johnson, *Writings of the New Testament* (Philadelphia, 1986), 67-83; for fuller treatments, see E.M. Smallwood, *The Jews under Roman Rule from Pompey to Diocletian* (Leiden, 1976), and V. Tcherikover, *Hellenistic Civilization and the Jews*, S. Appelbaum, trans. (New York, 1970).

[44] For a succinct treatment, see E.R. Goodenough, *An Introduction to Philo Judaeus*, 2d ed. (New York, 1963).

[45] See Simon, *La liberté de conscience*, 74: "La persecution était commencée, et l'intolerance civile entrait dans sa lutte sanglante contre l'intolerance religieuse, et du même coup contre la liberte de conscience."

If Jewish monotheism demanded of religious allegiance an "either/or" rather than a "both/and," nascent Christianity was even more exclusive in its proclamation. Now the One God of Judaism must be confessed according to the One Lord of the Christian *kerygma*. Christians increasingly claim not only that they represent the authentic people of God, but that they exclusively represent the people of God: that the confession of Jesus as Messiah is the necessary and non-negotiable point of access to the inheritance of Israel. Christians join to Judaism's exclusion of the nations its own exclusion of all other Jews.[46]

The subsequent history of Christianity, furthermore, can notoriously be read as a history of heresy, in which this fragmenting and absolutizing instinct is carried out to its extreme and absurd conclusion. It is not enough to confess Jesus as Lord, one must confess him properly as Lord; it is insufficient to be baptized, one must be baptized at the right time or at the right end or in the right season. And to show that it is the virus of intolerance at work in this constant process of exclusion, the claims are always absolute: the truth itself is at stake, salvation is at risk! Christianity was never so intolerant and merciless as to its own heretics. The reason, of course, is that the tradition of absolute claims and exclusivism is built into the canonical tradition: the battle against a latitudinarian Christian is continuous with the battle against the priests of Baal; a power struggle between preachers is warfare between light and darkness. And tragically often, the remedies recommended by Torah are followed: false prophets are killed in defense of true religion.

I am not suggesting that monotheism is necessarily exclusivistic and intolerant, but I do argue that the form of monotheism inherited and advanced by Christianity has tended to be both. And these tendencies have been given expression by forms of rhetoric that continue to shape the consciousness of Bible-reading Christians.

The Rhetoric of Intolerance. The world into which the New Testament was born was one of rhetorical hardball, and the earliest Christians learned to play it expertly. It was a world in which philosophical schools not only debated issues but engaged in slanderous attack. Teachers from rival schools were invariably guilty of vice as well as weak ideas; indeed, their shoddy theories were demonstrated by their shabby lives. All opponents were lovers of pleasure, lovers of possessions, and lovers of glory; all of them were guilty of hypocrisy. Such charges and counter-charges had a highly conventional character.[47] Slander against opponents

---

[46] Although R. Ruether's *Faith and Fratricide: The Theological Roots of Anti-Semitism* (New York, 1974) goes too far in suggesting that any Christology is inevitably anti-semitic (pp. 246-251), she does a brilliant job in locating Christian intolerance in its theological exclusivism.

[47] For examples, see Johnson, "The New Testament's Anti-Jewish Slander," 430-33.

was not taken so much as a literal description of fact as a warning against joining the opposition; its main function was to exhort insiders to a more fervent pursuit of virtue by presenting as a foil an exaggerated picture of the opponents' wickedness.[48]

Ancient critics of the Jews used this sort of rhetoric as did the Jewish apologetic literature which responded to such attacks. Rival schools within the philosophy called Judaism attacked each other with the same sort of rhetoric. And this is the style of rhetoric that we find in the New Testament's slanders against other forms of Judaism. The New Testament's language about scribes and pharisees is misunderstood if read as historical fact, but is rightly apprehended if read as the conventional way opponents were spoken of in that world.

Given the disproportionate size, influence, antiquity, and prestige of Judaism in the first century when compared to the nascent Christian movement, and given the fact that the literature of the New Testament was produced at a time when this movement was struggling both for existence and for some claim to the heritage of Israel, the polemic of the New Testament against Jews is—when compared to other samples from the same period, and despite its offensiveness to contemporary ears—relatively mild. It is certainly no more harsh than the language used by Platonists about Epicureans, or the language used by Pharisees about Sadducees, or the language used by Essenes about all other Jews.[49] However much the unbelieving Jews may be blamed for their failure to recognize the Messiah in Jesus, they were credited with worshipping the true God. As Paul declared, "I bear them witness that they have a zeal for God, but it is not enlightened" (Romans 10:2).

The problem with such language, of course, is that it was not read by subsequent Christians as the historical record of struggles for identity with Judaism, nor as language qualified by the rhetorical conventions of Hellenistic culture. Now located within canonical scriptures that were regarded as inspired by God and the very font of revelation, the New Testament's polemic against the Jews was read as stating propositional truth. The long history of Christian anti-semitism which based itself explicitly upon this language is sufficient testimony to the tragic consequences of this misreading.[50] Christian intolerance of Jews as people with a right to be Jewish according to their own choice is rationalized by the

---

[48] See, e.g., L.T. Johnson, "II Timothy and the Polemic Against False Teachers: A Re-Examination," *Journal of Religious Studies* 6/7 (1978-79): 1-26.

[49] Johnson, "The New Testament's Anti-Jewish Slander," 434-41.

[50] Its power is shown by the way in which a secular literary critic as sophisticated as Harold Bloom cannot detach himself from it. See, e.g., Harold Bloom, "'Before Moses was, I am': The Original and Belated Testaments," in H. Bloom, ed., *The Bible* (New York, 1987), 292-304.

claim that Christianity has used up all the authentic Judaism available. The Jews missed their chance, and the reason they did so was because they had all the characteristics the New Testament rhetoric ascribes to them: blindness, hypocrisy, love of money, envy, and the rest. The Christian God may wish Jews to survive for reasons of God's own, but there is certainly no legitimacy to Judaism as a religion, and no rights of Jews to practice that religion.[51]

The New Testament's language concerning Gentiles and their religious practices is even harsher. Christians had inherited from Judaism a well-developed contempt for Gentile idolatry, and like Jewish apologetics, was almost reckless in its wholesale condemnation of the majority of the Mediterranean world's population. It was axiomatic that Gentiles were "by nature" given to vice and ignorance and every sort of malice and depravity.[52] And although their "philosophy" was regarded as of little help,[53] their "religion" was considered to be the prime cause of their spiritual condition. They were lost in sin and vice precisely *because* of their worship of "dead gods." Idolatry represented not only an error in judgment, but a rebellion of the will, which led humans downward in a spiral of darkness, distortion, and destruction.[54] The ways of the Gentiles are ways of error, and their forms of religion are either pitiable or dangerous.[55]

There are some exceptions to this view, which will be noted later, some small recognition of the possibility for Gentiles to find God. But even these concessions are made despite their religion rather than through it. The most fateful step was taken when, building on the statement of Psalm 95:5 that "all the gods of the nations are demons," the writers of the New Testament simply identified pagan religion with the realm of the demonic. The equation can be detected sporadically beneath the exorcistic turf-battles between the kingdom of God and the counter kingdom of Satan that runs through Luke-Acts.[56] Particularly in Acts, the demonic role is played by forms of Gentile religion: magic, exorcism, prophecy. The Kingdom of God moves into the empire by destroying the

---

[51] That such views are not found only in the past or only among the uneducated is demonstrated by C. Klein, *Anti-Judaism in Christian Theology*, E. Quinn, trans. (Philadelphia, 1978).

[52] See Matthew 6:32; 1 Corinthians 5:1, 9; 6:10-11; 1 Thessolonians 4:5, 13; Ephesians 2:1-3, 11-12; Titus 1:12-13; 3:3; 1 Peter 1:14-18; 4:3-4; Revelation 17:1-18:20.

[53] On this, see P.W. Gooch, *Partial Knowledge: Philosophical Studies in Paul* (Notre Dame, 1987).

[54] See 1 Thessolonians 1:9-10; 1 Peter 1:14-17, and the *locus classicus*, Romans 1:18-32.

[55] See Matthew 6:7; 1 Corinthians 10:14-22; 12:1-2; Acts 13:6-12; 16:16-19; 19:11-20; 23-41.

[56] For this important aspect of Luke-Acts, see S.R. Garrett, *The Demise of the Devil: Magic and the Demonic in Luke-Acts* (Minneapolis, 1989).

power of Satan, exercised through pagan religion![57] Paul is thinking the same way when he declares in 1 Corinthians 10:20-23, "I imply that what pagans sacrifice they offer to demons and not to God [compare Deuteronomy 32:17]. I do not want you to be partners with demons. You cannot drink the cup of the Lord and the cup of demons. You cannot partake of the table of the Lord and the table of demons. Shall we provoke the Lord to jealousy? Are we stronger than he?"

I have called this step fateful, because it formed the basis for one of the most consistent themes in apologetic literature as Christianity moved into the wider world and sought its place there. The apologists of the second and third century were eager to place Christianity before the world as a philosophy,[58] and although they engaged in much of the detraction from other schools in the manner that was already conventional,[59] they were also sometimes willing to give credit to Gentile philosophy—while retaining the conviction that Moses was the best of philosophers and the source of the best of Greek philosophies,[60] that of Plato.[61]

In contrast, the apologists waged all out warfare against every form of Gentile religion. The only specific religious phenomenon for which I have found any positive acknowledgement was the Sybilline Oracle.[62] Otherwise, the view of Gentile religion is systematically skeptical and slanderous. There is no rumor too vague or scandal too small to report against its practitioners.[63] Idolatry is sometimes dismissed as fakery.[64] But when there are traditions of healing or prophecy that are impossible to dismiss, the power thus demonstrated is attributed to demons. Demons inhabited the shrines and seduced devotees. Demons worked wonders and prophesied, in order to deceive humans.[65] Demons spon-

---

[57] See Acts 5:1-11; 8:4-13; 13:4-12; 16:16-24; 19:11-20, and the discussion of them in L.T. Johnson, *The Acts of the Apostles* (Collegeville, 1992).

[58] See R.L. Wilken, "Collegia, Philosophical Schools, and Theology," in S. Benko and J. O'Rourke, eds., *The Catacombs and the Colosseum* (Valley Forge, 1971), 268-291.

[59] See, e.g., Tatian, *Address to the Greeks*, 2-3, 25; *Letter to Diognetus*, 8; Theophilus of Antioch, *To Autolycus* II, 4; III, 5-7; Clement, *Exhortation to the Greeks* V, 55.

[60] See Tatian, *Address to the Greeks*, 31; Origen, *Against Celsus*, VII, 42-45.

[61] See Clement, *Exhortation to the Greeks*, VI, 59; Origen, *Against Celsus*, VI, 3-19; VI, 47-54.

[62] Clement, *Exhortation to the Greeks*, VIII, 66; Theophilus of Antioch, *To Autolycus*, II, 9; II, 36; Justin Martyr, *Apology*, I, 20; Origen, *Against Celsus*, VII, 56.

[63] See, e.g., Clement, *Exhortation to the Greeks*, II, 13-14; II, 19; Theophilus of Antioch, *To Autolycus*, III, 8.

[64] See Clement, *Exhortation to the Greeks*, II, 13; Tatian, *Address to the Greeks*, 34.

[65] See Clement, *Exhortation to the Greeks*, I, 4; I, 7; II, 35; IV, 50; Lactantius, *Epitome*, 28 (a fuller development in *Institutes* II, 14-16); Tertullian, *Apology*, XXII-XXIII; *On Spectacles*, VIII; *To Scapula*, 2; Minucius Felix, *Octavius*, XXVII, 1-8; Tatian, *Address to the Greeks*, 9; Theophilus

sored the slanders against the Christian religion![66] The extent of this demonizing tendency is remarkable.

The implications of this rhetoric, I submit, are both obvious and
tragic. Demonizing other religions not only deprives them of any sacred
or revelatory value; it also deprives them of their properly human character, and makes them essentially a manifestation of enslavement rather
than of freedom. The people practicing such cults are held in thrall and
require exorcism. It is unthinkable to grant "religious freedom" to those
who are held captive by demonic forces. The demonization of other religions—indeed of heresies within the Christian tradition[67]—makes their
recognition as legitimate expressions of worship impossible.

I am suggesting that the grounds of Christian intolerance are imbed-
ded in the canonical texts and continue to shape Christian consciousness.
The tendency of Christian monotheism to absolutize religious commitment in an either/or, together with the tendency of Christian rhetoric to
demonize any form of religion not explicitly (and correctly) Christian,
combine in perpetuating intolerance toward religious diversity, and
therefore toward the religious rights of others. It is surely not by accident
that the Johannine literature, in which these tendencies converge most
dramatically,[68] is the touchstone of orthodoxy for those who consider
themselves to be truly "Bible Christians."

Exorcising the Demons of Intolerance in Christianity

Identifying the virus of intolerance latent within the biblical writings
will not by itself prevent its recurrence among Christians. A faithful and
critical hermeneutics must also provide an antidote, a reading of the New
Testament which counters its negative potential and at the same time
provides a positive basis for the Christian recognition of religious rights
as human rights. The appropriate beginning point for this critical and
constructive effort, however, is modesty. As John Courtney Murray
rightly notes, the attempt to ground religious liberty in the Bible is an
ambiguous one: "[I]t runs the risk of presenting religious freedom as
somehow a purely Christian invention, whereas every student of history

---

of Antioch, *To Autolycus*, I, 10; II, 8; Athenagoras, *Embassy*, 26-27; Justin Martyr, *Apology* I, 9;
56-57; Origen, *Against Celsus*, III, 3; III, 34-35; VII, 3-6; VII, 35; VII, 69; VIII, 13; VIII, 24.

[66] See Minucius Felix, *Octavius*, XXVIII; Justin Martyr, *Apology*, I, 14.

[67] Note that Justin Martyr attributes heresies to the demons. See ibid., I, 58.

[68] See W.A. Meeks, "The Man from Heaven in Johannine Sectarianism," *Journal of Biblical Literature* 91 (1972): 44-72.

knows that the idea has been developed and brought to realization also, and quite importantly, by the force of purely secular dynamisms."[69]

Indeed, the way of reading the canonical texts suggested here is in serious tension with the dominant tradition of Christian interpretation. It must be undertaken, therefore, not in a spirit of capitulation to the dominant ethos of the moment, or as a gesture of self-hatred, but rather in obedience to the guidance of God's Spirit as it has acted in our shared history, directing us in the light of centuries of tragic practice based on one way of reading to discern whether another way of reading may not be closer to the central principles of the Christian religion and perhaps even to the deeper meaning of the texts themselves.

The discipline of such re-reading is all the more necessary for those who are simultaneously committed to liberal social practices and their Christian identity, for if they are negligent in their reading of the text, or fail to base their practice in a spirit of fidelity to the text, they will fail to move less connaturally liberal Christians to this required *metanoia*, and will abandon the field of Christian hermeneutics to those with insufficient immunity to the text's latent virus of intolerance.

What reading of the texts, then, can be offered by way of antidote to Christianity's history of religious intolerance? In the following paragraphs, three basic approaches are suggested. They do not offer a comprehensive program, but only the sketch of how a serious hermeneutical engagement with this issue might proceed. I will consider in turn (1) the necessity of relativizing the polemical rhetoric of the New Testament; (2) the importance of hearing voices within the canonical texts that an earlier tradition of reading tended to suppress; and (3) the possibility of appealing to the central moral convictions of the New Testament as a guide to Christian attitudes concerning the religious rights of others.

Relativizing the Rhetoric. This first step has already been demonstrated by my earlier discussion. To read the polemic of the New Testament against Jews and Gentiles in terms of its historical circumstances and in terms of ancient rhetorical conventions is already to relativize its power. The reason is obvious: the texts are read not as unique and direct divine revelations expressing propositional truths about reality, but as human writings generated by specific social and historical circumstances and expressing truths of experience and conviction that possess revelatory value for subsequent readers only indirectly and through the mediation of interpretation. Precisely such a reading will be resisted by many biblicist Christians, whose allegiance to a "literal meaning" as the

---

[69] Murray, "Religious Freedom," 140.

basis for their Christian identity is absolute, and who regard any historical or literary contextualization as an attack on the authority of the text.[70]

Those of us who insist that taking the texts seriously implies precisely
the need for such a critical distanciation, and that the authority of the
texts is not diminished but enhanced by such interpretation, must recognize that at just this point, we face the absolutizing and exclusivistic tendencies I have earlier described. For such a view, it is not enough to
affirm the inspiration and authority of the text, or the value of a literal
rendering; each of those affirmations must also correspond with a specific interpretation of them, or be rejected as a faithless rejection of biblical authority.

The first hermeneutical battle within Christian communities on this
point, in other words—as on so many other points—focuses on the legitimacy of hermeneutics itself. And the very tendencies of the tradition
toward intolerance that this critical yet faithful hermeneutics wishes to
relativize will show themselves most powerfully and rigidly at this first
step. And with reason, for intolerance can thrive only in the world of absolutes. It recognizes that to render texts relative rather than absolute in
their force is already to concede the game. Many other things will follow.

Since in this chapter I *want* other things to follow, I will spell out the
first step, and then move on to the others. What does it mean to
"relativize the rhetoric?" Does it mean simply to deny the truthfulness of
scripture and rob it of its authority? Not at all. Rather, it means to gain
clarity on the sort of truthfulness such language contains, and to locate
more properly the authority of the text.

Ancient polemic has a sort of "truthfulness" that is appropriate to its
literary conventions and social context. In battles between rival groups,
such polemic (always read by insiders) served to encourage positive attitudes by exaggerating the wicked characteristics of the outsiders. Insider identity could be reinforced by means of contrast to outsiders, but it
could also be challenged by the suggestion that the evil traits of outsiders
might also be present among insiders.[71] Such language can serve a variety of legitimate literary functions that are "true." In Luke's Gospel, the
designation of the Pharisees as "lovers of money" (Luke 16:14) is literar-
ily "true," because in his narrative, those who oppose the prophet Jesus
are "the rich," and the Pharisees do reject the prophet Jesus.[72] To literalize

---

[70] See the thoughtful presentation of this approach by J.W. Cottrell, "The Nature of Biblical Authority: A Conservative Perspective," in C.R. Blaisdell, ed., *Conservative, Moderate, Liberal: The Biblical Authority Debate* (St. Louis, 1990), 21-40.

[71] For this function of polemical language in Matthew 23, with its vilifying of "Scribes
and Pharisees," see Johnson, "The New Testament's Anti-Jewish Slander," 433-34.

[72] See L.T. Johnson, *The Literary Function of Possessions in Luke-Acts* (Missoula, 1977), 109-
110.

and historicize such a characterization is both to rob it of its literary truth and to commit historical falsehood, for the Pharisees, on the evidence, were no more avaricious than other humans. Such literalization also deprives the text of its capacity to speak critically to insiders as "lovers of money" who reject prophetic speech.[73] It is possible, in a word, to deny the historical or propositional truth of ancient polemic regarding the Jews and the Gentiles without depriving the text of its more significant truthfulness, which has to do with its witness to authentic existence before God.

Defining the truth of scripture according to the literary conventions of the text seems a fairly obvious step.[74] But does it deprive the text of its authority? This would be the case only if scriptural authority is conceived of in simplistic terms. In fact, the authority of scripture for the life of the Christian community is part of an ongoing conversation which is always complex, most often indirect, and always mediated. To assert the authority of the scripture ought to mean that in every such conversation the words of scripture are taken with full seriousness. They cannot be taken with full seriousness unless they are considered in the light of their literary form and historical functions.[75]

To relativize the rhetoric of the New Testament concerning Jews and Gentiles is, I submit, both to take the truth and the authority of the scripture more seriously rather than less. The case can be made clearer by its contrary: to read the New Testament language about Jews and Gentiles of the past as though it spoke the literal truth about those who practice Judaism and other world religions today is to commit the New Testament to falsehood; to take that language literally as authorization for intolerance and persecution of Jews and other non-Christians today would be to falsify the authority of the scripture.

It is simply the case that the New Testament (like the Hebrew Scriptures) was written for a world considerably smaller than our own. Saint Paul could not have imagined the variety of ancient cultures and religious practices that might be included under the term "Gentiles," and could never have conceived that after twenty centuries there could still be humans who had never heard the Good News that Paul thought would shortly reach all people. If these texts are to speak to our own larger, more complex, and infinitely more pluralistic world, they must

---

[73] See R.J. Karris, "Rich and Poor: The Lukan Sitz-im-Leben," in C.H. Talbert, ed., *Perspectives on Luke-Acts* (Danville, 1978), 112-125.

[74] And taken as a necessary step in interpretation by Pius XII, *Divini Afflante Spiritu*, and the Second Vatican Council's *Dogmatic Constitution on Divine Revelation*, III.

[75] See L.T. Johnson, "Fragments of an Untidy Conversation: Theology and the Literary Diversity of the New Testament," in S. Kraftchick, ed., *Biblical Theology: Problems and Prospects* (forthcoming).

undergo more than a literal translation: they must be engaged in a way that allows their best and most enduring witness to Christian life to transcend those limitations that might, in other contexts, distort that witness.

I have dwelled at length on this first step, for it is of critical importance. It involves a sort of spiritual *kenosis* on the part of Christian readers, a modesty, if you will, before the mystery with which they have been entrusted. Choosing to dwell within the world of symbols shaped by Scripture, they take its strictures as addressed to their own hearts and not to other people; they repent of their own sins and do not count those of others; they celebrate the gift given them in the Lord Jesus and do not deliberate what gifts might be given others; they think it true that Jews have missed seeing Jesus as Messiah, but do not conclude that Jews have also thereby missed God; they think it right that idolatry as they have come to understand it leads people astray, but do not suppose that Hinduism is necessarily that sort of idolatry; they understand that spiritual forces can work for evil, but they take it as reckless impiety to suggest that the worship of a neighbor is demonic—unless, of course, the neighbor invites that description!

Relativizing Theological Claims. The application of literary and historical criticism to the rhetoric of the New Testament is a first step. But it does not go far enough, for the strain of intolerance in these texts derives not only from the language used about outsiders but also from the absolute character of its own theological claims. These resist historical relativization, and even gain greater force from their placement within the canon of scripture. The either/or character of Jewish-Christian monotheism appears even sharper when read outside the context of an ancient debate and as a uniquely inspired revelation. Approaching such language is therefore an even more delicate task, for attempts to soften that either/or can easily be regarded as a betrayal of Christian faith.

Nevertheless, the approach must be made, for the sake of full fidelity to the texts themselves, as well as for the health of the Christian confession. Two lines of reflection are suggested by the New Testament itself and can be indicated though not developed here.

The first begins with the recognition that the New Testament is not and has never claimed to be a description of objective reality, but rather a set of witnesses and interpretations of a community's faith. The very language of "confession" and "witness" indicates its intensely and irrevocably personal character. The statements made in the New Testament about God and about Jesus as Son of God, Lord, and Messiah, are statements that derive from specific and powerful human experiences of those realities. They witness to certain profound religious experiences, and they seek to interpret those experiences.[76] The "truth character" of the texts is found precisely in their subjectivity. For a religious community, this does not make them less but more valuable.

Confessional language can state truly what the community experiences and believes. Thus Paul in 1 Corinthians 8:5-6: "Although there may be so-called gods in heaven or on earth—as indeed there are many gods and many lords—yet *for us* there is one God, the Father, from whom are all things and for whom we exist, and one Lord, Jesus Christ, through whom are all things and through whom we exist." Certainly such language makes a claim to truth about the world as such; but the phrase "for us" recognizes that this claim is inextricably rooted in the subjective religious experience and commitment of the community, and that outsiders might be able to make a similar claim about "their" lord or god. The correlation of religious experience to confession is stated starkly by 1 Corinthians 12:3: "No one speaking by the Spirit of God says 'Jesus be cursed,' and no one can say, 'Jesus is Lord,' except by the Holy Spirit."[77]

What confessional language *cannot* truthfully do is deny the truth claims of other religious experiences or convictions. Once more, we return to the notion of an appropriate modesty before the mystery. The language of faith can celebrate the gift given this community. It cannot transcend itself also to be the adjudicator of other gifts given to other communities, or deny that other gifts might be given to other peoples. It is not given to humans to be both witnesses and judges.

I am suggesting that the monotheism Christianity inherited from Judaism with its strain of exclusivism and its demand for an either/or, can learn an important lesson from the more philosophical monotheism that encompassed a both/and. It could recognize the inevitable particularity and pluralism of religious expression without denying that only a single divine Person created, sustained, and governed the world. Schooled in this perception, Christians could read even the most exclusive and particularistic claims in the New Testament not as calls for intolerance, but as invitations to a more generous apprehension of God's activity among humans. Does Peter in Acts declare about Jesus, "there is no other name under heaven given among men by which we must be saved" (Acts 4:12)? Christians can assent to this wholeheartedly, for in fact this is the name by which they *are* "being saved." Does John have Jesus declare, "I am the way and the truth and the life; no one comes to the Father but by

---

[76] For this understanding of the New Testament, see Johnson, *The Writings of the New Testament*, 1-22, 530-51.

[77] Notice that this follows a polemical statement in 12:1-2 about being "carried away" by spiritual forces to idols; what is more interesting about the text is that it recognizes a commonality in religious experience beneath the difference in specific type.

me" (John 14:6)? The Christian finds no reason to question the truth of this, for to be a Christian means precisely to go to the Father through Jesus. But such language does *not* allow Christians to deny God other possibilities than the ones God has shared with them.[78]

Such modesty about the absolute claims in the New Testament is more than good manners. It is demanded by intellectual honesty. It is also supported by a second line of reflection on the theological language of the New Testament, which begins with the recognition that these writings also contain a number of powerful witnesses quite different from those used to support Christian intolerance. Allowing such statements to occupy a more central position is essential for changing the Christian mind concerning religious pluralism.

There are first those statements which stand in tension with the condemnation of Gentile religiosity by giving some positive recognition to the religious strivings and the moral character of the Gentile world. The most emphatic of these is found in Paul's Areopagus speech, which builds on the Athenian custom of erecting an altar to an "unknown God." Paul declares that he brings news of this God, "the one who made the world and everything in it. Since he is Lord of heaven and earth he does not dwell in temples made by hands. Neither is he served by human hands as though he needed anything, since he himself gives life and breath and everything to everyone." But Paul does not here despise their *deisidaimonia*,[79] or the ways in which humans throughout the world have sought and even found God: "From one human being he has made every nation of humans to dwell over the entire face of the earth. He has set apart designated seasons and the territories for their habitation, so that they might seek God, perhaps even sense and find him." The basis of this universal call to humans is creation itself: "Indeed he is not far from each one of us, 'For by him we live and move and are,' as even some of the poets among you have said, 'for we are also of his family'" (Acts 17:22-28). Although this speech obviously supplies the "explicit" for what they sought "implicitly," and concludes with the proclamation of Jesus, it is

---

[78] Circumspection is appropriate as well in making claims concerning other traditions from the perspective of Christian faith; one can appreciate the ecumenical impulses behind attempts to incorporate the world's peoples into an "anonymous Christianity," while still recognizing its inadequacy for the question facing us. See, e.g., K. Rahner, "Anonymous Christians," in *Theological Investigations*, K.H. and B. Kruger, trans. (New York, 1974), 6:390-98 and K. Barth, *Church Dogmatics* G.W. Bromiley and T.F. Torrance, eds. (Edinburgh, 1961) IV, 3, 1: The Doctrine of Reconciliation, 349-367.

[79] The term used by Paul in 17:22 is polyvalent; used negatively, it can mean "superstition" (Strabo, *Geography of Greece* 16, 2, 37), but used positively, it means "religious" (Dio Chrysostom, *Oration*, 61:9). The positive meaning is here intended.

nevertheless remarkably positive toward the legitimacy of Gentile religious longing.[80]

Of equal importance is Paul's own statement in Romans 2:1-16 concerning the status of Gentiles who have never heard the Law of God: "When Gentiles who have not the law do what the law requires, they are a law unto themselves, even though they do not have the law. They show that what the law requires is written on their hearts, while their conscience also bears witness and their conflicting thoughts accuse or perhaps excuse them" (2:14-15). We notice here the importance of acting according to "conscience" (*syneidesis*).[81] The radical character of Paul's statement lies in his placing both Jews and Gentiles on the same footing before God; not their religious confession but their deeds are what determine their place: "there will be tribulation and distress for every human being who does evil, the Jew first and also the Greek, but glory and honor and peace for every one who does good, the Jew first and also the Greek" (2:9-10). And Paul concludes this startling declaration with its theological warrant, "for God shows no partiality" (2:11).[82]

The theological principle of God's impartiality—that is, God's fairness toward all creation—is found in narrative form in Acts: Peter's invitation to visit the Gentile Cornelius leads him to perceive first that "God has shown me not to call any person common or unclean" (Acts 10:28), and then, "In truth, I am grasping that God is no respecter of persons. Rather, in every nation, the one who fears God and acts righteously is acceptable to him" (Acts 10:34).[83] This same principle of impartiality is the linch-pin of Paul's magisterial argument concerning the "righteousness of God" in his *Letter to the Romans*,[84] for Paul perceived that if God were truly One (that is, the source of all reality) and were truly righteous (that is, fair), then God must make available to all humans

---

[80] For the irenic and bridge-building character of the speech, see B. Gaertner, *The Areopagus Speech and Natural Revelation* (Lund, 1955) and F.G. Downing, "Common Ground with Paganism in Luke and Josephus," *New Testament Studies* 28 (1982): 546-59.

[81] This passage is one of the critical scriptural supports for the notion of "natural law," which plays a significant role in discussions concerning human rights. See, e.g., Thomas Aquinas, *Summa Theologica* I-II, q. 91, art. 2.

[82] The term *aprosōpolēmpsia* ("impartiality") is a New Testament neologism, deriving from the LXX translation, *prosopon labein* of the Hebrew *nasa panim*, ("to lift up a face"). The concept derives from passages like Leviticus 19:15: the just judge makes a decision based on the truth of the case and not on appearances.

[83] Peter's insight extends even further, to the recognition that Jewish Christians are "saved" on the same basis as the Gentiles, that is, by faith (Acts 15:11). For this whole development, see Johnson, *Decision-Making in the Church*, 59-87.

[84] On this, see J. Bassler, *Divine Impartiality: Paul and a Theological Axiom* (Chico, 1981) and H. Moxnes, *Theology in Conflict: Studies of Paul's Understanding of God in Romans* (Leiden, 1980).

some means of true response to God. Paul finds this in the response of faith. But, as many other recent critics have argued, Paul does not mean by faith first of all "faith in Christ," but rather "faith in God," which was brought to its supreme realization in Jesus' own faith (Romans 3:21-26).[85] Because Abraham had faith in God even when still a Gentile, he was counted as righteous (Romans 4:3-10), and became "the father of us all" (Romans 4:16).

Paul alone among the New Testament writers perceived the radical implications of the Gentile mission and the principle of righteousness by faith. If Gentiles can please God by following the law in their hearts apart from any "special revelation" through Torah, and if Abraham could be declared righteous by God through his obedient faith even before the Messiah, then the implications are profound: "We hold that a person is justified by faith apart from works of the law. Or is God the God of the Jews only? Is he not the God of Gentiles also? Yes, of Gentiles also, since God is One. And he will justify the circumcised on the grounds of their faith and the uncircumcised through their faith" (Romans 3:28-30). Christian theology has been slow to realize that, if taken seriously, Paul's dictum serves to relativize Christianity's absolute claims as well. Is God the God of the Christians only? No, for God is one. Then what follows?[86]

In Romans 9-11, Paul's midrashic argument concerning the ways in which God works dialectically through patterns of belief and unbelief among the world's nations expresses the same theological principle: even though the mystery of God's dealings are beyond human capacity to control or even to understand (11:33-35), the glimpses we have been given assure us that God's project is one that concerns all humans: "God has consigned all humans to disobedience, that he may have mercy upon all" (11:32).

The flat statement in 1 Timothy 2:3-4, that God "wills the salvation of all humans and that they come to the knowledge of the truth," is therefore not entirely isolated in the New Testament. There is a strong element of universalism to counter other more exclusive claims. In them, we see the development toward a monotheism that can celebrate the particularity of God's gift to this community in Christ the Lord, but uses that gift as the basis for positing a God sufficiently capacious in love to gift all humans in their own particularities, a God who "gives to all humans generously and without grudging" (James 1:5).

---

[85] See L.T. Johnson, "Romans 3:21-26 and the Faith of Jesus," *Catholic Biblical Quarterly* 44 (1982): 77-90.

[86] On this, see H. Boers, *The Justification of the Gentiles: Paul's Letters to the Romans and Galatians* (Peabody, 1994), 221-27.

Legitimating Religious Diversity. In the previous two sections, I have suggested ways in which tendencies in the New Testament leading to religious intolerance might be countered. Now I turn to a small group of texts which give direct support to religious liberty and diversity. The first set of statements are broadly acknowledged as Christianty's distinctive contribution to the development of religious rights; the second set of statements are perhaps as important, but are not usually read in the context of the present issue.

In two of his letters, Paul explicitly takes up the question of diversity of practice within the Christian community. In 1 Corinthians 8-10, the issue involves dietary regulations: are Christians allowed to purchase meat for their meals from pagan shrines, knowing that a portion of the animal had first been used in a religious ceremony ("offered to idols"), and are Christians allowed to take part in meals located at a pagan shrine?[87] The question of diet may appear to us as trivial, but it was not for the ancient world; matters of table-fellowship were of supreme importance in symbolizing one's spiritual allegiances. Paul's discussion is remarkable above all for its refusal to give a comprehensive answer: proper behavior depended on the circumstances, and the discernment of the circumstances in turn was the business of the individual's conscience (*syneidesis*).[88] In 8:7-13, Paul makes a series of statements that are literally of epochal importance. The morality of eating or not eating is not located in the objective facts of the case, but in the individual person's *perception* of those facts. It is the individual conscience which determines whether behavior is righteous or not. If I erroneously think something is wrong and do it, then I have done wrong: "But not all possess this knowledge [that idols are not real] . . . being hitherto accustomed to idols, eat food as really offered to an idol, and their conscience, being weak, is defiled" (8:7).

Paul's making the individual conscience the basis for righteousness before God within the messianic community is consistent with his insistence that the basis for Gentile righteousness before God is the "law written in the heart," that is, witnessed to by their conscience (Romans 2:15). It represents the fundamental shift from a heteronomous ethics to moral autonomy. And it provides the fundamental ground for religious liberty. If the determination of right and wrong is inward, it can be known only by the person's own conscience: "who knows a person's

---

[87] For the complexity of these issues in an intentional community, see G. Theissen, *The Social Setting of Pauline Christianity: Essays on Corinth*, J.H. Schuetz, trans. and ed. (Philadelphia, 1982), 69-144, and W.A. Meeks, *The First Urban Christians: The Social World of the Apostle Paul* (New Haven, 1983), 157-161.

[88] For a close analysis of his argument, see M. Mitchell, *Paul and the Rhetoric of Reconciliation* (Louisville, 1991), 237-257.

thoughts except the spirit of that person within" (1 Corinthians 2:11)? For
Paul, of course, the inner heart of a person is known even more truly by
God, which enables God to be the righteous judge unswayed by appearances and determining reward and punishment fairly by the actions
judged by the persons themselves to be right or wrong, "on that day,
when, according to my Gospel, God judges the secrets of men by Christ
Jesus" (Romans 2:14).

If one's ultimate destiny is to be determined by the discernment and
dictates of one's own conscience before God, it follows that conscience
must be free. It must not be subject to external tampering or manipulation. The coercion of authority or of societal pressure may force the body
to act in a certain way, but it must not force the mind to think a certain
way.[89] Liberty of conscience is the fundamental basis for religious freedom.[90]

At the conclusion of Romans, Paul expands the discussion of diversity in religious practice to include both diet and the observance of different days (Romans 14:1-5). Once more, he states the principle that it is the
individual conscience which determines the character of an act: "I know
and am persuaded in the Lord Jesus that nothing is unclean in itself; but
it is unclean for anyone who thinks it unclean" (14:14). It is important,
therefore, for each person to have a well-formed conscience: "let every
one be fully convinced in one's own mind" (14:5). Indeed, "the one who
has doubts is condemned, if that person eats, because of not acting from
faith; for whatever does not proceed from faith is sin" (14:23). Once more,
we see that the realm of conscience is a matter between the individual
person and God; it is a realm where human judgment is inappropriate
and unacceptable: "who are you to pass judgment on the servant of another? It is before one's own master that this one stands or falls. And he
will be upheld, for the Master is able to make him stand" (14:4). And
again, "Why do you pass judgment on your brother? Or you, why do you
despise your brother? For we shall all stand before the judgment seat of
God . . . so each of us shall give an account of oneself to God" (14:12).[91]

Underlying Paul's understanding of the primacy of conscience—
although remarkably left unexpressed—is the conviction that humans are
created "in the image of God" (Genesis 1:27), and are therefore of all

---

[89] This is precisely what is so profoundly offensive to genuine religious sensibilities
about any form of "programming" or mental manipulation.

[90] Compare this remarkable statement, in 1857, by L. Simon, "Tout cela . . . est compris
dans ce mot de liberté de conscience; il enferme tout à la fois le droit de penser, le droit de
prier, le droit d'enseigner et le droit d'user de cette triple liberté sans souffrir aucune dimi-
nution dans sa dignité d'homme et de citoyen." Simon, La Liberté de Conscience, 261.

[91] For the continuity in argument between the "theological" part of Romans and this
practical discussion of community life, see Johnson, Writings of the New Testament, 334-36.

creatures possessed both of special rights and responsibilities in relationship with creation and the creator.[92]

It is true that Paul's statements are directed in the first place to practices within the faith community, but they can be extrapolated into the wider arena of Christian attitudes toward other religious beliefs and practices. And even within the Christian community, one wonders why these words of Paul did not have a more restraining effect on heresiologists and inquisitors. Paul's statements on the inviolable rights of the conscience did have a great impact, nevertheless, on early Christian apologists. Even when they did not directly credit Paul, the principle that religious freedom is rooted in the liberty of conscience is a repeated theme. So Lactantius (250-325) declares: "[I]t is religion alone in which liberty has established her dwelling place. Beyond everything else, religion is a matter of free choice, nor can anyone be compelled to worship what he dislikes."[93] So Tertullian can state: "It is the law of mankind and the natural right of each individual to worship what he thinks is proper, nor does the religion of one man either harm or help another. But it is not proper for religion to compel men to religion, which should be accepted of one's own accord, not by force, since sacrifices also are required of a willing mind."[94]

In the medieval period, the comments of the *Glossa Ordinaria* on Romans 14:23 stimulated scholastic theologians to grapple with the concept of freedom of conscience in religion.[95] And in modern Christian declarations concerning the rights to religious liberty, the principle of the freedom of conscience, rooted in the understanding of humans as created in the image of God and therefore possessed of special and inalienable dignity, has played a pivotal role.[96]

In dealing with specific questions of religious diversity—differences in observance with regard to days and diet—Paul established a body of principles that could be extrapolated beyond those past, local, circumstances. Another set of statements in Paul also deals with religious diversity and deserves much closer attention than can be given them here.

---

[92] For the literature, see J. Jervell, *Imago Dei: Gen 1:26f in Spätjudentum, in den Gnosis, und in den paulinischen Briefen* (Göttingen, 1960).

[93] Lactantius, *Epitome*, 54; see also Tertullian, *Apology*, XXIV, 5-6; XXVIII, 1.

[94] Tertullian, *To Scapula*, 2; other texts which make appeal to conscience even when it flies in the face of custom or written laws, are Lactantius, *Epitome*, 55; Tertullian, *Apology*, XXVII, 1; Tatian, *Address to the Greeks*, 27; Justin, *Apology*, I, 2. In Origen, the appeal to conscience is connected explicitly to the notion of humans being created in the image of God; see *Against Celsus*, I, 4-5; V, 32-37.

[95] See L. Janssens, *Freedom of Conscience and Religious Freedom*, 21-53.

[96] Ibid., 120-24; Murray, "Religious Freedom," 138-39; Shupack, "The Churches and Human Rights," 149-53.

Once more, they are addressed to the local church at Corinth. This was, as we know, a church already fractious and on the verge of fragmentation, precisely because differences in opinion were hardening into mutually exclusive and intolerant parties. In the face of such refusal of diversity and willingness to divide, Paul's emphasis on the legitimacy of diversity is remarkable.[97] Of course he summons his readers to unity, but it is a unity of consciousness and commitment (1 Corinthians 10-3:4). On specific points, he regularly legitimates diversity of practice, so long as fundamental moral standards are met: he allows both marriage and virginity as legitimate forms of sexual expression (7:1-40); he can see circumstances where either participation or avoidance of idol-foods can be allowed (8:1-13); he acknowledges differences in ministerial style as legitimate (9:1-33).

Most striking, however, is Paul's explicit endorsement of the diversity of gifts and ministries within the community (12:4-31). What is impressive here is not simply the assertion that multiplicity is good and can work for the building up of the community of faith, nor even the metaphor of the messianic body, each of whose parts are essential and valuable for the life of the whole. What is most startling is that Paul roots this diversity in the life of God, the bestower of gifts: "There are varieties of gifts, but the same Spirit; and there are varieties of service, but the same Lord; and there are varieties of working, but it is the same God, who inspires them all in every one. To each is given the manifestation of the Spirit for the common good" (12:4-7). By using a three-fold designation for the cause behind a plurality of effects (Spirit, Lord, God), Paul plants the seed that will develop into the rich growth of Christian trinitarian thought. It reminds us that the Christian understanding of God as the source of all reality is, after all, not monadal but trinitarian, and that at the heart of God's own life there is both richness and diversity of expression—a unity all the more perfect because it encompasses difference. A deeper appreciation of trinitarian monotheism and of the richness of spiritual gifts such a prolifically alive God can bestow on humans, can go some way toward moderating the more exclusivist tendencies of Christianity's inherited monotheism.[98]

Living by Christianity's Moral Standard. What is perhaps most painful in Christianity's history of religious intolerance is the way in which it has failed to live by its own moral principles. Even if Christians

---

[97] A still valuable sketch of the factors leading to the composition of 1 Corinthians is J.C. Hurd, *The Origin of 1 Corinthians* (London, 1965).

[98] For the ways in which trinitarian thought can encompass a diversity of ways of speaking about God, see the important study by E. Johnson, *She Who Is: The Mystery of God in Feminist Theological Discourse* (New York, 1992).

cannot accomplish the mental *metanoia* necessary to perceive religious diversity as legitimate, and religious freedom as a fundamental human right, they can accomplish the moral *metanoia* demanded by their own tradition. Despite all the absoluteness of its theological claims, and despite its often harsh rhetoric against outsiders —the elements, we have seen, that enable the virus of intolerance to survive—the New Testament is unequivocally clear concerning the way humans are to act toward others.

The texts we have already surveyed insist that the religious choices made by humans are a matter between them and God—and must necessarily be so, since only they and God can know the basis of those decisions. They also insist that Christians are forbidden to judge those decisions made by others, much less to condemn them. Far from allowing Christians to coerce others, the texts caution even against influencing others in the delicate matters of conscience.

These same texts emphasize that the "mind of Christ" by which Christians are to live ought to impel them to lives of mutual upbuilding, that the exercise of one spiritual gift does not detract from or replace the exercise of another, and that diversity is the precondition rather than the opposite of true unity. And we do not have to search far to find moral principles that are of the most direct pertinence to the issue of religious rights. The most obvious is Jesus' commandment in Matthew 5:12: "Whatever you wish that men would do to you, do so to them; for this is the law and the prophets." It is a tribute to the power of religious intolerance that Christians who when in the minority and persecuted have asked that their freedom of conscience, their right to worship both privately and publicly, be granted, should so regularly have failed to grant that same right to others when they have been in the position to do so. But unless such behavior (every time it occurs) is recognized as a betrayal of the most fundamental moral standard of Christianity itself, then any notional assent to the principle of religious freedom is meaningless.

In its ideal, of course, Christianity seeks to adhere to a higher standard than even that of reciprocal respect for rights. Ideally, Christians see themselves summoned by Jesus to a love that transcends reciprocity: "You have heard that it was said, 'You shall love your neighbor and hate your enemy.' But I say to you, love your enemies and pray for those who persecute you" (Matthew 5:43). Ideally, Christians know that they are called to a standard exemplified by Jesus, who declared: "This is my commandment, that you love one another as I have loved you" (John 15:12). And Christians ideally understand that the one who "loved [them] and gave himself for [them]" (Galatians 2:20) also provided a pattern of that love which requires the most painful relativizing of one's own rights so that other may thrive. That is the ideal. And living by the ideal, Christians could combine their ecstatic celebration of the gifts given them with the joyful acknowledgement of the gifts given to others, having no need to suppress difference but rather to find in it the cause of ceaseless wonder at a prodigal God.

But since in every religious tradition the ideal is scarcely to be expected as a given, Christians might make a start with the Golden Rule as a minimum moral norm for behavior toward the religious practices of others. And against the backdrop of the language of their own tradition, Christians might do well to begin with speech, mindful of the words of James on the tongue: "With it we bless the Lord and Father, and with it we curse humans, who are made in the likeness of God. From the same mouth come blessing and curse. My brothers, this ought not to be so" (James 3:9-10).

Conclusion

In this chapter, I have suggested that the long history of religious intolerance among Christians suggests that a strain of intolerance is embedded in its normative texts, and that Christian affirmation of religious rights as humans rights requires in addition to a moral commitment a hermeneutical engagement with these texts. The virus of intolerance was located in the absolutizing and exclusivistic claims of the New Testament, and in its rhetoric about outsiders. I have argued that, though powerful, this strain is not so deadly as to vitiate the positive power of the New Testament. In addition to relativizing the rhetoric and the theological claims of the New Testament, therefore, primarily by paying close attention to the functions of the language expressing them, I have put forward witnesses in the New Testament that provide an opening to a more positive apprehension of religious rights of all persons. For Christianity, these are rooted in the principle that humans are created in the image of God, that the internal forum of conscience is inviolable to coercion, and that the richness of God's gifts to humans go beyond any tradition's capacity to comprehend. Finally, I appealed to the central moral principles of the Christian tradition as the most effective antidote to intolerance.

Christianity, like all religious traditions, is obligated by the exigencies of historical existence to renegotiate in every generation its normative texts in the face of an ever-changing world. The present chapter has had no other ambition than to offer a way of conceiving and considering the issue of "religious rights and Christian texts" in a world ever more obviously pluralistic. The premise of the chapter has been that the end of the

Constantinian era was far from the worst calamity to befall Christianity and may have been its greatest blessing, for it allows this tradition that has for so long been entangled in questions of politics and culture to rediscover once more the benefits of life in the diaspora.

The possibility has been extended for a fresh start on negotiating a place among the world's peoples and their religions. Perhaps this second time around Christians might learn from the more generous impulses glimpsed in texts from the time of its first diaspora, might be able to acknowledge more graciously the truths given to others by God,[99] and to breathe once more in rhythm with the most serene of Christian apologetic writings: "He came in gentleness and humility. He sent him as a king would send a son and king. He sent him as God for the sake of men. In sending him, he acted as a savior, appealing to persuasion and not to power—for it is not like God to use compulsion. He acted as one inviting, not as one pursuing; as a lover, not as a judge. . . ."[100]

---

[99] See, for example, the lovely testimony to the realization of religious truth among the nations—"even though they have been thought atheists"—in Justin Martyr, *Apology*, I, 41, and the acknowledgement of truths about God in the Greek poets, found in Clement, *Exhortation to the Greeks*, VII, 64, and Theophilus of Antioch, *To Autolycus*, II, 8.

[100] *Letter to Diognetus*, 7.

Religious Activism For Human Rights: A Christian Case Study

J. BRYAN HEHIR

Harvard University

I t is a simple task to demonstrate the substantial connection between the ministry of the Christian church, in its Catholic, Protestant, and Orthodox communities, and the defense and support of human rights today. A ministry of human rights is one of the explicit, public bonds which unites ecumenical Christianity in the last half of this often violent century. The common pursuit of human rights does not rule out a diversity of theological and philosophical traditions which contribute to the ministry; for the most part, a common witness often rests upon a pluralistic doctrinal foundation. Nor does a common witness translate directly into consensus about specific moral judgements made in concrete cases affecting human rights. The complexity and contingency of policy judgements on human rights would guarantee moral pluralism even if all the Christian communities worked from a unified theological-philosophical view of human rights.

One method of conceiving the topic would be to explore the diverse conceptions of the human rights ministry in the Christian church, testing the premises and patterns of moral reasoning which sustain a collaborative ministry in spite of theological and moral diversity. I have chosen not to pursue this road. Instead, in this chapter, I offer a case study of contemporary Catholicism's engagement with the issue of human rights. My hope is that it can serve as an example of how each major tradition within the Christian church could be analyzed in terms of its theory and policy.

In analyzing the relationship of the Catholic church to human rights, it is useful to acknowledge at the outset that the relationship has often seemed problematical, even to sympathetic analysts of Catholic life. In an article which ultimately draws a close and effective bond between the Catholic church and the promotion of human rights in the 1970s and

J. Witte, Jr. and J.D. van der Vyver (eds.), Religious Human Rights in Global Perspective, 97-119.
© 1996 *Kluwer Law International. Printed in the Netherlands.*

1980s, Professor Samuel Huntington begins his analysis with three commonly accepted reasons for suspecting a positive correlation of the Roman church and human rights. Citing Seymour Martin Lipset's observation that Catholicism "appeared antithetical to democracy in pre-World War II Europe and America,"[1] Huntington went on to specify "three plausible reasons" for expecting Protestant Christianity to be a more congenial setting for human rights principles and practice. Summarizing work in social science, Huntington found a doctrinal predisposition (the Protestant stress on individual conscience), an ecclesiological affinity (the democratic polity of Protestant communities), and a socio-economic tie (Weber's spirit of capitalism) between Protestant Christianity, human rights, and democracy.[2] On all counts Catholicism stressed different themes and values. The point of Huntington's research, however, was to highlight the central role of Catholicism in the struggle for human rights and democracy in the 1970s and 1980s. The thesis of this chapter is that the surprising correlation between contemporary Catholicism and human rights can be accounted for by developments in Catholic teaching and changes in both the world and the church. In this chapter, I shall first trace these themes and then seek to identify the emerging human rights challenges for the church in the decade of the 1990s.

Theory: The Rise of Rights in Catholic Teaching

When Professor Michael Walzer introduced his study of the just war theory, he forewarned his readers that he was writing a book of practical morality; he was not going to probe the "substructure of the ethical world," because it was a terrain of "apparently unending controversy."[3] I invoke Walzer's caution because I too must limit my purpose and intent in this analysis of human rights to "practical morality." The subtitle I have given to this section of the chapter, the *rise* of rights in Catholic teaching, implies the introduction of a new reality in Catholic thought in recent years. Whether the invocation of rights language in contemporary Catholic thought is an innovation or the reemergence of previously affirmed moral concepts is a topic which divides respected scholars of the Catholic tradition. To cite two, Professor Brian Tierney finds rights language in medieval thought in a way which Professor Ernest Fortin finds more apparent than real. I must leave the resolution of this argument to

---

[1] Samuel P. Huntington, "Religion and the Third Wave," *The National Interest* 24 (Summer, 1991): 30.

[2] Ibid., 30.

[3] Michael Walzer, *Just and Unjust Wars: A Moral Argument with Historical Illustrations* (New York, 1977), xv.

those with superior historical, linguistic, and philosophical skills. Walzer retreated from examining the substructure of the ethical world to a concern for "the present structure of the moral world."[4]

This chapter focuses upon the present structure and themes of Catholic social teaching. That body of socio-political doctrine has increasingly depended in the last thirty years on a rights-based analysis to defend human dignity, to evaluate national social policy, and to press for change in international politics.[5] The preeminent examples of a rights-based argument are John XXIII's *Pacem in Terris* (1963) and John Paul II's Address to the United Nations (1979) and his encyclical *Centesimus Annus* (1991). These texts should not, however, be read in isolation. They are part of a process of development in the moral categories and language of Catholic social teaching which is rooted in the social encyclicals of this century, achieves its most explicit form in the period between Pius XII's teaching and *Dignitatis Humanae* of Vatican II, and then moves in a more theological direction from the council through the teaching of John Paul II.

Plotting this process of development involves testing the relationship between the classical categories of natural law and natural rights theory. Catholic social and political thought has been effectively identified with a natural law vision of the moral universe.[6] The classical roots of Catholic social philosophy in Greek and Roman sources, and its contemporary expression in a text like John Paul II's *Veritatis Splendor* (1993) or the Congregation of the Doctrine of the Faith's text *Donum Vitae* (1986)[7] attest to the pervasive dependence of the Catholic moral tradition on a natural law ethic. The analytical question raised is how such a tradition comes to rely so heavily in recent years on human rights arguments.

At first glance any effort to relate the natural law and natural rights traditions faces formidable obstacles. They differ at the level of philosophical anthropology, in their theory of society, and in their doctrine of the state.[8] While cryptic contrasts tend to overstate an argument, it is not misleading to highlight how this three-dimensional difference between natural law and natural rights plays out. The fundamental division re-

---

[4] Ibid., xiii.

[5] For the principal documents of the recent tradition, see D.J. O'Brien and T.A. Shannon, eds., *Catholic Social Thought: The Documentary Heritage* (Maryknoll, 1992).

[6] For the role of natural law in Catholic moral theology, see C. Curran, *New Perspectives in Moral Theology* (Notre Dame, 1974), 1-46.

[7] John Paul II, *Veritatis Splendor* (Vatican City, 1993); Congregation for the Doctrine of the Faith, *Donum Vitae* (Vatican City, 1987).

[8] For the contrast of Catholic and Lockean conceptions of morality, see John Courtney Murray, *We Hold These Truths: Catholic Reflections on the American Proposition* (New York, 1960), 295-336.

sides in the concept of the person upon which each moral tradition is based. The natural law ethic holds tenaciously to a radically social concept of human nature. The person is social by nature, not by choice. From birth until death the person fits within a fabric of social ties which generate duties, but also provide support and protection for each person. The social context is intrinsically necessary for the full human development of the person; each person belongs, again by nature, to a multiplicity of social networks (family, nation, and human community). The philosophical anthropology of a natural rights ethic is grounded in a conception of the autonomous individual whose social relations and obligations arise from freely chosen contractual ties, not the dictates of nature or community. From this contrasting conception of personhood, the different theories of society logically follow. The social nature of the person finds expression in a natural law ethic in an organic model of society. The phrase organic model does not capture or convey the variations which are possible in such a conception of societal relations. It is a typology which can embrace the extensive social interrelations of medieval society or the more attenuated social fabric of contemporary communitarian theories. In either case, however, such a view of society is clearly different from the contractual model which complements the autonomous understanding of human nature. Again, the contractual model is a type; it finds expression in a different way in the work of John Rawls than its original expression in contract theories. The differing understandings of the person-society relationship yields the third contrast of natural law and natural rights theory, regarding the role and responsibilities of the state in society. The differences on this question are a matter of degree, but they do count. The natural law understanding endows the state with broadly defined responsibilities not only in the socio-economic order but also in the realm of culture. The natural rights conception presupposes an adversarial relationship of state and citizen which in turn yields a restrictive conception of the proper role of the state in society.

Given these profound differences between the tradition which has generated "rights talk" and the Catholic tradition, how have rights categories emerged so centrally in recent Catholic teaching? The process cuts across the twentieth century and involves three stages of development. It moves from the early social encyclicals of Leo XIII and Pius XI, to the period encompassed by the teaching of Pius XII, John XXIII and *Dignitatis Humanae*, and finally to the teaching of *Gaudium et Spes* and John Paul II.

Leo XIII and Pius XI. The early social encyclicals, *Rerum Novarum* (1891), and *Quadragesimo Anno* (1931), were clearly written in the framework of a natural law ethic; both explicit references and the implicit structure of each text attest to the natural law character of the teaching of

Leo XIII and Pius XI. Within this structure, however, both popes turned to the language of rights to defend workers against exploitation. The rights argument was neither comprehensive nor tightly systematic. Leo XIII focused on economic rights with no attention (at least in this text) to the more dominant focus in liberal cultures on political and civil rights. Moreover, as John Courtney Murray noted, Leo XIII revealed in *Rerum Novarum* a different conception of the role of the state than his writings on the political and cultural orders conveyed.[9] In the latter texts, Leo XIII favored an expansive, paternalistic conception of the state's role. In addressing the effects of the Industrial Revolution, Leo XIII wanted the state to protect workers, but he also wanted to sustain the notion of the economic order as a sphere distinct from the political order. Hence in *Rerum Novarum*, and even more explicitly in *Quadragesimo Anno's* principle of subsidiarity, the responsibility and reach of the state are restrained by institutions and by the civil law. If the logic of this position on the state had been followed consistently, it would have opened questions about rights of the citizen, and what role the state and the church should play in regard to them. This was left to Pius XII and John XXIII.

Pius XII and Dignitatis Humanae. In the development of Catholic human rights teaching, Pius XII is a transitional figure. The characterization is not meant to be critical. Essentially it is designed to show how Pius XII changed the content of Catholic teaching on rights, did not change the framework within which the teaching was held, and yet opened the door for further development by his successors and by Vatican II.

The major contribution of Pius XII involved the substance and scope of Catholic teaching on rights. He moved beyond economic rights to address political-civil rights and Catholic teaching on democracy. The driving forces in his teaching were his concern to elaborate a philosophy of citizenship and his urgent sense that the church had to confront the totalitarian state in the multiple forms in which it appeared in the interwar years. Both led him to acknowledge the value of democratic polity in a way which Leo XIII never did. Democratic polity was intrinsically related to the range of "modern liberties" (of speech, press, association) which Pius XII's nineteenth-century predecessors—including Leo XIII— found either ambiguous or dangerous. As Murray noted, the experience of twentieth-century totalitarian rule of left and right had the effect of joining the freedom of the citizen and the freedom of the church in the

---

[9] John Courtney Murray, "Leo XIII: Two Concepts of Government," *Theological Studies* 14 (1953): 551-560.

teaching of Pius XI and Pius XII.[10] Pius XII's second contribution to the teaching on human rights was his expansion of papal teaching beyond its focus on the nation to address the legal ordering of the international community. It might be argued that his emphasis was more on law than on rights, but the two were ultimately complementary.

While both of these moves by Pius XII significantly expanded Catholic teaching on human rights, he did not push beyond them to any systematization of the teaching.[11] He added to the content without reconceptualizing the teaching. In addition, he never moved from his expansion on political-civil rights and his concern to limit the reach of the modern state to the logical conclusion one could have drawn: a recasting of the Catholic position on religious freedom. On this vital issue of the 1950s, Pius XII went to the threshold of change, provided the concepts needed for change, but never stepped over the threshold. His famous address *Ci Riesce* (1953) epitomized his position; all the elements for a new conclusion on religious freedom were present, but it yielded only an argument about toleration of religious pluralism, something far less than affirming the right of religious liberty. In summary, all three of Pius XII's contributions—the inclusion of political-civil rights, the limits on the role of the state, and the international dimensions of human rights—stood in need of further development. He set the stage for John XXIII.

John XXIII and Pacem in Terris. John XXIII made a double contribution to the Catholic human rights ministry: the first was his encyclical *Pacem in Terris*; the second was his role in calling the Second Vatican Council. One product of the council was the document on religious freedom, *Dignitatis Humanae* (1965), which should be read in tandem with *Pacem in Terris*. Taken together, these texts establish John XXIII as the pivotal figure in the development of Catholic human rights theory.

David Hollenbach describes *Pacem in Terris* as "the most systematic of the modern papal statements on social and political questions."[12] *Pacem in Terris* was directly dependent on the teaching of Pius XII; the majority of the footnotes in John XXIII's text are taken from his predecessor. But *Pacem in Terris* locates the earlier teaching in a more structured, systematic context. The systematic treatment is evident in two ways. First, it provides a framework within which the socio-economic rights, which were the staple of the encyclical tradition, are woven together with the political-civil rights endorsed by Pius XII in his Christmas Messages of

---

[10] John Courtney Murray, "The Problem of Religious Freedom," *Theological Studies* 25 (1964): 546-547.

[11] See David Hollenbach, *Claims in Conflict: Retrieving and Reviewing the Catholic Human Rights Tradition* (New York, 1979), 59.

[12] Ibid., 64. I follow Hollenbach's views in this paragraph interpreting Pius XII.

the early 1940s. In endorsing this spectrum of rights, including rights which are immunities and those which are empowerments, the pope took the Catholic church into the heart of the United Nations human rights debates. The U.N. documents also encompass this broad range of rights, but there is little effort to provide a systematic foundation illustrating how these two distinct kinds of moral claims are coherently held together. For *Pacem in Terris*, the foundation and purpose of all rights is the dignity of the human person. The scope of the rights to be endorsed as legitimate moral claims is determined by the specific needs—material and spiritual—each person has to guarantee human dignity. At the time *Pacem in Terris* was written, debate was constant within the United Nations about which rights were to be given primacy, and whether all the claims found in U.N. texts were truly rights. The U.N. debate of the 1960s and 1970s reflected the broader ideological struggle of the Cold War. The socialist systems endorsed the socio-economic rights, and Western democracies gave priority to the civil-political rights. *Pacem in Terris* provided a different kind of voice and authority in setting forth a systematic interpretation of the range of human rights. It also provided an authoritative framework for an understanding of human rights within the church. While there is debate within the Catholic community about the ordering and ranking of rights, *Pacem in Terris* has set the horizon within which the debate has occurred for the last thirty years.

Both the style and substance of *Pacem in Terris* pointed beyond a systematic statement of rights to a broader and more ambitious goal. It is precisely in this document that the wider philosophical argument noted above, between the natural law and natural rights traditions, reaches a new stage of development. In the nineteenth century the papacy simply rejected the concept of "modern liberties" associated with the democratic revolutions; John Courtney Murray's work demonstrated that there were objective reasons for the church to oppose the philosophical foundations and political dynamic which animated liberalism in the last century. Murray also observed that the modern liberties contained truths which the church could assimilate in a less hostile political climate than the nineteenth-century papacy confronted.[13] Prior to *Pacem in Terris* the logic of Catholic teaching, from Leo XIII through Pius XII, slowly followed its own path of development. The explicit confrontation which marked the previous century was less visible, but there was little effort at any dialogue with the tradition which advocated the modern liberties.

Pacem in Terris is not an explicit appeal for dialogue on natural law/natural rights issues, but its endorsement of the spectrum of politi-

---

[13] Murray, "The Problem of Religious Freedom," 535-37, 548, and 504.

cal liberties, its conscious attempt to appeal across ideological lines, and its tone are all strikingly different from previous papal texts on human rights. In my view, John XXIII's document seeks to build a bridge, however narrow, between the contending traditions on human rights. Like most papal texts, it does not work out past controversies in the style of an academic moral philosopher. The pope simply states his expansive case for human rights, affirms much which had not been previously affirmed, and leaves the task of sorting out the deeper debate to others. My general assessment is that *Pacem in Terris* maintains a natural law framework and incorporates as much as is coherently possible from the natural rights tradition. I have no evidence that such a specific intention lay behind the encyclical. I am simply taking the text and searching for the rationale which sustains it.

Whatever the pope's intention, the question which *Pacem in Terris* leaves open is whether the final product is internally coherent. Commentators like Ernest Fortin are at least doubtful that even limited integration of the two traditions can be achieved.[14] While the encyclical endorses the concept of right as an immunity, affirms a role for freedom as a political value in stronger terms than any previous papal text, and reiterates Pius XII's support for the constitutional state whose powers are limited by law and by the rights of the citizen, the key to coherence, I believe, is that all these moves are made within the context of a natural law conception of the person and society. Specific rights are affirmed for each person, but the social fabric of interdependence is a characteristic of *Pacem in Terris*. Freedom is given a new status in the church's social ethic, but freedom is held in tension with the values of justice, love, truth, and order. The concept of the common good is a guiding principle of the entire encyclical at both the national and international levels of society. The concept of rights is held in tandem with specific duties, even if the priority of duty is not found as clearly here as in other magisterial texts.

It is true that Fortin's ultimate test question—how are rights and duties adjudicated when they are in conflict—is not answered in *Pacem in Terris*. My point, however, is that the overarching framework of the document and its classic Catholic themes of common good and social solidarity establish a context for adjudicating Fortin's question which does not put the natural law tradition in mortal danger.

A similar argument can and should be made about *Dignitatis Humanae*. Even more explicitly than *Pacem in Terris*, the conciliar text is in dialogue with the constitutional tradition of rights and liberties which affirmed the right of religious freedom, and stood in stark contrast to

---

[14] E. Fortin, "Human Rights and the Common Good," *CCIA Annual: Rights Authority and Community* 13 (Philadelphia, 1994): 1-7.

Catholic teaching from the sixteenth century. The Second Vatican Council's document formulates its own case for the right to religious freedom; its premises are not those of the argument which Leo XIII rejected in his nineteenth-century struggle with European liberalism. But the text does acknowledge other forces in society which have fostered the value of freedom, and, more importantly, it sets clear limits on the state's competence in the realm of religion.[15] By affirming the right to religious freedom in principle, by endorsing constitutional limits on the state and by joining religious freedom with other human rights, the Second Vatican Council moved beyond Pius XII and placed the church in support of the full panoply of freedoms needed in the political order for the defense of human dignity. Natural law is not forsaken, but it is developed in an argument joining constitutional ideas previously tolerated but not accepted by the church.

Vatican II and John Paul II. The period from 1940 to 1965 was a time of intense intellectual struggle within Catholicism concerning the issues of human rights, religious freedom, and democracy. The twin texts we have just examined established basic principles for the church on all three issues, bringing Catholic doctrine to a new stage of development and integration. A second conciliar text, *Gaudium et Spes* (1965), opened a new chapter on human rights, building upon the conciliar synthesis, but pressing it in a more theological direction. What the council began John Paul II continues; the post-conciliar development brings Catholic teaching on human rights to the 1990s.

The theological contribution of the council had two dimensions. First, on an ecclesiological level, *Gaudium et Spes* located the social ministry of the church and the protection and promotion of human rights solidly within the ambit of the church's religious ministry. The contrast with *Pacem in Terris* on this point is instructive. John XXIII's text is unmatched as a moral and political statement in defense of the human person. But the encyclical never explicitly connects its moral vision to the internal life of the church. The natural law character of the text renders it eminently useful in dialogue with secular political philosophy and law, but it does not relate its concerns to a wider theological understanding of the church. *Gaudium et Spes* provides the religious foundation and theological legitimation for Catholic involvement in the struggle for human rights. The consequences of this will be discussed in the next section of this chapter.

Second, *Gaudium et Spes*, again in contrast to *Pacem in Terris*, makes an explicitly theological argument for the ministry of human rights. The description of the person whose rights are to be protected is thoroughly

---

[15] Vatican II, *Dignitatis Humanae* (1965), in W.J. Abbott, ed., *The Documents of Vatican II* (New York, 1966), 678-696.

theological. The basic reason for personal dignity is our call to communion with God; the person is described in the categories of sin and grace, and the fulfillment of human nature can be understood only in terms of the risen Christ.[16] Both the theological anthropology which grounds human dignity and human rights, and the eschatological destiny of the person establish a context for human rights different from the philosophical arguments of Pius XII and John XXIII. The engagement of the church in the struggle for human rights is not only a moral and political task; it is part of the work of preparing a new heaven and new earth.

The theological foundation and framework which *Gaudium et Spes* established as the basis of the church's work in the struggle for human rights opened a path of theological reflection which many have pursued since the council. The discourse of the Theology of Liberation, for example, is much closer to the tone of *Gaudium et Spes* than it is to *Pacem in Terris* or *Dignitatis Humanae*. Other post-conciliar theological movements could be identified in the same way, but the most significant continuity with the theological case for human rights is provided by John Paul II. From the outset of his pontificate, human rights, in theory and in practice, have been a central characteristic of this pope's ministry. In 1979, a year after his election, his address to the General Assembly of the United Nations was an effort to interpret the entire range of world politics through the lens of human rights.[17] This address stood in the lineage of *Pacem in Terris;* it stayed within the framework of a philosophical argument, and it reaffirmed and broadened the earlier encyclical. The primary audience for this address virtually guaranteed that it would be philosophical in tone. But John Paul's pursuit of human rights, in his encyclicals and through his trips to the world's most conflicted areas, has taken on a thoroughly theological tenor. From his first encyclical *Redemptor Hominis* (1979) through *Sollicitudo Rei Socialis* (1987) to *Centesimis Annus* (1991) John Paul's social ethic—in which human rights are a central element—is rooted in a theological vision of the person, of history, and of the causes of injustice. To read these texts is to feel oneself much closer to Reinhold Niebuhr than to *Pacem in Terris*. The pope, a philosopher himself, is convinced that a purely philosophical analysis will not uncover the depth of the evil which must be addressed in the world today.

Christian anthropology therefore is really a chapter of theology, and for this reason, the church's social doctrine, by its concern for man, by its interest in him and in the way he conducts himself in the world, "belongs to the field . . . of theology and particularly of moral theology." The

---

[16] Vatican II, *Gaudium et Spes* (1965), in Abbott, *The Documents of Vatican II*, 220.

[17] John Paul II, *Address to the United Nations* (1979).

theological dimension is needed both for interpreting and solving present-day problems in human society.[18]

The journey of the last century for Catholic social thought has brought it from a human rights address to the socio-economic issues of the Industrial Revolution to a view of human rights which undergirds the church's engagement with politics, economics, and international relations. Along the way a working relationship was forged with many groups, and a limited but crucial link established between natural law and natural rights. By the time of the pontificate of John Paul II, a solid foundation for a ministry of human rights was established. He has used what he inherited and expanded it theologically and politically.

Change in the World and the Church: 1965-1990

This section of the chapter shifts the analysis from the content of Catholic teaching on human rights to the context, secular and ecclesial, within which the human rights ministry was exercised in the years between the close of the Second Vatican Council (1965) and the end of the Cold War (1990). The objective of this part of my wider argument is to trace a parallel pattern of change in world politics, on the one hand, and in the Catholic church, on the other. The argument advanced here is that these two independent processes converged to create an "open moment" for the exercise of the ministry of human rights. More specifically, the developments in Catholic teaching, examined above, provided the church with a renewed language of concepts, principles, and legitimation to engage the contemporary issues of human rights. Then the changing pattern of world politics in the 1970s and 1980s created a context for this ministry. The third element in the process was internal changes in Roman Catholicism, which equipped the church to grasp the opportunity of addressing human rights in the name of the dignity of the person. I shall try to capture this interplay of moral theory, political change, and ecclesiological reform under the rubrics of the "world," the "church," and the "policy."

The World. The post-World War II era gave birth to what Professor John Vincent once called "the human rights revolution."[19] The sources of the revolution were quite nonviolent texts, namely the United Nations documents on human rights adopted by the General Assembly. The three central texts are the Universal Declaration on Human Rights, the International Covenant on Civil and Political Rights, and the International

---

[18] John Paul II, *Centesimus Annus* (1991), in O'Brien and Shannon, *Catholic Social Thought*, 480.

[19] R.J. Vincent, *Human Rights and International Relations* (Cambridge, MA, 1986), 93.

Covenant on Economic, Social and Cultural Rights. The revolutionary impact of these documents was embodied in a fundamental principle. In the pre-war era, reaching back to international law in the nineteenth century, and even back to the legacy of the Westphalian order of international relations, human rights violations within states were regarded as matters of "internal jurisdiction." The categorization effectively ruled out political and legal responsibility of any external actors—states or others—for violations of human rights for anything short of genocide. The foundational U.N. human rights texts reversed the norm of internal jurisdiction. The effect of the U.N. texts was to establish, at least in principle, the responsibility of states for human rights violations within states. The responsibility was not spelled out, and enforcement mechanisms were virtually nonexistent, but a change had occurred which had the potential for broad consequences in international relations. It took over two decades after the Universal Declaration had been accepted by the United Nations for the international community to move from principle toward policies on human rights. But the principle of international responsibility had been substantially revised early in the post-war era, and it awaited the next step. Incremental changes were made between 1948 and 1970: regional forums responsible for human rights, like the European Court, were established; non-governmental organizations committed to the protection of human rights were formed; and a body of legal theory based on the premises of the U.N. Bill of Rights began to develop.

The next major phase of the human rights revolution, however, began in the 1970s. A two-dimensional process was discernible. First, in the life of the international community and in the discipline of international relations, the 1970s witnessed the growth of the transnational dimension of world politics. At the level of fact and experience, a combination of elements—communication, technology, mobility, and travel, an increasing number of international institutions and treaties, and, most powerfully, the integration of the global economy—served to establish bonds among nations and populations only some of which were consciously chosen. At the level of theory, a body of research, symbolized by the pathbreaking work of Robert Keohane and Joseph Nye, illustrated the limits of an exclusively state-centric view of world politics ("international relations") and began to develop the complementary idea of "transnational relations."[20] This combination of theory and practice sought to address the growing interdependence of the international community in spite of the fact that sovereign states remained (as Keohane and Nye always stressed) the basic unit of world politics.

---

[20] R.O. Keohane and J.S. Nye, *Power and Interdependence* (Boston, 1977); see also id., eds., *Transnational Relations and World Politics* (Cambridge, MA, 1970).

Research on interdependence and transnational flows of ideas, money, goods, and people produced specific studies on transnational problems and transnational actors. Both are relevant to the understanding of the role of human rights in world politics. Transnational problems have characteristics which mean that no single nation can address them effectively; they include issues as different as trade and monetary questions, environmental issues, and population policy. Transnational actors possess the following characteristics: they are based in one place, present in several others, possess a trained corps of personnel, a single guiding philosophy and a sophisticated communications system.[21] These characteristics can be found in institutions as diverse as global corporations and churches. The salient feature of transnational actors is that they understand the world and act in the world across national lines without needing the cooperation or permission of states. While the precise power relationship of sovereign states and transnational actors continues to be an object of intense study, the crucial feature of such institutions is that they require a different lens to understand world politics than a purely interstate perspective conveys.

The impact of the theory and practice of the politics of interdependence on human rights lay in the fact that human rights issues possessed most of the characteristics of a transnational problem, and human rights were the focus of some of the most effective transnational actors in the world. Increasing interdependence, a fact which states ignored at their political and economic peril, and the study of interdependence converged to move human rights issues toward the center of world politics, even in the midst of the Cold War politics of the 1970s and the 1980s.

The second contribution of the late 1970s to the human rights revolution was the engagement of the U.S. Congress, and, later, the Carter administration in its efforts to formulate a human rights policy. The explosive potential of the principles adopted in the Universal Declaration needed the engagement of states to move from principle to policy formation. Even committed non-governmental organizations were not able by themselves to press human rights on to the central agenda of world politics. Both the congressional policy of the early 1970s (adopted in part to rein in the *realpolitik* of Secretary Kissinger) and the Carter policy of the late 1970s had their limits, inconsistencies, and blind spots. But the effect of a joint legislative and executive branch address to human rights as a major goal of foreign policy opened new horizons for human rights policy in the international system. The priority given to human rights in the 1970s in U.S. policy was consciously eroded in the 1980s, and has not had

---

[21] See Samuel P. Huntington, "Transnational Organizations and World Politics," *World Politics* 25 (1973): 333-368; see also Keohane and Nye, *Transnational Relations*.

the same significance in the 1990s either, but the basic principles of the rights debate have stayed alive on the foreign policy agenda. Transnational actors remain often more interested than states in these issues, but the new status acquired by human rights questions since the 1970s leaves open new possibilities for the non-governmental organizations.

The Church. The development of Roman Catholic thought on human rights in the years prior to Vatican II prepared the church for an activist ministry in defense of the person. But more was needed, and it was supplied by the theology and reforms of the council. Theologically, the council called the church to deeper engagement in the world. Careful to maintain the distinction between the church and secular political organizations, the council defined a role for the church in the world of public affairs. The church's role was to stand as "a sign and safeguard of the transcendence of the human person."[22] The fulfillment of this vocation leads directly to a ministry of human rights. In a sense, what the conciliar teaching did was to tie the entire social tradition with its stress on social justice and human rights to the ministry of the church by defining that ministry in terms of defense of the person. This is clearly the intent of John Paul II when he defines the person as "the way for the ministry of the church."[23]

Having provided a basis for the work of human rights, the council took a major step in catalyzing that ministry by its teaching on the local church. There is hardly any doubt that the continuing stress in Catholicism on the universal scope of the church's life and its embodiment in the office and person of the pope has yielded benefits to the human rights ministry. But emphasis only on the center of the church's life (the papacy) can lose sight of the multiple possibilities which can never be touched directly from the center. This dimension of ecclesiology, a focus on the local church, had been neglected in Catholic theology for over a century. Usually the council's emphasis on the importance and irreplaceable role of the local church is seen as significant for the internal life of the church. In fact, however, an ecclesiology which addresses both the potential of the center of the church and the local church is strategically significant for the work of human rights. Ivan Vallier, in his early and important article on the Catholic church as a transnational actor, placed an almost exclusive emphasis on how the papacy shapes the life of local churches.[24] But there is another dynamic: some tasks *only* the local church can fulfill. This is particularly true when effective action on human rights

---

[22] *Gaudium et Spes*, 288.

[23] John Paul II, *Redemptor Hominis* (Washington, 1979), 44.

[24] Ivan Vallier, "The Roman Catholic Church: A Transnational Actor," in Keohane and Nye, *Transnational Relations*, 129-152.

requires tactical choices which only those with a detailed grasp of the concrete situation can make prudently and creatively. The council identified the local church as a legitimate source of initiatives in church life; Pope Paul VI invited the local church to exercise its creative role of relating the general teaching of the church to specific situations.[25] In the post-conciliar period, local churches from North and South America, Central Europe, the Philippines, and South Africa took the invitation seriously and made the kind of impact on human rights which attracted Huntington's analysis along with many others.

Finally, the council indirectly but effectively contributed to another factor in the human rights ministry. One initiative of Vatican II was to establish within the Roman Curia a Commission on Justice and Peace, an agency which was not part of the more traditional diplomatic service, yet was mandated to address issues affecting international justice and peace. One immediate fruit of this move was the creation within countries of similar commissions or offices, many of which became directly involved in the human rights issues affecting their countries. Particularly in religious communities, the establishment of justice and peace networks significantly expanded the work on human rights.

In summary, precisely when developments in international politics were highlighting both the place of human rights and the role of transnational institutions to address them, the Catholic church was reshaping the perspective and structure of one of the most experienced transnational networks in history. Substantively, Vatican II both legitimated a more activist Catholicism and provided resources for directing it. Structurally, the council's policy of decentralization both created new transnational networks in the church and urged initiatives adapted to the local level of the church's life. The combined effect of these conciliar actions was to impel Catholicism into human rights struggles throughout the international system in the next twenty years. Examples of that engagement constitute our next topic.

Policy. The objective of this section is to provide a sense of how the transnational church engaged the human rights issues. Rather than offer a detailed study of one or two cases, my method will try to find general themes which cut across cases and then to exemplify selected aspects of three locations in the church.[26]

---

[25] Paul VI, *Octogesima Adveniens* (1971), in O'Brien and Shannon, *Catholic Social Thought*, 266.

[26] For other examples of the church's involvement, see P. Nichols, *The Pope's Divisions: The Roman Catholic Church Today* (New York, 1981); A. Hastings, ed., *Modern Catholicism: Vatican II and After* (New York, 1991).

Generally speaking, the human rights ministry demonstrated the comparative advantage of the church's particular transnational structure. While sharing the basic characteristics of transnational actors, the church combined the capacity to act systemically (through the Vatican), nationally (through the local bishops' conference), and locally (through laity, priests, and religious directly involved in conflicted situations). While it would be claiming too much to see a developed strategy at work over the last twenty years, it is possible to identify how these distinct levels of the church collaborated in specific instances. The papacy could (and did at times) reinforce the witness of the local church, even protecting its members through papal visits. The local episcopal conferences could engage issues which would have been too specific for the Vatican to address, yet had great consequences for the local populace. The interaction among the distinct levels of this transnational actor were not always harmonious. Eastern European bishops sometimes found the Vatican too ready to strike a pragmatic agreement with the reigning communist regimes. The Holy See expressed concern at times that the grassroots initiatives could divide the church in a country. Several episcopal conferences sought to establish systematic working relationships on issues of international concern. The Vatican tolerated the moves, sometimes encouraged them, but also was cautious about losing its initiative on foreign policy issues.

While many forces were directing the church toward human rights from within, clearly one of the strongest influences on the life of Catholicism in the 1970s and 1980s was the rise of authoritarian regimes, particularly in developing counties. The dynamic of authoritarian rule which inevitably involved suppressing the independent sources of power in a country—the press, the legislature, the unions, the universities—often left the church in a classical posture of church-state confrontation, as the only institution capable of confronting unrestrained political power. As Huntington graphically puts it: "In country after country the choice between democracy and authoritarianism became personified in the conflict between the cardinal and the dictator."[27] Dramatic as that statement is, it should not be interpreted in a deterministic fashion. The simple structural confrontation of government versus church did not always yield an activist role for the church. The structural factors had to be matched with a certain theological and pastoral vision or the church remained silent, inert, and ineffective.

Moving beyond general characteristics to specific situations, the *Latin American* case should take precedence. On human rights issues, the Latin American "local church" led the way for the whole church. The conjunc-

---

[27] Huntington, "The Third Wave," 35.

tion of events was dramatic. Just as the Vatican Council was in session, the return of a military government in Brazil through a coup signaled the beginning of a process that would sweep across the continent. For the next twenty years, the Latin American church would live daily with authoritarian rule, torture, human rights abuse, and martyrdom in its struggle against the state.[28] The council had a profound effect on the Latin American church; it was the first "local church" to attempt a systematic application of the conciliar vision to a concrete situation.[29] The combination of external repression and an internal movement of reform (symbolized by the Medellin, Puebla, and Santo Domingo assemblies of bishops) produced in this local church three results.

First, the church in Latin America developed an authentically local theological perspective, the Theology of Liberation. The process by which it developed, the diverse modes of expression of the theology and the extended dialogue and debate about its method and content which has gone on in Latin America, and between the Holy See and its proponents, are all too complex to be accurately summarized here. But the fact that a specific style of articulating the Christian message did develop into a school of theology is a clear characteristic of the last three decades.[30] The content of the Theology of Liberation focused on themes directly related to human rights issues, although the theological vision was broader than simply a theology of human rights.

Second, both the theology arising from Latin America and the conflicted political setting in which the church found itself when faced with authoritarian military rule produced a pastoral method of shaping the local church, the Basic Ecclesial Communities. Like the Theology of Liberation, this pastoral style admits of much internal variation from country to country as well as changes in emphasis over time. But the way in which the church was organized "from below," building on the role of the laity, transforming the fact of a lack of clergy and religious into an asset, by using them strategically to build lay leadership, is one of the dominant themes of the church in Latin America since the 1960s.[31]

Taken together, the Theology of Liberation and the Basic Ecclesial Communities are two central features of how the church equipped itself

---

[28] D.H. Levini, "From Church and State to Religion and Politics," *World Affairs* 150 (1987): 93-108; C. Jerez, *Prophetic Possibilities for the Church in Central America* (London, 1987).

[29] Marcos McGrath, "The Impact of Gaudium et Spes: Medellin, Puebla and Pastoral Creativity," in J. Gremillion, *The Church and Culture Since Vatican II* (Notre Dame, 1985), 99-113.

[30] A.F. McGovern and T.L. Shubeck, "Updating Liberation Theology," *America* (July 16, 1988): 32-35, 47ff.

[31] M. DeC. Azevedo, "Basic Ecclesial Communities: A Meeting Point of Ecclesiologies," *Theological Studies* 46 (1985): 601-620.

to meet the challenge of Vatican II of entering more deeply into the life of the world as an evangelical presence.

The third feature of the Latin American church's engagement in the struggle for human rights and social justice was episcopal leadership. The three great ecclesial assemblies of Medellin, Puebla, and Santo Domingo symbolize the effort of the Latin American episcopate to move from the experience of Vatican II to a systematic application of it in the local conditions of Latin America. The episcopal leadership was not always simple to describe; there were struggles at a continental level, and there were difficult debates within countries. But if one tries to diagram the dynamic of the church in Latin America over the last thirty years, the movements from below, expressed in the Theology of Liberation and the Basic Ecclesial Communities, must be seen in tandem with a pattern of episcopal leadership from above.

These three factors produced a style of pastoral presence that was a central feature of the human rights struggle in Latin America from the 1960s through the 1980s. A complete account would require analysis of each country, and the record would be mixed. But in broad terms one can trace a movement of ecclesial leadership on human rights which is focused in the Southern Cone in the 1960s and 1970s, then moves to Central America in the 1980s. These areas were the most conflicted struggles, beginning in Brazil in the 1960s, moving to Chile in the 1970s, and then extending to Nicaragua, El Salvador, Guatemala, and Honduras in the 1980s.[32] The specific issues varied by country and region, but across the spectrum of this variety, the institutional church stood as the counterweight to state power. The activities engaging the church involved both a few high-level encounters of the "the dictator and cardinal," to use Huntington's phrase, and a multitude of more directly pastoral functions of gathering data on human rights abuses, staffing food centers and clinics, organizing workers, and maintaining contacts with local churches in countries which offered material and moral support in the human rights struggle.

In *Central and Eastern Europe* the church faced an entirely different human rights challenge than it did in Latin America. The pattern of repression was more long-standing and systematic, encompassing the entire era of the Cold War.[33] The confrontation between church and state in each country was directly linked to Soviet power exercised through client

---

[32] B.H. Smith, "Churches and Human Rights in Latin America—Recent Tends on the Subcontinent," in Daniel Levine, ed., *Churches and Politics in Latin America* (Beverly Hills, 1979), 155-193; and C. Jerez, *Prophetic Possibilities for the Church in Central America* (London, 1987).

[33] See H. Stehle, *Eastern Politics of the Vatican 1917-1979* (Athens, OH, 1981).

governments. (An analogy existed in Latin America because of U.S. support for military regimes.) The style of ecclesial resistance to state power and human rights abuses had a different character in Eastern Europe. Church posture and policy was directed from the top; internal ecclesial discipline was a more visible factor in the resistance than in Latin America. Contact with local churches was far more limited than was possible in Latin America. Ecclesial strategy in each country was usually shaped by a dominant figure in the hierarchy, pre-eminently by Cardinal Wyszynski in Poland. The complementary source of influence to local leadership was the detailed involvement of the Holy See in the Eastern European struggle of church and state. The Holy See's policy altered over time, from Pius XII's strategy of refusing contact with the regimes through the ecclesiastical *Ostpolitik* of John XXIII and Paul VI.[34] The Vatican-local church collaboration was both an essential aspect of a successful strategy of resistance to communist power and a complex relationship. On the one hand, the voice of Rome and the support Rome could muster from local churches (especially in Western Europe and the United States) through material, moral, and even political assistance to the church in Eastern Europe was a unique lifeline for embattled communities. On the other hand, when the Holy See's policy moved toward a model of limited dialogue with communist regimes, the local leadership of the church, particularly in Poland, was always concerned that a deal would be struck over the heads of local leadership.

The entire picture changed, of course, with the election of John Paul II. His impact on the position of the church in Eastern Europe, on the question of human rights, and even on the geopolitical power of the Soviet Union was the essential factor in the period from 1979-1989. Historians will have to sort out, in the long-term, the exact role he played. All analysts today, working with the data available, count him as an essential figure in the dismantling of Soviet power. Some, like Timothy Garton Ash, give his role a unique status.[35] By any account, a multiplicity of factors, some secular and others religious or moral, converged as the efficient cause of the collapse of communism. No account, however, could exclude either the role of the local church or the Polish pope.

Finally, then, it is useful to examine the human rights ministry as it took shape in the church in the *United States*. The particular contribution which such an examination can make to this chapter is to illustrate the transnationality of the church at work. In the cases highlighted thus far, Latin America and Eastern Europe, the ministry of human rights in-

---

[34] Ibid., 314-374.

[35] T.G. Ash, "Eastern Europe: Year of Truth," *New York Review of Books* (February 15, 1990): 17.

volved confronting issues within domestic societies. Obviously the United States has a host of issues which fall under the rubric of human rights problems: from race relations to issues of domestic poverty, to Native Americans and immigration policy, there is more than enough to engage the resources of this local church.

One of the characteristic responsibilities of this local church, however, is the continuing question of the U.S. role in the world. Human rights ministry for this local church must include both domestic and foreign policy issues. This responsibility can be understood easily enough by simply being conscious of the U.S. role, for good or ill, in the world. In addition, however, it is crucial to grasp that members of local churches are quite conscious of the U.S. role in their countries. They expect, therefore, a local church in the United States to be part of the process of examining and engaging human rights issues in U.S. foreign policy.

In both the regions discussed in this chapter, Latin America and Eastern Europe, as well as others as diverse as South Africa, South Korea, and the Middle East, there developed in the post-conciliar period an extensive network of ties among local churches, in which the U.S. church played a visible role. This network illustrates the multidimensional character of the church as a transnational actor. At one level the episcopal conferences were in direct and systematic contact, responding to events through statements, letters of support, and—here in the United States— congressional testimony and work on human rights legislation. A second level of contact was the role U.S. missionaries played; working in the ministry as a part of local churches, but being a part of this local church, the missionaries often were a catalyst, urging action here in the United States that could affect events they were confronting daily in their ministry of human rights. Third, there often was close collaboration between the church in the United States and secular human rights groups.

The record of this human rights engagement by the church in the United States is documented in a series of statements, testimonies, and policy initiatives reflecting the multi-faceted ministry of human rights which the universal church was pursuing through the Holy See and local churches. Beyond the political and moral dimensions of the human rights questions, this pattern of interaction among local churches—a pattern which always was overseen by the Holy See—is a case study in contemporary ecclesiology. In Catholic polity, the ties between a local church and the Holy See have always been direct and vital. The dynamics of the human rights ministry catalyzed an effort at horizontal collaboration in a worldwide church. As yet the full meaning of this style of being the church in the world is not clear. To some degree the very power of the ministry of John Paul II has tended to centralize even the human rights ministry. But over time, it would seem that the likely pattern of engaging all the resources of a transnational church will include strong vertical and horizontal ties to address the multiple issues which increasing interdependence poses for world politics and for a church committed to being in the world as a witness and agent of the gospel.

Human Challenges for Church and State: The 1990s

In a brief final reflection, my purpose is to sketch the changing context for human rights in both the world and the church in the 1990s. The kind of change introduced in world politics by the founding of the United Nations is at least being matched in depth and significance by the fundamental shifts of power and politics generated by the Post-Cold War world.[36] The full examination of the topic would have to address both the dramatic change in the structure of power created by the collapse of the Soviet Union and the communist ideology, as well as the more subtle shift in our understanding of principles of international order, particularly the role of state sovereignty and the issues of intervention. It is the intersection of these two major shifts, in my view, which creates the challenge of Post-Cold War politics.

The status and setting for human rights is only one dimension of this larger picture, but it is the only theme which it is possible to address in these closing reflections. First, the increasing role which human rights has played in world politics since the founding of the United Nations will continue to expand in the Post-Cold War world. Second, one consequence of the collapse of the bipolar struggle of the U.S. and the Soviet Union is that the pervasive security concerns which often corrupted human rights policies are now substantially diminished.[37] It is, therefore, possible to allow the issue of human rights to be examined on its own merits, distinct from questions of how this choice about rights could threaten the security interests of the United States. Third, the decline in the security competition has been matched by the rising saliency of economic issues in world politics. The integration of the world economy and the virtual impossibility of any state pursuing national goals without being engaged in the global economy means that the ties between human rights concerns and economic issues will increase. Fourth, the expansion of the democratization process, however imperfectly, into countries both enhances the possibilities of protecting human rights and makes it neces-

---

[36] J.L. Gaddis, "Toward the Post-Cold War World," *Foreign Affairs* 70 (1991): 102-122.

[37] See J. Bryan Hehir, "The United States and Human Rights," in K. Oye, R. Lieber and D. Rothchild, eds., *Eagle in a New World: American Grand Strategy in the Post-Cold War Era* (New York, 1992), 233-255.

sary to define more clearly what the human rights issues will be after democratization has begun. Finally, the paradox of the 1990s has been that the rapid decline of cosmic danger to the world in the Post-Cold War period has been accompanied by the explosion of ethnic, racial, and religious conflicts within states. Whether any causal relation exists here is not clear; what is lucidly evident is that the phenomenon of "failed states," which literally collapse politically and economically, is one of the human rights issues of the 1990s.

How are these changes likely to affect the ministry of human rights in the church? One certain feature of the new setting is the growing importance of non-governmental institutions in global politics, particularly organizations which address humanitarian and human rights issues. Their increasing significance arises from the hesitation of states to become involved in situations where a clear national interest (of security or economics) is lacking. Forced often by public opinion to do something in the face of widespread human suffering, but fearing direct involvement, states and international institutions are increasingly interested in the potential of non-governmental organizations. A host of questions then arises for church agencies about which alliances are appropriate, on what funding basis, with what guarantees that the church will be able to maintain an independent view of policy choices.

A second set of questions will arise within states as the human rights agenda changes. In Latin America, for example, the contributions which the church has made to the democratization process make it a continuing actor in the new stage of democratization-development issues facing Latin American economies. Questions which the church in developing countries has struggled with for decades about models of development, patterns of economic organization, and the impact on the poor now reappear in the context of increasing integration of the economy, the move to neo-liberal economic models across the globe and the consequences of these, not only for macro-economic questions, but for specific groups in the economy (peasants, laborers) with whom the church often has strong ties. In brief, human rights takes on the character of political economy at the global and local levels.

In Eastern Europe the democratization process has meant that the uniquely strategic role which the church had under communist rule is now in the midst of change. The opening of a democratic electoral process, the reemergence of groups in civil society, the inevitable opening of the culture of a country to outside influences of media, foreign investors, and international institutions pose issues for the church which are quite different from the stark, dangerous difficulties faced during a time of totalitarian rule.

Finally, as one looks at the world of the 1990s, the questions of human rights and principles of international order must be addressed. The declining security concerns in world politics make intervention in countries a less dangerous enterprise for large states than it used to be. The rising number of nations engulfed in civil conflict poses a major political-moral challenge to the international community. Is it wise to lower the barriers to intervention? If so, who does the intervening? If one fears a more interventionist world, especially for small states which are targets of intervention, how does one avoid a pattern where internal conflicts are simply "quarantined," that is, contained so they do not spread to states but not addressed with any outside assistance? These questions face a church whose conception of human rights has always been located in a broader concern for international order.

Human Rights in the Church

WILLIAM JOHNSON EVERETT
Andover Newton Theological School

T he advancement of human rights in civil society has been fostered as well as blocked by Christian churches. This ambivalence in the civil arena is mirrored within the churches as well. In this chapter I want to explore the relationship between legal processes within the churches and generally recognized human rights norms. From the outset it is clear that there is a variety of patterns in the life of the churches around the world. While we see clear efforts to suppress free speech in some churches, we also see agonized efforts to ensure representative governance and democratic decision-making in others. First, we need to understand how and why these various patterns arise. Second, we need to ask what we can learn from this encounter between the human rights movement and the churches.

Frame of Analysis

In order to analyze this complex situation, we can begin with a rough ordering of the factors shaping the way churches do or do not embody human rights norms in their internal life. We can then review the actual situations in the churches with these factors in mind. After reviewing some of these key areas of controversy, we can then return to this preliminary framework and refine our understanding of how and why these human rights issues arise and what they portend for the future of human rights.

Four fundamental factors seem to shape the way churches deal with human rights issues in their internal life: (1) the degree to which they have a codified internal law; (2) their ecclesiology, that is, their understanding of their purpose and proper internal structure; (3) their relation to environing governments; and (4) their relation to their environing culture.

J. Witte, Jr. and J.D. van der Vyver (eds.), Religious Human Rights in Global Perspective, 121-141.
© 1996 *Kluwer Law International. Printed in the Netherlands.*

Church Codification of Law. Churches vary greatly in the degree to which they have developed a complex internal legal structure. The Roman Catholic Church has the most highly developed tradition of Canon Law, stretching back at least to the codification of Roman-canon law in the eleventh and twelfth centuries.[1] All the European churches with a history of state sponsorship or close affiliation have an extensive corpus of law as well, either because of their internal size and complexity or the accumulation of legal agreements with their governments.[2] Even churches with no direct state ties have often developed very sophisticated bodies of internal law and legal procedure.[3] At the other end of the spectrum lies a multitude of smaller churches with little codified law, whether because of their theology, their charismatic mode of leadership, their parental pattern of governance, or their embeddedness in a subculture governed by tradition and custom.

Clearly, the way in which one might identify or evaluate human rights performance varies enormously depending on whether the church has a clear law and procedure. Informal or traditional churches may or may not conform to human rights norms. Highly legalized churches might have clear human rights codes on paper but fail to follow them in practice. In any case, since human rights norms generally have pushed for expression in covenants, constitutions, and codes, there is a tendency to assume that codification is good and that it reveals to a significant degree the extent of the church's conformity to human rights norms.

Type of Ecclesiology. The second factor is the type of ecclesiology shaping the church's internal life and external mission. A church's ecclesiology is shaped by theological principles, ethical values, and the cultural history of that church. Ecclesiology is the structural expression of that church's beliefs. The wide variety of ecclesiologies among Christians often surprises outsiders. That these ecclesiologies make a *theological* dif-

---

[1] For the current Code of Canon Law see Canon Law Society of America, *The Code of Canon Law: A Text and Commentary* (Mahwah, NJ, 1985). For a critical response see James Provost and Knut Walf, eds., *Canon Law Church Reality* (Edinburgh, 1986) .

[2] For instance, for Germany see the whole history of *Staatskirchenrecht* (State Church Law) in G. Schmidt Eichstaedt, *Kirchen als Körperschaften des Öffentlichen Rechts* (Köln, 1975); Hans Dombois (hrsg.), *Das Recht der Gnade: Ökumenisches Kirchenrecht* (Witten, 1961), vol. 1; Helmut Quaritsch and Hermann Weber (hrsg.), *Staat und Kirchen in der Bundesrepublik. Staatskirchliche Aufsätze* (Bad Homburg, 1967); Konrad Hesse, "Die Entwicklung des Staatskirchenrechts seit 1945," *Jahrbuch des Öffentlichen Rechts der Gegenwart, Neue Folge* 10 (1988): 1-80; Ernst Friesenhahn, Ulrich Scheuner and Joseph Listl (hrsg.), *Handbuch des Staatskirchenrechts der Bundesrepublik Deutschland* (Berlin, 1974-1975); Joseph Listl (hrsg.), *Grundriss des nachkonziliaren Kirchenrechts* (Regensburg, 1980).

[3] See the United Methodist *Book of Discipline*, which receives some alteration every four years through actions of its General Conference. The Presbyterian *Book of Order* exhibits a similar pattern.

ference is often seen by insiders as a perversion of the Gospel, with its apocalyptic critique of the institutions of Jesus's time. For these Christians *any* institutionalization of Christian life is suspect, if not anathema. However, the primordial fact that the early church preserved four Gospels and was purportedly constituted as twelve apostolic churches embeds this plurality and at least primitive institutionalization in the church's very beginnings if not in the will of its founding Rabbi.

These plural ecclesiologies have been variously classified. Some theologians, working in the tradition of Ernst Troeltsch, root their typology in the relation of the church to its culture. Others, such as Avery Dulles, seek it in terms of the church's understanding of its own highest value. Still others, such as Peter Rudge, anchor their typology in the affinity between theological categories and choices of organizational structure.[4] Each of these classification schemes illuminates different aspects of ecclesiology and helps explain differing facets.

In light of the issue of human rights in the church I would like to suggest that we ground our ecclesiological typology in the pattern of conflict over structure that goes back to Israelite origins and that was rehearsed in secular form by John Locke at the beginning of the modern movement for human rights. Namely, it is the conflict between patriarchal monarchy, on the one hand, and covenantal conciliarism on the other. In ancient Israel it was the conflict between the confederation of Israel gathered around the traveling Ark of the Mosaic covenant and the monarchy of David centered around the temple in Jerusalem. These very different conceptions of proper governance carried with them very divergent understandings of the rights of the people, differences which still reverberate in our debates.[5]

This conflict exploded again in the European recovery of this biblical dialectic in the sixteenth century. John Locke recast it in a partly secular form in his *Second Treatise on Government*, which was a trenchant attack on the whole ideology of patriarchy and a defense of the republican ideals rooted in Israel's covenantal and conciliar polity.[6] The individual lib-

---

[4] Ernst Troeltsch, *The Social Teachings of the Christian Churches*, Olive Wyon, trans. (New York, 1960); H. Richard Niebuhr, *Christ and Culture* (New York, 1956 [1951]); Peter Rudge, *Ministry and Management* (London, 1968); Avery Dulles, *Models of the Church: A Critical Assessment of the Church in All Its Aspects*, rev. ed. (Garden City, 1987).

[5] For a penetrating exploration of the Biblical roots see Daniel J. Elazar, *Covenant and Polity in Biblical Israel* (New Brunswick, NJ, 1995). For further Protestant developments see Max L. Stackhouse, *Creeds, Societies and Human Rights* (Grand Rapids, 1986).

[6] John Locke, *Two Treatises of Government*, Peter Laslett, ed. (Cambridge, 1960). For the theological dimension in Locke, see John Dunn, *The Political Thought of John Locke* (Cambridge, 1969). Republican readings of the Bible emerge in James Harrington, *Oceana*, in *The Political Works of James Harrington*, J.G.A. Pocock, ed. (New York, 1977); John Milton, "The Readie and Easie Way to Establish a Free Commonwealth and the Excellence Thereof Com-

erties necessary for participation in these emerging republics became the core of what the American and French revolutionaries later called human rights.

Locke's *Treatise* was a brilliant polemic which condemned any polity modelled after the patriarchal family in order to make way for the emergent republican aspirations of his time. However, humanity's ongoing need for familial care, socialization, nurture, and security have gradually brought back a modern form of the patriarch (and in this case matriarch) in the form of the welfare state and the "rights of entitlement" to care and sustenance, if not through limited associations then through the state. In this situation the "second table" of social, economic, and cultural rights can be set alongside the "first table" of political and civil rights as modern expressions of this tension between parental care and adult liberty.[7]

In this climate it might be possible to construct a simple ecclesiological typology on the basis of this distinction between "parentalist" and monarchical ecclesiologies, on the one end, and covenantal conciliar types, on the other. How a church manages these two values in its ecclesiology shapes how it looks from the standpoint of a theory of human rights. But this theory of human rights is, in turn, critically illuminated in terms of how it relates the rights contained in these modern "two tables" of civil rights and socioeconomic rights.

Relation of Church and Government. The third essential factor affecting the relationship of the church and human rights is the relation between a particular church and the governments of its civil environment. Many churches are transnational and so have numerous environments and governments to deal with. The church's search for internal consistency on a global basis perforce collides with the plurality of national laws and the way they may or may not incorporate human rights norms. To some extent these relationships arise from the church's ecclesiology and patterns of internal governance. To a large extent they arise from the constitutions, powers, and interests of governmental controls of their legal and political environment.

---

pared with the Inconveniences and Dangers of Readmitting Kingship in This Nation," in *Complete Prose Works of John Milton*, vol. 7, 1659-60, rev. ed. (New Haven, 1980), 407-463, and the famous "Putney debates" among Cromwell's soldiers. See *Puritanism and Liberty*, A.S.P. Woodhouse, ed. (Chicago, 1951).

[7] The United Nations Universal Declaration on Human Rights (1948) was followed in December 1966 by two U.N. Covenants spelling out political and civil rights (my "first table") and economic, social and cultural rights (my "second table"). The parallel with the two tables of covenantal law in the Bible draws me to this language. For the documents and a Reformed Christian response see Allen O. Miller, ed., *A Christian Declaration on Human Rights* (Grand Rapids, 1977). For further discussion of these international legal texts see the article by Natan Lerner in volume 2 of this collection.

In some regions, the churches are essentially "private" associations entirely separate from the civil law. The whole construct of human rights, which presumes the relatively involuntary environment of the civil state, may not even be valid for such voluntary associations. The right to join or leave a voluntary church preempts all other human rights claims within that church.

In other regions and churches, the church may be under the control of the state to some degree, as is still the case in many parts of Europe. Here, human rights in the church quickly becomes a matter relating to state policy. Within these situations of close accommodation between states and churches, churches may be "established," as in England, Norway, or Sweden, "public corporations" with a privileged status in law, as in Germany, or be governed by concordats with the state, as is the case with the Roman Catholic Church and Germany, Italy, and other countries. In this last case, the church seeks to be seen essentially as another state rather than an entity in any way subordinate to national law. How we view human rights in these churches will thus have a different cast, since their legal contexts of enforcement and the degree to which membership is voluntary vary substantially.

Relation of Church and Culture. Lastly, both the churches' ecclesiologies and their relation to governments is shaped by the dominant cultures and circumstances of their regions. Some churches find themselves in an overwhelmingly dominant position in a culture. In this situation of close accommodation or assimilation, the values of the dominant culture permeate the churches, shaping their appropriation and implementation of human rights norms. In other cases, they may be in an acute minority, whether persecuted, as in China of recent years, or preferred because of governmental interests in redressing past grievances, as with some Christian tribal peoples of India. The dominant culture shapes not only whether human rights are appropriated but also how the relation between the rights to liberty and the rights to care are balanced and integrated. The degree to which church membership brings social benefits or liabilities thus shapes the extent to which one may press for the exercise of certain rights within the church.

Contemporary Controversies

These four factors—the degree of legal development within the church, the type of ecclesiology, the church's relation to the state, and the cultural context of the church—help to orient the investigation of certain key human rights controversies within the churches. My investigation of these controversies is perforce illustrative, not exhaustive. I have not examined all Christian churches with a checklist to see how far they have incorporated human rights norms into their internal life. Nor have I surveyed the ways churches may have incorporated these norms without much controversy. Instead, I focus on the principal controversies over church discipline, governance, and administration that have divided church authorities and subjects—with illustrations drawn principally from India, Germany, and the United States. All four of the factors introduced in the foregoing section bear on the formulation, and resolution, of these controversies.

Church Discipline. Inasmuch as Christians are disciples of Jesus, seeking to follow "the Way" he set out originally, they are committed to some sort of discipline. The question is: Who interprets the discipline, and who enforces it? Churches vary widely in this respect, with some ecclesiologies supporting a clear central teaching authority and others leaving this interpretation to councils, congregations, and individuals themselves. The more this authority is removed from the immediate control of individuals the more questions of human rights may arise.

Membership. First, most churches with any degree of institutionalization must establish the limits of membership. Thus, they must reserve the right to dismiss members and to rule on their admission. Similarly, they tend to develop methods of behavioral control short of outright excommunication in an effort to redirect wayward members back to the path of discipline espoused by that church.

Very few people question the churches' need to discipline their members. Questions first arise, however, when that discipline carries with it civil or social penalties, especially where the church is closely tied to the state and the culture. Church discipline can damage people's reputations, social standing, or even eligibility for state-funded offices, as in European churches supported in some way by state funds. But this is not yet a question of human rights, unless the procedures followed in bringing to bear disciplinary sanctions violate human rights norms.

Assessment of questions of "due process" vary from region to region. American law differs from that of England and France. India has restricted its use by Constitutional means,[8] and other countries have other legal traditions which could still fall within general human rights norms. Some of the most famous cases in this regard have arisen in the Roman Catholic Church, whose central authorities have removed permission to

---

[8] Granville Austin, *The Indian Constitution: A Cornerstone of the Nation* (London, 1966), 73, 101.

teach in Catholic institutions from Stephan Pfürtner in Switzerland,[9] Hans Küng in Germany,[10] and Charles Curran in the United States.[11] The Dutch theologian Eduard Schillebeeckx also underwent disciplinary scrutiny.[12] Pfürtner, a Swiss Dominican, was deprived of his teaching duties at the University of Freiburg, because he raised in public profound questions about the Roman Catholic Church's approach to sexual ethics, including questions of birth control and homosexuality. Hans Küng, a leading Catholic theologian at the University of Tübingen in Germany, was subjected to numerous investigations by the Vatican offices during the decade following Vatican Council II. These resulted in the termination of his permission to teach Catholic theology in 1979, thus depriving him of his position at Tübingen. Charles E. Curran, a respected American theologian, was deprived of his permission to teach Catholic theology at Catholic University in Washington, after a seven year investigation of his teachings, especially those concerning sexual ethics.

In all of these cases the procedures themselves were characterized by a high degree of secrecy, though documents from them later emerged in the general public. Moreover, since they were ideological in character, the normal legal procedures involving guilt and innocence did not or could not come into play. Thus we have a question of whether questions of truth, which lie at the heart of theology and the ecclesiology growing out of it, can be dealt with in the same way as questions of guilt or innocence, which are the general concerns of a court of law.

Freedom of Speech in the Church. Do human rights norms require freedom of speech in the church, even by those who are employed to teach a received tradition? Some churches give wide latitude to freedom of speech, asking only that officials declare clearly whether they are speaking for the church or for themselves. For others, the whole person is absorbed into his or her office, leaving no room for such a distinction. Like soldiers, it is claimed, officers or teachers in the church have given up certain ordinary rights in order to carry out their assignments. Churches with a clear internal distinction between the public and private aspects of life can make a distinction between official and personal statements, but churches for whom a familial model is dominant have difficulty recog-

---

[9] Ludwig Kaufmann, *Ein ungelöster Kirchenkonflikt: Der Fall Pfürtner, Dokumente und zeitgeschichtliche Analysen* (Freiburg, 1987), and Hermann Ringeling, "Der Fall Stephan Pfürtner," *Zeitschrift für Evangelische Ethik* 32(4) (1988): 292-96.

[10] Leonard W. Swidler, ed., *Küng in Conflict* (Garden City, 1981), and United States Catholic Conference, *The Küng Dialogue: Facts and Documents* (Washington, 1980).

[11] William W. May, ed., *Vatican Authority and American Catholic Dissent* (New York, 1987).

[12] Leonard W. Swidler and Piet F. Fransen, eds., *Authority in the Church and the Schillebeeckx Case* (New York, 1982).

nizing such a distinction, just as parents do not recognize it in dealing with their children. In such a household model, there is no internal public where personal opinion can be given voice.

Many churches have experienced controversy of this kind. In the most notorious recent American case, many professors and administrators in schools controlled by the Southern Baptist Convention have been disciplined or dismissed on doctrinal bases.[13] This has resulted in disciplinary action from educational accrediting agencies though not from governments. Here again it is clear that the claim that human rights norms have been violated depends on holding an ecclesiology that maintains that the church itself, including its teaching offices, should be a free public similar to that envisioned in most human rights doctrines. However, those very doctrines of human rights would also contravene any requirement that churches must have such an ecclesiology. This would be a denial of religious freedom for religious groups and institutions. Moreover, it does not follow that the religious rights of individuals should be enforced by authorizing governments to intervene in those procedures to conform them to civil procedures incorporating human rights norms. Such a policy of intervention would reduce religious freedom solely to the beliefs and actions of individuals.

Confidentiality. A third area of discipline involves matters of confidentiality and pastoral care. Here no one is asking that matters of counseling and confession be public. The sphere of personal confession and counseling is inherently a private matter, as both churches and governments widely recognize. The point of contention arises when people wish to bring civil actions against churches for harms they allege to have suffered or might suffer in this confidential arena. This involves both the question of revealing evidence of child abuse as well as suffering from counselling which departs from acceptable professional norms.

For Americans, this was epitomized in the case of Ken Nally, whose parents sought to sue his church for being criminally responsible for his suicide.[14] Nally received counselling from the church's professional staff, who operated under the church's theological insistence that psychological distress is rooted in the person's sinfulness. Therefore, repentance must precede healing. Nally, his parents argued, was driven to suicide by this insistence, which only increased his guilt and self-hatred. The church claimed that it could not be prosecuted under secular counselling norms,

---

[13] Nancy Ammerman, *Baptist Battles* (New Brunswick, NJ, 1990); Morris Ashcraft, "Southeastern Seminary in Crisis: 1986–87," *Faith and Mission* 6(1) (Fall, 1988): 47-61.

[14] *Nally v. Grace Community Church of the Valley* (Cal. Sup. Ct., 1988). See Margaret P. Battin, *Ethics in the Sanctuary: Examining the Practices of Organized Religion* (New Haven, 1990), 206-53.

because its practices were protected aspects of its religious freedom. But the church's resistance to being sued could also be seen as an interference with the rights of Nally's parents to their day in court. American courts sided with the church, thus leaving a zone of freedom in which churches could both secure important human goods, such as spiritual growth, but also wreak unknown harms.

Most obvious among these harms are violations of ordinary norms of sexual behavior. Here many churches face increasing pressure to follow ordinary civil procedures in handling such cases or to face direct civil action regardless of any claims to immunity from state interference in these confidential arenas.[15] The Roman Catholic Church, the Episcopal Church, and other large historic American denominations have all taken steps recently to conform their laws and procedure to the civil models in the United States.

Church Marriage Law. The final contested arena in church discipline involves church governance of marital and family relations. For centuries, marital relations in Europe were governed by ecclesiastical law linking the marriage contract to the sacramental order of the church. While this legal arrangement may once have been an advance over earlier familial control of marriage, it eventually was attacked first in the Reformation and then in the republican revolutions of the eighteenth and nineteenth centuries. Gradually, the laws of marriage and family, including matters of inheritance, were removed from church control and placed in the hands of courts and governments, which consider them secular matters.

Today, any interference in marriage and family matters by churches seeking to maintain their own control can be seen as violations of rights that people have been guaranteed by the state. In secularized North Atlantic countries, human rights would imply the freedom to marry and divorce apart from all church or familial control. However, in regions where the state recognizes church law pertaining to marriage, the state's interference could be seen as restrictions on the freedom of religion, that is on the church's freedom to control marriage as a religious matter.

In India, for instance, there exist separate "personal codes" for each religious group, with an optional state code for those who seek it because of religious intermarriage or for personal reasons.[16] Here the clash be-

---

[15] Donald C. Clark, Jr., "Sexual Abuse in the Church: The Law Steps In," *Christian Century* 110 (April 14, 1993): 396-98; Marie M. Fortune, "How the Church Should Imitate the Navy," *The Christian Century* 109 (August 26/September 2, 1992): 765-66.

[16] E.D. Devadason, *Christian Law in India: Law Applicable to Christians in India* (Madras, 1974); Babu Mathew, et al., *Cases and Materials on Family Law I* (Bangalore, 1990); William E. Pinto, *Law of Marriage and Matrimonial Reliefs for Christians in India* (Bangalore, 1991); J. Duncan M. Derrett, *The Death of a Marriage Law: Epitaph for the Rishis* (New Delhi, 1978); N.

tween the human rights applicable to marriage and family and church law becomes sharpest. Since all these church codes reflect an earlier patriarchal model of family life they come into direct conflict with women's rights. In two cases, that of Shah Bano in Madhya Pradesh and Mary Roy in Kerala, Indian courts encroached upon discriminatory personal codes in favor of democratic values, only to produce a storm of protest.[17] In both cases the passionate support for these traditional personal codes reflects a situation in which the formal aspects of religion are embedded in a dense communal culture which finds its expression in terms of religious law. For the church or other religious organizations to introduce human rights values into their law requires that the whole sub-culture move with them.

In England, on a very different plane, the Anglican Church's law on divorce has deeply affected the life of the English monarchy. Should the church's law govern who is eligible to become the next English monarch or should the English people (and their monarchs) be entitled to follow a secular norm compatible with most human rights doctrines?

These cases illustrate that the way the church is or is not embedded in a wider community deeply affects how one approaches the role of human rights in the church. Either one presses to introduce human rights norms into a church which is deeply embedded in the society, or one seeks to separate the church from governance over family matters in order to resolve the conflict. Both directions imply a general model of social order as well as an ecclesiology.

Governance. Churches must also control who is allowed to set forth authoritative church teaching and carry on the general leadership of the churches, whether in congregations, missions, or schools. Some churches, such as those in the United States, are completely autonomous in their selection of leadership. Others must seek permission or confirmation from civil authorities, as with the Anglican Church in England, the

---

Khodie, ed., *Readings in Uniform Civil Code* (Bombay, 1975); Kavita R. Khory, "The Shah Bano Case: Some Political Implications," in Robert D. Baird, ed., *Religion and Law in Independent India* (New Delhi, 1993), 121-138; John H. Mansfield, "The Personal Laws or a Uniform Civil Code?" in Baird, ed., *Religion and Law in Independent India*, 139-178.

[17] *Mary Roy v. State of Kerala* (1986 Supreme Court 1011) and *Mohammed Ahmed Khan v. Shah Bano Begum and others* (1985 Supreme Court Cases 556). The *Shah Bano* decision precipitated riots leading to a parliamentary act overriding the court's decision. The *Roy* case had less violent, though still disturbing consequences. For Shah Bano, see Ali Asghar Engineer, ed., *The Shah Bano Controversy* (Bombay, 1987). For general discussion see William Johnson Everett, "Religion and Constitutional Development in India," *Journal of Church and State* 37(1) (1995): 61-85; Bruce Lawrence, "Woman as Subject/Woman as Symbol: Islamic Fundamentalism and the Status of Women," *Journal of Religious Ethics* 22(1) (Spring, 1994): 163-185. On inheritance matters (the *Roy* case), see Madhu Kishwar and Ruth Vanita, "Inheritance Rights for Women: A Response to Some Commonly Expressed Fears," *Manushi* 57 (March/April, 1990): 3-14.

Church of Sweden, and the Church of Norway. Less formal interference from state bodies in other countries can also affect these choices. Independent free churches are being pressured to democratize their selection procedures and to open eligibility not only to women and members of minority groups but also to homosexual persons or others who deviate from social norms but are otherwise prepared intellectually and spiritually for these positions. Major movements within the Roman Catholic Church have sought for some years to effect such changes, albeit with little success.[18]

Church Administration. The final arena of controversy involves persons employed in the church in a non-authoritative position. These have traditionally been the secretaries, custodians, administrators, and workers who run the institution on a daily basis. More recently, especially in regions experiencing a decrease in clergy, they have also held teaching and high level administrative positions. The thorny question is this: At what point should these employees lose rights they would have in secular employment simply because they work in a church trying to pursue a religious purpose? For instance, should they be able to form labor unions? American courts held in at least one case that church rights should take precedence over the right to form or join unions.[19] Absent labor unions, should employees still experience the same rights of liberty and care applicable to the general population? Here we reach difficult problems not only of how we construe human rights but of practical possibility, in terms of both resources and enforcement.

Efforts to extend ordinary interpretations of human rights to church employees have stressed the distinction between what is essentially religious in ecclesial institutions and what is secular. This implies that the "religious" aspects should be handled by clergy and the "secular" aspects can be handled by lay employees. This effort to drive a wedge between religious and secular realms within the church and between clergy and laity in church employment runs against the church claim that, regardless of ordination status, all employees are essential to its mission, which is a religious matter. The effort to extend rights to lay employees implies an

---

[18] See James Coriden, *We, The People of God* (Huntington, IN, 1969); James A. Coriden, ed., *The Case for Freedom: Human Rights in the Church* (Washington & Cleveland, 1969); id., ed., *Sexism and Church Law: Equal Rights and Affirmative Action* (New York, 1977); James Coriden, "Human Rights in the Church: A Matter of Credibility and Authenticity," in Alois Müller and Norbert Greinacher, eds., *The Church and the Rights of Man* (New York, 1979), 67-76; Leonard Swidler, "Demokratia, The Rule of the People of God, or Consensus Fidelium," in Swidler and Fransen, eds., *Authority in the Church and the Schillebeeckx Case*, 226-43; Dennis McCann, *New Experiment in Democracy: The Challenge for American Catholicism* (Kansas City, 1987); James Provost and Knut Walf, eds., *The Tabu of Democracy Within the Church Concilium* (London, 1992).

[19] *National Labor Relations Board v. The Catholic Bishop of Chicago, et al.* 440 U.S. 490 (1979).

ecclesiology which distinguishes between "secular" and "religious" dimensions of the church as institution, while the rejection of such efforts implies an ecclesiology which sees them as indivisible parts of one cloth. In traditional theological terms, the first ecclesiology is a "docetic" theory that separates the divinity and humanity in Christ, whose body is the church. The latter ecclesiology implies a highly incarnational theology in which these two dimensions are thoroughly merged in the church. Once again, the two camps are divided according to their theology and ecclesiology as well as their weighing of individual and institutional rights.

While many churches around the world are pressured to adopt the human rights norms established by local civil governments, European churches, which are closely related to the state, face a rather different pressure. For instance, German pastors are by law entitled to the same level of compensation and care as state officials.[20] Moreover, military chaplains in many countries have a governmental status that often involves privileges they would not enjoy in a normal church setting. In this case, the desire to follow a higher Gospel ethic leads many people to want to eliminate these privileges—privileges which to others might look like ordinary rights to liberty for soldiers or entitlements to care by church employees.[21] Whether these conflicts between a Gospel ethic and individual rights can be called human rights questions leads us back once again to the question of ecclesiology and normative models of church-state relations.

Toward an Understanding of the Differences

Having identified and ordered a number of cases of controversy, we can return to our preliminary list of factors shaping the question of human rights in the churches. We can explore their relative weight and how they interact to shape particular situations. Hopefully, we can isolate with more precision the key issues at stake in raising this fundamental question in the first place.

Degree of Internal Legal Development. The degree to which a church has a highly developed legal system does not seem to be a crucial variable. The Roman Catholic Church, with probably the most sophisticated canon law of all, is frequently involved in controversies over human rights within the church. Conversely, churches such as the Society of

---

[20] Wolfgang Bock, *Das für all geltende Gesetz und christliche Selbstbestimmung in Dienstrecht* (Ph.D. Diss., Frankfurt am Main, 1992).

[21] Karl Martin (hrsg.), *Frieden Statt Sicherheit: Von der Militärseelsorge zum Dienst der Kirche unter den Soldaten* (Gütersloh, 1989).

Friends have virtually no distinct legal structure, and yet they are almost never involved in these controversies.

What seems apparent is that legal development is shaped by theological convictions as well as size and length of history. The New Testament contains several passages attacking involved legal recourse, either inside or outside the church. A church's decision to have extensive legal forms involves theological decisions that require law, regardless of the claims of biblical origins. Neither course touches the question of whether human rights is protected or threatened in such a legal development.

What is clear is that to introduce more of a sense of individual rights into church life requires the elaboration of judicial processes to advance and protect such individual rights. If the church is to resist this legal approach to incorporating human rights, it has to discover some other credible way to guarantee human rights in the church. It may restrict the size of its organization, subject all decision-making to saintly judges or special councils or discover some other way. This choice returns us to questions of ecclesiology.

Ecclesiology. Ecclesiology is the bridge between fundamental theological values and practical organization. On the one hand, it is an expression of these values and, on the other hand, it is an expression of models of organization found adequate in the surrounding culture and adopted for church governance. In the case of human rights, Christian ecclesiologies can be seen on a spectrum between familial and conciliar models.

The familial model takes the parent-child relation as fundamental to human flourishing as well as to eventual perfection or redemption. Its dominant form not only in the West but in the East and South has been patriarchal and monarchical. The father rules and provides for the household. The wife and children obey and receive. When extended beyond the family as a model, it implies monarchy, as Robert Filmer and John Locke both knew.

This familial model stresses the values of care, control, nurture, transmission of heritage, and safeguarding of "the flock" (to draw on a related metaphor of care). When rights talk enters this model, it stresses the rights of the members to receive that care, to sustain their membership, to be fed spiritually, and to receive what they need for their spiritual growth from the church. Both Catholic and German Protestant formulations of "Rights in the Church" have stressed this set of values, though on distinctly different grounds.[22] Behind both of these traditions

---

[22] For instance, although Wolfgang Huber and Heinz Eduard Tödt, in their *Menschenrechte: Perspektiven einer menschlichen Welt* (Stuttgart, 1977), 204-208 stand clearly on the conciliar side of this debate, their list of ecclesial human rights begins with "access to faith." Ar-

lie strong parental and familial models of the church. For the Roman Catholic Church, this entails rule by the Pope, the "Papa" of the church. For the German church tradition it lies in the symbol of the "Landesvater," who combines the elements of rule and paternal care. In this model, church membership has about the same degree of voluntariness as does membership in a family. In this kind of church we are claimed by Christ and can secure this relationship only within the church. Thus, claiming adult participation in the church takes on much of the urgency of human rights demands in the relatively involuntary confines of membership within a national state. The claim of human rights participation is not trumped by the freedom to leave that church and join another.

This focus of rights talk echoes what I have called the rights to care in the "second table" of human rights—the economic, social, and cultural rights. Here we find not only the rights of individuals to fundamental security but also the rights of natural groups normally associated with providing this care, above all the family. What is at issue in these models is how the rights to care will be squared with the rights of these natural groups to preserve themselves and their traditions, even at the expense of any particular individual's right. The rights of women are frequently held in the balance within churches as well as in civil orders reflecting this model.

What is important to recognize is that from the inside of such an ecclesiology the rights question is largely one of serving the right to be nurtured by and within the group—the extended family of faith led by a father imbued with the spirit of the ancestral tradition. This is a particular view of the self, its rightful claims and also of the nature of faith and of the church.

The conciliar model takes as its point of departure the relations between adults in the public. It is rooted in covenants and contracts among adults rather than in the parental care invoked in familial ecclesiologies. When it comes to matters of human rights, it naturally focuses on the table of liberties necessary to enable people to engage in public argument and agreement. The fundamentally religious claims of the church arise

---

guing out of a German Protestant tradition, they emphasize that human rights values of participation, freedom, and equality have to be transformed theologically to find appropriate articulation in the church. Thus, for instance, freedom and equality have to be construed within the theological frame of neighbor love. For a Roman Catholic approach, in which sacramental participation historically plays a more important role, see Coriden, ed., *The Case for Freedom: Human Rights in the Church*, 12-14, and James Coriden, "Human Rights in the Church: A Matter of Credibility and Authenticity," in Alois Müller and Norbert Greinacher, eds., *The Church and the Rights of Man* (New York, 1979), 72-74.

more from the agreement among the people than from the tradition conveyed by the fathers of the church.

In this conciliar ecclesiology, our fundamental *"humanum"* is our adult capacity to enter into public friendships, arguments, and agreements with an inherently universal coverage that exceeds by far the bonds of family, ethnic community, and race. Salvation is not so much a matter of parental care by those who are wiser and more powerful; it is the illumination of conscience and its expression in the midst of others who can confirm, challenge, and expand our understanding. Freedom of speech is central to this ecclesiology just as admission to the nurturing grace of the sacraments is central to the familial model.

Obviously this latter model lies much closer to the rights of liberty stretching back to Locke. The readiness of churches shaped by this model to embrace the whole contemporary panoply of human rights seems largely determined by how much distance they want to maintain vis-à-vis their environing societies and governments. Their commitment to separation from the state may occlude their conformity to many human rights norms, as in the present battles over ordination of homosexual persons. This decision is shaped not only by other theological factors such as their eschatology but also by cultural factors such as their relative privilege or deprivation in the social order.

The Relation of Churches to Governments. Regardless of where churches find themselves on this ecclesiological spectrum, they must address the question of their relationships to governments. Here the crucial issues revolve around their degree of autonomy from governments and other powerful institutions, such as the business corporation or stock market.

First of all, who is accountable for securing these rights, or adjudicating their abridgement, however they might be construed? Is the church the sole judge? Are the civil courts or other governmental agencies? What would it mean to say that "humanity" or "God" is the judge? Churches differ sharply on this point. Some are willing to leave wide ranges of judgment to the civil courts, as when Protestant churches by and large leave matters of family law to them. German Lutheran churches have historically left much of church administration to the state, though that tradition has been substantially criticized since the Nazi era.[23]

---

[23] See the Barmen Declaration of 1934 in Arthur C. Cochrane, *The Church's Confession Under Hitler* (Philadelphia, 1962), 237-42. For an example of recent reflections on the implications of Barmen, see Alfred Burgsmüller (hrsg.), *Kirche als "Gemeinde von Brüdern" (Barmen III)* (Gütersloh, 1980), vol. 1.

By keeping some claim to self-determination in this judicial realm, the churches counter the often submerged tendency to make the nation-state the guarantor of human rights. That is, they take common cause with the claim that no institution can be entrusted with securing these rights. Only a society with genuine institutional pluralism of power can do so. This discussion of the political conditions for human rights cannot be followed here, though it is important to see how it intersects the subject before us.

If the decision is internal to the church, where should it reside? Does that choice reflect an ecclesiology as well as a theory of human rights? A familial model places these judgments with the parental figures in the church—those who bear the spirit of the ancestral deposit of faith. Those at the conciliar end ground it in the public debate of the assembly, often reduced to some form of public court.

On these points the human rights doctrines themselves exhibit a certain openness (or opaqueness), for they cannot give us detailed answers to matters of legal due process or the relative weighing of rights either between or within the two tables. The question posed for churches with both ecclesiological models is how they order their life to deal with these questions.

The second way the autonomy question arises is in ascertaining the degree to which ecclesiological models should conform to civil or public models of decision-making. Controversies over selection of leadership or over unionization rights bring us back to this point. Here we reach a fundamental dilemma, for the effort to change the practices of these churches to fit general human rights norms runs directly against other human rights provisions which defend the rights of churches to preserve their own beliefs and traditions—even if they violate human rights norms. But this is the rub: Are human rights really universal, or are they restricted to certain institutional arenas, namely the civil public? If restricted then they are better called civil rights. If universal then they deny the rights of persons to form associations that may dissent, indeed radically dissent, from the accepted norms of society.

This inherent tension in human rights doctrine cannot be pursued here, but it does point to the way that human rights doctrine has its own social, historical, and cultural location. Human rights doctrine has arisen to contest the patriarchal, monarchical, and feudal exclusion of persons from public life. It therefore is biased in favor of individual rights rather than the rights of associations. When religion is strictly a matter of individual belief and conduct, it will protect it. When it is a matter of institutional autonomy, it will seek to democratize that institution to reflect the democratic model of governance assumed in human rights doctrines. The only way these doctrines can remain internally non-contradictory is to remain at the level of the individual, leaving the state, in fact, as the only institution in the society. But this step would eviscerate most of the group rights, especially religious rights, which people would like to attribute to human rights.

This "rightful autonomy" of churches takes on different forms within different patterns of church-government relations.[24] In the "free church" pattern of the United States, for instance, churches struggle with the degree to which they can be reduced to the form and status of non-profit corporations. In a celebrated case, a California court held that the United Methodist Church is an hierarchical non-profit corporation, responsible for the actions of all its local "agents" despite clear and long established ecclesial statements to the contrary.[25] But if this direction is pushed far enough, the churches are robbed of their quality of being real publics, in which human rights doctrines are most applicable. They become a corporate version of the familial household under a hierarchical head.

In order for the churches in such a legal milieu to retain their special position as more than non-profit corporations, they must be clearly "religious" in a very goal-specific and delimited way, usually confined to some kind of cultic activity. To do more is to be involved in activity also pursued by purely secular institutions, whether for-profit or non-profit. These "secular" categories must then conform to general civil law—the usual medium for human rights norms. But this dissection of religious from secular aspects of the church betrays the very holistic and communal spread of religious concerns in Christianity as well as Judaism and Islam. To retain their autonomy in this situation, and with it their control over the application of human rights within their jurisdictions, they must be less than the holistic bodies they claim to be.

In situations where the churches are closely accommodated to the state, as among the German "public corporation" churches, governments may be able to introduce more human rights norms if that is the direction of governmental policy or constitutional requirement. Churches may likewise introduce their own conceptions of public civil rights norms into government policy. In Germany, high standards for employee treatment are shaped by government policy, while new understandings of the role of the military in society are being shaped by church initiatives in the

---

[24] Douglas Laycock, "The Right to Church Autonomy as Part of Free Exercise of Religion," in Dean Kelley, ed., *Government Intervention in Religious Affairs* (New York, 1986), 28-39.

[25] *Barr v. United Methodist Church*, 90 Cal. App. 3d 259 (1979), known as "the Pacific Homes Case." For discussion of the ramifications of the case, see Edward McGlynn Gaffney, Jr., Philip C. Sorenson, and Howard R. Griffin, *Ascending Liability in Religious and Other Non-profit Organizations* (Macon, GA, 1984).

wake of the recent German unification. Here the churches are made increasingly public but at the peril of their own future autonomy.

The concordat pattern introduces even more complications, for here the church—in this case the Roman Catholic Church—appears as a sovereign state in its relations with governments, even to the extent of claiming its own inviolable territory. Here the claim for autonomy reaches a kind of worldly apex by conceiving the church's exclusive loyalty to God in terms familiar to other states. In claiming its autonomy, in contrast to the free churches, it must claim to be more than a church. On the one hand, as a sovereign state it reaches the highest plateau of accountability for the incorporation of human rights norms, as its internal critics have hastened to point out. On the other hand, the point of this autonomy was precisely to avoid falling under norms extrinsic to the church's theology and ecclesiology. If we drive this paradox further we would have to ask of the Vatican that it subscribe to the United Nations covenants and extend these practices throughout its worldwide organization. If, however, it wishes to retain its ecclesial autonomy in other ways, it must give up the claim to state sovereignty. The general tendency by many states today to defer to the Vatican's claim only masks this internal contradiction. It does not resolve it.

Cultural Contexts and Human Rights in the Church. We turn now from conceptions of the church as a kind of corporation or even a kind of state to one in which the church is primarily a cultural entity. In this sense it is more than merely a corporation but less than a state. It is a "people." In contemporary parlance, it is an "ethnic community." This has deep Biblical roots as well as historic authenticity. Particular churches or denominations are often characterized by this ethnic homogeneity even if it is not part of their official self understanding.[26] Sometimes, these ethnic churches have a dominant position in the society, as in northern Europe. At other times, they are despised minorities, as is the case to some degree all over the world. At still other times, they may be the object of solicitous "uplift" by the government, as in the Indian case cited above.

What is peculiar to all these contexts is that the customs of the ethnic community tend to take precedence over norms that might support a widened public in the church community. Women, who might have exercised a powerful de facto role in the community, must then be seen as equals in a church public, contravening historic cultural views of their

---

[26] See Andrew Greeley, *The Denominational Society: A Sociological Approach to Religion in America* (Glenview, IL, 1972) for a discussion of the denominations as ethnic associations. The Church of Jesus Christ of Latter Day Saints is practically a state unto itself, while functioning totally within a seemingly secular state and federal constitution.

status. Government by consensus might be threatened by introduction of voting, with its tendency to move to majority rule. Patterns of inherited or charismatic priesthood might be displaced by rational elections according to "merit."

Most strikingly, where the church is legally vested with rights over marriage and family, the ethnic character of the church has an overwhelming impact on the presence of human rights norms in people's lives. The Indian case may be one of the more extreme, but it does not take long to find manifestations of it not only in European and South American contexts but in highly secularized countries, especially in matters of divorce and remarriage.

An additional element is introduced when the church becomes in effect the legal face of the ethnic community, which has no other standing before the state or corporations. Here the way the government treats the church is in fact the way it treats a whole ethnic community. I have already indicated some features of this in India, where tribal communities and religious communities evoke very different responses from the state. A different twist is given this in the United States, where the original inhabitants—the "American Indians"—have sought to preserve their communal autonomy under the umbrella of protecting their all-embracing traditional religion, even to the point of "establishing" it.[27] This is yet another coalescence of religious autonomy with ethnic national autonomy, with similar impacts on the way these groups might assimilate or reject human rights norms and practices.

This tension between "external" human rights norms and a people's customary integrity is not merely a matter of the autonomy of the ethnic church but also of the way norms of human rights are to be implemented within a jurisdiction. They involve not only the contrast between parental and conciliar ecclesiologies but also between informal and formal procedures, between tradition and "rational" choice.

Summary and Conclusions

The way human rights norms are implemented within churches is affected by their ecclesiologies and their relation to civil governments, by the degree to which they constitute an ethnic community and bear the traditions of that community, and by their internal degree of legalization. The central issue uniting these factors is their choice of ecclesiology, which brings with it a conception of the church's relation to government,

---

[27] See American Indian Civil Rights Bill (1976) and Sharon O'Brien, *American Indian Tribal Governments* (Norman and London, 1989).

family, and culture. This choice of ecclesiology rests in turn on a theological base which carries with it a particular conception of "the human."

The conception of the human has at least two issues that affect both ecclesiology and human rights theory. First, are human beings seen primarily as autonomous individuals who have rights prior to their communal relationships? This view is represented civilly by the liberal rights tradition and an ecclesiology rooted in voluntary association and congregationalism. Or, are human beings born out of a communal body of some kind, who have rights in order to participate effectively in that body? This is the assumption behind both socialist and traditional social theories and is echoed in a conception of the church as the Body of Christ or as a Mother from whom we emerge in faith.

The individualist conception of the human, anchored in the "first table" of political and civil rights, pits the individual against the state, depriving the multitude of intermediary institutions—including churches—of their legitimation and of human rights protection. The corporatist conception, anchored in the "second table" of social-economic rights, gives more protection to these intermediary institutions and communities but often at the expense of less powerful persons, especially women, within them. The question of the nature of the human is both ecclesiological and legal. A closer dialogue between ecclesiology and law may be able to lead us to more nuanced ways of linking them in a critical manner.

The second theological struggle over the meaning of "the human" highlights the difference between a parental and a conciliar ecclesiology, mirrored once again in the "two tables" of human rights. Here the root question emerges: Are human beings essentially stunted or corrupted and in need of the parental care of the bearers of historic wisdom and transcendental revelation? Or are human beings naturally oriented to the good, thus needing to have barriers to their growth toward adult citizenship removed by the state? Or are they both fallen and yet also redeemed, needing both a clear public space to express their goodness but also a differentiation of powers to keep their evil tendencies in check? Each of these perspectives gives rise to different emphases in both the conception, and securing of human rights.

The distinction between the rights to care and the rights to liberty, between the "second table" and "first table" rights, closely parallels the ecclesiological distinction between voluntarist and corporatist views of the church, between parental and conciliar ecclesiologies. An examination of the way churches appropriate or reject human rights norms challenges us to enter a more embracing dialogue between ecclesiology and human rights thought to see how these two "tables" of our modern human rights covenant might be conjoined for the sake of human beings within and outside the churches.

Thinking About Women, Christianity, and Rights

JEAN BETHKE ELSHTAIN
University of Chicago

W hat insights might be drawn from social and political theory in the matter of women and rights within Christian communities? This is a nearly impossible assignment for several reasons. First, Christianity is itself multiple, not monolith. Second, "women" constitute not one category but many. As with all human beings, women are divided by race, region, nationality, class, interests, passions, and what might be called the luck—or ill luck—of the historic draw. By that I mean that no one controls the time and place into which he or she is born and that historically-contingent dimension to our identities also plays a rather major role in determining how we think about communities, including the Christian community in its multiplicity, and the roles and rights of men and women within them. Perhaps the most one might expect, given the enormity and complexity of the issues involved, is that the social and political theorist helps us to "think what we are doing," in the words of political theorist Hannah Arendt. My task, then, will be one of conceptual clarification and sharpening. At stake are a number of vital and highly contested issues.

My reflections will be framed from a stance of skepticism about whether the language of rights is the most powerful and exigent way available to us to talk about our mutual participation and recognition within the body of the church. I begin with three interrelated questions. First, how do we understand human rights in general and the political, ethical, philosophical, and theological work this understanding does for us? Second, how do we think about rights within the body of a very particular community—the Church,[1] the body of Christ? Third, how does

---

[1] For the sake of brevity, I here refer to "Church" as a particular identity—something "new" in the antique world—knowing full well that the multiplicity of Christianity to which I refer is embodied in multiple ecclesial forms. This means, alas, that the term "Church," as

J. Witte, Jr. and J.D. van der Vyver (eds.), Religious Human Rights in Global Perspective, 143-155.
© 1996 *Kluwer Law International. Printed in the Netherlands.*

our understanding of rights presuppose a person of a particular sort or, more strongly, how do various understandings of rights help to constitute us as persons?

Male and Female

The best way to take up these matters is not from an abstract *a priori* stance outside and above them but to build from the ground up, so to speak. Consider, then, just how extraordinary was the shift from the presumptions and structures of the late antique world to those alternative commitments embodied in the Christian community. Welcomed into the new community, women shared in the activities and ideals that were its living tissue. The qualities most often associated with mothering—giving birth to and sustaining human life; an ethic of responsibility toward the helpless, the vulnerable, the weak; gentleness, mercy, and compassion— were celebrated. The realm of what the ancients called "necessity" generated its own sanctity. Women, like men, might be called upon to die for a cause, not as Homeric heroes wielding great swords, but as witnesses to the strength of their convictions.

Recall the rigidity of some classical presumptions, including a rather common anthropological assumption that women and men were confined to entirely separate spheres on the basis of what their innate being enabled them to realize. Christianity defied this rigid separation of human beings by declaring that every human being is equal in God's eyes: "there is neither Jew nor Greek, male nor female, free nor slave," in St. Paul's famous turn of phrase, "but all are one" in the new dispensation of Christ Jesus.[2] The new Christian community included, or incorporated, two groups excluded from the classical city—women and the poor. As Peter Brown argues, Christian women took on a public role in their own right in their relation to the poor and the sick. They founded shrines and poorhouses in their own names and were able to pick some of their own kin—their special saints—and to go into the public world out of devotion to these self-chosen kin.[3]

God's grace was available to all. God's love, Christian *Agape*, very different from classical *Eros*, infused human life. "We must love one another," was a core Christian commandment. We are, argued Augustine, well advised to judge ourselves and others not by our own acquisitions,

---

here deployed, takes on an unfortunate abstractness that, for the purpose of this chapter, is unavoidable. It should, nonetheless, be noted in light of my own objections to arguments that take place apart from, or without necessary reference to, certain concrete reference points.

[2] Galatians 3:28; Colossians 3:11.

[3] Peter Brown, *The Cult of the Saints* (New York, 1993).

or our power to compel, but by what it is we and they love. The new Christianity community was available to any who had a hunger and thirst for righteousness. The Christian of God on pilgrimage on this earth is "set apart by a holy yearning," in Augustine's phrase, and that yearning includes hope—hope lodged in the capacity of human beings to long for something different, to examine the nature of their relationship with their immediate environment, above all, to establish their identities by refusing to be engulfed in the unthinking habits of their fellows. The Christian recognizes an intimate dependence on the life around him or her and is aware of the tenacity of the ties that bind us to the world. What is our "business within this common moral life," Augustine queried, and it is with this question that all evaluations of women and rights within Christian communities should be situated. Men and women are not enemies but friends—brothers and sisters in communion.[4]

That, of course, is not all, for "male and female created He them."[5] How are we to understand "male" and "female"? Three positions have emerged.

Sex Polarity. I have already alerted us to one form of devaluation, a view widely held in classical antiquity and that continues to circulate even at present. This is the position of *sex polarity* that holds that male and female are unlike essences, something akin to different species. Although the antique view devalued the female in relation to the male, there is the mirror image of this devaluation in what might be called reverse sex polarity, or hostility on the part of female to male with the latter devalued in the overall scheme of things. Within the world of sex polarity, one sex is necessarily "better than" or a "victim of" the other. If one begins from the presumptions of sex polarity in either of its varieties, the only view of rights that is consistent with this ontological position is rights as adversarial, as a weapon one sex can, or should, use against the other.[6]

Sex polarists come in a number of historical and contemporary varieties. Whatever the source of philosophical inspiration, the outcome is an epistemological gulf—men and women "think differently"—that works to devalue one sex in relation to the other. Aristotle's dictum that women's rationality lacked the completeness and fullness of that of the male would be one example of this view. But there are harsher versions,

---

[4] This paragraph and the one preceding it are drawn from my essay, "Christianity and Patriarchy," *Modern Theology* 9(2) (April, 1993): 110, 112-113.

[5] Genesis 1:27.

[6] For the typology of male and female in relation to one another, I am indebted to Sr. Prudence Allen, *The Concept of Woman: The Aristotelian Revolution 750 B.C. - A.D. 1250* (Montreal, 1985).

those that begin with strong anthropological presumptions of the inferiority or superiority of one sex on the level of being itself. For example, in contemporary discussions of men, women, and war, it is striking how frequently the assertion that men are "by nature" violent, disorderly, the destroyers and violators of women, children, and all of nature is simply stated as a matter of fact. By contrast, women are identified with principles of care, peace-lovingness, and attunement with nature. In more polemical versions of a sex polarist argument, the universe itself is imperilled unless peaceful women somehow triumph over violent men. There is no room for mediating across this ontological divide. Beginning with a master/slave narrative in which all comes down, finally, to power, such sex polarists deploy rights as a weapon in what they unabashedly call the "sex war." This impugning of one sex to the advantage of the other is a long story, of course, as older misogynist narratives all too amply demonstrate. The difference between earlier generations of male disparagers of women and current disparagers of men by women is that the language of rights was not available as a central category in the rhetorical struggle. Rights, then, traffics as a variant on power-talk, as the emblematic relationship between male and female as separate categories is as that of oppressor and oppressed. Sex polarists cannot, by definition, think their way out of, or through, this static formulation. Or, perhaps better put, they can get out of the oppressor/oppressed and master/slave pairing only through the obliteration of one category: thus men must be "feminized," and the more virtuous and saintly sex must triumph for the scenario to play itself out to a desired end.

Sex Unity. A second position—sex unity—would seem to solve this problem of ontological inequality. Indebted to a literal rather than ironic reading of Book V of *Plato's Republic*, this position is one that obliterates difference in favor of the identity or unity of male and female. There are no differences that matter if one abstracts from embodiment, strips mothers and children of particular ties one to the other, and "mates" males and females (of the elite Guardian class) on principles of eugenic selection. A notion of rights flowing from sex unity would be a terribly abstract understanding of rights as part of an overarching structure and totalizing philosophy. In other words, we become equal to the extent that we are the same with our individualities rubbed off and our sexual identities a matter of indifference.

Oddly enough, sex unitists tended to wind up in an end-game similar to that of sex polarists who must vanquish the opposition or utterly transform "it"—another form of triumph through effacement. That is, the homogenizing urge, present at creation, so to speak, extends itself to political and theological projects that foresee the elimination of the whole category of gender, even the recognition of difference. All are "one," not in communion as a creedal body within which the distinctiveness of persons is preserved but, rather, are "one" in a politicized entity (whether a transformed polity, or family, or church) in which we are utterly indifferent to difference, having abstracted from our bodies so successfully that they are no longer a source of identity, no longer the object of epistemological wonder and understanding. Rights here would be the juridical identity of "species-beings," to borrow a Marxist term, who are not specifically bodies identified or tethered in a way that carries any theological, ethical, or political weight.

Sex Complementarity. Finally, there is sex complementarity, a vision of male and female in relation that emerged with distinctiveness within the Christian tradition. Sex complementarity begins from a stance of ontological equality and equal dignity that is nonetheless compatible with different roles and offices. Equality neither requires nor presumes homogenization; rather, sex complementarity affords a sense of partnership, of what it means to be in community and in communion. Framed with this understanding in mind, rights become signs of human dignity, marks of "the same" and "the distinct" simultaneously. This latter position is philosophically richer, but it complicates matters politically and requires a more nuanced understanding of the way rights structure our identities both with and against multiple bodies—family, church, neighborhood, and state. Rather than a presumptive and destructive abstraction from the body (sex unity), or a presumptive and destructive absolutizing of sex difference (sex polarity), one displays a view of embodied beings in relation.

My understanding of sex complementarity is indebted to the doctrine of creation, and it makes provision for both ontological distinctiveness and equality as well as for moments in which our differences are of lesser moment than our being at one in the body of Christ. This "at oneness" is not an obliteration of difference (as in sex unity), nor a destruction of the other (as in sex polarity) but a community that recognizes male and female sociality and friendship.[7]

The Language of Rights

With this backdrop in mind, I turn: first, to rights in general, second, to rights within the body of the church, and, finally, to the relationship between our understanding of rights and our view of the human person. Each of these topics deserves a much fuller discussion than this chapter

---

[7] I thank my colleague, William Schweiker, for urging me to stress this point and for other comments and criticisms.

can provide. But I hope that parsing matters in this way will help to open up debate. Because for many North Americans, at least, rights are trumps in political argumentation, helping to make more complex our discussion of rights is itself a contribution to a fuller and more interesting argument.

Rights are a Western invention, heavily indebted to Christian constructions of human ontological dignity as encoded over time in notions of natural law and right. Even prior to the emergence of Christianity, the ancients worked with complex distinctions between civil or what we might now call statutory or positive law and a more fundamental, basic underpinning, a law of all peoples, or a law transcending particular national differences. This *jus gentium* received powerful reinforcement from the Christian understanding of the human as created in the image of God. Medieval canonists and scholastics used the concept of *ius* to capture such immunities as the church's and clergy's claims to various exemptions, including exemption from military service and taxes, as well as a lower cleric's claims to protection against overbearing superiors in the hierarchy. (This by no means exhausts the medieval understanding of immunities, but it gestures toward the historic density of the idea.) To the extent that entitlements were involved, the concept of *ius* had to do with claims on charity or asylum, all claims based on a prior presupposition concerning Christian responsibilities toward "my neighbor" and hospitality toward "the stranger."[8] It is important to be clear that rights as thus construed are part of a deep and wide moral ontology in which rights do not exhaust the available moral vocabulary.[9]

Rights locate us within, rather than set us apart from, a community of a particular kind. Rights are inseparable from both our distinctiveness and our dignity. Over time, human rights as a philosophic given came to be understood, politically, as immunities that inhered in the person *qua* person. I have rights as a human person, not because my particular society has granted me a set of particular rights that are, in principle, revocable should the society change. Rights served as barriers to the depradations of the more powerful, as a bulwark against an overreaching or overarching political entity, the state. Rights as immunities do not place each human being in a "state of war" with each other. Such rights are a birth right, not a scarce resource available to some but not to all.

The influence of classical market economics helped to fuel a second understanding of rights and a shift of emphasis from rights as immunities to rights as entitlements. Entitlements place me in a different position towards both the state and my neighbor. Rather than serving an inter-

---

[8] See Brian Tierney's chapter included in this volume.

[9] Thanks to my colleague, Frank Gamwell, for urging me to make this point more prominent.

positional role—the state is not permitted to do certain things because so to do would violate human dignity—rights now affords us a way to couch a particular claim—"I" am entitled to certain things, because I belong to one of a proliferating number of possible human categories (male, female, young, old, handicapped, minority, etc.). Framed within a political economy of scarcity, rights as entitlements promotes a legalistic, adversarial, "zero-sum" approach to rights in general. I now compete in the marketplace of rights as entitlements, hoping that my claims will trump those of others. Tethered to an adamantly individualistic understanding of the human person, rights as entitlements denies any weight to principles of belonging, obligation, and community or communal identity. In this adversarial version of rights, the tethering of self to community is severed—at least in theory—and the transitive nature of rights is lost. Because we require "others" to be "ourselves, and to recognize our distinctiveness, that, too, is jeopardized. Lost in these possessive constructions of rights is a fundamental recognition of rights as transitive, as social, as the way we mark human dignity and the way persons have of acknowledging the dignity of others.

Hopefully, it is clear that rights within the body of the Church should drink most deeply from the well of rights as immunities rather than rights as entitlements, for the former view is not only dependent upon a genealogy of which Christianity is a central feature but is the understanding of human rights most coherently associated with the nature of the Church and of persons in communion. Here things get difficult, to be sure, but perhaps it helps to remember certain fundamental truths. The Church is not primarily a political institution; rather, it is the home of a pilgrim people. The Christian does not privilege political or civic identity above all other markers of identity; indeed, in cases of conflict, the name "Christian" should prevail over the name "American" or "Russian" or "Mexican." Christians have been on a collision course with state idolatry from the beginning.

Rights as immunities, as inherent markers of human ontological dignity, is the understanding of rights in general to which Christians are most indebted and toward which they can make the strongest contribution. Of course, this notion of rights bleeds over into rights as entitlements but reframes them. Now a right to a "just wage," for example, is not seen as a right that places me against the rights of others but as a way that we, together, claim a human birthright. This may, to be sure, underscore a politics of conflict to the extent that one group denies another a fundamental right. But the presuppositional end point is not a reversal in which those who were once privileged are now suffering and trampled upon and those who were ill-treated feast on the fruits of triumph; it is, rather, a world in which such harsh enmities have less scope for appearance and civic embodiment.

Ironically, to define the Church as a political institution in its very essence, and to go on to make claims within the Church using the contemporary language of rights as entitlements, pits Christians against one another in a world that presumes a scarcity of goods. No longer does the fullness of *Agape* prevail, but rather the penury of political economy, of zero-sum games. For rights as immunities, there are strong theological arguments to make. One begins with a being who is not the master of his or her own universe, not the creator of his or her own ground of being. But contemporary "rights talk" all too often bristles with a burgeoning panoply of human wants and starts from those wants rather than from dignities and immunities. Such versions of rights are, for the most part, explicitly extra-theological.

Not only that. A world defined by rights as adversarial possessions, increasingly lodged in a presupposition of pre-given "group identities" (by gender or race, for example), promotes or requires a flattening out of human identity. We are all bundles of needs and claims. What separates us one from the other is not our human distinctiveness but the fact that some are oppressors, others oppressed; some hegemonic, others abject. Rights are what we use to "get ours," as rights are displaced from the arena of human dignity as persons to the possessions of free-standing, self-sovereign selves. We lose a rich notion of human plurality in this process, a notion of human separateness and distinction that invites us into community and urges upon us a recognition of the dignity of each and all.

Rights and Personhood

How does our understanding of rights presuppose or help to constitute a person of a particular kind? I have already distinguished between rights as immunities and as entitlements. At this juncture, allow me to draw back into the picture the third of our alternative notions of sex identity, that of sex complementarity. The signs of this latter understanding are the inherent dignity of persons. The social and cultural implications are many. One would look to whether men and women are treated as by definition inferior in relation to superior; or as identical in a way that negates embodiment; or, alternatively, as analogical beings who work out their identities over time in relation. Here we must part company with those of our Christian forebears who saw in "man" the most perfect representation of what it means to be created "in the image of God." Sr. Prudence Allen, in an interesting article on "integral sex complementarity," writes: "It is in light of . . . contemporary understandings that the recent writings of Pope John Paul II are so illuminating, for he states explicitly that woman and man equally reflect the image of God."[10] Allen concludes that it is "hard to overestimate the significance of this shift in emphasis that Pope John Paul II is bringing to the Church's understanding of man and woman as persons."[11]

This shift is understanding is significant, because it gestures towards an understanding that puts together in a single frame rights as markers of human dignity and a view of male and female in relation. Mind you, my point here is not that every problem is hereby resolved; rather, my argument is that a theological basis for understanding rights is enhanced and proffered in a way that provides ample ground for disputation over the implications of this understanding for male and female standing, offices, and identities in the human story. This requires more fleshing out than I can here undertake in anything approaching adequacy. But a few more words are in order.

In his recent "World Day of Peace" message, John Paul II offered reflections on "Women: Teachers of Peace." His starting point was clear: "If, from the very beginning, girls are looked down upon or regarded as inferior, their sense of dignity will be gravely impaired and their healthy development inevitably compromised. Discrimination in childhood will have lifelong effects and will prevent women from fully taking part in the life of society."[12] The ground here laid is a clear ontology of human dignity that yields strong conclusions against invidious comparison and the ill use associated with discrimination (the old sex polarity position). This is a position that is at once old and new. It goes back to trinitarian understanding of a commune of separate yet one persons; it is more Augustinian than Thomistic in this sense. Male and female are from the beginning embodied beings who display the marks of "solitude" and "an inscrutable divine communion of persons."[13]

---

[10] Sr. Prudence Allen, "Integral Sex Complementarity and the Theology of Communion," *Communio* 17 (Winter, 1990): 523, 542-543.

[11] Ibid.

[12] Pope John Paul II, "Women: Teachers of Peace," *Origins* 24(28) (December 22, 1994): 465, 468.

[13] This is a citation from Pope John Paul II's homilies collected under the title, *Original Unity of Man and Woman: Catechesis on the Book of Genesis* (Boston, 1981) (quoted by Allen, "Integral Sex Complementarity," 543. Also important is Pope John Paul's much-maligned and, I believe, misunderstood—at least in North America—*Apostolic Letter on the Dignity and Vocation of Women* (Boston, 1988). My view that this document literally could not be "read" in a context in which rights are an adversarial possession of one against the other has become the dominant understanding of rights. Whatever one thinks of Pope John Paul's particular positions on, say, the ordination of women, this starting point he here sets forth offers what I have argued that we need: a rich parsing of rights tethered to an understanding of sex com-

Surely, Christians—of all people!—are obliged to take up the question of rights, sex, gender, participation, and power from a standpoint of theological distinction and argument. This argument is enriched, of course, with philosophy, including political philosophy. But if the argument is grounded in a narrowly political understanding, such as that of the "social contract," the deeper and richer ground I gesture towards in this chapter is lost altogether.

In another fascinating piece on the subject, Sr. Allen draws upon the words and witness of two quite different thinkers—Edith Stein and Hildegard of Bingen (1098-1179). Stein, of course, shares a great deal of philosophic ground with the current Pope, so it is no big surprise that their appreciation of human corporeality and male and female as analogical beings created in God's image should overlap. I will focus on Hildegard briefly because it helps to show the historic lineage of the modern view I am promoting. For Hildegard, men and women mirror one another. Hildegard thus establishes, in Allen's view, "a horizontal basis for complementarity between women and men, that is, that they are significantly different and simultaneously equal in dignity and worth."[14] Hildegard insists that men and women help to create one another; that each is "so involved with each other that one of them is the work of the other. Without woman, man could not be called man; without man, woman could not be named woman. . . . Neither of them could henceforth live without the other."[15] This is fascinating in part because Hildegard would seem to be working, at least tacitly, with an appreciation of human powers as plural, *potentia* rather than *potestas*. *Potestas* is a political construal of power as rule or dominion: power "over" others. *Potentia* points us towards something more open, less codified, from which our notion of potential is derived.

In our own time, rights have been driven more and more into a corner in which they are seen as a way to get and to hold power. I do not in any way want to disparage the claims of women within churches for equal dignity and respect; indeed, that is a direct outgrowth of the sex complementarity position. But I do want to challenge one version of the politicization of rights talk within the Church that tacitly presupposes as an essential description of male-female relationships an oppressor/oppressed scenario and that, further, flows from presuppositions that are sex-polarist or sex-unitist in nature. For these presuppositions

---

plementarity, of male and female as persons in community within a particular body called "Church."

[14] Sr. Prudence Allen, "Sex and Gender Differentiation in Hildegard of Bingen and Edith Stein," *Communio* 20 (Summer, 1993): 389, 402.

[15] Ibid.

flatten out distinctiveness; they push for a harsh politicization of all human relationships in line with the notion that plurality within various human communities is a bane not a blessing. Thus one "authority principle" must govern every arena of life, thereby undermining the dialogic "working" of men and women as creators and sustainers of one another under or within the frame of a transcendent principle that brings an appropriate humility to all human projects. Rights as markers of human dignity, while recognizing that political dominion does require that some hold office of a particular sort, nevertheless does not view rights as a vehicle to attain dominion. Rights, in fact, are the way we limit and chasten dominion. This more "horizontal" notion of rights is dependent upon a shared "vertical" relationship to God through Christ's incarnation and passion, through creation, fall, and redemption. In this world, men and women are different, yet equal in dignity and worth. And unjust rule is a form of dominion that privileges and dignifies one sex to the deprivation of the other. It signifies a fundamental disordering of human life.

The co-creation of man and woman in relation to one another (each as the "work" of the other, in Hildegard's happy term) is not an image of blissful harmony, an unlittered landscape of indistinguishable "oneness." Indeed, this latter view presupposes a sex unity posture that Christian theology challenges: we are equal in dignity and fundamental equality, but we are distinct one from the other as well; complementarity, not polarity, not unity. This relationship will, at times, be an antagonistic one as men and women "work" one another, struggling with and against sameness and difference. But within that particular community called "Church" this struggle is framed by a shared lineage. Given this lineage, this deposit of the centuries-old struggle of belief and unbelief, rights is a way we begin the discussion rather than a way we end the argument by defeating our pre-given sexual, racial, or class foes.

At this point, and in conclusion, I want to point to one further implication of this chapter. One might call this "humbling the United States." We Americans have a tendency to project both our power and our preoccupations. In the last quarter of a century, this country has done a tremendous amount of good by lifting up and sustaining a notion of human dignity and freedom abroad and going through agonies trying to achieve a "more perfect union" within. But there is, as always, a downside. We have tended to export not merely a general philosophic and political commitment to human dignity and freedom but, increasingly, to encase that understanding in an ever narrower and adversarial notion of rights. We have made strong claims that the equality of men and women necessarily demands no distinction whatsoever between offices, roles, and identities. Hence our preoccupation with "reproductive rights," especially abortion, and a strong tendency to see in this a necessary correlative of equality.

Confronted with concrete others—women in societies not our own who do not "fill in" rights and equality with this set of political commitments—there is an additional tendency to see their views as limited, unenlightened, a version of "false consciousness." A starting point in an adversarial construal of rights and a "wants-based" view of the human person permits very little by way a more generous interpretation of the needs and concerns of women who do not find this starting point at all self-evident.

For eight years now I have been conducting interviews with mothers' groups in a number of countries. Let me offer one piece of testimony, this from a woman who is one of the leaders of a group called "the Prague Mothers," a group of mothers organized around environmental issues. I asked her about her reaction to the presence of so many Americans in their midst post-1989 and, specifically, about the ways on which one version of North American feminism was being "exported" to her own society. In response, she said the following:

> We want to emphasize concrete problems not ideological attitudes or whatever you want to call them. We try to give objective arguments. Many feminists have tried to influence our position, but they consider us underdeveloped creatures who act as if we don't know what we are doing. But we are not interested in this new "feminist consciousness." We think we have a responsibility for children and for future generations. We must think globally. Everything is connected. We will stay as a mothers' organization because this is very powerful, this is who we are. We are in good contact with men in environmental politics. We do not see men as the enemy.[16]

For the Prague Mothers, rights is a way to talk about fundamental human dignity, not a way to position them against men *qua* men, but as a pathway toward fuller recognition and participation with like-minded men in a project of human possibility in light of inherent human dignity. How this will work itself out over time is, of course, a porous, open matter. Universal claims and particular outcomes and conditions emerge out of contestation, out of a process of debate, conflict, compromise. In that particular community we call "church," the fullness and completeness of being is by definition unattainable in the penultimate realm of human affairs. But rights is one way we honor and recognize our own dignity and that of others. Rights is a way we engage in communion, rather than a

---

[16] Interview with Anna Hradilkova, Prague, July, 1993 (unpublished).

way we separate in hostility. Rights is a way we try to stop depradations of power and chasten human arrogance. That women have suffered ill-dignities at the hands of men is undoubtedly the case. (Women, of course, are not innocent as perpetrators, but they have all too often been playing "defense" rather than "offense" in the historic story.) But this should yield not a politics of resentment for which "rights" becomes a justification but a politics of recognition, respect, and fairness in which rights plays a central role. If the Church fails in this regard, it suggests that the harsh view of a world in which all is power and possession is closer than ever to triumphing. Sad but true.

The Religious Rights of Children

JOHN E. COONS
University of California at Berkeley

A ny specifically Christian analysis of the religious rights of children is in short supply. Even the curators of the great Berkeley collection on religious law are unable to locate a single text; indeed, they find little in canonical sources about any aspect of childhood beyond the duties of parents regarding the sacraments and education. Of rights to be exercised independently by the child there is nothing. I hesitate to fall back on those scraps of scripture that favor minors. No doubt some lawyer could read Matthew 19:14 to establish a child's right of direct access to Jesus; and certain translations of the succeeding passage grant children a property right in heaven (in fee as tenants in common but defeasible upon their earthly survival to majority status). I assume that these rights would qualify as "religious," but somehow I think that the editors of this volume had something else in mind. In any case, claims of this sort remain unlitigated and undiscussed. Nor do I propose to disturb this tradition of restraint, but only to explain it, as I proceed to show why Christianity has encouraged adults to emulate children while specifying no juridical protections for the preferences of the little paragons themselves.

The reason for this reticence cannot be that Christians confuse children with puppies and porpoises, innocent creatures incapable of moral activity hence inappropriate subjects for rights. Man's amoral infancy is very brief; with the dawn of rationality comes moral (even legal) responsibility.[1] Christians are reminded of this not only by the Fourth Commandment but even by the civil law which also ordains the obedience of

---

[1] The full array of child-centered activities in the medieval church is presented in N. Orme, "Children and the Church in Medieval England," *Journal of Eccclesistical History* 45 (1994): 563. Several of the religious roles played by minors would fit into our subject if they were available for autonomous choice by individual children. Unfortunately there is no clear indication in Orme whether parents held a veto power over the child's participation, e.g., as a chorister or as a member of a youth guild.

157

J. Witte, Jr. and J.D. van der Vyver (eds.), Religious Human Rights in Global Perspective, 157-174.
© 1996 *Kluwer Law International. Printed in the Netherlands.*

children.[2] Such obligation assumes that children are free and rational actors; but, again, then, why have the Christians neglected to catalogue their corresponding rights? Even more irritating to the apologist, why have Christians left all the credit for the discovery of children's rights to secular advocates of the twentieth century with their laws, constitutions, international conventions, and legions of "child advocates." Every season produces a flood of mutually opposing works by liberationists and utilitarians telling us why children should (and should not) have the civil authority available to enforce their own wills.[3] One could suppose that respect for children had awaited the decline of the Christian community.

Happily there are more reasonable responses. The first is to deny the premise about the reforming genius of modern law. In fact, where the rights of children have expanded, this has occurred largely as a function of technological advance. These rights consist mostly of access to new techniques. As medicine, for example, masters a specific disease, children acquire a right to the cure. But this took only a modest change in legal theory. Granted, the verbal formula has shifted successively from father-right to mother-right and now to the "best interest of the child"; it is unclear that this alteration drove the results. Technology plus the availability and self-interest of bureaucratic delivery systems such as pediatrics, social work, mental hospitals and the whole professional edifice were the greater influence;[4] for the child *in extremis* these represent a set of institutional and medical possibilities that in prior generations were never an alternative. Until such remedies existed, there could be no right—legal or moral. Child advocates thus can be modest about the independent contribution of the law. Meanwhile such legal "advances" as no-fault divorce have taken their toll of the child's interest in an intact family. Whether the young are on the whole better off is anyone's guess (mine is no). By the way, these technological "rights" have all been of the sort chosen for them by adults; the child was seldom consulted. Later, this will be relevant to our definition of rights.

---

[2] By this, I mean that American law accepts that parents have the authority (however derived) to adopt and enforce positive and negative duties without the child's consent.

[3] Recent comments on these conflicting claims are E. Scott, "Judgment and Reasoning in Adolescent Decision Making," *Villanova Law Review* 37 (1992): 1607; M. King, "Children's Rights as Communication: Reflections on Autopoietic Theory and the United Nations Convention," *Modern Law Review* 57 (1994): 385; J. Coons, R. Mnookin and S. Sugarman, "Puzzling over Children's Rights," *Brigham Young University Law Review* (1991): 307. For a sustained analysis see L. Purdy, *In their Best Interest? The Case Against Equal Rights for Children* (Ithaca, 1992).

[4] For a general sense of the medical aspects of this point see R. Mnookin and D. Weisberg, *Child, Family and State*, 2d ed. (Boston, 1989), 455-592.

The second response to any charge of Christian indifference would focus upon our specific topic—the *religious* rights of the child. Let us be clear that both American law and the churches have recognized the independent religious rights of children exactly to the same extent—that is, not at all. Possibly I am missing something, but I have yet to encounter a case in which a child has successfully (or even unsuccessfully) invoked the guarantee of free exercise to overturn a decision of the parent.[5] Occasionally children secure their personal choice in respect to custody, abortion, or early emancipation but never, so far, on religious grounds. Conversely, we often have seen parents and their children allied to assert rights against the state. These federations have produced, in the United States, landmarks such as *Pierce*,[6] *Meyer*,[7] *Barnette*[8] and *Tinker*,[9] all of which allude to a child's right (to secure private instruction or to flout public school authority). However, even if these latter decisions had rested on the free exercise clause (they did not), they would establish no independent religious right of the child. We will know that such a thing exists when the Court orders a sheriff to escort the child to a church service that the parents have forbidden or to avoid one that they have commanded. This, of course, was Justice Douglas' point a generation ago in *Wisconsin v. Yoder*.[10] He saw plainly that vindication of the Amish parent could entail the religious subjugation of the Amish child. Nothing has changed (except for the general termination of minority at eighteen).

To extend the point outside our own legal system, I know of no treaty—including the *UN Convention on the Rights of the Child*[11]—that in-

---

[5] Nor has a 1986 article dealing with the very subject of this essay. L. Mueller, "Religious Rights of Children: A Gallery of Judicial Visions," *Review of Law and Social Change* 14 (1986): 323, however, leaves the vague impression that such rights may exist, and, except for the European phenomena reported in note 13, I see no evidence of them.

[6] *Pierce v. Society of Sisters*, 268 U.S. 510 (1925).

[7] *Meyer v. Nebraska*, 262 U.S. 390 (1923).

[8] *West Virginia State Board of Education v. Barnette*, 319 U.S. 624 (1943).

[9] *Tinker v. Des Moines Independent Community School District*, 393 U.S. 503 (1969).

[10] *Wisconsin v. Yoder*, 406 U.S. 205 (1972) (Douglas, J. dissenting).

[11] Granted, the language of Article 14 of the Convention is arresting:

> 1. States Parties shall respect the right of the child to freedom of thought, conscience and religion.

> 2. States Parties shall respect the rights and duties of the parents and, when applicable, legal guardians, to provide direction to the child in the exercise of his or her right in a manner consistent with the evolving capacities of the child.

And the preceding Articles 12 and 13 declare the child's right to express his or her views freely and to receive all manner of information. The reality, nonetheless, is that these "rights" depend upon the state of domestic law. This is made clear in King, "Children's Rights as Communication." King observes that the convention may be intended as a first step toward

sures a child's independent religious right, nor of any litigation in international forums that even raises the issue. The impending conflicts over gender distinctions that eventually may pit Islamic girls against state-subsidized religious schools in Western Europe are unlikely to change this. It is not at all clear that these children will be presenting a claim based upon religion. Just which religion would they be invoking as the basis of their access to co-education? Their real aim is to put an *end* to a specific religious practice, not to assert another with which it is in conflict.[12] The girls' theory must instead be that the principle of equal treatment in education outweighs the religious rights of its providers. So far as I am aware equality remains unrecognized as a religion. We seem to face the question of the religious rights of children in a rather abstract form.[13]

In truth, however, things are not so airy and academic. Children's independent rights—religious and other—do get adjudicated; it happens billions of times every day. Indeed, the third answer—and the one that will from this point occupy my full attention—is that there has long existed (and continues to exist) a practical regime of children's rights. These rights and the system that sustains them are in substantial part the artifact of Western religious dogma, tradition, and history. Though seldom noted in the codes or cases, Christian influence upon the status of childhood suffuses the positive law of all Western nations. And, specific to our present inquiry, the child's interest in religious liberty receives a greater practical protection under this cryptic regime than could ever be deliv-

---

the substitution of bureaucratic discretion for parental authority. As suggested below such a shift would not necessarily be a net gain for the child's liberty.

[12] The same would hold for either male or female circumcision. That is, the objection to the practice would probably not be based in religion, though the practice itself is. Hence religion will be invoked only in its defense (though it seems unlikely that a child will be the one to invoke it). An analogous religious right may well be advanced defensively in the hypothetical Islamic school case. It could be asserted by intervening Islamic boys invoking the Shari'a to support separate male instruction. But even such a distinctive religious child-right is likely to get diluted and denatured by parental alliance in the assertion of the claim. That alliance is likely to produce implicit or explicit judicial recognition of the adult right to direct their sons' education; and any parent who opposed a son's claim would in all likelihood prevail, at least until the age of fourteen (see note 13).

[13] Students from the gymnasium of Gelsenkirchen, Germany, have led me to one practical exception to the rule. From age 12 a child cannot be forced by a parent to change religion; and from age 14 a child has the right to choose his own religion. "Gesetz über die Religiöse Kindererziehung" (15 July, 1921; RGBI 939, 1263 (F5). My colleague Professor Stefan Riesenfeld recalls that his classmate Reimen, as an "Old Lutheran," successfully eluded the "reformed" curriculum, quite possibly by invoking this law (the views of Reimen's parents are unfortunately beyond recall). The implications for family integrity seem so significant that the dearth of comment is puzzling. I am credibly informed that a similar juvenile autonomy obtains in Italy and possibly elsewhere. Perhaps my perception of the risk to the family is a peculiar piece of Americana.

ered by statutory guarantees (though these too could have their place). This historic vindication of the child has simply been too subtle for the seculars.

Nor is it even so clear to the rest of us. It is the family that is the chief administrator of this system of children's rights and duties. By its nature, however, the family is pluralistic, plastic and private; it is thus difficult to locate precisely its place within a world of law that is typically rationalistic, rule-oriented, rigid, and public. My present commission, however, requires that this special realm of childhood jurisprudence be pinned somewhere on the legal map, and I will try.

Let me begin by specifying the problems created by the initial title of this chapter—"The Religious Human Rights of Children Within Christian Communities." To catalogue the "rights of children within Christian communities" threatened to lure me in more directions than I could possibly manage. The phrase could mean either "rights within" or "children within." The word "rights" could thus be understood either as (1) a religious autonomy of the individual child that the judiciary will enforce against all adults and the state; (2) a right of Christian parents to invoke civil authority to require a child to engage in (or refrain from) particular religious practices; or (3) a non-enforceable moral claim of the child himself against those adults (parents and others) who exercise authority within the church—one based upon purely Christian premises.

This third possibility would leave the state entirely out of the picture as either friend or foe of child or parent. Later, I will suggest that purely moral claims of this third kind do manage to penetrate the legal system in an interesting way. For the most part, however, I have decided to stick to the first two areas; here we find the enforceable relationships that involve all three potential players—child, parent, and state. A brief portrayal of the several species of enforceable legal rights is, therefore, necessary. This in itself presents some difficulty; of all the forms that rights may take, the idea of a child's right remains the most puzzling.

Oversimplifying a bit, adults hold four forms of legal rights. The first is a general right to do or attempt whatever is not specifically forbidden; call this *autonomy*. The second form consists of *negative* rights that constrain the violence, defamation, pollution, and treachery of others that injure our person and property. Third are the *positive* rights of every person to collective guarantees of minimal subsistence, legal aid, medical care and education (and for convenience we might locate here the rights of political participation). Fourth is the special form of right enjoyed by those adults who lose rationality and cannot conduct their own affairs; they are entitled to a *proxy* (anointed by the state) to make the decisions that the disabled right-holder would make if only he could. So we have rights to autonomy, to negative/positive protections, and to proxies.

Children enjoy rights to negative and positive legal protections. Once a child manages to exit the womb alive, even his mother and the doctor can no longer treat him as a non-person; and he has positive rights against both state and parent to welfare and education. What adults have and children still lack are the rights of proxy and general autonomy. Children enjoy very few autonomy rights; instead, their parents have plenary authority to choose for them from among the endless variety of lawful alternatives.[14] The parent selects exactly those activities which John and Mary will carry on today—and forbids the rest. Within the infinity of possibilities parents lay down the law of the family. You will eat oatmeal; you will not watch television; you will leave for church at 9:15. If a child violates these laws, she is subject to whichever form of corrective response the parent selects from yet another broad universe of possibilities; these include corporal and other punishments that the state could not impose even upon criminals. Of course, the familial discipline is commonly a good deal more restrained, consisting of temporary withdrawal of petty privileges, good advice delivered at various temperatures, or some subtler parental artifice.

Lacking the legal right of autonomy, children also lack (in general)[15] the right to a proxy. The proxy is a guardian who identifies with his client and wills as the client would will if he could (I concede the fictional aspect). The child and parent do *not* have such a relationship; parents are not bound by the strict limits set upon a proxy's authority. The proxy may not insist that his client read Milton Friedman or attend church. Parents by contrast can impose their *own* wills; thus they can convert Friedman and Islam into obligations of the child (both legal and moral). They decree and enforce the laws that regulate the daily lives of children. They are legislature, court, and sheriff. There are important theoretical disputes about whether they are mere delegates of the state or whether they constitute an independent legal sovereignty, but government they clearly are. And it is precisely as the lawgivers of childhood that parents might

---

[14] J. Coons, "Law and the Sovereigns of Childhood," *Kappan* 58 (1976): 19.

[15] Just who the court-approved child advocate is supposed to be speaking for in the cases of younger children can—e.g. in custody cases—be unclear. For the most part the abstract "best interest" standard controls; but lawyers generally try to learn the perspective of their young clients. In custody cases and other matters involving older children the law often gives considerable or even decisive weight to children's preferences; hence their lawyer is obligated truly to represent them. To that extent he is neither proxy nor parent (and the child becomes an authentic right-holder). See the discussion of these difficulties in K. Federle, "Looking for Rights in all the Wrong Places: Resolving Custody Disputes in Divorce Proceedings," *Cardozo Law Review* 15 (1994): 1523, 1550-1558.

(or might not) constitute a regime of children's rights—religious and every other. That they do create a zone of quasi-autonomy for the child will be my primary point. Indeed, being subject to the legislative authority of a parent (or parent figure) can be understood as the fifth form of legal right—the one specific to children. Let us call it the right to a parental sovereign. It is aggressively paradoxical in nature; for it is a "right" to be dominated by another.

Such a right, however, is not a simple contradiction, first of all because domination of the child by adults is in any case inevitable. Children do not arrive with the capacity for authentic autonomy. In their early teens some few acquire (and many do not) a maturity of personality that might support a broad self-determination. Even in cases of precocity, however, external adult forces—physical, intellectual, economic—render autonomy for most teenagers a thoroughly unrealistic ideal. Older people with superior experience, knowledge, size, and economic power would have the capacity to determine the external forms and possibilities of children's lives even if (especially if) children were allowed the broadest freedom. The teenage drug dealer is less an example of autonomy than he is the chattel of adult masters. But this example may mislead. The simple point is that, even in run-of-the-mill affairs that are entirely lawful the only practical question for most children will be which adult is allowed to set the boundary and meaning of liberty. Will it be the bureaucrat, the teacher, or the parent who will have authority to define the good life? Someone big will decide whether Alice goes fishing, goes to bed or goes to Sunday School.

The radical liberationist rejects the empirical premise, insisting instead that children *could* be effectively self-determining. The reason that children get dominated by others, they assert, is not that they are incapable of handling their own affairs. It is only because they have no autonomy rights that they are vulnerable. There is considerable literature devoted to this claim. This is not the place to recount all the practical hurdles that would make the adult form of self-determination a useless instrument for the child. I will rely upon the reader's own good sense and imagination to assess what real use a child could make of a freedom to quit school at age nine and take a job—or "divorce" her parents and live an "independent" life. I will go this far with the kiddie libbers: *the liberty of children is worth protecting*. That end, however, will not be secured by recognizing the legal right of the child to flout and dump the parent.[16]

---

[16] This is especially true if we assume a reciprocal liberation of the parent from the child; but, even if the parent remains the indentured provider and protector of the liberated

For the moment I use the expression "a child's right" to connote protection solely for the child's *self*-interest. This is distinct from the collective interest held by the rest of us in nourishing the competence of every young person as a citizen, worker, voter, and the like. My subject is not *duties* that the child owes to others and to the common good; it is rights enforceable against all others.[17] Keeping this in mind, we can say that broadly speaking there are two interests of the child that are candidates for rights; these are welfare and liberty. Welfare is a catch-all for clothing, food, shelter, education, and other essentials of material and moral flourishing. Liberty is the child's interest in exercising personal judgment and control in specific matters. Opportunities to decide for himself increase in practical importance to the child as he gradually matures and approaches the specific age of legal autonomy. Nevertheless, to have options is significant to a child at every moment from the onset of rationality. These choices come to the child only in the form of specific licenses granted by some adult regime. Parents or the state select those matters which the child may decide for himself. Today he is given the option to play, read or watch television; he may take the car, but only to the game; and he must be home by 10:30. These grants of partial self-determination I prefer to call "petty liberties"[18] (obviously they may be more than petty in significance to the child). They are limited in scope, and they are revocable by the adult authority.

(Parenthetically we should note that the welfare and liberty interests of a child often overlap. As the material well-being of a child increases or deteriorates, his real ability to exercise petty liberties is affected. The sick and hungry child can be licensed for a trip to the zoo that would exceed his physical, cognitive, social, or economic capacities.)

It is now time to emphasize that the importance of the child's experience of authentic liberty is a profoundly, if quietly, Christian notion. In the eyes of the Christian, children are moral beings from the age of reason. And whichever external sovereign may dominate his daily environment, in the crucial matter of conscience the rational child is a truly free agent. Though from inexperience (or from adult misinformation) the child may misperceive what is the objective good in a given situation, he remains responsible to keep on seeking that good and to pursue whatever he perceives it to be. This obligation of the child is identical to that of

---

child, the child's own autonomy remains at risk of domination by other adults—whether these be agents of the state or merely private predators and would-be philanthropists.

[17] My own definition of rights is, of course, parochial, and I do not suggest that it is useful outside the context of law. For a good non-technical alternative version of rights, see Gary Wills, *Inventing America* (Garden City, 1979), 214-217.

[18] See above note 14.

the adult; both are fallible, yet each remains capable of seeking the authentic good as the ideal. And whether one is a child or an adult, it is by the diligent quest for the good that moral self-perfection is achieved. Every rational actor, of every age thus is a full-fledged participant in the economy of salvation. Christians express this idea in different ways (and some reject it), but recognition of a plenary adult-like responsibility of the child is at least as old as Augustine. Any theory of childhood that would diminish moral responsibility (or reduce it to a duty of unquestioning obedience to adult authority) would be problematic to most Christians.[19]

This premise of moral accountability justifies expanding the zones of petty liberty as the child becomes competent in respect to specific matters. To be sure, limited self-determination regarding sports, hours, diet and the like may not in themselves raise issues of conscience, but the exercise of personal freedom, even in trivial matters, inevitably turns up moral challenge. Meanwhile, though the capacity to understand more complex moral issues continues to grow, it varies greatly from child to child at every age. And to inject a child into moral conflict beyond his grasp will seldom advance his general capacity for the social exercise of liberty. The trick then (in pursuing the child's interest in making practical choices) is to find the specific adult regime that will select and ration petty liberties in a manner that best nourishes the capacity of *this* child for moral autonomy now and for eventual participation in a free society as an adult. The obvious question becomes, just what sort of mature sovereign is best equipped to regulate this mix of freedom and dominion to be experienced by the individual child?

Three rough criteria help to identify the adult decision maker who can best determine the right blend for Mary Ann or George. These are *knowledge, caring, and accountability*, and I will consider them in order. The first comes in two relevant forms: personal knowledge of *this* child and professional knowledge of children as a class. Ordinarily these two forms of insight are held by different adults. The parent has the unsystematic and largely ineffable understanding of the child's hopes, fears, relationships, and moral environment. The professional, by contrast, knows that the child has a recognized disorder such as dyslexia for which a therapy may be selected from among competing scientific procedures. In general, it is possession of the parental form of knowledge which best equips the adult decider to choose the specific course of action. Professional opinion is important (even when the experts disagree), but it is the adult with personal knowledge of the child who—by uniting both forms of knowl-

---

[19] I have glided over the several dissenting views that cluster around well-known premises of human depravity and theological determinism. These would seem to imply a rather different theory of childhood responsibility (if any).

edge in herself—becomes the best chooser. The parent assimilates the opinions of the professionals and selects among the reasonable possibilities; she adds their wisdom to her own. By contrast, her special affective insight is less easily transferable to the professional. The parent, like the client of the lawyer or architect, is in a weaker position to identify the options—but in a superior position to decide. Professionals are more helpful as servants than masters.

By "caring" I mean the specific concern of the decision-maker for *this* child as distinguished from all children. I cannot demonstrate that caring makes for better decisions; in some instances the stress of caring may even produce irrationality, disqualifying the particular adult for decision. What is important in most cases, however, is the tendency of caring to focus the decider's powers and to keep them focussed so long as a problem continues. This constancy of attention is more true of adults who are linked to the child in a permanent and intimate relation. Professionals cannot afford such continuing intensity with each client; nor would such a relation be appropriate.

"Accountability" holds to the extent that the decision-maker is personally benefitted by any decision that is beneficial to the child and, correspondingly, is injured whenever the child suffers. It seems universally agreed that accountability, so defined, generally increases the chances for good decisions in individual cases. Who then has it? Though professionals and bureaucrats are marginally affected for good or ill by the fates of individual children whom they encounter professionally, it is obviously the parent who will continue to bear in a serious way the effects of any decision. Getting it right is a thousand times more consequential to the adult who must live with the child.

Overall it seems plain enough that the parent most nearly satisfies these three criteria of the good decider in the vast run of cases. There will be exceptions. Parents can have a powerful incentive, for example, to institutionalize the mentally defective child (that is, to avoid accountability by arranging for permanent separation); the exercise of this authority without societal oversight would be a considerable risk to the child, at least in respect of his liberty interest.[20] But at least in the day-to-day work of setting the boundaries of self-determination for normal children who are living at home and maturing at different rates, parents are the best bet. For it is in the parents' social, economic, and moral interest that the child advance toward autonomy; most will strive to dispense welfare and liberty accordingly.

---

[20] The unsettling example is *Parham v. J.R.*, 442 U.S. 584 (1979).

For a moment let us relax our focus upon rights and the child's self-interest. Critics of parental sovereignty need the chance to remind us that the good of the child is not the only good at stake. Occasionally they note that, though parental sovereignty is best for the child, it can conflict with the common good. Parents make socially "selfish" decisions such as sending their child to a private school (a favorite example).[21] I must not be drawn away from rights into a broad inquiry about the common good. Nonetheless, I can briefly observe that—among the alternative regimes—for two reasons the parental sovereignty is by far the most promising generator of civic virtue. The first is that children best learn the importance of commutative and distributive justice in an environment in which adults whom they know and trust are in command;[22] it is no surprise that children from the most disadvantaged homes who attend "narrow" religious schools rate higher on standard measures of tolerance, civic participation, and respect for law than children of similar circumstances who are forced by their poverty to study the politically determined curriculum of the government school.

The other reason is that, in a pluralistic society, there can be no collective vision of the good life. Outside Math and the Physical Sciences, the course of study in government schools—the civic catechism—will and must be confined to a narrow set of inoffensive ideas that can be squeezed through the lobbying process in Sacramento or Atlanta (and tomorrow, perhaps, Washington as we are given our national cognitive "Goals"[23]). The really interesting (and mutually conflicting) ideas about human flourishing must be politically censored to avoid offense (and, in some cases, the First Amendment).[24] The politically-minded teacher may still have some ideological elbow room, because there is a degree of de facto dominion inside the classroom. The overall tendency of the system, however, is to present the vanilla thesis that it is quite alright for the child—hence the citizen—to think and do whatever he or she pleases "so long as no one gets hurt"; students are assured that it is the object of a full life to invent one's own morality. Just how this indifferentism could

---

[21] H. Levin, "The Theory of Choice Applied to Education," in W. Clune and J. Witte, eds., *Choice and Control in American Education* (Bristol, PA, 1990), 1:247.

[22] "The strongest consciences . . . will be those with the most powerfully developed affiliation." J. Wilson, *The Moral Sense* (New York, 1993), 105. Wilson reiterates this theme at many points. Ibid., 47-48, 108, 114, 145, 157-158, 162-163, 226. Hegel observes that the family provides "the sound basis of a political edifice, the capacity of feeling one with a whole." *Reason in History*, chap. III, 3(b) entitled "Law as Realization of Freedom."

[23] Determined by the same educators from Sacramento and Atlanta. This particular form of orthodoxy is momentarily less threatening, but it is no monopoly of the Democrats.

[24] J. Coons, "Intellectual Liberty and the Schools," *Notre Dame Journal of Law, Ethics and Public Policy* 1 (1985): 495.

be a contribution to the common good is hard to understand. In a pluralistic society public values are best secured by a vigorous market in contrasting moral ideas taught in free institutions by adults who believe in
them. Children who accept the message that morality is a matter of private taste are the least likely to embrace civic responsibility. It is the child
imbued with strong ideas who will contribute most to an authentic social
dialogue about the common good. And the flip side of this truth is that
the adult regime that produces such focussed commitments to the common good simultaneously nourishes the individual child's capacity for
intellectual liberty.

I want now to show that broad parental sovereignty of this nature is
quite at home within the Christian commitment to moral liberty as it has
been expressed both in the secular and spiritual orders. In the West, the
temporal regime of most nations recognizably "Christian" has for centuries been suffused with what now is labeled "subsidiarity."[25] It is long accepted that in any community—civil or ecclesiastical—things tend to run
better when authority can be wielded by the persons within that social or
political unit who are the object of or most affected by its exercise. The
vague ideal is the preservation of an array of what Peter Berger has
dubbed "mediating structures"—collectivities with power dispersed
among them to make those decisions that can be made for the group
without posing a threat to other groups. Typical clusters of this sort are
labor unions, fraternal societies, trade associations, churches, and voluntary groups of every sort. But the quintessential unit, the one armed with
effective legal sovereignty, has been the family. Building upon and humanely tempering Hebrew and Roman foundations, Christianity has
gradually come to understand and to nourish parental sovereignty. It has
rejected categorically the systematically regimented childhood offered to
the West in Plato's *Republic*. Family autonomy had become the paradigm
of subsidiarity long before the word itself was coined.[26]

Because of its very familiarity, this fundamental attitude may appear
to be only marginally Christian in its roots. In most cultures decentralization of child rearing to the family level has proved a more socially efficient arrangement than the various versions of Plato's ideal; the

---

[25] This unlovely term seems to be a neologism of Pius XI in *Quadregesimo Anno* 79
(1931). By the 1990s it had become virtually epidemic in political and legal literature. See, e.g.,
G. Bermann, "Taking Subsidiarity Seriously: Federalism in the European Community and the
United States," *Columbia Law Review* 94 (1994): 331.

[26] This is made very empathetic by the examples in Orme, "Children and the Church in
Medieval England." Orme sums up as follows: "[T]he special education of children was left
to parents, godparents and school teachers. . . . Did the Church shy away from invading the
rights of parents over children? It certainly did not lay its hands on the process to the extent
that came to be felt desirable at the Reformation." Ibid., 585.

utilitarian justifications for family autonomy have been demonstrated by history's largest natural experiment. Nevertheless, Christianity played an historic role in making all these more mundane reasons seem natural and obvious to moderns; it acted from its own creedal imperatives, including a theology that recognized the authentic liberty of children. Further, it did so while preserving individual responsibility to an objective moral ideal. It is a theology in which human freedom—personal responsibility for salvation—has gradually emerged as the principal orthodox alternative among competing accounts of our justification. Fifteen hundred years of debate have left most Christians convinced that salvation is a process of cooperation in which God has made human consent a necessary element. The debate on this issue is not over, nor can it ever be. Nevertheless, one version of the answer has been regnant since at least the seventeenth century.

Let me restate this dogmatic consensus about freedom in capsule form: Every human person (of every degree of rationality) is invited to free association with God. The designated act of acceptance—our individual RSVP—consists in a diligent search for the divine will in specific matters. Though we cannot precisely identify the form in which the pagan and the atheist receive God's invitation, they too are fully included; recall that, along with the rest, they receive "the true light that enlightens *every man* who comes into the world." Hence they, too, may achieve justification simply by an honest struggle for the truth. Nor are Christians even in a favored position regarding the means of salvation. They, too, are responsible to seek the good of the objective moral order. In their quest for that good, they too are fallible; often they err despite their best effort to discover God's will. If they seek and act in good faith, however, they are justified and saved by the diligence of their search. That faithful quest for the good is sufficient to all—even to those who by honest error choose acts of objective immorality. As the present pope and Vatican II remind us, "It often happens that conscience goes astray through ignorance which it is unable to avoid, without thereby losing its dignity."[27] The new *Catechism* adds that "[e]very man who is ignorant of the Gospel of Christ and of his Church, but seeks the truth and does the will of God *in accordance with his understanding of it*, can be saved."[28]

If we are all rendered capable of salvation by a faithful quest for the good, it is not only the pagans who are our fellows.[29] The child's pros-

---

[27] The quotation is from *The Constitution on the Church (Gaudium et Spes)*, Article 16; John Paul II has most recently deployed it in the encyclical *Veritatis Splendor*, 62 and 63.

[28] *Catechism of the Catholic Church* (1994), 321 (emphasis added).

[29] That each individual enjoys the capacity to seek the good in the same degree is not, of course, demonstrable. Patrick Brennan and I will say what we can for the plausibility (and

pects, too, are identical to our own; for anyone who reaches the threshold of rationality recognizes, as specifically and clearly as the wisest adult, a personal responsibility to seek and attempt the good. This perception is inescapable; whether they like it or not, all minimally rational humans recognize their subordination to an order of obligation that is external to themselves. And, if self-perfection is achieved by the honest quest for the details of that obligation, this is a vocation for which children at the age of reason are as fully equipped as any moral philosopher. St. Augustine got that part right; when he stole his neighbor's pears for the sake of evil, he freely rejected the divine invitation.[30] The capacity to choose between self-perfection and self-corruption is democratically distributed. Children receive an adult share.

This sketch may resemble contemporary theological notions of a "fundamental option." Just what that embattled phrase entails seems to vary among the theologians who use it. Not all of its defenders would accept my description of orthodoxy, nor I theirs. Our differences will not be settled here. All I ask of the critic is to keep in mind my basic assumption that there exists an authentic and objective order of both natural and Christian morality. Such an order is necessary to the idea of the common good. The practical realization of that good by society would require that we discover its details. My point, however, does not concern the good of society. It is the very different proposition that *personal salvation* turns, not upon our getting the terms of this order of objective morality right, but only upon our subjective effort to do so. The effect of choices made is distinct in the inner and external realms. The recent papal encyclical *Veritatis Splendor* is consistent with this conclusion: Good intention and invincible ignorance cannot make an evil act good. But they can make the actor good.

By the way (*pace* Augustine) I take no position on the question of whether the deliberate choice of one objectively evil behavior constitutes the exercise of the "option"—the effective refusal of the divine invitation. Precisely in what the decisive act of assent or rejection does consist is beyond specification—at least by me. In respect to children I would be content to suppose that they can postpone that fateful commitment long past the onset of rationality. Whatever the case on that sub-issue, let us assume for the moment that I have stated what is roughly the Christian

---

implicit popular acceptance) of that proposition in a forthcoming work entitled *Created Equal: Was Jefferson Right?* A brief summary of our position will appear in 1995 in the *American Journal of Legal Philosophy* as part of an essay bearing the title "Natural Law and Human Equality."

[30] Augustine, *The Confessions*, II; IV-X.

view of the child's place in the economy of salvation. What adult sovereignty over their earthly affairs is then the Christian ideal?

Strictly speaking, so far as the child's own personal salvation is concerned, the form of the adult dominion appears at first to be a matter of indifference. So long as the minimum conditions of survival and rationality are maintained, all children who acquire reason will have the same opportunity. God does not strip the child of his full capacity to seek or reject the good merely because he or she becomes neglected or disadvantaged in the temporal order.[31] This ultimate moral invulnerability is sometimes misunderstood by critics of Christianity as a kind of moral escapism; and to be sure, it is a great consolation to the wretched of our species. In no way, however, does it diminish personal responsibility, nor does it allows us to finesse the problem of the proper distribution of authority over the child.

For, whatever his circumstances, there is no variation in the obligation of the rational child himself to continue seeking the objective good; nor is there variation in the obligation of the adult (if he would perfect himself) to seek that same good and, further, to assist the child in discovering that good for himself. Hence the question remains: Which adult sovereign will provide that specific mix of protection and freedom that will maximize the child's opportunity to grasp the content of the authentic good? It is in selecting that sovereign that we identify the most significant of all the rights that a child could enjoy and that adults must secure.

Here, again, we encounter paradox. We have just said that the most errant adult sovereign cannot diminish the child's capacity for moral self-perfection (salvation), because perfection turns solely upon the child's commitment and effort and not at all upon his specific perceptions and concrete realizations of the good. For the child, the only thing that is diminished by adult misinformation and abuse is the child's capacity to find (and thus to do) the objective good, and this capacity is quite distinct from the subjective power by which he commits to the search. One is tempted, then, to conclude that adult misinformation is no skin off the child's moral nose. That partial truth, however, would mislead, if it is also the case that the child has a moral imperative to be subject to that regime—whatever it is—which is most likely to transmit a true picture of the objective moral order. *But subjection to such a regime is the claim of his very nature, for to will it for himself is the condition of his own moral perfection.* Thus, as a matter of justice, the child presents a plausible claim to our securing for him in the legal order this very form of subordination, simply because his moral nature obliges him to commit to it. To achieve moral

---

[31] See the encyclical *Centesimus Annus* (1991), 34-35.

self-fulfillment he must willingly attach himself to his own best hope for moral truth; if we are to deny him what his own conscience would demand, there must be some countervailing social reason.

This truth-right of the child, then, must be given material content. In what regime is it best protected? My sense is that Christians, in general, suppose that it is the parent who most efficiently encourages the child to seek the objective good (whether conceived as a command of God, nature, or both). This natural imperative is best nourished in the family because of two observable characteristics of parents in their role as teachers of the specific good. First, on the negative side, the parent—in dealing with her own child—almost never denies the reality of an external and objective good; philosophical skepticism is a vice confined largely to professional elites and only when they are engaged in the instruction of audiences for whose moral welfare they have no personal concern. On the positive side every parent (including even the most cynical) promotes some version of a real good to her own child. While there is every danger that this message of the parent may be corrupt in its specific content, it almost never confuses the child's own preference with the ideal. Few parents transmit the individualist message that children invent their own good. With their own flesh all are moral objectivists. They tell the child to be good, because they cannot themselves stop believing that the good is something real.

We cannot expect all families to agree about the details of the good—nor even that children will agree with their own parents. Soon enough the child acquires reason and perceives that the parent is fallible about the content of the good life. In due course some children reject the parental code either in detail or altogether—temporarily or forever. What a child cannot escape while remaining within the jurisdiction of the family is the direct and constant experience of an adult who believes that *there is a good to be grasped* and who demonstrates this belief even (or especially) in the course of conflict with the child. Simply by insisting upon her own version of the good the parent furnishes the child the up-close, day-to-day reminder of the human duty to look outside our own egos. It is in this inescapable encounter that the child is constantly reminded that justice is an issue and comes face to face with the personal imperative to seek its content. In accepting or rejecting that basic human vocation the child moves toward or away from perfection.

So, in the end, what would count as a "child's religious right within a Christian community"? It is the socially protected guarantee of membership in a family or family-like environment including an adult or adults to whom the child is both close and subordinate. This subordination is the child's best hope of experiencing real, if petty, liberties that are coupled with the affirmation of an authentic good to be freely sought or rejected; both liberty and obligation will thus be presented to the child in specific and personal decisions made by an adult sovereign who has a profound practical and emotional interest in this child's ultimate moral autonomy.

Finally, I want to clarify the extent to which the adult sovereignty represents a practical risk of the moral and religious subjugation of the child. Justice Douglas is still correct.[32] Society has not yet recognized for the child any state-protected religious autonomy. Thus, the child who dissents from his family's religious convictions is, indeed, at risk of having his conscience violated by the big people. I see no clean escape from this, but at least three imperfect responses make this outcome tolerable.

First, the child's general obligation to obey the parent narrows the potential arena for legitimate moral and religious conflict. Apart from a few utilitarians this duty of obedience has received little attention from moral scholars.[33] Several millennia after the Fourth Commandment there is still no systematic Christian treatment of its content and boundaries.[34] I wish I were competent to rectify this oversight in moral philosophy. All I can offer is the broad line of analysis that seems most promising to an amateur. It begins with the observation that the child's duty to obey is conditional. Plainly, as a free moral agent, a child is bound to apply his own reason to moral issues and reach a personal decision; the duty to obey does not license servile participation in what the child perceives as wrongful acts ordered by adults. A parental command to despise your neighbor ought to be resisted by any child who sees clearly that it is evil. On the other hand, the child who embraces his primary obligation as a moral seeker, but who is unclear about the objective good in a given case, is entitled to (and *should*) give the parental command the benefit of a presumption. So long as there is room for doubt, the conscience of the obedient child should be clear. Hence cases of authentic moral conflict should be few.

The second imperfect justification for allowing parental authority to override the moral or religious dissent of children is the relative flexibility of the family (compared to the courts) in accommodating conflicting views without violating conscience. A child may feel a religious imperative to attend a racially integrated school; if the parent prefers the more convenient neighborhood school, something has to give. But a clean-cut rejection of conscience may be avoidable; for example, some alternative

---

[32] In his dissent in *Wisconsin v. Yoder*.

[33] See, e.g. Purdy, *In their Best Interest?*

[34] I would expect broad agreement that the example of the daughter of Jeptha the Galaadite would not be recommended to modern Christians. Judges 11:29-40.

experience of racial diversity may substantially satisfy the child's concern. The family is not a civil court which must utter a simple yes or no. It can temporize, adjust, and compromise; children sometimes change their minds; so do parents. We also learn from each other by hanging together even when we feel momentarily and mutually oppressed.

This suggests the third and related justification. If a system of rights were to make the parent hostage to the religious preferences of children, the identity of the family would be deeply compromised. It is one thing for the state to raise barriers against physical abuse and to protect the child when the family is already moribund. It would be quite another to strip ordinary parents of their authority to make the family into a representation of their own values. The family is for most of us *the* primary medium of moral expression. The parent experiences the child as both an audience and a message to the world. In a faint echo of the divine, children are the most important Word most of us will utter. I am willing to preserve that medium for adults (and in turn for their maturing children) at the cost of an occasional and temporary injustice to a particular child. For most children the family—autocratic and even arbitrary—remains on balance the best hope of authentic religious liberty.

Religious Human Rights In Judaic Texts

―❦ ❧―

DAVID NOVAK

University of Virginia

Rights of Religion and Religious Rights

I n speaking of "religious human rights," two different ideas come to mind. First, there is the idea of what is commonly called "religious liberty," that is, the duty of society to respect and protect the right of every human person to worship any god of his or her choice or no god at all (as long as the exercise of that right is not disruptive of the secular order of that society, of course). In other words, one of the primary duties of society is the duty to protect the right of religious liberty along with other human rights. But, second, there is the idea of what one could call "the religious foundation of human rights," that is, religious rights as the source of all other rights.

These two separate ideas are not mutually exclusive or incapable of ever being connected. Both could be seen as aspects of the more general issue of the relation of religion and society, which is certainly a perennial political issue. Nevertheless, being aspects of a larger issue does not resolve the tension that I perceive between these two ideas. There is a considerable difference between one who begins his or her reflection starting from the theme of religious rights *along with* other *human* rights, and one who begins his or her reflection starting from the theme of the religious *source of* rights, which must consider the question of rights from more than just a human perspective. In Judaism, Christianity, and Islam, which are religions of revelation, each of them sees its own truth as coming from God not man. Indeed, that stipulation is the only cogent distinction that can be made between a religion and a philosophy. Therefore, the distinction between beginning from one idea or the other involves real

175

J. Witte, Jr. and J.D. van der Vyver (eds.), Religious Human Rights in Global Perspective, 175-201.
© 1996 *Kluwer Law International. Printed in the Netherlands.*

differences in terms of the way we approach the whole issue of religion and society.

In fact, the difference between these two ideas is the subject of one of the great constitutional debates of our time, namely, the debate over the meaning of the so-called "religion clauses" of the First Amendment to the Constitution of the United States. It is to be recalled that there is not one clause of the First amendment pertaining to religion but two. "Congress shall [1] make no law respecting an establishment of religion or [2] prohibit the free exercise thereof." The question under such great debate today is whether the free exercise of religion clause follows from the disestablishment clause or vice-versa.[1] It is much more than an issue of syntactical analysis. Rather, the question is whether the exercise of religion is something the secular political authority having the power of lawmaking *subsequently entitles* the citizens of the polity to, or whether the citizens of the polity *already have the right* to exercise (that is, practice) their religion *before* the secular political authority makes any laws at all. In both options, the state is not to become the arbiter of which *one* religion is to be favored above all others. The difference here is that in the first option religion might very well be something *beneath* the domain of the state because it is too trivial for the state to want to legislate, whereas in the second option religion is something *beyond* the domain of the state because it is too important for the state to be able to legislate.

The difference between these two approaches to the First Amendment is nothing less than a political debate about whether religion requires a secular justification or whether the secular realm requires a religious justification. For religious people, it would seem that the practice of their religions must be the source of all other practices, including those practices involved in interhuman relationships that in and of themselves are not distinctly religious.[2] For secularists, though, religion can at best be a matter of tolerated taste. There is hardly an issue of political-moral dispute today—be it over abortion, euthanasia, criminal punishment, or war—into which this basic religious-secular dispute is not ultimately to be found at its core.[3] And, certainly, this is not the first time in human history when conflicting interpretations of an opaque text have been the locus of a great political debate.

---

[1] See Michael W. McConnell, "The Origins and Historical Understanding of the Free Exercise of Religion," *Harvard Law Review* 103 (1990): 1410ff.; Mary Ann Glendon and Raul F. Yanes, "Structural Free Exercise," *Michigan Law Review* 90 (1991): 477ff.; Michael Sandel, "Freedom of Conscience or Freedom of Choice?" in Os Guiness and James Davison Hunter, eds., *Articles of Faith, Articles of Peace* (Washington, 1990), 72ff.

[2] See Thomas Aquinas, *Summa Theologiae*, II/I, q. 94, art. 4 ad 1.

[3] For a full discussion of the ramifications of this *Kulturkampf*, see James Davison Hunter, *Culture Wars* (New York, 1991).

Without placing the presentations of texts from religious traditions in this political context, such presentations can be little more than "background music" for discussions of the real questions at hand in all their gravity. Thus some theoretical prolegomenon is a necessary condition for making the highly selective presentation of these texts an integral participant in the political discussion of rights today. This discussion is much too important theoretically and practically to bother with obscurantist scholarship. Only scholarship that truly *engages* is worthy of our political efforts here and now. And since my religious engagement is existentially prior to my engagement in any polity (the two only being identical when the Kingdom of God finally comes), in good faith I can only approach the question of religious human rights from the second standpoint, namely, religion as the source of *all* other rights.

The Basic Hermeneutical Question

A generation ago, in his introduction to an important volume of essays entitled *Judaism and Human Rights*, the Jewish political theorist Milton R. Konvitz correctly noted, "There is no word or phrase for 'human rights' in the Hebrew Scriptures or in any other ancient Jewish text. . . . Yet . . . the absence of these and related words and phrases does not mean the nonexistence of the ideals and values for which they stand or to which they point."[4] Konvitz was, of course, arguing against the kind of historicist reduction that would dismiss the question addressed in his volume and this volume by severing any connection between the issues of the present and the teachings of the past. Nevertheless, the other extreme to be avoided is simply to assume that ancient religious texts, in our case ancient Judaic texts, can function as precedents for moral principles that are already formulated fully in and for the present. For when this is done, the continuing moral necessity of rereading these texts becomes lost because the principles of which these texts are precedents are assumed to be true in and of themselves here and now. They are taken to be self-sufficient even if not always self-evident. And, indeed, anything but tangential concern with these ancient precedents might actually be practically counterproductive by diverting attention away from the real and pressing concerns to which moral principles are always to be addressed.

A good example of this latter fallacy, what might be called the "fallacy of immediate relevance," is the simple location in the Jewish tradition of precedents for democracy. Now certainly all of us who wish to

---

[4] Milton Konvitz, ed., *Judaism and Human Rights* (New York, 1972), 13.

strengthen the cause of religious liberty are well aware of the historical fact that religious liberty can only function in some sort of democratic polity today, especially where minority and individual (the greatest minority) rights are affirmed. And I cannot imagine any rational person wanting to live in anything but a democracy in the world today. The real alternatives are too horrible to entertain seriously. Jews, especially, have very good historical reasons for being in favor of democracy, even enthused by it. Jews have thrived in democracies and, conversely, they have frequently been major victims of the modern alternatives to democracy. This is why in the volume mentioned above, all the authors assume that Judaism is for democracy. However, without a critical role for Judaism in its relation to democracy in its current form, namely, a role where it attempts to re-think democracy as to what it is-to-be and not just to confirm it as-it-is, without that critical role I do not see how Judaism is not quickly turned into a matter of ultimately antiquarian interest, which is irrelevant when moral principles are practically *directed towards* the future and not just *traced from* the past parenthetically. In other words, unless Judaism can provide a basis for judging democracy and its rights talk, it becomes in the words of the great German Jewish philosopher of the early twentieth century, Hermann Cohen, only a historical origin (*Anfang*) of facts rather than a philosophical source (*Ursprung*) of concepts (*Begriffe*).[5] The task, then, is to look for a definition of rights that can bridge the gap between our modern limitation of that idea to *human* rights, that is, to the realm of intra-personal and inter-personal relationships, and the ancient Judaic inclusion of that idea into the relationship between God and humans.[6] When this is done, we will be in a better position to see the Jewish tradition in a critical relation to the reality of democracy and its concern for human rights, namely, how the Jewish tradition can provide an intelligent viewpoint from which not to just follow contemporary democracy and at best to be patronized by its adherents, but to judge and re-direct it. By so doing, we might actually find in and for contemporary democracy those practices that are indispensable for the conduct of a society worthy of the moral allegiance of rational human persons, and concurrently reject those practices in it and for it that make a society unworthy of such moral allegiance.

---

[5] Hermann Cohen, *Religion of Reason Out of the Sources of Judaism*, S. Kaplan, trans. (New York, 1972), 10, 63-64.

[6] See Mishnah Yoma 8.9 and Babylonian Talmud Yoma 87a re I Samuel 2:25, Isodore Epstein, trans. (London, 1987).

Rights, Duties, and Entitlements

The concept of rights can only be understood in correlation with the concept of duty. For the sake of greater clarity, let us assume that rights are claims, and duties are obligations. In the case of benevolence, which in the Jewish tradition is both a right of the less fortunate and a duty of the more fortunate (and hence not the arbitrary relation connoted by the usual word "charity"), it makes no sense to speak of my right to your support unless it can be assumed that you have a duty to support me.[7] Your duty is a recognition of my right just as my right is a recognition of your duty. Without the correlative duty for you to be benevolent, my claim is nothing but begging. And without my correlative right to your benevolence, your duty is nothing but largesse. The difference between begging and a right, and the difference between a duty and largesse, is that the former is justified whereas the latter is unjustified by a third party. Both rights and duties require enforcement to be cogent. That is, rights and duties are only intelligible in a social context where there is the rule of law. Accordingly, a right without a correlative duty has no socially sanctioned object for the exercise of its claim, and a duty without a correlative right has no socially sanctioned object for the exercise of its obligation. Thus it is the situation of claiming persons and obligated persons in a society which gives their respective rights and duties legal structure. Certainly in Judaism, rights and duties are the business of law.[8]

The question to be asked at this point is whether rights entail duties or duties entail rights. In democratic societies, it is usually assumed that rights entail duties. That is, human persons as individuals have inherent needs and powers. For the sake of the optimal fulfillment of these inherent needs that only collective power can opportune and protect, individuals contract over to society some of their inherent powers in return for these opportunities and protection. When this "social contract" is recognized, "natural rights" are then retroactively seen as its source.[9] Outside of society, however, there are only natural needs and powers that are sensed by individuals. "Rights" are constituted by reason, which is a linguistic/social phenomenon. Thus, in this view, individuals entitle the right of society to command its own duties in the form of public law. In other words, social duties are justified by individual rights. But, following this logic, society must be seen as an artificial construct, an epiphenomenon.

---

[7] See Babylonian Talmud Baba Batra 8b.

[8] See Babylonian Talmud Kiddushin 31a and parallels.

[9] See John Rawls, *A Theory of Justice* (Cambridge, MA, 1971), 27ff.

However, from a traditional Jewish point of view, this view is faulty for two reasons. First, it ignores the fact that human society itself is experienced as a natural phenomenon, as part of the order of creation itself. Humans have a need for society as the arena of communication over and above the need for society as a means to the fulfillment of selfish individual ends. As one of the rabbinic sages put it when he found himself in a community where he could no longer engage in discourse, "either fellowship or death" (*o haveruta o mituta*).[10] This is a more picturesque way of saying what Aristotle meant when he designated the human person as both "having speech" (*logon echn*) and "being a political animal" (*politikon zo'on*), which are actually two sides of the same coin.[11] Indeed, as many philosophers after Aristotle have seen, human society which is an essentially communicative reality has always been there in human life; it cannot be constructed *de novo*.[12] Furthermore, the very notion of a contract already presupposes the institution of society inasmuch as a contract is a *publicly* justified and enforced agreement. How could anyone know that a contract is to be kept (*pacta sunt servanda*) unless he or she already experienced the social order which contracts themselves presuppose? That is the philosophical problem. Second, the theological problem with social contract theory is that it assumes that the human individual is sovereign rather than God.[13] Thus social contract theory and its attendant notion of natural rights simultaneously involves an underestimation and an overestimation of the human condition. It underestimates the natural necessity of discursive community in human existence, and it overestimates the importance of human authority in the created order of the cosmos.

Nevertheless, the experience of tyranny in human history, especially the totalitarian tyranny that has so stained the twentieth century, correctly makes most of us wary of the other alternative, namely, that duties entail rights. For this notion seems to regard the claims of human persons to be subject to the will of the state, in the person of those who control it that is. The epitome of this approach can be seen in the doctrine of the Nazi state, enunciated early in its reign, that the right of humans to their

---

[10] Babylonian Talmud Ta'anit 23a. See Zevahim 117a re Leviticus 13:46.

[11] Aristotle, *Politics*, 1.1/1253a10-15.

[12] See, e.g., Max Scheler, *Formalism in Ethics*, M.S. Frings and R.L. Funk, trans. (Evanston, IL, 1973), 528ff.; Ludwig Wittgenstein, *Philosophical Investigations*, 2d ed., G.E.M. Anscombe, trans. (New York, 1958), 1.18, 8e.

[13] Even Kant, who posits the sovereignty of the human individual only as that of a rational being not acting out of sensual self-interest, still eliminates God's sovereignty either as the source or the end of the moral law. Thus the truly moral society can only be constituted by these rational self-legislating beings. Transcendence for Kant is that of reason over sense, not that of God over creation. See *Critique of Pure Reason*, B847; *Groundwork of the Metaphysic of Morals*, H.J. Paton, trans. (New York, 1964), 110-111. Cf. Martin Buber, *Kingship of God*, 3d ed., R. Scheimann, trans. (New York and Evanston, IL, 1967), 136ff.

very lives depends on whether the state decides that any human life is *Lebenswertesleben*, "life designated worthy of being allowed to live." Hence only those whom the state regards as duty-bound to remain present in the world for its sake may do so. Conversely, those whom the state regards as duty-bound to become absent from the world for its sake are to be killed (if they have not already committed suicide). They were designated *Lebensunwertesleben*, "life unworthy of life."[14] In this view, only the state has any real rights, and it alone may exercise them arbitrarily. When anything similar to this notion is put forth, I see the barbed wire of Auschwitz or the Gulag on the horizon.

The challenge for a presentation of religious human rights in the world today is to avoid the emptiness of individualistic rights talk without falling into the trap of the excesses of collectivism.

To present Judaism as a system founded on a notion of rights, however, is to run the risk of being challenged with the argument that empirically one can represent Judaism more convincingly as a system of duties. After all, whereas there is no real equivalent in classical Hebrew to our term "rights," there are certainly equivalents to our term "duty." The literary sources of the normative Jewish tradition continually speak of "commandments" (*mitsvot*) and "obligations" (*hovot*).[15] The closest term to our term "rights" is "permission" (*reshut*). But "permission" refers to those acts that the law has not yet ruled on and has thus left to the discretion of individuals. Nevertheless, considering the whole tendency of the normative Jewish tradition to expand rather than contract the range of the law, there are cases where areas formerly within the range of "permission" were reinterpreted to become areas of low priority obligations.[16] In the realm of the law, the area of "permission" is arbitrarily epiphenomenal. It is hardly the foundation for which we are still searching.

Yet to leave the description of the Jewish normative tradition at the level of duty alone begs the question. For as we have seen before, the very concept of duty cannot stand on its own without the correlative concept of rights. Afterall, a duty is something one *owes to someone else*. That someone else, therefore, has a *right to that duty*. Both "rights" and "duties" are bipolar terms. The contemporary French Jewish philosopher, Emmanuel Levinas, has made this relationship the cornerstone of his ethical philosophy. As he has powerfully described and argued, the very

---

[14] See Germain Grisez and Joseph M. Boyle, Jr., *Life and Death with Liberty and Justice: A Contribution to the Euthanasia Debate* (Notre Dame, 1979), 242ff.

[15] Generally, "commandments" are conditional norms, and "obligations" are unconditional norms. See Maimonides, *Mishneh Torah: Berakhot*, 11.2.

[16] See, e.g., Babylonian Talmud Betsah 36b.

presence of another person *(l'autre)* is itself a claim upon me, minimally obligating me to respect their right to life by not murdering them.[17] And here we see that although right and duty are correlative, the correlation begins from the point of rights and then extends to the point of duty, but not vice-versa. We might say that rights constitute the subject of human action and duty the object. Initially, it is the subject that acts upon the object by intending it before the object reacts upon the subject. Ultimately, then, it is a primary right/claim that creates a duty inasmuch as the right is related to the duty as a command. I differ with Levinas, however, in affirming with Jewish tradition that God, not man, is the One who makes the primary claim on our action in the world.[18]

Covenant: God, Persons, Community

If Judaism is for the most part a system of duties, and if duties imply rights, then it can be said with confidence that Judaism is a system of duties correlative with the supreme rights of God the creator. The system itself can then be understood as including the following relationships: (1) God to persons; (2) persons to God; (3) God to community; (4) community to God; (5) persons to persons; (6) persons to community; (7) community to persons. Explicating and illustrating these seven relationships will enable us to see the religious human rights that emerge from Judaism. And I hope it will also at least suggest why this system of relationships and the rights it includes offer a plausible alternative to the individualism and collectivism presently available in contemporary political theory.

God to Persons. It has been a major debate among biblical exegetes since the middle ages whether the traditional doctrine of *creatio ex nihilo* is actually taught in the text of the Bible, especially in the creation narrative at the very beginning of Genesis. "In the beginning God created the heavens and the earth. And the earth was an abyss *(tohu ve-vohu)* . . . and God said, 'let there be light,' and there was light" (Genesis 1:1-3). Now it could be inferred from this text that the "abyss" is some sort of primordial matter out of which God then created a world; or to use Platonic language, God engendered cosmos out of chaos.[19] If so, why did Judaism (and then Christianity and Islam) more and more insist that creation has no antecedents other than God? The answer I think is that only the doc-

---

[17] See Emmanuel Levinas, *Totality and Infinity*, trans. A. Lingis (Pittsburgh, 1969), esp., 187ff.

[18] See David Novak, *Law and Theology in Judaism* (New York, 1976), 2:15ff.

[19] See Plato, *Timaeus*, 29Eff.; also Jon D. Levenson, *Creation and the Persistance of Evil* (San Francisco, 1988), 3ff.

trine of *creatio ex nihilo* affirms the absolute authority of God. If there was anything else that shared God's transcendence of the world as we experience it here and now, then that would imply that God's authority is also shared with something that is not God.[20] *Creatio ex nihilo* is a corollary of the monotheism that Judaism saw as the alternative to the polytheism where each god's power and hence each god's authority are limited by the power and authority of some other god with whom he or she has to co-exist. In the primordial sense, God must be posited in the words of the kabbalistic mystical theology as *Ayn Sof*, "without limit" or "Infinite."[21]

At the most primary level, humans experience the power of God as unlimited. "See now that I, I am He and there is no other power *(elohim)* along with Me. I kill and I give life human; there is no one who can escape my hand" (Deuteronomy 32:39). "I am the first and I am the last, besides Me there is no power *(ayn elohim)*" (Isaiah 44:6). The response to God at this level is fear of God's absolute power. At this level, even human creatures have no rights at all inasmuch as they have no power to make any claims on God. As Marx correctly noted, rights without real power are meaningless.[22] Thus even when Abraham is arguing with God about the question of whether or not God is dealing justly with the people of Sodom and Gomorroh, he is forced to reiterate, "Here I presume *(ho'alti)* to speak to my Lord, even though I am but dust and ashes" (Genesis 18:27). And after God finally appears to Job after all his complaints and all the dialogues with his friends, Job is reduced to utter impotence by God's challenging question, "Where were you when I established earth?" (Job 38:4). Here the very ground under him, that which could be the basis of any claim, is bluntly reclaimed by the God who created the earth and Job in it, Job his creature who is now attempting to stand up against God on it. At this point Job is forced to conclude, "Therefore, I abase myself *(em'as)* and repent, being but dust and ashes" (Job 42:5). When faced by God directly, Job has no ontological foundation upon which any moral claim must ultimately rest.

At this most primary level, however, which must be reiterated whenever humans act as if they are equal let alone superior to God, God is not yet exercising his right as much as he is exercising his raw power. Such displays of primal power are so overwhelming that their object, man, is in no position to respond with anything but the inactivity of fear.[23] Man

---

[20] See Maimonides, *Guide of the Perplexed*, S. Pines, trans. (Chicago, 1963), 2.13.

[21] See Gershom G. Scholem, *On the Kabbalah and its Symbolism*, R. Manheim, trans. (New York, 1969), 73.

[22] See Karl Marx: *The Essential Writings*, F.L. Bender. ed. (New York, 1972), 53ff.

[23] See Jerusalem Talmud Berakhot 9.7/14b (Villna, 1907); also, Rabbi Obadiah Bertinoro, Commentary on the Mishnah: Avot 1.3.

at this level is in no position to respond with duty inasmuch as duty is essentially tangible action in the world. But at this level, man has no world in which to stand before God.

Persons to God. Nevertheless, Scripture also teaches that every human person is granted a special status by God in the created world. "And God created man in his image, in the image of God *(be-tselem elohim)* He made him, male and female He created them" (Genesis 1:27). There are various opinions about what is meant by the "image of God." Many have seen it to be some inherent characteristic of human nature like reason or free will. In other words, it is seen as the transfer of some divine power, be it reason or free will, to a special creature, one who is unlike any other creature. But the problem with seeing the image of God as an inherent characteristic of human nature is that such a characteristic can be constituted phenomenologically without reference to God. If God is only the external cause of reason or free will, essential insight into either of these phenomena does not require a causal explanation of how it originally came to be. What does saying "humans receive their reason or free will from God" add to the proposition "humans are rational or possess free will"?[24] In other words, these interpretations lose the intimacy *between* God and humans that is suggested by the opening words of God's creation of the human being, "Let us make the human *(adam)* in our image" (Genesis 1:26). The only way one can constitute the intimacy of the relationship *with* God that Scripture suggests is a possibility *for* humans from the very beginning and continually thereafter is to see the image of God as that which God and humans share in what they do *together*.[25] The Hebrew verb *"asoh"* as in *"na`aseh"* "let us make" means both making things and doing acts as, for example, "to do *(la`asot)* the Ten Commandments" *(aseret ha-devarim)* (Deuteronomy 4:13). Similarly, the Hebrew noun *"davar"* means both a thing and a word as, for example, "the word of our God *(devar eloheinu)* remains forever" (Isaiah 40:8).

Essential human action, which is the practice of the commandments, is unlike all other things that are *made by* the Creator. Rather, it is done *along with* the Creator. In rabbinic teaching, even God himself is imagined to observe the commandments of the Torah in order to share with his people the basic reality of their active life.[26] Thus the basis of a positive relationship between God and humans is the human capacity, designated as the image of God, to be able to respond to God's commandments with a sense of authentic obligation. Humans not only owe God everything for

---

[24] See David Novak, *Halakhah in a Theological Dimension* (Chico, CA, 1985), 96ff.

[25] See Franz Rosenzweig, *The Star of Redemption*, W.W. Hallo, trans. (New York, 1970), 154-155.

[26] See Jerusalem Talmud Rosh Hashanah 1.3/57a-b re Leviticus 22:9.

having made them, but more directly and more positively they owe God everything for descending from beyond to speak to them. Thus the first of the Ten Commandments, "I am the Lord your God who brought you out of the land of Egypt, out of the house of bondage" (Exodus 20:2), establishes God's commanding authority both on the basis of the good God has done for Israel by liberating her from slavery, and on the basis of the good God is doing and will do for Israel by giving her commandments that are in her best interest.[27] "And the Lord has commanded us to practice all of these statutes . . . for our own good *(le-tov lanu)* . . . it is beneficial for us *(u-tsedaqah tehiyeh lanu)* that we prepare ourselves to practice all these commandments *(ha-mitsvah ha-z'ot)* before the Lord our God as he has commanded us" (Deuteronomy 6:24-25).

This can be seen in the first explicit address of God to man after creation. "And the Lord God commanded *(va-yitsav)* the human being saying, 'from all the trees of the garden you may surely eat. But from the tree of the knowledge of good and bad you may not eat, for on the day you eat from it you shall surely die'" (Genesis 2:16-17). In rabbinic exegesis, the human being is both spoken *to* and spoken *about* in this statement. For the Hebrew reads *"al ha'adam,"* which means both "to the human being" and "about the human being." From this phraseology the Rabbis see an allusion to a prohibition of murder, which is of course needed at this point in the biblical narrative if Cain is to be held responsible by God for the murder of Abel.[28] Thus human dignity is affirmed by the teaching that all humans are capable in one way or another of being commanded by God, responding thereto, and being judged thereon. Accordingly, the ultimate indignity of death is that the dead person is now "free from the commandments," which means to be deprived of essential human nature, to be turned into something else, that is, "to return to the dust" (Genesis 3:19) from which one is made but not what one truly is, at least for "the shadow of our days on earth" (I Chronicles 29:15).[29] Human persons are regarded as sojourners in the world, who can only find their dwelling in the world when they realize that their authentic identity is neither derived from the world nor from themselves. That identity comes from being related to the One who himself transcends the world and directs it, the One to whom the world is always immanent.[30] "I am a sojourner *(ger)* on earth; do not hide your commandments from me" (Psalms 119:19).

---

[27] See Mekhilta: Yitro re Exodus 20:2, ed. Horovitz-Rabin, 219.

[28] Babylonian Talmud Sanhedrin 56b.

[29] Niddah 61b re Psalm 88:6.

[30] See Beresheet Rabbah 39.1.

The idea that God enables humans to be related to him by means of commandments leads to the idea that humans now have the right to justice both in their societies from each other and even more so in the cosmos from God. A relationship consisting of commandments and not just ad hoc commands involves an order.[31] That order includes God's action as the giver of commandments, the response of humans as keepers of commandments, and then the response of God in the ultimate consequences of either keeping or breaking the commandments. We can see this human right to justice, this claim of man upon the commanding God, throughout Scripture and the literature of the Rabbis.

At the time of the first crime, which was the murder of Abel by his brother Cain, Abel is depicted as claiming justice for himself from God. As God informs Cain, who at that moment is standing in trial before God, "the voice of your brother's blood cries to me from the soil of the earth *(min ha'adamah)"* (Genesis 4:11). The Rabbis point out that the word for "blood"—*"demei"*—is in the plural (literally, "bloods"), which means that Abel is not only claiming justice for his present that Cain destroyed by the act of murder, but also for his future, namely, the descendents that he could have had but will never hereafter have because of the murder.[32]

After the Flood, which was brought about because of the sin of public violence, God assures the survivors, Noah and his family, who are now the progenitors of restored humankind, that violence against them will not go unrequited. "Indeed, your lifeblood I shall claim *(edrosh)* from the hand of every beast I shall claim it, and from human hands I shall claim it, human life *(nefesh ha'adam)* even a man from his own brother's hand" (Genesis 9:5).[33] This last reference to fraternal violence seems to suggest the crime of Cain against Abel, and that violence is ultimately against our own kin in one way or another and not against total strangers.

Now, of course, this idea of divine justice for violence against innocent humans came to be questioned inasmuch as it is frequently the case that there is good cause to complain "Why does the way of the wicked prosper?!" (Jeremiah 12:1). As a result of such inherently legitimate complaints, the Jewish tradition developed the idea that the full consequences

---

[31] See David Novak, *Jewish-Christian Dialogue: A Jewish Justification* (New York, 1989), 153-154.

[32] Mishnah Sanhedrin 4.5.

[33] This verse is interpreted in the Talmud (Babylonian Talmud Baba Kama 91b) as including the prohibition of suicide, viz., God will avenge the blood of any victim, even when the victim and the perpetrator are one and the same person. In other words, there is no individual right to death. As for a communal right to inflict death for certain crimes, Scripture, of course, affirms it (see, e.g., Genesis 9:6). But, for the attempts of some of the Rabbis to so qualify this right as to make it in effect a null class, see Mishnah Makkot 1.10; Babylonian Talmud Makkot 7a; also, David Novak, *Jewish Social Ethics* (New York, 1992), 174ff.

of human justice or injustice are not to be expected in this world but, rather, in a world-yet-to-come *(olam ha-ba)*, which will be the Kingdom of God on earth *(malkhut shamayim)*.[34] Critics have long seen this type of answer to the question of absent divine justice to be in truth a begging of the question itself, a way of diverting attention away from a great theological embarrassment. Moreover, to follow the line of the Marxist designation of religion as the "opium of the people," such question-begging is seen as a way of enforcing the status quo, which is assumed to be the unjust exploitation of the masses by those with economic-political power over them.[35] However, in the Jewish tradition, this type of postponement of the question (which is not the same as begging it) has had very different results.

First, it has led to the emphasis of keeping the commandments for their own sake *(li-shmah)* rather than seeing them as instrumental for something else.[36] For as Aristotle wisely taught, the pursuit of a presently unattainable end cannot be a motivation for purposeful activity here and now.[37] Thus the final just reward or punishment for either keeping or breaking the commandments in this world is taken to be a future consequence of this action, essentially disjunct from the present, and thus not its actual present *telos*. The purposes of the commandments are seen as being for the sake of the present relationship with God and with fellow human beings. This led to the whole Jewish tendency to discover the "reasons of the commandments" *(ta`amei ha-mitsvot)*, that is, those intelligible ends for which the commandments are seen to function.[38] Indeed, here we see the theological connection with the interest by classical Jewish thinkers in the whole issue of natural law (which they often called by other names, however).[39]

Second, this affirmation of ultimate divine justice has functioned as an antidote to the despair that often comes when the quest for justice, the response to legitimate human rights, is based on human idealism. For the futility of the finite and mortal human situation taken in and of itself belies any idealism in the end. Indeed, total human efforts to bring about justice in the world have inevitably led to more injustice than they purport to cure. One need only think of the colossal fiasco of the utopian

---

[34] See Hullin 142a re Deuteronomy 22:7. Cf. Kiddushin 39b and Tosafot, s.v. "matnitin."

[35] See Karl Marx: *On Society and Social Change*, N.J. Smelser, ed. (Chicago, 1973), 13-14.

[36] See Mishnah Avot 1.3; Babylonian Talmud Rosh Hashanah 28a; Babylonian Talmud Nazir 23b.

[37] Aristotle, *Nicomachean Ethics*, 1.10/1100a10ff.

[38] See David Novak, *The Theology of Nahmanides Systematically Presented* (Atlanta, GA, 1992), 2ff.

[39] See Novak, *Jewish Social Ethics*, chaps. 1-3.

promises of Marxism in this century. The pursuit of justice for the sake of
human rights can only be maintained in good faith when those who seek
it see themselves as participants in a cosmic reality whose final outcome
transcends their own fragile efforts.[40] The final victory belongs to God
alone. For this reason, human prayer that God will do justice in his world
is as important as human efforts to effect justice in our own little domain
of activity in that world. It is not, however, a substitute for human efforts
which will be judged in the end.[41] As the Rabbis emphasized, prayer to
the merciful and gracious God is also to lead to the imitation of these
qualities by the humans who affirm them in prayer. "As He is merciful,
so you be merciful."[42]

Third, this postponement of ultimate divine justice to the messianic
future (l`atid la-vo) led to the emphasis on the practice of justice by hu-
mans here and now. For whereas God has all the time he wants to effect
justice in the world and can do so alone, mortal humans have only have
limited time to attempt to effect justice, always partial justice to be sure,
in situations at hand that call for justice to be pursued.[43] Furthermore,
they cannot do this alone. They require the help of others in society. And,
in order that human justice not be severed from divine justice, they require both divine guidance and divine example. This now leads us to
consider God's relation to human community and the rights and duties
that emerge here.

God to Community. In the biblical narrative, the original hope for a
united humankind, for one human city on earth, is dashed by the arrogant attempt of the builders of the Tower of Babel to unite humankind
against God.[44] According to one ancient tradition, this grandiose attempt
to solve the problem of human insecurity in the world also resulted in the
neglect of individual human claims for justice to be readily at hand.[45] As
a result, humankind is considered to be permanently fragmented; "the
Lord has scattered them over all the earth" (Genesis 11:9). This is to be
the human situation until the coming of the day "when the Lord will become king over all the earth" (Zechariah 14:9). At that time, God "will
turn to the peoples with a clear message (safah berurah), summoning all of

---

[40] Ibid., 163-164.

[41] See Mekhilta: Beshalah, 97 re Exodus 14:15 (Jerusalem, 1960).

[42] Babylonian Talmud Shabbat 133b re Exodus 15:2.

[43] See Mishnah Avot 2.15-16; Babylonian Talmud Ta'anit 21a.

[44] See Beresheet Rabbah 38.8 re Genesis 11:4.

[45] See Louis Ginzberg, *The Legends of the Jews* (Philadelphia, 1909), 1:179.

them in the name of the Lord to serve him with one accord" (Zephaniah 3:9).[46]

Because of the inherent fragmentation of humankind in this world, the biblical narrative quickly turns to God's relationship with one particular community. In God's choice of Abraham and his descendents, God's direct covenant with at least some humans for the time being is now Scripture's primary concern. The more indirect covenant with the earth and its natural order that came with Noah and humankind that survived the Flood becomes the background for the prime divine-human reality in the world. The Noahide covenant and its law are the minimal conditions for the emergence and development of this more specific covenant, but they are not rich enough in detail and intensity to suffice for the fuller life with God on earth required by the historicity of the human condition. That historicity consists of singular events and their celebration that can only be the subject of the memory of a singular community among others in the world. The Noahide covenant involves the generality of nature; it does not supply content. It presents negative limits but not the positive claims that can only be made by persons historically situated in a community.[47] Nevertheless, this covenant is considered to be ultimately for all of humankind. Thus God informs Abraham at the very moment of his initial call to him that "all the families of the earth shall be blessed through you" (Genesis 12:3). The covenant is of universal significance, even if at present it is only a matter of local experience and practice. Minimally, this means that the moral standards of this community are defensible as being in the interest of universally valid human rights.

In the biblical narrative, the covenantal relationship between God and the Abrahamic community (eventually the people Israel) becomes more exact in terms of its significance for the issue of justice in the world, which takes the form of concern for the human right to justice. God invites Abraham to a dialogue with him concerning the proposed punishment of the evil cities of Sodom and Gomorroh and all their citizens. The dialogue is initiated by God as follows:

> How can I hide from Abraham what I am about to do? And Abraham is to be a great and important nation through whom all the nations of the earth are to be blessed. For I know him intimately (yeda`tiv) and this is to lead (lema`an) to his commanding his children and household to follow after him, that they might

---

[46] See Maimonides, *Mishneh Torah: Melakhim*, chap. 11, uncensored ed. (Jerusalem, 1983).

[47] See Novak, *Jewish Social Ethics*, 70ff.

> keep the way of the Lord to practice righteous judgment (*tsedaqah*
> *u-mishpat*). This is to lead (*lema`an*) to the Lord's bringing about
> all that he has spoken about him (Genesis 18:17-19).

First, there is the question of why God must inform Abraham of what
he plans to do with the two cities. The answer to this seems to be that
unless Abraham and the community around him (at that time beginning
with his own domestic circle) have actually been assured of God's most
elemental justice, they could not possibly model their own practice of
justice on it. For justice to be more than a human pursuit, it must be connected to "the way of the Lord." And for the way of the Lord to be a
model for human practice, it must be minimally consistent in its application. That is, the innocent and the guilty must not be confused, and the
punishment must be appropriate to the crime.[48]

It is not that justice is prior to God. For something to be prior to or
even coequal with God, as we have seen when noting the traditional
doctrine of *creatio ex nihilo*, would make God inherently limited. But a
limited God is not greater than that which necessarily limits it. Instead,
the text seems to teach that *if* God wants to maintain a relationship with a
community on earth, and *if* that relationship is to be concerned with the
human condition itself, which most basically involves the rights of *any*
human person to justice, *then* God should act justly. God's autonomous
moral authority, which he need not exercise primordially if he does not
wish to do so, entails this much responsibility now that he has chosen to
exercise it. The "justice" (*that*) that Abraham confronts God about is not a
primordial reality in which even God has to participate, as was the case
in Plato's constitution of the relation of God and justice.[49] It is, rather, a
self-imposed modification of divine activity; it is to be translated by the
adverb "justly" to avoid any notion that it is more than the action which
it modifies. "Will the judge of all the earth himself not do justly?"
(Genesis 18:25). Such unjust action admitted by God in his own words
with Abraham (as opposed to action whose justice is unknown as was
the case with Job) would make God's claims "obscene" (*halilah*), that is, it
would mark God's authority as the arbitrary exercise of power so familiar from the political experience of all nations.[50] Man, on the other hand,
being thrown into the world already before having to make any existential choices, has no such primordial choice, therefore. Whereas God does

---

[48] See *Sifre: Devarim*, L. Finkelstein, ed. (New York, 1969) 303 re Deuteronomy 25:1;
Babylonian Talmud Sanhedrin 90a.

[49] See *Euthyphro*, 10Aff.; also, David Novak, *Suicide and Morality* (New York, 1975),
31ff.

[50] See Rashi, *Commentary on the Torah*, M. Rosenbaum and A.M. Silvermann, trans.
(London, 1946), Genesis 18:25.

not have to make any choice at all, humans do. Thus if humans are to do justly, they must indeed participate in the justice that is not of their own making. Humans are essentially responsive and thus not autonomous in any foundational sense, contrary to the rights theory that found its most profound enunciation in Kant.[51]

Second, the text from Genesis 18 indicates that the greatness and importance of the Abrahamic nation is not to be a matter of material or military might. The greatness in the eyes of the world is to be moral. "Not by military power *(hayil)* and not by material strength *(koah)*, but by my spirit says the Lord" (Zechariah 4:6).[52] Minimally, that would mean that God's relation to this community results in a system of law in which the concern for human rights would impress anyone having a similar concern. Thus Moses tells the people of Israel poised to enter the Promised Land of the universal significance of the law God has given them.

> For it is your wisdom and understanding in the eyes of the nations that will hear all these statutes and will say, 'surely this nation is a wise and discerning people.' For what great nation has God so close to them as we do when we call upon the Lord our God? And what great nation has such righteous statutes *(huqqim)* and ordinances *(mishpatim)* as this whole Torah.... (Deuteronomy 4:6-8).[53]

Indeed, part of the messianic vision is that the nations of the world will eventually come to Jerusalem for their claims to be adjudicated. They will say "let us go up to the mountain of the Lord, to the house of the God of Jacob, and He will direct us from his ways and we will walk in his paths . . . he will judge between the nations and arbitrate *(ve-hokheah)* for many peoples" (Isaiah 2:3-4).[54]

Because of God's claim on his covenanted community to exercise their duty to deal justly, communally as well as individually, the greatest indictment of this community and its institutions by the prophets was perversion of the rights of the most helpless citizens of the polity by those with the power to do otherwise. Political destruction is promised unless "you seek justice *(that)*; rectify oppression; champion *(shiftu)* the orphan and plead the cause of the widow" (Isaiah 1:17).[55] Because the covenant is with the all-seeing God, no perversion of rights can hide behind the ano-

---

[51] See Kant, *Groundwork of the Metaphysic of Morals*, 78-79. Cf. Novak, *Jewish-Christian Dialogue*, 148ff.

[52] Cf. Deut. 8:17-18.

[53] See Maimonides, *Guide of the Perplexed*, 3.31 (Chicago, 1972).

[54] See Tosefta Sotah 8.6 re Deuteronomy 27:8 (New York, 1957).

[55] See Babylonian Talmud Sanhedrin 32b re Deuteronomy 16:20.

nymity of faceless institutions. God's concern for the welfare of every human created in God's image gives him the right to demand proportional concern on behalf of the covenanted community especially. They are to imitate God in his role as "father of orphans and judge for widows" (Psalms 68:6).

That concern for justice is to include just dealings with those outside the community itself; indeed, injustice towards the gentiles, for the Rabbis, entails the sin of "profanation of God's name" *(hillul ha-shem)*.[56] Such injustice prevents the gentiles from admiring the inherent justice of the Torah and to praise the God who gave it as well as to desire to appropriate it. Such injustice would not inspire them to come to Jerusalem, literally or figuratively, for the just response to their rights claims.

God's rights and God's championing the rights of those who need justice the most creates numerous duties for the community. But the issue of the just adjudication of rights claims is something that transcends the actual political institutions of the covenanted community. Thus in rabbinic jurisprudence, when the Jewish authorities are unable to properly adjudicate the rights of persons in their own domain, even Jews are allowed to go to gentile authorities with their rights claims, provided that these authorities practice a law with due process.[57]

Community to God. God's right to command numerous duties to his elect community, prominent among them being the duty to "pursue justice" (Deuteronomy 16:20), does not, however, mean that the covenanted community has no rights itself in its relationship with God. Since God has voluntarily chosen to covenant himself with Israel (as he voluntarily chose to create the world solely by himself *ex nihilo*), Israel has the right to demand that God not abandon them by annulling the covenant. The people's claim on God's faithfulness is as indissoluble as God's claim on theirs. Thus the validity of the covenant is irrevocable even though Israel's disloyalty to it regularly occurs. This comes out in the way the Talmud interprets Moses' dialogue with God after Israel has worshipped the Golden Calf.

"Remember Abraham, Isaac and Israel your servants to whom you yourself took an oath. . . ." (Exodus 32:13). What does "you yourself" *(bakh)* mean? Rabbi Eleazar said that it means that Moses really said the following to God: "Master of the universe, if you had taken an oath to them in the name of heaven and earth, I could say that just as heaven and earth are perishable *(betelim)* so is your oath *(shevu`atekha)* perishable. But now you have taken an oath by your own great name. Therefore, just as

---

[56] See Babylonian Talmud Baba Kama 113a-b.

[57] See Babylonian Talmud Baba Batra 54b and parallels; Maimonides, *Mishneh Torah: Sanhedrin*, 26.7.

your great name lives and endures forever so must your oath endure forever."[58]

This theological homily is based on the legal fact that in Jewish law only an external authority can annul an oath, thus freeing the person who took it from the obligation to fulfill it. The assumption is that this external authority is higher than the person taking the oath.[59] But God has not recognized any external authority in promising to be covenanted to Israel. Rather, God has based his oath on his own imperishable being, his own unique name. Therefore, there is no way that even God can release himself from the covenant. All he can do in good faith is chastise Israel in the hope that such chastisement will awaken her from her illusions and turn her back to her only authentic covenant partner.

Much of Jewish communal prayer in the form of requests (baqashah) is the claim on God perpetually to remember just who his people is. Although Israel is for the most part obliged to recognize her own difficulties as stemming from unfaithfulness to the covenant and praise God for his mercy (hoda'ah), there are times when Israel has the right to express her anger with God for what seems to be unjustified harshness. "See O Lord and look at whom you have done this, women even eat their own children!" (Lamentations 2:20).[60] In fact, the only limit on this expression of anger is the prohibition of blasphemy, the curse that wishes God to be dead.[61]

This right of the covenanted community to be angry with the presently unjustified ways of God assumes special importance for the Jewish people after the Holocaust, particularly as regards their duty to pursue justice and champion human rights. For there is the great temptation to turn away from God for not rescuing so many of his people from the murderers. Part of that turning away from God is to conclude that there is no justice at all in the cosmos. But if there is no justice at all in the cosmos, then to maintain human justice as a tiny island in a sea of absurdity seems futile. Jewish abandonment of the universal God because of the experience of gross injustice can quickly lead to the conclusion that justice is not to be done because it has nothing in which to endure. At this point, survival itself becomes the only task. But in extremis there are no moral restraints.[62] Everything becomes a matter of self-defense, which is the one area where fear of consequences can justify even killing. Even for

---

[58] Babylonian Talmud Berakhot 32a; also, Novak, *Halakhah in a Theological Dimension*, 126ff.

[59] Babylonian Talmud Nedarim 27b.

[60] See Babylonian Talmud Gittin 56b re Exodus 15:11.

[61] See Mishnah Sanhedrin 7.5.

[62] Babylonian Talmud Sanhedrin 72a. See also Novak, *Jewish Social Ethics*, 167ff.

those who still want to cling to the ancient tradition of God-talk, without
the affirmation of cosmic justice as a reality and an irrevocable (although
humanly partial) task, the god they affirm is for all intents and purposes
a tribal deity, one who is incapable of judging them but only judges their
enemies. Their god becomes a projection of themselves and their power.
Such a god is neither the source nor the protector of human rights.

Persons to Persons. The rights persons claim from each other and the
duties they owe to each other emerge from the common world that per-
sons have to share with each other. Not only is "the earth the Lord's"
(Psalms 24:1), but even in the limited sense that "the earth is given to
humans" (Psalms 115:16), the earth does not belong to any one of them.[63]
The theme that guides discussion in this area is basic human reciprocity.
Thus the Rabbis speculated that the quarrel that led to Cain's murder of
Abel was that Cain as the "tiller of the ground" and Abel as "shepherd"
(Genesis 4:2) fought over who had absolute title to the earth. Cain
claimed that the ground belonged to him and thus demanded that Abel
forfeit any right to it; Abel claimed that all moveable things belonged to
him and thus demanded that Cain forfeit any right to even the clothes he
was wearing.[64] Instead of going to God or to their parents to adjudicate
this dispute, Cain seized the initiative and thought he eliminated Abel's
claim by eliminating him. Conversely, Abraham and the Philistine chief-
tain Abimelech "take an oath to each other, and conclude a covenant"
(Genesis 21:31-32) because of peace in the land in which they both are
living so closely proximate.[65]

The idea of basic human reciprocity with its rights and correlative
duties comes out in one of the most famous passages in the Talmud.
When a gentile asks Hillel the Elder to "convert me to Judaism on the
condition that you teach me the entire Torah while I stand on one foot,"
the sage answers, "what is hateful to you do not do to your fellow."[66] Of
course, there is much more to the entire Torah than just that, but what
this text suggests is that the rights and duties that emerge out of basic
human reciprocity are the place to begin to appreciate the fuller range of
rights and duties with which the Torah is concerned. This is what is
meant by the sage's concluding words to the would-be convert, "This is
the entire Torah and the rest is commentary. Now go learn." In Jewish
tradition, though, the commentary often surpasses the immediate text at
hand.[67] Furthermore, someone without this most basic moral sense is

---

[63] See Jerusalem Talmud Berakhot 6.1/9d re Psalm 24:1.

[64] Beresheet Rabbah 22.7.

[65] See Jerusalem Talmud Shevi'it 6.1/36c.

[66] Babylonian Talmud Shabbat 31a.

[67] See Mishnah Hagigah 1.8.

hardly going to be interested in the much more stringent requirements of the entire Torah.[68]

The essential concern with reciprocity found in this text comes out in a comment by the twelfth century theologian Maimonides on a text in the Mishnah that speaks of acts "for which the fruit is consumed in this world even though the principle endures in the world-to-come."[69] Maimonides applies this text to those commandments that pertain to what is "between humans" *(bein adam le-havero)*.[70] Unlike those commandments that pertain to what is "between humans and God," whose consequences are transcendent, interhuman commandments have immanent consequences inasmuch as what I do on behalf of someone else is done with the expectation that as much will be done on my behalf.

Human sociality can only develop when there is this general openness to interpersonal mutuality and reciprocity. This seems to be what Aristotle meant when he said that "friendship *(philia)* also seems to be the bond that holds communities together" and that it is "considered to be justice in the fullest sense . . . not only a necessity but something desirable per se."[71] Friendship is greater than justice, because it includes justice's negative claims and engenders positive duties as well. In other words, concern with human rights must not remain at the level of a simple demarcation of claims but it must lead to the emergence of a society in which a common life is developed, one that is beyond but not at the expense of these human rights exercised by individuals.[72] Persons have duties to the community itself. Indeed, without these communal duties human rights would quickly lose the only context in which they can be exercised with true protection. Concern for the common good enhances human rights by teaching those virtues that include respect for the human dignity of each and every person *(kevod ha-beriyot)*.[73]

Persons to Community. In the Jewish tradition, society functions as much more than the mere arbitrator of the conflicting claims of individuals. The good of society is something worthy in itself and not just instrumental for something else. Being a community, this entity has rights that claim the duty of individuals who live and flourish there as the social beings they are by nature.

---

[68] See Babylonian Talmud Yevamot 22a.

[69] Mishnah Pe'ah 1.1.

[70] *Commentary on the Mishnah*: Pe'ah 1.1, Jerusalem Talmud Kafih, ed. (Jerusalem, 1976), 1:55.

[71] *Nicomachean Ethics*, 8.1/1155a20.

[72] Ibid., 8.1/1155a25-30. See Babylonian Talmud Baba Batra 100a and David Novak, "Is There A Concept of Individual Rights in Jewish Law?," *Jewish Law Association Studies* (Atlanta, 1994), 129ff.

[73] See Babylonian Talmud Berakhot 19b and parallels.

Jewish law is replete with duties that the community claims from individuals.[74] Most of these duties are formal legal obligations, that is, there are sanctions for the refusal to obey them. Some of these duties involve the community removing certain rights that individuals previously had.[75] Such removal is always justified by considerations of the common good that are considered to override the private good that the exercise of an individual right intends. An example of this transfer of rights, so to speak, is the following:

> Ulla said that the literal law of Scripture is that a debtor may pay his debt even with the poorest quality produce (*ziburiyot*), as it says: "you [the claimant] are to stand outside [the dwelling of the debtor] and the man whose debt you are claiming shall bring the pledge out to you" (Deuteronomy 24:11). Now, what does one usually bring out, is it not the least valuable stuff among his things (*pahot she-ba-kelim*)? Therefore, what is the reason the sages rule that a debtor is to be paid with at least medium quality produce (*beinonit*), is it not so that (*kedei*) the door will not be closed in the face of borrowers?[76]

This is one of several rabbinic rulings that in effect removed a Scripturally granted right to an individual for the sake of the economic good of the entire community.[77] The assumption is that the full exercise of the right of debtors basically to unload merchandise that is difficult to sell as repayment of their debts will in the end stifle the ready lending of money.[78] Those who have money to lend will regard lending as entailing just too much trouble to want to bother with it at all. Such a breakdown of communal responsibility on the part of borrowers will have bad consequences for the entire community.

What we have just seen is how the transfer of a right was formally legislated. However, there are some cases where the transfer of a right is not legislated but only encouraged. The following is an example of this type of voluntary transfer of an individual right for the sake of the common good:

> Rabbi Eliezer the son of Rabbi Yose the Galilean says that it is forbidden to submit one's case to arbitration (*asur li-vetsoa*) and whoever does so is a sinner . . . but let the legal ruling (*ha-din*)

---

[74] See, e.g., Babylonian Talmud Shabbat 23a. For the criteria for making these new duties, see Babylonian Talmud Avodah Zarah 36a-b.

[75] See, e.g., Mishnah Arakhin 5.6 and Mishnah Gittin 9.8.

[76] Babylonian Talmud Baba Kama 8a.

[77] See, e.g., Babylonian Talmud Yevamot 89b.

[78] Cf. Babylonian Talmud Gittin 36a.

pierce the mountain. . . . Rabbi Joshua ben Korhah says that it is meritorious (mitsvah) to submit one's case to arbitration as Scripture says: "True and peaceful judgment (that shalom) you shall adjudicate in your gates" (Zechariah 8:16). But is it not so that when there is judgment there is no peace and when there is peace there is no judgment? So what kind of judgment contains peace? That is arbitration.[79]

The phrase used by the first opinion, "let the legal ruling pierce the mountain" means that whereas it is easier to go around a mountain, the most direct way to get beyond it is to go through it. In other words, the law is to be upheld without regard for social consequences. In this case, the law is for the sake of the rights of the litigant judged by the authorities to be the innocent party in a case. He benefits; the litigant judged to be the guilty party suffers.

However, in the second opinion there is the political issue of the peace of the community over and above the legal issue of whose individual rights are to be enforced and whose are not to be enforced. In this opinion, the authorities must combine concern for individual claims (that) with concern for the common weal (shalom). The only way this can be done with legal integrity is if, before any decision is made in a private monetary dispute, both parties themselves agree to waive their respective right to the possibility of total legal victory and thus agree that neither of them will win and neither of them will lose. Both are willing to compromise (pesharah) for the sake of the common weal from which both they and everyone else in the community ultimately benefits.[80] Now even though no one is literally obligated by the law to agree to arbitration in lieu of a formal trial, the later Jewish authorities urged more and more that litigants be subjected to at least social pressure to do so.[81] That social pressure is to be persuasion on the basis of the essential reasonableness of naturally social beings rising above the level of even legitimate private interest for the sake of what they should deem more important in the end.[82]

Nevertheless, in our century especially, when we have seen how the rights of individuals have been crushed under the weight of collectivist regimes, many have good reason to be suspicious of a system that seems

---

[79] Babylonian Talmud Sanhedrin 6b.

[80] For the right to not exercise, i.e., waive, one's right, see Babylonian Talmud Kiddushin 32a; Babylonian Talmud Sotah 25a.

[81] See Maimonides, Mishneh Torah: Sanhedrin, 22.4-6, Isodore Twersky, trans. (New Haven, 1976); Tur: Hoshen Mishpat, 12 (Jerusalem, 1992).

[82] See Babylonian Talmud Baba Metsia 48b.

to always place *bonum commune* over *bonum sibi*, that is, the notion that man is made for the state rather than the other way around.

Community to Persons. The debate over how much weight should be placed on individual rights as opposed to communal duties and vice-versa is currently being waged by those who call themselves "liberals," on the one side, and those who call themselves "communitarians," on the other side.[83] The preponderance of data from the Jewish tradition, certainly from the Jewish legal tradition, would seem to place this tradition within the communitarian camp. The question is how one can have a generally communitarian perspective and still maintain an important role for individual rights, even when at times they are at odds with the claims of the community.

One can, of course, simply argue for some sort of balance between the two claims. However, the problem with such a stipulation is that in particular instances one never knows for sure just which side to emphasize. Thus without a middle term to mediate between these two disjuncts, we do not seem to see how they can function in essential harmony. Is not leaving the matter at this level like agreeing to agree?

It seems to me that if one looks more carefully at the idea of the covenant *(ha-berit)*, the essential harmony needed between individual rights and communal duties can be found in Judaism. For in the covenant both individuals and the community as a whole are directly related to God.[84] The community does not mediate that relationship between God and individual persons anymore than individuals create the community as an instrument for the fulfillment of their own private needs. Thus the Torah as the constitution of the covenant addresses its commandments both to the community and to the various individuals in it. Both of them have the duty to enhance the rights/privileges *(zekhut)* of the other to practice more and more of the commandments of the Torah. Each is, therefore, responsible for the other.[85] As the Mishnah puts it: "God wanted to privilege *(le-zakot)* Israel, therefore He increased the number of commandments for them."[86] From this we can see how one of the main duties of the community is to enhance the right of as many of its members as possible to practice more and more of the commandments of the Torah. Thus individuals, over and above the usual bodily and property

---

[83] For a good discussion of this debate as it relates to Judaism, see Alan Mittleman, "From Private Rights to Public Good: The Communitarian Critique of Liberalism in Judaic Perspective," *Jewish Political Studies Review* 5 (1993): 79ff.

[84] Even that quintessential modern apostate from Judaism, Baruch Spinoza, was favorably impressed by this aspect of the covenant. See *Tractatus Theologico-Politicus*, chaps. 16-17.

[85] See Babylonian Talmud Shevu'ot 39a re Leviticus 26:37.

[86] Mishnah Makkot 3.16.

rights they expect society to protect, also have a covenantal claim on the community. And it is a matter of common good itself for the community to act on behalf of these individual rights. The following is a vivid example of this covenantal process at work:

> An instance about Rabbi Eliezer: Once when he entered the synagogue and did not find ten [the quorum required for public worship]. So he freed his slave on the spot so that he could be the tenth. . . . But how could he do this? Didn't Rav Judah say that whoever frees his slave violates the positive commandment "you shall enslave them forever" (Leviticus 25:46)? But this was a matter of fulfilling a commandment *(le-dvar mitsvah)*. Yet doesn't this consist of a commandment whose condition is a sin [and hence not the valid practice of the commandment]? No, a public commandment *(mitsvah de-rabbim)* is different.[87]

To appreciate the dialectic in this Talmudic discussion, one must be aware of how much the institution of slavery developed from the time of the proof text from Leviticus to the time of Rabbi Eliezer (first century C.E.). In biblical times, it seems as though gentile slaves of Jews were only considered to be part of the covenanted community in the sense that certain legal restrictions, such as working on the Sabbath, also applied to them.[88] They were primarily chattel, although their basic human right to bodily integrity was legally enforced.[89] But by rabbinic times they were considered to be quasi-members of the covenanted community. Thus both male and female slaves had to undergo the same rites of initiation required of a convert.[90] The only difference between a slave and a convert was that a convert had all the rights of a native born member of the community (with a few minor exceptions) whereas a slave had virtually none of them.[91] Certainly, one of the greatest of these rights is the right to be counted as part of the quorum for public worship. Nevertheless, looked at only on the level of individual rights, the Scripturally based law that applies to the community regarding holding slaves might still take precedence. However, when the community itself needs the participation of a slave for purposes of the common good, then its interest and that of the slave actually coincide. A task for the community's religious

---

[87] Babylonian Talmud Berakhot 47b. Cf. Babylonian Talmud Sukkah 30a and parallels.

[88] See Exodus 20:10.

[89] See ibid., 21:20, 26-27. See, also, Jerusalem Talmud Ketubot 5.5/30a re Job 31:15.

[90] See Babylonian Talmud Shabbat 135b; also, Novak, *Law and Theology in Judaism*, 2:87ff.

[91] The question of whether slaves themselves regarded their status as beneficial or detrimental depended on whether a slave valued physical security (of slavery) over communal rights (of freedom) or vice-versa. See Babylonian Talmud Gittin 12b.

authorities might well be to look for ways to legally expand the range of such social needs for the inclusion of more and more persons in the authentic life of the community.[92]

The institution of slavery is, of course, something that has happily disappeared from our world today. I cannot think of anyone who could put forth a morally persuasive argument to look upon it with favor, let alone advocate its return. But what we see from this Talmudic text is typical of the way the Jewish tradition more and more made slavery a thing of the past. The way this was done was to see the slave's right to freedom as his or her claim to be a full participant in the life of the community, someone given the opportunity to contribute to the common good. In the case of public worship, we have the best example of the harmony between the private and the public, the individual and the communal. For public worship includes personal prayer just as personal prayer finds a deeper context when it is part of public worship.[93] Being communal is different from being collectivist. Indeed, when worship becomes collectivist, it loses the personal devotion (kavvanah) that is considered to be its very essence.[94]

Conclusion

At the beginning of this chapter, I emphasized how the mandate of this volume actually deals with two different questions: first, the question of religious liberty; and second, the question of the religious foundation of human rights. There I indicated my preference for the second question. Nevertheless, the two are closely related. For without the emphasis of religious liberty in a society that is secular by definition, those who see a religious foundation for the human rights a secular society such as ours affirms have no entry into the moral discourse of the public square. The task of religious believers who wish to enter this moral discourse (although there are quite a few who regard such entry more dangerous to their religious integrity than beneficial to it and thus opt for sectarian seclusion) is to persuade others that a religious foundation for human rights can respect the realm of the secular where so many of these rights are exercised far better than "secularism" can respect the realm of the religious. In other words, the task of the religious believer—Jewish, Christian, or Muslim—is to provide a better foundation for the moral claims of a secular realm where the vast majority of whose citizens profess relig-

---

[92] See, e.g., Mishnah Bikkurim 1.4; Jerusalem Talmud Bikkurim 1.4/64a re Gen. 17:5; Maimonides, *Mishneh Torah: Bikkurim*, 4.3.

[93] See Babylonian Talmud Rosh Hashanah 34b.

[94] See Babylonian Talmud Ta'anit 2a re Deut 11:13.

ious belief and, indeed, see their very allegiance to that secular realm as itself being religious.[95]

---

[95] See Richard John Neuhaus, *The Naked Public Square* (Grand Rapids, 1984), esp. chap. 1.

Forming Religious Communities and Respecting Dissenter's Rights: A Jewish Tradition For A Modern Society

MICHAEL J. BROYDE

Emory University

aw is one of the ways that groups of people cohere and form a society.[1] Religion is another.[2] The complex intersection of these two ways of social formation in the Judaic tradition is a critical part of the Jewish understanding of "religious human rights."

This chapter focuses first on the legal process Jewish law[3] uses to form communities and to exclude people from them.[4] It addresses the

---

[1] For a review of the recent literature on this issue see, Lawrence M. Friedman, "The Law and Society Movement," *Stanford Law Review* 38 (1986): 763.

[2] For a detailed discussion of the impact religion has had on the formation of society, see Jerold S. Auerbach, *Justice Without Law* (Oxford, 1983). The thesis of Auerbach's book—that many religious systems can create justice without any formal system of law—is quite debatable, and beyond the scope of this paper. It is clear that Jewish law is not such a system, although, as Auerbach notes, it is a system of justice without lawyers, which is not the same as a system of justice without law. Justice without law and justice without lawyers are by no means identical, although to those involved in the common law model of justice it might appear that they are the same. The Jewish legal system certainly had all of the apparent indicia of a legal system (unlike the Amish, who, Auerbach maintains, lack a legal system) although the Jewish tradition had no lawyers as part of its legal system. For more on this issue see, my forthcoming work *The Jewish Perspective on Practicing Law* (Yeshiva University Press, 1995). The confusion that results from comparing a system of law without lawyers (such as Jewish law), with a system of justice without law (such as Amish society) can sometimes be found in Auerbach's book.

[3] Jewish law (called *halacha* in Hebrew) is the term used to denote the entire subject matter of the Jewish legal system, including public, private, and ritual law. A brief historical review will familiarize the new reader of Jewish law with its history and development. The Pentateuch (the five books of Moses, the *Torah*) is the historical touchstone document of Jewish law, and according to Jewish legal theory was revealed to Moses at Mount Sinai. The Prophets and Writings, the other two parts of the Hebrew Bible, were written over the next 700 years, and the Jewish canon was closed around the year 300 B.C.E. From the close of the canon until 250 C.E. is referred to as the era of the *tanaimim*, the redactors of Jewish law, whose period closed with the editing of the *mishnah* by Rabbi Judah the Patriarch. The next five centuries was the epoch in which the two Talmuds (Babylonian and Palestinian) were

203

J. Witte, Jr. and J.D. van der Vyver (eds.), Religious Human Rights in Global Perspective, 203-233.
© *1996 Kluwer Law International. Printed in the Netherlands.*

sources within Jewish law for the power to shun or excommunicate[5] people and the goals of such practice. It then discusses the Jewish legal problems raised when excommunication and shunning are used in a modern secular community, whose primary means of self-classification is not normally through religion.

This chapter then analyzes illustrative American, British, and Canadian cases that have reviewed the use of such excommunication and shunning. None of these legal systems, ultimately, provides satisfactory protection for the right and rite of excommunication. The chapter thus proposes a number of changes in prevailing secular laws to protect the community's right to form itself and to define its membership, and the

---

written and edited by scholars called *amoraim* ("those who recount" Jewish law) and *savoraim* ("those who ponder" Jewish law). The Babylonian Talmud is of greater legal significance than the Palestinian Talmud, and is a more complete work.

The post-talmudic era is conventionally divided into three periods: the era of the *gaonim*, scholars who lived in Babylonia until the mid-eleventh century; the era of the *rishonim* (the early authorities), who lived in North Africa, Spain, Franco-Germany, and Egypt until the end of the fourteenth century; and the *achronim* (the latter authorities), which encompass all scholars of Jewish law from the fifteen century up to this era.

From the period of the mid-fourteenth century until the early seventeenth century, Jewish law underwent a period of codification, which led to the acceptance of the law code format of Rabbi Joseph Caro, called the Shulchan Aruch, as the basis for modern Jewish law. Many significant scholars—themselves as important as Rabbi Caro in status and authority— wrote annotations to his code which made the work and its surrounding comments the modern touchstone of Jewish law. The most recent complete edition of the Shulchan Aruch (Vilna, 1896) contains no fewer than 113 separate commentaries on the text of Rabbi Caro. In addition, hundreds of other volumes of commentary have been published as self-standing works, a process that continues to this very day.

For a more literary history of Jewish law, see Menachem Elon, *Jewish Law: History, Principles and Sources* (Philadelphia, 1994); and for a shorter review of the literary history of Jewish law, see Suzanne Last Stone, "In Pursuit of the Counter-text: The Turn to the Jewish Legal Model in Contemporary American Legal Theory," *Harvard Law Review* 106 (1992): 813, 816 n.13.

[4] Classically, this is known as shunning and excommunication. The term "excommunication" has its origins in the exclusion of a person from the Christian right to communion, and thus, the term is not itself of Jewish origins. See James H. Provost, "Excommunication," in Mircea Eliade, ed., *Encyclopedia of Religion* (New York, 1987), 5:218. Notwithstanding its origins, it has become the accepted term to use to refer to this status. The adoption of legal phrases with origins antithetical to a particular religious practice of rabbinic Judaism, and then their subsequent incorporation into the literature of rabbinic Judaism has precedent; see, e.g., Aaron Kirschenbaum, "The Good Samaritan: Monetary Aspects," *Journal of Halacha & Contemporary Society* 17:83 (1989): 84-87.

[5] In Hebrew, the word *cherem* means to destroy; see Exodus 22:19 and Deuteronomy 13:16. However, in modern and rabbinic Hebrew it means to excommunicate; see Rabbi Jacob Karo, Shulchan Aruch, *Yoreh Deah* 334:1. This isolation is sometimes also expressed as through the term *nidui* or *shamta*. The precise linguistic differences between these various terms is beyond the scope of this paper. For more on this, see "Cherem," *Encyclopedia Talmudit* (Jerusalem, 1976), 16:326.

individual's right to leave such communities. Current secular law doctrine in these three countries does neither well.

The conclusion notes that exclusions from religious sub-communities are not only fundamental to the ways in which a religious community forms itself, but profoundly compatible with general moral and legal notions of minority rights, and represents the most equitable way a religious community can form itself in a modern society.

Jewish Law on Excluding

Classical Jewish law offers a broad variety of penalties for those who violate the law. The Bible has four different types of death penalties[6] for a variety of offenses, some of which one could hardly describe as "criminal."[7] Generally, those offenses for which death is not the prescribed punishment, were punished by whipping according to Jewish law.[8] A small number of offenses were punished by *karet*, a divinely-mandated punishment which humans had no hand in. Some violations were not punished at all.[9] Beyond those penalties found explicitly in the Bible, a Jewish court had available *makot mardut*, literally the whipping of a rebel—a process that allowed the court to punish a person who defied the law—through judicially-mandated beatings.[10] So, too, a Jewish court had available the *kipah*, a Jewish version of "three strikes and you're out," where a repeat offender could be (informally) killed if he violated the law with impunity.[11]

Despite these classical formulations, Jewish law has not had the judicial authority to inflict any of these punishments for nearly two thousand years.[12] Indeed, Jewish law has functioned for the past two millennia

---

[6] Stoning, burning, slaying and strangling; see Deuteronomy 17:17; Leviticus 10:2; and Deuteronomy 13:16.

[7] See Maimonides, *Sanhedren* 14:1 and 15:3, Isodore Twersky, trans. (Jerusalem, 1976), who lists the 36 different offenses for which there is a death penalty.

[8] See, e.g., ibid., 16:1, 18:1-2 listing 207 different violations for which lashes are mandated. The codifiers after Maimonides declined to cite these punishments in their codes precisely because they felt them to be inapplicable in modern times. Thus, no listing of death penalty or lashing cases is even found in the classical code of Jewish law, the Shulchan Aruch.

[9] Ibid., 18:1-3.

[10] See Rabbi Chezkeya Demedina, *Sedai Chemed* 4:287-288 (New York, 1960) for more on this issue. As a matter of legal theory, Jewish courts might still be entitled to use this punishment; see Menachem Elon, *Principles of Jewish Law*, (Jerusalem, 1974), 534-35. However, it is clear that Jewish courts do not *ever* order this punishment in modern times, and it is thus considered a punishment no longer applicable.

[11] Babylonian Talmud, *Sanhedren* 81b. This penalty is also inapplicable in modern times.

[12] Formal jurisdiction ended forty years prior to the destruction of the Second Temple. Ibid., 41a. While perhaps some sort of criminal jurisdiction might have been granted to the

with only two real jurisdictional bases to punish violations—the "pursuer" grant of jurisdiction, and excommunication or shunning.[13] The pursuer rationale (*rodef*) is the jurisdictional source of power for a Jewish court or community to intervene to prevent a murder—by force if need be, and even if that use of force violates the rules of the host country.[14] This area of Jewish law is widely known and much written about.[15] It is irrelevant to the formation of a sub-society in modern times, since the cases it governs are crimes that are nearly always also violations of basic general moral principles and thus subject, on a practical level, to concurrent jurisdiction of the secular government. Thus the normal response— even in a very insular, fastidiously observant, Jewish society—to a murder would be to call the police.[16]

The remaining power Jewish courts are left with to address the routine problems involved in formation of a sub-society is that of excommunication and shunning.[17] The power to form a sub-community and to exclude people from that sub-community is a power that can frequently

---

Jewish community in Spain in the 1300s and in various other times in Jewish history by the civil government, even that jurisdiction was not directly based on Jewish law and involved punishments unheard of in Jewish law. For a further discussion of this issue, see Elon, *Principles of Jewish Law*, 529.

[13] Perhaps there is also some emergency jurisdiction, although this author is inclined to view this form of jurisdiction in post-Talmudic times as a broad manifestation of the pursuer rationale. See further, H. Ben-Menahem, *Judicial Deviation in Talmudic Law* (Boston, 1991). Essentially complete civil jurisdiction is still part of Jewish law, and is beyond the scope of this paper.

[14] Thus, for example, if one saw "A" going to murder "B" in Atlanta, Jewish law would allow one to kill "A" if that is the only way to prevent the crime. In fact, the scope of the pursuer rationale is quite a bit broader than that case, and it perhaps provides the governing jurisdictional grant (and perhaps the substantive laws) for such areas of abortion, spousal abuse, armed robbery and other violent crimes; for more on this, see *Shulchan Aruch, Choshen Mishpat*, 425:1-3 (Jerusalem, 1992).

[15] See further, Marilyn Finkelman, "Self-Defense and Defense of Others in Jewish Law: The Rodef Defense," *Wayne State Law Review* 33 (1987): 1257.

[16] See, e.g., *People v. Drelich*, 506 N.Y.S.2d 746 124, A.D.2d 441 (2d App. Div. 1986).

[17] One other significant power is present, which is the religious authority to exclude people from the privileges Jewish law mandates that one adherent extend to another. For example, in a society where the secular law does not mandate that one return lost property to its rightful owner, Jewish law directs that one nonetheless return such property to a fellow Jew who observes Jewish law. This type of privilege also can be used to create communities and exclude individuals. This author has argued elsewhere that these privileges are in fact quite similar in purpose—to create a community committed to a similar level of observance— to excommunication, but are used on a much higher level. See Michael J. Broyde and Michael Hecht, "The Gentile and Returning Lost Property According to Jewish Law: A Theory of Reciprocity," *Jewish Law Annual* (forthcoming). Thus, as will be shown later in this chapter, excommunication and shunning were used only to prevent public defiance of community norms, whereas these remaining reciprocal privileges were used to distinguish personal observance. This is a quite difficult topic, and the conclusion found in that paper could be contested.

encourage conduct in ways that formal law itself either cannot or will not accomplish. Jewish law and culture was quite aware of that fact, and designed within its legal and ethical system rules that relate to the use of social pressure.

A recent case arising in the rabbinical courts of Israel demonstrates this well, and presents itself as a modern—but classical—example of the power of a Jewish court to order social shunning of a person whose conduct is not in full compliance with the ethical dictates of Jewish society. The Supreme Rabbinical Court in Israel is discussing what to do in a situation where a divorce seems proper, and is desired by the wife, but yet the husband will not co-operate in the processing of the divorce.[18] The court states:

> In the appeal[19] which was presented before us on January 7, 1985, the court did not find sufficient cause to compel[20] the husband to divorce his wife. The Court did, however, try to persuade the man, who is religiously observant, that he follow the proper path and to obey the decision of the court [that it is proper for him to issue the divorce], for it is a good deed to heed the words of the Sages who religiously obliged him to divorce his wife and that he has chained his wife needlessly.[21]

The court gave the husband an extension of three months within which to grant a divorce to his wife. However, when the Court saw that three months passed without a response, they declared:

> [W]e instituted the separations of Rabbenu Tam as found in the Sefer HaYashar (*Chelek HaTeshuvot* 24) which states: Decree by force of oath on every Jewish man and woman under your jurisdiction that they not be allowed to speak to him, to host him in their homes, to feed him or give him to drink, to accompany him

---

[18] For more on this topic, see Irwin H. Haut, *Divorce in Jewish Law and Life* (Targum, 1983), 18 and Irving Breitowitz, "The Plight of the Agunah: A Study in Halacha, Contract, and the First Amendment," *Maryland Law Review* 51 (1992): 312.

[19] For a discussion of the appellate process in Jewish law, see Eliav Shochetman, *Civil Procedure in Jewish Law* (Jerusalem, 1994), 443-71.

[20] In Jewish divorce law, a court has three choices. It can compel the issuing of a divorce (and in such a situation, Jewish law would allow court-ordered compulsion to force a bill of divorce to be written). However, there are few grounds for such an order—essentially adultery or serious marital misconduct. Alternatively, a court can rule that one is "religiously obliged" to participate in a divorce. In such a situation, judicial force cannot be used. The grounds for such an order are numerous, and that was the order in this case. Finally, it can rule that a divorce is not mandated by Jewish law, and should only be given with the full and complete consent of both parties. See generally *Shulchan Aruch Even Haezer*, 154.

[21] Jewish courts, unlike common law courts, not only decide cases but give moral advice based on the teachings of Jewish law and ethics. See Menachem Elon, *Jewish Law: History Sources, Principles IV* (Philadelphia, 1994), 1863-71.

or to visit him when he is ill. . . .

> We added to these strictures that no sexton of any synagogue in the area where the husband resides be allowed to seat him in the synagogue, or call him to the Torah, or ask after his welfare, or grant him any honor. All people are to distance themselves from him as much as possible until his heart submits and he heeds to voices of those instructing him that he grant his wife a divorce.

> And so it was done, at which time the husband submitted and granted his wife a divorce.[22]

This case involved the use of the communal sanction of mild shunning to encourage a person who wished to be part of the religious community in Israel[23] to obey the mandates of Jewish law and ethics. A person who felt no desire to belong to the community, and thus was not threatened by the possibility of exclusion from it, would not have reacted in the manner this person did. The sanction would have had no effect.

One should not think that such methods of persuasion occur only in Israel. For example, in the case of *Grunwald v. Bornfreund*[24] the plaintiff sought an injunction from a United States District Court prohibiting the "Central Rabbinical Congress of the United States and Canada, its Rabbinical Court and its members (the 'Rabbinical Congress'), and defendants from making any efforts to have plaintiff withdraw his action from this Court and submit it to a rabbinical or ecclesiastical court and from temporarily or permanently excommunicating plaintiff, his counsel, and staff."[25] Modern rabbinical courts can and do excommunicate. Indeed, excommunication and its lesser cousin, shunning, remain valid expres-

---

[22] Like many opinions of the Supreme Rabbinical Court, this case was initially published as part of the Responsa literature of its judges, see Rabbi Obadiah Yosef, *Yabia Omer*, VII:23 (Jerusalem, 1993) (Even HaEzer) and Rabbi Eliezer Waldenberg, *Tzitz Eliezer*, VII:53 (Jerusalem, 1989).

[23] Note how the court states: "We did, however, try to persuade the man, *who is religiously observant*, that he follow the proper path and to obey the decision of the court, for it is a mitzvah to heed the words of the Sages who obliged him to divorce his wife. . . ." *Yabia Omer* VII: 23 (emphasis added).

[24] 696 F. Supp. 838 (E.D.N.Y 1988).

[25] The affidavit submitted described the consequences of this excommunication as follows: "plaintiff may be totally excluded from the community, he will not be able to shop at the stores of members of the community, his zizzitt, a fringed garment worn by observant Jews, may be cut off, the mezuzah, religious verses in a container, may be removed from his door, and there will be no religious prohibition on injury to his property or, indeed, his murder." Ibid. at 839. The movant's affidavit is clearly incorrect as a matter of Jewish law. As noted by the Court, it mixes the legal sanctions for excommunication with that of informing, a far more serious violation of Jewish law and ethics. The Jewish tradition simply excluded people when excommunication was ordered. No other penalty should be imposed.

sions of religious will within the Jewish community to this very day, and they are used to express communal disdain for a person's actions.

The Power and Purpose of Exclusion. The Talmud discusses the legal rules related to shunning in some detail,[26] and over time the legal rules have grown in detail and purpose.[27] One overarching theme emerges from the legal discussion: unlike the many forms of punishment found in classical Jewish law, the purpose of the exclusion process is to deter future violations of Jewish law—primarily by other members of society, but also by the excluded person. Punishment and retribution as aims were not thought to be part of the process, as they were in classical Jewish criminal law.[28]

Any analysis of the rules relating to excluding people raises two questions. First, may one shun or excommunicate a person when the shunning process might (or will) drive this person completely away from the religious community or religious observance?[29] Second, may one shun or exclude the relatives of a person in order to encourage the person to cease his or her activities? These two questions are central to the seminal issue of this chapter: *what is the purpose of excluding people from the community?*

The problem of excluding people from the community when they will abandon religious observance in response is part of a very important discussion as to whom Jewish law is seeking to deter through the process of excommunication. Is it the person who is flaunting community standards, or is it the community at large that will witness the person's exile from the community, and thus be deterred? If it is the former, then one does not shun a person who will abandon the faith when shunned. If it is

---

[26] Babylonian Talmud *Mo'ed Katan* 14b-17b.

[27] Perhaps one could suggest that as other remedies were abolished in response to societal concerns, the uses of exclusion to form a community increased. Thus, it is quite reasonable that Rabbi Asher ben Yecheil (Spain, 1300s) can essentially abandon the use of exclusion as a punishment (see *Responsa of Asher* 43:9) as the Jewish community in Spain at that time had criminal jurisdiction over the Jewish community, including the statutory authority to execute. See *Responsa of Asher* 17:1 (Jerusalem, 1991); *Responsa of Yehuda ben Asher*, 75 (New York, 1957).

[28] See generally Elon, *Principles of Jewish Law*, 469-475.

[29] At first glance this might seem like a peculiar question. After all, is not the goal of excommunication to remove the person from the community? It is clear that in Talmudic times that was not the goal. For example, the great sage, Rabbi Eliezer was excommunicated by the Talmudic Sages for defiance of the majority on a particular issue. Notwithstanding his excommunication, he remained one of the premier Talmudic scholars of his time, to whom other scholars went to hear lecture—all the while making sure that they stayed more than four cubits away from him, as required by Jewish law. He was excommunicated to indicate that his view on a particular topic was wrong, and his defiance was unacceptable. However, he clearly remained in the faith-group of rabbinic Judaism. For more on this, see *Bava Metzia* 59a-b.

the latter, then that factor is not relevant. Indeed, this discussion reflects the ultimate reality concerning all shunning cases: in modern times and in democratic countries, the penalty of exclusion works on the one being shunned only if the person desires the approbation of the faith that is excluding him or her.

This fact itself reflects a profound historical change in the purpose of excluding people from the community. Classical Jewish law held "that a person on whom an excommunication ban lies can be regarded as dead."[30] Indeed, flogging was perceived as a more merciful punishment than excommunication in classical Jewish law.[31] In a closed and tightly knit community, surrounded by a generally hostile society, exclusion from the Jewish community was a very severe penalty. Many classical Jewish law authorities would thus not shun or excommunicate under any circumstances.[32] This has changed in post-emancipation times. As noted by a secular critic: "Shunning and excommunication became so common in the later centuries that they no longer made any impression and lost their force [to the uncommitted]. They became the standard rabbinic reaction to all forms of deviation or non-conformity considered incompatible with or dangerous to Orthodoxy. As such, they are sometimes imposed by extreme Orthodox authorities at the present day, but as neither the person afflicted nor the public at large regard them as bound by them, they have ceased to be a terror or have much effect."[33] Particularly today, a person who is shunned can simply leave the community and join a different community adhering to different religious principles.

Rabbi Moses Isserless, one of the codifiers of Jewish law, writing in his glosses on *Shulchan Aruch*, resolves the issue of the purpose of exclusion by stating:

> We excommunicate or shun a person who is supposed to be excommunicated or shunned, even if we fear that because of this, he will bring himself to other evils [such as leaving the faith].[34]

---

[30] Elon, *Principles of Jewish Law*, 543.

[31] Jacob ben Asher, *Tur Yoreh Deah* 334 (Jerusalem, 1992).

[32] See Rabbi Jacob Moellin, *Minhagai Maharil*, 34 (Jerusalem, 1991).

[33] Haim Cohen, quoted by Elon, *Principles of Jewish Law*, 544. It is worth noting that (notwithstanding their ineffectiveness) the British Mandate law governing Palestine appeared to outlaw these pronouncements as a form of criminal conspiracy; see *Criminal Ordinances of Palestine* Sect. 36. I am inclined to disagree with Cohen's thesis as to the cause of the ineffectiveness of the current penalties. While Cohen appears to maintain that the penalty became ineffective because of overuse by the "extreme Orthodox," I am inclined to maintain that the penalty became ineffective due to the emancipation and the general change in social status of the Jewish community. Once one can legally move out of the Jewish district/ghetto and avoid the community's sanction, excommunication becomes a much weaker penalty.

[34] *Yoreh Deah* 334:1.

The rationale for this is explained clearly by later authorities. The purpose of the shunning or excommunication is to serve notice to the members of the community that this conduct is unacceptable, and also, secondarily, to encourage the violator to return to the community. In a situation where these two goals cannot both be accomplished, the first takes priority over the second.[35] This is true even in situations where there is a reasonable possibility that the person will leave the Jewish faith completely and simply abandon any connection with the community to avoid the pressures imposed on him. The shunning and excommunication can be said to have accomplished its goals in such a situation— even if the shunned person continues in the path of defiance and leaves the faith community.[36] Not unexpectedly, the vast majority of civil suits related to excommunication involved people who have left the faith community in response to their exclusion.

It is worth noting that there is a minority opinion to the contrary which rules that one should not shun or excommunicate a person who will leave rather than be excommunicated. Rabbi David Halevi, writing in his commentary *Turai Zahav*, states that he disagrees with the approach of Rabbi Isserless, and in his opinion it is prohibited to shun a person when one suspects that the person shunned will withdraw from the Jewish community in response.[37] However, many commentators, while noting his remarks, make a crucial distinction as to why people might be excluded. They note that while as a matter of theory one could be shunned or excommunicated merely for violating any law, or even for avoiding a financial obligation,[38] in fact, that is not how and why exclusion is used. Exclusion, these authorities state, is used as a deterrent, to

---

[35] See comments of Rabbi Shabtai ben Meir Hacohen, *Nekudat Hakesef*, 334:1; Rabbi Yair Bachrach, *Responsa Chavat Yair*, 141 (Jerusalem, 1968); Rabbi Yakov Emden, *Responsa Yavetz*, 1:79 (Lemberg, 1887); Rabbi Avraham Yitzchak Kook, *Da'at Cohen, Yoreh Deah* 194 (Jerusalem, 1983); Rabbi Moses Feinstein, *Iggrot Moshe Yoreh Deah*, 1:53, OC 2:33 (New York, 1959); Rabbi Yizchak Isaac Herzog, *Hechal Yitzchak OC*, 30(3) (Jerusalem, 1961) and *Pitchai Teshuva* commenting on *Yoreh Deah*, 334(1).

[36] These dual goals of shunning and excommunication are found in religions other than Judaism. For example, a recent court case discussed the process of withdrawal of fellowship from the Church of Christ. It noted: "Withdrawal of fellowship is a disciplinary procedure that is carried out by the entire membership in a Church of Christ congregation. When one member has violated the church's code of ethics and refuses to repent, the elders read aloud to the congregation those scriptures which were violated. The congregation then withdraws its fellowship from the wayward member by refusing to acknowledge that person's presence. *According to the Elders, this process serves a dual purpose: it causes the transgressor to feel lonely and thus to desire repentance and a return to fellowship with the other members; and secondly, it ensures that the church and its remaining members continue to be pure and free from sin.*" *Guinn v. The Church of Christ of Collinsville*, 775 P.2d 766 n.2 (Okl. 1989) (emphasis added).

[37] Commenting on *Yoreh Deah*, 334:1.

[38] Indeed, this is quite clearly stated in *Shulchan Aruch Yoreh Deah*, 334:1.

prevent other people from violating the law, and is no longer used as a method of punishment. Thus, these authorities note that Rabbi Halevi's point is true, but inapplicable. In a case where a person is violating the law, and the punishment imposed will drive him further away—but there is no other community value at stake—it might be that Rabbi Halevi's point is correct that it is prohibited to punish by exclusion. However, such is no longer the purpose of shunning and excommunication; inevitably, more is at stake than this single person's violation.[39]

The process of shunning or excommunicating individuals relates not solely to their violation of religious law, but also to their apparent status as members of the community in good standing. For example, Jewish law reserves the right, as a matter of jurisdiction, to assert that any Jew who willfully deviates from Jewish law may be excluded. However, the law is established that such shunning or excommunication does not, in fact, occur unless it is actually pronounced by a Jewish court, and such pronouncements are not forthcoming unless the person started as a member of the faith community and now is publicly deviating from it in a way designed to hinder communal organization.[40] Thus, in modern times vast numbers of Jews are distant from any version of traditional Judaism, happy with that status, and yet are not under any decree of excommunication;[41] the few who are excluded, appear to be people who are deeply insiders within the faith but yet are actively dissenting.[42]

The legal status of a "non-member" of the Jewish community is considerably better than that of one who joins and is expelled or wishes to leave.[43] This is consistent with the essential purpose of shunning and ex-

---

[39] Indeed, this remark is part of a broader posture of modern Jewish law that the punishment of criminals for any reason other than deterrence of future crime is no longer within the jurisdiction of Jewish law. Just as the pursuer rationale permits only the use of force to prevent crime, and not to punish it, so too, the essential goal of the shunning process is to deter future violations (either by this person or others). It is not to punish.

[40] See *Shulchan Aruch* 334:12 and commentaries ad locum; see also comments *of Nekudat HaKessef* on *Taz Yoreh Deah*, 334(1).

[41] For a discussion of levels of observance in the Jewish community, see Harold Dellapergola and Uziel Schmelz, "Demography and Jewish Education in the Diaspora," in H. Himmelfarb and S. DellaPergola, eds., *Jewish Education Worldwide: Cross Cultural Perspectives* (Lanham, MD, 1989), 43, 55.

[42] Thus, for example, the three court cases discussed in this paper that address legal aspects of excommunication within the Jewish tradition all are clearly concerned with insiders who are flouting the will of the community, and yet wish to remain part of that community.

[43] Within the Jewish tradition, one who was never part of the community almost inevitably has the status of a "child who was kidnapped" from the faith, and is thus excused from any penalty for his violation based on his complete lack of familiarity with the faith. The Jewish tradition directs that one must befriend such persons to bring them closer to the faith; certainly such people cannot be shunned. See further Maimonides, *Mamrim*, 3:3 and Rabbi Abraham Isaiah Karletz, *Chazon Ish, Yoreh Deah*, 1(6), 2(160), and 2(28) (Bena Brak, 1962).

communication in the Jewish tradition—to establish a religious community. Non-members do not disrupt such a community: dissenters do.[44]

The second issue that needs to be addressed within the Jewish tradition is whether one may shun the relatives of a person in order to encourage the person to cease his disruptive activities. This situation also crystallizes the purpose of this treatment. As a general matter, classical Jewish law prohibits punishing an innocent person as a way of punishing another person for a violation of the law.[45] Thus, the question is whether shunning is really a form of punishment, or is it some other type of activity not bound by the jurisprudential rules of punishment?

Once again, Rabbi Isserless adopts the legal rule that posits that punishment is not the goal. He states:

> It is within the power of a Jewish court to order [as part of a shunning] that a violator's children not be circumcised, that his dead not be buried, that his children be expelled from the school, and that his wife be removed from the synagogue until he accepts the ruling of the court.[46]

Thus, Rabbi Isserless endorses exclusion not only of those who defy the community, but also recognizes that people can be excluded from the community when their inclusion, through no fault of their own, will prevent the formation of the community.[47] Letting the close family of an excluded person participate in the religious sub-community—using its synagogue, cemetery, or schools—still allows the "excluded" person to be part of the community although he is "excluded."

This is, by no means, the only ruling, possible. Commenting on this phrase, Rabbi David Halavi, writing in his classical commentary Turai Zahav, states: "Heaven forbid this. The world is only in existence because of the studies of children in school. It makes sense to prohibit circumcising children, as that obligation is solely the father's;[48] the same is true for burying his dead. . . . However, studying by children has no restitution. . . . So, too, to exclude his wife from the synagogue is impro-

---

[44] This is hinted at in Robert Bear's recounting of his exclusion from the Reformed Mennonite Church. He states "Because I have been excommunicated I am considered to be more sinful than if I had never known 'the truth'." Robert Bear, *Delivered Unto Satan* (Philadelphia, 1974), 10.

[45] Deuteronomy 24:16.

[46] *Yoreh Deah*, 334:6, quoting from a responsa of Rav Palti Gaon (9th century).

[47] It is important to realize that Rabbi Isserless is not discussing the exclusion of the relative who assists in the disruption. Rather he permits the exclusion from the community of people who, if allowed to remain, will cause disruption through their mere presence.

[48] Until children reach adulthood, the primary obligation to circumcise is limited to the father; see *Shulchan Aruch Yoreh Deah*, 360:1.

per; if he sinned, what was her sin?"[49] Clearly this approach assumes that excommunication and shunning are a form of judicial punishment, subject to the general rules regulating the fairness and propriety of any punishment. This ruling is consistent with Rabbi Halavi's analysis, discussed above, which prohibited exclusion when the person will leave the community in retaliation. It is predicated on a judicial model of exclusion bound by the rules of punishment.

Rabbi Isserless, and those authorities who follow his view, simply assume that the normal rules regulating judicial punishment do not apply in the case of shunning and excommunication—not because on a practical level the innocent person is unhurt, but because on a philosophical level, exclusion is not punishment. Rabbi Hershel Schachter, agreeing with Rabbi Isserless's ruling, states that the one being shunned "would agree to obey the law, in the particular area which he is remiss, in order to afford his wife and children a proper religious environment. *Using the children as leverage is not to be confused with punishing them unjustly.*"[50]

The question is why is leverage not to be confused with punishment? Certainly the children or spouse would feel that they are—for all apparent purposes—being punished. Rabbi Schachter's point goes to the purpose of the shunning or excommunication, rather than to its apparent impact—to compel communal cohesiveness and to exclude people who prevent it. In a situation where shunning relatives would have no impact on the conduct of the principal and would not.admit the person to the community, such conduct is prohibited.[51]

In summary, Jewish law has an institution called shunning and excommunication whose goal is to exclude from the community people who seek to dissent from central tenets of the community. However, it is not used as a form of punishment and does not have its origins in any judicial institutions. It is designed to encourage people to conform to communal norms or cease to be part of the religious sub-community.[52]

---

[49] Actually, he is quoting from the works of the Rabbi Shlomo Luria, *Yam Shel Shlomo*, a major scholar of Jewish law who lived two generations prior to Rabbi Halevi.

[50] Rabbi Hershel Schachter, "Synagogue Membership and School Admission," *Journal of Halacha and Contemporary Society* 12(50) (1986): 64 (emphasis added).

[51] Ibid.

[52] This raises the issue of recognized diversity within a particular religious faith. Within Judaism there are certain well-established differences of practice, custom, and law that are based on the historical separation and isolation of certain geographical groups. Thus, for example, there are Eastern European Jews, commonly called *Ashkenazim* and Oriental Jews, commonly called *Sefardim*; these two groups have their own customs, and frequently also their own laws, that govern many matters. There is a considerable body of literature discussing the establishment of practices within the community when the "community" is made up of members with different customs, traditions and laws.

Shunning: For What Offenses. Having established the legal basis for shunning and excommunication, it is now necessary to determine the offenses that merit such exclusion. As noted above, the theoretical Talmudic law is clear: "[O]ne who violates any prohibition may be shunned."[53] That is, however, only the beginning of the rule. One of the commentators immediately notes that this is limited to a situation where the person has already been formally warned that his public conduct violated Jewish law.[54] So, too, one may not excommunicate or shun a person who unintentionally violated Jewish law; indeed, one may not—Jewish law rules—shun a person who is aware of what the rule of law is, tries to observe it, and occasionally slips.[55]

The classical code lists specific offenses for which shunning is proper. All involve breaches of community discipline. For example, the classical code lists as one who ought to be shunned a person who denigrates a community scholar, or an agent of the Jewish court while he is doing his job, or a person who mocks—not who violates—one of the rules of Jewish law. Other offenses include desecration of God's name[56] or refusing to accept the jurisdiction of the Jewish court system.[57] Such offenses hinder

---

In a nutshell, Jewish law recognizes not only the right of a community to exclude people from the sub-society who are in deviation from the basic tenets of the community in violation of Jewish law, but also to compel members of a different recognized Jewish community to adhere to the norms of the majoritarian Jewish practice in the community where they reside. Thus, for example, a Jew of Eastern European descent who would normally follow the rites and laws of the *Ashkenazic* Jewish community must publicly follow the strictures of the Oriental (*Sefardic*) community were he to reside in such a community. Of course, Jewish law would recognize the right of this person to form his own community following the Ashkenazic rite when a mass of such people were present. However, the Jewish tradition clearly grants to the majority community the right to insist that all of the participants in its community adhere to the same public rites on significant issues—or leave the community to form its own religiously separate community (which is perfectly proper). It matters not at all whether the deviation from communal norm is one that is "historically legitimate" or not. For a recent Hebrew work on the issue of interactions between various communities in Israel, see Tal Doar, *Tal Amarti* (Jerusalem, 1992), 1-26.

[53] *Shulchan Aruch, Yoreh Deah,* 234:1.

[54] See comments of Rabbi Shabtai ben Meir Hacohen, *Seftai Cohen, Yoreh Deah,* 334:2.

[55] *Shulchan Aruch, Yoreh Deah* 334:38, and see comments of Rabbi David Halevi (*Taz*), n.18. The classical example of that is the case of a person who is aware that it is wrong to use God's name in vain, generally abstains from so doing, but occasionally in moments of frustration does so. Such a person cannot be excluded.

[56] *Yoreh Deah,* 334:43.

[57] A Jewish court would not order exclusion as an economic remedy for such a violation—indeed, it cannot. See *Shulchan Aruch Chosen Mishpat* 13. It would only order exclusion if the one who lost the case defied the court and declined to implement the economic remedy ordered by the Jewish court. In that case, exclusion might be ordered; it, however, is not an economic remedy, but rather a form of contempt of court, whose punishment bears no relationship to the underlining issues in the case.

the creation or maintenance of a community, and can destroy the community if not stopped.

The Jewish tradition thus differs significantly from various Christian practices of using shunning to enforce observance of the details of the law and to supervise the private conduct of its members. That was never its use in the Jewish tradition. Adultery, polytheism, Sabbath violations, ritual violations, and other central tenets of the faith, which were grounds for excommunication from the Christian community, were never subject to shunning by the Jewish tradition unless the person engaged in this conduct in a public manner intended to indicate defiance of the Jewish tradition.

The differences between Jewish and Christian views of shunning can be seen in cases brought before American courts by disgruntled excommunicants. While there are a wealth of American tort cases involving shunning and excommunication by various Christian denominations, these are categorically different from excommunication cases involving Jewish law. A brief summary of the allegations contained in these cases is itself worthwhile, as it highlights uses by different faiths of exclusion and excommunication. Of the reported American cases[58] that deal directly with a suit related to an excommunication or a shunning by a Christian denomination, four allege that a religious denomination publicized the sexual practices of one of its congregants or former congregants in the process of excommunication.[59] Four cases allege alienation of affection from spouses based on religiously-motivated abandonment because of one partner's lack of observance which resulted in excommunication.[60] Three cases allege that the church engaged in financial slander against a member when it publicized an alleged fiscal impropriety of the member in the process of excommunication.[61] Four cases allege financial

---

[58] As of September 1, 1994, on Westlaw.

[59] *Guinn*, 775 P. 2d at 775 (excommunication based on fornication); *Ventimiglia v. Sycamore View Church of Christ*, 1988 WL 119288 (Tenn. Ct. App. 1988) (excommunication resulting from adultery); *Hadnot v. Shaw*, 826 P.2d 978 (Okla., 1992) (excommunication based on fornication); *Synder v. Evangelical Orthodox Church*, 264 Cal. Rptr. 640, 216 Cal. App. 3d 297 (Cal. Ct. App. 1989) (excommunication based on adultery).

[60] *Hester v. Barnett*, 723 S.W.2d 544 (Miss. Ct. App. 1987) (alienation of affections suit resulting from excommunication ordered by pastor); *O'Neil v. Schuckardt*, 733 P.2d 693 (Idaho 1986) (alienation of affections suit resulting from excommunication ordered by denomination); *Radecki v. Schuckardt*, 361 N.E. 543 (Oh. Ct. App. 1976) (same); *Carrieri v. Bush*, 419 P.2d 132 (Wash. 1966) (alienation of affections suit resulting from excommunication ordered by church).

[61] *Molko v. Holy Spirit Association for the Unification of World Christianity*, 252 Cal.Rptr 122 46 Cal. 3d 1092, 762 P.2d 46 (1988) (allegation of financial fraud as the cause of an excommunication); *Bear v. Reformed Mennonite Church*, 462 Pa. 330, 341 A.2d 105 (1975) (financial ruin resulting from allegation of fraud leading to excommunication); *Lide v. Whittington*, 573

claims relating to misappropriating church funds by church officials, resulting in excommunication by the one alleging the impropriety (or otherwise protesting a fiscal practice of the church).[62] Two cases deal with excommunications as a result of attempts to fire the pastor.[63] Only in one case does the plaintiff pose a general challenge to the practice of shunning without a specific allegation of impropriety.[64] The cases reflect both the routineness of the excommunication process in these denominations, and its general use as a method of governance in the community.

The only two American cases that discuss the Jewish excommunication process reflect the different interest associated with the Jewish use of excommunication. In one case, a member of a Chasidic Jewish community was suing the educational institution of his community alleging systemic corruption on the part of the institution against the government and various students.[65] He was excommunicated for bringing forth that violation.[66] The second case involved a witness in a grand jury proceeding who was set to testify against a Jewish institution, alleging systemic fraud by the institution. He wished to avoid testifying, based on the fact that he would be excommunicated if he did so.[67] Both of these cases raises the specter of "community issues" that go far beyond the question of the propriety of an individual person's conduct. These cases are typical of the issues that result in removal from the community. *Exclusion is not for the "garden variety" sin in the Jewish tradition.*

Indeed, the differing approaches to exclusion reflect a deeper difference concerning the more general issue of non-compliance with religious obligations by members of one's faith. How does a faith go about forming its own sub-community? Does it, as the Church of Christ does, seek only to have the already committed join the faith, and then use the proc-

---

S.W.2d 614 (Tex. Ct. App. 1978) (excommunication resulting from an allegation of business misconduct and slander).

[62] *Lozanoski v. Sarafin*, 485 N.E.2d 669 (Ind. App. 1985) (excommunication resulting from church financial dispute); *Macedonia Baptist Foundation v. Singleton*, 379 So.2d 269 (La. App. 1979) (excommunication resulting from inter-church dispute about fund-raising matters); *Davis v. Church of Jesus Christ of Latter Day Saints*, 258 Mont. 286, 852 P.2d 640 (Mont. 1993) (allegation of fraud and breach of fiduciary duty leading to excommunication resulting from medical injury in a church building); *St. John's Greek Catholic Hungarian Russian Orthodox Church of Rahway v. Fedak*, 96 N.J.Super. 556, 233 A.2d 663 (N.J.Super. A.D. 1967) (excommunication resulting from property dispute in church).

[63] *Bowen v. Green*, 275 S.C. 431, 272 S.E.2d 433 (S.C. 1980) (excommunication resulting from attempt to fire pastor); *Bentley v. Shanks*, 48 Tenn.App. 512, 348 S.W.2d 900 (Tenn. App. 1960) (excommunication resulting from firing of pastor).

[64] *Paul v. Watchtower Bible and Tract Society of New York, Inc.*, 819 F.2d 875 (9th Cir. 1987) (excommunication resulting from disfellowship of parents).

[65] *Grunwald*, 696 F. Supp. at 838.

[66] Ibid., 839.

[67] *In re Fuhrer*, 419 N.Y.S. 426 (1979).

ess of shunning and excommunication to enforce discipline among the already committed?[68] Or does it adopt the policy of the modern Catholic Church which automatically excommunicates for serious violations, and in addition, reserves the right to excommunicate for political or public defiance of the church.[69] Classical Judaism adopted neither of these policies. It excommunicated *only* for public violations of the law and only when these violations were designed to undermine the community or the ability to form a community. Thus, as a general matter, Jewish communities are made up of people of various levels of observance. Shunning and excommunication are not used as a method to encourage observance, but to exclude people from the community who did not accept and vocally disagreed with the communitarian tenets of the group.

Exclusion and Secular Law

The choices a religion makes concerning the exclusion policy it enforces affect the nature of the community that is formed. So too, does the secular law of the society it lives in. The next section of this article will address the impact of American, British, and Canadian law on Jewish (and, by comparison, other religious) doctrines concerning exclusion.

Exclusion and American Tort Law. Religious doctrines do not live in a vacuum. The way American tort law rewards or punishes certain behavior—including religious behavior—affects the frequency and form of the behavior. As the United States Court of Appeals for the Ninth Circuit put it: "Permitting prosecution of a cause of action in tort, while not criminalizing the conduct at issue, would make shunning an 'unlawful act.' Imposing tort liability for shunning on the Church or its members would in the long run have the same effect as prohibiting the practice and would compel the Church to abandon part of its religious teachings."[70] Jewish communities frequently confronted this issue in Eastern

---

[68] *Guinn*, 775 P.2d at 768-69.

[69] Thomas J. Green, "Future of Penal Law in the Church," *The Jurist* 35 (1975): 212-275. See generally, The National Conference of Catholic Bishops, *Resolution of National Conference of Catholic Bishops* (Washington, 1989) and Ari L. Goldman, "O'Connor Warns Politicians Risk Excommunication Over Abortion," *New York Times* (June 15, 1990): A1, B2 ("Catholics in public office must also have this commitment to serve the state; but service to God must always come first.").

[70] *Paul*, 819 F.2d at 877. There are a few examples of excommunications having unquestioned secular law consequences. One such case is *Borntrager v. Commissioner*, 58 T.C.M. (CCH) 1242 (1990) which involved the rights of an excommunicated member of the Old Order Amish to keep his religious exemption from Social Security benefits, taxes or even having a Social Security number. The court ruled that the statutory exemption of the Amish was at least in part based on the Amish community's self-sufficiency in caring for its members; since Borntrager was no longer a member in good standing in the Amish community, and would

Europe, whose governments generally outlawed the use of excommunication and shunning. Not surprisingly, when confronted with significant governmentally-imposed sanctions against this practice, the Jewish authorities ceased using exclusion as a method of community formation or maintenance.[71]

American cases on excommunication and shunning have raised two related issues: (1) may courts impose damages against religious communities for torts such as the intentional infliction of emotional distress that impose liability for a plaintiff's non-physical damages, such as alienation of affection or interference with a contractual relationship? or (2) do the First Amendment religion clauses immunize religious groups from such tort suits? These two doctrines are the counterbalances that form American tort law in this area.

The reader is entitled to one caveat. The religious parameters relating to excommunication and shunning differ from religion to religion. It is vitally important to grasp that these same terms mean drastically different forms of treatment towards shunned and excommunicated individuals depending on the faith group. For example, the Church of Scientology of California at one point—and perhaps still[72]—adopted a policy of "fair game" towards individuals who are excommunicated. One court described the doctrine as follows: "Under Scientology's 'fair game' policy, someone who threatened Scientology by leaving the church may be deprived of property or injured by any means by a Scientologist. . . . [The targeted defector] may be tricked, sued or lied to or destroyed."[73] The state interest in protecting an excluded member from such practices clearly is greater than the interest in protecting a person from the more common version of religious shunning, which the Ninth Circuit described as follows: "Members of the Jehovah's Witness community are prohibited—under threat of their own disfellowship [shunning]—from

---

not be assisted by the Amish communal welfare system should he need it, he is not entitled to social security exemption.

[71] For a Jewish law discussion of the issues raised by a governmental ban on excommunication, see Rabbi Yecheil Michael Epstein, *Aruch HaShulchan Yoreh Deah* 334 (preface and section 42) (Habokin, 1992). In my opinion, the material in the preface is not an authentic representation of the position of Jewish law, but was placed there for the purpose of permitting the publication of the work in response to censorship by the Czarist government. An examination of the *Aruch HaShulchan Choshen Mishpat* indicates that this was his method of speaking exclusively to the censor. His actual explanation for the legal basis for not using the power to exclude when prohibited by the secular government from using it, is found in *Yoreh Deah* 334:42, buried among other issues in a way that the censor, most likely not completely familiar with Hebrew, would not find.

[72] See *Hart v. Cult Awareness Network*, 13 Cal. App. 4th 777, 16 Cal. Rptr.2d 705 (Cal. Ct. App. 1993) which discusses the doctrine of "fair game" in some detail.

[73] *Wollershein v. Church of Scientology*, 212 Cal. App. 3rd; 260 Cal. Rptr. 331 (1989) (brackets are in the original opinion).

having any contact with disfellowshiped persons and may not even greet them. Family members who do not live in the same house may conduct necessary family business with disfellowshiped relatives but may not communicate with them on any other subject."[74] Indeed, this is similar to the manner a person would be treated if excluded from the Jewish community, which sought to punish only through the removal from the community.[75]

The numerous cases that address the problems of religious exclusion, shunning and excommunication apply one of three categories of legal rules. First, some courts hold as a matter of law that religious discipline can never be actionable when the disciplined member remains a member of the religious organization that is disciplining him or her.[76] In this theory, consent proves to be the underlying defense to allegations of tortious misconduct by a religious organization. Absent membership in the faith, or after withdrawal from membership, the activities of the church are no different from any other organization in terms of tort law treatment.[77]

The essential failure of this theory, in my opinion, is that it focuses on the status of the person being injured and misses one of the fundamental purposes of church discipline: to inform the faithful that a person's conduct violated the religion's tenets, and thus they have been excluded.[78] To allow lawsuits, particularly for the intentional infliction of emotional distress or similar torts for the use of this information (even after resig-

---

[74] *Paul*, 819 F.2d at 877. The court went on to describe how such a person would be treated: "[A shunned person] visited her parents, who at that time lived in Soap Lake, Washington. There, she approached a Witness who had been a close childhood friend and was told by this person: 'I can't speak to you. You are disfellowshiped.' Similarly, in August 1984, [defendant] returned to the area of her former congregation. She tried to call on some of her friends. These people told Paul that she was to be treated as if she had been disfellowshiped and that they could not speak with her. At one point, she attempted to attend a Tupperware party at the home of a Witness. [Defendant] was informed by the Church members present that the Elders had instructed them not to speak with her."

[75] *Shulchan Aruch, Yoreh Deah* 334:2-11. Exclusion in the Catholic canon aw tradition contains within it a number of different levels of varying severity, none of which permit violence against the person. See Green, "Future of Penal Law in the Church."

[76] See *Guinn*, 775 P.2d at 767-69.

[77] See Comment, "Religious Torts: Applying the Consent Doctrine as Definitional Balancing," *University of California at Davis Law Review* 19 (1986): 949, 975-83 for a list of such cases. The earliest of the American cases defends this theory by stating: "[t]hey joined the church, with a knowledge of its defined powers, and as the civil power cannot interfere in matters of conscience, faith or discipline, they must submit to rebuke or excommunication, however unjust, by their adopted spiritual rulers." *Gartin v. Penick*, 68 Ky. (5 Bush) 110, 120 (Ct. App. 1869) (Robertson, J.), quoted in *Chase v. Cheney*, 58 Ill. 509, 539 (1871).

[78] Thus, in *Guinn*, the court held actionable the fact that: "Parishioner was publicly branded a fornicator when the scriptures she had violated were recited to the Collinsville Church of Christ congregation on October 4. As part of the disciplinary process the same information about Parishioner's transgressions was sent to four other area Church of Christ congregations to be read aloud during services." *Guinn*, 775 P. 2d at 768.

nation), deprives the religious organization of its ability to standardize the conduct of its members by publicizing cases of exclusion. The community is formed by publicly establishing norms of conduct. Such cannot be done under this legal rule, since the moment a person resigns from the church, the church loses any ability to announce their exclusion.

Second, some courts have held that the "religiously motivated disciple is entitled to First Amendment Protection and cannot form the basis"[79] for a suit in tort.[80] These courts, including the United States Court of Appeals for the Ninth Circuit, rule that: "Because the practice of shunning is a part of the faith of [a religion], we find that the 'free exercise' provision of the United States Constitution . . . precludes the plaintiff from prevailing. The defendants have a constitutionally protected privilege to engage in the practice of shunning."[81]

The most significant failure of this approach is that it places outside the scope of governmental regulation potentially egregious conduct. Indeed, a very strong case can be made that the current interpretation of the First Amendment does not require that government immunize religion from tort laws that are generally applicable. Whatever the merits of *Employment Division v. Smith*[82] in the context of criminal law, one could see very significant problems developing were religions granted general tort law immunity for all conduct which is religiously directed or compelled.[83] Even limiting such an immunity to "intangible or emotional harm"[84] provides a level of immunity to a religious practice that would leave many uncomfortable and a license to injure enjoyed by no one else. Notwithstanding one commentator's endorsement of this "First Amend-

---

[79] Hayden, "Religiously Motivated Conduct," 642-43

[80] *Paul*, 819 F.2d at 875 and *Burgess v. Rock Creek Baptist Church*, 734 F. Supp. 30 (D.D.C. 1990).

[81] *Paul*, 819 F.2d at 876. I have deleted the court's discussion of the constitutional law of the State of Washington.

[82] 494 U.S. 872 (1990).

[83] Indeed, the United States Supreme Court's ruling in *Employment Division v. Smith*, 494 U.S. 872, 879 (1990), which states that "the right of free exercise does not relieve an individual of the obligation to comply with a 'valid and neutral law of general applicability,'" undercuts the whole validity of *Paul*, which compels a religiously motivated exception to a tort law doctrine. See Douglas Laycock, "The Remnants of Free Exercise," *Supreme Court Review* (1990): 45-46. However, the application of these principles to cases that call for the application of general tort law rules is quite unclear. Indeed, a claim could be made that *Smith* has overruled any dicta to the contrary which implies a heightened governmental deference to religious claims in the face of a neutral state law, such as its tort law. Of course, if tort law doctrines were specifically modified to prohibit a particular religious activity, that would lead to a much stronger First Amendment challenge; see *Church of Lukumi Babalu Aye, Inc. v. City of Hialeah*, 113 S.Ct. 2217 (1993).

[84] *Paul*, 819 F.2d at 883.

ment" approach of complete immunity for religious organizations,[85] the fact remains that the granting of immunity in the face of religiously-motivated tortious conduct can produce profoundly negative consequences.

Third, some courts rule that shunning or excommunication can be—by itself—tortious conduct subject to liability. This theory assumes that the state interest in preventing shunning and excommunication is strong enough to allow state interference in all of these decisions. The first American case to adopt this posture, *Bear v. Reformed Mennonite Church* advanced this argument in its simplest form, arguing that the church's shunning practice[86] "may be an excessive interference within areas of 'paramount state concern,' i.e. the maintenance of marriage and family relationship, alienation of affection, and the tortious interference with a business relationship, which the courts of this Commonwealth may have authority to regulate, even in light of the 'Establishment' and 'Free Exercise' clauses of the First Amendment."[87] Other courts have also agreed with this basic approach, and ruled that shunning and excommunication are actionable conduct even when it is unaccompanied by any other activity.[88]

This approach has the potential to limit vastly the scope of religion's right to self-associate and exclude others. If in fact, as *Bear* rules, the Constitution provides no protection from tort law liability for interfering with a spousal relationship when a minister announces that associating with a particular person—even by that person's spouse—violated the rules of the Faith, tort law has accomplished what no other set of legal rules can do under the Constitution. It has prevented a Faith from announcing its opinion on the ethical conduct of a portion of society, even when the faith makes no attempts to coerce compliance with its doctrines or punish adherents of other faiths.

---

[85] Hayden, "Religiously Motivated Conduct," 653.

[86] The court earlier had described the practice as: "[T]he church and bishops, as part of the excommunication, ordered that all members of the church must 'shun' appellant in all business and social matters. ('Shunning,' as practiced by the church, involves total boycotting of appellant by other members of the church, including his wife and children, under pain that they themselves be excommunicated and shunned.)." Ibid.

[87] *Bear*, 341 A.2d at 105.

[88] *Van Schaick v. Church of Scientology*, 535 F.Supp. 1125 (D.Mass. 1982). This can also be implied from *Christofferson v. Church of Scientology*, 644 P.2d 577 (Or. Ct. App.), petition denied, 650 P.2d 928 (Or. 1982), which held that there was no liability, but implied that liability was possible, as a matter of law. This lack of protection can also be derived from a long line of cases that deny any First Amendment immunity to recruitment practices of faiths; see *Murphy v. I.S.K.Con. of New England, Inc.*, 571 N.E.2d 340 (Mass. 1991); *McNair v. Worldwide Church of God*, 242 Cal. Rptr. 823 (Ct. App. 1987); and *Molko v. Holy Spirit Ass'n*, 762 P.2d 46 (Cal. 1988).

Exclusion and the Financial Ramifications: The British and Canadian Approaches. A much more problematic case of exclusion, and the judicial response to it, occurs when the faith that is doing the excluding bundles religious rights with financial claims. A classical case of that is the division of property by a religious commune when it orders the excommunication of members, and the forfeiture of those members' property rights. There are no United States cases addressing this issue, for the Supreme Court has ruled that ecclesiastical disputes command secular court abstention if called upon to resolve matters of religious belief or governance. As stated in *Serbian Eastern Orthodox Diocese v. Milivojevich*: when "hierarchical religious organizations . . . establish their own rules and regulations for internal discipline and government, and . . . create tribunals for adjudicating disputes over these matters, [then the] . . . Constitution requires that civil courts accept their decisions as binding *upon them.*"[89]

Such is not the case in many other common law countries, which will freely review such determinations. Indeed, an example of the problems faced by a court in such a case can be found in *Lakeside Colony of Hutterian Brethren v. Hofer*, issued by Canadian Supreme Court.[90] In this case, the Court confronted the excommunication (and expulsion) of the Hofer family from a colony of the Hutterian Church of Canada for pressing a patent claim against another colony of the Church. Under relevant Church doctrine, which was codified in the articles of incorporation of the commune, expelled members lost their financial claim to the asserts of the commune.[91] After reviewing the actions of the Church for conformity to Canadian corporate law and adherence to its own associational by-laws, the Supreme Court announced that expulsions from these types of religious associations are also governed by "natural justice." The Court stated: "The content of the principles of natural justice is flexible and depends on the circumstances in which the question arises. However, the most basic requirements are that of [1] notice; [2] opportunity to make

---

[89] *Serbian Eastern Orthodox Diocese v. Milivojevich*, 426 U.S. 696, 724-25 (1976) (emphasis added). While American courts will hear the fiscal aspect of these cases, they will not (and cannot) review, in any form, the ecclesiastical determinations. See also *Jones v. Wolf*, 443 U.S. 595 (1979).

[90] 97 D.L.R. 4th 17; 36 A.C.W.S. (3d) 512 (1992). This case in an appeal from the judgment of the Manitoba Court of Appeal, 77 D.L.R. (4th) 202, 70 Man. R. (2d) 191, 25 A.C.W.S. (3d) 2, dismissing an appeal from a judgment of Ferg J., 63 D.L.R. (4th) 473, 62 Man. R. (2d) 194, 18 A.C.W.S. (3d) 117, declaring that the defendants were no longer members of a Hutterian community and that there excommunication was valid.

[91] The legality of that contractual arrangement had been affirmed in *Hofer v. Hofer*, 13 D.L.R. (3d) 1 (1970). The dissent in this case indicates that this precedent is ripe to "revisit." Ibid., 64.

representations; and [3] an unbiased tribunal."[92] The Court then determined that the notice provided to the excommunicated members by the
Church was insufficient and that the expulsion and excommunication
were thus void. The Court ordered the excommunicated individuals returned to the colony as members.[93]

This Canadian approach to the problems of exclusion is no better, in
my opinion, than its American counterparts. Under the guise of reviewing a property settlement, the court imposed substantive requirements of
"natural justice" that might be completely foreign to any particular religious tradition's system of laws. Based on these laws of "natural justice," the Court will reverse a determination that a particular form of
conduct merited excommunication from a particular religious denomination.[94] These types of judicial determinations should, simply put, be
beyond the scope of any secular court. To allow procedural review of an
ecclesiastical court's determinations in the context of the property rights
of the excommunicated has a certain amount of validity, as that property
ownership issue is at its core secular. However, the question of membership in the colony of the Church should be beyond review of a secular
court. The rights of the faithful to excommunicate for violations of religious doctrine—without conforming to Canadian notions of due process—
would seem to be protected. Any restrictions on that religious right
should be incompatible with freedom of religion and association guaranteed in the Canadian Bill of Rights.[95] One cannot help but recall the
words of the learned Zechariah Chafee who observed: "In very many instances the courts have interfered in these [ecclesiastical disputes], and
consequently have been obliged to write very long opinions on questions
which they could not well understand. The result has often been that the
judicial review of the highest tribunal of the church is really an appeal

---

[92] Ibid., 36

[93] Ibid., 58.

[94] Indeed, the failures of this three-part test of natural justice is recognized in the Canadian Supreme Court's own discussion of the third prong of the test, the requirement of an
unbiased tribunal. The Court stated: "There is no doubt that an unbiased tribunal is one of
the central requirements of natural justice. However, given the close relationship amongst
members of voluntary associations, it seems rather likely that members of the relevant tribunal will have had some previous contact with the issue in question and, given the structure of
a voluntary association, it is almost inevitable that the decision-makers will have at least an
indirect interest in the question. Furthermore, the procedures set out in the rules of the association may often require that certain persons make certain kinds of decisions without allowing for an alternate procedure in the case of bias." Ibid., 37. These issues are even further
compounded when the issues are theological in nature. Is it really possible to produce an
"unbiased tribunal" to discuss an issue of theology?

[95] The dissent correctly noted that the proper way to resolve the property claims of the
excommunicated would be for that group to make a claim "for a division of the assets and
judgment for their share." Ibid., 63-64.

from a learned body to an unlearned body."[96] Such is certainly the case when a court reviews ecclesiastical determinations for conformity with the ethereal requirements of "natural justice."

A better example of how a court should address this type of challenge to exclusion can be found in the case of *Regent v. Chief Rabbi of the United Hebrew Congregations of Great Britain and the Commonwealth (Ex parte Wachmann)*[97] concerning the authority of the Chief Rabbi of Great Britain to defrock a clergyman for sexual misconduct. The clergyman appealed the decision to the Queen's courts, which ruled that the ecclesiastical functions of the Chief Rabbi, in determining who was religiously fit and who was not, were religious in nature and thus not subject to any secular review. This is true, the Court ruled, even though the declaration on the unsuitability of the applicant to occupy a position as a rabbi resulted in the applicant being "unemployable as a rabbi and is stripped of all religious status."[98] The Court spurned the plaintiff's arguments from "natural justice": "[Plaintiff] would be prepared to rely solely upon the common law concept of natural justice [to overturn the decision of the Chief Rabbi]. But it would not always be easy to separate out procedural complaints from consideration of substantive principles of Jewish law which may underlie them."

Jewish law does not recognize the elaborate requirements of natural justice in these types of cases,[99] and the British Court rightly recognized that the exclusion of a person from a particular ecclesiastical function, or an exclusion of a person from a particular faith group, is itself not subject to any judicial review external to the faith that makes that determination.[100] Of course, as noted by the British Court, this determination of ecclesiastical exclusion by the Chief Rabbi would have no relevance to a determination of a breach of contract, or other financial rights and duties

---

[96] Zechariah Chafee, "The Internal Affairs of Associations Not For Profit," *Harvard Law Review* 43 (1930): 993, 1024.

[97] [1993] 2 All ER 249 (QB).

[98] Ibid., 253. This religious status granted him certain rights under British law, including the right to perform marriages.

[99] As there is no "right" to be a congregational rabbi.

[100] Indeed, the essence of plaintiff's claim was that the Chief Rabbi did not conform to the substantive requirements of Jewish law which, in plaintiff's opinion, require that this type of determination be made by three *dayanim*, sitting Jewish law judges, in the context of a formal *beit din*, a Jewish court, and not as an administrative determination by the Chief Rabbi. Ibid., 255. I am inclined to agree with the posture of the Chief Rabbi that such determinations need not be made by a formal *beit din*. The rationale for such an informal procedure is that a determination of actual sexual impropriety and the legal consequences of such conduct can only be made by a Jewish court. However, a rabbi can be defrocked by the much lower mere standard of appearance of impropriety (see Rabbi Moshe Isserless (*Rama*) *Choshen Mishpat*, 25:2), which is an administrative determination. One thing is clear, the British Court correctly realized that the proper standard to use is beyond the determination of the Queen's Bench.

owed by one party to another.[101] Those determinations would be made by the secular courts, independent of the ecclesiastical rules of the Chief Rabbi.

The Value of Excluding. This author is inclined to look at the fundamental values encapsulated by the practices of religious discipline, and determine which of these central values are worthy of governmental protection, and limit the privilege to cases where those values are furthered. As noted, the Jewish tradition recognizes two possible theoretical models for religious discipline: punishment of the offender and formation of a community through exclusion.[102] The Jewish tradition opted for the second model as the jurisprudential basis for its practice of exclusion.

Of these two models, only the second is worthy of tort law immunity and First Amendment protection. Punishment of individuals for violations of the law (religious or otherwise) is to be left to the governmental authorities (and to God). Attempts by religious groups to use their many members or their economic might to punish people for violations should not be protected as a religious value. These are fundamental governmental prerogatives which should not, and may not, be delegated.[103] That is not, of course, to say that such conduct is always tortious; rather, as conduct by a religious group it should have no First Amendment protection. The assertion that a person who is punished by his former co-religionists for a violation of religious law is entitled to any less protection of his rights than others is difficult to support. In one case the court stated: "[Plaintiff] did not suffer his economic harm as an unintended byproduct of his former religionists' practice of refusing to socialize with him any more. Instead he was bankrupted by a campaign his former religionists carefully designed with the specific intent to bankrupt him. Nor was this campaign limited to means which are arguably legal such as refusing to continue working at Wollersheim's business or to purchase his services or products. *Instead the campaign featured a concerted practice of refusing to honor legal obligations . . . owed [plaintiff] for services and products they already had purchased.*"[104]

Religious conduct with the intent to punish—if protected by tort or criminal immunity—delegates to the sectarian community a core governmental authority. As noted by the Supreme Court: "At the time of the

---

[101] *Chief Rabbi*, 2 All ER, 255. In this case the Court seems to find that there was no employment contract, and thus no breach of secular law. Ibid., 255-256.

[102] Subsumed within this second justification is the possibility that the person will repent and wish to return to the community.

[103] See generally *Larkin v. Grendel's Den, Inc.*, 459 U.S. 116 (1982).

[104] *Wollersheim v. Church of Scientology*, 212 Cal. App. 3d 872, 890, 260 Cal. Rptr. 331, 343 (Cal. Ct. App. 1989).

Revolution, Americans feared not only a denial of religious freedom, but also the danger of political oppression through a union of civil and ecclesiastical control."[105] Laurence Tribe in his treatise on American constitutional law elaborates on this problem: "Even if a state ceded power to a church in a way that avoided any ongoing administrative entanglement, the action would be unconstitutional. . . . [Under] the vesting entanglement[106] test, breadth is irrelevant so long as the power remains a traditionally governmental one. . . . Thus, *any* degree of vesting entanglement —not merely excessive entanglement—is prohibited."[107] More generally, government has an interest in preventing religion from punishing people who leave it; absent such protection, the freedoms of the First Amendment appear vacuous. *The right of religious dissent is no less precious than the right of religious conformity.*[108]

In my opinion, a solid middle ground is implied in many of these cases. This middle ground provides a doctrinal basis for discussing secular legal responses to shunning and excommunication that neither protects religious rights to oppress those who scorn or violate the faith, and yet grants legal protection to a faith community's right to form its own insular sub-group and exclude people who violate the rules of the community.

The First Amendment should only protect the right of a faith community to exclude members; thus shunning, excommunication, and other methods of isolation are all protected only when they are used to exclude. However, claims based not on the need of the faith community to exclude, but on its need to convince the "unfaithful" to return, or to punish them for their violation, should be subject to scrutiny of tort and criminal law and enjoy no protection. This approach can be found implicitly in a number of cases, although this distinction is not found as the controlling rule in any single case. For example, in *Guinn*, the Supreme Court of Oklahoma, after ruling that the crucial feature in determining protected status is membership, goes on to note:

---

[105] *Larkin*, 459 U.S. at 126, n.10.

[106] Vesting entanglement is the term used for the problem that results when the government delegates its authority to an ecclesiastical group.

[107] Laurence Tribe, *American Constitutional Law*, 2d ed. (St. Paul, MN, 1988), 1229 (notes omitted, emphasis in original).

[108] This is consistent with Supreme Court precedent which has repeatedly declined to recognize "religious group rights" as a value higher than the aggregate of individual group rights. See *Ohio Civil Rights Commission v. Dayton Christian Schools, Inc.*, 477 U.S. 619 (1986) and *Corporation of the Presiding Bishop v. Amos*, 483 U.S. 327 (1987). For an article arguing that "religious rights should be recognized as of a higher value", see Fredrick Gedicks, "Toward A Constitutional Jurisprudence of Religious Group Rights," *Wisconsin Law Review* (1989): 99.

> For purposes of First Amendment protection, religiously-motivated discipli-
> nary measures that merely exclude a person from communion are vastly dif-
> ferent from those which are designed to control and involve. A church
> clearly is constitutionally free to exclude people without first obtaining their
> consent. But the First Amendment will not shield a church from civil liability
> for imposing its will, as manifested through a disciplinary scheme, upon an
> individual who has not consented to undergo ecclesiastical discipline.[109]

A similar result was reached in *Gruenwald v. Bornfreund*.[110] After discussing the protected status of a mere act of exclusion by any religious
organization, the Court indicates that were the defendant to have proven
that he would suffer "battery, trespass, or theft," or any other tortious act
as a result of the excommunication or other conduct by a religious group,
it would enjoin this conduct.[111]

The virtues of this "middle ground" approach are clear. First, religious adherents must have the right to form their own sub-society. While
the melting pot may be some people's image of an ideal American society, the rights of those who do not wish to melt but wish to keep their
own unique identity must be protected. These people have not only the
right to avoid governmentally-compelled blending, but also to avoid the
internal confusion of allowing multiple voices to speak in the name of its
faith-group. However, granting religious groups unfettered rights to stifle internal dissent creates the possibility that religions will use that right
to compel religious orthodoxy or adherence to its religious norms. Such
action also is contrary to (at the least) the spirit of the First Amendment.
Focusing on the purpose of the exclusionary act forces the courts—and
thus eventually the faiths themselves—to ask why a particular person is
being excluded.[112] Once a clear understanding of why people are ex-

---

[109] *Guinn*, 775 P.2d at 780.

[110] 696 F.Supp. at 839.

[111] Sifton states: "To the extent that the Weg affirmation alleges that plaintiff will suffer
battery, trespass, or theft in the absence of a religious prohibition against those acts, plaintiff
has failed to show that such injury is imminent or likely. The harm which will give rise to an
injunction must be not remote and speculative but actual and imminent."

[112] This fits in well with the purpose of the Restatement also. Once the purpose of the
excommunication is not to hurt or punish the person but simply to exclude him, the tort of
intentional inflection of emotional distress is inapplicable. *Restatement (Second) of Torts* (1965):
46(1) now states: "One who by extreme and outrageous conduct intentionally or recklessly
causes severe emotional distress to another is subject to liability for such emotional distress,
and if bodily harm to the other results from it, for such bodily harm.

"There are three basic elements that must be shown in order to allow a recovery under
this tort: (1) Defendant must have intended to inflict severe emotional distress; (2) The conduct must be 'extreme and outrageous'; (3) severe emotional distress must result."

A religion that announces a violation of its norms of conduct, without any intent to
punish the violator, or otherwise cause that person harm—but whose motives are merely to

cluded is articulated by each faith, tort law can grant or deny protection to those exclusions whose purpose is consistent with the protected First Amendment values of forming a religious sub-community.[113]

Second, this "middle ground" approach is superior in application to any of the three tests found in the various court opinions. It is simply more nuanced than either the blanket First Amendment protection granted by the *Paul* case or the generic non-protection advocated by the *Bear* case. Both of these cases appear to adopt standards that are too easily prone to abuse. *Bear* creates civil liability for core religious functions, and contains the capabilities of destroying any faith's exclusionary policies. Once one allows a civil action for alienation of affection when a minister advises a spouse to leave a marriage on religious grounds (as *Bear* does), there is little sacred religious advice that is not actionable in tort.[114] The potential to destroy religious communities is clear. *Paul* allows religious communities to persecute those who leave a faith. This simply cannot be tolerated in a free society. *Paul* also appears to allow, or at least could be read to allow, such practices as "fair game" or "freeloader debt" that can be used to prevent people from exercising their right to leave a religion and not be part of the community.[115]

More significantly, this test is superior to the more nuanced "consent test" advocated by *Guinn*. There are crucial problems with this test. Most significantly, *Guinn* allows people to be disciplined based on their apparent consent, when they join the Church. While this theory might have a certain amount of validity in a highly organized and well-disciplined church as was the case in *Guinn*, this test has little validity for the many faiths where synagogue or church membership is by no means a commitment to observance of the normative rules of the faith. To assert, for example, that mere membership in the Catholic church would give the local parish the right to publicize who is using a prohibited method of birth control, or membership in a synagogue would give the rabbi the

---

tell the faithful what conduct conforms to the norms of the faith—will never "intend to inflict severe emotional distress" and thus will never be liable under this tort. The purer the religious motives are, the less likely a recovery will be allowed.

[113] Of course, religions with unprotected motives will not likely announce their motives as such. However, once a legal test of purpose is announced, religious exclusion practices—whatever their "true" motives—will have to craft themselves around the fact that excommunication and shunning practices that appear designed to punish will probably not be granted tort law immunity. Eventually, such practices will cease.

[114] Thus, for example, there are situations where Jewish law encourages divorce; indeed, Jewish law categorically prohibits reconciliation in certain circumstances. Accepting the test used in *Bear*, one could easily conclude that a rabbi who informs a congregant of the position of Jewish law, and tells him that the Creator desires him to obey, is liable.

[115] Tribe correctly classifies these rights as "rights of religious autonomy." See Tribe, *American Constitutional Law*, 1154. The crucial insight is autonomy, and not coercion of others.

right to announce who does not keep kosher, misses the fact that these religions do not use membership as a litmus test of full observance. The *Guinn* court has taken a very specific rule of the Church of Christ and turned it into a general rule of law when it should not have.[116]

Moreover, the consent test allows the church to punish violators, even if they clearly do not wish to have that done against them. The whole notion of consent, even in a situation where the church uses membership as a litmus test of observance, is suspect. Thus, even in *Guinn*, it is clear from the facts of that case, that the woman did not wish to have information concerning her sexual life publicized to church members.[117] Whether she was or was not a member at the time of the publication, *it is clear that she did not consent* to be disciplined.

So, too, Professor Hayden's assertion, in defense of the consent rule, is debatable. Professor Hayden writes:

> A second related strength of the consent theory in this context derives from the nature of free exercise itself: individuals should be free to practice one religion or another, or none at all. When a person has chosen one organized belief structure, he should be held to it until he chooses to withdraw, and therefore he should not be able to sue his fellow members for disciplining him in accordance with church doctrine and policy. As soon as that person chooses to leave one religion, however, either to join another or to join none at all, the government has an interest in the individual's free exercise of that choice to leave.[118]

Why should the government allow religions that have organized belief structures to punish people who wish to belong to the faith, and yet violate its rules? It makes more sense to limit the faith's rights to actions which exclude these people and not actions designed to punish them. Carried to its logical conclusion, Professor Hayden's analysis would permit even physical disciplining of members, and not limit immunity to the tort of "intentional inflection of emotional distress" but to such crimes as assault. It is clear that the consent obtained is not genuine.

The consent doctrine, in short, is at best a narrow doctrine suitable for only select faiths, and at worst a fiction that allows religions to publi-

---

[116] A modified version of the *Guinn* test can be found in Comment, "Religious Torts," 975-83, which argues that membership in a religious faith creates a rebuttable presumption that one consents to the faith's rules. The problem is that this consent is simply untrue when it comes to religious discipline. People rarely if ever consent to public humiliation. Particularly in situations where the one being punished by the faith employs a lawyer to deter the faith's activity, the "consent through membership" doctrine is simply inapplicable.

[117] For example, see *Wollersheim v. Church of Scientology*, 260 Cal. Rptr. 331 (Ct. App. 1989) which rules that all discipline is in fact non-consensual.

[118] Hayden, "Religiously Motivated Conduct," 651.

cize private details of people lives against their will. This problem clearly comes to the fore when one examines the difficulties later cases have had in applying the test developed in *Guinn*.[119]

The same values that would seem to preclude most damage awards for excommunication and shunning in tort law would prevent judicial review of the merits of excommunication through the guise of resolving a property law dispute. The approach of the Canadian Supreme Court in *Lakeside Colony of Hutterian Brethren*, which allows for judicial review of orders of expulsion and exclusion to ensure their conformity with natural justice would seem to be unwise, for it evaluates the "correctness" of what are core theological determinations when these same factors can be avoided and the property law dispute be resolved independent of a merit determination of the correctness of the faith's exclusion. A better rule would be either to adopt the American approach enunciated in *Milivojevich* which mandates complete abstention, or the British approach in *Chief Rabbi* which allows formally for review, but with a completely deferential standard of review.

This chapter started with a Jewish perspective on shunning and excommunication, and it argues that Jewish law in this area is respectful of both minority and majority rights and gives each the ability to form its own exclusive community. The common law of torts and constitutional law should aim to do the same. The goals of such doctrines and practices should be to allow the formation of self-selected sub-communities sharing common religious values, which are protected in their right to exclude, but prevented from harassing in the name of religion. The law must reflect both of these goals, and it currently does not.

Conclusions

Painting with a broad brush, certain conclusions can be drawn as to the nature of shunning, excommunication, and other exclusionary practices devised by Jewish and other religious communities to allow them to form a sub-community within modern secular society.

Many religious communities cannot be fully open to any and all conduct by its members. Jewish communities established a mechanism and procedure for the exclusion of members of the faith who reject basic tenets of the community or faith. Such mechanisms include partial shun-

---

[119] For example, in *Hadnot v. Shaw*, 826 P.2d 978, (Okla. 1992), the Oklahoma Supreme Court had to address the issue of constructive withdrawal and implied consent. Indeed, it appears that the court allowed post-withdrawal action needed to re-enforce discipline under some form of a consent theory, even when it was clear that the disciplined individuals considered themselves free from the religious dictates of the church, and did everything except actually send in a letter of withdrawal.

ning, complete shunning, and in rare situations, excommunication. Others faiths uses comparable processes in different ways to shape their communities. These mechanisms of exclusion should be allowed to affect only people who wish to remain part of the religious sect that issued the shunning. People should be free to leave the faith group and avoid the penalty.

Government has a regulatory interest in governing these religious—and all other—collective groups that engage in activity designed to exclude people from a particular benefit. Government is (or should be) precluded on various freedom of religion grounds, however, from regulating purely ecclesiastical or faith matters.[120] These grounds should also be understood as precluding the government from preventing faith groups from forming their own special sub-communities, which excludes based on religious criteria. In that way, religious groups are entitled to more protection than mere commercial enterprises.[121]

The right to religious exclusion cannot, however, rise to the level of implicit (or explicit) coercion to religious conformity. This issue was clearly noted in a discussion within Jewish law concerning coercion, and minority rights. Writing in the early 1600s, Rabbi Shabtai ben Meir Ha-Cohen protested against a particular form of shunning and asserted that in the social framework of Eastern Europe in the seventeenth century it is tantamount to coercion and should not be allowed.[122] Essentially, he stated that in an insular and thoroughly intertwined Jewish community, which was the norm in the pre-emancipation communities of Eastern Europe, shunning was a form of compulsion and was thus only permitted when actual physical force was legally permitted according to Jewish law. Absent continuous interaction with the community, a single person who wishes to rebel would perish. Shunning was coercion in that social setting. In such a society, religious minority rights disappear if even low level exclusion is allowed, and government must interfere to protect people's freedom of religion.

Such an intertwined society does not exist in America and other democratic polities. Shunning and excommunication as practiced by

---

[120] *Milivojevich*, 426 U.S. at 724-25.

[121] Thus, for example, government clearly can prevent a non-denominational social club from limiting, based on religious faith, its membership. A religious social club should have that right. See *New York State Club Association, Inc., v. City of New York*, 487 U.S. 1 (1988).

[122] Rabbi Shabtai ben Meir Hachohen, *Gevurat Anashim* 72 cited in *Pitchei Teshuva Even Haezar*, 154:30 (Gush Etzion, 1990). Many commentaries on the *Shulchan Aruch* other than *Pitchei Teshuva* express dissent to *Gevurat Anashim's* rule. See *Aruch Hashulchan, Even Haezer* 154:63; *Maharam M'Lublin* 1 and 39 (Jerusalem, 1960), *Eliyahu Rabbah* 1-3; *Rav Betzalel Ashkenazi* 6 and 10; Chief Rabbi Yitzchak Isaac Halevi Herzog, *Techuka Liyisrael Al Pi Hatorah* III:202 and 209).

many faiths, including Judaism, are no longer designed to compel or force observance by the shunned one. The pressures imposed will no longer prevent a person from functioning or cause him or her to starve. Rather the process of shunning and excommunication creates a choice. It forces people to decide in which society they wish to reside. Only coercion to choose is involved. It does not, in its modern form, actually compel any particular activity. Just as a person has the right to remove himself or herself from a particular religious society, that society has a right to remove itself from him or her. Minority rights in the context of religious freedom has to include the right to leave a sect. It does not, however, include the right to remain part of a group, while defying that group's wishes.

Ultimately, religious freedom has to include the right to choose and to form one's own co-religionists and religious community members. This is the best protection government can give to religious minorities and still maintain a freedom of religion.

Jewish NGOs And Religious Human Rights: A Case-Study

IRWIN COTLER[*]

McGill University, Montreal

This volume and its sequel are emerging at a critical juncture in the struggle for human rights in general, and religious human rights in particular. On the one hand, there has been a literal explosion of human rights. Human rights have become an organizing idiom of our political culture, indeed, the new secular religion of our times. At the same time, however, in the dialectics of revolution and counter-revolution in human rights, violations of human rights continue unabated. The homeless of America, the hungry of Africa, the imprisoned of Asia and the Middle East can be forgiven if they think the human rights revolution has somehow passed them by, while the silent tragedy of the Kurds, the ethnic cleansing in the Balkans, the horror of Sarajevo, the agony of Angola and Rwanda are metaphor and message of the assault upon, and abandonment of, human rights in our time.

What is true of the human rights revolution and counter-revolution in general, in this Dickensian era with its best of times and worst of times, is also true of the state of religious human rights. On the one hand, freedom of religion is one of the most fundamental human rights, anchored in, and given expression in contemporary international law. It is enshrined in Articles 1(2) and 55(c) of the UN Charter, Article 18 of the 1948 Universal Declaration of Human Rights, Article II of the Convention on the Prevention and Punishment of the Crime Genocide, Article 9 of the 1950 European Convention for the Protection of Human Rights and Fundamental Freedoms, Article 1 of the 1950 UNESCO Convention

[*] This chapter represents the tentative conclusions of the author's work in progress, and is printed herein absent footnotes. For references and related discussion, the reader is directed to the author's writings listed in the "biographical sketches" section and to the chapters by David Novak, Michael J. Broyde, and Michael S. Berger and Deborah Lipstadt herein, and to the chapters by Natan Lerner, Asher Maoz, and John Witte and M. Christian Green in the companion volume. —The Editors

235

Against Discrimination in Education, Article 4 of the 1965 International Convention on the Elimination of all Forms of Racial Discrimination, Article 18 of the 1966 International Covenant on Civil and Political Rights, Article 12 of the 1969 American Convention on Human Rights, Principle VII of the 1975 Final Act of the Helsinki Conference on Security and Cooperation in Europe, Article 8 of the 1981 African Charter on Human and Peoples' Rights, Article 7 of the International Convention on the Elimination of All Forms of Discrimination Against Women, Article 1 of the 1981 Declaration on the Elimination of All Forms of Intolerance and of Discrimination Based on Religion or Belief, and Article 14 of the 1989 Convention on the Rights of the Child. The special status of freedom of religion in international human rights law is further buttressed by the fact that it is non-derogable even in times of emergency under Article 4(2) of the CP Covenant, as well as Article 27(2) of the American Convention.

Notwithstanding this "critical mass" of protections for freedom of religion in international law, however, freedom of religion remains "the most persistently violated human right in the annals of the species." Indeed, "religious intolerance has generated more wars, misery and suffering than any other type of discrimination or bias," and is not unrelated to much of the ethnic, tribal, "civilizational," conflict of our day.

Interestingly enough, this dialectical character of religious human rights—with its consecration in law and its massive violations—finds expression in the historiography of the Jewish religion and the experience of the Jewish people.

On one level, the Jewish religion and Jewish religious rights are at the core, the foundation, of universal human rights as a whole. In a word, if human rights has emerged as the new "secular religion" of our time, then the Jewish religion is at the core of this new "secular religion" of human rights—the whole symbolized by the normative exhortation in the Jewish religion of *"Tikun Olam,"* the responsibility to "repair the world." This responsibility, as well as the notion of *"B'Tselem"*—that we are all created in the image of G D—is the essence of a religion organized around the inherent dignity of the human person, and the equal dignity of all persons. Jewish lore has often elaborated on this theme, as reflected in the following story from the Talmud: "What is the most important verse in the whole Bible?" asked a Talmudic sage, Ben Azai. His answer: "The verse from the Book of Genesis that says: 'Man was created in the Divine image'." That verse establishes for Jews the fundamental relationship between one person and another. All were created in the image of God. Therefore, all are entitled to equal respect for their dignity and worth. Similarly, the Talmud provides that when a witness in a capital case comes to the witness stand, he must be admonished in the following words: "A single man was created in order to teach you that if one destroys a single person, it is as though he had destroyed the population of the world. And if he saves the life of a single person, it is as though he had saved the whole world."

And yet, notwithstanding this profound commitment to human rights anchored in the Jewish religion, in the very history of the Jewish people and in the prophetic tradition (or perhaps because of it, as Cahn put it in his insightful work "Warrant for Genocide"), violations of Jewish religious rights—be they through forced conversions, expulsions, inquisitions, pogroms, and yes genocide—have been one of the most persistent and enduring hatreds in all of human history.

It is not surprising, therefore, that Jewish NGOs, as legatees of the Jewish past and trustees of the Jewish future, should have committed themselves to the promotion and protection of human rights in general, and religious rights in particular and to combatting human rights violations in general, and the violations of freedom of religion and Jewish rights in particular.

Defining Jewish NGOs and Their Agendas

A word about definition. In referring to "Jewish" NGOs in this chapter, I have adopted a definition of the term "Jewish" which is anchored both in a more inclusive notion of what being Jewish means, as well as in an appreciation of what Jewish NGOs in fact do. More particularly, I have not restricted or limited the term "Jewish" to its religious or sectarian definition of a Jew as a person born of a Jewish mother or who has converted to Judaism. Rather, the term "Jewish" will refer to the intersecting religious, cultural, ethnic, and national identities whose composite defines what it means to be Jewish. This in fact is the mosaic that defines Jewish NGOs, or the mosaic by which these NGOs define themselves, and that defines the Jewish agenda or mission statements of the major, and mainstream Jewish NGOs reflected in its variegated forms.

Another way of describing this mosaic—of Jews as a religion, a culture, an ethnic group, a people, a nation—in terms even of the category of religion alone, and as an example of the multiple configurations involved, is as follows: (1) the religious rights of Jews as individuals involved in the free exercise of religion; (2) the religious rights of Jews as a group where the free exercise of religion can only be exercised in community with others; (3) the religious rights of Jews as a community with respect to, among others, the responsibilities of Jews as a community or collectivity in the Diaspora; (4) the religious rights of Jews as a culture, referring to the transmission of ideas, heritage, values, norms, morals, and the like that make up the composite of a culture; (5) the religious rights of Jews as a people, where such rights are inextricably bound up with the Jewish right of self-determination; and (6) the religious rights of the Jews as a nation in their homeland Israel, particularly respecting those rights that may be fulfilled only in Israel, and referring, conversely, to the centrality of Israel to the Jewish people.

Similarly, if one is to approach the meaning of the term "Jew" from the perspective not of freedom of religion, but of freedom from discrimination on grounds of religion, that is, Jewishness, a similar configuration emerges. As Natan Lerner put it: "In the case of the Jews, ethnicity, religion, and culture are inextricably interwoven, in the self-perception of the victims of anti-semitism as well as in the perceptions of the anti-semites."

If one links this "typology" of being Jewish, to the "typology" of Jewish NGOs, the universe of Jewish NGOs may be characterized as follows:

(1) There are religious or sectarian Jewish NGOs that represent or advocate denominational or sectarian interests only—or even a particular feature of the sectarian or denominational interest. Among these are religiously Orthodox, Conservative, or Reform Jewish NGOs, devoted to the promotion and protection of their particular sectarian interest. One example is the religiously Orthodox Jewish NGO Agudath Israel which is devoted to protection of the religious rights of observant Jews in the matter of Kashruth.

(2) There are secular and liberal Jewish NGOs—sometimes referred to as Jewish "human rights" NGOs—that concern themselves with the promotion and protection of religious human rights from a constitutional or "rights" perspective, and who, among others, use "church-state" litigation as a main prong in their strategic advocacy. This litigation strategy is often deployed more in the defense of non-Jews than in the defense of Jews, on the principle that "there cannot be security and freedom for Jews unless there is security and freedom for persons everywhere."

(3) There are Jewish "human rights" NGOs—which include also the Jewish NGOs in Category 2, but which themselves do not belong to Category 2—that are particularly concerned with protecting Jews from discrimination in general and from "Jew hatred" in particular. For these groups, Holocaust remembrance is an organizing idiom, Holocaust denial a "clear and present" danger, and bringing Nazi war criminals to justice a special responsibility.

(4) There are "international" human rights NGOs such as the World Jewish Congress that serve as the "diplomatic" arm of the Jewish people,

and whose mission "is to address the interests of Jews and Jewish communities all over the world." Indeed, the mission statement of the World Jewish Committee is expression and example of the integrative advocacy of international Jewish NGOs organized around the concern for Jews and Judaism in their religious, cultural, ethnic, and national configurations, including the notion of the centrality of Israel to the Jewish people.

Indeed, the increasingly intersecting and interlocking nature of what it means to be a Jew—and the increasing transnational character of this mosaic—is finding enhanced expression even among the major "national" Jewish NGOs whose advocacy is increasingly being internationalized.

(5) There are "international" Jewish NGOs, such as the American Jewish Joint Distribution Committee (JDC), whose ongoing mission is the relief, rescue, and reconstruction of Jews and Jewish communities in distress, and whose mission statement cites the Mishnaic injunction that "to save one person is to save a world." They are often joined in their efforts by another international Jewish NGO, the World ORT Union, whose object is "the amelioration of the economic and social status of Jews and other persons through vocational training and technical education in countries where the need exists"; and by national networks of immigrants and refugee rights NGOs, such as the Jewish Immigrant Aid Services (JIAS) of Canada, "dedicated to facilitating the lawful entry of Jewish refugees and immigrants into Canada," and which include thereby, the protection of their religious human rights.

(6) There are general purpose, grass roots, mass membership, integrated Jewish NGOs. The best example is B'nai B'rith—the name meaning sons (children) of the covenant—the "oldest and largest in the world." Its emblem is the seven-headed candlelabra, its motto has a clearly religious cast. Another example is the Women's International Zionist Organization, which like B'nia Brith enjoys consultative status at the United Nations and engages in a myriad of Israeli-centered education, humanitarian, and cultural activities.

(7) One of the oldest NGOs and the oldest Jewish human rights NGO is the Paris-based Alliance Israeliese Universielle. Founded in 1866, this organization, together with the Anglo-Jewish Association and the Board of Jewish Deputies, made an important contribution to the early development of human rights law, particularly religious rights law. Over the years, it emerged as a prototype of an "educational-cultural" NGO, responsible for establishing schools and other institutions for Jewish communities in distress.

(8) There are "Jewish" NGOs who are almost exclusively devoted to a universalist agenda, as in the work of those NGOs that operate to allevi-

ate hunger in the developing world, or whose humanitarian work is largely in "countries without Jews," inspired by the injunction of *"Tikun Olam."*

(9) There are "legal" or "juridical" Jewish NGOs such as the International Association of Jewish Lawyers and Jurists, that seek to act as "Counsel to the Jewish people," including the promotion and protection of their religious human rights.

(10) There are "single issue" or special purpose Jewish NGOs that have organized themselves around a particular, and compelling issue, such as the struggle for Soviet Jewry. Indeed, during the period that the Soviet Jewry issue became a major human rights issue on the East-West agenda, NGOs like the National Conference on Soviet Jewry or the Union of Councils of Soviet Jews had a major impact on the development of a U.S. human rights foreign policy.

(11) There are Jewish women NGOs—of both a national and international character—engaged in the struggle for Jewish human rights in general and women's rights and the rights of Jewish women in particular. Some of these organizations including Jewish religious rights NGOs, have had to challenge violations of Jewish women's rights carried out ostensibly in the name of religion itself, such as in the case of *Agunot.*

(12) The mission statements of all the major international—and national—Jewish NGOs include reference, in some form, to the "survival, security, and well-being of the State of Israel." Indeed, to the extent that Israel has emerged as the "civil religion" for organized Jewry—and to the extent that the "existential" relationship between Israel and the Jewish people embraces the panoply of identities and rights described earlier, including religion and religious rights—the agenda of many national and international NGOs reflect and represent these values.

Having regard to this preamble, this chapter will be organized around the following seven themes or questions:

First, what has been the contribution of Jewish NGOs to the development of international law in the matter of religious human rights? Here I propose to offer a snapshot of the history of—indeed one might almost say historic—Jewish NGO contributions at various historical junctures in the development of international human rights law.

Second, what has been the contribution of Jewish NGOs to the development and critique of domestic constitutional and statutory law? Here I propose to offer a comparative perspective of the involvement of Jewish NGOs in the development of constitutional and statutory law in both Canada and the United States, which may be instructive not only about their respective perspectives on religious human rights but their distinctive legal cultures and Jewish sensibilities.

Third, what has been the role of Jewish NGOs in combatting violations of religious human rights in the domestic arena, that is, the adage that "petitioners must come with clean hands"? Here I will identify areas where Canadian and American Jewish NGOs have made a significant contribution to the protection against discrimination on grounds of religion, with particular reference to the divergent and contrasting positions taken by these NGOs in Church-State issues as well as in the hate speech controversies.

Fourth, what strategies have Jewish NGOs engaged in—and indeed sometimes pioneered—in exposing violations of religious human rights, and in combatting their violation? Here the chapter will focus on the struggle for oppressed Jewry—particularly Soviet Jewry not only as a case-study of the role of Jewish NGOs in the promotion and protection of religious human rights, but as a model for strategic advocacy by NGOs in the matter of redressing violations of religious human rights generally speaking.

Fifth, what has been the role of international Jewish NGOs in the protection against discrimination in the international arena? Here the chapter will focus on three case-studies—reclamation of Jewish communal property in Eastern Europe and the former Soviet Union, redressing the historic "teaching of contempt" in the context of Christian-Jewish dialogue, and combatting the "new anti-semitism" in the international arena—and the related founding of three international Jewish NGOs to address these concerns.

Sixth, are there distinctive features of the general panoply of religious human rights protections about which Jewish NGOs are particularly concerned, and how have these concerns shaped their advocacy and activism respecting religious human rights?

Finally, what has the role of Jewish NGOs in the promotion and protection of religious human rights taught us about the importance of religious human rights in the pantheon of human rights, and about the importance of religious human rights to the agenda of Jewish NGOs?

The Contribution of Jewish NGOs to the Development of the International Law of Religious Human Rights

The following is a snapshot of the contribution of Jewish NGOs in the development of international human rights law before and after World War II. During the 19th century, and up to World War II, Jewish NGOs were instrumental in the development of five fundamental principles which constitute the foundation of contemporary international human rights law; after World War II, these groups made notable contributions to the creation of important instruments of international human rights law. The role of Jewish NGOs in this process is little known, but it is a matter of great historical moment in the emergence of what is generally referred to as the "international law of human rights."

From the Congress of Vienna in 1815 to the Paris Peace Conference and the Minorities Treaties in 1921. Although contemporary international human rights law is popularly regarded as a post-World War II phenomenon or "United Nations Law" as it is sometimes characterized, the "historic antecedents" of international human rights, as Thomas Buergenthal put it, are rooted in developments that found expression from the Congress of Vienna in 1815 to the Treaty of Berlin in 1878; from the American intervention on behalf of Romanian Jewry in 1902 to the U.S. intercession in the Kishinev Pogrom of 1905; and from the Treaty of Paris of 1919-20 to the Minorities Treaties of 1921.

Admittedly, on the level of Jewish experience during this century, it was yet another century-long example of Jewish persecution, or what Robert Wistrich has called the "enduring hatred" of the Jews. On another level, however, this century constituted—as Professor Feinberg pointed out in a brilliant but largely unknown article called "The International Protection of Human Rights and the Jewish Question"—an historic watershed in the development of international human rights law in general, and religious human rights in particular. And so while contemporary international human rights law has met with a "consistent pattern of gross violations of human rights" in spite of the international human rights legal regime, the century from 1815 to 1921 witnessed the reverse: the development of international human rights law in response to the violations of that period.

Indeed, as Professor Feinberg points out, "the oppression, persecutions, and sufferings which were the lot of Jewry in many lands stirred the conscience of the world," and led to the conceptualization of five international legal doctrines that were to form the foundation of contemporary international human rights law, particularly in the area of religious human rights.

The *first* such doctrine was the *doctrine of humanitarian intervention*— the principle that a state may intervene in the affairs of another state if that other state engages in inhumane or uncivilized conduct that shocks the conscience of mankind. While the moral and legal authority of this doctrine has been undermined or blunted by its manipulation for political purposes, it has of late been reasserted with uncommon juridical vigor in its invocation by the United Nations Security Council in the 90s to authorize humanitarian intervention in Somalia, Bosnia-Herzegovina, Rwanda, and Haiti. Indeed, it appears to be a little known, though not unimportant datum, that the roots of this doctrine can be traced to humanitarian intervention on behalf of Jews and Christians in the 19th century; that these interventions were inspired by concern for the religious human rights of Jews and Christians; and that, in the case of interventions on behalf of Jews, they were quintessentially and prototypically humanitarian, inspired only by concern for the religious human rights of Jews and no other political or partisan design. They represented therefore the classical and original conception of the doctrine of humanitarian intervention as it was meant to be, rather than what it subsequently became.

Moreover, as Feinberg alludes to in the double entendre of the title of his article, not only does the "Jewish Question"—or the persecution of Jews—constitute a case study in the violation of international law in general, and religious human rights in particular; it also represents an historic watershed in the contribution of Jewish NGOs to the development of international human rights law in general and Jewish religious rights in particular. For during this 19th century period, Jews were not only the object of humanitarian interventions, they themselves were, at the same time, a most important factor in moving the great powers to take action on their behalf. Almost every one of the humanitarian interventions for the benefit of Jews was the result of petitions and appeals of Jewish organizations such as l'Alliance Israelite Universelle, the Board of Deputies, and the Anglo-Jewish Association. As Feinberg put it: "Worthy of special mention is the fact that the most significant achievement in the field of the international protection of human rights in the 19th century was to a very large, perhaps even decisive extent, the outcome of Jewish endeavours." Feinberg is here referring to the Congress of Berlin in 1878, at which Rumania, Serbia, and Montenegro were granted independence "on the condition that they undertook to eschew discrimination between their subjects on grounds of religion and to guarantee them equal rights and freedom of worship." The guarantee of rights in Serbia, Montenegro, and particularly Russia concerned the Jews above all, and it was the Jews who fought this issue at the Congress of Berlin.

It was the "Jewish" connection—both as prospective victims of discrimination and as petitioners for redress—that led to a *second* important, and historic, doctrinal development: the principle that the *recognition of the independence of a state is contingent upon that state's guarantee of freedom of religion and eschewal of discrimination on the grounds of religion*. "By defending—and vindicating—the cause of the Jews of Rumania, Serbia and Bulgaria before the Congress," wrote Saint Vallier, the second French delegate at the Congress, to l'Alliance Israelite Universelle, "we have defended the cause of justice, humanity and civilization."

This principle of state responsibility in turn led ineluctably to a *third* major doctrinal development or principle—*the protection of minorities*—which found expression at the Paris Peace Conference in 1919-20, where the Minorities Treaties were drafted and which Feinberg described as a historic step "towards the recognition of human rights as an integral part of international law." He summed up this historical development and the role Jewish NGOs played in it as follows:

> The demand for guarantees of the rights of the Jewish communities in East, Central and Southern Europe was brought before the Conference by the Committee of Jewish Delegations, set up in Paris in the very days when the Conference was being assembled, and composed of delegates from those communities, and representatives of Jewish communities in the United States, Canada, Palestine and Italy and representatives of the Zionist Congress and the B'nai B'rith Order. It is worthwhile noting that, in its memorandum to the Conference, the Committee did not demand special rights or privileges for the Jews alone; it presented a proposal for the general settlement of the minorities problem, to be applied to all minority groups in all the countries in question.

The *fourth* doctrinal development, writes Feinberg, is the principle of *universalization of rights*—including religious human rights—and the *very idea of a United Nations*. This principle and idea grew out of the Minorities Treaties themselves. Indeed, in 1926 the Institute of International Law—and in 1927 the International Diplomatic Academy—asked that "a Universal Treaty for the Protection of the Fundamental Rights of Man" be drawn up.

Finally, out of the doctrine of humanitarian intervention —the protection of vulnerable peoples from actions that "shock the conscience" of mankind—emerged a *fifth* international legal doctrine, namely, the principle of *accountability for crimes against humanity*, which became the cornerstone of the Nuremberg Principles following World War II. As Henri Rolin put it, the concept of crimes against humanity from an historical point of view, is "the logical outcome of the humanitarian intervention by States against certain odious acts which rouse the conscience of the civilized world." Albert de la Prudelle adds: "Where once the law of nations knew only humanitarian interventions—be it that of the United States in Kishinev or the great powers in Rumania—it hereinafter recognized the subjection of those guilty of inhuman persecutions to an [international] criminal jurisdiction."

In summary, five great doctrines, organized around, if not inspired by, religious human rights, emerged from the Congress of Vienna to be reconsidered or reasserted at the Paris Peace Conference, and to thereby comprise the "historic antecedents" of contemporary international human rights law—the doctrine of humanitarian intervention, the principle of state independence conditioned on guarantees of freedom of religion and protection against discrimination on grounds of religion, the principle of minorities rights (including religious human rights on an individual and collective level), the principle of the universality of rights as the best guarantee for (religious) human rights, which was the forerunner of the United Nations itself, and the principle of accountability for crimes against humanity. As to the role of Jewish organizations in this process, Feinberg's comments are particular relevant:

> The oppression, persecutions and sufferings which were the lot of Jewry in many lands stirred the conscience of the world in the period between the Congress of Vienna and the Paris Peace Conference and prompted the Great Powers to intervene from time to time on their behalf. Throughout that period, and at the Conference itself, the Jews applied all their energy and initiative in the international arena to the struggle against oppression and for the assurance of Jewish rights and of respect for Jewish dignity. In doing so, they made a noble contribution to the furtherance of fundamental human rights and Man's basic freedoms, and to the development of public international law.

Post-World War II Developments. Given this moral and jurisprudential legacy, it is not surprising that Jewish NGOs should have made a notable contribution to the creation of five important post-World War II international human rights instruments, including, in particular, provisions relenting religious human rights. For reasons of economy, I will but enumerate these agreements and identify the contribution of Jewish NGOs.

First, Jewish NGOs were critical for *the development of the United Nations Charter* of 1945. Jewish NGOs were not only "present at the creation," but played a formative role in the organization of the San Francisco Conference in 1945 and the formulation of the U.N. Charter itself. As Natan Lerner put it, "the WJC, the American Jewish Conference and the Board of Deputies of British Jews made joint representations to the San Francisco Conference, while their representatives approached delegations, expressing their concern that an effective system of human rights should be adopted." Indeed, "the fate of the Jews at Hitler's hands was a major impetus for the decision to make the protection of human rights a principal purpose of the United Nations." And so, in the ashes of the Holocaust, and in the wake of the collapse of the special guarantees in the

Minorities Treaties and the like, Jewish NGOs were prominent among those organizations who, even before the United Nations founding Conference in San Francisco, joined in publishing in December 1944 a "Declaration of Human Rights" asserting that "an International Bill of Human Rights must be promulgated." In language reminiscent of contemporary international human rights law doctrine, they affirmed that "no plea of sovereignty shall ever again be allowed to permit any nation to deprive those within its borders of those fundamental rights." They affirmed their belief in "the equal and inalienable rights of all members of the human family." And, in the words of Sidney Liskofsky, they acted on the credo "that the human rights of Jews would be respected and secured in the degree that the rights of all men were honoured and safeguarded."

In a word, for Jewish NGOs the protection of human rights was held out as a principal purpose of a United Nations; the notion of "state sovereignty" was not to be used as an exculpatory defense or immunity for human rights violations; and the United Nations was to be the guardian and protector of universal human rights. And so they pleaded for the adoption of a comprehensive Bill of Rights—with requisite implementation measures—together with the Charter of the United Nations itself.

Regrettably, however, from the outset, the major Western countries, including the United States and the USSR, were reluctant to assume specific legal commitments. Accordingly, while the United Nations Charter declares as one of its purposes "to promote respect for human rights and fundamental freedoms for all without distinction as to race, sex, language or religion," it eschewed a legally binding Bill of Rights; instead, a nonbinding Universal Declaration of Human Rights was adopted—the first component of a three-part project that was to include the Declaration, a binding Covenant, and a system of implementation measures for the Covenant.

First, Jewish NGOs were critical for *the development of the Universal Declaration of Human Rights* of 1948. Because the Declaration was generally considered to be without legal force, and perhaps because the Cold War had not yet begun, the Universal Declaration as "a common standard of achievement for all peoples and nations" was completed and adopted with remarkable speed. Two provisions were included that were of particular concern to Jews and the theme of this chapter. The first was Article 12, which recognized "the right of everyone to leave any country, including his own." This *"Grundnorm"* right, which is intimately bound up with the exercise of all other rights, including in particular freedom of religion, became the moral and juridical clarion call for oppressed Jewry. Accordingly, not only was the inclusion of this right important to Jewish NGOs at the time, but it became the organizing theme of Jewish NGO advocacy in the 1970s and 1980s with respect to oppressed Jewry in general and Soviet Jewry in particular. A second provision of importance to the Jews, found in Article 19 of the Declaration, spoke of the right of everyone, "alone or in community with others, and in public or private, to manifest his religion or belief in teaching, practice, worship, and observance," and which became the precursor of similar provisions from the CP Covenant to the Helsinki Final Act.

Third, Jewish NGOs were critical to the development of *The Convention on the Protection and Punishment of the Crime of Genocide* of 1948. Just one day before the adoption of the Universal Declaration of Human Rights—and no less inspired by the horrors of the Holocaust—the Genocide Convention was adopted. The document was very much the handiwork of Jewish NGOs like the World Jewish Congress, and the unrelenting commitment of a single Polish Jew—Rafael Lemkin. It was Lemkin who named it and Jewish NGOs who helped nurture it to creation. Indeed, in 1947, a WJC memorandum "had urged the ECOSOC to outlaw genocide as a non-political crime, whether committed in times of war or peace. Congress urged its affiliates to approach their governments in order to obtain their endorsement of the Convention." Regrettably, it was to take the United States another 40 years before it ratified the Convention, notwithstanding that its essential juridical—and existential core—was the right of groups to be protected against acts committed with intent to destroy, in whole or in part, a national, ethnical, racial, or religious group as such. It constitutes, therefore, among others, an existential protection for religious human rights.

Fourth, Jewish NGOs played a part in the development of the *International Covenant on Political and Civil Rights* and the *International Covenant on Economic and Social Rights*, both of 1966. It was to take close to 20 years for these two International Covenants to be adopted, during which time, as Liskofsky has written, "Jews stood in the vanguard of those advocating additional human rights laws of general applicability and stronger measures of enforcement." Indeed, during the period of preparation, the WJC made oral and written submissions at every single meeting of the Commission on Human Rights and the ECOSOC NGOs Committee. In particular, the WJC argued the case for the inclusion in the Covenants of a non-discrimination clause, and the prohibition of incitement to national, racial, or religious hatred. It submitted "that no real equality could be achieved unless dissemination of racial or religious hatred and intolerance were prohibited, and freedom of speech was not abused in order to incite hatred."

Moreover, as soon as the drafting committee of the Human Rights Commission was established in 1947, the WJC urged it to take measures providing for the recognition of the right of petition for individuals and non-governmental organizations, and for the establishment of appropriate machinery to implement substantive principles, such as those relating to discrimination and religious human rights. While both Covenants— particularly the International Covenant on Civil and Political Rights— contain express reference to religious human rights, the implementation provisions were weakened, with the Right of Petition made optional and relegated to a separate Protocol.

Finally, Jewish NGOs worked for the development of *The International Convention on the Elimination of All Forms of Racial Discrimination* of 1966 and the *Declaration on the Elimination of All Forms of Religious Discrimination or Intolerance* of 1981. NGOs in general, and Jewish NGOs in particular, were active early on in pressing for action on the prevention of discrimination. As early as 1953, the WJC had asked for a special covenant outlawing the advocacy of national, racial, and religious hatred and intolerance, and was among the promoters of the Geneva Conference of Non-Governmental Organizations interested in the Eradication of Prejudice and Discrimination in 1955 which adopted a number of resolutions relating to discrimination.

Accordingly, after a wave of swastika daubings in 1960 in Germany and elsewhere, the American Jewish Committee and the World Jewish Congress urged the United Nations to draft the appropriate international instruments to address such manifestations. The United Nations decided to split the focus, preparing one instrument on racial discrimination and a second on religious freedom.

The American Jewish Committee, the World Jewish Congress, and other Jewish NGOs were very much engaged in the preparation of these and other U.N. instruments through convening meetings of legal experts; preparing and submitting proposed draft language to government delegates and independent experts serving on the relevant U.N. bodies; critiquing new and revised proposals; advocating adoption of the instruments, among other means. Later, they also assisted in efforts to ensure implementation of the instruments, both by monitoring procedures developed by the supervising body for CERD, and by taking a leadership role in defining and refining ways to implement the Declaration. For example, in the 1980s, the American Jewish Committee commissioned the preparation of a legal commentary (guide) to the 1981 U.N. Declaration on Religious Intolerance, the principal intergovernmental instrument guaranteeing protection of religious freedom. This commentary, now nearing completion, was the basis for the preparation of a draft "General Comment" detailing government responsibilities to assure religious freedom as interpreted by Article 18 of the International Covenant on Civil and Political Rights, to which the U.S., Canada and some 130 other nations are now parties. In an age of growing challenges to religious freedom by religious extremists and governments alike, the adoption, in 1993, of this "General Comment" by the Human Rights Committee is an important, internationally respected, and authoritative counterweight to the otherwise continued limitations placed on religious freedom by new U.N. instruments.

The Contribution of Jewish NGOs to Constitutional Law of Religious Human Rights

I will now offer a comparative perspective of Jewish NGO involvement in the United States and Canada which may be instructive not only in the legal cultures of the two countries, but in their respective perspectives on religious human rights as well.

Jewish NGOs in the United States. The activities of Jewish NGOs in the United States in the formulation of constitutional and statute law regarding religious human rights have been organized around three basic themes: (1) ensuring guarantees of the freedom to manifest and maintain one's own belief (without coercion); (2) ensuring maintenance of the boundaries between religion and politics—that is, the separation of church and state—in accordance with the United States Constitution; and (3) ensuring the right to equality, equal citizenship, and non-discrimination in matters of religious human rights.

The activities of three major U.S. "Jewish defense organizations" in the promotion and protection of religious human rights—largely though not exclusively through the courts, and largely, though not exclusively, in relation to issues of separation of church and state—are a case-study of the role of Jewish NGOs in the promotion and protection of religious human rights in general; and a case-study of their organizing principle—of "promotion and protection"—"that the rights of Jews would only be secure when the rights of people of all faiths were equally secure." Indeed, the three Jewish NGOs have filed more *amicus curiae* ("friends of the court") briefs on behalf of the rights of non-Jews than of Jews.

What follows is a snapshot of the advocacy of the American Jewish Committee in this regard, offered with three caveats. First, it is a snapshot of the litigation strategy which, while crucial to Jewish NGOs in the protection of religious human rights, is not the only strategy deployed. Second, in many of these cases, the American Jewish Committee was joined by the other two major Jewish NGOs—the Anti-Defamation League and the American Jewish Congress. Third, more recently, in the last ten years in particular, the shared, albeit distinctive perspectives and litigation strategy of these three Jewish NGOs have increasingly been challenged by religiously orthodox Jewish NGOs. In particular, the Commission on Law and Public Affairs, the litigation arm of Agudath Israel, has filed opposing amicus briefs in matters pertaining to the litigation of religious human rights in general, and matters of separation of church and state in particular.

As it happened, the first major case in which the American Jewish Committee (hereinafter the AJC), the ADL, and the American Jewish Congress filed a legal brief—*Pierce v. Society of Sisters of the Holy Names of Jesus and Mary*—had nothing to do directly with the religious human rights of Jews. The AJC filed a brief in the *Pierce* case to challenge an Oregon law, inspired by the Ku Klux Klan, that required all children to attend public schools. The real intent—and ultimate prospective effect—of the law was to put Catholic parochial schools out of business. There were no Jewish parochial schools in Oregon, and one might wonder what the "nexus" of this case was to a Jewish NGO. But this case was to emerge as a "defining moment" in the litigation strategy of the AJC—and that of its associated sister organizations. For it was through this case that these Jewish NGOs were to declare and establish the underlying theme of their litigation strategy as set forth earlier—that religious rights of Jews would only be secure if the religious rights of people of other faiths were equally secure. Hence, even though there were no Jewish parochial schools in Oregon at that time, AJC filed its brief on the side of the Catholic schools. The Supreme Court unanimously struck down the law holding that, among others, it interfered with the liberty of parents to educate their children as they wished. This decision, as Samuel Rabinove, legal counsel to the Committee put it, "has been termed the Magna Carta of Parochial Schools."

The *Pierce* case was the first of a series of cases in which the AJC was to uphold religious rights, freedoms and practices for people of all faiths. For example, in the 1943 case of *West Virginia v. Barnette*, the compulsory "flag salute" case, the AJC supported the right of Jehovah's Witness children, in accordance with their parents' religious convictions, to refuse to salute the flag in public school. Justice Robert Jackson, speaking for the Court, directly addressed the constitutional guarantee of religious freedom and pluralism: "If there is any fixed star in our constitutional constellation, it is that no official, high or petty, can prescribe what shall be orthodox in politics, nationalism, religion, or other matters of opinion or force citizens to confess by word or act their faith therein. If there are any circumstances which permit any exception, they do not occur to us."

In the 1963 landmark case of *Sherbert v. Verner*, the AJC filed a brief in support of the right of a Seventh-Day Adventist to receive unemployment compensation benefits when she had refused to accept employment requiring her to work on Saturday. The Supreme Court held that for the state to disqualify Mrs. Sherbert for such benefits solely because she refused to work on Saturday, a decision based squarely on her religious beliefs, imposed an unconstitutional burden on her free exercise of religion. As Justice Brennan, writing for the majority, put it: "To condition the availability of benefits upon this woman's willingness to violate a cardinal principle of her religious faith effectively penalized the free exercise of her constitutional liberties."

In a remarkably similar case in 1987, *Hobbie v. Unemployment Appeal Board of Florida*, the AJC filed an amicus brief, together with the Baptist Joint Committee on Public Affairs and the Christian Legal Society, on behalf of Mrs. Hobbie, who had converted to the Seventh-Day Adventist faith during her employment. The Supreme Court's tough standard, articulated in *Sherbert*, requiring "strict scrutiny" of state actions that infringe on religious liberty unless the state can show a "compelling interest" in so doing, was significantly reinforced by its decision in the *Hobbie* case.

In *Wisconsin v. Yoder* in 1972, the AJC joined Jewish and Christian groups in supporting the rights of Amish parents to limit their children's education to the eighth grade which conflicted with Wisconsin's compulsory school attendance law (requiring attendance until age 16). In 1986, in the case of *Witters v. Washington Department of Services for the Blind*, the AJC supported Witters in his claim for government aid to the handicapped, which he had chosen to use for training to become a Christian minister. The U.S. Supreme Court unanimously held that the state program of aid to the handicapped clearly had a secular purpose, i.e., to aid a particular category of persons not defined by religion, to become productive citizens. In the case of *Goldman v. Weinberger*, also in 1986, AJC joined with the Christian Legal Society in upholding the right of an Orthodox Jew in the Air Force to wear his yarmulke indoors while on duty.

While the AJC and its sister NGOs have been "vigorous proponents of the free exercise of religion" they have opposed, no less vigorously any state "entanglement" with religion "or breach in the wall of separation between Church and State," be it by way of religion in the public schools, or government aid to religious schools, or religious symbols on public property. For example, the AJC filed amicus briefs in a series of cases involving state-sponsored organized prayer and bible reading in public schools. These cases are compelling examples not only of the church-state "separation" controversy in the U.S., but of the adherence of the major liberal and secular Jewish NGOs to the "separationist" ideology. The issue came to a head in the landmark cases of *Engel v. Vitale* and *Abington*

School District v. Schempp, where the Supreme Court held that such state-sanctioned conduct violates the Establishment Clause. While in *Engel* the Court struck down a state-composed prayer for public school use, *Schempp* went beyond that to rule that state-sponsored recitation of *any* prayer, or devotional reading from the Bible, breached the Establishment Clause. The decisions, which caused a furor at the time, and were widely denounced as being anti-religious, anti-Christian, and un-American— engendered a certain backlash against the Jewish NGOs, who were accused, along with the Supreme Court, of trying to remove G D from the classroom. While subsequent attempts during the Reagan and Bush administrations to amend the United States Constitution to permit organized school prayer have not been successful, the recent Republican "Contract with America," supported by a Republican-controlled Congress, might make it a reality. Jewish NGOs are once again at the forefront of the opposition.

As for government aid to religious schools, just as there are those who believe that the Establishment Clause does not prevent state-organized prayer in the public schools, there are also those who believe that it does not bar a state from subsidizing parochial schools, even if their reason for being is to propagate a religious faith. Indeed, the U.S. Supreme Court has upheld certain kinds of state aid to religious schools in the form of bus transportation (the *Everson* case), secular textbooks loans (the *Allen* case), and services for the health and welfare of the student (the *Wolman* case), provided the performance of these services is essentially secular.

At the same, the Court has said, and the three Jewish NGOs have so argued, that it is not a proper function of government to advance the religious mission of parochial schools, and so it has struck down state attempts to fund specific educational activities within parochial schools. As the AJC has put it, "the predominant view of the Jewish Community is that all religions will flourish best if government keeps its hands off, neither to hinder nor to help them." In 1993, however, in the case of *Zobrest v. Catalina Foothills School District*, the Supreme Court ruled (5-4) that the Establishment Clause does not bar using government money to pay for a sign language interpreter to accompany a deaf student in a parochial school. This decision marked the first time that the Court has allowed a public employee to be part of a religious school's instructional program.

It now appears that the major "parochaid" battleground in the years immediately ahead is likely to be the issue of tax-dollar vouchers for parents to enrol their children in any school they may wish, including denominational schools. AJC, ADL, and the American Jewish Congress are opposed to such vouchers for religious schools as well as for private schools, both on constitutional and public policy grounds. COLPA, the litigation arm of Agudath Israel, and other Orthodox religious Jewish NGOs are in favor. The Supreme Court has never ruled squarely on the constitutionality of such tax-funded vouchers for religious schools. But with the various initiatives now pending, it may be just a matter of time before one is passed and a litigation challenge to vouchers for such schools reaches the Court. As a review of the cases would indicate, each side in this battle can cite case law in its favor, and each side would be supported by, if not spearheaded by, Jewish NGOs.

In the matter of religious symbols on public property, the AJC in *Lynch v. Donnely* (1984) joined other Christian and Jewish groups in filing amicus briefs opposing government-sanctioned religious symbols on public property. The U.S. Supreme Court upheld (5-4) the constitutional right of a city to erect a nativity scene as part of its annual Christmas celebration. The result, in the eyes of some Jews, was so insensitive to any religious sensibility that they said it was a mistake for the ACLU to have brought this "hard" case in the first place—and an even greater mistake for Jewish organizations to have participated in it. But in 1989 the ACLU—joined by the Jewish NGOs—was back in court again, in the dual case of *County of Allegheny v. ACLU*, this time to challenge not only the display of a creche in a courthouse, but also a Menorah display, which was provided by Chabad, a branch of Lubavitch Chasidic movement. This time, the secular and liberal Jewish NGOs challenging the displays were opposed by Chabad and Orthodox Jewish NGOs supporting them. It is a pattern that is increasingly going to characterize First Amendment litigation in the United States. In a dual—and ambivalent ruling—the Supreme Court (5-4) declared the nativity scene unconstitutional (an improper "endorsement of religion"), but upheld the Menorah (which had been placed alongside a Christmas tree) as a "secular expression."

Jewish NGOs in Canada. The Canadian experience, and the role of Canadian Jewish NGOs in the matter of religious human rights, contrasts sharply with the situation in the United States. This contrast reflects not only the different "rights cultures" of the two countries, but the different "rights perspectives" of Jewish organizations in the U.S. and Canada. These differences find expression in the manner in which, both through litigation strategy and otherwise, Jewish NGOs in the two countries have adopted dramatically different—if not opposite—principles and policies. Indeed, the "constitutionalist" and normative perspectives of Canadian Jewish NGOs invites one to ask some serious questions about the seemingly "self-evident truths" as held out by the American Jewish organizations.

First, a word about constitutionalism and context. It should be noted that, for the first 115 years of the Canadian constitutional experience, Canada, unlike the United States, did not have any entrenched Bill of Rights. Indeed, any inquiry into the Canadian constitutional process in the first 115 years of Canadian constitutional history, from 1867 to 1982, would reveal a continuing preoccupation with the powers of government at the expense of the rights of people. More particularly, traditional constitutional analysis and reform revolved around the division of powers between the federal government and the provinces—otherwise known as "legal federalism"—as distinct from the American preoccupation with limitations on the exercise of power, whether federal or state, otherwise known as "civil liberties." The result was that the powers of government tended to precede, if not obscure, the rights of people, when the rights of the people ought to have preceded the powers of government. The outcome was a political or legal theory in which the constitutional discourse was about federalism or "power," and not about "rights" or people.

In a word, constitutional law developed in Canada as a "powers process," a battle of "sovereign jurisdictional rivalry" between the federal government and the provinces, with the courts as the arbiters of that process, rather than as a "rights process" with the courts as the guardians of those rights. It is not surprising, therefore, that while in the United States the popular metaphor of the American Constitution—"life, liberty and the pursuit of happiness"—is a rights-oriented, people-oriented metaphor, the popular metaphor in the Canadian constitution—"peace, order, and good government"—is a power-based, government-oriented metaphor, with a clear federalist—if not centralist—orientation. Professor Bora Laskin, later Chief Justice of the Supreme Court of Canada, summed up this constitutional experience in one pithy sentence: "The basic constitutional question was which jurisdiction should have the power to work the injustice, not whether the injustice itself should be prohibited." Or, as he otherwise put it: "the constitutional issue is simply whether the particular suppression is competent to the Dominion or the Province, as the case may be."

This historical obsession with the division of powers not only obscured the claims to protection of civil liberties, but very often determined the disposition of the claims themselves. In a word, and ironically enough, legal federalism became the "looking glass" for the determination and disposition of civil liberties issues. Accordingly, whenever a federal or provincial statute appeared to offend against civil liberties, the central question for judges became, "is the alleged denial of civil liberties within the legislative competence of the denying legislature?" Sometimes this "jurisdictional" technique worked, more often it did not. If it did not work, that was the end of the matter, however much this analysis may have obscured, let alone denied, the civil liberties issue. And even when it worked, it left the disturbing inference that if the same offensive legislation had been passed by the competing, yet competent, legislative jurisdiction, that legislation under this "jurisdictional" logic, would have necessarily been held to be valid.

And so it was then, that legislation offending religious human rights was either upheld or invalidated on jurisdictional grounds only, that is, impugned not on the grounds that the legislation was offensive, but that the wrong legislature enacted it. Accordingly, in the *Saumur* case, a Quebec City by-law which effectively prohibited Jehovah Witnesses from distributing their religious tracts was struck down on the grounds that it trespassed on federal jurisdiction in relation to criminal law, that is, the wrong jurisdiction enacted it. At the same time a long line of cases held that "Sunday Observance" legislation is within the exclusive federal jurisdiction over criminal law.

With the adopting of the Charter of Rights in 1982, and the constitutionalization of rights in Canada, any law that affected freedom of religion was now vulnerable to challenge under S.2(a) of the Charter, which guarantees to everyone the "fundamental freedom" of "freedom of conscience and religion." In 1985—three years after the adoption of the Charter—the Supreme Court of Canada, in *R. v. Big M Drug Mart*, struck down the Lord's Day Act, the federal Sunday Observance legislation which mandated store closings on Sundays and on Christian holidays— an Act that for 75 years had withstood any constitutional challenge until the advent of the Charter. Dickson CJ. offered the following definition of freedom of religion: "The essence of the concept of freedom of religion is the right to entertain such religious beliefs as a person chooses, the right to declare religious beliefs openly and without fear of hindrance or reprisal, and the right to manifest religious belief by worship and practice or by teaching and dissemination." In 1988, in the *Zylberberg* case, the Ontario Court of Appeal struck down an Ontario regulation mandating religious exercises, including prayer in the public schools, on the grounds that it "imposed Christian observances upon non-Christian pupils, and religious observances on non-believers." In 1990, in *C.C.L.A. v. Ontario*, the same court struck down another regulation requiring a public school to devote two periods per week to religious education on grounds that this was "Christian" education. Ontario did not appeal these decisions, while the Canadian Jewish Congress had intervened in both cases to challenge the Ontario legislation.

Admittedly, the Charter has wrought a constitutional revolution in Canada to the point that, as Madame Justice Claire L'Heureux-Dubé of the Supreme Court put it in 1987: "[T]he Court has stretched the cords of liberty more in five years than the U.S. Supreme Court has in 200." The Court has struck down Sunday legislation, legislation mandating "religious exercises," including school prayer, and regulations requiring religious education. But, for all the recent similarity in result between Canadian and American case law, the protection of religious human rights—and the role of Jewish NGOs—has otherwise been remarkably different in Canada than in the United States.

First, while American Jewish NGOs have gone to court to challenge government-sanctioned religious symbols on public property, Canadian Jewish NGOs have avoided controversial "creche" cases in Canada. On the contrary, they have supported, for example, the building of a Succa (symbolic shelter marking the Jewish holiday of Succot) at City Hall in Toronto, or a Chai Menorah on the grounds of the Manitoba Legislative Assembly to mark the holiday of Chanukkah, while being singularly unconcerned with a Christmas tree on a City Hall Plaza.

Second, while American Jewish NGOs have challenged any government aid to Jewish education, Jewish NGOs have supported such government assistance in Canada; indeed, Jewish NGOs like the Canadian Jewish Congress have even gone to court to secure government support for Jewish education precisely on the grounds that the absence of such support constitutes a denial of *both* the "freedom of religion" and the "equality" provisions of the Canadian *Charter of Rights and Freedoms*. In this sense, then, Jewish NGOs in Canada have interpreted the promotion and protection of religious human rights in the matter of government aid to education in a manner exactly opposite to their counterparts in the United States.

Third, while Jewish NGOs in the United States have been steadfast in limiting government aid to public schools only—and have eschewed any government recognition of a state-supported private school system on both constitutional and policy grounds—Jewish NGOs in Canada have sought equal standing for Jewish schools within, for example, the Quebec school system—on the grounds that the public school system in Quebec and Ontario under the Canadian Constitution is effectively confessional, i.e., it authorizes government aid to Catholic and Protestant denominational schools. In other words, rather than challenge the constitutionality of the "confessionality" principle in the Quebec public school system, they have sought to be recognized as another component of it; while in Ontario, Jewish parents supported by the Canadian Jewish Congress, have now gone to court to secure standing and assistance for Jewish parochial schools in Ontario not unlike that which has been part of the "constitutional practice" in Quebec.

Fourth, while American Jewish NGOs have filed amicus briefs challenging a variety of breaches of the "wall of separation," Canadian Jewish NGOs have not espoused any constitutional principle of "separation." Indeed, S.29 of the Canadian Charter of Rights—which expressly incorporates the "confessionality" principle from S.93 of the B.N.A. Act—effectively constitutionalizes the role of the state in religion; Canadian Jewish NGOs are now seizing on this principle—and the equality rights principle in S.15 of the Charter—to seek support for government assistance to Jewish schools.

Why these profound difference in the approach of Jewish NGOs to the protection of religious human rights in the United States and Canada? The answer may well lie in the different political and legal cultures of these two countries. First, the United States is organized around an "individual rights" theory and culture; Canada is organized around group rights and communitarian sensibilities as well as individual rights—a "culture" reflected both in the provisions protecting group rights and individual rights in the Canadian Charter of Rights and Freedoms, as well as in the case law interpreting and applying the Charter. Second, the United States eschews any relationship between church and state. For the mainstream Jewish rights organizations, this notion of "separationism" emerges as much an article of "faith" as a principle of constitutionalism. In Canada, the Charter of Rights acknowledges the relationship or co-mingling of the two—certainly as far as denominational rights in education are concerned—and the Supreme Court of Canada has upheld this "relational" principle. Third, the socio-cultural imaging of the United States has been that of a "melting pot" or at least, a legal culture uncomfortable with the recognition of "multiculturalism" as a cultural, let alone juridical norm; in Canada the socio-cultural legal imaging has been that of a "mosaic," while "multiculturalism" is entrenched as a constitutional norm in Section 27 of the Canadian Charter of Rights and Freedoms. Fourth, the United States Constitution makes no reference to G D, while the Canadian Charter of Rights—in its opening Preamble—speaks of a Canada founded upon principles that recognize the "supremacy of G d and the rule of law." Fifth, as sociologists are fond to point out, the organizing idiom of American constitutionalism is that of "the right to life, liberty, and the pursuit of happiness"; the organizing idiom of Canadian constitutionalism, if not Canadian culture, has been that of "peace, order and good government," reflective, as Edgar Friedenberg pointed out, of the Canadian "deference to public authority"—at least in the pre-Charter culture. Sixth, Americans, born of revolution—and having endured the ravages of a Civil War—tend to regard their government as more adversary than ally; Canadians, products of a

Parliamentary system and spared the fall-out of revolution, tend to regard their government as more ally than adversary, though the rights
culture is admittedly modifying that notion.

But leaving different constitutions and legal cultures aside in Canada
and United States, there is also a different Jewish sensibility regarding
religious human rights. For example, in the United States the notion of
separation of church and state not only protects Jews from "established"
religion, but protects them from their own inner religious establishment
as well. In Canada, Jews have been more generally responsive to a traditional sensibility, which influences their approach and sensibility regarding religious human rights as a whole. Furthermore, in the United
States, Jewish NGOs have been largely activist secular organizations—
and even religiously Jewish NGOs have been predominately associated
with Reform Judaism. In Canada, Jewish NGOs, while also secular activist organizations, tend to have a more "traditionalist" sensibility, while
religious Jewish NGOs tend to be more orthodox.

The Role of Jewish NGOs in Combatting Religious Discrimination in the United States and Canada

Again, for purposes of economy, I will summarize, rather than elaborate upon, nine areas of Jewish NGO activity. And while the description
of the Jewish NGO contribution in the development of constitutional and
statute law in the promotion and protection of religious human rights—
the subject matter of the previous section —focused largely on the role of
the American Jewish NGOs as a case-study, with contrasting references
to Canada, this discussion will focus mainly on the role of Canadian
Jewish NGOs as a case-study, with contrasting references to their American counterparts.

Canadian Anti-Discrimination Law. The first human rights case in
Canada in which any NGO was accorded standing to intervene was one
involving religious discrimination, the *Drummond Wren* case in 1945. The
first NGO ever to be given standing in a Canadian court was a Jewish
NGO, the Canadian Jewish Congress, one of the oldest of Canadian human rights NGOs. The case concerned a challenge to an Ontario restrictive covenant purporting to prohibit "the sale of land to Jews or persons
of objectionable nationality." The Ontario High Court, invoking the U.N.
Charter's commitment to the protection of human rights from discrimination on grounds of religion—and citing pronouncements of political
leaders such as Roosevelt, Churchill, and De Gaulle in their condemnation of anti-semitism—held that the legislation was void because it offended public policy. In so doing, the case became the first Canadian case

to grant relief from discrimination on grounds of religion—in this case to those of "Jewish nationality." The outcome of the case was not unrelated to the intervention by a Jewish NGO, for the reference to the U.N. Charter and the condemnations of anti-semitism by world leaders as exemplary of public policy, were contained in the submissions of the CJC. Moreover, the reference by the Court to the horrors of the Holocaust and the dangers of racism were not unlike the argument made by the CJC itself.

If the intervention by a Jewish NGO helped bring about the first case ever in which a Canadian court awarded relief from religious discrimination, Jewish NGOs also had played a role in the conception, drafting, and enactment of the first anti-discrimination statute to be passed in Canada, the Ontario *Racial Discrimination Act* of 1944. Indeed, the Court in *Drummond Wren* had relied on the prohibitions contained in this legislation in voiding the discriminatory restrictive covenant in the case. For the Act prohibited the publication, display or broadcast of anything indicating an intention to discriminate on the basis of race or creed. The statute was designed to remedy the "Whites Only," "Gentiles Only" or "No Jews or Dogs Allowed" signs which once littered beaches and shop windows in Ontario. Not surprisingly, Jewish NGOs lobbied for the enactment of this legislation, as well as for the Acts respecting fair employment and accommodation which came into force in some provinces in the 1950s. But the real revolution in the protection of religious human rights in Canada came with the enactment of comprehensive Human Rights Acts and the provision of full-time commissions. The first such statute was the Ontario Human Rights Code of 1962, which prohibited discrimination on the grounds of race, creed, color, nationality, ancestry or place of origin. Today, all Canadian provinces, the Northwest Territories, the Yukon Territory and the federal government have anti-discrimination legislation. The legislation prohibits, among other things, discrimination because of race, religion or creed, color, nationality, ancestry and place of origin; and Jewish NGOs, particularly in Quebec, Ontario and Manitoba, advocated for, lobbied, and helped bring about this legislation.

Constitutionalization of Freedom of Religion and Protection Against Religious Discrimination. Canadian Jewish NGOs played a formative role in the adoption of the Canadian Charter of Rights and Freedoms, and the constitutionalization thereby of both the principles of "freedom of conscience and religion" in Section 2 of the Charter, and that of equality rights and the prohibition against discrimination on grounds of religion, including a provision for affirmative action in S. 15(1) and (2) of the Charter.

The adoption of the Canadian Charter of Rights and Freedoms was heralded by the then Justice Minister, Mark MacGuigan, as "the single most significant legal development in Canada and in the second half of the 20th century," while the Chief Justice of Canada, Antonio Lamer, speaking at the 10th Anniversary of the Charter, likened it to a "revolutionary" act "comparable to the discoveries by Pasteur in science."

The Canadian Jewish Congress, having a prescient sense of the revolutionary character of those changes—and what it might portend for Jews as well as others—developed a strategy designed to maximize the Jewish voice in the conception, drafting, and enactment of the Charter. First, the CJC established in May 1980 a Select Committee on the Canadian Constitution, composed largely of leading Canadian constitutional law scholars, and presided over by one of Canada's most distinguished scholar-advocates, Professor Maxwell Cohen, former Dean of Law at McGill University and Judge Ad Hoc of the International Court of Justice. Second, it authorized the Select Committee to review the various drafts and related *traveaux preparatoires* of a proposed Charter of Rights, and to engage in a clause-by-clause analysis of such a Charter. Third, it requested the Committee to identify the areas and issues of particular concern to Jews, and to report back to the CJC both as to its overall conception of the Charter, and its recommendations respecting prospective CJC submissions on particular subject-matter areas. Finally, the Committee was to invite submissions from Canadian Jewry which would be factored into its analysis and recommendations.

In November 1980, pursuant to the Canadian Supreme Court's having upheld the constitutionality of the "people's package," or proposals for constitutional reform—including its "centrepiece" the Charter of Rights—the draft Charter of Rights was submitted to a newly established Joint House Senate Committee on the Constitution for a clause-by-clause review. Submissions were also invited from interested members of the Canadian public and NGOs. Although the time frame for preparing and making such submissions was less than a month, hundreds of organizations lined up to make written, and if permitted oral, submissions on the proposed Charter. The parliamentary hearings were packed, the atmospherics heady, the media provided saturation coverage, and there was a felt sense by all participants that they were partaking of a great historical drama.

In what was characterized as an "historic CJC forum on the Charter," the Canadian Jewish Congress set aside a full day to discuss whether CJC, through the Select Committee, should make any submissions to the Joint House Senate Committee on the Constitution, and if so, what those submissions might be. After protracted and heated debate, the CJC voted to authorize the Select Committee to make a comprehensive submission on the whole of the draft Charter, with specific recommendations in the following areas and subject-matters: first, in the area of Fundamental Freedoms or political rights, to support the references to freedom of conscience and religion and freedom of expression, and to recommend the specific exclusion of hate speech from the ambit of expression; second, to include a clause constitutionalizing the domestic prosecution of war criminals; third, to constitutionalize equality rights and protection against discrimination, with particular reference to discrimination on grounds of race, religion, or gender; fourth, and the subject of particular debate at the CJC meeting, to recommend, in the area of equality rights, the constitutionalization of affirmative action; fifth, to support minority language rights in education; sixth, to recommend the entrenchment of multiculturalism; and finally, with regard to the overarching balancing principle of Section One, to require that any purported limits on the guaranteed rights be required to be "reasonable, prescribed law, as can be demonstrably justified in a free and democratic society"—the contemplated analogue to the American "strict scrutiny" principle.

The CJC was one of the first NGOs invited to appear before the Parliamentary Committee, where it both submitted a written brief, and made oral arguments in support of the above recommendations. As it happened, the final draft of the Charter incorporated all the recommendations made by the CJC, save for the recommendation that hate speech be excluded from the ambit of protected expression; and these recommendations were to prove to be of crucial importance in the historic case-law interpreting and applying the Charter. But if the CJC made an important—indeed historic—contribution to the adoption of this revolutionary rights Charter, its involvement in court challenges under the Charter, in the "litigation of the values of the nation," was less involved and sustained.

First, the mandate of the CJC Select Committee was not renewed after a new CJC administration was elected in 1983, reflecting thereby a change in the perceived purposes as well as priorities of CJC. More particularly, CJC was prepared to consign "human rights" advocacy to other human rights NGOs, reserving for itself a more narrow, and limited, conception of its role in Charter litigation to one where there was a direct "Jewish nexus." Effectively, then, it eschewed the principle that guided American Jewish NGO involvement in religious liberty cases, namely, that the human rights of Jews would be respected and secured in the degree that the rights of all people were safeguarded and respected.

Second, by absenting itself from human rights litigation where it did not discern a Jewish nexus, it unsuspectingly acquiesced in the "adverse impact" of this litigation for matters of Jewish concern, such as in the Equality Rights litigation.

Third, and perhaps most important, there did not appear to be a clear strategy on these issues. There were times when the CJC did not intervene in cases even where a Jewish nexus was discernible, such as in the historic "Sunday Observance" cases, which had a direct interest for Canadian Jewry; yet it did intervene to challenge religion in the public schools, and to support government aid to Jewish education.

To be fair to the CJC, like any NGO, it had to adjust commitments to capacities; and, in the absence of any legal department, such as exists with the American Jewish NGOs, involvement was much more restrained. And while it did not appear to map out its interventions in the matter of equality rights and religious liberty as part of an over-all strategy—as did the Women's Legal Education and Action Fund (LEAF) on equality and gender issues—it did make an important contribution in cases and areas where it did intervene.

In particular, mention must be made of two areas where it applied for standing and did intervene in the major litigation engaging these areas— hate speech and the bringing of Nazi war criminals to justice. Given the importance of these issues in the panoply of Jewish human rights, they will now be treated separately, albeit briefly, below.

Constitutionality of Anti-Hate Legislation. If there is a single issue that has galvanized Canadian Jewish NGOs, it has been the right of minorities to protection against group vilifying speech; and while the proximate cause of the passage of hate propaganda legislation in Canada was the report of the Special Committee on Hate Propaganda (hereinafter the Cohen Committee), demands for legislation of this kind predated the establishment of the Cohen Committee. Indeed, "it is fair to say that the Canadian Jewish Congress (CJC) was the leader in bringing the problem of hate propaganda, particularly anti-semitic literature largely originating in the United States, to the attention of the government authorities, and requesting remedial legislation. For the CJC was convinced, following a careful analysis of existing Criminal Code provisions, that there was no legal basis to fight hate propaganda in the criminal courts, and for years, beginning in the early 1950s, and through the 1960s, it lobbied for legislative reform."

In the meantime, a series of events converged in support of the enactment of anti-hate legislation. First, a growing human rights movement had mobilized across Canada and attracted considerable public support for the passage of all sorts of remedial legislation to combat discrimination of various kinds. Second, international treaties were being signed committing signatory states, including Canada, to the enactment of measures against racist hate speech. Third, a number of foreign states had turned their attention to the problem of hate propaganda and were enacting anti-hate legislation; while in Canada there was a growing belief—and evidence—that the dissemination of hate propaganda was on the rise. Moreover,

> the mass dissemination of vituperative materials appeared to accelerate in early 1964, and in March of that same year the *Toronto Star* editorialized about the "stream of violently anti-semitic and anti-Negro material... circulating through the mails in Toronto," including the notorious Nazi newspaper, *Der Sturmer* containing an account of "Jewish ritual murder." At the same time, and from across the country came demands from organizations as diverse as the Manitoba Bar Association, the Canadian Federation of University Women, and the National Convention of the Royal Canadian Legion for government action to halt the attacks. Some commentators called for a "test case" to deal with the use by hate propagandists of the mails, while Jewish NGOs felt the time was propitious to enact anti-hate legislation.

But it was the dramatic findings in the unanimous Report of the Cohen Committee in 1965, and the prestige of its membership, that became the catalyst for action. In the words of the Cohen Committee, and later to be invoked by the Supreme Court of Canada in upholding the constitutionality of the anti-hate legislation, the potential for psychological and social damage of hate propaganda, both to a desensitized majority and to sensitive minority target groups, is incalculable. As Mr. Justice Jackson of the United States Supreme Court wrote in *Beauharnois v. Illinois*, such "sinister abuses of our freedoms of expression . . . can tear apart a society, brutalize its dominant elements, and persecute even to extermination, its minorities."

Accordingly, the Cohen Committee recommended in 1965, and the Canadian Parliament in 1970 enacted, anti-hate legislation closely modelled on the CJC recommendations of the 1960s. In particular, the provisions enacted prohibited the advocacy or promotion of genocide, the communication of hatred against an identifiable group that was likely to lead to a breach of the peace, and the wilful promotion of hatred in a public place against an identifiable group, with a series of defences to safeguard the rights of the accused.

In a major forum on "Freedom of Expression and Hate Propaganda" at a "Nuremberg" Conference at McGill University in 1987, Professor Maxwell Cohen in a retrospective on the Report, summed up the dilemmas faced by his Committee—and subsequently by the Canadian courts—as follows:

> The Report on Hate Propaganda was published in November of 1965—twenty-two years ago. It dealt with the classic dilemmas in this field. "Sticks and stones may break my bones but names will never hurt me" had become, in the light of the increasing sensibilities of people everywhere, an impossible cliché with which to live. It may have suited an older, fairy-tale time; it was impossible in the post-Nuremberg generation in which we lived. So, we faced the classic philosophical dilemma of determining the limits on free speech, when speech is not directed to a serious political debate as such, but is directed to race or to religion in some unpleasant, intentionally hurtful way.

As it happened, all the major Canadian Jewish NGOs supported the enactment of the anti-hate laws—as they had supported earlier federal and provincial anti-discrimination legislation—and saw the anti-hate legislation as part of the "genre" of legislation protecting, among others, against religious discrimination. Indeed, they have intervened in support of the constitutionality of the legislation in every hate speech case that has come before the Supreme Court of Canada, including the criminal law remedy or "group libel" legislation prohibiting the public and wilful promotion of hatred against an identifiable group; the federal anti-discrimination remedy in the Canadian Human Rights Act which prohibits the repeated use of telephonic communications for the propagation of hatred against an identifiable group, which is defined as a discriminatory practice; and provincial anti-discrimination remedies such as those found in the Quebec Charter of Human Rights and Freedoms, whose parallel provisions are even broader than the federal.

Admittedly, American Jewish human rights NGOs might be surprised to learn that their Canadian counterparts were largely responsible for the enactment of Canada's anti-hate legislation to begin with, let alone the intervention of Canadian Jewish NGOs in all the "hate speech" cases in support of the constitutionality of such legislation; for unlike the Canadians, all the major American Jewish NGOs regard hate speech as protected speech under the First Amendment, and have filed amicus briefs in support of the constitutionality of hate speech or have challenged legislation seeking to combat it.

Hate Crimes Legislation. While American Jewish NGOs eschewed any support for the criminalization of hate speech, they have been at the forefront of national and state efforts to counter hate motivated crimes. In particular, from the time the Anti-Defamation League (ADL) conceived, drafted, and proposed model hate crimes legislation for adoption some 14 years ago, the response has been nothing short of dramatic.

More than half of the states have now enacted laws based on, or similar to, the ADL model, and almost every state has some form of legislation which can be invoked to redress bias-motivated crimes. The United States Congress has also taken steps to enact a federal hate crime statute, with both the House of Representatives and the Senate recently voting to include a penalty-enhancement provision in their respective versions of the omnibus crime bill. Furthermore, in a landmark decision in the struggle against bias motivated criminal conduct in June 1993 in Wisconsin, the U.S. Supreme Court in a unanimous decision upheld the constitutionality of Wisconsin's penalty-enhancement hate crimes statute, which was based on the ADL model.

Indeed, the ADL had filed an amicus brief in support of hate crimes legislation before both the Wisconsin and United States Supreme Courts, where it described the compelling need for such legislation, and explained how the Wisconsin law comported with the First Amendment. The brief maintained that the core of the legislation is a "penalty enhancement" concept whereby the defendant is subject to an enhanced penalty if his crime is motivated by an intent to harm based on the victim's race, religion, or similar characteristics, and which thereby acts upon the entire community as well as the victim. As the amicus brief put it, "enhancing the penalty also serves to give a message as to the seriousness with which society judges bigotry that takes the form of criminal conduct directed toward certain groups, and acts as a deterrent to such conduct." The brief affirmed that the statute was not criminalizing hate speech, which was protected by the First Amendment; it merely enhanced the penalty for crimes where bias was the principal motivating factor.

The ADL model statute also includes an institutional vandalism or "religious rights" section which increases the criminal penalties for vandalism aimed at houses of worship, cemeteries, schools, and community centers, and seeks to deter attacks against the most common targets of vandalism: churches, synagogues and religious schools. The statute requires knowledge of the character of the property but does not require proof of motive for the vandalism, making convictions easier to obtain.

Another provision of the model legislation creates a civil action for victims. While these activities might presently be actionable in a common law tort suit, this provision makes it explicit. Additionally, this section provides for additional forms of relief, such as recovery for actions by minors, which is generally not permitted under most states' common law tort actions. These additional forms of relief can have a significant deterrent value, and should also encourage victims to consider bringing civil suits.

The ADL model legislation also includes a section on bias crime reporting and training. Experience has shown that accurate, comprehensive, and comparative data concerning the number, location and types of bias crimes is essential to combat hate crimes. The enactment of the federal Hate Crime Statistics Act in 1990 demonstrated widespread recognition of the necessity of gathering data on crimes motivated by bigotry and prejudice in order to be able to combat hate crimes.

Religious Discrimination in Employment. In June 1994, in an important case involving "adverse impact discrimination," the Supreme Court of Canada reversed a lower court opinion which had upheld the refusal of a Catholic School Board to compensate Jewish teachers for loss of pay for not working on Yom Kippur. In doing so, the Court relied on a line of precedents and principles in anti-discrimination law in the matter of religion which Canadian Jewish NGOs had helped establish through their interventions in the cases. In particular, the Court held that adverse impact discrimination will arise where an employer for genuine business reasons adopts a rule or standard which is on its face neutral, and which will apply equally to all employees, but which has a different and discriminatory effect upon another employee or group of employees based on religion, a prohibited ground of discrimination. This principle and proposition can be expected to guide the court in cases of this kind.

Trans-National Discrimination by Foreign Governments: The Arab Boycott. In 1977, the Report of the Commission on Economic Coercion and Discrimination exposed a pattern of compliance and complicity with the Arab Boycott in Canada in both the private and public sectors. It concluded that the notion of an "Arab Boycott" was a misnomer; that what really was taking place was a "Canadian boycott," that is, the acquiescence by Canadian corporations in the extra-territorial application of foreign law to Canada purporting to dictate, through a restrictive covenant, the terms of commerce between Canada and a friendly state, the terms of commerce between Canadian corporations themselves, and worst of all, purporting to dictate in Canada the terms of employment on grounds of religion. In other words, Canadian corporations, as a condition for doing business with an Arab country, had to undertake not to do business with Israel (secondary boycott) or with another *Canadian* corporation that did business with Israel (tertiary boycott) or not to employ or promote Canadians of the Jewish religion. The evidence in the Commission's Report established that both *government* Crown corporations and leading Canadian corporations had knowingly complied with both the secondary and tertiary boycotts, and in some instances, had refused to hire or promote Canadians because they were Jews.

While these dramatic disclosures were taking place in Canada—and Canadian Jewish NGOs were seeking to get anti-boycott, anti-discrimination legislation enacted— similar revelations in the United States had already resulted in U.S. Congressional Hearings on the impact of the Arab boycott in America; in the enactment of comprehensive federal anti-boycott legislations mandating disclosure of requests to comply with the boycott while prohibiting actual compliance itself; in the establishment of a "Boycott Watch" monitoring unit and newsletter by the American Jewish Congress; in the initiation by American Jewish NGOs of a Business Roundtable with leading American corporations to secure their support for a strong anti-boycott stance; and in authorizing a "right of action" in U.S. courts for American citizens to seek redress for any damages caused through the discriminatory application of the Arab Boycott in America.

Indeed, the ADL has filed amicus briefs in support of a private right of action in American courts for victims of the Arab boycott. The briefs document the inception, expansion, and growing impact of the Arab boycott of Israel; the methods by which the boycott has been enforced by the Arab League, and its discriminatory effects on companies and individuals; and the enactment of the federal anti-boycott provisions, which Congress enacted primarily to deal with the unfairness and discrimination implicit in these restrictive covenants. In particular, as the amicus briefs demonstrate, the anti-boycott legislative provisions were intended to protect the civil rights of a special class—people discriminated against on the basis of race, religion, sex, or national origin; nationals, residents and business concerns of boycotted countries; and American Jews as well as U.S. companies employing American Jews or supporting Jewish organizations, indicating the clear nexus to discrimination on grounds of religion. The briefs conclude by recalling that "the EAA's anti-boycott provisions were intended to protect victims of the Arab boycott, both by permitting them judicial redress and by prohibiting any further participation in the boycott. These purposes can only be served by recognition of a private right of action under the EAA."

While the Jewish NGOs in the U.S. helped secure the enactment of comprehensive anti-boycott legislation, filed amicus briefs in support of victims of the Arab boycott seeking redress in American courts, and had been instrumental in a host of initiatives as set forth above, Canadian Jewish NGOs were markedly less successful in developing any parallel initiatives in Canada. Part of the reason was that all this was taking place in the pre-Charter era, before a "rights culture" had taken hold in Canada. A more important reason—and one which demonstrates the importance of rights-based arguments—was that the advocacy for anti-boycott legislation and related measures in Canada was being advanced by the Canada-Israel Committee (CIC), the lobby group for Israel in Canada, rather than the CJC or B'nai B'rith, Canadian Jewish human rights NGOs. In other words, the advocacy by CIC took a Canadian rights issue of anti-discrimination law and made it appear as a political issue related to the Arab-Israeli conflict; in contrast, the advocacy by major Jewish human rights NGOs in the U.S.—in concert with American civil liberties groups—resulted in the issue in the U.S. being perceived for what it was—a human rights issue involving discrimination on one or more prohibited grounds of discrimination, namely religion. As a human rights, anti-discrimination issue it resonated in the court of American public opinion; as a perceived political, Middle-East issue in Canada it never seriously got off the ground.

Domestic Enforcement of International Human Rights Norms Against Religious Persecution. *Siderman v. Argentina* concerned the confiscation of property and acts of torture committed against the Siderman family in Argentina by the Argentine military junta which seized power in 1976. The Sidermans were among the many victims of the Argentine military, whose rule from 1976 to 1983 was characterized not only by a virulent anti-Semitism, but also by kidnappings, torture, and the "disappearances" of thousands of Argentine citizens.

José Siderman was a prominent Argentine Jew who miraculously survived being kidnapped, beaten, and tortured. After he and his family fled to the United States—where they found a safe haven—their assets, including the largest hotel in northern Argentina and other significant real estate holdings, were confiscated. When their initial efforts to obtain redress in Argentina failed, the Sidermans initiated a lawsuit in the United States. At that time, ADL supported their complaint in federal district court with an amicus brief that detailed a pattern of anti-Semitism in Argentina and argued that U.S. courts have jurisdiction to redress injuries such as those the Sidermans suffered.

In 1984, the U.S. District Court issued a default judgment in favor of the Sidermans. However, that judgment was vacated a year later when a representative of the Argentine government appeared in court for the first time in the case and invoked the Foreign Sovereign Immunities Act. The Sidermans chose not to appeal the decision immediately. Instead, they again sought to obtain redress in Argentina, where the military was no longer in power. However, after several years their efforts proved fruitless, prompting a decision to return again to the U.S. courts.

In ADL's brief supporting the Sidermans' appeal to the United States Court of Appeals, the focus again was on anti-Semitism in Argentina, both historically and specifically under the rule of the military junta. In addition, the ADL brief argued that the facts of the *Siderman* case brought it within an exception to the Act of State doctrine and consequently the district court erred in applying that doctrine. In a word, the judicially created Act of State doctrine allows U.S. courts to abstain from deciding a case involving an international transaction on the grounds that one of the actors in the transaction is a foreign state; but what has come to be known as the *Bernstein* exception to the doctrine precludes its application by the courts if the U.S. State Department informs the court that the executive branch has determined application of the doctrine to be unnecessary.

In its brief, ADL contended that *Bernstein* stands for the general proposition that the Act of State doctrine does not bar claims in U.S. courts for property seized by a foreign government based on *religious discrimination*. Furthermore, the brief pointed out that the Sidermans' property was confiscated by a regime no longer in power, and therefore "it can hardly be argued that a court's consideration of this case could embarrass the Executive's conduct of foreign affairs." Finally, the brief noted that the treatment of the Sidermans was also a violation of international law which U.S. courts should redress.

Judgment in the case is still pending. But the importance of the case lies in the principle that U.S. domestic courts may be resorted to for the enforcement of international human rights against a foreign government in matters of religious discrimination, demonstrating again the importance of religious discrimination as a matter of *jus cogens* in international law.

Gender-based Discrimination Under Cover of Religion. Canadian Jewish NGOs have challenged attempts to use religion as an exculpatory defense to a gender-related human rights violation—for example, where the country of origin supports the practice of female genital mutilation as a "religious" responsibility—and Jewish NGOs have gone to court to support the claim for refugee status on grounds of gender-specific persecution.

In a landmark immigration ruling, Canada has granted refugee status to a Somalia woman who fled her country with her 10-year-old daughter, because she feared that the daughter would face ritual genital mutilation. In one of the rare times that any Western nation has specifically cited the threat of this ancient custom, widely practised in Africa, as a reason for granting asylum, a panel of Canada's Immigration and Refugee Board said the daughter's "right to personal security would be grossly infringed" if she were forced to return.

A case similar to the one just described in Canada came up recently in the United States. A federal immigration judge ruled in March 1994 that a Nigerian woman living illegally in Portland, Oregon would not be deported to her native country because her two young daughters would probably face genital mutilation if they accompanied her. The Portland judge's ruling was not as sweeping as that of the Canadian panel; the judge did not grant a request for asylum, which would have broken new ground, but merely annulled an expulsion order.

Both the American and Canadian judges have put foreign governments on notice that religion will not avail as a cover for human rights violators; and Jewish NGOs in Canada and the United States have been active in securing the enactment of guidelines that would authorize the conferral of refugee status on the basis of gender related persecution on grounds of religion.

Holocaust Remembrance and War Crimes Justice: The Right to Memory as a "Religious" Right. Being Jewish has been described as an exercise in "collective memory." Indeed, for Jews, memory itself is almost a religion, and Holocaust remembrance a religious right—even duty. For the Holocaust, as Nobel Laureate Elie Wiesel has reminded the world again and again, was a war against the Jews in which not all victims were Jews, but all Jews were victims. "Zachor"—remember—has become for Jewish NGOs not only a moral exhortation, but a "right to memory," a religious commandment. Holocaust denial, then, is regarded by Jewish NGOs not only as an assault on memory, on truth, but as the "killing of the victims a second time"—the ultimate assault on Jewish sensibility. At the same time, bringing Nazi war criminals to justice is seen as much as a matter of fidelity to Holocaust remembrance as it is fidelity to the rule of law.

Thus, for American, Canadian, European and Latin American Jewish NGOs, fidelity to Holocaust remembrance, combatting Holocaust denial, and bringing Nazi war criminals to justice is seen as the ultimate protection of religious human rights—the Jewish NGO sword and shield against defamation—the existential antidote to injustice. Indeed, it has been a centerpiece of the work of international Jewish human rights NGOs like the World Jewish Congress, or national human rights NGOs like the ADL, just as it is the *raison d'être* of the Simon Wiesenthal Centre, the fastest growing Jewish human rights membership NGO of the past decade. It has likewise been the inspiration behind the building of Holocaust Memorials such as the Simon Wiesenthal Centre Museum of Tolerance in Los Angeles, the U.S. Holocaust Museum in Washington, or the Holocaust Memorial Centre in Montreal.

For Canadian Jewish NGOs, these issues have not only been priorities on the "Jewish" rights agenda, but they have sought to make them priorities on the Canadian justice agenda. Accordingly, these NGOs have played a crucial role in the enactment of anti-hate legislation to combat Holocaust denial and protect the integrity of memory; in the enactment of war crimes legislation to authorize the domestic prosecution of Nazi war criminals in Canada; and in having included in the Canadian Charter of Rights a provision to constitutionalize prosecution of war criminals—to insure that "retroactivity" shall not avail as a defence against prosecution.

Jewish NGOs have appreciated that these issues are inextricably intertwined. As the Ontario Court of Appeal put it: "[T]he Holocaust did not begin in the gas chambers, it began with words—those are the chilling facts of history." For those NGOs then, the first order of justice was combatting this racist incitement; as well, every time NGOs bring a Nazi war criminal to justice, they strike a blow against the Holocaust denial movement.

Canadian Jewish NGOs have not only played a crucial role in public advocacy on these matters, but they have gone to court to secure the application of these laws. In a word, these NGOs have intervened in every major war crimes case before the Appellate and Supreme Courts of Canada. For the Jewish human rights NGO for whom memory is itself almost a religion, Holocaust remembrance and bringing Nazi war criminals to justice are regarded as profound statements—and actions—in the promotion and protection of religious human rights.

Strategies and Models of Advocacy by Jewish NGOs in the Promotion and Protection of Religious Human Rights

There is perhaps no single issue of the violation of religious human rights around which Jewish NGOs coalesced more than the situation of oppressed Jewry around the world. Indeed, the plight of Soviet Jewry in the 1970s and 1980s, and, somewhat belatedly, that of Syrian and Ethiopian Jewry in the 1980s, dominated the Jewish and human rights agenda of every major Jewish NGO, while spawning the emergence of single issue Jewish NGOs dedicated to the struggle for Soviet, Syrian and Ethiopian Jewry. Some of these "single-issue" Jewish NGOs—such as the National Conference on Soviet Jewry and the Union of Councils for Soviet Jewry—became major Jewish and human rights NGOs in their own right and helped to influence the course and conduct of both American foreign policy and the Helsinki process throughout most of the 1970s and 1980s, as the situation of Soviet Jewry was a watershed issue in East-West relations themselves.

What follows is an identification of the role played—and strategies deployed—by Jewish NGOs in addressing—and seeking to redress—the violations of religious human rights, using Soviet Jewry as a case-study. What emerges is a prospective model for strategic advocacy by religious NGOs, or human rights NGOs generally speaking, in the matter of redressing violations of religious human rights or human rights at large.

Reports of Violations. One of the most important, indeed crucial, NGO functions—and one indispensable to the promotion and protection of religious human rights—is the investigation, documentation, exposure, and denouncing of violations of religious human rights and the violators themselves. As Professor John Humphrey put it, the "mobilization of shame against human rights violators" is the ultimate sanction. Or, as Professor Mullerson has said: "[M]onitoring is the very essence of human rights enforcing." That "the whole world is watching" tends to concentrate the minds of human rights violators wonderfully.

Accordingly, whether we are speaking about the human rights of Jews in the Soviet Union, Syria, or Ethiopia, the evidence is compelling that this fact-finding function is crucial to the promotion and protection of human rights. Indeed, governments themselves have become increasingly dependent on the fact finding of NGOs; while the intergovernmental machinery, such as the U.N. Commission on Human Rights, or the Human Rights Committee under the International Covenant on Civil and Political Rights, would be "virtually incapacitated" in the absence of NGO briefs, petitions, documentary evidence, legal analysis, written and oral interventions.

But if fact finding and human rights monitoring by NGOs is crucial to the promotion and protection of human rights generally, the "mobilization of shame" by Jewish NGOs against the Soviet Union's violations of the rights of Soviet Jews is dramatic evidence of the efficacy of this fact finding and monitoring NGO strategy. For it was the exposure of the Soviet Union's systematic denial of the right to emigrate for Soviet Jews that led to the enactment of the Jackson-Vanick Amendment conditioning the conferral of U.S. trade benefits on the rate of Jewish emigration from the U.S.S.R. It was the documentation of the Jewish Prisoners of Conscience in the U.S.S.R.—people who like Josef Begun were fired from their job for desiring to emigrate and then charged with parasitism for not having a job—that exposed the full brutality of the Soviet Union and isolated them in the court of world public opinion. It was the massive evidence of the corresponding denial of the religious rights of Soviet

Jews—the right to the free exercise of their religion, the right to teach and learn the Hebrew language and basic tenets of their faith and culture, the right "to worship or assemble in connexion with a religion or belief," the right to visit, and be visited by their co-religionists abroad—that culminated in the "shame" which is the international community's chief enforcement weapon; while the denial of these religious rights—coupled with the denial of the right to emigrate—regarded as tantamount to the denial of the right to life itself—led to the international sanctions regime—including the "linkage" under the Helsinki Final Act.

Legislative Lobbying. It might seem paradoxical to attribute a legislative role to NGOs. But increasingly, and in the international arena in particular, NGOs are playing a formative role in the initiation, drafting, interpretation, and application of international human rights agreements and standard-setting generally. So, whether it be the International Covenants on Civil and Political Rights, and Economic Social and Cultural Rights, or the International Convention on the Elimination of all Forms of Racial Discrimination or the Convention on the Elimination of Discrimination Against Women, or the recent Convention on the Rights of the Child, NGOs have played an important legislative role.

What is true of the legislative role of human rights NGOs in general, is particularly evident in the legislative contribution of Jewish NGOs in the matter of religious human rights in particular. For it was Jewish NGOs who were responsible for the inclusion of the "religion" provisions in the U.N. Charter and in the Universal Declaration of Human Rights; who ensured that Article 18 respecting freedom of religion was included in the ICCPR; who lobbied for and helped bring about the Genocide Convention; who made a substantial contribution to the provisions respecting discrimination in the Convention on the Elimination of All Forms of Discrimination and the UNESCO Convention; who played a formative role in securing the provisions relating to religion in the Helsinki Final Act let alone the Declaration on the Elimination of All Forms of Religious Intolerance.

Indeed, the Copenhagen Conference on the Human Dimension is an excellent case-study of the role and efficacy of Jewish NGOs. For the National Conference on Soviet Jewry, the Union for the Councils for Soviet Jews, the World Jewish Congress and others, in concert with the American Delegation to the C.S.C.E. Conference, played an important role in the identification and drafting of "those principles of justice which form the basis of the rule of law . . . and which are essential to the full expression of the inherent dignity and of the equal and inalienable rights of all human beings." The Canadian Helsinki Watch Group, and the Canadian Committee on Soviet Jewry, working closely with both the Canadian and

Soviet Delegations, contributed to the inclusion for the first time in a
C.S.C.E. Concluding Document of a joint proposal by Canada and the
U.S.S.R. to combat racial incitement including a specific condemnation of
anti-semitism itself. The Proposal, in part, reads as follows:

> (40) The participating States clearly and unequivocally condemn
> totalitarianism, racial and ethnic hatred, anti-semitism, xenopho-
> bia and discrimination against anyone as well as prosecution on
> religious and ideological grounds.

They declare their firm intention to intensify the efforts to combat these
phenomena in all their forms and therefore will:

> (40.1) take effective measures, including the adoption, in confor-
> mity with their constitutional systems and their international ob-
> ligations, of such laws as may be necessary, to provide protection
> against any acts that constitute incitement to violence against
> persons or groups based on national, racial, ethnic or religious
> discrimination, hostility or hatred, including anti-semitism.

Humanitarian Assistance to Victims. NGOs are playing an increasingly important, if not indispensable role in rendering a variety of forms
of humanitarian assistance to victims of human rights abuses and their
families, including, for example, tracing disappeared persons as in the
case of the inquiry into the fate and whereabouts of Raoul Wallenberg;
visiting detainees in prison as in the visits to the Chistopol prison by
members of Helsinki Watch Groups; securing humane conditions of confinement through representations made within the C.S.C.E. Conferences;
and providing material and moral assistance to their families and the
like. This humanitarian assistance may involve not only representations
to the human rights violator government, but to one's own government,
to other governments, to inter-governmental bodies and international organizations.

Jewish NGOs are a dramatic example of this strategy as they served
as a vital lifeline for Jewish refuseniks, prisoners of conscience, and other
victims of human rights violations in the Soviet Union. They saw to it
that every prisoner of conscience—indeed every refusenik family—was
adopted by some Jewish organization, synagogue, or family in the West;
that children of prisoners of refuseniks were similarly "adopted"; that
whole Jewish communities in the U.S.S.R. were "twinned" with munici-
palities, provinces or states, in the U.S., Canada, Europe, and elsewhere;
that food parcels, mail, reading materials and the like were sent to the
"Sharanskys," "Nudels," "Beguns," languishing in the Soviet Gulag; that
prayer books, matzos on Passover, and other religious articles and neces-

sities were delivered to synagogues in the Soviet Union; that regular visits to refuseniks and families of political prisoners would take place from
their co-religionists abroad; that refusenik cancer patients would have
special attention so that they might secure the best medical care that
could be made available to them, and, if they had to die, that their dignity and religious sensibility would be protected as best it could; that, in
a word, as the Talmud instructs, and which is the guiding credo for Jewish NGOs engaged in humanitarian assistance, "all Jews are responsible
one for another."

Legal Representation to Victims of Human Rights Abuses. This is,
admittedly, a difficult and somewhat complex role, but a particularly
compelling one for NGOs. For legal representation not only helps to secure redress for victims of human rights violations, it serves a number of
collateral functions at the same time. Indeed, the work of Jewish NGOs is
not only a case-study of this NGO strategy, but in many ways Jewish
NGOs and the lawyers associated with them pioneered in the development of this legal strategy itself, and the collateral benefits that attended
it.

In particular, Jewish NGOs and their respective attorneys inspired
the mobilization of shame against the USSR violator regime through
public legal petitions to the Procurator-General of the USSR; prepared a
documented set of testimonies to the innocence of the accused through
the collection of witness testimony and documentary evidence; organized
what was effectively a critical mass of human rights advocacy on behalf
of refuseniks and political prisoners through petitions to inter-
governmental fora, including the U.N. Human Rights Committee (where
appropriate), the I.L.O., and U.N.E.S.C.O.; utilized the complaints procedure and "open forum" of the Helsinki process; used domestic courts to
enforce international human rights norms; and exercised the U.N. 1503
procedure in cases of a "consistent pattern of gross violations of human
rights," such as in the denial of the right to emigrate for Soviet Jews. Indeed, the advocacy work of the Jewish NGOs is a case-study of the use
and efficiency of a myraid of procedures and remedies under both domestic and international human rights law.

Human Rights Education. This educational process involves
"conscientization," as some in the human rights movement call it—or
"sensibiliser" as the French put it—in order to create a culture of human
rights—with particular respect for religious human rights.

The work of Jewish NGOs in the matter of education for tolerance—
or education against religious intolerance—is a case-study of this strategy, particularly in the example of the American Jewish Committee. Indeed, the American Jewish Committee's Jacob Blaustein Institute for the

Advancement of Human Rights (JBI) has made the subject of religious intolerance—its dimensions, root causes, and possible remedial measures—a major focus of its activities; while the international affirmation of "religious human rights" has been a focal point of its research and advocacy projects. Thus the Institute has worked to assure the adoption and later the implementation of the Declaration on the Elimination of All Forms of Religious Intolerance. It launched a series of colloquia in the 1970s and 1980s that brought together prominent international scholars and jurists to examine the central elements of religious freedom; the essays and publications that were produced helped equip scholars, international experts, diplomats, and practitioners who in turn advocated, analyzed, or sought to implement "religious human rights," including in particular, the characterization of the right to leave as the most fundamental of rights.

Although the Institute, as the American Jewish Committee itself, was particularly concerned with the fate of the Soviet Jews who were barred from leaving their country, it perceived the problem of "the right to leave" as a far more universal one, affecting many people across the globe. For a country's arbitrary refusal to permit its nationals to emigrate was a standing violation of one of the most hallowed rights in international human rights law.

Accordingly, from its earliest days, the Institute embarked upon a continuing educational effort to ensure the observance of this freedom in international law, while demonstrating how the denial of this freedom was tantamount to the denial of the right to liberty—including religious liberty—if not the right to life itself. In June 1972, the Jacob Blaustein Institute, together with the International Institute of Human Rights in Strasbourg, France, and the Faculty of Law of the University of Uppsala, Sweden convened some 70 scholars and human rights experts from 25 countries to discuss the right to freedom of movement throughout the world in what has come to be known as the Uppsala Colloquium.

By exposing the devices some governments used to circumvent freedom of emigration, and by developing recommendations for international safeguards, the Uppsala Declaration adopted at the gathering focused world attention on this fundamental right. Widely disseminated to scholars and practitioners in the human rights field, the Declaration was translated into several languages and published in numerous journals. It helped serve as a resource for the drafters of the Jackson Amendment to the Trade Reform Act of 1974, which linked most-favoured-nation trade status with free emigration, and had an important impact on the Helsinki Conference on Security and Cooperation in Europe. Indeed, in the historic Final Act (Accord) of that conference in 1975, 35 nations, including the United States, Canada and the Soviet Union, pledged to respect basic human rights and freedoms, including freedom of religion and belief and freedom to leave and to return. The colloquium proceedings, with background papers and recommendations, were published in a bilingual volume (French and English) titled, *The Right to Leave and to Return*; the publication and Declaration are still used as basic educational resources—perhaps the most thorough on the subject—by scholars and officials.

The U.N. Subcommission on the Prevention of Discrimination and Protection of Minorities, which for years was prevented from dealing with the right to leave by the Soviet bloc, finally initiated a study of the subject in 1982 and designated a special rapporteur to implement it. To provide guidance for the rapporteur, the Blaustein Institute commissioned Hurst Hannum, Director of the Procedural Aspects of International Law Institute, to produce the widely used guidebook, *The Right to Leave and Return in International Law and Practice* (1987). The JBI then helped to arranged three conferences of experts on the subject. The special rapporteur's final draft declaration, issued in June 1988, was modeled on a proposed text developed at one of these conferences. The draft declaration was further considered at subsequent conferences in New York and Strasbourg in 1989, both arranged by the Institute, and it served as a basis for the first Declaration in 1989 on *The Right to Leave* ever adopted at a USSR conference in Moscow co-sponsored by a group of Jewish NGOs.

Expressing Solidarity with Indigenous NGOs. This role involves not only providing a *moral/physical* lifeline to victims and their families, but also a moral juridical support system to indigenous human rights NGOs in the human rights violator countries who may be jeopardizing not only their organizational status but also the lives of their members. Accordingly, while human rights struggles are fought and won for the most part in the national arenas, the international NGO support system provides not only promotion of, but protection for, that human rights struggle.

Again, the role of Jewish NGOs in the matter of the struggle for Soviet Jewry provides an illuminating case-study of this basic strategy. For it was the international solidarity and support system developed by these Jewish NGOs that provided a protective umbrella for the Soviet Helsinki Watch Groups and the even more fledgling—and vulnerable—Jewish organizations and groupings in the USSR. In a word, the reality that "the whole world is watching" gave credence to the Camus pledge that "we cannot prevent children from being tortured—but we can prevent less children from being tortured." Jewish NGOs—like NGOs generally—could not prevent Helsinki Monitors from being arrested or Jewish refuseniks from being imprisoned—but they were able to prevent less Monitors from being arrested, and less refuseniks from being imprisoned.

Again, the Concluding Document of the Copenhagen Conference gives expression and effect to this NGO support system within the Helsinki process. For in Article 10 of the Concluding Document—which the Helsinki and Jewish NGOs themselves helped draft as part of their legislative role—the participating States reaffirm "their commitment to ensure effectively the rights of the individual to know and act upon human rights and fundamental freedoms, and to contribute actively, individually or in association with others, to their promotion and protection."

Public Advocacy, "Shame," and the Role of the Media. While acting as Counsel to Soviet Prisoners of Conscience like Anatoly Sharansky—and to NGOs who had taken up their cause—I had occasion to meet with Soviet dissident Andrei Sakharov in the Soviet Union in 1979. It turned out to be a fateful meeting, as I was expelled from the Soviet Union the next day—with my meeting with Sakharov described as one of my "criminal" activities—and with Sakharov himself forcibly exiled shortly thereafter to Gorky.

But the words—the message of that encounter—were indelibly imprinted on my psyche—and advocacy—forever. As Sakharov put it, "I do not know what will help the cause of human rights—I do know that it will not be helped by silence." And as if to buttress his remarks—and the need to combat the Soviet violations of religious human rights—he added the following: "Anti-semitism in the Soviet Union has been raised to the level of a state religion in a Godless society." Public advocacy, for Sakharov, was an essential ingredient in the "mobilization of shame" against the Soviet Union. "Shame," as Sakharov put it, was the best sanction we had, for the Soviet Union was preoccupied with its legitimacy, and the media, as Sakharov concluded, was the carrier, the instrument, of this mobilization of shame. The Sakharov dictum was translated into Jewish NGO strategy for whom public advocacy, the mobilization of shame, and the exposure by the media were guiding principles.

Similarly, the case of Soviet Prisoner of Conscience Josef Begun emerged as a *cause celebre* for the cause of human rights in general and religious human rights in particular in the Soviet Union. Begun, one of the first to learn and to teach Hebrew in the USSR, became also a case-study of Catch-22 Gulag Justice in the matter of Jewish refuseniks in the Soviet Union. Fired from his job for desiring to emigrate, he was then charged with parasitism for not having a job, and threatened with psychiatric confinement for the treatment of the condition of parasitism. Having served his sentence for parasitism, he was charged with unlawful

residency upon his return to Moscow; finally, he became the first refusenik ever to be subjected to "triple jeopardy" when he was charged
and convicted for "anti-Soviet slander and agitation" for seeking nothing
else but to exercise his rights under Article 18 of the ICCPR—to which
the USSR was a State Party—"to individually or in community with others and in public or private, to manifest his religion or belief in worship,
observance, practice, and teaching."

The Jacob Blaustein Institute for the Advancement of Human Rights,
in concert with the International Human Rights Law Group, the International Human Rights Committee of the American Bar Association Section
of International Law and Practice, and the American Association for the
Advancement of Science convened an international seminar of legal experts in early 1984 to discuss how to use existing U.N. procedures in
cases such as that of Begun for the promotion and protection of the human rights of prisoners of conscience in general and their religious human rights in particular. The legal scholars at the seminar drafted a
memorandum to the Procurator-General of the Soviet Union seeking a
reversal of Begun's conviction on the grounds that it violated both Soviet
and international law. This document was also forwarded to the
UNESCO director-general with the request that he intercede with the Soviet authorities as the violations cited involved rights protected under the
UNESCO Convention; to the U.N. Human Rights Committee as it involved a direct violation of Article 18 of the CP Convention; and to the
ILO as evidence of a policy and practice of discrimination in employment
prohibited under the ILO Convention.

Both the seminar and the memorandum attracted wide media coverage, heightening international awareness of the plight of Soviet Jews and
the dismal state of human rights in the USSR. Indeed, it became one of
the few instances where the Soviet Union was called to account by the
U.N. and its specialized agencies like UNESCO and the ILO, and a case-
study of the value of NGO coalition strategy and the efficacy of international advocacy.

The Role of International Jewish NGOs in the Promotion and Protection of Religious Human Rights

The "Teaching of Contempt" and Catholic-Jewish Dialogue. The
birth of Christian anti-semitism, the "teaching of contempt," has long
been regarded by Jews—and now acknowledged by Christians themselves—as having been a major source of Jewish suffering through the
ages. Indeed, the notion that anti-semitism "had deep theological roots in
Christianity"—that the assault on the religious human rights of Jews was

being made in the name of the Christian religion—began to be recognized by both Jewish and Christian NGOs as being as prejudicial to the cause of religious human rights in general as it was to Jewish human rights in particular.

This led to the founding in 1968 of a major international Jewish NGO, the International Jewish Committee for Inter-religious Consultations (IJCIC) on behalf of world Jewry, with representatives from the World Jewish Congress, the Synagogue Council of America, B'nai B'rith/Anti-Defamation League, the American Jewish Committee, and the Israel Jewish Council for Interreligious Relations. Since the mid-1960s, and the founding of the ICJIC, Christian-Jewish relations in general, and Catholic-Jewish relations in particular, have evolved dramatically. In particular, the relations are no longer characterized by a tradition of mutual antagonism, exacerbated by an absence of dialogue, or a *dialogue des sourdes*. What follows is an enumeration of the dramatic developments in the past 30 years, where ICJIC has played an important participatory, deliberative, and at times initiatory role in an historic inter-faith dialogue that has remained largely unknown, except to the cogniscenti.

The first step came in 1965 at the end of the Second Vatican Council with the repudiation of the traditional Catholic teaching of continuing Jewish guilt for the death of Jesus, and a rejection of anti-semitism. Following the Council, the Church began to speak of the Jews in completely new terms, recognizing Judaism as an ongoing, valid religion as opposed to the former teaching of its dimunition and loss of validity since the coming of Jesus.

Shortly after the founding of the IJCIC, the Vatican established a Commission for Relations with Judaism and since 1970 has maintained a dialogue with it. Two central documents, published in 1974 and 1985, set down the new doctrines of the Catholic Church towards Jews and Judaism. In particular, the documents—and doctrines—laid emphasis on the Jewish roots of Christianity, the Jewishness of its founders, and the statement that G D's covenant with the people of Israel remained unbroken.

Most important for Jews was the complete change of the Church concerning anti-semitism. The Church, "instead of being part of the problem, became part of the answer." Anti-semitism was condemned, with the Church taking an active role in combatting all instances of anti-semitic manifestations and, for example, sending a joint Catholic-Jewish team to Eastern Europe to examine the situation there and to decide jointly how to fight it. At a joint conference held in 1990, the Vatican representatives spoke of the need for the Church to do *teshuvah* —repentance, for which the Church used the Hebrew word—for the wrongs it had committed against the Jewish people, and this statement was subsequently repeated by the Pope.

The regular meetings between the Vatican Commission and the IJCIC had succeeded in addressing—and for the most part resolving—a host of contentious issues. By the 1980s the major divisive item remaining on the agenda was the relationship between the Vatican and the State of Israel. Edgar Bronfman, President of the World Jewish Congress and elected Chairman of IJCIC, was to affirm and reaffirm the shared consensus of all Jewish NGOs that "there can be no normalization of relations between the Catholic Church and the Jewish people, as long as the Church refuses to recognize and establish diplomatic relations with the State of Israel," making it clear that Israel was central to the Jewish people, and normalization therefore of Catholic-Jewish relations depended upon normalization of relations between the Catholic Church and Israel.

In 1994, with the Vatican-Israel Agreement, that normalization was achieved. According to the Agreement, which includes a preamble and 15 Articles, the Vatican and the State of Israel agreed fully to normalize relations, including the exchange of ambassadors within four months of the signing of the agreement. Among the Articles was a joint commitment to cooperate in combatting all forms of anti-semitism, and in promoting mutual understanding among nations, tolerance among communities, and respect for human life and dignity. In particular, the Holy See reiterated its condemnation of hatred, persecution, and all other manifestations of anti-semitism directed against the Jewish people; as well, it expressed its condemnation of attacks on Jews and desecration of Jewish synagogues and cemeteries, which offend the memory of victims of the Holocaust. Those undertakings towards protecting the religious rights of Jews—set down in an agreement with Israel—constituted an acknowledgement by the Holy See of the centrality of Israel for the Jewish people. As well, the State of Israel recognized the right of the Catholic Church to carry out its religious, moral, educational, and charitable functions, and to have its own institutions. Both parties to the Agreement recognized the need for dialogue and cooperation, while the State of Israel guaranteed the freedom of Catholic worship and affirmed its continuing commitment to maintain and respect the status quo in the Christian holy places.

The signing of the Agreement, the recognition of the State of Israel by the Vatican, as well as the establishment of diplomatic relations, symbolize, according to former President of Israel, Chaim Herzog, "an historic Jewish victory against an institution that has shown extreme hostility toward the Jewish people throughout the generations. . . . We are speaking about historic recognition from the spiritual leadership of the Christian world, a recognition that the State of Israel, the state of the Jews, is an accomplished fact, a country with standing and value in the community of nations."

In addition to this historic agreement, in 1992, the Catholic Church issued a new Universal Catechism which appeared in English two years later. As the catechism is an authoritative doctrinal Church document, Jews examined it with interest for its teachings relating to Jews and Judaism. Most of the progressive steps that had been stated in Church documents over the past thirty years were integrated, including the rejection of collective Jewish guilt for the death of Jesus; the Jewish roots of Christianity and of its founders; and the Jewish roots of the Catholic liturgy. In particular, genocide, persecution, and discrimination "by race or religion" are condemned, and the document incorporates the Pope's statement, which is revolutionary in the light of previous teaching, that the covenant between God and the Jews has not been broken and retains its validity. At the same time, however, the new Catechism affirms the belief that the importance of the Hebrew Scriptures is that they prefigure the events of the New Testament, a teaching which is obviously objectionable to Jews.

IJCIC and Jewish-Protestant Relations The IJCIC has been engaged in a dialogue not only with the Catholic Church, but also with the Protestant world. In that context, an important declaration was issued in 1994 by the Evangelical Lutheran Church in America. This is a sequel to the declaration adopted at a meeting between IJCIC and representatives of the World Lutheran Federation in Sweden in 1983, wherein the Lutheran participants repudiated the anti-Jewish teachings of Luther which declaration was endorsed in 1984 by the Assembly of the Lutheran World Federation. Similarly, the new American Lutheran Church declaration, addressed to the Jewish community, "rejects Luther's violent invective against the Jews and expresses deep and abiding sorrow over its tragic effects on subsequent generations." In particular, it deplores the appropriation of Luther's words by modern anti-semitism and undertakes increasing cooperation and understanding between Lutheran Christians and the Jewish community, with IJCIC playing an increasing role in this inter-faith dialogue.

Restitution of Jewish Property and the Reclamation of Jewish Religious Patrimony. The Holocaust—the genocidal murder of six million Jewish men, women and children simply because they were Jews—is clearly the greatest tragedy to have befallen the Jewish people, if not the cause of religious human rights, in this century. What may not be so well known—and what constitutes a continuing violation of religious human rights and unrequited war crime—has been the "despoliation of victims of mass murder, or their heirs" through the seizure of Jewish property, much of it communal religious property. For, in addition to the murder of the six million, the murderers and their accomplices helped themselves to vast amounts of Jewish property, public and private, movable and immovable. In fact, the prospect of seizing that property was often a tempting incentive for local people to assist in, or even orchestrate, the murder of their Jewish neighbors. During the war, certain states retained nominal independence and allied themselves with Germany. Others were directly occupied or annexed. But irrespective of who was responsible for the actual seizure, the bulk of stolen property devolved to the state, or to the entities or persons occupying the assets.

Even before the end of the hostilities in Europe, the World Jewish Congress (WJC) had initiated activity aimed at the recovery of Jewish property, and published an extensive study on the subject by Dr. Nehemiah Robinson. Nahum Goldmann, co-founder of the WJC, raised the issue at the War Emergency Conference in Atlantic City, in November 1944, when he declared: " The principle that Jewish assets must be given back to their legitimate holders wherever possible must be regarded as inviolable."

However, in the period immediately after the Second World War, survivors who attempted to secure the return of their property were sometimes killed by those who had enriched themselves—while these deaths intimidated others from making such claims. At the same time, new legislation made it exceedingly difficult to recover plundered property. In some countries, inheritance was limited to lineal relatives, and very short claims deadlines were imposed. Still others, like Hungary and Romania, who by virtue of the peace treaties they had signed with the Allied and associated powers, were compelled to turn over heirless Jewish property to organizations working toward the rehabilitation of Jewish survivors, refused to do so.

The collapse of Communism and the "defrosting" of history has now presented Jews with an opportunity to renew efforts to reclaim Jewish property in Central and East Europe. In 1992, leading Jewish NGOs, including the World Jewish Congress, B'nai B'rith, Joint Distribution Committee, the Jewish Agency, and survivors' groups created the World Jewish Restitution Organization (WJRO). WJRO activities are focussed on the coordination of claims for the return of communal property and the transfer to the Jewish people of heirless holdings. The organization also aims to secure for individual Jews, whether resident in the countries in question or not, the same rights as those of local citizens.

In November 1992, WJC President and WJRO Chairman Edgar Bronfman and the Israeli Minister of Finance Avraham Shohat signed a memorandum in which the State of Israel's special interest in the restitution of Jewish property was established. The memorandum recognized that "the State considers itself to be the natural and principle heir to Jewish public property and where there is no other heir, to Jewish private property, together with local Jewish communities and the Jewish people." Similarly, the WJRO has concluded agreements with Jewish communities in order to coordinate restitution efforts.

Regrettably, the emerging democracies of Eastern Europe continue to block restitution of Jewish property to their rightful owners, just as their predecessor regimes had done at the end of the Second World War. And while the situation varies from country to country, a disturbing pattern of state-sanctioned discrimination can be discerned. The discrimination may not be apparent on its face, as the governments have seemingly enacted "neutral" legislation providing for the restoration of property seized by post Second World War communist regimes; but the legislation affects adversely Jewish claimants, who are effectively barred from having their property restored.

First, according to the legislation, foreign citizens not domiciled in the country are ineligible to reclaim their assets. This provision would effectively extinguish any Jewish claim, as most survivors left their countries of origin (in part due to the prevalent atmosphere of anti-semitism in those countries *after* the war) before they could reclaim their assets.

Second, and having regard to communal religious property, the legislation limits its restitution only to communities and churches which have enjoyed an uninterrupted existence since the war. For Jewish communities, this constitutes a "double killing": first, they were murdered, and their property plundered; now they are to be punished because they were murdered. Indeed, many of those who directly and indirectly benefitted from plundered Jewish property have expressed opposition to the restitution of this property to Jews.

Third, while the governments of the Eastern European emerging democracies have been disposed to return communal religious property to churches, they have refused to return the restitution of Jewish communal religious property to the Jews. This discrimination is particularly disturbing in a country like Poland, where the government has enacted legislation providing for the restitution of property to the Roman Catholic Church and other Christian churches, but has refused to do so in the case of the Jewish community; yet the pre-War Jewish community in Poland numbered 3,300,000 Jews—85% of whom were murdered—with the magnitude of their holdings valued in billions of dollars.

Fourth, in many countries the disposition of Jewish property has been left in the hands of local authorities to whom it devolved. These authorities have shown little inclination to returning the property—indeed, they often have a vested interest in blocking the restitution or in attaching such conditions that would make it impossible (or attractive) for the Jewish community to repossess it. In the Czech Republic, for example, local authorities have displayed a tendency to return to Jewish communities neglected burial grounds and synagogues which require a significant Jewish investment (and even those concessions were only granted after local authorities were subjected to pressure from the Czech government). They are not prepared to return potential lucrative income-producing properties such as buildings in the center of Prague.

Accordingly, representatives of the WJRO have met with leaders of East European governments with a view to securing agreements with them on restitution. They have also worked to implement the agreements so secured; and have enlisted the support of the U.S. Congress and government in their efforts. In a letter of April 10, 1995, Congressional leaders urged the U.S. Secretary of State Warren Christopher to take action in this matter: "It should be made clear to the countries involved . . . that their response on this matter will be seen as a test of their respect for basic human rights and the rule of law, and could have practical consequences on their relations with our country. It is the clear policy of the United States that each should expeditiously enact appropriate legislation providing for the prompt restitution and/or compensation for property and assets seized by the former Nazi and/or Communist regimes. We believe it is a matter of both law and justice."

Religious Human Rights and the New Anti-Semitism: Founding a New International NGO. In July 1992, the World Jewish Congress convened an International Conference in Brussels on "Racism, Anti-Semitism, Xenophobia and other Forms of Intolerance." The Conference brought together an unusual international consortium of political leaders, scholars, and NGO activists to consider the explosive question of racial and religious hatred which was stalking across Europe and other global stages. One of the panels addressed the question of the development of a "new anti-semitism," and the anchorage of that anti-semitism in the United Nations itself. As one of the participants put it:

> What Jewish NGOs are witnessing today—and which has been developing incrementally, almost imperceptibly, for some 25 years now—is a new anti-semitism—grounded in classical anti-semitism, but distinguishable from it; anchored in the "Zionism is Racism" Resolution but going beyond it; a new anti-semitism which almost requires a new vocabulary to define it—but which can best be defined as the discrimination against, or denial of,

national particularity anywhere, whenever that national particularity happens to be Jewish.

In a word, classical anti-semitism, is the discrimination against,
or denial of, the right of individual Jews to live as equal members
of a free society; the new anti-semitism involves the discrimination against, or denial of, the right of the Jewish people to live as
an equal member of the family of nations. What is indigenous to
each form of anti-semitism—and common to both—is discrimination. All that has happened is that it has moved from discrimination against Jews as individuals—a classical anti-semitism for
which there are indices of measurement—to discrimination
against Jews as a People—the new anti-semitism—for which one
has yet to develop indices of measurement.

It is not surprising therefore, that if classical anti-semitism—anchored
in religious discrimination against Jews—has been a centrepiece of Jewish NGO concern, that the new anti-semitism—or discrimination against
Jews as a people—should emerge as a priority on the Jewish NGO
agenda. As the Conference panelists demonstrated, "the most distinguishing feature of this new anti-semitism has been its anchorage in the
very body created to combat racial and religious discrimination—the
United Nations."

As the witness testimony and documentary evidence revealed, the
U.N., founded as an alliance against racism and anti-semitism, had been
converted into a forum for the very dissemination of hatred itself; while
Jewish NGOs, for whom the United Nations was sword and shield
against religious discrimination, now found themselves having to challenge the very integrity of the U.N. itself.

Accordingly, the Brussels Conference recommended the establishment of a new NGO—to be called "United Nations Watch"—whose
mandate would be to "monitor the United Nations and to measure that
organization's performance by the yardstick of the U.N. Charter." In
particular, U.N. Watch would investigate the "new anti-semitism"—the
singling out of Israel for differential and discriminatory treatment by the
U.N.—as a case-study of U.N. compliance with its own Charter. As U.N.
Watch's founding statement put it: "We believe that the U.N.'s treatment
of Israel is an important test of how the U.N. is complying with its Charter."

It might be useful, therefore, to identify the several varieties, or indices, of this new anti-semitism as described at the WJC Conference, in order better to appreciate the mandate of this new NGO, as well as
appraise the U.N. not only as a case-study of this new anti-semitism but
as repository and instrument for its expression.

First, there is *political anti-semitism*, involving the discrimination against, or denial of, the legitimacy, if not existence, of the state of Israel. This is the contemporary analogue of classical or theological anti-semitism, which discriminated against, or denied the very legitimacy of, the Jewish religion. In each instance the essence of anti-semitism was the same—an assault upon whatever is the core of Jewish self-definition at any given moment in time—be it the Jewish religion at the time of classical anti-semitism, or the State of Israel as the "civil religion" of the Jewish people under the new anti-semitism. Indeed, to the extent that Israel has emerged as the "civil religion" of world Jewry—the organizing idiom of Jewish self-determination as Schlomo Avineri has put it—this new anti-semitism is a *per se* assault—in contemporary terms—on the religious sensibility of the Jewish people.

Second, there is *ideological anti-semitism*, the "demonizing" of Israel, the attribution to Israel of all the evils of the world, the portrayal of Israel as the enemy of all that is good and the repository of all that is evil, not unlike the medieval indictment of the Jew as the "poisoner of the wells." In other words, in a world in which human rights has emerged as the new secular religion, the portrayal of Israel as the metaphor for a human rights violator in our time exposes Israel as the "new anti-Christ," with all the "teaching of contempt" for this "Jew among the Nations" that this new anti-semitism implies.

There are a number of additional indices by which this new anti-semitism can be identified, if not measured. These include: ideological anti-semitism, in the form of the "Zionism is Racism" indictment, and the singling out of Israel's ideological *raison d'être* for discriminatory treatment. They include the denial to Israel of "international due process" in the international arena, as in the singling out of Israel for differential if not discriminatory treatment amongst the family of nations, and where Israel emerges, as it were, as "the Jew among the Nations." They include the international "legal" character of this anti-semitism, wherein a kind of Orwellian inversion of law and language, human rights becomes the mask under which this "teaching of contempt" is carried out. They include the economic coercion and discrimination practised through the Arab boycott which emerges as the contemporary economic analogue of classical economic anti-semitism. Classical economic anti-semitism involved discrimination against Jews in housing, education, and employment; the new economic anti-semitism involves the extra-territorial application of an international restrictive covenant against Jews, wherever they may be, with a "chilling" effect against persons who would seek to do business with them. The cutting edge of this new anti-semitism in the form of Holocaust Denial, which moves inexorably from denying the Holocaust, to accusing Jews of fabricating the "hoax" of the Holocaust, to indicting Jews for extorting false reparations from the innocent German people in order to build their "illegal" State of Israel on the backs of the real indigenous owners, the Palestinians.

All this is not to suggest, nor would the Jewish NGOs who have addressed this phenomenon wish to have it inferred, that Israel is somehow above the law, or that Israel is not to be held accountable for any violations of law. On the contrary—Israel is accountable for any violations of international law or human rights like any other State, and the Jewish people are not entitled to any privileged protection or preference because of the particularity of Jewish suffering. But the problem, as U.N. Watch has put it, is not that Israel as the "Jew among Nations" seeks to be above the law, but that it has been systematically denied equality before the law; not that Israel must respect human rights—which she should—but that the human rights of Israel have not been respected; not that human rights standards should be applied to Israel—which they must—but that these standards have not been applied equally to anyone else.

Jewish NGOs on the Principles of Religious Human Rights

An appreciation—or distillation—of the foregoing discussions in this chapter—having regard to the Jewish NGO agenda in the matter of the promotion and protection of religious human rights—and the strategies developed to secure that protection—would suggest the following salient features and corresponding advocacy as hereby enumerated.

Religious Liberty as "First Liberty." If there is one right or freedom that is regarded by Jewish NGOs—no less than their non-Jewish counterparts—as the basis for all other freedoms it is that of religious liberty. Indeed, the characterization of religious liberty as the "first liberty" and the "first freedom" underlay the founding of, as it is the *raison d'être* for the major—and mainstream—Jewish NGOs; and it is this generic and fundamental right of religious liberty which was at the heart of "a number of enduring and interlocking principles . . . of liberty of conscience, free exercise of religion, pluralism, equality, separationism, local regulation of religion, and disestablishment of religion."

Liberty of Conscience and Free Exercise. If there was one cardinal principle in the panoply of religious human rights for Jewish NGOs it was that of the free exercise of religion, which was inextricably bound up with that of liberty of conscience. John Witte has aptly summarized this relationship—this "organic linkage [between] religious belief and religious action"—as follows: "Liberty of conscience was a passive guarantee: the right to be left alone to choose one's beliefs. Free exercise of religion was an active guarantee: the right to act publicly on the choices of conscience once made."

Indeed, the free exercise of religion was not only a *Grundnorm* of religious liberty for Jewish NGOs; it was the defining principle for the work of all Jewish NGOs—sectarian and secular, conservative and liberal. It was not only a "first freedom" for Jewish NGOs, but a unifying one; and it inspired Jewish NGO advocacy, designed to protect the panoply of what Witte has termed "essential rights and freedoms"—the related principles—bound up with this cardinal principle.

Accordingly, as set forth earlier herein—Jewish NGOs filed amicus briefs in support of the principle of equality, as in their support of the religious activities of groups singled out for discriminatory treatment by odious municipal and state ordinances; in support of the principle of liberty of conscience, as when Jewish NGOs supported the right of children of Jehovah Witnesses—in accordance with their parents' religious convictions—to refuse to salute the flag in public school; in support of the principle of pluralism, as in the amicus brief supporting the right of Amish parents to limit their children's education to the eighth grade; and, most notably, perhaps, in the landmark cases of *Sherbert v. Verner*, in support of what came to be known as the principle of strict scrutiny or the "compelling state interest" test, which, as Witte put it, "drew together the classic principles of liberty of conscience, free exercise, equality, pluralism, and localism, and accorded free exercise protection to both religious individuals and religious groups."

Indeed, when the use of the compelling state interest test in the adjudication of free exercise claims was subsequently undermined in the *Employment Division v. Smith* case, a "wall-to-wall" consortium of Jewish NGOs supported—and indeed were legally instrumental in the drafting and enactment of—the 1993 American *Religious Freedom Restoration Act*. It marked one of the few occasions in recent years when the secular and liberal NGOs such as the American Jewish Congress and the American Jewish Committee joined together with sectarian and conservative NGOs like Agudath Israel and its Commission on Law and Public Affairs; and when the principle draftspeople of the Act were representatives from both sets of NGOs.

Free Exercise, Disestablishment, and Separationism. If Jewish NGOs, regardless of religious and political ideology, have been united in their support for the "free exercise of religion" principle and clause—and the multiple and related principles bound up with it—they have increasingly been divided with respect to the establishment clause and its single underlying principle of separationism, or "wall of separation between Church and State." Accordingly, when the secular and liberal

American Jewish NGOs join other American Christian groups in filing amicus briefs opposing government sanctioned religious symbols on public property, the sectarian and conservative American Jewish NGOs file amicus briefs in their support, while the matter is a non-issue in Canada. When secular and liberal American Jewish NGOs file amicus briefs in opposition to a Rabbi leading prayers at a school graduation ceremony, American Orthodox Jewish NGOs like Adgudath Israel support the clergy-led prayer. When the secular and liberal American Jewish NGOs file amicus briefs opposing aid to religiously related schools, including voucher systems and other "choice" programs, the American sectarian and conservative NGOs support "properly drawn education choice programs [that] can constitutionally and equitably provide funds for non-public school students," while all Canadian Jewish NGOs support government aid to Jewish parochial schools, and, as we have seen, are going to the Supreme Court of Canada to seek its validation.

Jewish NGOs and the "Report Card" on Religious Freedom. In 1987 the American Jewish Congress established the Kahn Religious Liberty Resource Centre to evaluate the status of religious liberty in the United States. In 1992 it began to publish the *Report Card on Religious Freedom*—an annual report on judicial trends in interpreting the free exercise and Establishment Clause of the First Amendment. Religious liberty experts from across the country are asked to evaluate judicial trends in five areas—corresponding to the five principles respecting religious human rights: (1) freedom from *explicit government discrimination against individuals due to their religious beliefs*, such as rules prohibiting people of a certain religion from holding public office; (2) freedom from *indirect government burdens or restrictions on religious practices*, including laws that impinge upon an individual's religious practices or beliefs; (3) freedom from *government promotion of religion*—government-sponsored religious services, the display of religious symbols at government sites, etc.; (4) freedom from *government inculcation of religion in public schools*, including organized prayer, religious pageants and religious songs at public schools; and (5) freedom from *government financial entanglements with religious institutions*, including financial aid (particularly in the form of direct payments), grants, tax credits and vouchers.

While the first two principles involve the free exercise of religion and therefore represent features or principles of religious human rights that would be supported by all Jewish NGOs the last three—organized around the principle of separationism—enjoy the support only of the liberal and secular NGOs, and not the conservative and sectarian ones.

Protection Against Discrimination on Grounds of Religion. This principle—which enjoys support amongst all Jewish NGOs—protects against discrimination based, *among others*, on religion, based on the following principle: "Discrimination shall mean any distinction, exclusion, restriction or preference based on race, colour, religion or belief, descent, ethnic origin, language, or sex, which has the purpose or effect of nullifying or impairing the recognition, enjoyment or exercise, on an equal footing of human rights and fundamental freedoms in the political, economic, social, cultural or any other field of life."

In particular, such a provision protects against "classical antisemitism," that is explicit government or private discrimination against Jews on grounds of their religion, such as rules prohibiting people from a certain religion from holding office, or renting an apartment, or securing employment, or serving in the military and the like, whether they be explicitly discriminatory or fairly neutral and impact adversely on Jews. As well, Jewish NGOs have invoked this principle to protect against the "new anti-semitism," which involves the discrimination against, or denial of, national particularity anywhere whenever that national particularly be Jewish, be it in the extraterritorial and discriminatory provisions of the Arab boycott; or the "Zionism is Racism" Resolution; or the singling out of Israel or the Jewish people for differential and discriminatory treatment in the international arena; or the persecution and denial of religious human rights of oppressed Jewish minorities; or the seizure and plunder and non-restitution of Jewish religious property.

Restitution of Jewish Religious Communal Property. If actions intended to damage, profane, or destroy objects of religious worship are prohibited as a matter of domestic criminal law, the seizure and plunder of both individual and Jewish religious communal property during World War II was a clear violation of the "laws and customs of war"—a clear "war crime" in the context of the crime of genocide. The restitution of that religious communal property—whose seizure and plunder constituted a massive violation of religious human rights—is regarded by Jewish NGOs entrusted with their restitution not only as the protection of religious human rights, but as tantamount almost to a religious duty, as set forth earlier in the separate treatment of this subject. Accordingly, one can expect the issue of this reclamation of Jewish heritage—of the protection of memory—to be a priority issue for international Jewish NGOs in the protection of religious human rights.

Religious Rights of Jewish Women. The notion of "Agunot" (chained women), described elsewhere in this volume, may not yet be a household word amongst Jewish NGOs, let alone the Jewish community in general. But it has inspired the creation of a newly formed International Jewish Women's Rights NGO—the International Coalition for Agunot Rights (ICAR)—whose *raison d'être* is the plight of these "forgotten" women, and who declared 1994 to be "the Year of Freedom for *Agunot*." If nothing else, it has been the year when the issue finally made it onto the Jewish religious and human rights agenda, though it has yet to become a priority for the mainstream Jewish "human rights" NGOs in Canada, the United States, or Israel, the country constituencies of ICAR.

Conclusions

What has the role of Jewish NGOs in the promotion and protection of religious human rights taught us about the importance of religious human rights in the panoply of human rights, and about the importance of religious human rights to the agenda of Jewish NGOs?

First, the foregoing analysis confirms the anchorage of religious human rights in the pantheon of international human rights law—which cynics and skeptics alike will regard as trite law and trite observation—and demonstrates the persuasive authority of international law in the matter of religious human rights, and the efficacy that can be made of it. In a word, whether it be the struggle for the religious human rights of oppressed Jewry abroad, or the constitutionality of anti-hate legislation at home, international human rights law in the matter of religious human rights has had a significant impact.

Second, religious human rights are not only bound up with the protection of all other rights—and often the condition for their enjoyment—but they are an indispensable part of the Jewish NGO agenda. Indeed, the major national and international Jewish NGOs not only have the protection of religious human rights as a priority on their agenda, but they have actually been founded for that purpose, as their respective mission statements reveal.

Third, for both national and international Jewish NGOs the adjectival "Jewish" referant is to be construed broadly as containing not only Jewish concerns of a sectarian character, but ethnic, cultural, national, indeed, existential concerns of a "people." Indeed, Jewish NGOs regard themselves—though they may not always be so regarded by others—as representing and advocating on behalf of a "people," not just a religion, or a religion that must be construed as bound up with the identity of a People. Accordingly, the broad construction that is to be put on both the terms "Jewish" and "religious" in the discussion of "Jewish NGOs and religious human rights" ensures not only that religious human rights will be at the core of the struggle for human rights, but at the core of the Jewish NGO agenda.

Fourth, the protection of religious human rights is not only part of the larger agenda of human rights—and at the core of the Jewish NGO agenda. The State of Israel is the organizing idiom of Jewish self-definition—the "civil religion" of the Jewish people—and is thus central to their human rights struggle as well. This is seen in the quest for restitution of Jewish property seized and plundered in the Second World War and in the struggle to reach agreement between the Vatican and Israel to spurn anti-semitism and to recognize Israel. For both national and international Jewish NGOs, Israel is central to Jewish identity, to the Jewish people, to the Jewish NGO agenda; it is inextricably bound up with the promotion and protection of religious human rights as part of the larger agenda for human rights.

Fifth, the principle of separation of church and state is as much culture-bound as it is rights-based. American and Canadian Jewish NGOs have come down on opposite sides of the issue in the matter of state aid to religious education. For the Canadian Jewish NGO, it is a matter both of the free exercise of religion and of the equality of all religions, and should be supported. For the American Jewish NGO, it is a matter of the establishment of religion and should be rejected. One thing, however, is clear: For both sets of NGOs, church-state issues are part of the larger struggle for human rights, and central to their respective agendas.

Sixth, similarly, the contrasting Canadian and American NGO approaches to the constitutionality of anti-hate legislation—reflected in the earlier snapshot of the syntax of opposing legal arguments—represent not only "two views of liberty," but different views of equality.

Seventh, the inarticulate—or unarticulated—major premise for Jewish NGO advocacy in the matter of religious human rights reposes in the teachings of the Jewish religion itself. Indeed, in the uniqueness of its particularity can be found the universality of its vision.

Eighth, the advocacy and litigation strategy of the major Jewish human rights NGOs in the matter of religious human rights proceeds from the assumption that the "human rights of Jews would be respected and secured to the degree that the rights of all people were safeguarded and respected." Again, this not only reaffirms the importance of religious human rights to the larger agenda of human rights but the importance of religious human rights to the Jewish NGO agenda. Accordingly, most of the cases in which Jewish NGOs filed amicus briefs were on behalf of non-Jews. But while this principle is to be welcomed, it can also be a double-edged sword. To the extent that the Jewish NGO intervenes to challenge the constitutionality of policies and practices that are part of the mainstream Christian sensibility, they run the risk not of being respected for their intervention, but of being resented for it.

Tenth, anti-semitism continues to be history's "longest hatred" as it is history's first "hate crime." But anti-semitism, as Per Ahlmark has continuously emphasized, is not so much a Jewish problem as a non-Jewish responsibility and that, as Jean Paul Sartre put it, "if the Jew did not exist, the anti-semite would create him." But if a struggle against anti-semitism must be seen as part of the larger agenda of human rights, so must any religious or racial hatred be seen as a universal responsibility, and is part of the Jewish NGO agenda.

Eleventh, the internationalization of human rights—or humanization of international law—has been paralleled by the internationalization of Jewish NGO advocacy; indeed, it is arguable that it was the early internationalization of Jewish NGO advocacy around religious human rights that may have inspired the Jewish contribution to the development of international human rights law as a whole. As well, in an increasingly interdependent universe, transnational public advocacy may be the defining characteristic of the human rights NGO of the twenty-first century; accordingly, trans-national Jewish NGO advocacy in the promotion and protection of religious human rights may serve as both case-study and model for strategic advocacy by human rights NGOs in the matter of the promotion and protection of human rights generally.

Twelfth, the struggle for Jewish religious rights in the decade ahead will contain its own internal struggle for gender equality. Indeed, while the plight of "Agunot" is more a struggle for equality than it is for religion, this denial of equality is rooted in religion itself—a matter which may presage the struggle for equality in all religions as part of the larger struggle for human rights itself—and central to the NGO role in the promotion and protection of religious human rights.

Women In Judaism From The Perspective of Human Rights

MICHAEL S. BERGER *and* DEBORAH E. LIPSTADT
Emory University

"He dreamt that he saw a ladder, which rested on the ground with its top reaching to heaven, and angels of God were going up and down on upon it." Genesis 28:12

T he title of this volume and its sequel, *Religious Human Rights in Global Perspective*, presents us with both an anomaly and a challenge. On the one hand, the term "religious," at least in the Western experience, inclines one to look to the heavens for the source of correct action.[1] Obligations stem from a lawgiving deity whose will has become known to us through various forms of revelation. On the other hand, the word "human" is not simply an adjective describing the kind of rights being discussed, as opposed to, say, animal rights. Emerging in the early Enlightenment, the notion grounds our obligations to one another in the individual's humanity, an aspect of the person independent of his or her race, religion, or ethnic identity. The universalism inherent in this idea is one of the hallmarks of modernity, serving as the benchmark for treatment of minorities, prisoners of war, and criminals.[2] Therefore the term "religious human rights" strikes us as a virtual oxymoron, for while religions focus on the top of Jacob's ladder, Enlightenment philosophers and ethicists are exclusively concerned with Jacob at its base.

---

[1] The Eastern religious traditions, both in their polytheistic and non-theistic forms, provide very different models for understanding human rights in a religious context. See the essays on Hinduism, Buddhism, and especially Confucianism in Leroy S. Rouner, ed., *Human Rights and the World's Religions* (Notre Dame, 1988). Rouner's introductory essay (ibid., 1-14) is very helpful in comparing and contrasting the western and eastern approaches to human rights.

[2] See Jacob Katz, "Post-Emancipation Development of Human Rights: Liberalism and Universalism," in David Sidorsky, ed., *Essays on Human Rights: Contemporary Issues and Jewish Perspectives* (Philadelphia, 1979), 282-96.

J. Witte, Jr. and J.D. van der Vyver (eds.), Religious Human Rights in Global Perspective, 295-321.

Nevertheless, many of us, whether secular scholars of religion or religiously-committed scholars and laypersons, are involved in this project
precisely because we do not see such an abyss separating the two realms.
In our perception, there is a close, intimate connection between human
rights and religion. Violations of human rights, whether locally or across
the world, offend many of us as morally and religiously repugnant. On
the positive side, advocates of human rights frequently link arms with
priests, ministers, and rabbis, joining in common cause, such as in the
American civil rights crusade of the 1960s. The dreams and goals of those
who pursue and defend human rights are clear echoes of ancient prophetic voices which also hoped for an ideal society based on justice and
truth. In short, the challenge of this volume and its sequel is that we want
to be those angels, ascending and descending the ladder, some more easily than others, in an effort to better understand the connections and relationships between the two spheres.

This chapter concerns women's rights within Jewish communities.
One way of approaching this subject is simply to list a woman's rights
and obligations according to halakhah (Jewish law): what she is obligated
to do for others, such as her spouse, children, and parents, and how, in
turn, others are obligated to act with respect to her. As in any legal system, there will be privileges as well as restrictions which developed over
time, and which need to be seen from precisely that historical perspective. This, in itself, would be an ambitious project, and indeed is the necessary backdrop for any informed discussion of the topic. But if we are to
be true to the challenge we believe this project sets before us, then we
must sketch out, however theoretically, the potential contribution of
viewing the issue from the perspective of human rights.

We should state, from the outset, that we are not merely engaged in
the critical review of Jewish law by contemporary canons of human
rights. This project was not established to expose aspects of religious traditions which affront and even violate accepted standards of recent human rights commissions and conventions. Not only would that
undermine the spirit of cooperation which distinguishes this project, it
would necessarily put the various religions on the defensive, forcing an
apologetic posture that would preclude any openness and candor crucial
to our enterprise.

Nor is our aim to show, in the classical tradition of apologia, that a
particular religious tradition anticipated or even served as the source of
modern human rights, essentially claiming that contemporary views are
simply redundant. Rather, our aim is to lay bare some of the assumptions
and premises of each system, and then examine if any fruitful intersection is possible. We begin with a brief analysis of the different notions of

rights in each tradition, followed by an overview of laws relating to women in halakha. We then take a particular case, considerably pressing on the contemporary Jewish scene, and explore some ways that our discussion might illuminate that issue.

Jewish Law and Human Rights

The overlap of Jewish law and human rights in practical terms is an important starting point for our analysis of the respective assumptions of each system.[3] *Prima facie*, the Jewish Bible's persistent concern for "the stranger, the orphan, and the widow"[4] as well as for the poor person, is an expression of the basic moral posture of Jewish law, insuring the care and equal treatment due every member of society regardless of economic condition or social status.[5] The Rabbis continued in this vein, instituting laws and practices that would prevent abuses of these disadvantaged classes.[6] Medieval Jewish communities were almost universally characterized by locally supported institutions and funds established and maintained to help widows, orphans, and the poor—features that still distinguish modern Jewish communities across the spectrum. For those interested in human rights, Jewish history appears to stand proudly by its record of concern for the disadvantaged and unfortunate.

---

[3] The attention this subject has received over the last twenty years is impressive, producing a staggering number of articles, books, and symposia on the relationship of Jewish law and human rights. S. Daniel Berslauer has recently collected the extensive literature in *Judaism and Human Rights in Contemporary Thought: A Bibliographical Survey* (Westport, 1993). The comprehensive introduction reviews the theoretical axes along which the various approaches to the subject can be organized.

[4] The three-part formulaic expression appears no less than ten times in the Book of Deuteronomy alone: 14:29; 16:11,14; 24:17,19,20,21; 26:12,13; 27:19.

[5] There are many scholars who see in the Bible and rabbinic literature a clear and unequivocal emphasis on ethics. See, e.g., Louis Jacobs, "The Relationship Between Religion and Ethics in Jewish Thought," in Gene Outka and John P. Reeder, eds., *Religion and Morality* (New York, 1973), reprinted in Menachem Marc Kellner, ed., *Contemporary Jewish Ethics* (New York, 1978).

[6] For instance, measures were taken to insure *she-lo tin'ol delet bifnei lovin*, literally "that the door should not be locked in the face of the borrowers," who were generally poor. In other words, when legal procedure or even biblical law could serve as an excuse not to lend money to the poor, the Rabbis eased the requirements or found a way to circumvent the law. Thus, Jewish law requires, according to one opinion, three ordained judges to adjudicate a dispute in civil suits. The Rabbis allowed three knowledgeable laymen to comprise the court to make it easier for the lender to sue for his money, thus removing a technical obstacle from the initial act of lending. *Babylonian Talmud* Sanhedrin 2b-3a, Isadore Epstein, trans. (London, 1987). Hillel's prosbul, which allowed lenders to collect their loans even after the sabbatical year which biblically cancelled all debts, was intended to benefit the poor who found it increasingly difficult to borrow money as the seventh year approached. Babylonian Talmud Gittin 36a-b; cf. *Jerusalem Talmud* Gittin 4:3 (Villna, 1907).

However, this practical intersection belies a fundamental theoretical difference between Jewish law and modern notions of human rights.[7] Borrowing Robert M. Cover's phrase,[8] the "narrative" behind the "nomos" of halakha is two-fold: first, it is the idea that all humans are created in the image of God, an idea which itself has two corollaries. One is that everyone is endowed with a measure of absolute worth, even sanctity, which obligates people to act with a basic degree of respect toward each other. The Genesis story refers to the first human as created with a divine image (1:26-27), and that this creation was "very good" (1:31). The Torah's imperative to "love your neighbor" (Leviticus 19:18) is predicated on the equal worth of every human being. For the Rabbis, this principle served as an indication of the infinite value of human life; thus, witnesses in capital crimes were warned by the judges: "Anyone who destroys the life of a single person, it is as if he destroyed an entire world."[9] When testimony is to have such potentially grave consequences, it is crucial to underscore the infinite worth of each individual. In rabbinic literature, the commandment not to leave an executed criminal hanging until dusk (Deuteronomy 21:22-23) is presented as a basic expression of the divine image of the person, even one who violated the law.[10]

The notion that mankind is created in God's image has a further, perhaps more significant, corollary for human action: the imperative to imitate God. As beings with a divine aspect,[11] persons are enjoined to live up to their potential and act in divine ways toward one another. The Pentateuchal injunction "You shall be holy, for I, the Lord your God, am holy" (Leviticus 19:2) is an echo of this notion, as is the rabbinic interpretation of Exodus 15:2: "Just as He is merciful and compassionate, so you shall be merciful and compassionate."[12] These are the clearest expressions of the idea that human beings are under the obligation to actualize their own divine image by acting ethically.[13]

---

[7] Much of this analysis is based on Lenn Evan Goodman's penetrating yet brief "Equality and Human Rights: The Lockean and the Judaic Views," *Judaism* 25 (1976): 357-62. See also Ze'ev W. Falk, *Law and Religion* (Jerusalem, 1981), 75-89, esp. 79-86.

[8] Robert M. Cover, "Nomos and Narrative," *Harvard Law Review* 97 (1983): 4.

[9] Mishnah Sanhedrin 4:6.

[10] Babylonian Talmud Sanhedrin 46b.

[11] This notion is expressed in Psalms 8:5: "What is man that You should remember him, but You made him little less than a god (or angels)."

[12] Babylonian Talmud Shabbat 133b. Cf. Babylonian Talmud Sotah 14a which actually enumerates specific activities which God performed and persons should emulate: clothing the naked, visiting the sick, comforting mourners, and burying the dead.

[13] Maimonides, when discussing the treatment of slaves, also refers to the dual notion of every person's worth and the commandment to imitate God. *Mishneh Torah*, Laws of Slaves, 8:9, Isadore Twersky trans. (New Haven, 1976). However, S.D. Goitein, who also saw in Maimonides a dual ground for the treatment of slaves, understood the first notion to be

Secondly, the biblical account of the exodus from Egypt functions, already in the Torah itself, as the ultimate equalizer. As an epilogue to a lengthy chapter on how one is to treat the poor, especially those who are forced to sell either their inherited land or even themselves, the Torah states: "for it is to Me that the Israelites are slaves, they are My slaves, whom I brought out of Egypt; I am the Lord your God" (Leviticus 25:55). Economic lordship is the most common form of "subjugation" in a society; the law insists on protecting the dignity of those who are forced to depend on others. For a nation which owes its collective existence to a benevolent and undeserved act of divine redemption, all members stand in equal relation to God. With God at the vertex, all Jews are equal.

These two *religious* conceptions of equality are in marked contrast to the philosophical basis of modern human rights. For while the opening sentence of the American Declaration of Independence, in a deistic mimickry of the biblical stance, states "All men are created equal," in fact the 18th century notion of mankind's equality was simply the latest incarnation of an idea which traces its origins to the Greek Sophists, and whose heirs were Machiavelli, Hobbes, and Locke. Broadly speaking, all these thinkers express the idea that the basic equality of people is their capacity—and willingness—to destroy everyone else in the unchecked pursuit of each person's own self-interests. Hobbes' famous description of humanity's pre-civilized state as "the war of all against all" is the necessary consequence of seeing people as individuals engaged in the ceaseless and relentless pursuit of power.[14] Echoing the Sophists, Locke as well asserts that the sole significance of a person as regards others is his or her being a source of potential danger. The critical corollary for Locke is that the primary function of government (and law) is to protect citizens from one another, restraining the innate but subdued aggression which is constantly threatening to surface. This pessimistic, naturalistic view of humankind is in stark contrast to the predominant view in Judaism which both sees the person as a being with divine qualities, and portrays the role of law and government to be the nurturing of a person's moral character within a society actively cooperating to attain a higher ideal.[15]

---

the *unity* of mankind, not the infinite worth of the individual. See S.D. Goitein, "Human Rights in Jewish Thought and Life in the Middle Ages," in Sidorsky, ed., *Essays on Human Rights: Contemporary Issues and Jewish Perspectives*, 254.

[14] Thomas Hobbes, *Leviathan* Part I, chap. 11.

[15] We say "predominant view" because rabbinic literature does contain expressions of the Sophist position: "R. Hanina, the priestly understudy, says: 'One should pray for the welfare of the government [*malkhut*, literally, 'monarchy'], for were it not for the fear of [government], people would swallow one another alive." *Mishnah Avot* 3:2, Herbert Darby, trans. (London, 1944). Babylonian Talmud Avodah Zarah (4a) sharpens the image further,

In this light, the modern notion of human rights is not just a reconceptualization of an ancient moral impulse, formulated in immanent
rather than transcendent terms. The descent down Jacob's ladder from
religious obligations to human rights suggests a fundamental transformation of the social significance of persons. For the biblical worldview,
humans are created in the divine image and as such deserve dignity and
respect as equals to every other person. People are obligated to help one
another both to improve collective conditions and to assist in the other's
material and spiritual development.[16] In contrast, for the modern *Weltanschauung*, "human rights" refers to one's claims against society—a men-
acing group of self-interested individuals who literally endanger one's
well-being. For obvious reasons, minorities, women, children, and the
handicapped require the protection of human rights, for they are most
vulnerable in a society formed solely to prevent the natural aggression of
which all humans are capable and which they are willing to use.[17]

We now turn to the issue of the rights of women in Jewish law. We
will briefly sketch the general contours of women's rights and obligations, highlighting the rules and procedures which were instituted over
time both to insure a woman's dignity and to protect her from potential

---

depicting people as fish of various sizes, with the larger ones swallowing the smaller ones,
were it not for the presence of government. This is certainly an echo of the pessimistic view of
human beings found later in Hobbes and Locke. Nevertheless, one must be careful to note
that in his comment, R. Hanina is referring to a foreign government, in this case, the Roman
governorship of Judea. While there were many in the land of Israel at the time who prayed
for the government's downfall for a variety of political reasons, R. Hanina reminded them
that the very presence of the government insured some measure of law and order in an otherwise anarchic society, and should thus be supported. (Josephus attests to the priestly allegiance to the Roman authorities; see *Antiquities of the Jews*, Book XX, ch. 10.) Moreover, R.
Hanina is not referring to law, but to the system of government which administers justice and
metes out punishment, a function which the Jewish court system did not significantly perform during the later years of the Second Temple period. R. Hanina's comment cannot be
seen as a general view of the purpose of Halakha, or Jewish law as a legal sytem.

[16] While there seems to be ample evidence of the moral character of Jewish law, a thorough analysis would require examining the *vitality* of ethics within Jewish law. In other
words, even as many laws achieve what we would identify as moral ends, the legal exegesis
and discussion within the sources of Jewish Law themselves rarely if ever invoke ethical
principles. See Sid Z. Leiman's "Critique of Louis Jacobs" in Menachem Marc Kellner, ed.,
Contemporary Jewish Ethics (Brooklyn, 1978), 58-60; Gerald J. Blidstein, "Moral Generalizations
and Halakhic Discourse," *S'vara* 2(1) (1991): 8-12.

[17] Strict capitalism is, of course, the economic equivalent of this conception of human
value. A person's worth is his labor, self-interest propels the system, and those who are not
successful are deemed either incompetent, or simply not actualizing the aggressive potential
with which each person is naturally endowed. Governmental interference is therefore
shunned and even feared as introducing an unfair factor into the "natural state" of men:
those most aggressive will "naturally" succeed. The contemporary debate about "rights" to
health insurance, retirement benefits, and other forms of welfare is an effort to superimpose
the Lockean model of government on the economic state of society.

abuses implicit in the unequal relationships in which most women found themselves: father-daughter and husband-wife.

Women in Jewish Law: An Overview

"I find women more bitter than death" (Ecclesiastes 7:26). "He who finds a wife has found happiness" (Proverbs 18:22). These two biblical passages from the Ketuvim (the Writings) alert us to the multiplicity of voices contained in the Jewish tradition. Rarely does one find only one opinion on a subject within the sources of Judaism, even on such fundamental issues as idolatry or martyrdom. From a methodological standpoint, then, it is difficult to draw general conclusions about any subject from traditional Jewish law. Its authoritative texts span millennia, from the Bible to contemporary codes and rabbinic responsa.[18] The tradition is self-consciously exegetical and interpretive, using careful analysis of prior texts and codes to yield solutions to any problem. Historically, the majority of Halakha's earliest and most authoritative sources date from the rabbinic period, roughly spanning from about the second century B.C.E. to the sixth or seventh century C.E. During this time, an immense body of legal material evolved in the oral culture of the academies, initially summarized in the Mishnah in the late second-early third century C.E. by the patriarch Rabbi Judah, and later redacted with greater detail and commentary in the Palestinian and Babylonian Talmuds. We shall focus on these sources in reviewing the legal status of women in Jewish law.[19]

In matters of civil or criminal law, men and women are essentially equal, whether they be victim or criminal. Thus, Halakhah forbids harming a man or a woman, and both are held liable for assault.[20] The consequences of harming a slave were identical whether the slave was male or female.[21] According to biblical law, both parents were due equal respect, and striking either parent was punishable by death.[22] Both part-

---

[18] For an overview of the history of Jewish law, see David Feldman, *Marital Relations, Birth Control and Abortion in Jewish Law* (New York, 1974), 3-18, reprinted in Menachem Marc Kellner, ed., *Contemporary Jewish Ethics*, 21-40.

[19] Two main works that summarize this particular realm of law are Judith Hauptman, "Images of Women in the Talmud," in Rosemary Radford Ruether, ed., *Religion and Sexism* (New York, 1974) and Judith Romney Wegner, *Chattel or Person? The Status of Women in the Mishnah* (New York, 1988). As the respective titles imply, each book focusses on a different rabbinic legal text as its source.

[20] See, e.g., Exodus 21, *passim*. In general, the *midrishei halakha* go to great exegetical lengths to ensure that all torts laws apply equally to men and women. See, e.g., *Mekhilta de-rabbi Yishmael* to Ex. 21:18ff., Horovitz-Rabin, trans. (Jerusalem, 1960).

[21] Exodus 21:26-7.

[22] Exodus 20:10; 21:15.

ners to an illicit sexual union were executed,[23] and in contrast to other ancient Near Eastern codes, such as that of Hammurabi, neither the class nor the sex of the victim affected compensation.

While women enjoy access to all legal forms of redress, they are restricted from its process. They can serve neither as witnesses in criminal proceedings nor as judges in any court of law.[24] This exclusion from public life extends to all areas of communal service in its official forms.[25] Historically, however, women were not absent entirely from the public sphere. Both Talmuds are replete with legal cases involving women engaged in serious, even large-scale business transactions, and are often represented as possessing their own land.

It is with respect to ritual law where the clearest distinction between men and women is evident. According to the Mishnah, women are exempt from all positive laws which are of a time-bound nature.[26] This encompasses most festival laws unless a specific exegesis re-obligates women in the observance, such as eating unleavened bread at the Passover seder. This exemption had wide-ranging consequences, for according to Jewish law, in "verbal" laws such as prayers and blessings, one can discharge one's responsibility by listening to another recite the required formula as long as the two persons were of equal obligation. While women were permitted to recite the prayers, the time-bound nature of praying (morning, afternoon, and evening) meant that women were essentially exempt, and thus could not discharge a male's obligation. Women were not counted in the quorum for prayer, thus excluding them from synagogue services except as spectators. According to the Talmud, women were allowed to be called up to the Torah when it was publicly read, but subsequent rabbinic legislation excluded them from this sphere as well due to "the congregation's honor," a vague yet certainly unflattering notion.[27]

---

[23] *Sifra* to Lev. 19:29.

[24] The source of their disqualification as witnesses is an exegesis found in *Sifre* to Deuteronomy 19:17 (New York, 1969); cf. Mishnah Shevuot 4:1 and Babylonian Talmud Shevuot 30a. This exclusion, as noted, was limited to criminal cases; in ritual matters, women's testimony was accepted to establish the status of certain objects, whether they were permissible or not. Regarding women's inability to serve as judges is derived from a mishnaic identity between eligibility to testify and eligibility to serve as a judge. See Mishnah Niddah 4:4. Women were, however, permitted to render halakhic decisions in an extra-judicial capacity; see Pitchei Teshuvah to *Shulhan Arukh*, Hoshen Mishpat 7:4 (Jerusalem, 1992).

[25] Babylonian Talmud Yevamot 45a. Cf. Sifre to Deut. 17:15.

[26] Mishnah Kiddushin 1:7.

[27] Babylonian Talmud Megillah 23a. The exact quote is as follows: "Our rabbis taught: All are qualified to be among the seven [who read the Torah], even a minor and a woman, but the Sages said that a woman should not read because of the congregation's honor." Some interpret this to mean that someone might enter the service and, seeing a woman reading, would conclude that no male present is capable of reading from the Torah scroll, a genuine

This exemption from time-bound commandments is generally taken to be based on the social need to have the woman available at all times to meet the needs of her husband and children. Imposing an additional set of demands would simply be unfair. However, even this theory, reasonable from a socio-historical standpoint, is not universally accepted. Given a woman's obligation in several time-bound commandments, such as hearing the Scroll of Esther on Purim, lighting Hanukkah candles, and others, this explanation is not adequate. Moreover, this account should lead to the conclusion that single women, or elderly women with no children or husbands any longer, should still be obligated. Due to these objections, Saul Berman has argued that what truly underlies this exemption is the perceived needs of Jewish society, which the rabbis believed were best served by keeping women in the family context.[28] The critical distinction between the commandments, according to Berman, is those which can be performed at home and those which must be performed in the communal sphere. The primary goal of this exemption was family stability, a goal best achieved if the woman was not given the chance to choose between familial duties and communal performances.[29]

Berman's theory may also account for the other significant exemption of women in Jewish law: they are not obligated to study Torah. For traditional Jews, the Torah is not merely a set of rules and laws, but the embodiment of the divine word, the record of God's revelation to the Jewish people. The oral traditions which developed around it are the essence of rabbinic Judaism, and being left out of the enterprise could, arguably, deprive a Jew of connecting with her people's spiritual heritage. Nevertheless, Torah study, particularly in the rabbinic period, left the familial realm of parent to child (Deuteronomy 6:7, 11:19) and entered the academy, where one first heard *tannaim* recite the oral traditions of previous generations, and then personally debated its meaning with contemporary scholars. Torah was no longer a family affair but a communal one, and, once again, women were excluded from that sphere.

Even this explanation, however, does not explain why the exemption was extended to all women, even those who presently are not, or are no longer, in the context of the traditional family. Moreover, given the temperament of many men today, these fathers' involvement in family duties

---

skill given the absence of vowels or punctuation in the Torah text. The term "the congregation's honor" is used on several occasions in the Babylonian Talmud, each with a different connotation. See, e.g., Babylonian Talmud Megillah 24b. It is therefore difficult to retrieve the precise meaning of this source.

[28] Saul Berman, "The Status of Women in Halakhic Judaism," in Elizabeth Koltun, ed., *The Jewish Woman: New Perspectives* (New York, 1976), 114-128.

[29] Ibid., 123.

should exempt them as well from some time-bound commandments.[30] Rather, what we have here is, as Berman suggests, a fundamental split between the private and the public spheres. However, when this functional distinction is mediated through laws and is expressed in legal language (the only one available to the rabbis), many consequences which flow from the original distinction are sacrificed to create a clear and easily implemented system. These legislative concerns led the rabbis to exclude all women from the public realm in order to facilitate the situation of most of them—a concern law school professors often appreciate but the man (sic) in the street does not.[31]

Thus, in certain respects, women enjoyed the same rights as men, while in others, particularly in ritual and academic settings, women were excluded and consigned to the home. This mixed image, where women and men are sometimes treated equally by the law and sometimes not, is even more noticeable in the next realm we will examine: marriage and divorce.

Marriage and Divorce

"A bad wife is as hard (to bear) as a stormy day."[32] "If your wife is short bend down to listen to her."[33] As these two passages indicate, an analysis of Jewish attitudes and practices in the realm of marriage and divorce demonstrates there has been significant development over the centuries, virtually all of it designed to enhance the status of the woman and to make her less vulnerable. These changes reflect both the dynamic quality of Jewish law and a basic attitude towards the woman as a person. As will be demonstrated, this almost inherent dynamic quality has not been marshalled to address a situation in which many Jewish women today suffer abuse and extortion to simply bring an end to their marriages.

The first chapter of Mishnah *Kiddushin*, which deals with issues of betrothal and property, opens with the statement that a women is "acquired by three different means: money, document, or sexual intercourse."[34] Some contemporary scholars, focusing on the word "acquired" (*niknait*) and the first two transactional means mentioned in this Mish-

---

[30] The single father with custody of his children, or even when he has visitation rights, are situations which immediately come to mind.

[31] See Saul Berman's response to Pnina Lahav in *S'vara* 3(1) (1993): 51-54, esp. at 52.

[32] Babylonian Talmud Yevamot, 63b.

[33] Babylonian Talmud Baba Metzia 59a.

[34] M. Kiddushin 1:1. By the early amoraic period, the Rabbis opposed using sexual intercourse as a means of effecting a marriage. See Babylonian Talmud Kiddushin 12b.

nah, have argued that this rendered the woman a form of property.[35] There was, they contend, virtually no difference between acquiring a woman and acquiring other kinds of property. Their argument is strengthened by the fact that the subsequent paragraphs in this chapter of the Mishnah deal with the acquisition of other forms of property, such as slaves, animals, real estate, and portable objects.

One can only speculate about the nature of marriage in pre-rabbinic times; there are simply too few sources of only dubious reliability. In any event, by the time of the Mishnah's redaction, the Rabbis had already significantly moved away from the concept of women as chattel, if it ever obtained at all. They did so in a number of ways. First, the amount which was used to effect the marriage was so minimal that it is hard to consider this transfer of funds a purchase.[36] It was in essence a symbolic payment to recognize the man's "acquisition." What the husband was acquiring in this transaction was the sole right to have sex with this woman. In contrast to the purchase of property, before a marriage could be arranged, the consent of the woman had to be obtained.[37] Moreover, the man could not sell a woman he acquired for a wife, nor could he compel her against her will to do certain things, as was the case of English law until the end of the nineteenth century. Nor could he treat her as an animal: though wife beating was recognized as a form of chastisement, it was considered by many Rabbis as grounds for compelling a man to divorce his wife.[38]

Furthermore, on two occasions, the Bible records the payment of a bride-price (*mohar*) to the father for his daughter.[39] This seems to reflect the prevalent custom in the ancient Near East custom of actually buying a bride.[40] In the Second Temple period, however, economic conditions prevented young men from amassing sufficient sums to pay the *mohar* in advance. This led to the conversion of the *mohar* into a marriage settle-

---

[35] Wegner, *Chattel or Person*, 43, 227, n.84.

[36] The School of Shammai argued that a *denar* was a sufficient amount. The School of Hillel, whose view was accepted, argued that it was only a *prutah*, the eighth part of an Italian issar. Though we are not sure of the exact equivalent, we do know that these were exceptionally minimal amounts. A *prutah* might well be the contemporary equivalent of a penny. Even a *dinar* was not more than the contemporary equivalent of five dollars. M. Kiddushin 1:1.

[37] Babylonian Talmud Kiddushin 41a.

[38] An eleventh century rabbi ruled that a man who beat his wife was to be treated more severely than a man who beat another man, because he was not obligated to honor his fellow man but he was obligated to honor his wife more than himself. For additional discussion of this point see Rachel Biale, *Women and Jewish Law: An Exploration of Women's Issues in Halakhic Sources*, (New York, 1984), 93-96.

[39] According to the Bible, her father received the bride-price from a man who violated or seduced his daughter. Exodus 22:15-16; Deuteronomy 22:28-29.

[40] Hauptman, "Images of Women in the Talmud," 185.

ment for the *bride* (*not* her father) providing for her in the event of divorce or widowhood. R. Simeon ben Shetah, the leader of the Pharisees in the Hasmonean period (mid-second century B.C.E.) strengthened the settlement by introducing the husband's pledge of all his possessions as security. The substance of the settlement is embodied in the marriage contract (*ketubah*) which witnesses sign before a wedding, attesting to the husband's acceptance of the obligation. In general, the sum of the settlement is roughly the equivalent of living expenses for one or two years. Subsequent rabbinic legislation insured the protective capacity of this settlement by prohibiting any couple from marrying without a *ketubah*; if it were later lost, rabbinic law forbad their living together until a new one was written and signed by witnesses. Furthermore, if the *ketubah* had to be collected, she was to receive the money before any other distributions were made from his estate. If the inheritance was insufficient, the rabbis ruled that the sons were to go begging, allowing the mother and the daughters to be maintained by whatever funds were available in the estate.[41] These enactments collectively had the impact of rendering marriage easier and divorce more difficult.[42]

Finally, the paragraph in Kiddushin which speaks of the "acquisition" of the wife is, in fact, the last time the Mishnah uses the term *niknait*, "acquired," in reference to a marriage. All subsequent references use the term *kiddushin*, "exclusively designated," but also connoting an aura of holiness. In Judaism something that is holy is set aside for special use. In terms of marriage, *kiddushin* denotes exclusivity. According to the Rabbis the man was sanctifying the woman to himself, that is, for his sole access to her sexual functions.[43] While this was the husband's privilege, it was not his prerogative to allow others to "use" his wife, even by the seemingly legitimate means of divorce and subsequent remarriage.[44]

While the rabbinic portrayal of *betrothal* was clearly dissimilar to the acquisition of chattel, it was particularly the rabbinic understanding of *marriage* and the mutual obligations it entailed that reveal true sensitivity and concern for protecting the woman. The Mishnah enumerates and the Gemara expands upon an entire series of rights and protections accorded the wife. Recognizing that from a social and economic perspective, the

---

[41] M. Bava Batra 9:1.

[42] Babylonian Talmud Ketubbot 82b; Jerusalem Talmud Ketubbot 8:11; Eliot N. Dorff and Arthur Rosett, *A Living Tree: The Roots and Growth of Jewish Law* (New York, 1988), 443.

[43] Biale, *Women and Jewish Law*, 48.

[44] Deuteronomy 24:1-4. See the *Commentary of Nachmanides*, Charles Chavel, trans. (New York, 1971) and *Commentary of Sforno* (Jersualem, 1981), *ad loc*, and the explanation in the *Sefer ha-Hinukh*, commandment 580 (Jerusalem, 1991).

wife was the dependent partner in the relationship, the tradition provided her with a host of protections. When a wife fell sick the husband had to provide for her.[45] Should he die she could not be evicted from the marital residence.[46] Most significantly, the Mishnah recognized that she has certain emotional and social needs. Her husband could not arbitrarily prevent her from visiting her parents or attending community gatherings such as weddings or funerals. If he did attempt to do so, he was obligated to grant her freedom by divorcing her and granting her the funds promised her in the *ketubah*.[47] One thousand years later, Maimonides, who insisted on her right to visit her parents' home as well as her friends and neighbors observed that "she is not in a prison from which she cannot come and go."[48] Most importantly, her husband was liable for her support, burial, and ransom should she be kidnapped.[49] All these practices are manifestations of her dependency on him and his responsibilities towards her.

A wife had certain reciprocal obligations towards her husband. According to the Mishnah, she was obligated to wash his face, hands, feet, make his bed, and pour his wine.[50] The Talmud expanded and contracted these to reflect those acts which according to local custom are performed by a wife for her husband. Thus, today washing feet would *not* be included. In certain places, she was obligated not only to raise the children and perform household duties, but also to spin, weave, and sew the family's clothing. If she had the means, either from her husband's wealth or her own assets, she was allowed to hire others to do these chores for her,[51] though Rabbi Eliezer cautioned that she should not remain idle but should be compelled, if necessary, to undertake certain tasks because "idleness leads to promiscuity."[52]

---

[45] M. Ketubot 4:9.

[46] M. Ketubot 4:12.

[47] M. Ketubot 7:4,5.

[48] To this, Maimonides appended the following comment: "On the other hand, it is unseemly for a woman to be constantly going out abroad and into the streets, and the husband should prevent his wife from doing this and should not let her go out, except once or twice a month, as the need may arise." *Mishneh Torah*, Laws of Marriage 13:11. This comment of Maimonides must be seen in light of contemporary Islamic law; see Goitein, "Human Rights in Jewish Thought and Life in the Middle Ages," 256.

[49] M. Ketubot 4:4. While she could relieve him of certain obligations towards her, such as the responsibility to feed and clothe her, she could not waive his obligation to ransom her. See Samuel Morrell, "An Equal or a Ward: How Independent is a Married Woman According to Rabbinic Law?" *Jewish Social Studies* (Summer/Fall, 1982): 190.

[50] Babylonian Talmud Ketubot 61a.

[51] M. Ketubot 5:5.

[52] M. Ketubot 5:5. The Talmudic discussion of this view does not indicate whether Rabbi Eliezer's opinion is normative, although Maimonides does codify it. See ibid., 21:2. This sort of rabbinic suspicion of female sexuality is not uncommon in rabbinic literature.

Furthermore, the husband's financial responsibilities to his wife granted him rights to her earnings while they were married, and to the usufruct from the fields she brought into the marriage.[53] But even in this regard, the husband's rights were limited. In contrast to Anglo-American law, any assets she brought to the marriage remained her property and were returned to her in the case of a divorce. While he controlled what was done with these during the marriage, he could not sell them without her consent.[54]

Perhaps the true test of a woman's rights within society according to Jewish law is the status of the *unmarried* woman. In contrast to the traditional patriarchal system, there are entire classes of Jewish women who have total control over all aspects of their lives. While the dependent women—the minor daughter, wife, and levirate widow[55]—have a nexus of rights, some of which have been enumerated here, their person is greatly controlled by the men upon whom they depend. In contrast, the divorcee, the widow, and the adult unmarried daughter (after age twelve) are totally independent. There is extensive anecdotal evidence of these women arranging their own marriages, conducting business affairs, and functioning in all but the realm of ritual as autonomous and independent beings. Though a wife was forbidden from selling her own property without her husband's permission, a divorcee could have the court compel her former husband to sell his property in order to gain what is due her as enumerated in the *ketubah*. The widow had even greater latitude. Not only did she control her own property, but she did not need court approval to sell portions of her late husband's estate. Moreover, a widow who was not a levirate could marry whomever she wished.[56] The adult single daughter could engage in all sorts of business transactions without obstacle, for she had sole claim to her property. This belies claims made by those such as Simone de Beauvoir that Judaism is a pure patriarchal system.[57] Only in the realm of ritual and Torah study were these otherwise independent women curtailed in their activities.

Perusal of both the laws and the general statements about marriage in the Talmud offers valid grounds to argue that the tradition considered marriage as a complex set of entitlements and obligations each partner

---

[53] M. Ketubot 4:4, 6:1.

[54] M. Gittin, 5:6.

[55] The levirate widow was a woman whose husband died without leaving any male children. She was to marry her brother-in-law so that he could perpetuate his brother's line. If he does not wish to marry her, he must perform a ceremony releasing her. If he does neither she remains an *agunah*, unable to marry anyone else, until his death.

[56] Wegner, *Chattel or Person*, 170.

[57] Simone de Beauvoir, *The Second Sex* (New York, 1974). See generally Wegner, *Chattel or Person?*

had towards the other. As Judith Hauptman concludes, the Talmud considered marriage to constitute a relationship between two human beings each with his or her own set of needs and responsibilities. The man was clearly the dominant partner in this relationship, owing to a variety of social, economic and religious reasons. But her personal rights were protected in a sophisticated arrangement of reciprocal duties and privileges.[58]

Reciprocity, however, does not imply equality, and this is the crux of the matter. In the biblical and rabbinic conception, marriage is not the union of two adults mutually consenting to spend their lives together—although the Rabbis did insist that both partners agree to the marriage.[59] Rather, marriage is the man's acquisition of exclusive legal claim to his wife's sexual function. The only Pentateuchal reference to either marriage or divorce is significant in this regard:

> When a man takes a wife and has intercourse with her, and if she fails to please him because he finds something obnoxious about her, he should write her a bill of divorce, hand it to her and send her away from his house. She will leave his household and [may] become the wife of another man. [If] this latter man rejects her, writes a bill of divorcements, hands it to her, and sends her away from his house, or [if] the man who married her last dies. Her first husband who divorced her shall not take her to be his wife again. . . .[60]

The expression in the first verse, "and has intercourse with her," is the essence of the marital relationship. In Hebrew, the words for husband derives from the same root as "to have intercourse"—*b.'a.l.* To be sure, even these rights were limited by Halakhah: rabbinic tradition recognized rape within marriage, and forbad it.[61] Even more far reaching was the notion that intercourse was a wife's right and a husband's duty,[62] and

---

[58] Hauptman, "Images of Women in the Talmud," 186.

[59] Babylonian Talmud Kiddushin 41a warns that a man should not marry off his minor daughter, but should wait until she matures and can express her own opinion about whom she wanted to marry. Nor should a man betroth a woman without seeing her first, lest he subsequently find her repulsive. It is interesting that the Talmudic justification for this is that he may subsequently come to hate her, thus violating the biblical command "Love your neighbor as yourself" (Leviticus 19:19). Samuel Morrell points out that this Talmudic teaching is significant because it treats the woman purely as a person and not as a wife. See Morrell, "An Equal or a Ward," 189.

[60] Deuteronomy 24:1-4.

[61] Maimonides writes: "[a husband] must not rape her by having intercourse against her will, but rather [let him perform the act] with her consent and in mutual arousal and joy." Ibid., 15:17.

[62] Ketubot 47b, 56a.

a man could not withhold conjugal rights as part of a stipulation of marriage[63]—in sharp contrast to other ancient Near Eastern traditions.

What these verses make clear is that the model of marriage was unilateral acquisition of sexual rights, perhaps requiring (as the Rabbis later did) the woman's consent. And if this is how marriages are forged, then there exists only one way to dissolve them: the man must surrender the rights he possesses and return them to the woman. This explains why the verse concentrates on the husband's dissatisfaction with his wife (for whatever reason), and not the reverse; only he can initiate a divorce, so only he can initiate a marriage.

Once again, it is rabbinic tradition which went very far in protecting the woman from the abuses inherent in a system where only one party has control. Even a brief survey of Jewish divorce law will reveal that the rabbis acted to enhance her clearly vulnerable position by making it harder for him to divorce his wife. The Rabbis conceived of a variety of avenues to safeguard a wife from a capricious and vengeful husband who, because of jealousy or instability, would try to wreak havoc with her life. The harder it was to divorce her, presumably, the more protected she would be.

The vast majority of the tractate of the Mishnah on divorce is concerned with the technical matter of standardizing the *get*, the writ of divorce. The bill had to be written with certain kinds of ink, on particular forms of paper, and by a scribe. These various requirements were apparently intended to prevent the husband from sitting down in anger and simply scribbling a few lines which would radically affect his wife. It is striking that in rabbinic law, marriage entails far fewer technical details than divorce, reflecting both the preference for marriage (and the desire to facilitate it), as well as the bias against divorce and the belief that the woman needed protection.

According to Jewish law, a married woman who committed adultery was executed, and if there were children from the act, they had the status of a *mamzer*, which prohibited them from marrying anyone but another *mamzer*. Given these serious consequences, the rabbis went to pains to make sure that the divorce was genuine and that the woman was clear about her own status. Rabban Gamliel, patriarch of the second century C.E., therefore enacted that if a man sends a *get* through an agent to his wife (a common practice if he happened to be far away from her), he is not allowed to cancel that agency in a court.[64] The Mishnah declares that Rabban Gamliel did this "for the betterment of the world" (*tikkum 'olam*),

---

[63] Babylonian Talmud Kiddushin 19b.
[64] Mishnah Gittin 4:1.

and the Talmud offers two reasons for this enactment. One opinion maintains that if the nullification of the agency were allowed to be valid, then the wife might receive the divorce, mistakenly assume it was valid (even though it had been cancelled), and proceed to marry someone else. The children of this second marriage would then be *mamzerim*, a consequence to be avoided at all costs. The other possible situation, maintained by a different scholar, was that women, fearful that their husbands have cancelled the writ, might be paralyzed into inaction after receiving *any* writ of divorce through an agent. These women might never re-marry, fearful that they were still legally married to their first husbands.[65] It is not at all clear whether this was a prevalent practice, or whether Rabban Gamliel was merely preventing an anticipated abuse. In any event, according to one view, it was the woman's future which was the patriarch's primary concern.

Nor could the husband's control extend beyond the termination of the marital relationship. Thus, once a woman had her *get*, she was free to marry whomever she wished. Her first husband could not stipulate either during the marriage or in the *get* that he divorced her on the condition that she would not marry a specific person.[66] Divorce meant total liberation from the first husband.

The Rabbis of the Babylonian Talmud, concerned to produce greater equity in the entire procedure, established a means for the woman to sue for divorce. In a variety of situations, she could turn to a Jewish court and ask it to force her husband to grant her a divorce: if her husband was afflicted by a physical condition which made him repulsive to her, if he did not uphold his obligation to maintain or support her as he stated he would in the *ketubah*, or if she found him sexually repulsive and could not have relations with him.[67] Maimonides' formulation vividly portrays the Halakha's sympathy for the woman caught in an unbearable marital bond:

> [She] should be questioned as to the reason for her rebelliousness [that is, her refusal to have relations with her husband]. If she says, "I have come to loathe him and I cannot willingly submit to his intercourse," he must be compelled to divorce her immedi-

---

[65] Babylonian Talmud Gittin 33a.

[66] The Talmud's exegesis (Babylonian Talmud Gittin 82b) is clear that this would not constitute a genuine divorce: "'And he shall give her a writ of *keritut* (severence)'—we require total severence, and there is none [in this case]." In other words, if even after divorce, the former husband controlled her choice of a second spouse, then the woman was not entirely her own mistress.

[67] Babylonian Talmud Ketubot 63b, 70a-77b; Hauptman, "Images of Women in the Talmud," 189.

ately, for she is not like a captive woman who must submit to a
man who is hateful to her.[68]

Medieval rabbinic authorities added other grounds on which to sue for
divorce, such as wife-beating or the husband's frequenting prostitutes.[69]
Divorce initiated by the man, however, was strictly a matter of individual
judgment and discretion.[70]

But even this rabbinic effort to redress the inequity of divorce proceedings could not change the biblical character of divorce: a unilateral
action by the husband. At best, the court could compel him to give her
the *get* if it found her suit legitimate. The man's consent was the *sine qua
non* of the entire process.

Two other steps were taken in the early Middle Ages to balance the
powers in divorce, and both are credited to Rabbi Gershom of Mainz
(960-1028): One banned polygamy on penalty of social excommunication
(*herem*), the other forbad divorcing a woman against her will.[71] These two
rulings marked the end of the man's absolute right of divorce, for not
only was her consent now necessary, but the man no longer had the option of ignoring his first wife and marrying another woman. Divorce had
to be effected before he could move on with his life. Prior to this ruling,
the only leverage available to the woman was the financial consequences
of divorce for the husband, the amount having been pre-set in the
ketubah. In general, only the wealthy could afford a divorce, since the
ketubah granted her the legal right to claim her dowry even if it meant
"taking the shirt off his back."[72]

However, the method by which Rabbi Gershom instituted these rulings inherently contained a loophole: a rabbinic ban can be overridden if
the dispensation of one hundred rabbis (*heter me'ah rabbanim*) is obtained.
Thus, if a man's wife became mentally unbalanced, preventing her from
accepting a *get*,[73] the husband could secure the agreement of one hundred
rabbis and marry a second wife, provided his first wife's needs were met.
This strategy is, in fact, available to any man whose wife refuses to accept

---

[68] Mishneh Torah, Laws of Marriage, 14:8.

[69] Rabbi Moses Isserles to *Shulhan Arukh, Even ha-Ezer*, Laws of Divorce 154:3.

[70] For a summary of this discussion see Biale, *Women and Jewish Law*, 73-79. The Rabbis
believed that if marital infidelity was the sole reason for a divorce the husband might be
tempted to simply be unfaithful as a means of causing the divorce to proceed.

[71] There is evidence that these rulings were in effect even before Rabbi Gershom. See
Ze'ev W. Falk, *Jewish Matrimonial Law in the Middle Ages* (Oxford, 1966), 13-18; Blu Greenberg,
On Women and Judaism: A View from Tradition (Philadelphia, 1981), 130.

[72] Babylonian Talmud Yevamot 63b; Babylonian Talmud Gittin 58a; M. Nedarim 9:5;
Falk, p. 115.

[73] In Jewish Law, the receipt of a *get* is taken to be a type of transaction, and thus requires the mental competence of both parties, as in any transaction.

the bill of divorce for what are deemed illegitimate reasons, a decision rendered by the rabbinical court involved. In this scenario, the husband actually writes a *get* and deposits it in the court, appointing the members of the court as his proxies to deliver the *get* to his wife whenever she chooses to come to the court and accept it. Thus, the *heter me'ah rabbanim* does not leave her chained, but allows him to go on with his life even if she is recalcitrant and refuses to accept the *get*. No such recourse, however, is open to her; if her husband was beset by a mental illness, or refused to write the bill of divorce, she became an *agunah*, a chained woman, unable to remarry.

The unfortunate situation of the *agunah* is well-known in Jewish law, and was already addressed by the rabbis of the Mishnah. The typical case was a husband who never returned from travelling abroad, and while the precarious nature of travel justified a presumption of death, hard evidence was lacking which would clearly establish this fact and free her to re-marry. To prevent this, some Rabbis suggested writing a conditional form of divorce, whereby the writ would become valid if the husband did not return by a specified time.[74] In the event that the husband did not have this foresight, the Rabbis were prepared to relax the rules of evidence, which normally require two witnesses to establish fact,[75] and accept the testimony of only one witness.[76] The Rabbis were even willing to accept the testimony of those who would, under normal circumstances, be disqualified, such as a woman, a minor, or even the wife herself despite her vested interests.

The more insidious type of *agunah* is the woman whose husband refuses to grant her a divorce. Whether out of anger, revenge, or spite, he will not give her the document which will allow her to terminate the marriage and re-marry. Traditionally, rabbis treated this situation, known as "the recalcitrant husband," with familiar and tested methods to force him to divorce his wife. Various social pressures, ranging from public declarations and humiliation in the synagogue to outright social excommunication, were at a rabbi's disposal to compel the husband to release his chained wife. These options, however, were effective when Jewish communities were fairly independent entities with virtually complete control over their internal affairs. If a man did not grant his wife her freedom, the court could socially excommunicate him and make it impossible for him to live in that community. Because people were far less mobile, the community could also more easily monitor his movements and warn other communities not to have any dealings with this married

---

[74] M. Gittin 6:5.

[75] See Deuteronomy 17:6; 19:15.

[76] Mishnah Yevamot 10:1.

man who refused to accede to the court's ruling and issue his wife a divorce. Today, however, when the rabbinic courts do not possess such power, and men are free to travel far to communities unaware of their recalcitrance, the plight of the *agunah* has become quite severe. Even in the State of Israel, where rabbinic courts enjoy exclusive jurisdiction over marital matters, including the right to jail recalcitrant husbands,[77] there are nevertheless men who prefer to suffer this punishment rather than issue their wives a *get*.[78] To be sure, for many cases it might be a simple matter of legislation, enacting a law which makes the consequences of recalcitrance much more severe, such as freezing assets, garnishing wages, and the like. Nevertheless, the procedural rules of divorce themselves prevent rescuing the woman whose husband ignores all these punitive measures and remains recalcitrant. He, alone, can grant her freedom to re-marry, and his refusal to grant the *get* necessarily chains her to him for life.

More significantly, many women are able to secure a divorce only by meeting the extortionate demands of their husbands. Thus, women regularly find themselves subject to severe financial, custodial, and other sorts of stipulations in order to have their husbands agree to grant them a divorce. To avoid becoming permanent *agunot*, some women agree to pay their spouses exorbitant sums of money or to forgo child support. Inequitable divorce settlements are reluctantly agreed to, at times involving serious and delicate custody issues, in order to secure the *get*. Most regrettably, some rabbis have even come to see this kind of conduct by the husband as acceptable, providing the demands are not extraordinary. This kind of abuse is endemic to a divorce procedure which places the full responsibility of divorce on one party alone, and given today's world, social pressure will solve only a handful of the most severe *agunah* cases. The overwhelming majority of women will either capitulate to their husbands' demands or suffer in silence and solitude.

---

[77] Part of the problem is the unwillingness of the rabbinical courts to use the power they have on the men, preferring to advise the couple to work things out rather than separate. While in some cases this is justified, and reflects a healthy effort to see divorce as a quick and easy solution to any marital strife, the rabbinical courts at times refuse to recognize cases of abuse from which the woman needs immediate recourse. Between 1948 and 1986, the rabbinical courts in Israel only used compulsory *get* measures on recalcitrant husbands fourteen times; between 1980 and 1985, ninety-five men whose wives refused to accept a divorce were given permission to take second wives. The tendency of the court, however, to use its power to compel the husband to give his wife a divorce is increasing. In 1992 alone it used that power five times. See Naomi Grossman, "Women Unbound: Breaking the Chains of Jewish Divorce Law," *Lilith* (Summer, 1993): 8-10.

[78] Recently, the newspapers reported that a man in Israel who had been incarcerated since *the early 1960s* for not giving his wife a *get*, died in jail. All this time, his wife could not remarry.

There are, in essence, two sets of problems here: attitudinal and *halakhic*. For a long time, the traditional community denied that there was a problem. As recently as the late 1970s, many modern Orthodox rabbis and much of the Orthodox community dismissed the problem as one of little significance.[79] Today, however, increasing numbers of rabbis are willing to acknowledge that this is a serious problem.[80] In part, their recognition of the problem is rooted in the fact that their daughters and granddaughters have faced this difficult situation.[81] The problem of the recalcitrant spouse has increasingly been recognized by Orthodox rabbis as a problem which must be resolved. There are still those who believe that, while it is a tragedy, nothing essentially can really be done to change the situation. Men must simply be pressured to agree to the Rabbinic Court's ruling. Some of the rabbis who take this position argue that the woman who finds herself in this situation somehow deserves it.[82] In contrast, one rabbi publicly conceded that this situation was a tremendous *Hillul Hashem*, a desecration of God's name.[83]

Rabbis of the Conservative movement have adopted their own solution. They have relied on the conditional divorce, inserting a clause in the marriage agreement which makes the marriage null and void if a civil divorce is not followed by a Jewish divorce within six months. The other Conservative strategy has been to have the rabbinic court annul the marriage if they deem it necessary to do so in the interests of justice. They justify this action on the passage in the Talmud "everyone who betroths does so at the discretion of the Rabbis."[84] This is understood to mean that there is an implicit condition in every Jewish marriage that it is subject to

---

[79] Conversation with Rabbi Saul Berman, September 3, 1994.

[80] Blu Greenberg, "Woman Today—An Orthodox View," in Steven Katz, ed., *Frontiers of Jewish Thought* (New York, 1992), 76-81.

[81] The publisher of a major Jewish newspaper in New York which caters to the Orthodox community refused the request of a number of organizations to publish the names of men who had refused to accede to the court's directive to issue their wives gets. However, when his daughter was subjected to the blackmail of a recalcitrant husband who demanded an interest in the paper in exchange for issuing the get, the publisher's attitude changed. He now publishes the list and has become a major supporter of legislation by the State assembly to strengthen the position of Jewish women facing a divorce.

[82] One of the apologists referred to at the outset of this paper wrote in 1986 that "in the case where a wife is oppressed or remains an *agunah*, one may say that it is the divine will, for whatever reasons He deemed fit." H.E. Yedidiah Ghatan, *More Precious than Rubies: The Unique Status of Women in Judaism* (New York, 1986), 135.

[83] Basil Herring, "Putting an End to the Agunah Problem," *Amit* (September, 1994): 18-19.

[84] Babylonian Talmud Gittin 33a and parallels. According to the medieval Franco-German Tosafists, this idea came to be expressed in the betrothal formula "Behold you are betrothed to me with this ring *according to the laws of Moses and Israel.*" Thus, rabbinic approbation is a condition of every marriage. See ibid., s.v. *kol*.

annulment by Jewish legal authorities.[85] The Reform movement has simply done away with the need for a religious divorce altogether.

The Orthodox community does not accept the validity of the Conservative movement's solutions, finding technical *halakhic* difficulties both in the concept of a conditional marriage, and in the applicability of the Talmudic prerogative of annulment which, admittedly, was only rarely used historically.[86] Many within the Orthodox rabbinate diagnose the problem in a much different way. The fault lies not in the *halakhic* system per se; the fact that a large number of *agunot* have appeared only recently is evidence that the existing system is sufficiently viable. What these Orthodox leaders bemoan is the changing conditions which have rendered traditional methods of coping with this problem essentially useless. The reliance on social pressure assumes both a tight-knit community and the individual's need for a community to supply his identity. Neither of these conditions obtain for the average Jew, excepting those who have chosen to live in the ultra-Orthodox community, particular the Hassidic sects. Given the mobility of people and their willingness either to join a different community or simply not to identify with an Orthodox community altogether, the old strategies will no longer work. New methods must therefore be proposed to meet the challenges posed by the *agunah* problem.

Since secular governments have assumed many of the legal and social functions previously held by the autonomous community, the Orthodox rabbinate naturally first turned to these authorities to address the problem of *agunot*. This approach was tried in the State of New York which, given the large population of Orthodox Jews, heard many cases of *agunah*. The New York legislature passed a law that would withhold a civil divorce from a couple until "all barriers to the other party's remarriage" are resolved. Barriers to remarriage specifically include "any religious or conscientious restraint or inhibition imposed on a party to a marriage, under the principles of the denomination of the clergyman or minister who has solemnized the marriage, by reason of the other party's commission or withholding of any voluntary act." In 1992, this law was expanded to permit judges of civil courts to take into consideration a husband's refusal to grant a *get* when deciding the distribution of marital

---

[85] Dorff and Rosett, *The Living Tree*, 526.

[86] See David Novak, *Law and Theology in Judaism* (New York, 1974), 31-54; J. David Bleich, "The Device of the 'Sages of Spain" as a Solution to the Problems of the Modern Day Agunah," in id., *Contemporary Halakhic Problems* (New York, 1989), 3:329-343.

assets. A judge could withhold portions of the assets from the husband until he grants the divorce.[87]

This New York law on divorce, however, has been challenged as unconstitutional. Moreover, other states have refused to adopt such legislation precisely because it compels a party to engage in a religious act on pain of withholding civil relief—a *prima facie* violation of the religion clauses of the First Amendment to the United States Constitution.[88]

The opposition to this solution is not just constitutional in nature. Many Orthodox feminists find the efforts to rely on the secular authorities "insufficient" at best and a *Hillul Hashem* (desecration of God's name), at worst. These women, many of whom have been deeply involved in the struggle on behalf of *agunot*, regard reliance on secular authorities as a concession that Jewish law is incapable of ensuring justice for Jewish women.[89] They also contend that turning to the secular authorities for help is a strange decision for a community which has always believed its legal system to be the keystone of an all encompassing way of life.

Over the years, segments of the Orthodox community have proposed a range of solutions, many of which have not been widely accepted.[90] Recently, the pre-nuptial agreement, used by couples on an ad hoc basis for years, has been standardized and adopted by the Rabbinical Council of America, the organization of Orthodox rabbis. Under the terms of this agreement, the husband commits to maintain and support his wife until such time as the marriage is properly terminated. Both spouses agree to let the rabbinic court adjudicate any attempts to dissolve the marriage. (That provision protects the husband from a wife who procrastinates in order to be supported.) The major advantage of such an agreement is that it avoids the court as an instrument of religious coercion; the secular authorities are involved only in the enforcement of a civil contract signed by two parties. However, all rabbis must demand that every couple sign such an agreement before marrying for this to serve as an even partial solution. Some rabbis are uncomfortable raising such practical concerns related to divorce with a couple presently planning a life together; some

---

[87] Rivka Haut, "The Agunah and Divorce," in Debra Orenstein, ed., *Lifecycles* (Woodstock, 1994), 198.

[88] Dorff and Rosett, *The Living Tree*, 547.

[89] Haut, "The Agunah and Divorce," 199.

[90] For a description of these attempts see Moshe Meiselman, *Jewish Women in Jewish Law* (New York, 1978), 103-115. Over the years, various *halakhic* solutions have been offered by rabbinic legal scholars such as Emanuel Rackman, Ze'ev Falk, Shlomo Riskin, and Eliezer Berkovits. See Irwin Haut, *Divorce in Jewish Law and Life* (New York, 1983); Shlomo Riskin, *Women and Jewish Divorces, the Rebellious Wife, The Agunah and the Right of Democracy to Initiate the Divorce in Jewish Law, A Halakhic Solution* (Hoboken, 1989).

couples even refuse to listen. More significantly, the pre-nuptial agreement nevertheless requires the woman to hire a lawyer to sue her husband for the conditions stipulated in the contract. This is an expense which, in addition to all the expenses of a divorce, may make the prenuptial agreement of little value for some women in economic distress. Furthermore, this arrangement obviously leaves out all those women who were married without such an agreement but who nevertheless find themselves *agunot*. Thus, this new strategy must be tested over time to see if it will achieve serious results in even a majority of *agunah* cases.

Understanding the Jewish Response to the Agunah

In light of our earlier analysis of human rights, the situation of the *agunah* and the rabbinic responses to her plight point to a disturbing trend in contemporary Jewish law. In a word, contemporary halakha has become increasingly Lockean. For much of its formative history, halakha had operated with the self-conscious aim of leading the community to a higher plane of mutual respect and concord. It not only anticipated abuses that lay in the technicalities of law and pre-empted them; it also prescribed actions that were deliberately designed to improve the interpersonal relations between men and women, between adults and minors (particularly orphans), and between Jews and non-Jews. To be sure, there were rabbinic enactments that only addressed specific inequities once they had been perpetrated, although the historical extent of these abuses is rarely clear and usually incapable of verification.[91] Nevertheless, the overall trajectory of Jewish law, particularly in the rabbinic period, was to create a covenantal society guided by the revealed law of God and predicated on the infinite worth of the individual who was created in the divine image. This, as we explained earlier, was in sharp contrast with the Hobbesian-Lockean pessimism regarding human nature.

In recent years, Jewish law has seen its role as primarily reactive, a trend the case of the *agunah* highlights quite well. Rather than preventing

---

[91] Thus, in connection with Hillel's prosbul, the Babylonian Talmud (Gittin 36a) describes the situation that "the people ('am) had refrained from lending." Whether this was a widespread phenomenon, or merely some of the people did not lend remains an open question. Certainly, if Hillel did not act until the abuse was rampant, then there seems to be precedent for the more conservative position which is reluctant to make any sweeping reforms. Two important qualifications to this case must be noted, however. First, Hillel's enactment was to have the practical effect of nullifying a Torah law, viz., the cancellation of all debts in the sabbatical year. Second, in the Babylonian Talmud's formulation, Hillel saw that the people were violating another biblical prescription: not to be close-fisted as the sabbatical year approached and to lend freely (Deuteronomy 15:9-10). Hillel's choice was thus between enacting a measure which would circumvent one law or allow the "rampant" violation of another law to continue. For a discussion of these sources, see *Svara* 2:2 (1991): 61-73

abuses which are only theoretically possible, many halakhic authorities wait until a problem reaches a certain intolerable level, and then address it, if at all. Obviously, there are exceptions, such as Rabbi Abraham Kook's *heter mekhirah* which allowed Jewish farmers to work the soil of Israel during the sabbatical year, a year during which the land is required to lie fallow.[92] However, most rabbinic leaders (across the denominational divide) have allowed certain conditions which they acknowledge as lamentable to continue even as many Jews—usually in the minority— suffer. For instance, families willingly subject themselves to extreme economic hardship in an effort to conduct family celebrations at a level of extravagance dictated by social custom and pressure. The increased affluence among Jews, especially in America but now even in Israel, has created a materialistic bent that imperils the more traditional values of modesty and humility, and more seriously forces those less endowed to forgo their dignity and seek assistance just to prevent the greater embarrassment in their own communities of having a sub-standard affair. Many rabbis address these regrettable social developments in sermons and other exhortatory media, but they remain reluctant to institute measures that could genuinely reverse these disturbing trends.[93] In a liberal, capitalistic environment, where all pursue their own desires unfettered by moral restraints or social considerations, law is seen as interfering in the individual's freedom to spend money as he or she wishes, unless actual aggression or harm is being caused. But this is far from the ideal of nurturing a holy community, the traditional task of Halakha.

Of course, there are many reasons which may account for this passivity: rabbinic authority is in fact a small shadow of what it once was, regrettably forcing many rabbis to consider popular opinion before enacting certain rulings; the lack of institutional and social cohesion in the Jewish community makes it very difficult to implement significant changes or monitor their observance;[94] and within Orthodoxy, which has defined itself over and against the Reform and Conservative denominations precisely in its commitment not to change the law, there is self-

---

[92] For a review of the relevant issues, see Yitzchak Gottlieb, "Understanding the Heter Mechira," *Journal of Halakha and Contemporary Society* 26 (1993): 5-57.

[93] For a parallel in the rabbinic period, see Babylonian Talmud Ketubot 8b, where costs of a funeral reached such a prohibitive level that some mourners simply left their dead and fled rather than suffer the embarrassment of a simple funeral. Rabban Gamliel deliberately ordered his own funeral to be as simple as possible, and the populace followed in his footsteps.

[94] Some ultra-orthodox communities, which are much more insular and cohesive, have been able to apply some restraint on spending, since affiliation defines the identity of the members. The leaders of some Hasidic groups—the Gerrer rebbe is perhaps the most noted in apocraphyl anecdotes which circulate among the ultra-orthodox—have enacted some measures to curb the trend.

imposed restraint to implement any far-reaching halakhic changes, as necessary as they may be.[95] Furthermore, we cannot discount that the Jews' very presence in a Lockean system, especially in America, has influenced their views of Halakha. In defending Jewish law before the bar of contemporary culture, many have adopted the terminology and conceptual apparatus of secular law in their apologia.[96] For most legalists, Jewish law is no different from American law (or any secular, liberal system), and it need only intervene when the level of aggression of one against another becomes intolerable.

While many of these factors are external to halakha, it is noteworthy to mention a possible internal cause: the increased codification of Jewish law. When discussing the history of halakha, one must be aware that the legal and textual landscape did not remain the same. Aside from the relative social insularity of medieval Jewish communities, the halakhic system itself was extraordinarily pluralistic, with toleration of virtually any opinion which could find support or sanction in the rabbinic sources. In fact, it is not clear that one can refer to a "halakhic system" at all during this period. There was wide latitude within Jewish law, and some rabbis employed this latitude to institute rules and laws which would benefit their communities.

However, already during the Middle Ages, there were attempts to reduce the diversity of halakha and to codify only one or two positions on a given subject. Given the multiplication of views, this is quite understandable; limiting options helps to unite a community and to sharpen its self-definition, particularly in the face of schismatic challenges. Codes were also preferred within Islam, inclining those in its orbit to pursue a similar enterprise. Thus, in the twelfth century, Maimonides composed a a major code of Jewish law, partially intended to emulate his Muslim peers, and partially intended to delegitimize the Karaites who rejected many rabbinic interpretations of the Torah. The codificatory trend continued (interestingly in Spain and the Middle East but not in Northern

---

[95] Jacob Katz was one of the first to point out that "Orthodoxy" is as modern a phenomenon as Reform, and its claims to preserve the old traditions were simply part of its anti-Reform polemic. See Jacob Katz, "Orthodoxy in Historical Perspective," *Studies in Contemporary Jewry* 2 (1986): 3-17. See also Moshe S. Samet, "The Beginnings of Orthodoxy," *Modern Judaism* 8 (1988): 249-69. The reluctance of the ultra-Orthodox in Hungary even to *portray* Judaism as halakhically pluralistic, let alone dynamic and evolving, is well documented by Michael K. Silber, "The Emergence of Ultra-Orthodoxy: The Invention of a Tradition," in Jack Wertheimer, ed., *The Uses of Tradition: Jewish Continuity in the Modern Era* (New York, 1992), 23-84.

[96] One exception is Dr. Isaac Breuer, who insisted on the fundamental differences of Jewish and secular law, which necessarily lead to conflicting implications. See Isaac Breuer "The Philosophical Foundations of Jewish and Modern Law," in Jacob S. Levinger, ed., *Concepts of Judaism* (Jerusalem, 1974), 53-81.

Europe) with the Arba'ah Turim of Jacob Ben Asher in the fourteenth century, and the Shulhan Arukh of Joseph Karo in the sixteenth century. Due to a variety of reasons, Karo's code, combined with the glosses of Moses Isserles,[97] within a century of its initial printing achieved world-wide acceptance as the authoritative code of Jewish law. On most issues, only one or two positions are cited, thus removing other opinions from the domain of "legitimate," that is, normative, views.[98] Attempting to enact rulings which are not explicitly sanctioned in Karo's code is systemically difficult, inclining contemporary authorities to seek only those solutions which have some basis in the codes. Given the dramatically different set of religious and social circumstances, it is unlikely that an answer will be found that addresses the widespread abuses of the agunah in a fundamental way.

Over the last several decades, divorce rates have steadily increased throughout the industrialized world, and the religiously-committed community has not been immune to this trend. Unfortunately, in the Jewish case, the legal fallout of this phenomenon has been the widespread use of extortion by the husbands before granting their wives the *get* they so desperately need in order to close this agonizing chapter in their lives and move on. The worst tragedy is the *agunah* who remains in perpetual limbo, married yet single, unable to enter serious relationships because her prior marriage has not been officially terminated.

The aim of this chapter has not been to offer practical solutions to a clearly vexing problem. We chose not to review the legitimacy of existing legal options or to propose new ones, for that is neither within our expertise nor appropriate to this forum. Rather, in the spirit of this project, we have sought to shed light on a contemporary crisis within the Jewish community by informing an otherwise insular discussion with the philosophical reflection and comparative analysis which a meeting of scholars affords. For only by greater insight and deeper understanding will Jacob be able to ascend the ladder hitherto reserved for angels alone.

---

[97] See Isadore Twersky, "Shulhan 'Aruk: Enduring Code of Jewish Law," *Judaism* 16 (1967): 141-58, reprinted in Isadore Twersky, *Studies in Jewish Law and Philosophy* (New York. 1982).

[98] On the normative preference the ultra-Orthodox gave the *Shulhan Arukh* precisely because it generally codified only one opinion, see Silber, "The Emergence of Ultra-Orthodoxy, 48ff.

The Duty To Educate In Jewish Law: A Right With A Purpose

ᦒ

MICHAEL J. BROYDE
Emory University

J ewish Law[1] demands of society that certain basic rights be provided for all children. Most of these rights are intuitive. There is an obligation to feed and care for children, to refrain from abusing children, and, to the extent a legal system can mandate, to love one's children.[2] This chapter explores an area of obligation not generally considered a "human right," but which Jewish law views as a fundamental obligation that a parent (and society) owes to a child: the duty to educate children. Jewish law mandates that a parent—and if a parent cannot, then society—provide for the religious, moral, and secular education of children.[3] This obligation is as much a part of the parental duty as the obligation to feed and clothe. Indeed, according to many, the duty to educate is the basis for the right of parents to have custody of their child, and even custody rights can be affected by abandonment of the duty to educate.

It is the thesis of this chapter that the duty to educate—both oneself and one's children—is fundamental within the Jewish tradition. However, this right to an education is categorically different from the right to an education that one currently encounters in modern international law and in various states in America. Jewish law imposes a duty to educate children so that they—when becoming adults—will be equipped with the skills and knowledge to fulfill their own duty to be educated, as adults also are obligated to educate themselves according to the Jewish tradi-

---

[1] On the meaning of Jewish law (called *halacha* in Hebrew) see my chapter herein "Forming Religious Communities and Respecting Dissenter's Rights," at note 3.

[2] For a general and popular survey of the child-parent relationship in Jewish law, see Shoshana Matzner-Bekerman, *The Jewish Child: Halakhic Perspectives* (Hobokin, 1984).

[3] Indeed, to this very day, American constitutional law does not mandate that government provide for the education of children, although once it provides for the free public education of some, it must do so for all; *Plyler v. Doe*, 457 U.S. 202 (1982). As noted in *Plyler*, 220, as late as 1960 there were areas of the United States where no public education was provided.

J. Witte, Jr. and J.D. van der Vyver (eds.), Religious Human Rights in Global Perspective, 323-335.

tion. International law and the various states in America that have granted children "rights" to an education have done so without imposing any duty on these children when they are adults to continue their own education.

The Duty to Educate Children: A Religious Education

Jewish law, like Christian canon law and Islamic Shari'a law, rules that there is a duty to provide for a religious education. The classical code of Jewish law, the Shulchan Aruch,[4] written by Rabbi Joseph Caro, codi-fied the rule when it states:

> There is an obligation upon each person to teach his son Jewish law; if the father does not teach him, the son is obligated to teach himself. . . . One is obligated to hire a teacher to teach one's chil-dren. . . .[5]

Indeed, it is quite impossible to imagine a faith group not imposing an obligation upon its adherents to seek out a religious education. Two recent commentators expressed very similar notions when explaining the duty to educate in canon law and Islamic law. Father James Conn stated: "The relevant legislation on the issue of [the] right to be educated is found in the most recent Code of Canon Law, based on the teaching of the popes and of the Second Vatican Council. Specifically, there are six-teen canons that enumerate the obligations and rights of the Christian faithful. For example, Canon 217 assures all members of the Church "the right to a Christian education by which they will be properly instructed so as to develop the maturity of a human person and at the same time come to know and live the mystery of salvation."[6] Professor Azizah Y. al-Hibri summarized the Islamic position by stating: "Many Islamic jurists viewed education as either completely or practically compulsory based on an *ayah* (*Qur'anic* verse) that states: "[T]hose who conceal [from peo-ple] the clear Signs and Guidance which we revealed, after we have made them clear to people in the Book [the *Qur'an*], shall be cursed by God and others who [are entitled to] curse."[7]

---

[4] Israel, 1488-1575.

[5] Shulchan Aruch Yoreh Deah 245:1. In the Jewish tradition, a number of authorities note that even when, for one technical reason or another, the formal verse-based obligation to educate one's children is inapplicable, there is an intuitive obligation to propagate the faith by teaching religious tenants to adherents. "Chinuch," *Encyclopedia Talmudica* 161-201 (Jerusalem, 1978), 16:165.

[6] James Conn, "Symposium on Religious Law," *Loyola of Los Angeles International & Comparative Law Journal* 16 (1994): 9-106, at 13.

[7] Azizah Y. al-Hibri, in ibid., at 23.

In the Jewish tradition, the duty to provide for the education of children is discussed in considerable detail. Jewish law explains that the obligation to "teach" a child is not limited to reading and text skills, but also includes rudimentary Jewish philosophy and theology:

> When does one begin to teach a child? When he begins to speak one teaches him that God commanded Moses on the Mount with the Law (*Torah*) and the principle of the unity of God. Afterwards one teaches him a little bit until he is six or seven at which point one sends him to elementary school.[8]

The Code also mandates that a Jewish school system be established in every community:

> Every community is obligated to have an elementary school, and every community that does not have an elementary school should be shunned [until one is established] . . . since the world only exists out of the merit of the discourse found when small children study.[9]

Indeed, that broad mandate to educate is not the end of the discussion. The Code addresses the details of classroom management also. For example, it states:

> Twenty-five children to a teacher. If there are more than twenty-five students and less than forty, one must provide a teacher's aid; when there are more than forty students, a second teacher must be provided.[10]

Finally, unlike other areas of Jewish law which impose some limits on the competitive nature of business,[11] in the area of education, Jewish law endorses only competition:

> One landowner in a courtyard who wants to establish a school in his residence cannot be stopped [through zoning ordinances] from doing so. So too, when one teacher opens a school next to

---

[8] Shulchan Aruch Yoreh Deah 245:5.

[9] Shulchan Aruch Yoreh Deah 245:7. Islamic law adopts a very similar principle. Islamic law accepts that if the members of one community in a Muslim state agree to abandon education of their children, the ruler—by force if needed—can compel the establishment of an elementary school; see Azizah Y. al-Hibri, "Symposium on Religious Law," 23, n.9.

[10] Shulchan Aruch Yoreh Deah 245:15.

[11] For a survey of this area, see Aaron Levine, *Free Enterprise and Jewish Law* (New York, 1980).

another school, so as to encourage the students to go to this institution [and not the first one], one cannot stop this conduct.[12]

In short, the Jewish tradition is unambiguous that there is a duty placed on parents to educate children. Furthermore, it seems clear that when that duty can not or will not be fulfilled by parents, there is a community-wide obligation to provide for the education of children.[13]

The purpose of this duty to educate is not merely an abstract commitment to aid in the acquiring of knowledge. Rather, as one recent article noted: "Jewish law imposed a duty to educate a child in those duties [and laws] that he will be obligated in as an adult, in order that he should be prepared and familiar with the commandments. . . . Even though a minor is not obligated to observe the law, he should do so as a form of preparation for adulthood. . . . The same is true for the study of religious texts. The early authorities note that the biblical verse 'and you should teach your children to speak about [Jewish law]' requires that one familiarize one's children with the study of Jewish law."[14]

Given this educational framework, a focus on childhood education in preparation for adulthood, the parental duty to educate has a significant impact on other parental rights and privileges. One of the classical examples of this is in the area of child custody law. Rabbi Asher ben Yecheil, one of the premier medieval commentators on Jewish law,[15] in the course

---

[12] Shulchan Aruch Yoreh Deah 245:22. This stands in contrast to the general rule of Jewish law, which would allow competition in the same general geographical locale, but would prohibit competition "on the same block."

[13] Babylonian Talmud Bava Batra 21b, Isidore Epstein, trans. (London, 1987) and commentaries *ad locum*. There is a very interesting dispute within the Jewish tradition as to how exactly this societal duty should be fulfilled. Most authorities maintain that the duty to educate, when it would not be fulfilled by the parents, was then a duty of the court system (in Hebrew, *beit din*), and the courts were directly responsible for the education of those children whose parents would not educate them. This was part of the duty of the court to "orphans." For an exposition of this theory, see Tosafot, comment on Nazir 28b s.v. *beno*; Rabbi Abraham Gambeiner, *Magen Avraham* 640:3; Rabbi Isaac Bruna, *Terumat Hadeshen* 94 (Jerusalem, 1989); and Rabbi Abraham Danzig, *Ha'ai Adam* 66:3 (Jerusalem, 1991). The other approach argues that the court's duty was limited to appointing guardians for children to provide for their education. The courts did not supervise the educational process for these children. That obligation was, in essence "privatized." For an exposition of this approach, see Maimonides, *Inheritance* 11:1; Rabbi Jacob Reisher, *Chak Yaakov*, Orach Chaim 434:15 (New York, 1961); and perhaps Shulchan Aruch Choshen Mishpat 290:15. While the theoretical differences between these two approaches are small (as in the end, all authority resides in the court system), the practical differences are quite significant in terms of how these children are educated.

[14] "Chinuch," 161-162 (quoting Deuteronomy 11:19). Indeed, the Hebrew term used to discuss children's education reflects this notion. The term used (*chinuch*) means "beginning" or "preparation," as the focus of Jewish law's educational policies is to prepare children for their roles as adults. For more on this, see Maimonides, *Commentary on the Mishnah*, Minachot 4:5.

[15] Germany and Spain, 1250-1327.

of discussing the custody of children, asserts the theory that the right of parents to custody of their children appears to be a manifestation solely of the duty to educate one's children.[16]

Rabbi Asher states that since the Talmud ruled that one must educate children, it is intuitive and obvious that this "duty" to educate gives rise to a "right" of custody, which is necessary to fulfill the duty to educate.[17] He then asserts that one should use this obligation to educate to determine which parent should receive custody in cases where the marriage has ended. In those cases where the mother bears the primary duty to educate, the mother has the right of custody.[18] In those cases where that duty falls primarily on the father, the father receives custody. When the duty to educate ends—at the age of legal adulthood[19]—the concept of "custody" (like the duty to educate) disappears as a matter of law, and children are placed with whichever parent or stranger they wish to be placed with.[20]

A Moral Education in the Jewish Tradition

As noted by the medieval authority Rabbenu Manoach[21] the obligation to provide for the religious education of one's children has two different components to it. The first is to raise one's children "on the straight

---

[16] Rabbi R. Asher ben Yecheil, *Responsa of Asher (Rosh)* 17:7 (New York, 1957); see also Rabbi Judah ben Samuel Rosannes, *Mishnah Lemelech*, Eshut 21:17 (Jerusalem, 1992).

[17] *Responsa of Asher*, 82:2. Support for this approach can be found in other early authorities; see e.g. Rabbenu Yerucham ben Meshullam, *Toldat Adam veChava* 197a, in the name of the gaonim; Rabbi Yitzchak deMolena, *Kiryat Sefer* 44:557, in the name of the gaonim; and Rabbi Yosef Gaon, *Ginzey Kedem* 3:62. Of course, all of these authorities would agree that in circumstances in which the parents are factually incapable of raising the children—are legally unfit—they would not be the custodial parent. However, Asher appears to adopt the theory *that parents are custodial parents of their children based on the obligations to educate*, subject to the limitation that even a natural parent cannot have custody of children if unfit to raise them.

[18] For reasons that relate to the presence of a "tender years" doctrine, the mother also has custody rights in small children. The details of this are beyond the scope of this article. For more on this, see Michael J. Broyde, "Child Custody: A Pure Law Analysis," *Jewish Law Association Studies VII: The Paris Conference Volume* (Atlanta, 1994), 1-20.

[19] Twelve for a girl and thirteen for a boy; Shulchan Aruch Orach Chaim 55:9 and Even Haezer 155:12. This age also requires signs of physical maturity. Ibid.

[20] For a longer discussion of this issue, see the responsa of Rabbi Ezekiel Landau, *Nodah BeYehudah E.H.* 2:89 (New York, 1955), and Rabbi Isaac Weiss, *Minchat Yitzchak* 7:113 (New York, 1992), where these decisors explicitly state that in a case where the mother was assigned custodial rights, but the father was granted the right to educate (an unusual arrangement), and this right was incompatible with the mother's custody claim, his rights and obligations to educate supersede hers and custody by the mother will be terminated.

[21] Narbonne, end of 13th century to mid-14th century. Much of Rabbenu Manoach's life remains clouded in mystery; for more on this, see "Rabbenu Manoach of Narbonne," *Encyclopedia Judaica* 11 (Jerusalem, 1973): 892.

and narrow path" of life and to convey to them the imperatives of moral people. This is the primary educational obligation of a parent. Secondarily, one is under a duty to provide for one's children's formal education in technical religious law and observances. This obligation, however, is secondary in nature.[22] Indeed, Rabbi Joseph Kaphach, writing for the Rabbinical Court of Appeals in Israel, notes that in modern times the technical aspects of education are almost always delegated to educational institutions, and the primary job of parents is to provide for the moral, rather than the textual, education of their children. He states:

> Even if neither parent will educate the children in the study of Jewish law . . . still a parent owes his children—and children should receive from their parents—a close and robust relationship through which a child can develop into an adult with adult characteristics and an adult demeanor.[23]

In sum, the Jewish tradition mandates a duty to educate oneself and one's children in religious law, religious observances, ethical principles, and theology.

The Duty to Educate Children: A Secular Education

The parental duties to educate are by no means limited to a religious (or moral) education. The Talmud, writing nearly 1700 years ago, is quite explicit that there is a duty to teach one's children a way to earn a living.[24] The Talmud recounts:

---

[22] Rabbenu Manoach, *Shevitat Haessor* 2:10 (Lemberg, 1881). Similar such observations can be found in Rabbi Naphtali Tzvi Yehuda Berlin, *Meshech Chachma* (Jerusalem, 1949); Genesis 18:19; and Rabbi Chaim Or Zaruah, *Or Zaruah* 2:48 (Jerusalem, 1963). The correctness of this observation of Rabbenu Manoach is quite significant, as it affects the practical obligations toward children in many cases. For example, Rabbi Meir Schlessenger, in "The Duty to Educate," *Sha'alei Da'at* 1 (Israel, 5749), ponders what educational policy should one adopt when the secondary duty to teach technical religious law conflicts with the primary duty to teach moral behavior—such as the case when too much pressure is exerted upon a child to conform to the details, thus causing the child to abandon the faith completely. Rabbi Schlessenger asserts, based on an insight of the late Rabbi S.Z. Auerbach, that one must insure that the primary obligation is not abandoned in the process of teaching the secondary requirements—technical religious law. The duty to educate needs an assessment of what maximizes the total amount of proper behavior rather than what fulfills the technical obligations.

[23] Pseudonymous case, 9 Piskei Din Rabaniyim [Israeli Rabbinic Court] 251, 259 (1974).

[24] Indeed, more generally, parents are under an obligation to teach children "survival skills" for life. Thus, the Talmud, Kiddushin 29b, recounts that parents are obligated to teach children to swim, as a child who cannot swim is lacking a basic skill necessary to survive. Other authorities have understood the Talmud phrase "to swim" as an idiom directing a parent to teach children all things needed for survival. For more on this, see "Av," *Encyclopedia Talmudica* (Jerusalem, 1948), 1:16-18.

> Rabbi Judah states: Anyone who does not teach his children a
> profession, it is as if he has taught them robbery.[25]

The later Jewish law authorities note that the Talmud does not call for a parent to provide a child merely some method to earn a living or simply a gift of money. Rather Jewish law requires that a child be taught a "profession."[26] As noted by Rabbi Joshua Boaz,[27] a parent does not fulfill this obligation merely by providing a child with an ongoing source of income, such as a trust fund, or even with an income-producing business that the child cannot run, but merely derive income from.[28] The obligation to provide a trade or a skill—rather than just a source of income—is elaborated on by Rabbi Shlomo Yitzchaki (Rashi)[29] in his commentary on the Talmud. He states that Rabbi Judah's ruling that a profession need be taught was predicated on the belief that absent work to occupy one's time, a person might turn to mischievousness—or even crime—out of boredom.[30] Thus, a parent must provide a child with the skills that groom the child towards becoming a fine, upstanding adult.

In short, Jewish law requires that one teach his progeny a profession, and that this duty is part of the parent's general obligation to educate one's children.[31] How precisely to teach a child to earn a livelihood, particularly when the needs to earn a living conflict with the obligation or inclination to study Jewish law or other aspects of Judaism, is itself unclear.[32] So too, what particular type of secular education to provide for each child is left to the discretion of the parents. In the details of this,

---

[25] Babylonian Talmud, Tractate Kiddushin 29a, 30b.

[26] A "profession" (in Hebrew, um'nut) appears to mean more than a way to earn a living—it denotes specific skills.

[27] Spain and Italy, c. 1470-1557.

[28] Sheltai Gibborim, commenting on Kiddushin 12a(1) (Rif pages).

[29] France, 1040-1105.

[30] Commenting on Kiddushin 30b; see also comments of Rabbi Abraham Gumbiner, Magen Avraham, on Shulchan Aruch Orach Chaim 156. This obligation, however, is not so narrow that it forces a parent to pick a particular profession. Thus, providing a child with the skills needed to be a farmer, rather than just giving them an income-producing farm, would certainly fulfill this obligation.

[31] See generally, "Chinuch," 162. It is worth noting that the rule requiring that one teach his child a trade is not cited explicitly in either Maimonides' code or Shulchan Aruch. As demonstrated by Rabbi Jacob Emden, this does not mean that these authorities do not accept that there is such an obligation; see Rabbi Jacob Emden, Responsa Shelat Yavetz 2:68 (Lemberg, 1881), and Rabbi Ovadia Yosef, Responsa Yachave Daat 3:75 (Jerusalem, 1989).

[32] See Rabbi Ovadia Yosef, Yachave Daat 3:75, where the author addresses the issue of whether one should send a child to a trade school or an institution of higher study of Judaism. Rabbi Yosef concludes that the obligation to teach a child about Judaism supersedes the obligation to teach them to earn a living.

Jewish law provides little definitive direction. However, it is clear that there is an obligation.[33]

The Duty to Educate: The Obligation of an Adult

Unlike modern common or international law, which limit the right to an education to children, Jewish law does not confine the duty to receive an education to children only. In the chapter immediately following the rules related to teaching children, the classical Jewish law code, the Shulchan Aruch states:

> Every Jew is obligated to study Judaism whether he be rich or poor, healthy or sick, single or married. . . . All are obligated to set aside a time for study every day and night.[34]

Adults, like children, have a duty to spend time educating themselves and have the right to receive an education. For example, the Shulchan Aruch states:

> A person [adult] must trifurcate his study and spend a third of his time on the study of the twenty-four books of the Hebrew Bible; a third of his time on mishnah, which is the oral law; and a third of his time on Talmud, which involves investigating and comprehending matters from beginning to end and being able to analogize from one matter to another . . . until one understands the essence of the law.[35]

When a Jewish society allocates resources to education, adult education is no less a priority than children's education.[36]

Indeed, it is an open issue, how, in the Jewish tradition, parents are supposed to balance their own needs to study with the needs of their children. A person who cannot afford for himself to study and also to pay for the education of his child is only supposed to assign a higher priority to his child's education if he feels that the child will derive more benefit

---

[33] It is beyond the scope of this article to explore the more general question of the theoretical relationship between advanced secular education and Jewish theology and philosophy; for more on this topic see Norman Lamm, *Torah Umaddah* (Northvale, NJ, 1992).

[34] Shulchan Aruch Yoreh Deah 246:1.

[35] Shulchan Aruch Yoreh Deah 246:4. The code continues this discussion by addressing under what circumstances a person may change this division of topics, and the proper balance between economic and educational needs.

[36] Indeed, when the Shulchan Aruch discusses the laws of education, it has some sections that discuss the problems of educating adults (Yoreh Deah 246:7-17) and some sections discussing the problems of educating children (Yoreh Deah 245:9-20).

from that education than he will.[37] (However, even in a case where the parent's formal allocation of resources is to educate himself, and not his children, it is clear that the obligation to provide a moral and religious education for one's children still applies.)

This right of adults to an education leads to one of the significant differences between Jewish law and the current approach of many countries. There is little doubt that modern international law recognizes the right of children to an education. For example, Article 28 of the United Nations Convention on the Rights of the Child declares:

> States parties recognize the right of the child to education, and with a view to achieving this right progressively and on the basis of equal opportunity, they shall, in particular:
>
> (a) Make primary education compulsory and available free to all;
>
> (b) Encourage the development of different forms of secondary education, including general and vocational education;[38]

So too, Article 29 of this same convention tells us the purpose of this right to an education:

> States parties agree that the education of the child shall be directed to:
>
> (a) The development of the child's personality, talents and mental and physical abilities to their fullest potential;[39]

However, international law imposes no duty on an educated child when he becomes an adult to continue that education, and no duty on society to foster the education of adults. There is no obligation to help adults in the development of their "personality, talents and mental and physical

---

[37] Shulchan Aruch Yoreh Deah 245:2. It is worth noting that most authorities rule that there is no duty on a minor child to educate himself; the duty is solely on the parent to educate the child; see comments of Rashi, Berachot 48a (s.v. *ad*), Ritva, *Responsa* 97 (Jerusalem, 1973), and "Chinuch," 162.

[38] United Nations Convention on the Rights of the Child, Article 28. U.N. Doc. A/Res/44/23 (1989). For a discussion of this document's integration into American law, see Roger Levesque, "International Human Rights Grow Up: Implications for America Jurisprudence and Domestic Policy," *California Western International Law Journal* 24 (1994): 193-240. For an intellectual history of this document, see Sharon Detrick, *The United Nations Convention on the Rights of the Child: A Guide to the Travaux Préparatoroires* (Dordrecht/Boston, 1992), 382-403.

[39] United Nations Convention on the Rights of the Child, Article 29.

abilities to their fullest potential" in international law. It is a right *only* to a child's education.[40]

The same result is reached by modern American common law. While there has been a vast expansion of the rights of a child to an education in the last decade in America, this has been nearly[41] exclusively limited to the redefining of the state's or parent's duty to children.[42] There is no mention of the duty of adults to receive an education. When the requirement of parents or society to educate children ceases, the obligations of education cease, as the young adult is under no obligation to self-educate.

Indeed, American common law has repeatedly recognized this as an issue and has struggled with it. The most common area of difficulty is in the area of college education. Elementary and (early) high school education are mandatory; post-high school education is not.[43] Logic would indicate that when a young adult wishes to receive such an education, he must negotiate with his parents over cost issues, and parents are fully within their rights to decline to pay for the college education of their children. Indeed this is the law.[44] However, this line has been increasingly expanded in the context of divorced parents, with many courts imposing a duty on parents to assist in the college education of their

---

[40] Indeed, others have noted that the United Nations Declaration on the Rights of the Child sometimes grants children more rights than they have as adults; see Donna Gomien, "Whose Right (and Whose Duty) Is It? An Analysis of the Substance and Implementation of the Convention on the Rights of the Child," *Human Rights* 7 (1989): 161, 162-165.

[41] "Nearly" is used because there is one clear exception. States have created adult educational programs as a remedy to the victims of racial discrimination who are now adults but who were deprived of education as children. See *Regents of the University of California v. Bakke*, 438 U.S. 265 (1978). This is the exception that proves the theme of this article. Even when American society does mandate adult education programs and might consider it a "right" and a "duty," *it is only as compensation for one who was illegally deprived of a child's right to an education.* In the Jewish tradition, these two duties are essentially independent of each other. Immediately after the classical Code states that "there is an obligation on a person to educate his children," it states "if one's father does not teach one, one must teach oneself;" Shulchan Aruch Yoreh Deah 245:1.

[42] See, e.g., Alexandra Natapoff, "1993: The Year of Living Dangerously: State Courts Expand the Right to Education," *Education Law Reporter* 92 (1994): 755-787, which documents the vast increase in the right to education given to children within the last ten years. This fine article, with its state-by-state survey of the changes wrought by educational reform, makes no mention of any concept of an adult's right to an education.

[43] *Quinn v. Johnson*, 589 A.2d 1077 (Sup. Ct. N.J. 1991) (noting that an adolescent who graduates from high school prior to reaching the age of majority is under no obligation to attend college, although divorced parents are under an obligation to support such an education if desired by the child).

[44] See Kathleen Conrey Horan, "Postminority Support for College Education—A Legally Enforceable Obligation in Divorce Proceedings?" *Family Law Quarterly* 20 (Winter, 1987): 589, 590.

children, even though these "children" are under no obligation to receive such an education.[45]

Simply put, the modern common law has increasingly stretched the duty of parents to educate, so as to insure that *someone* is still responsible for the furthering of the "child's" education. In the Jewish tradition, the duty of a parent to educate his children certainly ceases at the time when the child enters legal adulthood.[46] *However, the moment the obligation of the parents ceases, the obligation resides directly on the adolescent himself.* Jewish law can just as easily force the adolescent to comply with its mandate that he receive an education, as it can force a parent to comply with the mandates of Jewish law to educate a child.

However, the Jewish tradition recognizes the economic reality of modern times, which is that it is exceedingly difficult for one to adhere to a rigorous duty to provide for one's own education without some financial assistance.[47] In various times and in varies communities, different supplements were provided. For example, in 1944 the Chief Rabbinate of Israel decreed that:

> Whoever looks at this fairly will conclude that the situation [regarding support for adolescents] requires appropriate remedial legislation. In our time, even adolescent children (girls as well as boys) under the age of fifteen face serious moral dangers if their support is not assured on a legal basis.[48]

Thus, the rabbinical courts in Israel mandate support until the age of fifteen.

Other authorities, based on the obligation of a person to give charity, have argued that parents are under an obligation to give charity to their children who are engaged in study before the parents be allowed to engage in any other charitable giving, and that a court can compel this distribution if the parents have any money available.[49] So too, many

---

[45] Richard C. Rusk, "Educational Obligations for Children of Dissolved Marriages," *Res Gestea* 36 (October, 1992): 156-162.

[46] Rabbenu Asher, commenting on Nazir 29b.

[47] Indeed, the Talmud (Ketubot 49a) clearly notes that there is a religious obligation to support one's children when possible.

[48] Decrees of the Rabbinical Court of Israel, 1944, reproduced in Menachem Elon, *Jewish Law: History Sources and Principles* (Philadelphia, 1994), 831-832.

[49] Justice Menachem Elon of the Israeli Supreme Court described the process of forcing parental support as follows:

> The law prescribes that the giving of charity can be compelled, i.e., when a court is convinced that an individual is financially able to give charity and there are people dependent on charity funds, the court . . . may compel the individual to give charity in an amount that it determines he is able to pay. The law relating to charity contains an addi-

authorities recognize that grandparents have an obligation to provide for the education of their grandchildren (when parents cannot) before they can engage in other charitable activities.[50]

More generally, the support of higher-learning institutions is perceived as a form of charity. Unlike alms-giving, which actually supports the impoverished, the Jewish tradition recognizes that one who cannot himself pursue his own education, shares in the education of others by providing for the support of those who are studying. Thus, the Shulchan Aruch states:

> One who cannot study, either because he is completely ignorant or because he is busy, can support others who are studying.[51]

Rabbi Moses Isserless,[52] in his classical glosses on this code adds:

> Such a person [who supports others who are studying] is considered as if he himself is studying. A person can arrange a partnership in which one studies and the other supports, and they will split the rewards [the divine rewards of education and the profits from the business].[53]

In sum, Jewish law provides for a right to an education for adults as well as children and created support mechanisms to encourage adults to educate themselves or support other adults who were being educated.

Professor Robert Cover of Yale Law School noted a crucial difference between the rights-based approach of common law countries and the duties-based approach of Jewish law. He remarked:

> Social movements in the United States organize around rights. When there is some urgently felt need to change the law or keep it in one way or another a "Rights" movement is started. Civil rights, the right to life, welfare rights, etc. The premium that is to be put upon an entitlement is so coded. When we "take rights seriously" we understand them to be trumps in the legal game. In

---

> tional rule that establishes priorities of entitlement for recipients. That rule states: "The poor of one's household have priority over the poor of one's town, and the poor of one's own town have priority over the poor of any other town." The combination of these two rules yielded the conclusion that a father could be subject to legal sanctions for failure to support his children, because such support is the highest form of charity.

Elon, *Jewish Law*, 116-117 (footnotes omitted).

[50] Rabbi Shabtai ben Meir, *Seftai Cohen*, Shulchan Aruch Yoreh Deah 245:1-3.

[51] Shulchan Aruch Yoreh Deah 245:1.

[52] Crakow, 1520-1575.

[53] Comment of Rabbi Moses Isserless, Shulchan Aruch Yoreh Deah 245:1.

Jewish law, an entitlement without an obligation is a sad, almost pathetic thing.[54]

The difference in the rights and duties surrounding education between Jewish and common law is as clear an example of this phenomenon as one can encounter. International law and the law of many states in America recognize a child's "right" to an education. However, from a Jewish perspective, this type of right would be a lonely right, as it is not connected to any duty imposed on the child to be educated. It gives a child the right to something that this child will not have when he becomes an adult.

Such is not the approach of Jewish law.[55] The Jewish tradition recognizes a child's right to an education. However, this right is part of a broader picture within the Jewish tradition that focuses on the duty of each and every person to be educated. Children possess a right to be educated so that they can be in the best position to fulfill their duty to continue that education as adults. In sum, in Jewish law, there is a duty to be educated that is applicable to adults and children. According to international and common law, the right to an education is "child's play."

---

[54] Robert M. Cover, "Obligation: A Jewish Jurisprudence of the Social Order," *Journal of Law and Religion* 5 (1987): 65, 67 (footnotes omitted).

[55] Nor, for that matter, of canon or Islamic law; see the discussion in text accompanying notes 6 and 7. Jewish, Christian, and Islamic religious legal systems mandate a duty on people (adults and children) to be educated.

Islamic Foundations of Religious Human Rights

ABDULLAHI A. AN-NA'IM[1]

Emory University

F ollowing an introduction of the terms of reference and thesis of this chapter on the Islamic foundations of religious human rights, my discussion will fall into three parts. First, I will offer an outline of the origins, nature, and development of Islamic law and theology, and their modern influence. The second section will focus on the nature and circumstances of discourse about rights and responsibilities in the Islamic world today. In that light, I will suggest in the third section a theory of Islamic foundations of religious human rights, as can be perceived in the modern context.

Introduction: The Imperative of Resolving a Paradox

Within the framework of this book as a whole, this chapter is sup-posed to discuss Islamic legal and theological foundations of religious human rights and responsibilities, and the influence of an Islamic dis-course about rights in more recent Islamic legal life. As a matter of termi-nology, however, no distinction was made in the work of early Islamic scholars, or in the minds of their followers, between law and theology. Subject-matters ranging from legal, in the modern sense of the term, to that pertaining to belief and doctrine, ethics and morality, religious ritual practices, style of dress, hygiene, courtesy, and good manners, were all seen as falling within the domain of *Shari'a*, the divinely ordained way of life.[2] Accordingly, I will use the term Shari'a in the following discussion.

---

[1] I prepared the first draft of this chapter while a guest researcher at the Norwegian In-stitute of Human Rights. I also wish to acknowledge thankfully the instructive continuing discussions with Tore Lindholm, Senior Researcher at the Institute, over some of the issues discussed in this chapter.

[2] For analysis of the development of the concept of Shari'a see Fazlur Rahman, *Islam* (Chicago, 1979), 101-109.

J. Witte, Jr. and J.D. van der Vyver (eds.), Religious Human Rights in Global Perspective, 337-359.
© 1996 *Kluwer Law International. Printed in the Netherlands.*

The phrase "religious human rights," as used in this chapter, refers to those rights which pertain to freedom of belief and conscience, including religious dissent, conformity or lack thereof, and tolerance, as *human rights*.[3] That is to say, I am concerned with religious rights as conceived, articulated, and applied within a "human rights" paradigm, rather than within a particular religious or other frame of reference or legal system. The conception and implementation of religious rights as human rights is both necessary and paradoxical in that the two can neither be easily joined nor separated.[4]

The connection is difficult to make, on the one hand, because of the inherent tension between the underlying premise of universality of human rights and the specificity of religious foundations for those rights.[5] Since the universality of human rights means the validity and application of these rights to all human beings throughout the world, they must apply regardless of whether or not they are perceived to be founded in the religious beliefs of a given community. Universality of human rights is particularly challenged by religious activists, such as Islamist groups in several Islamic countries today, who claim that their religious belief requires the establishment of a "theocratic" state to enforce their vision of the sacred law. Yet, it is imperative to maintain the universality of human rights against such claims precisely because of the exclusive and abusive nature of a theocratic state, against believers and non-believers alike.

On the other hand, it is difficult to separate religion and human rights, because they both not only operate on the same moral plane of justification, but also overlap and interact in content. Both normative systems are premised on the same moral precepts of human relations,

---

[3] Human rights are those claims to which every human being is entitled by virtue of his or her humanity, without distinction as to race, color, sex, religion, language, or national origin. The current formulation of these rights is to be found in the 1948 Universal Declaration of Human Rights and subsequent international instruments, but I do not take these sources to be either definitive or exhaustive. New formulations can and should emerge, and old ones should remain open to revision, elaboration, and reformulation.

[4] On various aspects of this necessary but problematic relationship see generally Abdullahi Ahmed An-Na'im, et al., eds., *Human Rights and Religious Values: An Uneasy Relationship?* (Grand Rapids, MI, 1995); Leonard Swidler, ed., *Religious Liberty and Human Rights in Nations and Religions* (Philadelphia, 1986). For a discussion of some of the issues in relation to the subject-matter of this book, see, generally, Daniel G. Ashburn, ed., *"The State of Religious Human Rights in the World: Preliminary Consultation*, Preliminary Documents of Religious Human Rights Project 2 (1993).

[5] The basis of universality of human rights and practical criterion for their identification is in the Golden Rule or the principle of reciprocity, that is, these are rights which I claim for myself as a human being, not by virtue of any legal or other status and must therefore concede to others by the same token because that is the basis of my claim. See Abdullahi Ahmed An-Na'im, *Toward an Islamic Reformation: Civil Liberties, Human Rights and International Law* (Syracuse, 1990), 162-63.

and while believers are moved to uphold human rights norms out of religious conviction, the protection of the right to hold and act on those convictions is integral to the fundamental concept of human rights. Since believers will always make the connection, whether positively or negatively, it is better for human rights advocates to acknowledge and respond to it rather than pretend that it does not exist.

Failure to resolve the apparent paradox between religion and human rights, I maintain, is detrimental from both perspectives. Unless common ground can be found whereby people would uphold human rights as a matter of, or at least without violation to, their religious conviction, they would be expected to make a choice between the two "creeds."[6] In that case, I argue, the cost to the community or person making such a choice is not only in the loss of some or all of the benefits of the abandoned creed, but also in relation to the value of the adopted or preferred one. If a community opts for upholding what it believes to be the precepts of its religion over a commitment to human rights norms, then the community and its members will lose from a religious as well as a human rights point of view. Opting for human rights over religious precepts, on the other hand, would entail loss from a human rights as well as a religious perspective.

Loss of the benefits of the abandoned creed may be obvious, but how does a choice between the two creeds diminish the value of the adopted one as well? In my view, a commitment to human rights enhances the quality of religious belief and the relevance and utility of its precepts to the lives of its adherents. By its very nature, and in order to influence effectively the moral convictions and daily behavior of those who subscribe to it, religious belief must be voluntarily adopted and maintained. Coerced belief is a contradiction in terms, and can only breed hypocrisy, social corruption, and political oppression.

Moreover, as can be seen from the history of every major religion, internal disagreement is essential for the rejuvenation of belief and rectification of practice among its adherents. The survival and renewal of every major religion was ensured by the convictions and insights of its dissidents as much as by the conformity of its orthodoxy. In the Islamic context, for example, every form of Sunni, Sufi (mythic), or Shi'a belief held by its adherents today as "orthodox" was, at some point in history, a dissident view which survived against the opposition of the "orthodoxy" of that time. By protecting the right to dissent within a religious community, human rights norms and mechanisms safeguard the prospects of

---

[6] Taken as a set of fundamental beliefs or principles, human rights can certainly be described as a creed. But I use the term here for a short-hand reference, without necessarily implying or rejecting the validity of its application to human rights.

spiritual growth of any religion and the practical utility of its precepts to the lives of its adherents.

Yet, as can also equally be seen from the history of every major religion, dissident religious views were always persecuted and repressed in the name of protecting the integrity of the faith, the community, and/or the moral well-being of others. While such concerns should be taken seriously because of their legitimate importance to believers, they should never be allowed to contradict or undermine the facts of religious and political plurality, or diminish the commitment of the community to recognize and respect them in the shared public domain. The present reality and future prospects of religious and political plurality must be fully acknowledged and catered for as integral to, and essential for the legitimacy and integrity of, the faith and/or the community.[7] Otherwise, claims of acting in the interest of protecting the integrity of the faith and community will be nothing more than a pretext for political and religious domination by certain elites or groups of believers.

From a human rights perspective, while a religious motivation to uphold human rights enhances the prospects of voluntary compliance and the emergence of the political will to enforce them, resistance to these rights from a religious point of view is extremely difficult to overcome. Muslim believers, for example, "cannot conceive of nor accept a system of rights which excludes religion. Religion for them suffuses every facet of life and no system of rights that ignores this fundamental axiom is worthy of adoption and enforcement."[8] Religious experience is therefore not only an indispensable resource for enlisting the support for human rights among believers, especially in forging the rational linkage of rights to responsibilities as people experience them in their everyday life,[9] but also a rich and valuable source of the content of those rights. Moreover, as noted earlier, these connections are being made by believers and must be acknowledged and responded to as such.

Thus, despite their difficult and paradoxical relationship, religion and human rights must not only be reconciled, but indeed support each other. This can and should be achieved, I believe, through efforts on both sides of the issue. Secular human rights advocates, on the one hand, must transcend an attitude of indifferent tolerance of religion to a moral recognition of religious faith and serious engagement of religious perspectives.

---

[7] The fundamental fact and legitimacy of necessary and permanent plurality is emphasized by the Qur'an itself, in verse 13 of chapter 49 which I would translate as follows: "We [God] have made you [all human beings] into peoples and tribes so that you may get to know each other and cooperate. Those who are most honored by God are the pious and righteous ones."

[8] John Witte, Jr., "Introduction" herein.

[9] Ibid.

Those who take religion seriously, on the other hand, must see human rights as integral to their belief or concern, rather than as a purely secular system to be accommodated. I see this chapter, and the book as a whole, as an effort to find such a common ground for mutual support.

In seeking to explore the prospects and problems of finding Islamic foundations for human rights, this chapter does not claim to offer a comprehensive discussion of the issues in relation to every aspect of Islamic history or all parts of the Islamic world. It is simply not possible to capture the full richness and complexity of many centuries of the history of major and highly diverse parts of the world in a single work. Instead, my purpose here is to distill the most pertinent features of that history, and to draw on some of the experiences of Islamic communities, in order to develop a coherent theory of Islamic foundations of religious human rights.

As elaborated later, this theory is premised on two main principles. First, with respect to "internal" freedom of belief and dissent among Muslims, since identity and its normative system can only be meaningful and useful in historical context, Islamic identity and Shari'a must remain open to renegotiation and reconstruction by each community in its own particular circumstances. Given the fact that human agency is unavoidable in the interpretation and implementation of religious texts, every formulation of Islamic identity and articulation of Shari'a is necessarily a product of human reason and action. As such, no formulation or articulation should be allowed to monopolize religious authenticity and authority to the exclusion of others. Alternative formulations and articulations should be allowed to compete for acceptance by the community as the practical arbiter of Islamic authenticity. Freedom of belief and dissent must therefore be safeguarded among those who identify as Muslims in order to ensure the vitality and integrity of this process of renegotiation and reconstruction of religious identity and law.

Second, with respect to religious human rights of non-Muslims, modern circumstances of permanent religious and other pluralities of national and international political communities require equal respect for the religious human rights of all members of the community as the basis of the demand of Muslims themselves to those rights. Moreover, the recognition of the fact of plurality and its consequences is not only supported by scriptural Islamic sources, as noted earlier, but also sanctioned by the historical experience of Islamic communities.

Shari'a, Past and Present

I would not restrict a discussion of Islamic foundations of religious human rights to the basis of those rights, or lack thereof, under Shari'a. Other aspects of Islamic consciousness, such as perceptions and experiences of piety and spirituality, as well as socio-economic and political factors, are always integral to an understanding of Muslim beliefs and behavior. Indeed, I maintain that the origins, nature, and context of the development of Shari'a was itself conditioned by the historical context of early Islamic societies of the Middle East.[10] In due course, local context also strongly influenced the adoption and adaptation of Shari'a in other parts of the Islamic world.

By the same token, historical contexts are affecting, and will continue to affect, the understanding and implementation of Shari'a as part of the foundations of religious human rights in Islamic societies. Local context and socio-economic and political factors influenced the displacement of Shari'a during the colonial and early independence era in most Islamic countries, as well as its recent resurgence as a framework of discourse about rights and human rights.

In this light, I will now offer a brief outline of the origins, nature and development of Shari'a as a theoretical model for an Islamic way of life. Although this ideal model was rarely fully implemented in the actual lives of Islamic communities and individuals, it remains a powerful symbol and source of motivation and framework for action to the present day. This section will therefore conclude with an evaluation and discussion of the role of Shari'a in modern Islamic discourse about rights and responsibilities.

The primary sources of the conceptual frame of reference and detailed content of Shari'a are the Qur'an and Sunna of the Prophet Muhammad.[11] Traditions of the earliest generations of Muslims were also

---

[10] An-Na'im, *Toward an Islamic Reformation*, 52-62.

[11] The Qur'an is the written text of what Muslims believe to be the final and conclusive record of divine revelation. The Qur'an was delivered by the Prophet and memorized by the first generation of Muslims until it was collected in a written text about two decades after the Prophet's death. Except for minor differences in the style of recitation, that text of the Qur'an, known as *Al-Mushaf Al-Uthmani*, is acknowledged by all Sunni Muslims as the only valid text of the Qur'an. The version of the text of the Qur'an accepted by Shi'a Muslims is slightly different, but not in ways which are significant for purposes of this chapter. See generally John Burton, *The Collection of the Qur'an* (Cambridge 1977).

Sunna of the Prophet were oral traditions of his verbal utterances and living example which were collected in written compilations for the first time during the second and third centuries of Islam, eighth and ninth centuries, A.D. The authenticity and relative authority of some texts of Sunna continue to create controversy among Sunni as well as Shi'a Muslims to the present day. On the concept and process of collection of Sunna and sources of contro-

taken as authoritative sources of Islamic guidance in popular practice. Throughout the first century of Islam, Islamic communities and individuals referred to these sources for guidance in their daily lives, in light of their own recollections of the living example of earlier generations and understanding of the message of Islam. The process of consulting scholars who were believed to be knowledgeable of the text and interpretation of the Qur'an and Sunna, and of the history and relevance of the traditions of early Islamic communities, gradually evolved into a practice of following a set of general principles and specific rulings attributed to a particular master or teacher and his leading disciples.

By the end of the second century of Islam, and beginning of the third (eighth and ninth centuries A.D.), the practice of adherence to a preferred scholar developed into a systematic and consistent following of what came to be known as his school of jurisprude, *madhhab*. For the next millennium, and largely to the present day, the development of Shari'a has been structured and governed by the methodology, principles, and rules set by the founding teachers, their immediate disciples, and subsequent scholars of the major surviving schools of Islamic jurisprudence, *madhahib al-fiqh al-Islami*.[12] Much of the legal and theological life of Islamic communities occurred within the framework of the school prevailing in a given community, often within a sub-division or line of thinking and authority.[13] However, the extinction of some schools, and shifts of territorial influence among the surviving schools, testifies to a dynamic of discourse and choice by Islamic communities according to the sense of each community of which school (or sub-school) is more responsive to its needs and interests at a given time.

Several features of the formative stage of Shari'a, in contrast to subsequent developments and more recent trends, should be noted here. First, the founding scholars were engaged in a process of derivation of general principles and specific rules for the guidance of their communities, responding to queries and requests or elaborating on hypothetical questions to clarify theoretical and methodological principles as they

---

versy, see, Rahman, *Islam*, chap. 3 and Ahmad Hasan, *Early Development of Islamic Jurisprudence* (Islamabad, 1970), chap. 5.

[12] Rahman, *Islam*, 81-83.

[13] Thus, each of the surviving four Sunni schools (Maliki, Hanafi, Shafi'i and Hanbali—named after their founding scholars of the eighth and ninth centuries), tends to have a certain territorial sphere of influence within the Islamic world. Whereas the Maliki school, for example, is now generally more prevalent in North and West Africa, the Hanbali school is followed in Saudi Arabia, at least as the "official" doctrine of the Kingdom. But in the Saudi Arabian case, it is the Wahabi interpretation of the Hanbali school which prevails, rather than that of the other scholars of the school as a whole. Shi'i schools also have a similar territorial spread, the Ja'fari school in Iran, Zaiydi in southern Arabia, the Isma'ili among the Shi'a of the Indian sub-continent, and so forth.

deemed necessary and useful for the community. Thus, the founding scholars and their immediate disciples were not, and did not see or present themselves as, establishing separate or distinctive, let alone immutable, schools of thought. Yet, one school or another came to be rigidly followed as the only valid articulation of Shari'a. A more integrated approach appears to be emerging today as a result of the intellectual and political context of the modern Islamic movement, but automatic observance of the accepted school or scholar(s) continues to be the norm.

Second, the elaboration of Shari'a by the founding scholars through the interpretation of Qur'an and Sunna, in light of the living traditions of the early Islamic communities, was initially a spontaneous and unstructured process. To early Muslims, all divine guidance was contained in the Qur'an and Sunna, which were rendered in their own Arabic language and exemplified in the then oral history of their recent forefathers. Rigorous methodology for the derivation of Shari'a principles and rules evolved gradually in response to certain developments.[14] The evolution of rigorous and systematic methodology was also probably prompted by the growing maturity and complexity of Shari'a itself.

In response to these and other factors, scholars began to develop technical rules and criteria for the interpretation of the Qur'an, the authentication and recording of Sunna and its reconciliation with the Qur'an, the relevance and use of early traditions of Islamic communities in relation to the Qur'an and Sunna, and so forth. This occurred within each of the schools, but *al-Safi'i* is generally credited with the most systematic and influential methodological development of what came to be known as *ilm usul al-fiqh al-Islami*, the science of the foundations of Islamic jurisprudence.[15] But, over time, that legitimate and necessary

---

[14] With the spread of Islam east into Persia and India, and west through North Africa to Spain, the many diverse peoples who embraced the faith or came under the domain of its political power, did not know the Arabic language or the history of early Islamic communities. Moreover, those peoples had their own pre-Islamic cultures, some had ancient and highly developed civilizations, including their distinctive legal and theological systems, and social, political, and economic institutions. The interaction and cross-fertilization of Islamic principles and rules with pre-Islamic norms and institutions of the then newly Islamized communities was expected, as indeed had already happened in Arabia and the Middle East, but that had to be in accordance with Islamic criteria as developed by the early more authoritative scholars and model communities.

[15] On the formative stages of Islamic jurisprudence and methodological developments, see Joseph Schacht, *An Introduction to Islamic Law* (Oxford, 1964), 45-48, 58ff.; Majid Khadduri, trans., *Islamic Jurisprudence, Shafi'i's Risala* (Baltimore, 1961), 40-84; Hasan, *Early Development of Islamic Jurisprudence*, chap. 8; Noel Coulson, *A History of Islamic Law* (Edinburgh, 1964), chap. 4; George Makdisi, "The Juridical Theology of Shafi'i: Origins and Significance of Usul Al-Fiqh," *Studia Islamica* 59 (1984): 5-47.

methodological regulation became too inhibiting for, indeed detrimental to, the further development of Shari'a, especially in the modern era.[16]

This is particularly true and clear, in my view, in relation to the nature and role of *ijtihad*, literally self-exertion or effort, but referring in this sense to the exercise of deliberate juridical reasoning to derive principles and rules of Shari'a. Although technically understood by Islamic jurists as applying only to matters on which there is no clear and categorical text in the Qur'an and Sunna, *ijtihad* was clearly applied to those fundamental texts themselves. Community leaders and scholars were always exercising ijtihad in relation to the Qur'an and Sunna because they had to rely on their own judgment in deciding which provisions of the Qur'an and Sunna applied to a given situation or question, and in interpreting and applying the text(s) they deemed relevant. With the development of *usul al-fiqh*, however, *ijtihad* was regulated and restricted to the point of extinction, and remains extremely problematic to the present day.[17] But since *ijtihad* was defined and regulated through human reason in the past, rather than being the direct product of divine revelation as such, it can be re-defined and re-regulated through human reason today and in the future.

A third significant feature to note about the formative stages of Shari'a is that while the scholars were elaborating and perfecting an ideal and comprehensive normative system, the affairs of the state were conducted more in accordance with pragmatic political expediency than with the dictates of that system. For much of Islamic history since the Amawy dynasty (661-750 A.D.), there existed "an uneasy truce between *ulama* [scholars of Shari'a] . . . and the political authorities.... As long as the sacred law [Shari'a] received formal recognition as a religious ideal, it did not insist on being fully applied in practice."[18] But the dichotomy between theory and practice should neither be exaggerated nor simplified in terms of secular and religious characterizations—an important point to note in relation to current Islamic discourse as indicated later.

For one thing, this dichotomy varied from time to time and from one field of Shari'a to another in ways that maintained the credibility of the appearance of allegiance to the ideal model from both the scholarly and political points of view. Second, the "light and distant" nature of government and administration in the imperial states of the past, coupled with the diffusion of Shari'a in inaccessible treatises and commentaries,

---

[16] An-Na'im, *Toward an Islamic Reformation*, chap. 3.

[17] Coulson, *A History of Islamic Law*, 80-81; Schacht, *An Introduction to Islamic Law*, 69ff.; An-Na'im, *Toward an Islamic Reformation*, 27-29. Cf. Wael B. Hallaq, "Was the Gate of Ijtihad Closed?" *International Journal of Middle Eastern Studies* 16 (1984): 3.

[18] Joseph Schacht, *The Origins of Muhammadan Jurisprudence* (Oxford, 1959), 84.

were not conducive to rigorous systematic implementation. Communities were left to conduct their daily affairs in accordance with their own local customary or traditional practices that included Shari'a norms, but not in a coherent and formal sense of codes of law in the modern sense of the term.

More significantly from the point of view of current debates about human rights in the Islamic world, the ideal of Shari'a has remained very much alive in the hearts and minds of Muslims, even when they lived under colonial administrations which sought to displace Shari'a by modern notions of law and government in formal and systematic ways.[19] As explained by Anderson:

> To a Muslim, it has always been a far more heinous sin to deny or question the divine revelation than to fail to obey it. So it seemed preferable to continue to pay lip-service to an inviolable Shari'a, as the only law of fundamental authority, and to excuse departure from much of it in practice by appealing to the doctrine of necessity (*darura*), rather than to make any attempt to adapt law to the circumstances and needs of contemporary life.[20]

But this traditional attitude is presently being challenged by Islamic activists who are saying that Muslims are now free to implement the totality of Shari'a after several decades of political independence as nation-states. It is far from clear, and extremely doubtful to my mind, whether the modern Islamists' project will lead to the implementation of Shari'a as articulated by the founding scholars and known to Islamic communities through the ages. In addition to the incompatibility of fundamental aspects of Shari'a with the modern circumstances of living in pluralistic nation-states in a globalized and interdependent world,[21] the very effort of codification and enforcement by centralized coercive authority contradicts the nature of Shari'a and the mainstream of Islamic history. Nevertheless, I would insist that the Islamists' project must be taken very seriously because of its drastic consequences to human rights, and religious human rights in particular.

---

[19] On the process of displacement of Shari'a by Western laws during the colonial period, see Herbert Liebesny, *The Law of the Near and Middle East* (Albany, 1975), 56; James Norman D. Anderson, *Law Reform in the Muslim World* (London, 1970), 1-2, 33.

[20] Anderson, *Law Reform in the Muslim World*, 36.

[21] For a critique of the theoretical model of a Shari'a state in the modern context, see, generally, An-Na'im, *Toward an Islamic Reformation*, chaps. 4-7.

Nature and Circumstances of The Present Discourse

It is difficult to generalize about the modern discourse of rights and responsibilities in all Islamic countries. Even in relation to certain regions or countries, one can identify several stages and forms of discourse. Generally speaking, however, this discourse tends to fall within two main stages, at least in relation to the countries of the Middle East and North Africa. During the struggle for independence, and immediately after it was achieved, the debate was focused upon nationalist projects whether liberal (such as that of Bourgiba in Tunisia), Arab/socialist (such as that of Nasir in Egypt), or socialist (such as that of the FLN in Algeria). Those projects were explicitly or implicitly secular in orientation with little reference, if any, to the role of Shari'a or an "Islamic ideology." However, upon the failure of the proponents of those projects to deliver the promised benefits, a variety of Islamist groups appear to have succeeded in seizing the initiative and re-defining the terms of discourse. I will focus on this second stage because of its significance to the subject of this chapter, without claiming that the "Islamization" of discourse is either total or irreversible throughout the Islamic world, or parts thereof.

In my view, discourse between Islamists and their opponents,[22] especially in the Middle East and North Africa, is complicated by contextual and operational factors and characterized by conceptual confusion. The reasons for this include the political and historical conditions under which discourse is taking place, the orientation and power relations of the participants as well as the subject-matter and terms of reference of the discourse itself. What is of particular concern for the subject of this chapter, however, is the conceptual confusion of this discourse.

On the Islamist side, the present discourse is apparently "modern" in its form and techniques, using to great effect sophisticated methods of organization, mass media and communications technology. These modern forms and techniques are being deployed in pursuit of the declared objective of recapturing and resurrecting an idealized vision of a past "Golden Age" of a powerful civilization. But that objective is usually presented as an ideological slogan, without a clear statement of how a

---

[22] These two groups are certainly too diverse to be subsumed under single terms, even within the same country at a given time. While noting the variety of discourses and diversity of participants and contexts, the following analysis will focus on discourse about the role of Islam as political ideology and the definitive framework of constitutional and legal systems. In this light, I will use the term Islamists to refer to those who present themselves as such, and deliberately employ Islamic concepts and terminology in their discourse. Since those who do not present themselves as Islamists and do not use Islamic concepts and terminology as a matter of preference are united in their opposition to the Islamists, I will refer to them as such.

Shari'a model might be reconciled with the realities of a modern multi-religious nation-state or of international relations.

Despite these obvious problems with the Islamists' side of the discourse, their opponents appear to be in disarray and generally on the defensive. Possible reasons for this include such political factors as being associated in the public eye with the previous discredited nationalist, post-independence project, both liberal and socialist. Leftist Muslims appear to be demoralized and suffering a loss of ideological inspiration, especially after the collapse of the Soviet bloc and the general retreat of socialism in Europe. Liberal Muslims seem to suffer from perceptions of American patronage, which is seen as a liability in itself, in addition to its negative association with perceptions of total American bias in favor of Israel in the Arab-Israeli conflict.

The discourse is also distorted by prevailing conditions of political oppression in many countries of the region, which in turn inhibit communication and public debate, especially with respect to any subject-matter deemed by security forces to be "sensitive" or controversial. Denied access to the mostly state-owned media, the Islamists seek political support for their cause by preaching at mosques and other "religious" locations and occasions, as well as using their own media (tapes and publications). Islamists are also very effective in generating support through the provision of social and health services to the target communities. Their opponents lack the organization and orientation to use these means, but may have better access to newspapers, as and when permitted by the government, which are not read by the illiterate majority of the population. Thus, the two sides rarely interact directly between themselves, or with each other's constituencies among the public at large.

A sense of mutual hostility and suspicion is intensified, it seems, by a lack of conceptual common ground: while Islamists speak of Shari'a and the revival of the glorious Islamic tradition, the frame of reference of their opponents is modern notions of constitutionalism, democracy, and human rights. Consequently, there is not only growing polarization and mis-communication between the two sides, and between each of them and the public constituency of the other, but their respective positions are also likely to be seen as contradictory or irreconcilable. The Islamic public at large is therefore presented with a stark choice: either Islam and Shari'a or democracy and human rights, without discussion or explanation of why there must be a choice, and why in these terms in particular.

Moreover, perceptions of a wider context of a historical confrontation with the West seem to reinforce this stark choice. Islamists tend to point to Western support for democracy and human rights as a ploy of exploitation and domination. Liberal Muslims, on the other hand, are discouraged by Western double-standards, as reflected, for example, in its domineering behavior in the Gulf War of 1991 in contrast to its failure to act in Bosnia.

The most significant consequence of this wider context for our purposes here is that issues of identity and authenticity are seen as of paramount importance in a fundamental geo-political confrontation. Thus, the Islamists' discourse often seems to be more about the *right* to define the identity of the community, and the duty to protect it against hostile non-Muslims aliens and, perhaps more importantly, against subversion by corrupt Westernized elites or heretics and renegade Muslims, than about the actual meaning of that identity and its relevance in the modern national and international context. Having succeeded in emphasizing the "Islamic" dimension of that identity over all other ethnic, cultural, economic, and political elements, the Islamists now claim a monopoly over Islamic authenticity and authority to define and defend the identity of the community in those terms.

In their present defensive mode, on the other hand, opponents of the Islamists appear to be more concerned with defending themselves against charges of treason and subversion than with contesting the Islamists' right to define and defend the identity of the community in question. The very act of contesting the Islamists' definition of the identity of the community and monopoly of Islamic authenticity is seen as confirmation of the charge, rather than an attempt to incorporate other elements which may have been integral to that identity, or to oppose its political manipulation. In this way, the boundaries become more important than the content, and those threatened with exclusion become more concerned with asserting their conformity with the criteria of inclusion than with contesting those criteria and the way they are applied.

This confrontational and unproductive state of discourse, I suggest, is compounded further by two conceptual confusions, one over the relationship between religion and the state in the Islamic context, and the other pertaining to the relationship between rights and responsibilities in connection with conceptions of the individual and the community. The first is more explicit and visible; the second is more implicit in the first and less appreciated as a separate issue.

It is not possible to trace here the precise sources and chronology of the confusion about the relationship between religion and the state. It is clear, I would suggest, that this confusion evolved through a dialectical process since the middle of the last century when Muslim reformers began debating whether it is desirable to separate religion and state, or Islam and politics, in order to achieve rapid modernization. While the advocates of separation, which came to be known as secularism (*al-*

ilmaniya) cited lessons from European history and quoted Western political theory in support of their position, its opponents claimed that Islam
allowed no distinction between religion and state.

The coercive and intrusive manner in which secularization was imposed by authoritarian regimes in Turkey and Iran after the end of the
First World War, and attempts to do so in other parts of the Islamic
World after the Second World War, aggravated the confusion and intensified the controversy over the issue. At present, Islamists present secularism as an anti-religious concept designed to alienate Muslims from
their religion and thereby secure and perpetuate their domination and
exploitation by the West. Those who advocate separation of Islam and
politics, they allege, are anti-Islamic subversive agents of alien cultures
serving the interests of foreign powers. In this way, the Islamists seek to
discredit their opponents while installing themselves as the acknowledged guardians of Islamic identity and authenticity.

Liberal and socialist Muslims, on the other hand, have traditionally
failed to take an Islamic discourse seriously or to educate themselves in
its concepts and techniques. Whether this was due to a belief that it was
unnecessary to engage in such discourse, or because of a fear that to do
so would mean conceding the legitimacy and authority of the Islamists'
frame of reference, the fact of the matter is that an Islamic discourse has
become, or is becoming, unavoidable in many Islamic countries. It is
therefore important to clarify the relationship between religion and the
state from an Islamic point of view.

The other serious conceptual confusion pertains to the relationship
between rights and responsibilities in connection to conceptions of the
individual and community. Following their premise of seeking modernization through the application of European models and political theory,
Muslim reformers emphasized earlier in the twentieth century the need
to protect individual liberties against encroachment by the state and
community at large. To counter that claim, Islamists now tend to emphasize the interests of the community over the rights of the individual.

This confusion is closely related to issues of identity as well as the
relationship between religion and politics with direct consequences to
freedom of belief. According to the Islamists, since Islam is the sole foundation of the identity of the community, the state must "regulate" freedom of belief as the essential criterion of membership in the community.
By disputing this in favor of protecting individual freedom of belief, they
charge, their secular (read anti-Islamic) opponents are weakening the Islamic identity of the community and undermining the Islamic nature of
the state.

In this way, confrontational discourse faces modern Islamic communities with a compounded stark choice between "secular" individualism and "Islamic" communitarianism. As I will argue in the next section, the sharp dichotomy implicit in this choice is neither necessary from an Islamic religious point of view, nor realistic or useful to make in practice.

Foundations of Religious Human Rights

In light of the previous discussion, it is clear that freedom of belief ought to be supported from an *Islamic religious* point of view, because it is essential for the authenticity of religious belief and experience as such and for the vitality and relevance of an Islamic normative system to the lives of Muslims today. An equally valid and fundamental reason for such support is that freedom of belief is essential for the peace and stability of necessarily and permanently pluralistic national and international political communities.

The task set for this chapter is to examine both the positive and negative aspects of an Islamic frame of reference for religious rights *as human rights*. This should be done, first, with a view to evaluating the existence or absence, adequacy or inadequacy, of Islamic foundations for these rights. The second purpose of such an evaluation, I believe, is to seek ways of developing Islamic foundations for freedom of belief, to the extent they are absent, and of promoting them to greater adequacy and stronger influence on Islamic law and behavior.

There is an obvious "advocacy" element in my perception of the second purpose of this task (also implicit throughout my analysis) in that I am not concerned with an "objective" or "impartial" evaluation of the situation, but rather with changing or supporting it in favor of better protection of human rights, including religious human rights. From my perspective as a Muslim who not only takes both Islam and human rights seriously, but also believe them to be mutually supportive normative systems, that is the point of the whole exercise.

The background, context, and some of the premises of my approach to this task have already been explained in the preceding sections. This final section offers a two-fold discussion. First, I shall briefly review the status of religious rights under Shari'a as commonly conceived in Islamic discourse today and assess that conception from a human rights point of view. Second, I will elaborate on a theory of stronger Islamic foundations for religious human rights with a view to promoting and enhancing the protection of these rights in Islamic countries today.

On the first count, the Shari'a scheme of religious rights provides that a person is essentially "free" to adopt or reject Islam, but certain consequences will follow from his/her choice:[23]

(1) If a person chooses to become a Muslim, or is born and raised as a Muslim, then he or she will have full rights of citizenship in an Islamic state, subject to limitations against the rights of women as conceived in modern constitutional and human rights law. However, once a Muslim or officially classified as such, a person will be subject to the death penalty if he or she becomes an apostate, that is, one who persists in repudiating his or her faith in Islam. An apostate is also subjected to forfeiture of property, nullification of marriage, and other legal consequences.

(2) If a person chooses to be or remain a Christian, Jew, or believer in another scriptural religion, as defined by Shari'a—one of *ahl al-kitab*, the People of the Book or believers in divine scripture who are called *dhimmis*—he or she will suffer certain limitations of rights as a subject of an Islamic state. There are differences as to the scope and extent of these limitations among various schools of thought and individual scholars of Shari'a, and the practice has also varied over time. The essential point is that *dhimmis* are not supposed to enjoy complete legal equality with Muslims.

(3) If a person is neither a Muslim nor one of *ahl al-kitab*, as defined by Shari'a, then that person is deemed to be an unbeliever (*khafir* or *mushrik*). An unbeliever is not permitted to reside permanently, or even temporarily according to stricter interpretations, in peace as a free person within the territory of an Islamic state except under special permission for safe conduct (*aman*). In theory, unbelievers should be offered the choice of adopting Islam, and if they reject it they may either be killed in battle, enslaved, or ransomed if captured.

Compared to the legal and theological systems of other "state religions" of the past, it is clear that the Shari'a scheme of religious rights was superior from a modern perspective of freedom of belief. Moreover, except for minor exceptions or relatively brief periods, such as the early Fatimi dynasty in Egypt in the tenth century A.D., past and present Islamic states have generally tended to adopt the least restrictive interpretation of these principles, or to disregard them in favor of relatively greater freedom of belief.

But when judged by modern standards of human rights, the Shari'a scheme is objectionable not only because of its limitations on freedom of belief for Muslim and non-Muslims alike, but also in view of its very con-

---

[23] For elaboration and documentation of the Shari'a scheme, see An-Na'im, *Toward an Islamic Reformation*; id., "Religious Minorities under Islamic Law and the Limits of Cultural Relativism," *Human Rights Quarterly* 9(1) (1987): 1-18.

ception of civil and political rights on the basis of a religious classification of people. To illustrate briefly the first point, the capital crime of apostasy not only violates the right of a Muslim to adopt another faith or belief, but can and has been used to punish Muslims who express unorthodox views which are deemed to be a repudiation of belief in Islam.[24] While limitations on the rights of non-Muslim believers clearly constitute serious discrimination on grounds of religion, the possibility of death or enslavement for an unbeliever is a total nullification of any notion of human rights in principle and content.

Moreover, the very notion of basing civil and political rights on a religious classification is inherently inconsistent with the premise of the universality of human rights, however "insignificant" the legal consequences of that universality may appear to be. I would therefore conclude that although there are foundations for some religious rights in Shari'a and in the practice of Islamic states past and present, that level of protection of freedom of belief does not offer a sufficient foundation for religious *human* rights.

Nevertheless, I suggest that it is possible to construct a coherent and conceptually valid theory of Islamic foundations of religious human rights based on the following elements. First, since Shari'a is a historically-conditioned *human* interpretation of the fundamental sources of Islam, alternative modern interpretations are possible. Second, a reconstruction of Shari'a in support of Islamic foundations for religious human rights is imperative in view of the need for contesting and renegotiating Islamic identity and its normative system in the present circumstances of plurality of national and international political communities. Third, such a theory will be fully Islamic, because it would be based on the text of the Qur'an as interpreted and accepted by Muslims in the present context, instead of applying Shari'a principles which were the product of interpretation by earlier Muslims in their own historical context. To clarify further these elements, it is necessary to outline the hermeneutical premise of this theory.

Hermeneutics may be defined as the art or science of interpretation, especially of scriptural texts. In view of the inevitability of using human reason and action in understanding and implementing any text, as noted earlier, a hermeneutical process is necessary for understanding the purpose and normative content of a text like the Qur'an or Bible.[25]

---

[24] For a recent example of this, see Abdullahi Ahmed An-Na'im, "The Islamic Law of Apostasy and its Modern Applicability: A Case from the Sudan," *Religion* 16 (1986): 197-223.

[25] For an elaboration on this point and the following remarks see Abdullahi An-Na'im, "Toward an Islamic Hermeneutics for Human Rights," in An-Na'im, et al., eds., *Human Rights and Religious Values: An Uneasy Relationship?*, 229-42.

Each religion, or specific tradition within a religion, is supposed to have its own distinctive set of interpretative techniques and their underlying assumptions which are accepted as valid or authoritative by the adherents of the religion or tradition in question. In reality, however, there will be more than one competing hermeneutical framework, each of which is open to mutual challenge and reformulation among cobelievers. Thus, for example, the diversity of Sunni, Shi`a, and Sufi Muslim schools of thought signify differences in the hermeneutical framework, not only among Muslims in general but also among those who belong to each of the Islamic traditions.

Although the proponents of one Islamic interpretative framework would normally tend to characterize those of others as invalid or illegitimate, even un-Islamic, the only reasonable and practical way to settle such differences is for each side to present its case to the relevant community of believers as the ultimate arbiter and mediator between competing frameworks. This would usually happen in the process of seeking the support and allegiance of the community, and the issue would be settled over time through the community's adoption or rejection of one point of view or another. But how does a particular type of Islamic interpretative framework emerge and prevail over others at a certain time?

The emergence of a new interpretative framework, I suggest, is normally a function of individual and collective orientation, that is to say, the conditioning of the existential or material circumstances of the person and the community in relation to the text. A Muslim, for example, would understand the text of the Qur'an, and derive its normative implications, in terms of his or her knowledge and experience of the world, including perceptions of self-interest in political, economic, and social context, and of the realities of inter-communal and/or international relations. A similar process, I maintain, operates at the communal level in that the prevalence or demise of an interpretative framework is normally a function of the collective orientation of the community as defined above, that is to say, the conditioning of the existential or material circumstances of the community at a given time.

This does not mean that the process is either completely deterministic in that interpretations are automatically determined by settled and immutable orientations, or wholly relativistic in opening religious texts to all and every type of interpretation. The process is not deterministic because individual and collective orientations are sometimes influenced by visions of change and transformation beyond the immediate conditioning of circumstances as perceived by the general population. Otherwise, there would be no opportunity for the emergence of radical ideas and social movements capable of transcending the conditioning of individual and communal circumstances, and indeed eventually transforming those circumstances themselves. Individuals and communities do exercise a choice in articulating, adopting, or rejecting one interpretative framework or another.

The process is not arbitrary and relativistic because the validity of a proposed interpretation is judged by a living community through serious discussion and deliberation. The proponents of each interpretation will, of course, seek to win the support of the community through the use of what they claim are Islamic concepts and arguments, but it is the community which will ultimately make that determination. In practice, the community may follow the advice of its political or opinion leaders, and those whose proposals were thereby rejected should accept that decision until they can either win those leaders over or persuade the community not to follow their advice. The alternative is to seek to impose their interpretation on the community which will only be counter-productive in the end.

In the process of emergence and adoption or rejection of interpretative frameworks there is the factor of "historical contingency," which refers to the notion that an idea will not emerge or prevail prematurely. But since historical contingency can only be judged in retrospect, who is to predict whether or not an idea is in fact premature and how can that be done with certainty? The emergence of an idea and the ability of its proponents to propagate it are indications of the ripening of historical contingency, but only time will tell whether or not the circumstances of the period were conducive to the conditioning and/or individual and collective choice that would allow it to prevail. In fact, as illustrated by the history of major religions, including Islam, social and political resistance are to be expected, and should not be taken as conclusive evidence of the final rejection of an idea, however radical or innovative it may appear to be.

To illustrate briefly the application of this analysis to the subject of Islamic foundations of religious human rights, I would cite verse 137 of chapter 4, which can be translated as follows:

> Those who believed, then disbelieved, believed again and disbelieve once more, and become even more disbelieving, God shall not forgive them or guide them on the right path.

Although the majority of early Islamic scholars interpreted this verse as consistent with the imposition of the death penalty for apostasy,[26] I would see it as conclusively excluding any possibility of punishment for

---

[26] See, e.g.,*Tafsir al-Tabari*, 9:314-18 (*Dar al-Ma'arif bi-Masr*, not dated).

disbelief in this life, since there is no mention of such punishment in this verse or anywhere else in the Qur'an. The difference between my understanding of this verse and that of early scholars, which is still advocated by some Islamists today, reflects divergence in interpretative frameworks, but neither is more or less Islamic because of that reason alone. Disagreement between these frameworks and their normative implications should be settled by the community of Muslims at large in light of the Islamic argumentation presented on behalf of each position.

The example of apostasy is particularly appropriate for the purposes of my analysis, because it also involves the conceptual confusions mentioned earlier, namely, the question of the relationship between Islam and the state and that between rights and responsibilities. In the absence of Qur'anic authority, as noted earlier, the punishment of apostasy under Shari'a is based on reports of Sunna. But the support of Sunna for this punishment is valid only on the assumption of a certain type of unity of Islam and the state and a particular view of rights and responsibilities that conditions the former on performance of the latter. Sunna can be understood to support imposing the death penalty for apostasy only if disbelief is equated with high treason on the assumption that citizenship is based on belief in Islam. That assumption, in turn, is valid only under a view of entitlement to the rights of citizenship on the condition of satisfactory performance of the responsibilities of belief as a pre-requisite of membership of the community whose members enjoy those rights.[27] Moreover, this reasoning is premised on a conception of freedom of belief as a conditional right of citizens and not as a human right to which all human beings are entitled.

While this reasoning and its underlying premise were valid, in my view, in the historical context of the formative stages of Shari'a, they are no longer valid today. The individual and collective orientations of Muslims today, I believe, are probably different from those of earlier generations because of the radical transformation of existential and material circumstances of today compared to those of the past. In contrast to the localized traditional existence of past Islamic societies, Muslims today live in multi-religious nation-states which are fully incorporated into a globalized world of political, economic, and security interdependence, and constantly experiencing the effects of mutual social/cultural influence with non-Islamic societies. While some individual Muslims may still choose to advocate traditional notions of community and conditionality of rights, the reality of the pluralistic national and international political communities of today support entitlement to freedom of belief as a hu-

---

[27] See An-Na'im, *Toward an Islamic Reformation*, 86-87.

man right rather than a conditional right of membership of a religious community.

In support of the view that freedom of belief is a human right to which all human beings are entitled by virtue of their humanity, rather than a right conditioned upon the performance of certain responsibilities of membership in a community, I would note that the right is needed and useful only in the former rather than the latter sense. If the benefits of freedom of belief is available only to believers who are accepted as such, what is the rationale for having a right to freedom of belief at all? The right to freedom of belief is needed, and can be claimed, only by non-believers and believers who are not accepted as such by the community in question. I would also recall here the argument made earlier about the importance of freedom of belief, including the right of dissent, for the vitality and relevance of the religion itself and its normative system.

Finally, I wish to add the following suggested clarification of the above-mentioned conceptual confusion of the relationship between religion and the state and that of the individual and community in the Islamic context. In my view, notions of complete unity of religion and state, on the one hand, and their strict separation in a community of believers, on the other, are both conceptual fallacies which also lacks support in Islamic history, including the articulation and implementation of Shari'a itself.

The organic relationship between religion and *politics* is too obvious to deny, and is not problematic except when it results in restrictions on the legal and human rights of citizens on the ground of their faith or belief. Even with regard to the state, religion can legitimately play a ceremonial or symbolic role in public life. What is objectionable is for religious beliefs to be constituted as the basis of political authority and legal system of a nation-state in ways which, for example, condition or base legal and human rights on faith or belief or gender. To do so would immediately repudiate the survival of the political community as well as undermine the integrity and authenticity of religious belief and practice.

It is important to inject this clarification in current discourse about rights and human rights in Islamic countries today, because, as indicated earlier, the protagonists tend to misconceive the issues and unduly restrict the options open to Islamic societies. Instead of facing Islamic societies with a false stark choice between total unity or complete separation of Islam and politics/state, participants in the discourse should seek to clarify and articulate a formulation of the relationship in ways which satisfies an Islamic sense of identity and self-determination without violating internationally-recognized human rights norms.

It is also important to emphasize that secularism, as practiced in many parts of the world (and not only the West), is not anti-religion. On the contrary, secularism was conceived and applied in parts of Western Europe and the United States in order to protect freedom of belief and promote religious piety.[28] Moreover, there is nothing in the concept and practice of secularism to justify associating it as such with the exploitation and domination of others. Western powers did not colonize, and now seek to dominate, Islamic countries *because* the former were/are secular, or *through* secularizing the latter countries. Nevertheless, the existence of these misconceptions must be acknowledged and addressed by those who are concerned that the relationship between Islam and politics or the state is not only compatible but also fully supportive of universal human rights, including religious human rights.

Conclusion: Realities and Prospects

Islamic Shari'a and history present a mixed picture regarding foundations of religious human rights, whereby the theory of the freedom of belief was comparatively superior to those of other state-religions in the past and the practice was generally better than the theory, but both are no longer acceptable from a modern human rights point of view. Strong Islamic foundations for religious human rights are conceptually possible, but their practical prospects depend on the outcome of the current discourse in Islamic countries.

Although I strongly believe in the Islamic validity of the theory presented in this chapter, I would neither suggest that it is the only possible Islamic foundation of religious human rights nor claim that it is necessarily widely accepted as such in practice. In my view, the more Islamic foundations for religious human rights one can find, the better, for these multiple foundations will support and reinforce each other in promoting these rights as universal human rights. My theory may not be consciously accepted as such, but all its factual elements and essential logical premises are familiar to educated Muslims and scholars of Islam.

By addressing it to Muslims, I hope that my theory will contribute to promoting an Islamic commitment to religious human rights, and thereby influence current and future practice in favor of greater respect and protection of these rights in Islamic countries today. A better understanding by non-Muslims of the prospects and problems of Islamic foun-

---

[28] For a concise clarification prompted by the needs of an Islamic discourse without being part of it see, Helge Hoibraaten, "Secular Society: An Attempt at Initiation," in Tore Lindholm and Kari Vogt, eds., *Islamic Law Reform and Human Rights: Challenges and Rejoinders* (Oslo, 1993), 231-57.

dations for religious human rights, together with efforts from other religious perspectives contained in this book and its sequel, should also
contribute to enabling believers and non-believers alike to collaborate in
a global project to protect and promote universal religious human
rights.[29]

---

[29] I see this process as integral to the project of promoting universal cross-cultural le-
gitimacy of human rights. See, generally, Abdullahi A. An-Na'im and Francis M. Deng, eds.,
Human Rights in Africa: Cross-Cultural Perspectives (Washington, 1990); Abdullahi A. An-
Na'im, ed., *Human Rights in Cross-Cultural Perspectives* (Philadelphia, 1992).

Rights of Women Within Islamic Communities

RIFFAT HASSAN

University of Louisville

B efore I address the issue of the human rights of women within Islamic communities, I consider it necessary to reflect on two areas of concern which have—in my judgment—a critical bearing on the human rights debates in the present-day Muslim world. The first area of concern relates to some widely-held assumptions regarding human rights and to the secular nature of the human rights discourse which has developed within the framework of the United Nations. The second area of concern relates to the perception of Islam and Muslims, in and by the West, and the image of Muslim women which has become prevalent in Western societies.

Some Assumptions About "Human Rights"

In the contemporary world, the term "human rights" has become a fad, and it is often used rather glibly. Underlying this usage is the assumption that everyone knows what "human rights" are and from whence they came. Another widespread assumption is that human beings do, in fact, possess "human rights." If the latter assumption were valid, that is, if "human rights" were a universal human possession, there would not be significant numbers of persons in virtually every society in the world struggling, either openly or surreptitiously, to secure their "human rights."

It may be argued, on a philosophical plane, that "human rights" do exist, though they are not exercised by all or even most human beings. This argument leads, however, to the question: If "human rights" exist though they are not being exercised by all or most human beings (many of whom would be astonished to know that they had any such "rights"), then in what sense do these "human rights" *exist*? It is an historical fact

361

J. Witte, Jr. and J.D. van der Vyver (eds.), Religious Human Rights in Global Perspective, 361-386.
© 1996 *Kluwer Law International. Printed in the Netherlands.*

that "human rights" have never been, nor are they now, the universal possession of humankind, although the United Nations adopted the International Bill of Human Rights containing the Universal Declaration of Human Rights in 1948.

It may also be argued that, though all or most human beings do not exercise their "human rights," these rights remain intact since human beings can exercise them whenever they choose to do so, because these rights are universally recognized and enforceable by courts of law. In answer to this argument (besides remembering the words of Shakespeare regarding the delays of justice), I would like to cite the words of an eminent Muslim jurist:

> It would be pointless to detail the progressive erosion of human rights in so many contemporary constitutions around the world. Against the rising tide of governmental interference and despotism, they are proving like dikes of straw. Under the guise of creating a "welfare state" or" an egalitarian society," most rights have been deprived of all meaning or significance. In some parts of the world they are directly suspendable and often remain suspended. In states that claim socialist objectives, many of these rights are deprived of enforceability through independent courts; in some constitutions they have been made subject to so many constitutionally authorized inroads as to become devoid of all reality. Even in countries where they do not suffer from any of the above limitations, judicial interpretation has, in deference to the idea of State activism and the welfare of the people, severely limited their scope. Perhaps never before has man enjoyed so great a capacity for good and for bad as today; yet never before has an individual felt, as now, so helpless in confrontation with the power and weight of faceless governmental agencies. Power like wealth accrues in the hands of those who wield it. The constitutional limitations of the free world appear to provide little safeguard or guarantee against the continuation of this trend.[1]

The Universal Declaration of Human Rights. Though the Universal Declaration of Human Rights is called "universal," it "was articulated along the lines of historical trends of the Western world during the last three centuries, and a certain philosophical anthropology of individualistic humanism which helped justify them."[2] The Declaration simply as-

---

[1] K.M. Ishaque, "Islamic Law—Its Ideals and Principles," in A. Gauher, ed., *The Challenge of Islam* (London, 1980), 57.

[2] Raimundo Panikkar, "Is the Notion of Human Rights a Western Concept?" *Breakthrough* 31 (Spring, 1989).

sumed a universal human nature common to all the peoples, the dignity of the individual, and a democratic social order.[3]

In the decades since the Declaration, the term "human rights" has become an integral part of both political and popular discourse, particularly amongst Western, and Western-educated, persons. Until very recently most of this discourse has been largely in secular terms. In fact, it is frequently assumed, and stated, by many advocates of human rights, in both Western and non-Western (including many Muslim) countries, that human rights can exist only within a secular context and not within the framework of religion.

Underlying the stance that the concept of human rights is fundamentally secular, and, therefore, outside of, and even antithetical to, the worldview of religion, is—of course—a certain view of religion in general, or of particular religions. In Muslim countries such as Pakistan, for instance, it is often remarked by secular-minded proponents of human rights that it is not meaningful to talk about human rights in Islam because as a religious tradition, Islam has supported values and structures which are incompatible with the assumptions which underlie the Universal Declaration of Human Rights.

What needs to be pointed out to those who uphold the Universal Declaration of Human Rights to be the highest or sole model of a charter of equality and liberty for all human beings is that given the Western origin and orientation of this Declaration, the "universality" of the assumptions on which it is based is—at the very least—problematic and subject to questioning. Furthermore, the alleged incompatibility between the concept of human rights and religion in general, or particular religions such as Islam, needs to be examined in an unbiased way.

A Popular Muslim Reaction. Muslims, reacting to the charge that human rights can only exist within a "Western" and/or "secular" society, are apt to make statements such as the following by A.K. Brohi, a legal scholar and philosopher who served as a Federal Minister in the Pakistan government:

> There is a fundamental difference in the perspectives from which Islam and the West each view the matter of human rights. The Western perspective may by and large be called anthropocentric in the sense that man is regarded as constituting the measure of everything since he is the starting point of all thinking and action. The perspective of Islam on the other hand is theocentric— God-conscious. Here the Absolute is paramount, and man exists only to serve his Maker, the Supreme Power and Presence which

---

[3] Ibid.

alone sustains his moral, material and spiritual make-up, secures
the realisation of his aspirations and makes possible his transcendence. . . . [In the West] the rights of man are seen in a setting
which has no reference to his relationship with God, but are posited as his inalienable birthright. The student of growth of Western civilization and culture notices throughout that the emphasis
is on human rights within an "anthropocentric" perspective of
human destiny. Each time the assertion of human rights is made
it is done only to secure their recognition from some secular
authority such as the state itself or its ruling power. In marked
contrast to this approach the strategy of Islam is to emphasize the
supreme importance of our respect for human rights and fundamental freedom as an aspect of the quality of religious consciousness that it claims to foster in the heart, mind and soul of
its followers. The perspective is "theocentric" through and
through. . . . It seems at first sight, therefore, that there are no
human rights or freedoms admissible to man in the sense in
which modern man's thought, belief and practice understand
them; in essence, the believer has only obligations or duties to
God since he is called upon to obey the Divine Law, and such
human rights as he is made to acknowledge stem from his primary duty to obey God. Yet paradoxically, in these duties lie all
the rights and freedoms. Man acknowledges the rights of his fellow men because there is a duty imposed on him by the religious
law to obey God and the Prophet and those who are constituted
as authority to conduct the affairs of state. In everything that a
believer does his primary nexus is with his Maker, and it is
through Him that he acknowledges his relationship with the rest
of his fellowmen as even with the rest of creation. In the words of
the Qur'an, "Man has been created only to serve God."[4]

While Brohi is correct in saying that the perspective of Islam is God-
centered, his generalization that the Western perspective is "anthropocentric" needs to be seriously qualified. The viewpoint of many Christians and Jews who form a significant component of the Western world
is, in fact, similar to that of Brohi. For instance, writing on *The Judeo-
Christian Heritage and Human Rights*, Carl F.H. Henry, a Protestant theologian and founding editor of *Christianity Today*, states:

Though it may at first seem astonishing to the contemporary
mind, Jewish law, as Haim Cohn remarks, embraces no concept
of human rights in the modern sense. The Bible stresses "not
rights but duties—and these were essentially duties to God,"

---

[4] A.K. Brohi, "Islam and Human Rights," in Gauher, ed., *The Challenge of Islam*, 179-181.

Louis Henkin reminds us, "although fellowman was the benefi-
ciary of many of them". . . . The Bible has a doctrine of divinely
imposed duties; what moderns call human rights are the contingent flipside of those duties. . . . To be sure, many biblical duties—if not all—imply a corresponding enforceable right. The
divine prohibition of theft or of removal of a landmark implies
an unstated right to property and possession.[5]

Henry goes on to make a comparison between the Biblical approach
to human rights and the Universal Declaration of Human Rights—a
comparison which would be echoed by many Muslims including Brohi.
Henry writes:

The Universal Declaration of Human Rights (1948) presents a
panorama of human rights while it says very little about human
duties and nothing at all about duties to God. Only Article 29,
which limits the exercise of rights by reciprocal rights and a regard for morality, public order and general welfare, refers to
human duty, and even here the context is anthropological. Although the stipulated rights are considered the generally acknowledged norms of modern civilization, none is legally
enforceable since the Declaration wholly ignores the subject of
ultimate source and sanction of rights and does not even obligate
states to enact the stipulated rights. The Bible, by contrast, has no
notion of publicly unobligated individuals who are beneficiaries
of rights—claims, or of ultimate rights formulated and conferred
by earthly institutions, let alone of civil government existing only
as a humanly devised option. "Do unto others," said Jesus, "as
you would that they do unto you" (*Matthew* 7:12).[6]

The fact that the Universal Declaration of Human Rights does not acknowledge religion as a source of human rights points to what I consider
a critical flaw in the orientation of the United Nations. It is understandable why in 1948, against the backdrop of massive human conflicts, the
United Nations would want to distance itself from any sort of identification with religion which has, historically, contributed significantly to
much divisiveness and strife in the world. However, it is much less understandable how the United Nations could become so trapped in its
secular discourse that it would persist in its refusal to deal with the fact

---

[5] Carl F.H. Henry, "The Judeo-Christian Heritage and Human Rights," in Carl H. Esbeck, ed., *Religious Beliefs, Human Rights and the Moral Foundations of Western Democracy*
(Columbia, MS, 1986), 29-30, quoting Haim Cohn, *Human Rights in Jewish Law* (New York,
1984), 17ff. and Louis Henkin, *The Rights of Man Today* (Boulder, CO, 1978), 1.

[6] Henry, "The Judeo-Christian Heritage and Human Rights," 30.

that for millions of human beings whose lives are rooted in belief rather than unbelief, human rights become meaningful only when they are placed within the framework of their belief-system.

The United Nations may well be coming to that realization. In the document produced at the conclusion of the United Nations International Conference on Population and Development, held in Cairo in September 1994, "religion, ethics, and culture" were considered to be factors which are relevant in population planning and development. This recognition of the place of religion marks a shift, which is radical enough to be called a paradigm shift, in the orientation of the United Nations. This shift away from a wholly secular mindset is likely to make the United Nations much more effective in reaching out to masses of people in many parts of the world.

While it is necessary, in my opinion, to recognize the importance of religion as a major, if not *the* primary, source of human rights for a large number of human beings, including the majority of Muslims, in the world, I have great difficulty in accepting as valid or normative Brohi's statement that "Man acknowledges the rights of his fellow men because this is a duty imposed on him by the religious law to obey God and the Prophet and those who are constituted as authority to conduct the affairs of state." Certainly, modern Islam's most outstanding thinker, Muhammad Iqbal, who spent his whole life teaching Muslims how to develop their selfhood and who believed that "art, religion and ethics must be judged from the standpoint of personality,"[7] would have challenged the idea that the highest human morality consisted either in obedience to a law which was externally imposed or in doing one's duty to one's fellow beings only from a sense of religious constraint. In Iqbal's own words, "There are many who love God and wander in the wilderness; I will follow the one who loves the persons made by God."[8]

For hundreds of years now, Muslims have been taught that they were created to serve God by obeying those in authority over them and by enduring with patience whatever God willed for them. For hundreds of years, Muslim masses have patiently endured the grinding poverty and oppression imposed on them by those in authority. Not to be enslaved by foreign invaders whose every attempt to subjugate them was met with resistance, Muslim masses were enslaved by Muslims in the name of God and the Prophet, made to believe that they had no rights, only responsibilities; that God was the God of Retribution, not of Love; that Islam was an ethic of suffering, not of joyous living; that they were determined by

---

[7] Muhammad Iqbal, quoted by R.A. Nicholson, *The Secrets of the Self*, translation of *Asrar-e-Khudi* (Farsi) (Lahore, 1964), xxii.

[8] Muhammad Iqbal, *Bang-e-Dara* (Urdu) (Lahore, 1962), 151.

"Qismat" or Fate, not masters of their own fate. The heroic spirit of Muslim thinkers such as Syed Ahmad Khan and Iqbal, who were born in India in the last century—products not only of a pluralistic society but also of an East-West synthesis—brought about a Renaissance in the Muslim world and liberated Muslims from the multi-faceted bondage of colonialism. Their work, however, was not completed, since the traditionalism which has been eating away at the heart of Islam for several centuries continues to hold sway over most of the Muslim world. What we are witnessing today in the Muslim world is of extreme interest and importance, for we are living in an age of both revolutions and involutions, of both progression and retrogression, of both great light and great darkness. It is imperative for Muslims that they rethink their position on all vital issues, since we can no longer afford the luxury of consoling ourselves for our present miseries and misfortunes by an uncritical adulation of a romanticized past. History has brought us to a point where rhetoric will not rescue us from reality and where the discrepancies between Islamic theory and Muslim practice will have to be accounted for.

Having drawn attention to aspects of the on-going debate on human rights in the contemporary world which seem to me to be highly relevant in understanding the issue of human rights in the context of the Muslim world, I turn to my second area of concern which relates to the way Islam and Muslims are perceived in the West. This perception along with the way in which Muslim women are commonly portrayed in Western societies, also plays—I believe—a crucial role in the evolving discussion on human rights in many Muslim communities throughout the world.

Western Perceptions of Islam (and of Muslim Women)

Since the 1970s, there has been a growing interest in the West in Islam and Muslims. Much of this interest has been focussed, however, on a few subjects such as Islamic Revival, Islamic Fundamentalism, The Salman Rushdie Affair, and Women in Islam, rather than on understanding the complexity and diversity of the World of Islam. Not only the choice of subjects, but also the manner in which these subjects have generally been portrayed by Western media or popular literature calls into question the motivation which underlies the selective Western interest in Islam and Muslims. It is difficult to see this interest as being positively motivated given the widespread negative stereotyping of Islam and Muslims in the West.

Though there are a number of Americans who had not paid any serious attention to Islam or Muslims until the Arab oil embargo of 1973 or the Iranian Revolution of 1979, propaganda against Islam and Muslims is nothing new in the West. It is as old as the first chapter of Islamic history, when the new faith began to move into territories largely occupied by Christians. Dante, the great poet of medieval Christianity, perceived the Prophet of Islam as the divider of the world of Christendom and assigned him to all but the lowest level of hell for his grievous "sin." St. Thomas Aquinas, the most outstanding Scholastic philosopher who owed such profound debt to the thinkers of Muslim Spain, described Islam as nothing but a construct to accommodate the lust of Muhammad.[9] What far-reaching shadows were cast upon the future by powerful Christian voices such as those of Dante and Aquinas can be glimpsed from Thomas Carlyle's historic lecture on "The Hero as Prophet. Mahomet: Islam" in the series entitled *On Heroes, Hero-Worship and The Heroic in History.* Writing in the mid-nineteenth century, Carlyle urged his fellow Christians to dismiss *"our current hypothesis* about Mahomet, that he was a scheming Imposter, a Falsehood Incarnate, that his religion is a mere quackery and fatuity."[10]

Given the reservoir of negative images associated with Islam and Muslims in "the Collective Unconscious" of the West, it is hardly surprising that, since the demise of the Soviet Empire, "the World of Islam" is being seen as the new "Enemy" which is perhaps even more incomprehensible and intractable than the last one. The routine portrayal of Islam as a religion spread by the sword and characterized by "Holy War," and of Muslims as barbarous and backward, frenzied and fanatic, volatile and violent, has led, in recent times, to an alarming increase in "Muslim-bashing"—verbal, physical, and psychological—in a number of Western countries.

In the midst of so much hatred and aversion toward Islam and Muslims in general, the outpouring of so much sympathy, in and by the West, toward Muslim women appears, at a surface level, to be an amazing contradiction. Are Muslim women also not adherents of Islam? Are Muslim women also not victims of "Muslim-bashing"? Few of us can forget the brutal burning of Turkish Muslim girls by German gangsters or the ruthless rape of Bosnian Muslim women by Serbian soldiers. In what way, then, am I—a Muslim woman—to interpret the "sympathy" shown to Muslim women by the popular rhetoric of the West?

As a Muslim woman who has lived for the greater part of her life in the West, I find it difficult to believe on the basis of my experience, that

---

[9] Quoted by E.W. Fernea in "Roles of Women in Islam: Past and Present" (unpublished paper presented at The Ta'ziyeh Conference held at Hartford Seminary, Connecticut, May 2, 1988).

[10] Thomas Carlyle, "The Hero as Prophet. Mahomet: Islam," in id., *On Heroes, Hero-Worship and the Heroic in History* (New York, 1903), 43 (emphasis added).

there is much genuine concern for Muslim women in many Western countries or peoples. The concern which exists in a country with a large Muslim population—such as England—is that the cultural norms and values of British society not be jeopardized or compromised by "foreigners" like the Muslims. A large number of Muslims living in England happen to be blue-collar workers who are devout religiously and highly conservative insofar as attitudes toward women are concerned. This was the case when I was a student at the University of Durham in England during the 1960s. At that time neither the religious devotion of the Muslims nor their attitude toward women caused much concern to British society. But things changed radically and dramatically after the publication of *The Satanic Verses* by Salman Rushdie, in the fall of 1989. The intense reaction of the Muslims to this book which degraded, with a calculated deliberateness, that which was most sacred to them in their religious tradition, caused grave alarm to the British who began to see the Muslims in Britain as a threat to their "secular democracy."[11] One very effective way to get back at the Muslims was to hit them where it would hurt the most—by politicizing the issue of Muslim women. Images of "poor, oppressed" Muslim women began to attract more and more publicity, not only in England but also in other Western countries with sizeable Muslim minorities, as Muslims generally were denounced as anti-Western, anti-rational, anti-modern, even anti-human.

The Qur'an and Human Rights

Since the modern notion of human rights originated in a Western, secular context, Muslims in general, but Muslim women in particular, find themselves in a quandary when they initiate, or participate in, a discussion on human rights whether in the West or in Muslim societies. Based on their life experience, most Muslim women who become human rights advocates or activists feel strongly that virtually all Muslim socie-

---

[11] At a conference on the theme of "Religious Fundamentalism and Western Secular Democracy," sponsored by the Anglo-American Ditchley Foundation and held at Oxfordshire in England, in Spring 1991, Sir Geoffrey Howe, who was the former deputy Prime Minister of England, said that Muslims in Britain had become a threat to the "secular" "democratic" values of British society. He cited two major examples to illustrate his contention—the way in which Muslims behaved with regard to Salman Rushdie, and the way Muslim women were treated by the Muslim community. A Member of Parliament from a district in London which has a large Muslim population cited many cases of the maltreatment of Muslim women mainly by their families, but when I offered to make some suggestions as to how the situation of Muslim women in England could be improved, he was not at all interested in hearing these suggestions. It became obvious that he was interested in quoting the statistics of how many Muslim women were being maltreated and not in finding ways to help Muslim women change their conditions of life.

ties discriminate against women from cradle to grave. This leads many of
them to become deeply alienated from Muslim culture in a number of
ways. This sense of alienation often times leads to anger and bitterness
toward the patriarchal structures and systems of thought which dominate most Muslim societies. Muslim women often find much support and
sympathy in the West so long as they are seen as rebels and deviants
within the world of Islam. But many of them begin to realize, sooner or
later, that while they have serious difficulties with Muslim culture, they
are also not able to identify with Western, secular culture. This realization leads them to feel—at least for a time—isolated and alone. Much attention has been focussed, in the Western media and literature, on the
sorry plight of Muslim women who are "poor and oppressed" in visible
or tangible ways. Hardly any notice has been taken, however, of the profound tragedy and trauma suffered by the self-aware Muslim women of
today who are struggling to maintain their religious identity and personal autonomy in the face of both the imperialism of Western, secular
culture and the intransigence of Islamic traditional culture.

We need to clarify the term "the Islamic tradition." The Islamic tradition—like other major religious traditions—does not consist of, or derive
from, a single source. Most Muslims, if questioned about its sources, are
likely to refer to more than one of the following: the *Qur'an* or the Book of
Revelation which Muslims believe to be God's Word transmitted through
the Agency of Angel Gabriel to the Prophet Muhammad; *Sunnah* or the
practical traditions of the Prophet Muhammad; *Hadith* or the oral sayings
attributed to the Prophet Muhammad; *Fiqh* (Jurisprudence) or *Madahib*
(Schools of Law); and the *Shari'a* or code of law which regulates the diverse aspects of a Muslim's life. While these "sources" have contributed
to what is cumulatively referred to as "the Islamic tradition," they are not
identical or considered to be of equal weight. Of all the sources of the Islamic tradition, undoubtedly, the most important is the Qur'an which is
regarded by Muslims in general, as *the* primary, and most authoritative,
source of normative Islam.

Given the centrality of the Qur'an to the lives of the majority of the
more than one billion Muslims of the world, the critical question which
has been the subject of my reflection for many years is: What, if anything,
does the Qur'an say about human rights? On the basis of my research
and reflection, as well as my deepest faith, I believe that the Qur'an is *the*
Magna Carta of human rights and that a large part of its concern is to free
human beings from the bondage of traditionalism, authoritarianism
(religious, political, economic, or any other), tribalism, racism, sexism,
slavery or anything else that prohibits or inhibits human beings from

actualizing the Qur'anic vision of human destiny embodied in the classic proclamation: Towards Allah is thy limit.[12]

In this section, I offer an account of the Qur'an's affirmation of fundamental rights which all human beings ought to possess because they are so deeply rooted in our humanness that their denial or violation is tantamount to a negation or degradation of that which makes us human. From the perspective of the Qur'an, these rights came into existence when we did; they were created, as we were, by God in order that our human potential could be actualized. These rights not only provide us with an opportunity to develop all our inner resources, but they also hold before us a vision of what God would like us to be: what God wants us to strive for and live for and die for. Rights created or given by God cannot be abolished by any temporal ruler or human agency. Eternal and immutable, they ought to be exercised since everything that God does is for "a just purpose."[13]

Right to Life. The Qur'an upholds the sanctity and absolute value of human life and states in Surah 6: *Al-An'am*: 151:

> do not take any human being's life—(the life) which God has declared to be sacred—otherwise than in (the pursuit of) justice: this has He enjoined upon you so that you might use your reason.[14]

In Surah 5: *Al-Ma'idah*: 32, the Qur'an points out that, in essence, the life of each individual is comparable to that of an entire community and, therefore, should be treated with the utmost care: "We ordained for the Children of Israel that if anyone slew a person unless it be for murder or for spreading mischief in the land it would be as if he slew the whole people: And if any one saved a life, it would be as if he saved the life of the whole people."[15]

Right to Respect. In Surah 17: *Al-Isra'*:70, the Qur'an says: "Now, indeed, We have conferred dignity on the children of Adam."[16] Human beings are deemed worthy of esteem because of all creation they alone chose to accept the "trust" of freedom of the will (Surah 33: *Al-Ahzab*: 72). Human beings can exercise freedom of the will because they possess the rational faculty, which is what distinguishes them from all other crea-

---

[12] Reference here is to Surah 53: *An-Najm*: 42; the translation is by Muhammad Iqbal, *The Reconstruction of Religious Thought in Islam* (Lahore, 1971), 57.

[13] Reference here is to, Surah 15: *Al-Hijr*: 85; Surah 16: *An-Nahl*: 3; Surah 44: *Ad-Dukhan*: 39; Surah 45: *Al-Jathiyah*: 22; Surah 46: *Al-Ahqaf*: 3.

[14] Translation by Muhammad Asad, *The Message of the Qur'an* (Gibraltar, 1980), 188.

[15] Translation by 'Abdullah Yusuf' Ali, *The Holy Qur'an* (Brentwood, 1989), 257.

[16] *The Message of the Qur'an*, 429.

tures (Surah 2: *Al-Baqarah*: 30-34). Though human beings can become "the lowest of the lowest," the Qur'an declares that they have been made "in the best of moulds" (Surah 95: *At-Tin*: 4-6), having the ability to think, to have knowledge of right and wrong, to do the good and to avoid the evil. Thus, on account of the promise which is contained in being human, namely, the potential to be God's vicegerent on earth, the humanness of all human beings is to be respected and considered to be an end in itself.

Right to Justice. The Qur'an puts great emphasis on the right to seek justice and the duty to do justice. In Surah 5: *Al-Ma'idah*: 8, it tells the believers:

> O you who have attained to faith! Be ever steadfast in your devotion to God, bearing witness to the truth in all equity; and never let hatred of any one lead you into the sin of deviating from justice. Be just: this is the closest to being God-conscious.[17]

And again, in Surah 4: *An-Nisa'*: 13f; the Qur'an emphasizes the importance of upholding justice:

> O ye who believe! Stand out firmly for justice, as witnesses to Allah, even as against yourselves, or your parents, or your kin, and whether it be (against) rich or poor: for Allah can best protect both. Follow not the lusts (of your hearts), lest ye serve, and if ye distort (justice) or decline to do justice, verily Allah is well-acquainted with all that ye do.[18]

In the context of justice, the Qur'an uses two concepts: "`adl*" and "*ihsan.*" Both are enjoined, and both are related to the idea of "balance," but they are not identical in meaning. "`*Adl*" is defined by A.A.A. Fyzee, a well known scholar of Islam, as "to be equal, neither more nor less." Explaining this concept, Fyzee wrote: "in a court of Justice the claims of the two parties must be considered evenly, without undue stress being laid upon one side or the other. Justice is introducing the balance in the form of scales that are evenly balanced."[19] "`*Adl*" was described in similar terms by Abu'l Kalam Azad, a famous translator of the Qur'an and noted writer, who stated: "What is justice but the avoiding of excess? There should be neither too much nor too little; hence the use of scales as the emblems of justice."[20] Lest any one try to do too much or too little, the Qur'an points out that no human being can carry another's burden or attain anything without striving for it (Surah 53: *An-Najm*: 38-39).

---

[17] Ibid.

[18] *The Holy Qur'an*, 228-229.

[19] A.A.A. Fyzee, *A Modern Approach to Islam* (Lahore, 1978), 17.

[20] Ibid.

Recognizing individual merit is a part of *"`adl,"* the Qur'an teaches that merit is not determined by lineage, sex, wealth, worldly success, or religion, but by righteousness. Righteousness consists of both right "belief" *("iman")* and just "action" *("`amal")* as clearly indicated by Surah 2: *Al-Baqarah*: 177, which states:

> It is not righteousness that ye turn your faces towards East or West; but it is righteousness to believe in God and the Last Day, and the Angels, and the Book, and the Messengers; to spend your substance, out of love for Him, for your kin, for orphans, for the needy, for the wayfarer, for those who ask, and for the ransom of slaves; to be steadfast in prayer, and practice regular charity; to fulfill the contracts which ye have made; and to be firm and patient, in pain (or suffering) and adversity, and throughout all periods of panic. Such are the people of truth, the God-fearing.[21]

Surah 49: *Al-Hujurat*: 13 tells us: "The most honoured of you in the sight of Allah is (he who is) the most righteous of you."[22] While Surah 4: *An-Nisa'*: 95 distinguishes clearly between passive believers and those who strive in the cause of God:

> Such of the believers as remain passive—other than the disabled—cannot be deemed equal to those who strive hard in God's cause with their possessions and their lives. God has exalted those who strive hard with their possessions and their lives far above those who remain passive. Although God has promised the ultimate good unto all (believers), yet has God exalted those who strive hard above those who remain passive by (promising them) a mighty reward—(many) degrees thereof—and forgiveness of sins, and His grace; for God is indeed much-forgiving, a dispenser of grace.[23]

Just as it is in the spirit of *"àdl"* that special merit be considered in the matter of rewards, so also special circumstances are to be considered in the matter of punishments. For instance, for crimes of unchastity the Qur'an prescribes identical punishments for a man or a woman who is proved guilty (Surah 24: *An-Nur*: 2), but it differentiates between different classes of women: for the same crime, a slave woman would receive half, and the Prophet's consort double, the punishment given to a "free" Muslim woman (Surah 4: *An-Nisa'*: 25; Surah 33: *Al-Ahzab*: 30). In making such a distinction, the Qur'an while upholding high moral standards,

---

[21] *The Holy Qur'an*, 70-71.

[22] Ibid., 1343.

[23] *The Message of the Qur'an*, 123-124.

particularly in the case of the Prophet's wives whose actions have a normative significance for the community, reflects God's compassion for
women slaves who were socially disadvantaged.

While constantly enjoining "`adl," the Qur'an goes beyond this con-
cept to "ihsan," which literally means, "restoring the balance by making
up a loss or deficiency."[24] In order to understand this concept, it is necessary to understand the nature of the ideal society or community
("ummah") envisaged by the Qur'an. The word "ummah" comes from the
root "umm" or "mother." The symbols of a mother and motherly love
and compassion are also linked with the two attributes most characteristic of God, namely, "Rahim" and "Rahman," both of which are derived
from the root "rahm," meaning "womb." The ideal "ummah" cares about
all its members just as an ideal mother cares about all her children,
knowing that all are not equal and that each has different needs. While
showing undue favor to any child would be unjust, a mother who gives
to a "handicapped" child more than she does to her other child or children, is not acting unjustly but exemplifying the spirit of "ihsan" by
helping to make up the deficiency of a child who is unable to meet the
requirements of life. Thus "ihsan" shows God's sympathy for the
"disadvantaged" segments of human society (such as women, orphans,
slaves, the poor, the infirm, and the minorities).

Right to Freedom. As stated earlier, the Qur'an is deeply concerned
about liberating human beings from every kind of bondage. Recognizing
the human tendency toward dictatorship and despotism, the Qur'an says
with clarity and emphasis in Surah 3: *Al-'Imran*: 79:

> It is not (possible) that a man, to whom is given the Book, and
> Wisdom, and the Prophetic Office, should say to people: "Be ye
> my worshippers rather than Allah's." On the contrary (He would
> say): "Be ye worshippers of Him Who is truly the Cherisher of
> all."[25]

The institution of human slavery is, of course, extremely important in
the context of human freedom. Slavery was widely prevalent in Arabia at
the time of the advent of Islam, and the Arab economy was based on it.
Not only did the Qur'an insist that slaves be treated in a just and humane
way,[26] but it continually urged the freeing of slaves.[27] By laying down, in
Surah 47: *Muhammad*: 4, that prisoners of war were to be set free, "either

---

[24] G.A. Parwez, *Tabweeb-ul-Qur'an* (Lahore, 1977), 1:78.

[25] *The Holy Qur'an*, 148.

[26] See, e.g., Surah 4: *An Nisa'*: 36.

[27] See, e.g., Surah 2: *Al-Baqarah*: 177; Surah 4: *An-Nisa'*: 92; Surah 5: *Al-Ma'idah*: 89; Surah
9: *At-Tawbah*: 60; Surah 24: *An-Nur*: 33; Surah 58: *Al-Mujadalah*: 3.

by an act of grace or against ransom,"[28] the Qur'an virtually abolished slavery since "[t]he major source of slaves—men and women—was prisoners of war."[29] Because the Qur'an does not state explicitly that slavery is abolished, it does not follow that it is to be continued, particularly in view of the numerous ways in which the Qur'an seeks to eliminate this absolute evil. A Book which does not give a king or a prophet the right to command absolute obedience from another human being could not possibly sanction slavery in any sense of the word.

The greatest guarantee of personal freedom for a Muslim lies in the Qur'anic decree that no one other than God can limit human freedom (Surah 42: *Ash-Shura*: 21), and in the statement that "Judgment (as to what is right and what is wrong) rests with God alone." (Surah 12: *Yusuf*: 40).[30] As pointed out by Khalid M. Ishaque, an eminent Pakistani jurist:

> The Qur'an gives to responsible dissent the status of a fundamental right. In exercise of their powers, therefore, neither the legislature nor the executive can demand unquestioning obedience. . . . The Prophet, even though he was the recipient of Divine revelation, was required to consult the Muslims in public affairs. Allah addressing the Prophet says: ". . . and consult with them upon the conduct of affairs. And . . . when thou are resolved, then put thy trust in Allah" (Surah 3: *Al-'Imran*: 159).[31]

Since the principle of mutual consultation *("shura")* is mandatory (Surah 42: *Ash-Shura*: 38), it is a Muslim's fundamental right, as well as responsibility, to participate in as many aspects of the community's life as possible.

The Qur'anic proclamation in Surah 2: *Al-Baqarah*: 256: "There shall be no coercion in matters of faith"[32] guarantees freedom of religion and worship. This means that, according to Qur'anic teaching, non-Muslims, living in Muslim territories, should have the freedom to follow their own faith-traditions without fear or harassment. A number of Qur'anic passages state clearly that the responsibility of the Prophet Muhammad is to communicate the message of God and not to compel anyone to believe.[33] The right to exercise free choice in matters of belief is unambiguously endorsed by the Qur'an in Surah 18: *Al-Kahf*: 29, which states: "The Truth is

---

[28] *The Message of the Qur'an*, 778.

[29] G.A. Parwez, *Islam: A Challenge to Religion* (Lahore, 1968), 346.

[30] *The Message of the Qur'an*, 343.

[31] Ishaque, "Islamic Law—Its Ideals and Principles," 157.

[32] *The Message of the Qur'an*, 57.

[33] See, e.g., Surah 6: *Al-An'am*: 107; Surah 10: *Yunus*: 99; Surah 16: *An-Nahl*: 82; Surah 42: *Ash-Shura*: 48.

from your Lord: Let him who will believe, and let him who will, reject (it)."[34]

The Qur'an also makes clear that God will judge human beings not on the basis of what they profess but on the basis of their belief and righteous conduct, as indicated by Surah 2: *Al-Baqarah*: 62 which states: "Those who believe (in the Qur'an) and those who follow the Jewish (scriptures), and the Christians and the Sabians, any who believe in God and the Last Day, and work righteousness, shall have their reward saith the Lord; on them shall be no fear, nor shall they grieve."[35]

The Qur'an recognizes the right to religious freedom not only in the case of other believers in God, but also in the case of non-believers in God (if they are not aggressive toward Muslims). For instance, Surah 6: *Al-An'am*: 108 states:

> Revile not ye those whom they call upon besides God, lest they out of spite revile God in their ignorance. Thus have We made alluring to each people its own doings. In the end will they return to their Lord, and We shall then tell them the truth of all that they did.[36]

In the context of the human right to exercise religious freedom, it is important to mention that the Qur'anic dictum, "Let there be no compulsion in religion"[37] (Surah 2:*Al-Baqarah*: 256) applies not only to non-Muslims but also to Muslims. While those who renounced Islam after professing it and then engaged in "acts of war" against Muslims were to be treated as enemies and aggressors, the Qur'an does not prescribe any punishment for non-profession or renunciation of faith. The decision regarding a person's ultimate destiny in the hereafter rests with God.

This right to freedom includes the right to be free to tell the truth. The Qur'anic term for truth is *"Haqq"* which is also one of God's most important attributes. Standing up for the truth is a right and a responsibility which a Muslim may not disclaim even in the face of the greatest danger or difficulty (Surah 4: *An-Nisa'*: 135). While the Qur'an commands believers to testify to the truth, it also instructs society not to harm persons so testifying (Sura 2: *Al-Baqarah*: 282).[38]

---

[34] *The Holy Qur'an*, 716.

[35] Ibid., 33-34.

[36] Ibid., 325-326.

[37] Ibid., 106.

[38] G.A. Parwez, "Bunyadi Haquq-e-Insaniyat (Urdu)," in *Tulu'-e-Islam* (Lahore, November, 1981), 34-35.

Right to Privacy. The Qur'an recognizes the need for privacy as a human right and lays down rules for protecting an individual's life in the home from undue intrusion from within or without.[39]

Right to Protection from Slander, Backbiting, and Ridicule. The Qur'an recognizes the right of human beings to be protected from defamation, sarcasm, offensive nicknames, and backbiting (Surah 49: *Al-Hujurat*: 11-12). It also states that no person is to be maligned on grounds of assumed guilt and that those who engage in malicious scandalmongering will be grievously punished in both this world and the next (Surah 24: *An-Nur*: 16-19). Urging throughout that human beings should treat others with sensitivity and compassion, the Qur'an points out in Surah 4: *An-Nisa'*: 148-149:

> God loves not that evil should be noised abroad in public speech, except where injustice hath been done; for God is He who heareth and knoweth all things. Whether ye publish a good deed or conceal it or cover evil with pardon, verily God doth blot out (Sins) and hath power (In the judgment of values).[40]

Right to Acquire Knowledge. The Qur'an puts the highest emphasis on the importance of acquiring knowledge. That knowledge has been at the core of the Islamic world view from the very beginning is attested to by Surah 96: *Al-`Alaq*: 1-5, which Muslims believe to the first revelation received by the Prophet Muhammad. This passage reads:

> Proclaim! (or Read) in the name of thy Lord and Cherisher, who created, created man, out of a (mere) clot of congealed blood. Proclaim! And the Lord is Most Bountiful. He who taught the (use of) the pen taught man that which he knew not.[41]

Asking rhetorically if those without knowledge can be equal to those with knowledge (Surah 39: *Az-Zumar*: 9), the Qur'an exhorts believers to pray for advancement in knowledge (Surah 20: *Ta-Ha*: 114). The famous prayer of the Prophet Muhammad was "Allah grant me knowledge of the ultimate nature of things" and one of the best known of all traditions ("*ahadith*") is "Seek knowledge even though it be in China."

According to the Qur'anic perspective, knowledge is a prerequisite for the creation of a just world in which authentic peace can prevail. The Qur'an emphasizes the importance of the pursuit of learning even at the

---

[39] See, e.g., Surah 24: *An-Nur*: 27-28, 58; Surah 33: *Al-Ahzab*: 53; Surah 49: *Al-Hujurat*: 12.

[40] *The Holy Qur'an*, 232-233.

[41] Ibid., 1672-1673.

time, and in the midst, of war, as indicated by Surah 9: *At-Tawbah*: 122, which states:

> With all this, it is not desirable that all of the believers take the field (in time of war). From within every group in their midst some shall refrain from going to war, and shall devote themselves (instead) to acquiring a deeper knowledge of the Faith, and (thus be able to) teach their home-coming brethren, so that these (too) might guard themselves against evil.[42]

Right to Leave One's Homeland Under Oppressive Conditions. According to Qur'anic teaching, a Muslim's ultimate loyalty must be to God and not to any territory. To fulfill his Prophetic mission, the Prophet Muhammad decided to leave his place of birth, Mecca, and emigrated to Medina. This event *("Hijrah")* has great historical and spiritual significance for Muslims who are called upon to move away from their place of origin if it becomes an abode of evil and oppression where they cannot fulfill their obligations to God or establish justice. In a powerful passage in Surah 4: *An-Nisa': 97-100,* the Qur'an states:

> When angels take the souls of those who die in sin against their souls, they say: "In what (plight) were ye?" They reply: "Weak and oppressed were we in the earth." They say: "Was not the earth of Allah spacious enough for you to move yourselves away (from evil)?" Such men will find their abode in Hell—What an evil refuge!—except those who are (really) weak and oppressed—men, women, and children who have no means in their power, nor (a guide post) to direct their way. For these, there is hope that Allah will forgive for Allah doth blot out (sins) and forgive again and again. He who forsakes his home in the cause of Allah, finds in the earth many a refuge, wide and spacious: Should he die as a refugee from home from Allah and His Messenger, his reward becomes due and sure with Allah: And Allah is Oft-Forgiving, Most Merciful.[43]

Right to Develop One's Aesthetic Sensibilities and Enjoy the Bounties Created by God. As pointed out by Muhammad Asad, "By declaring that all good and beautiful things of life, i.e., those which are not expressly prohibited are lawful to the believers, the Qur'an condemns, by implication, all forms of life-denying asceticism, world-renunciation and self-mortification."[44] There is a great difference between the spirit of clas-

---

[42] *The Message of the Qur'an,* 285.

[43] *The Holy Qur'an,* 217-218.

[44] *The Message of the Qur'an,* 207, n.24.

sical Greece with its contempt for sense-perception and the Qur'an which regards physical phenomena as "Signs of God." Some of the most memorable passages in the Qur'an point to the insight and wisdom which can be gained by reflecting on the myriad manifestations of God's creative activity all around us. The Qur'an tells Muslims that monasticism was not prescribed by God (Surah 57: *Al-Hadid:* 27). Though they are to remember that the hereafter is more important than the life on earth, Muslims are told to reject the negative view that it is wrong to enjoy the beauty and bounty of God's creation.

In Surah 7: *Al-A`raf:* 32, the Qur'an states:

> Say: "Who is there to forbid the beauty which God has brought forth for His creatures, and the good things from among the means of sustenance?"

> Say: "they are (lawful) in the life of this world unto all who have attained to faith—to be theirs alone on Resurrection Day."[45]

The right to develop one's aesthetic sensibilities so that one can appreciate beauty in all its forms, and the right to enjoy what God has provided for the nurture of humankind, are, thus, rooted in the life-affirming vision of the Qur'an.

Right to Sustenance. As pointed out by Surah 11: *Hud:* 6, every living creature depends for its sustenance upon God. A cardinal concept in the Qur'an which underlies the socio-economic-political system of Islam is that the ownership of everything belongs not to any person, but to God. Since God is the universal creator, every creature has the right to partake of what belongs to God (Surah 6: *Al-An am:* 165; Surah 67: *Al-Mulk:* 15). This means that every human being has the right to a means of living and that those who hold economic or political power do not have the right to deprive others of the basic necessities of life by misappropriating or misusing resources which have been created by God for the benefit of humanity in general.

Right to Work. According to Qur'anic teaching, every man and woman has the right to work, whether the work consists of gainful employment or voluntary service. The fruits of labor belong to the one who has worked for them—regardless of whether it is a man or a woman. As Surah 4: *An-Nisa':* 32 states: "to men is allotted what they earn, and to women what they earn."[46]

Right to "The Good Life." The Qur'an upholds the right of the human being not only to life but to "the good life." This good life, made up

---

[45] Ibid., 207.

[46] *The Holy Qur'an,* 194.

of many elements, becomes possible when a human being is living in a just environment. According to Qur'anic teaching, justice is a prerequisite for peace, and peace is a prerequisite for human development. In a just society, all the earlier-mentioned human rights may be exercised without difficulty. In such a society, other basic rights such as the right to a secure place of residence, the right to the protection of one's personal possessions, the right to protection of one's covenants, and the right to move freely, also exist.[47]

Other Rights. Since Qur'anic teaching embraces every aspect of human life, it contains references to more human rights than can be mentioned in this short summary. Reference has been made in the foregoing account to the human rights which figure most importantly in the Qur'an and which continue to be of on-going interest and importance in contemporary Muslim societies. In addition to the rights mentioned in the foregoing, reference may also be made to the following: (1) the right to social and judicial autonomy for minorities; (2) the right to protection of one's holy places; and (3) the right to return to one's spiritual center.[48] According to Surah 3: *Al-'Imran:* 96, Surah 5: *Al-Ma'idah:* 97, and Surah 22: *Al-Hajj:* 25, the *"Ka'ba"* in Mecca is the spiritual center of all humankind. It was here that the Prophet Ibrahim proclaimed the pilgrimage to all humankind, as pointed out by Surah 2: *Al-Baqarah:* 125, Surah 3: *Al-'Imran:* 96, and Surah 22: *Al-Hajj:* 26.

Rights of Women: Qur'anic Ideals Versus Muslim Practice

Muslim men never tire of repeating that Islam has given more rights to women than has any other religion. Certainly, if by "Islam" is meant "Qur'anic Islam," the rights that it has given to women are, indeed, impressive. Not only do women partake of all the general rights mentioned in the foregoing section, they are also the subject of much particular concern in the Qur'an. Underlying much of the Qur'an's legislation on women-related issues is the recognition that women have been disadvantaged persons in history to whom justice needs to be done by the Muslim *"ummah."* Unfortunately, however, the cumulative (Jewish, Christian, Hellenistic, Bedouin, and other) biases which existed in the Arab-Islamic culture of the early centuries of Islam infiltrated the Islamic tradition, largely through the Hadith literature, and undermined the in-

---

[47] In this context, reference may be made to several Qur'anic verses. See, e.g., Surah 2: *Al-Baqarah:* 229; Surah: *Al-'Imran:* 17,77; Surah 5: *Al-Ma'idah:* 1; Surah 17: *Al-Isra':* 34; Surah 67: *Al-Mulk:* 15.

[48] In this context, reference may be made to number of Qur'anic verses. See, e.g., Surah 5: *Al-Ma'idah:* 42-48; Surah 9: *At-Tawbah:* 17.

tent of the Qur'an to liberate women from the status of chattels or inferior creatures and make them free and equal to men.

A brief review of Muslim history and culture brings to light many areas in which—Qur'anic teaching notwithstanding—women continued to be subjected to diverse forms of oppression and injustice, often in the name of Islam, and, what is far worse, in the name of a just, merciful, and compassionate God. While the Qur'an, because of its protective attitude toward all downtrodden and oppressed classes of people, appears to be weighted in many ways in favor of women, many of its women-related teachings have been used in patriarchal Muslim societies against, rather than for, women. Muslim societies, in general, appear to be far more concerned with trying to control women's bodies and sexuality than with their human rights. Many Muslims when they speak of human rights either do not speak of women's rights at all,[49] or are mainly concerned with how a woman's chastity may be protected.[50] (They are apparently not very worried about protecting men's chastity).

Women are the targets of the most serious violations of human rights which occur in many Muslim societies. Muslims say with great pride that Islam abolished female infanticide; true, but it must also be mentioned that one of the most common crimes in a number of Muslim countries (for example Pakistan) is the murder of women by their husbands. These so-called "honor-killings" are, in fact, extremely dishonorable and are frequently used to camouflage other kinds of crimes.

Female children are discriminated against from the moment of birth, for it is customary in Muslim societies to regard a son as a gift, and a daughter as a trial, from God. Therefore, the birth of a son is an occasion for celebration while the birth of a daughter calls for commiseration if not lamentation. Many girls are married when they are still minors, even though marriage in Islam is a contract and presupposes that the contracting parties are both consenting adults. Even though so much Qur'anic legislation is aimed at protecting the rights of women in the context of marriage[51] women cannot claim equality with their husbands. The husband, in fact, is regarded as his wife's gateway to heaven or hell and the arbiter of her final destiny. That such an idea can exist within the framework of Islam—which, in theory, rejects the idea of there being any intermediary between a believer and God—represents both a profound irony and a great tragedy.

---

[49] For example, R.A. Jullundhri, "Human Rights in Islam," in A.D. Falconer, ed., *Understanding Human Rights* (Dublin, 1980).

[50] For example, A.A. Maududi, *Human Rights in Islam* (Lahore, 1977).

[51] See, e.g., Surah 4: *An-Nisa'*: 4,19; Surah 24: *An-Nur*: 33; Surah 2: *Al-Baqarah*: 187; Surah 9: *At-Tawbah*: 71; Surah 7: *Al-A raf*: 189; Surah 30: *Ar-Rum*: 21.

Although the Qur'an presents the idea of what we today call a "no-fault" divorce and does not make any adverse judgments about divorce[52] Muslim societies have made divorce extremely difficult for women, both legally and through social penalties. Although the Qur'an states clearly that the divorced parents of a minor child must decide by mutual consultation how the child is to be raised and that they must not use the child to hurt or exploit each other,[53] in most Muslim societies, women are deprived of both their sons (generally at age 7) and their daughters (generally at age 12). It is difficult to imagine an act of greater cruelty than depriving a mother of her children simply because she is divorced. Although polygamy was intended by the Qur'an to be for the protection of orphans and widows,[54] in practice Muslims have made it the Sword of Damocles which keeps women under constant threat. Although the Qur'an gave women the right to receive an inheritance not only on the death of a close relative, but also to receive other bequests or gifts during the lifetime of a benevolent caretaker, Muslim societies have disapproved greatly of the idea of giving wealth to a woman in preference to a man, even when her need or circumstances warrant it. Although the purpose of the Qur'anic legislation dealing with women's dress and conduct,[55] was to make it safe for women to go about their daily business (since they have the right to engage in gainful activity as witnessed by Surah 4: An-Nisa': 32) without fear of sexual harassment or molestation, Muslim societies have put many of them behind veils and shrouds and locked doors on the pretext of protecting their chastity, forgetting that according to the Qur'an[56] confinement to their homes was not a normal way of life for chaste women but a punishment for "unchastity."

Despite the fact that women such as Khadijah and "A'ishah (wives of the Prophet Muhammad) and Rabi'a al-Basri (the outstanding woman Sufi) figure significantly in early Islam, the Islamic tradition has, by and large, remained rigidly patriarchal until now, prohibiting the growth of scholarship among women particularly in the realm of religious thought. This means that the sources on which the Islamic tradition is mainly based have been interpreted only by men who have arrogated to themselves the task of defining the ontological, theological, sociological, and eschatalogical status of Muslim women. It is hardly surprising that until now the majority of Muslim women have accepted this situation passively, almost unaware of the extent to which their human (also Islamic,

---

[52] See, e.g., Surah 2: *Al-Baqarah*: 231, 241.

[53] The reference here is to Surah 2: *Al-Baqarah*: 233.

[54] The reference here is to Surah 4: *An-Nisa'*: 2-3.

[55] See, e.g., Surah 24 *An-Nur*: 30-31; Surah 33: *Al-Ahzab*: 59.

[56] The reference here is to the Qur'an, Surah 4: *An-Nisa'*: 15.

in an ideal sense) rights have been violated by their male-dominated and male-centered societies. Kept for centuries in physical, mental, and emotional bondage, and deprived of the opportunity to actualize their human potential, even the exercise of analyzing their personal experiences as Muslim women is, perhaps, overwhelming for these women. (Here it needs to be mentioned that while the rate of literacy is low in many Muslim countries, the rate of literacy of Muslim women, especially those who live in rural areas where most of the population lives, is amongst the lowest in the world.)

Much of what has happened to Muslim women becomes comprehensible if one keeps one fact in mind: Muslims, in general, consider it a self-evident fact that women are not equal to men, who are "above" women or have a "degree of advantage" over them. There is hardly anything in a Muslim woman's life that is not affected by this belief; hence it is vitally important, not only for theological reasons but also for pragmatic ones, to subject it to rigorous scholarly scrutiny and attempt to identify its roots.

The roots of the belief that men are superior to women lie, in my judgment, in three theological assumptions: (1) that God's primary creation is man, not woman, since woman is believed to have been created from man's rib, and is, therefore, derivative and secondary ontologically; (2) that woman, not man, was the primary agent of what is customarily referred to as "Man's Fall" or the expulsion of man from the Garden of Eden, and hence "all daughters of Eve" are to be regarded with hatred, suspicion, and contempt; and (3) that woman was created not only *from* man, but also *for* man, which makes her existence merely instrumental and not of fundamental importance.

I have been engaged for more than a decade in research which offers compelling proof on the basis of an analysis of the Qur'anic text and teaching, that the three assumptions on which the superstructure of the idea of man's superiority to woman has been erected, not only in the Islamic but also in the Jewish and Christian tradition, are unwarranted. First, the myth that Eve was created from the rib of Adam has no basis whatever in the Qur'an which, in the context of human creation, speaks always in completely egalitarian terms. In none of the thirty or so passages that describe the creation of humanity (designated by generic terms such as *"an-nas," "al-insan,"* and *"al-bashar")* by God in a variety of ways, is there any statement which asserts or suggests that man was created prior to woman or that woman was created from man. If woman and man were created equal by God—and this is clearly and unambiguously the teaching of the Qur'an—they cannot become unequal *essentially* at a subsequent time, since God is the ultimate arbiter of value. This means that the inequality of women and men in almost all Muslim (and many other) societies cannot be seen as having been willed by God, but must be seen as a perversion of God's intent in creation. All this notwithstanding, the ordinary Muslim continues to believe, with ordinary Jews and Christians, that Adam was God's primary creation and that Eve was made from Adam's rib, hence can never be equal to him.

Second, in the context of the story of the "Fall," it needs to be pointed out that the Qur'an provides no basis whatever for asserting, suggesting, or implying that "*Hawwa*" (Eve) was tempted by "*ash-Shaitan*" (the Satan), in turn tempted and deceived Adam, and led to his expulsion from "*al-jannah*" (the Garden). Yet many Muslim commentators[57] have ascribed the primary responsibility for man's "Fall" to woman and have branded her as "the devil's gateway."[58] Though no "Fall" occurs in the Qur'anic narrative, as pointed out by Iqbal,[59] and though there is no doctrine of original sin in Islam, patriarchal Muslim culture has used the Biblical myth to perpetuate the myth of feminine evil, particularly in order to control women's sexuality which it associates, like St. Augustine, with "fallenness."

Third, the Qur'an, which does not discriminate against women in the context of creation or the "Fall" story, does not support the view—held by many Muslims, Christians, and Jews—that woman was created not only *from* man, but also *for* man. That God's creation as a whole is "for just ends" (Surah 15: *Al-Hijr*: 85) and not "for idle sport" (Surah 21: *Al-Anbiya*: 16) is one of the major themes of the Qur'an. Humanity, fashioned "in the best of moulds" (Surah 95: *At-Tin*: 4) has been created in order to serve God (Surah 51: *Adh-Dhariyat*: 56). According to the Qur'an, service to God cannot be separated from service to humankind, or, in Is-

---

[57] For instance, al-Tabari.

[58] This expression comes from Tertullian (A.D. 160-225), a Church Father from North Africa who wrote: "And do you not know that you are (each) an Eve? The sentence of God on this sex of yours lives in this age: the guilt must of necessity live too. You are the devil's gateway; you are the unsealer of that (forbidden) tree: you are the first deserter of the divine law, you are she who persuaded him whom the devil was not valiant enough to attack. You destroyed so easily God's image, man. On account of your desert—that is, death—even the Son of God had to die." Tertullian, *De culte feminarum* 1.1, quoted in Leonard Swidler, ed., *Biblical Affirmations of Woman* (Philadelphia, 1979), 346.

[59] In *The Reconstruction of Religious Thought in Islam*, 85, Iqbal writes: "[The] Qur'anic legend of the Fall has nothing to do with the first appearance of man on this planet. Its purpose is rather to indicate man's rise from a primitive state of instinctive appetite to the conscious possession of a free self, capable of doubt and disobedience. The Fall does not mean any moral depravity; it is man's transition from simple consciousness, a kind of waking from the dream of nature with a throb of personal causality in one's own being. Nor does the Qur'an regard the earth as a torture-hall where an elementally wicked humanity is imprisoned for an original act of sin. Man's first act of disobedience was also his first act of free choice; and that is why according to Qur'anic narration, Adam's first transgression was forgiven. . . ."

lamic terms, believers in God must honor both "*Haquq Allah*" (rights of God) and "*Haquq al-'ibad*" (rights of creatures). Fulfillment of one's duties to God and humanity constitutes the essence of righteousness. That men and women are equally called upon by God to be righteous and will be equally rewarded for their righteousness is stated unambiguously in a number of Qur'anic verses.[60] Not only does the Qur'an make it clear that man and woman stand absolutely equal in the sight of God, but also they are "members" and "protectors" of each other. In other words, the Qur'an does not create a hierarchy in which men are placed above women (as they are by many formulators by the Christian tradition), nor does it pit men against women in an adversary relationship. They are created as equal creatures of a universal, just and merciful God whose pleasure it is that they live—in harmony and righteousness—together.

In spite of the Qur'anic affirmation of the equality of man and woman, Muslim societies in general have never regarded men and women as equal, particularly in the context of marriage. Fatima Mernissi's observations on the position of a Muslim woman in relation to her family in modern Morocco apply, more or less, to Muslim culture generally:

> One of the distinctive characteristics of Muslim sexuality is its territoriality, which reflects a specific division of labor and a specific conception of society and of power. The territoriality of Muslim sexuality sets ranks, tasks and authority patterns. Spatially confined the woman was taken care of materially by the man who possessed her, in return for her total obedience and her sexual and reproductive services. The whole system was organized so that the Muslim "ummah" was actually a society of male citizens who possessed among other things the female half of the population. . . . Muslim men have always had more rights and privileges than Muslim women, including even the right to kill their women. . . . The man imposed on the woman an artificially narrow existence, both physically and spiritually.[61]

Underlying the rejection in Muslim societies of the idea of man-woman equality are the three deeply-rooted beliefs mentioned earlier, namely, that women are inferior to men in creation (having been created from a crooked rib), and in righteousness (having helped ash-Shaitan in defeating God's plan for Adam), and in having been created mainly to be of use to men who are superior to them.

---

[60] See, e.g., Surah 3: *Al-'Imran*: 195; Surah 4: *An-Nisa'*: 124; Surah 9: *At-Tawbah*: 71-72; Surah 16: *An-Nahl*: 97; Surah 23: *Al-Ahzab*: 35.

[61] Fatima Mernissi, *Beyond the Veil* (Cambridge, 1975), 103.

Woman and man, created equal by God and standing equal in the sight of God, have become very unequal in Muslim societies. The Qur'anic description of man and woman in marriage reads thus: "They are your garments/And you are their garments" (Surah 2: *Al-Baqarah:* 187) implies closeness, mutuality, and equality. However, Muslim culture has reduced many, if not most, women to the position of puppets on a string, to slave-like creatures whose only purpose in life is to cater to the needs and pleasures of men. Not only this, it has also had the audacity and the arrogance to deny women direct access to God. It is one of Islam's cardinal beliefs that each person—man or woman—is responsible and accountable for his or her individual actions. How can the husband become the wife's gateway to heaven or hell? How can he become the arbiter not only of what happens to her in this world but also of her ultimate destiny? Surely such questions must arise in the minds of Muslim women, but so far they have not been asked aloud. My own feeling is that not only Muslim men, but also Muslim women—with a few exceptions—are afraid to ask questions the answers to which are bound to threaten the existing balance of power in the domain of family relationships in most Muslim societies.

Despite everything that has gone wrong with the lives of countless Muslim women through the ages due to patriarchal Muslim culture, I believe strongly that there is hope for the future. There are indications from across the world of Islam that an increasing number of Muslims are beginning to reflect seriously upon the teachings of the Qur'an as they become disenchanted with capitalism, communism, and Western democracy. As this reflection deepens, it is likely to lead to the realization that the supreme task entrusted to human beings by God, of being God's deputies on earth, can only be accomplished by establishing justice which the Qur'an regards as a prerequisite for authentic peace. Without the elimination of the inequities, inequalities, and injustices that pervade the personal and collective lives of human beings, it is not possible to talk about peace in Qur'anic terms. It is important to note that there is more Qur'anic legislation pertaining to the establishment of justice in the context of family relationships than on any other subject. This points to the assumption implicit in much Qur'anic legislation, namely, that if human beings can learn to order their homes justly so that the human rights of all within its jurisdiction—children, women, and men—are safeguarded, then they can also order their society and the world at large, justly. In other words, the Qur'an regards the home as a microcosm of the *"ummah"* and the world community, and emphasizes the importance of making it "the abode of peace" through just living.

The Treatment of
Religious Dissidents Under Classical
and Contemporary Islamic Law[1]

DONNA E. ARZT

Syracuse University

W ith the possibility of a final settlement to the Arab-Israeli conflict on the horizon, with the realignment of Muslim states and
movements in the wake of the Soviet Union's demise and the
Persian Gulf War, and with fears of "Islamic fundamentalism" replacing
"the Communist threat" in the popular Western psyche, there is hardly a
more timely topic than that of religious dissent in Islam. This chapter examines the doctrinal and historical treatment of those who deviated from
Islamic orthodoxy, either deliberately or inadvertently, in both the pre-
modern and modern eras. Given the frequent difficulty in ascertaining
the true motives behind religious persecution, the topic by necessity also
considers how Islam and Islamic law have been used to justify repression
of actual and perceived political opponents to Muslim regimes. As Islam
scholar Ann Elizabeth Mayer notes, Islam is only one factor in the reception of human rights in the Middle East. One must distinguish between
the prescriptive norms of the religion and the actual practices of modern
Muslim states, which may be motivated by multiple factors, including
nationalism and Muslim ambivalence about Westernization.[2]

It is hoped that the norm/practice distinction—as well as the evolu-
tionary changes over close to 1400 years of Islamic history—can be drawn
by careful separation of the classical origins and the contemporary manifestations of the Islamic approach to religious dissent. This chapter is accordingly divided into three major parts. Part I raises methodological

[1] The research for this study was supported by a summer grant from the Syracuse University College of Law. The author would like to thank Michael Dufault and Tracy Zagroba
for their invaluable research assistance.

[2] Ann Elizabeth Mayer, *Islam and Human Rights: Tradition and Politics* (Boulder, 1991), xi-
xiv, 11-21. See also John L. Esposito, *The Islamic Threat: Myth or Reality?* (New York, 1992), 65.

J. Witte, Jr. and J.D. van der Vyver (eds.), Religious Human Rights in Global Perspective, 387-453.
© 1996 *Kluwer Law International. Printed in the Netherlands.*

issues, inherent in a study of this kind, concerning the use of definitions, its scope and source material, and the standards of international and regional law by which religious human rights in the Islamic world are implicitly, if not explicitly, judged. Part II examines religious dissent under classical Islamic law, beginning with an overview of the structure of Islamic law, and followed by the specialized topics of apostates and blasphemers; heretics and renegades; and non-Muslims and infidels. Part III explores the same set of specialized topics under contemporary Islamic law, prefaced by a discussion of constitutional, statutory, and international law in modern Islamic states. The chapter concludes by reference to the conflict between secularism and Islamic revivalism (often mislabeled "fundamentalism") over the future identity of Muslim states.

Methodological Issues

Given the nature of such a study as this—an unavoidably selective survey of Islamic religious principles, policies, and practices by a Western-educated, non-Muslim, non-Arabic[3] speaking, Jewish non-cleric—it is important to begin by identifying the premises, preconceptions, and other strictures that might underlie an author's perspective (some would say bias). The most obvious of these concern terminology.

Definitions. Some of the terms used quite habitually within the human rights movement present a special perplexity in the context of Islam.

Dissident. For instance, the word "dissident" (literally meaning, "to sit apart," from the Latin *dis* and *sid*) became popular during the 1970s as a Western label for activists in the Soviet and Eastern European human rights movements. More than simply adherents to a form of opposition, deviance or non-conformity, dissidents invoke a special "dedication to liberty of conscience, intellectual freedom, and the right of free expression."[4] Soviet dissidents themselves defined the term as "someone who disagrees in some measure with the ideological, political, economic or moral foundation that society rests on,"[5] and as "those people (a small minority) who refused to accept the basic principle of totalitarianism—suppression of the individual's right."[6] Though their specific causes dif-

---

[3] Translations of any type, and not infrequently from Arabic into English, can be subject to distortion, sometimes inadvertently, sometimes perhaps deliberately. Mayer notes, for instance, some misleading divergences in the English and Arabic versions of the Universal Islamic Declaration of Human Rights. Mayer, *Islam and Human Rights*, 27.

[4] C. Robert Cole and Michael E. Moody, eds., *The Dissenting Tradition* (Athens, OH, 1975), ix.

[5] Roy Medvedev, *On Soviet Dissent: Interviews with Piero Ostellino*, George Sanders, ed. (New York, 1980), 1.

[6] Valentine Turchin, *The Inertia of Fear and the Scientific Worldview* (New York, 1981), 25.

fered, the various Soviet and Eastern European dissident movements shared common methods of action: public expression of their views, non-violence, and insistence on compliance with international law.[7]

These very definitions reveal their Western, secular roots. They derive from a liberal belief in individualism, including the separation of public and private realms of thought and action, and in the right to disagree with the collective authority. By contrast, Islam, for all its internal cultural and political diversity, is rooted in a radically different consciousness toward community and authority. "Islam," which literally means "submission to the will of God" (and "Muslim," "one who submits"), provides a comprehensive code of law, covering the social, political, and economic life of the community as well as rituals of worship. There is no separation of "mosque and state" in Islam. Religion is pervasive, not compartmentalized into one day of the week as in most modern Western societies. Moreover, as Lisa Anderson has written of the Middle East, "Opposition has little place in a system where the ruler is accountable only to God and where it is the ruler's responsibility to guarantee the continued harmonious integration of each individual and group into the community."[8] In this context, is the study of "religious dissidents in Islam" another legacy of Western colonialism, if not an oxymoron?

As this chapter will show, there is indeed an Islamic tradition of individual dissent, as well as more collective reform and revival movements. (Some students of Islam identify a right, or even a duty, of disobedience to a ruler who has transgressed God's law.[9]) Moreover, in order to include within its scope non-Muslims, who by their very existence "sit apart" from the Muslim world, this study will dispense with the qualification that dissidents must deliberately and publicly express their opposition. Simply by their presence, and their commonplace desire to live as a distinctive community, non-Muslims are considered "non-harmonious" and accordingly treated under separate rules of Islamic law.

At the other end of the spectrum, what of radical movements such as Islamic Jihad which deliberately resort to violence as a method of opposition? Are they to be considered to fall within the category of "dissident"—assuming that violence is indeed justified under Islamic law?[10] In demarcating the term "dissident," this chapter follows the defi-

---

[7] See generally Ludmilla Alexeyeva, *Soviet Dissent: Contemporary Movements for National, Religious, and Human Rights* (Middletown, 1985).

[8] Lisa Anderson, "Lawless Government and Illegal Opposition: Reflections on the Middle East," *Journal of International Affairs* 40 (1987): 219, 221.

[9] Bernard Lewis, *The Political Language of Islam* (Chicago, 1988), 70, citing a *hadith* in which Muhammed said, "Do not obey a creature in transgression against the Creator."

[10] A popular Western notion of Islam is that it is inherently militant and violent. While this may be a view grounded in ignorance, the use of force by some groups of Islamists

nition of "prisoner of conscience" adopted by the non-governmental human rights organization, Amnesty International, which excludes persons who have "used or advocated violence."[11] This exclusion is consistent with the dissident methodology employed by the Soviet and Eastern European prototypes. However, like Amnesty, this author opposes the use of torture, extrajudicial execution, "disappearance," disproportional punishments or other unfair treatment of any person, regardless of whether he or she has used or advocated violence.[12] That is, no government, Muslim or otherwise, is justified in abusing the human rights of persons who oppose it, even if they adopt the use of violence in the course of such opposition. While states are entitled—in fact, even obligated[13]—to protect their citizenry and the public order against acts of violence, they are still required to give due process to the suspected perpetrators.

Religious. The next term, "religious," as a modifier of dissent and dissident, raises a host of questions. To avoid the conundrum over what exactly constitutes religion, this essay will adopt the approach of international law, which includes both "religion and belief" in the same set of provisions. "Religion and belief" includes theistic, non-theistic, and

---

serves to bolster this distorted image. However, according to Abdullah Omar Naseef, Secretary-General of the Muslim World League, among numerous others: "It is totally unIslamic to use violence. Islam teaches that people should talk in a democratic way. . . . We should open a dialogue and try to understand what [the young militants] want, because the use of force and aggression will not solve the problem." Clare Pedrick, "Muslim World League Chief Naseef Asks Pope to Intercede Over Bosnia," *Moneyclips* (March 18, 1993).

[11] "[T]he imprisonment, detention, or other physical restrictions imposed on any person by reason of his or her political, religious or other conscientiously held beliefs or by reason of his or her ethnic origin, sex, colour or language, provided that he or she has not used or advocated violence (hereinafter referred to as 'prisoners of conscience')." Statute of Amnesty International (as amended by the 20th International Council, meeting in Yokohama, Japan, August 31 - September 7, 1991), article 1(a).

[12] Ibid., articles 1(c) and 1(d). On the numerous examples of governmental violations of the procedural and other human rights of militant Islamists, see, e.g., Amnesty International, "Algeria: Deteriorating Human Rights Under the State of Emergency" (March, 1993); id., "Egypt: Grave Human Rights Abuses Amid Political Violence" (May, 1993); id., "Tunisia: Heavy Sentences After Unfair Trials" (October, 1992); Middle East Watch, "Human Rights Abuses in Algeria: No One is Spared" (January, 1994); id., "Egypt: Trials of Civilians in Military Courts Violate International Law; Executions Continue, No Appeal of Death Sentences to Higher Court" (July, 1993); id., "Egypt: Human Rights Abuses Mount in 1993" (October 22, 1993); id., "Tunisia: Military Courts that Sentenced Islamist Leaders Violated Basic Fair-Trial Norms" (October, 1992); Helsinki Watch, "Human Rights in Uzbekistan" (May, 1993). One of the implicit messages of these reports is that attempts by Muslim governments to suppress Islamic militantism seem only to fuel it.

[13] It has been held that international human rights law requires states to prevent human rights violations that are committed by private actors such as armed opposition groups, vigilante death squads and the like. See Velasquez Rodriguez Case, Inter-American Court of Human Rights (Judgment of July 29, 1988), Series C, No. 5.

atheistic beliefs, as well as the right not to profess any religion or belief. Moreover, the phrase is not limited to traditional or ancient religions,[14] so it applies to relatively new faiths such as the Baha'i.

More troublesome is the question of what constitutes "religious dissent" in societies which organically combine political and religious solidarity, rejecting the separation of church and state commonly found in countries with predominantly Christian populations. For instance, are the Shi'ites of Southern Iraq in fact religious dissenters from the nominally Sunni regime of Saddam Hussein, or really a geo-political threat to his rule, given their affinity with Iran? When is political opposition legitimately labeled heresy or apostasy? Similarly, how does one separate Islamic revival movements from Pan-Arab or Pakistani or Indonesian nationalism, or from anti-Westernization, when in each instance Islam may in fact have been used as a symbol of national or cultural unity rather than an integral part of group ideology?[15]

Each of these questions will be kept in mind at relevant stages of this inquiry. As stated above, the study will examine the use of religious justifications for repressive measures, even if the actual motive is political or otherwise secular.[16]

---

[14] General Comment Adopted by the Human Rights Committee under Article 40, Paragraph 4, of the International Covenant on Civil and Political Rights, U.N. Doc. CCPR/c/21/Rev. 1/Add. 4, September 27, 1993, 1. See, e.g., Article 18(1) of the International Covenant on Civil and Political Rights, 999 U.N.T.S. 171, 6 I.L.M. 368 (1967) ("Everyone shall have the right . . . to manifest his religion or belief in worship, observance, practice and teaching"). See also Article 1(1) of the UN Declaration on the Elimination of All Forms of Intolerance and Discrimination Based on Religion of Belief, G.A. Res. 55 (XXXVI)(1981), 21 I.L.M. 205 (1982), which inserts the word "whatever" before the word "belief." See also the chapters of Natan Lerner and David Little included in the sequel to this volume, John Witte, Jr. and Johan van der Vyver, eds., *Religious Human Rights in Global Perspective: Legal Perspectives* (The Hague/Boston, 1995).

[15] For instance, according to one scholar, "The Islamic Revolution in Iran, no matter how it appeared to the West at the time, was not the work of the priests but rather the product of an overwhelming wish by the Iranian people to regain their cultural identity and to liberate themselves from foreign domination." Mina Reeves, *Female Warriors of Allah* (New York, 1989), 133. Islamic revival movements often use the language of anti-Westernism when in fact their real opponent is their own country's secular or Western-leaning government.

[16] The term "secular," which will be used throughout this essay, requires its own definition. The dictionary definition—"indifference to or rejection or exclusion of religion and religious considerations"—is not very helpful, though it implies a contrast between temporal and sacred, this-worldly v. other-worldly, human-centered as opposed to God-centered. *Webster's Ninth New Collegiate Dictionary* (Springfield, 1990), 1061. Derived from the Latin, "saeculum," meaning "age," the term literally means "of this [present] age." The term "secularism" was coined by G.J. Holyoake in his 1854 work, *Principles of Secularism*, to mean, "a certain positive and ethical element, which the terms 'infidel,' 'skeptic,' [and] 'atheist' do not express"—even though the latter terms have been used interchangeably with secularism by religious detractors of the concept. See Mehrzad Boroujerdi, "Can Islam be Secularized?" in M.R. Ghanoonparvar and Faridoun Farrokh, eds., *In Transition: Essays on Culture and Identity in Middle Eastern Societies* (Laredo, TX, 1993), 57, citing Tamara Sonn, "Secularism and

Other Terms. By necessity when translating from one cultural context to another, terms can only be used in a rough approximation of equivalency. While it may be technically inaccurate in the context of Islam to use terms such as "blasphemy" and "fundamentalism," which have particular Christian connotations,[17] English-speaking readers can be forewarned to approach these parallels as inexact similes.

Finally, for purposes of this essay the term "classical Islam" will refer to the period from 622 C.E., when the Prophet Muhammed and his followers left Mecca to establish the first Islamic community in Medina, until the tenth century, with the "closing of the door of *ijtihad*" (reasoning and interpretation of Islamic law). While "contemporary Islam" can be said to have begun in the mid-nineteenth century, when reformers again called for the "reopening of the door of *ijtihad*" (and which, not coincidentally, also marked the beginning of European colonialism), for the sake of brevity, the "contemporary" period will for the most part in this study be confined to the era of independent nation-states, from approximately the end of World War II to the present, and most frequently, the last fifteen years, beginning with the 1979 Islamic revolution in Iran.

Scope and Sources. The Muslim world, which consists of one billion people constituting the majority population in over forty states, ranging beyond the Middle East and North Africa to South Asia and the non-Slavic former Soviet republics of Central Asia, is by no means a cultural, racial, linguistic, or jurisprudential monolith. Over as important a matter as the duty of *jihad*, for instance, interpretations vary widely: it can mean the moral struggle to follow the path of God, or the necessity of armed struggle against the enemies of Islam, or various postures in between. The most militant view is itself restricted in some interpretations only to defensive battles, while others consider armed *jihad* equally just in an offensive posture.[18] State structures themselves vary from those officially

---

National Stability in Islam," *Arab Studies Quarterly* 9 (Summer, 1987): 302. As a philosophy, secularism has also been associated with concepts such as pluralism, progressivism and the separation of church and state. Boroujerdi, "Can Islam be Secularized?" 57.

[17] See Leonard W. Levy, *Blasphemy: Verbal Offense Against the Sacred, From Moses to Salman Rushdie* (New York, 1993). "Fundamentalism" was an early twentieth century Protestant movement advocating the literal interpretation of the Bible. See Lawrence Kaplan, ed., *Fundamentalism in Comparative Perspective* (Amherst, MA, 1992). Esposito regards "fundamentalism" as "too laden with Christian presuppositions and Western stereotypes, as well as implying a monolithic threat that does not exist." He prefers "Islamic revivalism" or "Islamic activism," the former of which will be used here. Esposito, *The Islamic Threat*, 7-8.

[18] Ibid, 32-33; Majid Khadduri, *The Islamic Conception of Justice* (Baltimore, 1984), 180; Ibrahim Malik, "Jihad—Its Development and Relevance," *Palestine-Israel Journal* No. 2 (Spring 1994): 26; Chris Hedges, "In the Sudan, Islamic Leader Talks of Tolerance," *The New York Times* (December 6, 1994): A6. See also Judith Miller, "Faces of Fundamentalism: Hassan al-Turabi and Muhammed Fadlallah," *Foreign Affairs* (November/December, 1994): 123.

proclaimed as Islamic, where Shari'a (Islamic law) is a formal source of law, to secular countries with majority Muslim populations, where Islamic norms may operate in an indirect manner.[19] While most Islamic regimes follow the Sunni schools of Islamic jurisprudence, Iran is not the only country with a majority of Shi'ites.

While this wide scope poses practical problems for a chapter-length survey, it attempts to avoid the resort to stereotypes and demonized caricatures, simplistic equations of Islam with violence, and other examples of the "ignorance of triumphant imagination."[20] It is also important to use a balance of Muslim and non-Muslim sources to obviate both Western biases and Eastern apologetics.[21]

In one sense, the scope of this study will be artificial: because other chapters in this volume cover women and children in Islamic law, most of the "dissidents" described here will, by default, be adult males. This constriction is not incongruent with the nature of Islamic societies, how-

---

[19] In this chapter, the term "Islamic states" shall refer to those countries, which include Saudi Arabia, Egypt, Malaysia, Iran, and Iraq, that have officially proclaimed Islam to be the state religion or for which Islamic law is a formal source for legislation. The term "Muslim states" shall refer to the "Islamic states" *as well as* countries whose Muslim population forms a majority (50% or greater) but which have not officially made Islam the state religion or source of law. Examples of the latter include Djibouti, Senegal, and Turkey. Population figures are based on *The World Almanac and Book of Facts 1994* (Mahwah, NJ, 1993), 736-825. On the effect of Islamic norms in the latter type of state, see Abdullahi Ahmed An-Na'im, "Islam, Islamic Law and the Dilemma of Cultural Legitimacy for Universal Human Rights," in Claude E. Welch, Jr. and Virginia A. Leary, eds., *Asian Perspectives on Human Rights* (Boulder, 1990), 31.

The Organization of the Islamic Conference, a non-governmental organization established in 1965 for the promotion of Islamic solidarity among its member states, had 51 members as of December, 1994. *Reuters World Service* (December 11, 1994). The membership includes some states with fewer than 50% Muslims (for instance, Chad, Sierra Leone, and Uganda) which are not included in the term "Muslim states" as used in this chapter. See N.J. Reneger, *Treaties and Alliances of the World* (Essex, 1990), 562.

See note 107 for a full list of the 43 states which constitute the group of "Muslim states" as used herein.

[20] Esposito, *The Islamic Threat*, 45, quoting R.W. Southern, *Western Views of Islam and the Middle Ages* (Cambridge, MA, 1962), 28. On the Western conflation of images of "Islamic fundamentalist" and "terrorist," see Ileana M. Porras, "On Terrorism: Reflections on Violence and the Outlaw," *Utah Law Review* (1994): 119, 134-138.

[21] The reader will note that many of the citations in the third main part of this chapter concerning contemporary examples of human rights violations are to the publications of Western-based organizations such as Amnesty International and Human Rights Watch. These organizations strive to base their information on the first-hand reports of dissidents who are indigenous to the country under investigation and who, by the very nature of their vulnerable status, are unable to issue their own publications. In fact, as these two organizations frequently note, repressive governments often undertake campaigns to stop the flow of information outside the country by oppressing the monitors of human rights. See, e.g., *Amnesty International Annual Report 1987* (London, 1988), 4-5; and *Human Rights Watch World Report 1994* (New York, 1993), xxi-xxiii.

ever, given the traditional prohibition on women's ability to engage in public activities and discourse, essential elements of the dissident.

Legal Standards. In the course of a study of this kind, judgments and critical appraisals will inevitably be made. It is proper, therefore, to identify those external standards which the evaluator relies on as the basis for judgment. Those are the provisions of regional and international human rights law pertaining to religious freedom and the rights of religious minorities. The international law of religious freedom encompasses both "hard" law, that is, norms that are legally binding on states either because they have ratified them or because they have been so widely adopted as to have risen to the level of customary international law, and "soft" law, those emerging norms that are hortatory though not yet legally binding, but because of endorsement by respected and representative groups, are likely to become so in the future.[22] Where they codify already existing norms of customary international law, it is expected that "soft" law provisions are to be complied with. Included here in the discussion of "soft" law are two regional declarations adopted by intergovernmental organizations composed of Muslim states, in addition to one regional treaty formally adopted by African states. The two most relevant international documents have been discussed elsewhere in this volume and its sequel[23] and will therefore only be mentioned briefly here.

The International Covenant on Civil and Political Rights, a treaty which entered into force in 1976, has been adopted by 125 countries, including 23 Muslim states.[24] Freedom of thought, conscience, and religion are guaranteed by article 18. Another provision of this same Covenant, article 27, prohibits states from denying religious minorities the right, in community with other group members, to enjoy their own culture, profess and practice their own religion, or to use their own language.[25]

---

[22] See Louis Henkin, Richard Crawford Pugh, Oscar Schacter and Hans Smit, *International Law: Cases and Materials*, 3d ed. (St. Paul, 1993), 126-143.

[23] See the chapter of Natan Lerner included in the sequel to this volume, Witte and van der Vyver, eds., *Religious Human Rights in Global Perspective: Legal Perspectives*.

[24] The following Muslim states were parties to the International Covenant on Civil and Political Rights as of December 31, 1993: Afghanistan, Albania, Algeria, Azerbaijan, Bosnia-Hercegovina, Egypt, Gambia, Guinea, Iran, Iraq, Jordan, Lebanon, Libya, Mali, Morocco, Niger, Nigeria, Senegal, Somalia, Sudan, Syria, Tunesia, and Yemen. *Multilateral Treaties Deposited with the Secretary General: Status as at 31 December 1993* (New York, 1994), 124-125.

[25] As the UN Human Rights Committee, created under article 40 of the Covenant, has commented, the fact that a religion is recognized as an official or state religion or that its followers constitute the majority of a state's population, is not a lawful ground for impairing any rights under the Covenant, including rights under articles 18 and 27, of anyone who does not accept the official ideology or even outright opposes it. General Comment Adopted by the Human Rights Committee, para. 9, p. 4. See also article 5(d)(vii) of the International Convention on the Elimination of All Forms of Racial Discrimination, 660 U.N.T.S. 195, 5 I.L.M. 352 (1966), which prohibits discrimination on the basis of race or national or ethnic origin in

The Declaration on the Elimination of All Forms of Intolerance and of Discrimination Based on Religion or Belief,[26] a United Nations General Assembly resolution adopted in 1981 (without a vote), extends in greater detail the relevant norms of the International Covenant. The UN's Special Rapporteur on this issue, Elizabeth Odio Benito, has concluded that the phrase "intolerance and discrimination based on religion and belief" encompasses not only discrimination which infringes on freedom of thought, conscience, religion, and belief, "but also acts which stir up hatred against, or persecution of, such persons or groups." After closely examining the Declaration, the Covenant, and a comparable provision on religious freedom in the Universal Declaration of Human Rights, the Special Rapporteur also concluded that all three of these international documents mean "that everyone has the right to leave one religion or belief and to adopt another, or to remain without any at all."[27] As discussed below, these conclusions are relevant to the widely known Islamic belief that a Muslim who rejects Islam is an apostate, for whom the penalty is often said to be death.

A regional treaty that constitutes "hard law" in a region that includes Muslim states is the Organization of African Unity's African Charter on Human and Peoples' Rights, which entered into force in 1986.[28] Article 8 states: "Freedom of conscience, the profession and free practice of religion shall be guaranteed. No one may, subject to law and order, be submitted to measures restricting the exercise of these freedoms." The Charter also imposes on every individual, in article 28, "the duty to respect and consider his fellow beings without discrimination, and to maintain relations aimed at promoting, safeguarding and reinforcing mutual respect and tolerance."

Although it is not binding law and has not been widely commented on, the Organization of the Islamic Conference adopted the Cairo Declaration on Human Rights in Islam in 1990.[29] Article 10 states: "Islam is the

---

exercise of the right to freedom of thought, conscience and religion. (Note, however, that "religion" is not a protected category within the Convention's article 1(1) definition of discrimination.) As of December 31, 1993, 28 Muslim states were parties to this Convention. Turkey was a signatory but not a party. *Multilateral Treaties Deposited with the Secretary-General*, 99-100.

[26] G.A. Res. 55 (XXXVI)(1981), 21 I.L.M. 205 (1982).

[27] Ibid., par.21. The relevant provision in the Universal Declaration of Human Rights is article 18.

[28] O.A.U. Doc. CAB/LEG/67/3/Rev.5, 21 I.L.M. 58 (1982). The following Muslim states are parties to the African Charter on Human and Peoples' Rights: Algeria, Comoros, Djibouti, Egypt, Gambia, Guinea, Libya, Mali, Mauritania, Niger, Nigeria, Senegal, Somalia, Sudan, and Tunisia.

[29] Reprinted in *Twenty-Four Human Rights Documents* (Center for the Study of Human Rights, Columbia University, New York, 1992), 180-183. See Ann Elizabeth Mayer, "Universal

religion of unspoiled nature. It is prohibited to exercise any form of compulsion on man or to exploit his poverty or ignorance in order to convert him to another religion or to atheism." While the Declaration announces in its last article that it is based solely on the Shari'a, its numerous references to "every human being" seem to indicate that it applies to the treatment of non-Muslims as well as of Muslims. However, the combination of these two sentences in article 10 may mean that it is prohibited to use compulsion or exploitation to convert someone from Islam to another religion or atheism, but not the reverse.

Other Cairo Declaration provisions which similarly appear to operate in one direction only include article 22(b): "Everyone shall have the right to advocate what is right, and propagate what is good, and warn against what is wrong and evil according to the norms of Islamic Shariah"; and the less ambiguous article 22(a): "Everyone shall have the right to express his opinion freely in such manner as would not be contrary to the principles of the Shariah." The Declaration contains no explicit references to the rights of non-Muslims, nor does it include a general right to "freedom of thought, conscience, and religion" as found in the international agreements. Perhaps not so surprisingly, the Cairo Declaration has been strongly endorsed by Iran and Saudi Arabia but has not received widespread support in the Muslim world generally.[30]

By contrast, the Universal Islamic Declaration of Human Rights ("UIDHR"), adopted by the Islamic Council in 1981, does contain the references found in the discourse of international law.[31] Article X, titled "Rights of Minorities," states: "The Quranic principle 'There is no compulsion in religion' shall govern the religious rights of non-Muslim countries. In a Muslim country, religious minorities shall have the choice to be governed in respect of their civil and personal matters by Islamic Law or by their own laws." Article XIII provides every person with the right to freedom of conscience and worship in accordance with one's religious beliefs, while article XII(e) forbids ridiculing, holding in contempt, or inciting public hostility against the religious beliefs of others.

Versus Islamic Human Rights: A Clash of Cultures or a Clash with a Construct?" *Michigan Journal of International Law* 15 (Winter, 1994): 307, 327-350, for an analysis of the 1990 Cairo Declaration on Human Rights in Islam.

[30] Ibid., 350, 375-377.

[31] Reprinted in C.G. Weeramantry, *Islamic Jurisprudence: An International Perspective* (New York, 1988), 176-183. This book also contains a 1979 resolution by the First International Conference on the Protection of Human Rights in the Islamic Criminal Justice System. Ibid., 184-5. A Draft Charter on Human and People's Rights in the Arab World was approved by Arab experts meeting in Siracusa, Italy in 1986 under the auspices of the International Institute of Higher Studies in Criminal Sciences. See also the Hammamat Declaration of 1983, reprinted in *MERIP Middle East Report* (January, 1984), 23.

The UIDHR is not without its own qualified passages. Although article XII(a) provides every person with the right to express his thoughts and beliefs, it is only "so long as he remains within the limits prescribed by the Law," which, in the Arabic version, reads, "the Shariah," the particular word for Islamic law.[32] Moreover, no one "is entitled to disseminate falsehoods or to circulate reports which may outrage public decency, or to indulge in slander, innuendo or to cast defamatory aspersions on other persons." These limitation provisions may explain why the Islamic Council did not intervene on behalf of author Salman Rushdie when the Ayatollah Khomenei ordered his execution in a 1989 *fatwa* (formal juristic opinion).[33]

Like the Cairo Declaration, the UIDHR was drafted in response to the purported tendency among Western rights advocates and scholars to "exclude Islam from the cultural domain where human rights were conceived and proclaimed and where they retain meaning."[34] (Indeed, the UIDHR's seemingly oxymoronic title conveys either a deliberate ambiguity or a ridicule of the term "universal.") While on first glance both documents appear to replicate the international agreements, on closer review they diverge quite self-assuredly, if subtly. Whether conflicts between international and regional norms are to be decided in favor of the former or latter has not been formally adjudicated within international human rights law. Indeed, as the next section of this chapter demonstrates, this question reflects one of the most hotly contested and unresolved disputes in the field of human rights. For these purposes, we should note that although the Cairo and Universal Islamic Declarations are not legally binding, they do portray different approaches to the reconciliation of Islamic law with international human rights law. To the extent that they conflict, they illustrate the lack of a consensus within even the modern Islamic world on the question of religious human rights.

Westernization and Cultural Relativism. The underlying tension between divergent international and regional norms of what constitutes human rights surfaced quite unmistakably at the U.N.'s World Conference on Human Rights, held in Vienna in the summer of 1993. Not sur-

---

[32] See Mayer, *Islam and Human Rights*, 87-88 on the differences between the English and Arabic translations. See also ibid., 86-89, 120-128, 153-155, and 173-175, for an extensive commentary on the UIDHR.

[33] Ibid., 241 n.37. See also Bassam Tibi, "The European Tradition of Human Rights and the Culture of Islam," in Abdullahi Ahmed An-Na'im and Francis M. Deng, eds., *Human Rights in Africa: Cross-Cultural Perspectives* (Washington, 1990), 104, 117-123.

[34] Mohammed Arkoun, *Rethinking Islam: Common Questions, Uncommon Answers* (Boulder, 1994), 106. According to Arkoun, the UIDHR was constructed from Sunni rather than Shi'ite interpretations of Islamic law. Ibid.

prisingly, Muslim countries—most prominently Iran, Syria, Yemen, Pakistan, Indonesia, and Malaysia—among other developing nations, loudly attacked the popular Western notion that human rights are universal. In preparatory regional meetings held in advance of the Conference, African states declared that "no ready-made model [of human rights] can be prescribed at the universal level since the historical and cultural realities of each nation and the traditions, standards and values of each people cannot be disregarded,"[35] while Asian states implicitly criticized Western hegemony in the statement that "the promotion of human rights should be encouraged by cooperation and consensus and not through confrontation and the imposition of incompatible values."[36] Speaking for the proponents of universalism, the United States Secretary of State responded to these challenges: "We cannot let cultural relativism become the last refuge of repression."[37]

Indeed, there is a strong correlation between the advocacy of cultural relativism and abuse of human rights. As noted by Mayer, many Muslim states "had been guilty of egregious violations of human rights. It was therefore in their political interest to find rationales for asserting the nonapplicability of international rights norms."[38] Yet it must be borne in mind that the repressive policies of militant Islamic regimes have been imposed top-down, by the unelected (even where they claim to be "the elect"). They are not by any means a reflection of the will of the Muslim

---

[35] Tunis Declaration on Human Rights, par. 5 (Nov. 6, 1992)(published by the United Nations Department of Public Information, DPI/1346-93 13777-April 1993-7M). Similar language made its way into the final document of the World Conference in a compromise with the Western position: "All human rights are universal, indivisible and interdependent and interrelated. The international community must treat human rights globally in a fair and equal manner, on the same footing, and with the same emphasis. *While the significance of national and regional particularities and various historical, cultural and religious backgrounds must be borne in mind*, it is the duty of States, regardless of their political, economic and cultural systems, to promote and protect all human rights and fundamental freedoms." Vienna Declaration and Programme of Action, par. 5 (June 25, 1993), A/CONF.157/23, p. 5 (emphasis added). The Western view held the dominant position: "The universal nature of these rights and freedoms is beyond question." Ibid., par. 1, p. 4. However, the developing states were successful in preventing the conference from adopting effective human rights enforcement machinery, which was the original purpose of the conference.

[36] Bangkok Declaration on Human Rights, preamble (April 2, 1993)(published by the United Nations Department of Public Information, DPI/1346-93 13777-April 1993-7M). A similar view was expressed by the Sudan when it withdrew from participation in the 1994 U.N. Cairo Conference on Population. The Sudanese Minister of Culture and Information described his state's decision to boycott the conference as "a kind of holy war against the new hegemony which some seek to impose on us," referring to the Clinton Administration's ostensible campaign to use the conference to promote Western values. "The Sudan Withdraws From U.N. Cairo Conference on Population," *The New York Times* (August 31, 1994): A9.

[37] Quoted by Elaine Sciolino, "U.S. Rejects Notion that Human Rights Vary with Culture," *The New York Times* (June 15, 1993): 5.

[38] Mayer, "Universal versus Islamic Human Rights," 373.

people. Torture and summary executions are not an "Islamic tradition" in the legal sense any more than they are "Catholic" when they occur in Latin American countries. For every Salman Rushdie condemned in the East, the West has had a Socrates, a Galileo, a Voltaire, and, in the present century no less, a James Joyce, a D.H. Lawrence, and a Henry Miller.

Thus, governmental strategies that stifle free expression, ban access to outside information,[39] and punish dissent "are not in any way distinctively 'Islamic,'"[40] despite efforts by Muslim regimes to rationalize and insulate their abuses through the invocation of ostensibly authoritative Islamic doctrines. Furthermore, to insist—as Islam's Western apologists often do—that international human rights norms do not apply to Muslims is to adopt a patronizing, racist stereotype that Muslims are barbaric and inferior to Westerners, "undeserving" of international law's protection, or that Islam is monolithic and that repression is the Muslim norm.

Because of the apparent failures of secular liberalism and nationalist socialism—both movements of Western origin—to propel Muslim states into an economic and political par with the West, the current retreat of the Islamic world into a defensive, reactive, and "fundamentalist" mode, particularly one that emphasizes cultural distinctiveness, is not at all inexplicable.[41] Frustration and feelings of powerlessness are often channeled into a radical, even militant backlash against the external forces that can be blamed for the defeat. Where, as here, the backlash appears[42] to be directed against Western domination that is not coincidentally secular, Muslim disdain for the "Godless," culturally and ethically "barren" West is almost inevitable. Hence, the emphasis on the inseparability of politics and religion, perhaps the most central characteristic of Islam.

---

[39] Islam is often invoked as an excuse for shielding Muslims from outside ideas. For instance, in March, 1994 the Saudi Ministerial Council banned the importation, sale and use of satellite television dishes on the grounds of protecting "the religious and social values of the country." Violators will be fined and their equipment confiscated. "Saudi Arabia: Satellite Dish Ban," *The Article 19 Bulletin*, Issue 20 (June 1994): 5.

[40] Mayer, "Current Muslim Thinking About Human Rights," in An-Na'im and Deng, eds., *Human Rights in Africa*, 149. As King Hussein of Jordan recently said of terrorist attacks against Jewish and Israeli targets in London and Buenos Aires, "Nothing irritates me more or is more painful to me than to witness and see acts and attitudes attributable to Islam that have nothing to do with Islam, my faith and my religion." Douglas Jehl, "3 Leaders Angered by New Terrorist Attacks," *The New York Times* (July 27, 1994): A8.

[41] See Abdullahi An-Na'im, "What Do We Mean by Universal?" *Index on Censorship* 23 (September/October, 1994): 120, 122.

[42] Some would argue that while the rhetoric of Islamism is anti-Western, in political terms it in fact "is directed primarily against a [Muslim] country's own government, which the fundamentalists hope to topple and supplant." Arnold Hottinger, "The Real Perils of Islamism: How a Minority Can Prevail," *Swiss Review of World Affairs*, translated and reprinted in *World Press Review* (May, 1994): 12.

But cultural diversity is not incompatible with human rights; it is one of the byproducts, one of the purposes of human rights, particularly of religious human rights. Pluralism is inseparable from the liberty that induces it. When universalists invoke international human rights law, the focus is as much on the "law" and the "human" as it is on the supposed global consensus that achieved it. What is universal in all societies is the need for the rule of law and the belief in human dignity. What differs from culture to culture is how and why one gets to those conceptions.

One purpose of this chapter is to demonstrate that Islam is itself culturally relative and pluralistic. It has always been subject to various interpretations, schools of thought, sects and subsects, depending on what Muslims of any given time and place have believed.[43] Moreover, like most religions, it has evolved over the centuries not only due to internal debate, but also because of interactive influences from the cultures it enveloped, whether Greek, Christian, Judaic, Persian, Byzantine, or other. The twentieth century's version of intercultural influence, that which takes place on the global level of international consensus-building around law, is simply another example of this mutual enrichment process. While there is a great need for intercultural dialogue in order to grant the "margin of appreciation"[44] that each culture deserves, there is also a need to know what is authentically Islamic so one can detect when Islam is being exploited or distorted as a convenient rationale for repression.

Religious Dissent Under Classical Islamic Law

The Structure of Islamic Law. This section of the chapter sets the context for the discussion of religious dissidents by briefly mentioning some of the basic concepts and relevant categories of Islamic law. More detailed explanations are set out in other chapters of this anthology.[45]

Islamic law, like Jewish law, is a comprehensive and organic body of religious duties governing political, economic, and social life as well as the spiritual realm of worship and ritual—that is, behavior as well as belief. Law and theology are inseparable in Islam, as are the spiritual and the temporal realms of human life. The term for Islamic law, "Shari'a,"

---

[43] See An-Na'im, "What Do We Mean by Universal," 123.

[44] "Margin of appreciation" is a doctrine employed by the European Court of Human Rights to allow governments the room to restrict freedom of expression when local interests and necessity in good faith demand it. A government's estimate of that necessity is entitled to some, but not absolute, deference. See Mark W. Janis and Richard S. Kay, *European Human Rights Law* (Hartford, 1990), 114-115, 244-258.

[45] See the chapters by Abdullahi A. An-Na'im and Riffat Hassan included herein. See also Donna E. Arzt, "The Application of International Human Rights Law in Islamic States," *Human Rights Quarterly* 12 (May 1990): 202.

literally means "the way" or "road" to follow (not unlike the Jewish term, "Halakah"), or more loosely, "the discipline." Shari'a is comprised of two categories of sources, the primary, which consists of the Qur'an (the collection of recitations that Allah revealed to Muhammed) and the Sunna (the collection of traditions about the conduct and sayings of Muhammed), and the secondary sources, *Ijma* and *Qiyas*, which are not per se sources but rather methods of discovering Shari'a.[46]

Supremely authoritative and infallible, as it is the word of God, the Qur'an cannot be altered. "There is no changing the words of Allah" (10:65).[47] When the Qur'an is silent, one turns to the Sunna. Together, the Qur'an and Sunna are said to constitute an integrated whole, though in cases of conflict, the former prevails. When neither of the two primary sources offer a relevant passage, a third source, *Ijma* ("consensus"), provides a body of fixed rules reflecting the unanimous agreement of Islamic scholars, so long as their collective view did not conflict with the Qur'an and Sunna. Finally, when none of these three revealed or communal sources provide a relevant rule, individual Islamic scholars can derive one through logical inference from the primary sources and reasoning by analogy (*Qiyas*), much as common law jurists do. The mental exertion involved in this interpretive process, which requires special training, is called *Ijtihad*. Thus, through *Ijma* and *Ijtihad* the community of Islam over time was able to develop the law to meet evolving needs, despite the formal notion that Shari'a is rigid and immutable.[48]

Despite the emphasis in Islam on submission and unanimity, a variety of schools of interpretation or jurisprudence developed across the geographically wide and philosophically diverse range of Muslim societies, each with its own body of literature. "A tree, whose network of branches and twigs stems from the same trunk and roots; a sea, formed by the merging waters of different rivers; a variety of threads woven into a single garment; even the interlaced holes of a fishing net: these are some of the metaphors used by Muslim authors to explain the phenomenon of *ikhtilaf*, or diversity of doctrine," in Islamic law.[49]

---

[46] See generally Weeramantry, *Islamic Jurisprudence.*

[47] Chapter (*Sura*) 10, verse 65. Unless quoting the Qur'an from a secondary source, this essay follows the English translation in Marmaduke Pickthall, *The Glorious Koran: A Bi-Lingual Edition with English* (London, 1976). Pickthall is both a Muslim and a native English speaker who consulted Egyptian experts in rendering his translation. According to Islamic law, the Qur'an should not be read in translation because to do so is to alter Allah's revelation. Ibid., vii. Different editions and translations use different numbering systems for the verses, but they are usually within one or two verses of each other.

[48] See generally Weeramantry, *Islamic Jurisprudence*, 40-45.

[49] N.J. Coulson, *A History of Islamic Law* (Edinburgh, 1964), 86.

Today, the schools of orthodox (or Sunni, from the word Sunna) Islam are mutually respected but in their formative years were hostile and competitive. The four major schools are the Hanafi, which is dominant today in Afghanistan, Pakistan, Turkey, and Egypt; the Shafi, found in Indonesia and East Africa; the Maliki, dominant in North Africa; and the Hanbali, which predominates in Saudi Arabia. Each has its own method of *ijma*. For instance, the Hanafis accept the opinions of Islamic scholars from any time period if based on principles of equity. The Malikis accept only the *ijma* of the Medina scholars, and only on the basis of public interest, while the Hanbalis follow only the consensus of the companions of Muhammed.[50] This diversity of interpretive approaches belies the popular stereotype of a monolithic Islam.

The distinctions between the two major Islamic sects are even more pronounced than those between the Sunni schools. Shi'ite Muslims, considered heretical by Sunnis, have always been a numerical minority within Islam. They too have their own schools of jurisprudence, including the Ithna 'Ashari or Imamis, the Ismaili, Alawi, Druze, and Zeydi. Their split from orthodox Islam began as a political dispute and only later took on theological aspects. Shi'ites believe that the Imam[51] or leader of the community must be a descendant of Ali, the fourth Khalifah and Muhammed's son-in-law who died in 661, thereby repudiating the first three Khalifahs, recognized as leaders by the Sunnis, who select any member of Muhammed's tribe for the chief leadership position. While Sunnis believe that the Khalifah is a servant of the law, serving only as a temporal leader, chosen by community consensus, required to seek scholarly consultation and removable for misconduct, the Shi'ite Imam is a sinless interpreter of the law, both a spiritual and a political leader, installed by prophetic designation, infallible and singularly capable of unitary leadership. Shi'ites accept the Qur'an and Sunna as sources of law, but not as the sole source of truth; the pronouncements of the

---

[50] Weeramantry, *Islamic Jurisprudence*, 40; Coulson, *A History of Islamic Law*, 36-52; Rene David and John E.C. Brierley, *Major Legal Systems in The World Today* (New York, 1985), 457-62.

[51] For Shi'ites, the title "Ayatollah" refers to a teacher while an Imam is a teacher who has achieved a semi-divine status as an intermediary with God. In Iran, the highest ranking Ayatollah (such as Khomeini) is an Imam, given the title Grand Ayatollah. The "Twelfth Imam," according to Shi'ites, will be a descendant of Ali, Muhammed's son-in-law. Related Shi'ite terms include *ulam* (religious scholar), *faqih* (jurisprudence expert), and *mujtahid* (scholar licensed to exercise *ijtihad*). *Mujtahids* are distinquished through additional titles according to their erudition and following. See Gregory Rose, "*Velayat-e Faqih* and the Recovery of Islamic Identity in the Thought of Ayatollah Khomeini, in Nikki R. Keddie, ed., *Religion and Politics in Iran: Sh'ism from Quietism to Revolution* (New Haven, 1983), 168, n.11. *Velayat-e Faqih* means "governance of the jurisprudence," the *Shi'ite* concept that the Muslim state shall be run by the clerics.

Imams, even if in conflict with scholarly consensus, are also authoritative.[52] But this results in a Shi'ite concept of law that is, according to at least two modern scholars, "more authoritarian and far more detached from social reality than the Sunni concept."[53]

Categories of Religious Dissidents. When addressing particular issues involving types of religious human rights, one must keep in mind that the idea of human rights is a fairly recent addition to Western thought; in transplanting and grafting it onto the much older legal tradition of classical Islamic law, incongruities are bound to appear. For instance, Islam predates not only the modern, democratic notion of popular sovereignty, it also predates the medieval concept of royal sovereignty. "Since it recognizes only the sovereignty of God and does not believe in unrestricted man-made laws, its object is to put an end to the rule of human beings over other beings."[54] While the abolition of domination is a noble ideal, it is ultimately incompatible with the central tenet of the human rights movement: the inherent freedom and equality of all persons, which can only be achieved through the rule of (man-made) law.

Nevertheless, Majid Khadduri, a leading Islamic law scholar, has identified the five most important principles of Islamic human rights: (1) dignity and brotherhood; (2) equality among members of the community, without distinction on the basis of race, color, or class; (3) respect for the honor, reputation, and family of everyone; (4) the presumption of innocence; and (5) individual freedom.[55] These can be deduced from the basic Islamic principles of the unity of God and Allah's command for justice and equality.[56] Khadduri acknowledges, however, that upon closer examination, the five principles are less than absolute. "Dignity and brotherhood," for instance, not to mention "equality," are the "privilege only of persons of full legal capacity," which means free Muslim adult males. Thus, non-Muslims and slaves, as well as women and children, receive

---

[52] Weeramantry, *Islamic Jurisprudence*, 47-49; Mayer, *Islam and Human Rights*, 47-50. Sufism, sometimes mistakenly called a third major sect of Islam, is a mystical, intuitive movement responding to the intellectualism and formalism of orthodox Islam. It includes both Sunnis and Shi'ites. Early Sufi devotees were considered heretics, but by the twelfth century Sufi monastic orders had spread to all parts of the Muslim world. See William Stoddart, *Sufism* (Wellingborough, 1982).

[53] Abdullahi Ahmed An-Na'im, *Toward an Islamic Reformation: Civil Liberties, Human Rights, and International Law* (Syracuse, 1990), 31, 199, n.87, quoting Majid Khadduri, "Nature and Sources of Islamic Law," *George Washington Law Review* 22 (1953): 22.

[54] Amir Hasan Siddiqi, *Non-Muslims Under Muslim Rule and Muslims Under Non-Muslim Rule* (Karachi, 1969), 1.

[55] Khadduri, *The Islamic Conception of Justice*, 236-7.

[56] James P. Piscatory, "Human Rights in Islamic Political Culture," in Kenneth Thompson, ed., *The Moral Imperatives of Human Rights: A World Survey* (Washington, 1980), 153, paraphrasing Muhammad Khalaf Allah Ahmad.

only partial protection of the law or have no legal capacity at all.[57] Put less charitably by scholar and human rights activist Abdullahi Ahmed An-Na'im, "Categorization and discrimination on grounds of religion or belief is fundamental to traditional Shari'a law."[58] Khadduri also notes that procedural protections for criminal defendants are not fully guaranteed.

In the next three subsections, this chapter explores the classical Islamic law concerning three categories of religious dissidents: (1) apostates and blasphemers; (2) heretics and renegades (or reformers); and (3) non-Muslims and infidels (and the related topic of jihad against enemies of Islam). These distinctions may seem artificial; indeed, the categories often overlap as they are all, in one way or another, challenges to orthodoxy and the cohesion of community. (For instance, orthodox Muslims may treat Baha'is and Ahmadis as apostates and heretics whereas these groups consider themselves non-Muslims and Muslims, respectively.) Perhaps the tripartite division is best understood as constituting expression of these three aspects of religious human rights: (1) freedom from the religion; (2) pluralism within the religion; and (3) equality and tolerance for non-members of the religion. In terms of categories of persons, the division would roughly cover: (1) non-believing former members; (2) non-orthodox believing members; and (3) non-believing non-members. Note that these labels are from the perspective of the orthodox believer;

---

[57] See Majid Khadduri, "Human Rights in Islam," *Annals of the American Academy of Political and Social Science* 243 (1946): 79; Bernard Lewis, *Race and Slavery in the Middle East* (New York, 1990). The Islamic rules governing the status of slaves have been abolished through secular law in most states but never formally repudiated within Shari'a. Although slavery in Islamic countries is supposed to be non-existent today, there are occasional reports of its occurrence. For instance, the U.S. State Department reports that despite the fact that slavery has been abolished several times in the Islamic Republic of Mauritania, most recently in 1980, somewhere between 30,000 and 90,000 people are being forced to perform compulsory labor there, both in urban areas and isolated communities, including in the homes of prominent government officials. Department of State, *Country Reports on Human Rights Practices for 1993* (Washington, 1994), 185. The Maurs, the Arabic-speaking, dominant ethnic group, "are used to this tradition of having Black Africans as slaves—slaves they have inherited from their fathers and families," according to Mocktar Toumbou, a Mauritanian economist who defected in 1991. Miriam Feldman, "Arab Regime Keeps Black Slavery Alive in Mauritania," *Near East Report* 38 (February 14, 1994): 28. On reports of slavery in the Sudan, see Ken Ringle, "The Next Rushdie? Gaspar Biro Spoke Out. Sudan's Government Condemned Him," *The Washington Post* (March 26, 1994): D1.

The following Muslim countries are not parties to either the 1953 Convention to Suppress Slavery or the 1956 Supplementary Convention on the Abolition of Slavery: Azerbaijan, Comoros, Indonesia, Kazakhstan, Kirghizistan, Lebanon, Oman, Qatar, Somalia, Tajikistan, Turkmenistan, United Arab Emirates, and Uzbekistan. *Country Reports on Human Rights*, 1403-1406.

[58] Abdullahi Ahmed An-Na'im, "Religious Freedom in Egypt: Under the Shadow of the Islamic *Dhimma* System," in Leonard Swidler, ed., *Religious Liberty and Human Rights in Nations and in Religions* (Philadelphia, 1986), 55.

persons labeled apostates and heretics often consider themselves more pious than their accusers.

Apostates and Blasphemers. Freedom of religion has been said to encompass not only the freedom to hold theistic beliefs but also the freedom to hold non-theistic beliefs as well as the freedom to change one's religion or belief, all without coercion or discrimination.[59] It should follow then that criticism of religion, whether expressed verbally or through an act tantamount to the rejection of one or more religions, must be protected as an individual's human right. Because orthodox Muslims consider Islamic law to constitute, comprehensively, the Whole Duty of Mankind, and to be divine, eternal, correct, and immutable, any allegation that all or any aspect of it is less than ideal would inevitably be seen not only as an affront, but as a disloyal act of treason against Allah and against the unity and eternal values of the believing community.[60] Such allegations must, therefore, be resisted and punished, in order to protect believers not only from injury but also from the possibility of change, which challenges to immutability represent.

Accordingly, in classical Islam, those Muslims who renounced their belief in Islam—who "disbeliev[ed] after having believed"[61]—were considered apostates. On the basis of the Qu'ranic verse, "Whoso judgeth not by that which Allah hath revealed: such are disbelievers" (Qur'an 5:44), some Islamic scholars placed any Muslim who refused to judge or be judged by Shari'a into that category.[62] Apostasy (*ridda*) was one of the seven *hudud* offenses against God, the mandatory punishment for which involved physical pain; the six others were theft, armed robbery, drinking alcohol, adultery, slanderous claims of unchastity, and armed rebellion against the leadership. Apostasy could be committed by word (blasphemy),[63] by deed, or by omission of a duty, so long as the offender

---

[59] Oldrich Andrysek, "Non-believers: A New Aspect of Religious Intolerance?" *Conscience and Liberty* 2 (1990): 15, 22, citing reports of the Special Rapporteur on Intolerance and Discrimination in Matters of Religion or Belief of the U.N. Commission on Human Rights, U.N. Doc. E/CN.4/1990/46, page 60, para. 113.

[60] See Kanan Makiya, *Cruelty and Silence: War, Tyranny, Uprising and the Arab World* (New York, 1993), 90; David Lawton, *Blasphemy* (Philadelphia, 1993), 13.

[61] Abdulaziz A. Sachedina, "Context for the Ayatollah's Decree: The Religious and Political in Islam," in Appignanesi and Maitland, eds., *The Rushdie File* (Syracuse, 1990), 223.

[62] Abdullahi Ahmed An-Na'im, "The Islamic Law of Apostasy and its Modern Applicability: A Case from the Sudan," *Religion* 16 (1986): 197, 213. Some scholars insisted that such rejection of Shari'a must be based on the belief that non-Islamic rules are better and more just than Islamic rules. Ibid.

[63] Islam has no precise equivalent to the term blasphemy, which is derived from the Greek "to hurt" and "to speak" and used as the opposite of "euphemy," the source of "euphemism". See Lawton, *Blasphemy*, 14. Traditionally in Christianity and Judaism, blasphemy meant speaking profanely or impiously of the sacred. Just as Islam makes no firm distinction between religion and state, it draws no sharp line between the sacred and the pro-

intended the word, act, or omission with awareness of the penalty, death.[64] The *hudud* crimes were those acts that infringed not only on religion but also threatened community interests in public order, thereby requiring state control. For instance, the Qur'an calls for the death, mutilation, or expulsion of those who take up arms against Allah, create discord on earth, and strive after corruption (Qur'an 5:33).

However, no passage of the Qur'an actually specifies any penalty per se for apostasy. The closest approximations state: "And for those who disbelieve in their Lord there is the doom of hell, a hapless journey's end" (Qur'an 67:6). "And whoso seeketh as religion other than the Surrender to Allah (*Islam*), it will not be accepted from him, and he will be a loser in the Hereafter" (Qur'an 3:85). Numerous other verses cajole the Muslim into adhering to the faith, to avoid the temptation (posed particularly by the People of the Book) to convert, but the exhortation is moral, not penal. Moreover, during his lifetime, Muhammed is said never actually to have executed persons who, once having adopted Islam, later renounced it.

Nevertheless, conversion to another religion was considered apostasy and may in practice have carried the death penalty. The Qur'an orders those who "turn back" (to enmity) to be slain, "wherever you find them" (Qur'an 4:89). This verse may have justified Muhammed's victory over pagan tribes when he returned to conquer Mecca between the years 624 and 630. More directly, Muhammed is reported to have said that "he who changes his religion must be killed,"[65] unless he repents. This is a *Hadith*,

---

fane, making blasphemy against Islam impossible in the Christian and Jewish sense. More broadly, however, blasphemy is rhetorical desecration of any orthodoxy, not only religious ones. Under Lawton's definition of blasphemy as an affront not against God but against a fundamentalist community, ibid., 141, secular communities of a fundamentalist nature could also be blasphemed. Given Islam's insistence on obedience, its concern for protecting community security, and its sanctification of scripture, many dissidents were labeled apostates for utterances that in Christian lands, or in a later era, might have carried the label of blasphemy. The Islamic concept of "apostasy by word" could thus be translated as "blasphemy".

[64] See Aly Aly Mansour, "*Hudud* Crimes" in M. Cherif Bassiouni, ed., *The Islamic Criminal Justice System*, (London, 1982), 195, 197; Taymour Kamel, "the Principle of Legality and Its Application in Islamic Criminal Justice," in ibid., 150, 163-166. Some jurists omit rebellion from the list of seven *Hudud* offenses, while others also omit wine-drinking and apostasy, as neither the Qur'an nor Sunna prescribed specific penalties for them. Ahmad Abd al-Aziz al-Alfi, "Punishment in Islamic Criminal Law," in ibid., 227.

[65] Piscatory, 145, citing Majid Khadduri, *War and Peace in the Law of Islam* (Baltimore, 1955), 150. The Hanbali school put apostates to death immediately, while the other three Sunni schools of jurisprudence gave apostates three days to reconsider, after which, if they refused to retract their apostasy, they were executed. The Hanafis did not execute women apostates, presumably because women would not engage in war against Muslims. See Mohammed Talbi, "Religious Liberty: A Muslim Perspective," in Swidler, ed., *Religious Liberty and Human Rights*, 182-183, n.16. Talbi states that until the execution of Mahmoud Taha in Sudan in 1985, and recent threats against Copts in Egypt and atheists in Tunisia, he knows of

rather than a Qu'ranic verse, first compiled during the wars of apostasy after Muhammed's death, when some of the previously converted Arab tribes in Medina renounced Islam by refusing to pay the alms tax. The first Khalifah, Abu Bakr, who was keen on legitimizing his authority as successor, violently subdued the tribes after reminding them of their agreement with God's prophet. He may have relied as precedent on Muhammed's order to dismember and slowly kill a band of apostates who murdered Muslim herdsmen and stole their cattle.[66] Some modern scholars, however, believe that Abu Bakr was committing a political act of counter-rebellion for which a *hudud* sanction was invoked collectively and which was not intended to be applied to "pure" cases of individual apostasy. Similarly, Muhammed's order may have been imposed for murder and theft, not apostasy. Alternatively, it is possible that the early Muslim leaders and jurists were confused over the Qu'ranic tension between religion and politics, thereby improperly treating disobedience, communal betrayal, murder, theft and perhaps mere breach of contract as apostasy.[67]

The Quranic statement, "There is no compulsion in religion" (Qur'an 2:256), is often cited to support the view that death was not an authorized punishment for conversion. However, the remainder of that same verse implies that the non-coercion rule applied only to those who convert *to* Islam, not those who leave it: "There is no compulsion in religion. The right direction is henceforth distinct from error. And he who rejecteth false deities and believeth in Allah hath grasped a firm handhold which will never break. Allah is Hearer, Knower" (Qur'an 2:256). This would constitute a double standard. Although conversion to Islam must be freely chosen, without fear and without coercion, "it is practically impos-

---

"no implementation throughout the history of Islam of the law condemning an apostate to death." Ibid., 183. This is probably not a precisely accurate statement. See, for instance, note 151 below.

[66] See An-Na'im, "The Islamic Law of Apostasy," 211-212.

[67] Khadduri, *The Islamic Conception of Justice*, 238. As the apostates in this situation had taken up arms against the Muslims, the death penalty could be considered an act of self-defense in wartime. Talbi, "Religious Liberty," 183. Therefore, it should not even be cited as a case of apostasy, though it often is. Abdulaziz A. Sachedina, "Freedom of Conscience and Religion in the Qur'an," in David Little, John Kelsay and Abdulaziz Sachedina, eds., *Human Rights and the Conflict of Cultures: Western and Islamic Perspectives on Religious Liberty*, (Columbia, SC, 1988), 80-82; Abdulaziz A. Sachedina, "Al-Bukhari's *Hadith* on 'Killing Those Who Refuse to Fulfill the Duties Enjoined by God and Considering them Apostates'," in ibid., 97. See "As the World Turns: The Islamic Awakening's Second Wave," *New Perspectives Quarterly* 9 (Summer, 1992): 52, 54. See also Muhammad Zafrulla Khan, *Islam and Human Rights* (London, 1967), 112-120, who argues that neither apostasy nor change of faith entailed a temporal punishment; and Mayer, *Islam and Human Rights*, 170 on the views of Lebanese scholar Subhi Mahmassani.

sible," according to modern scholar Mohamed Talbi, "once inside Islam, to get out of it."[68]

Regardless of the actual punishment rendered, about which there may have been no consensus, it is fair to conclude that conversion to a religion other than Islam was treated as apostasy, a crime. And if the apostasy was deemed to constitute an outright act of rebellion or sedition, it could, with Qur'anic sanction, be punished by death. Short of physical death, apostates who did not repent suffered various elements of "civil death," including suspension of the right to dispose of property and to inherit property. Marriage contracts were dissolved upon the apostasy of either spouse, and their children were declared illegitimate.[69]

Heretics and Renegades. While apostasy, in the mind of the orthodox, is a rejectionist's act of unbelief, and blasphemy is injurious rhetoric ("form or sound or interference"), heresy is more about content: false belief, or the denial of orthodox belief by a rival school of thought.[70] Just as criticism or rejection of religion could be labeled as apostasy, attempts to reform or revise it could be considered heresy. In the case of a scripture that is held to be sacrosanct and immutable, non-orthodox interpretations are vulnerable to the charge. Of course, one group's heresy is another group's innovation.

Unlike apostasy, which is definitely, if ambiguously, proscribed in the Qur'an and Sunna, heresy is a concept derived from Muslim history rather than Islamic legal texts. Muhammed, in fact, is reported to have said, "Difference of opinion among my community is a sign of the bounty of God."[71] The Islamic concept of heresy (*kufr*) must be traced to the early conflict between the Sunni, Shi'ite, and Kharijite communities over the legitimate successor to Muhammed, with the result that each sect regarded the others as heretical. Under Sunni rule, the leaders of Shi'ite and other heterodox sects were persecuted and executed for "subversive activities," a charge often based on slim evidence. An outright civil war erupted in the years 656-661 between supporters of the Sunni Khalifah Mu'awiya and those backing Ali, who later became the Shi'ites.

---

[68] Talbi, "Religious Liberty," 182 and 182 n. 15. "God is merciful and quite tolerant with regard to conversion to Islam, whereas God is severe and intolerant with regard to conversion from Islam to another religion." Masao Abe, "A Buddhist Response to Mohamed Talbi," in Swidler, ed., *Religious Liberty and Human Rights*, 189, 190. See also Sachedina,"Freedom of Conscience and Religion in the Qur'an," 67-68.

[69] An-Na'im, "The Islamic Law of Apostasy," 212. See also Mayer, *Islam and Human Rights*, 178, on the "civil death" of Baha'is in Iran.

[70] Lawton, *Blasphemy*, 15-16.

[71] Coulson, *A History of Islamic Law*, 102.

A third sect, the Kharijites ("seceders"), who believed that leaders should be democratically elected on the basis of piety and personal ability alone, was hostile to both communities. The Kharijites assassinated Ali and attempted to kill the Sunni leader, Mu'awiya. Ali's son (and Muhammed's grandson), Hussein, was thereafter brutally massacred along with his followers by Sunni troops.[72] This latter event came to symbolize, for the Shi'ites, the persecution they suffered under the orthodox majority. The first eleven of their Imams or leaders, beginning with Ali and Hussein, were murdered. The twelfth, who mysteriously disappeared, will someday return as a messiah, according to Shi'ite (sometimes called "Twelver") legend. In the meantime, Shi'ite ritual, belief, and conduct is focused upon the theme of martyrdom and intense reverence for their Imam.

While the autocratic Shi'ites were arrayed to the right of the Sunni majority, the democratic Kharijites stood to the Sunnis' left, which made them enemies of all Muslims. They believed that beyond one's degree of God-fearing, all people are equal before Allah. The Kharijite leader's legitimacy depended on his commitment to justice; if he was corrupt, unjust and ineffective, the community could remove him, an option not available to Shi'ites and Sunnis. Eventually, they contended, when everyone becomes a true believer, the need for an Imam and even for the state would "wither away," a doctrine that anticipated the Marxist version by twelve centuries. Influenced by the Greek philosophy they encountered in Syria, the Kharijites also advocated the doctrine of *qadar* (will-power), a form of free will, which led them to criticism of repressive government and into questions of human responsibility for choosing between justice and injustice. Anathema to Sunnis, who believed in the doctrine of *jabr* (compulsion or involuntarism) and the theory that all human acts were predicated by Allah, *qadar*'s advocates had to be persecuted in order to prevent disobedience to God—and to Sunni hegemony. Like all heretics, they would be punished by eternal fire in hell. *Qadar* was attractive to Shi'ites as well, as it justified their opposition to Sunni rule.[73]

The Kharijites were by no means humanists, however. Militant and puritanical, they had their own concept of heresy, which required capital punishment, and believed in the prosecution of war against unbelievers. Other Muslims, repelled by the violence that accompanied these politico-religious battles, called for moderation, tolerance of differing opinions, and the separation of religious and moral questions from political de-

---

[72] Ibid., 103-119; Khadduri, *The Islamic Conception of Justice*, 20-38. For the sake of simplification, the names of particular dynasties engaged in these internecine conflicts have been omitted.

[73] Ibid.

bates. Called *Murjiites*, they advocated the doctrine of suspension of judgment on political issues and the view that each Muslim had the right to his own opinion and should be immune to charges of heresy, so long as he was a monotheist and believed in the message of Muhammed. Not a distinctive sect or school of jurisprudence, the Murjiites laid the groundwork for other more tolerant heterodoxies, such as that espoused by al-Hasan al-Basri in Southern Iraq during the late seventh and early eighth centuries. Additional groups, such as the *Najdites*, advocated anarchism, arguing that inward belief in Islam's religious and moral obligations can supersede discord and obviate the need for government.[74]

After the eleventh century, the only significant rival sect that survived, either corporeally or philosophically, was the Shi'ite. For instance, Kharijite doctrine is little known today because most of its writings were destroyed by opposing sects. Because of violent persecution, remnants of the Kharijites were forced to flee to remote outposts. Today they are found only in Oman, the official faith of which is *Ibadi*, a Kharijite subgroup, and in isolated areas of North Africa.[75] Nevertheless, their existence, along with that of the Murjiites, demonstrates that almost from its very start, Islam contained a tradition of dissent and pluralism, even if it was inhibited from flourishing. As noted by Ann Elizabeth Mayer, if the Kharijites and their thought had become "better known and more widely accepted by Muslims than they presently are, it might be said that the Islamic tradition from the earliest stages has included ideas that anticipated some of the democratic principles that underlie modern human rights norms."[76]

Non-Muslims and Infidels. "Minority rights, it has been suggested, function at the limits of the international law of human rights by testing States in their humanitarian concerns."[77] The manner in which a society treats its ethnically, racially, religiously or linguistically diverse minorities—that is, any uniquely identifiable, non-dominant, and hence vulnerable group—may serve as a litmus test of its commitment to human rights. Accordingly, while members of such groups may not consciously choose to become dissidents, nor conceive of themselves in that way, by very reason of their subordination they may be forced into the role of human rights advocates.

---

[74] Ibid. The mystical *Sufis*, particularly those with pantheistic views, were condemned by early orthodox Muslims. The Persian Hallaj was executed for heresy in 922. See note 52 above.

[75] See Sayed Hassan Amin, *Middle East Legal Systems* (Glasgow, 1985), 292-294.

[76] Mayer, *Islam and Human Rights*, 50, 223 n.18.

[77] Patrick Thornberry, *International Law and the Rights of Minorities* (Oxford, 1991), 394.

Classical Islam saw the world as a battleground where Muslim believers and unbelieving infidels waged war and accordingly divided it into two parts: the territory under Islamic rule, called *dar al-Islam*, and the rest of the world ruled by non-Muslim powers, called *dar al-Harb*, or the territory of war. There was no such state as that of neutrality. A *harbi*, or member of the *dar al-Harb*, was an unsubjugated unbeliever and by definition, an enemy of Islam. According to Majid Khadduri: "The territory of war was the object, not the subject, of Islam, and it was the duty of the Imam, head of the Islamic state, to extend the validity of its Law and Justice to the unbelievers at the earliest possible moment. . . . The instrument through which Islam sought to achieve its objectives was the jihad."[78] Jihad, which literally means "effort," "sacrifice," or "exertion" in the path of God, was a religious and legal duty of each Muslim to combat evil and corruption, to claim the earth for Allah and to spread his word. "Ye should believe in Allah and His messenger, and should strive for the cause of Allah [jihad] with your wealth and your lives" (Qur'an 61:11). Intended to protect the welfare of the Muslim community against enemies, jihad might be analogized to the modern concept of "national security" as a justification for state action. That is, though realistically needed to protect the state, as a concept it could also be abused in the form of imperialism abroad and human rights violations at home.

While often defined as "holy war," a term equivalent to the Western religious concept of "just war," jihad did not necessary require violent military conduct. While dying in battle was considered the highest form of witness to Allah, for which one would attain paradise in the hereafter,[79] the duty could be exercised not only through armed struggle but also through preaching and example, not to mention psychological warfare. If a community of *harbis* agreed to accept the Islamic order, a peace treaty—never to exceed ten years—could be established with them. Only overtly hostile infidels had to be vanquished; thus, jihad, according to some schools of jurisprudence,[80] was only to be invoked defensively.

---

[78] Khadduri, *The Islamic Conception of Justice*, 163, 164.

[79] Esposito, *The Islamic Threat*, 33. However, Shari'a forbid non-*jihad*-justified wars, the killing of non-combatants, and other inhumane acts of combat. See An-Na'im, "Islamic Law, International Relations and Human Rights," 326; Khadduri, *War and Peace in the Law of Islam*, 102-105.

[80] Khadduri notes that early scholars, such as Abu Hanifa and Shaybani who stressed tolerance toward non-believers, "made no explicit declarations that the jihad was a war to be waged against non-Muslims solely on the grounds of disbelief." However, Shafi'i formulated the doctrine that *jihad* was to be waged on unbelievers for reason of their disbelief, not only when they openly fought Muslims. See Shafi'i, *The Islamic Conception of Justice*, 165-166. After the classical period, when Islamic power began to decline, scholars construed *jihad* as only a defensive duty, dormant until actual danger loomed. Ibid., 168-170. Sa'id Hawa, a member of the Muslim Brotherhood movement in Syria, derived five varieties of *jihad* from the Qur'an

Given the Qu'ranic principle, "no compulsion in religion," *harbis* were not necessarily forced to convert to Islam.

But state expansion was another matter. As Abdulaziz Sachedina has noted: "Undoubtedly there were many instances of *jihad* in Islamic history in which the actual motivation was an interest in territorial expansion."[81] Islam was not only to be defended but to be spread. Because of its early history as an expansionary power, the Islamic empire came to dominate a diverse array of other cultures. In the first two decades alone after Muhammed's death, Arab armies conquered Syria, Jerusalem, Persia, Iraq, and Egypt. Within the first century they had reached Spain and North Africa to the West, Byzantium to the North, and India and present-day Afghanistan to the East.[82] In these provinces, Muslim military governors were appointed and poll (*jizya*) and land taxes were imposed on non-Muslim subjects who did not convert to Islam. Local civil control, however, was usually left to the non-Muslims.

Within the *dar al-Islam*, in the civilizations which developed in these wide-ranging imperial territories, four socio-economic classes were identifiable. In descending order of status, they consisted first of the Muslim Arab rulers, who lived in garrisoned residences, paid only a religiously-mandated alms tax, and received a regular payment from the imperial treasury. (Within this class, Muslim men outranked Muslim women.) The second highest class was the non-Arabs who had converted to Islam with such alacrity that they far out-numbered the ruling Arab class and often caused fiscal crises by becoming exempt from the poll taxes. They tended to have originated as pagans, who lacked the Jewish and Christian traditions of martyrdom for their faith. Despite Muhammed's proclamation that "all Muslims are brothers," the converts were not always received wholeheartedly. "Although better educated, they were rarely accepted socially and had to attach themselves to an Arab family or tribe as clients (*mawali*). In the West, the *mawali* became Arabicized," causing the term itself to disappear by the eleventh century. "But in the East the Arabs were ultimately absorbed by their subjects, and while Islam remained the

---

and *Hadith*: jihad through language; jihad through learning; jihad through body and mind; political jihad; and financial jihad. Malik, "Jihad—its Development and Relevance," 32-33. On the duration of peace treaties with non-Muslims, see Majid Khadduri and Herbert J. Liebesny, eds., *Law in the Middle East* (Washington, 1955), 367.

[81] Sachedina, "Freedom of Conscience and Religion," 84. See also Khadduri, *The Islamic Conception of Justice*, 164-170.

[82] See Philip Khuri Hitti, *History of the Arabs* (London, 1937); Khalid Yahya Blankinship, *The End of the Jihad State: The Reign of Hisham Ibn Abd al-Malik and the Collapse of the Umayyads* (Albany, 1994).

dominant religion, Iranian, Turkish, Berber and Indian characteristics prevailed."[83]

Third came the "People of the Book" or those whose faith was based, like Muslims, on revealed scripture (*ahl al-kitab*, thus the name *kitabi*, also known as *dhimmi*, which means "guaranteed"), the Jews and Christians whom Muhammed had decreed be treated with tolerance. "Lo! those who believe, and those who are Jews, and Sabaeans, and Christians— whosoever believeth in [God][84] and the Last Day and doeth right—there shall be no fear come upon them, neither shall they grieve" (Qur'an 5:69). Moreover, *hadiths* report the Prophet as stating: "Whoever wrongs a *dhimmi* or lays on him a burden beyond his strength, I shall be his accuser on the Day of Judgment."[85] The third *Khalifah*, Umar, added the Zoroastrians of Persia to this classification; Mandaeans[86] and others were added later. The justification was that monotheistic, revelatory religions which originated before Islam were embryonic, incomplete, and flawed if not distorted versions of Islam itself, but deserving of at least a limited tolerance.

Dhimmis were conquered peoples who had agreed to submit to Muslim rule. Offered a compact or covenant of protection (*dhimma*, often called the "Pact of Umar" after the Khalifah who originated it), *dhimmis* were permitted certain privileges, including the autonomy to practice their faith, in exchange for payment of the *jizya* tax (by non-indigent, able-bodied males between 16 and 50, fixed according to financial position), certain restrictions on their freedom, and a commitment to live peacefully. A typical *dhimma* contract offered the following privileges:[87] The contract provided protection of *dhimmi* land, crops and livestock,

---

[83] Maan Z. Madina, "The Disruption and Decline of the Arab Empire," in John A. Garraty and Peter Gay, eds., *The Columbia History of the World* (New York, 1972), 271, 267-279.

[84] Pickthall translates this as "Allah," but the sense of the verse is that the People of the Book worship God, the same God as the Muslims, albeit of a different name. Pickthall, *The Glorious Koran*, 103.

[85] Weeramantry, *Islamic Jurisprudence*, 86. Weeramantry also notes a tradition that Muhammed lodged several members of the tribe of Thaqif, who were "unbelievers," in his own mosque. Ibid., 85-86, citing S.A. Ali, *The Spirit of Islam* (London, 1896). See also Bernard Lewis, *The Jews of Islam* (Princeton, 1984), 11 and Siddiqi, *Non-Muslims Under Muslim Rule*, 6.

[86] Mandaeans, also called Subba or John the Baptist Christians, are found in present-day Iraq. Colbert C. Held, *Middle East Patterns: Places, Peoples and Politics* (Boulder, 1994), 283.

[87] See Weeramantry, *Islamic Jurisprudence*, 90-91; Siddiqi, *Non-Muslims Under Muslim Rule*, 5-9; Abul A'la Maududi, *Rights of Non-Muslims in Islamic State* (Lahore, 1961), 10-13; Raphael Patai, *The Seed of Abraham: Jews and Arabs in Contact and Conflict* (New York, 1986), 45-46. A category of persons related to *dhimmis* was the *musta'min*, a *harbi* who lived temporarily in Muslim territory and who was granted an *aman*, or "safe conduct" visa, for entry and temporary residence. While exempt from *jiyza*, a *musta'min* was permitted to practice his religion and engage in an autonomous form of community according to his own laws. Diplomats typically fit into this category. See Lewis, *The Political Language of Islam*, 77-78.

property, life and honor against attack. It offered full rights of inheritance if heirs could establish their right under Islamic law, and full powers of acquisition, sale, transfer, grant and mortgage of land. It offered exemption from military service (or exemption[88] from *jizya* for those willing to render such service). It offered maintenance of *dhimmi* indigents through funds provided by the *zakat* tax paid by Muslims (and not by *dhimmis*). It offered freedom to worship their religion, including protection from desecration of existing holy sites, autonomy in appointment of religious leaders, and freedom from pressure to convert—though scholars differ over whether they had freedom to engage in practices that conflicted with Islam, such as the consumption, sale, and production of alcohol.[89] Finally, the contract offered juridical autonomy (exclusive jurisdiction) in civil matters according to their own laws, and equality of punishment and restitution in criminal matters according to Islamic law (for instance, the same punishment, death, and the same blood-money for murder of both *dhimmis* and Muslims).

These benefits carried concomitant burdens, the badges of *dhimmis'* second-class status. *Dhimmis* could not hold political or judicial office outside their local community structure and could not testify in litigation involving Muslims. They could not marry Muslim women and were forbidden to carry arms, to ride horses or mules, to walk in the middle of the street, to sell their books or religious articles in marketplaces, to raise their voices during worship, or to build churches, tombs, or houses higher than those of Muslims. *Dhimmis* were required to wear distinctive clothing and hair styles, which set them apart from Muslims, and to stand in the presence of Muslims. They were not to convert Muslims to their religion nor prevent one of their own from converting to Islam.[90] Moreover, if the People of the Book refused the *dhimma* compact, they had only the choice of death or converting to Islam—willingly, or after their defeat in war. Hence, scholars such as Lewis and An-Na'im consider the *dhimma* contract to constitute coerced submission rather than a

---

[88] An-Na'im states that exemption from *jizya* in exchange for military service was "rather exceptional and contrary to the predominant practice." Abdullahi Ahmed An-Na'im, "Islamic Law, International Relations and Human Rights: Challenge and Response," *Cornell International Law Journal* 20 (1987): 317, 331 n. 82.

[89] See Weeramantry, *Islamic Jurisprudence*, 86, stating that they had to yield to Islamic law in matters of morality (such as adultery, as well as intoxication), even if their own religion dictated the contrary; compare Siddiqi, *Non-Muslims Under Muslim Rule*, 9, stating that full liberty was granted regarding games of chance and usurious contracts, as well as intoxication. Maududi, *Rights of Non-Muslims*, 13 concurs that they were exempt from punishment for drinking wine and, citing Imam Malik, possibly adultery too. Bernard Lewis states that *dhimma* covenants required refraining from usury. Lewis, *The Jews of Islam*, 11.

[90] See Khadduri and Liebesny, eds., *Law in the Middle East*, 363-364; Patai, *The Seed of Abraham*, 45-46; An-Na'im, *Toward an Islamic Reformation*, 88-91, 144-149.

charter of rights.[91] Lewis would concede, though, that while *dhimmis* were treated in a discriminatory manner, they were not subject to outright persecution.[92]

The fourth and final class consisted of *harbis* who had been made slaves: Greeks, Turks, Armenians, Kurds, Spaniards, Berbers, Africans, and other polytheists and idolators who had been captured as prisoners of war rather than slain in or after battle. Spurning slavery but unable to outlaw it, Muhammed had decreed that slaves be treated the same as their masters in regard to food, clothing, and shelter. Unlike the slaves of ancient Greece or Rome or, indeed, the United States, they could hold property and were supposed to have equal rights before Muslim courts in matters of criminal law. Moreover, they could seek their freedom in court on grounds of cruelty, harsh treatment, or failure to provide maintenance.[93] Nonetheless, outside of these privileges, they lacked the freedom of Muslims and even *dhimmis*. They had the choice only of slavery, conversion to Islam, or death. "Then, when the sacred months have passed [when a treaty with idolators has expired], slay the idolators wherever ye find them, and take them (captive), and besiege them, and prepare for them each ambush. But if they repent and establish worship and pay the poor-due [that is, convert], then leave their way free. Lo! Allah is Forgiving, Merciful" (Qur'an 9:5).

The Islamic toleration of slavery offered various advantages: "economically, through the profitable slave trade, socially through the institution of concubinage and the harem, and politically as individual slaves gained power as favorites, bodyguards, and rulers."[94] But like the *dhimma* compact that established a *de jure* segregation of Muslims and non-Muslims, with clearly inferior status for the latter, it could also be justified on theological grounds:

> Since the Islamic state is basically an ideological state, only those persons are to be primarily entrusted with its administration who believe in its ideology, are conversant with its spirit, and have dedicated themselves to the promotion of the objectives of the state. . . . This does not mean that the Islamic state taboos the utilization of non-Muslims in the service of the state. This only

---

[91] "Since non-Muslims were given the choice between embracing Islam, becoming *dhimmis* and paying *jizya* if they qualified for that status, or fighting the Muslims, it cannot be said that there was no compulsion in religion," states An-Na'im, referring to verse 2:257 of the Qur'an. An-Na'im, *Toward an Islamic Reformation*, 149. See Lewis, *The Jews of Islam*, 10.

[92] While virtually every Western scholar of this subject concedes that Jews were treated more humanely in Islamic lands than in Christian ones, some note that Muslims treated Christians better than they did Jews. See, for instance, Patai, *The Seed of Abraham*, 48.

[93] Weeramantry, *Islamic Jurisprudence*, 139.

[94] Madina, "The Disruption and Decline of the Arab Empire," 271.

means that while availing of the services of non-Muslims, due care should be taken that the Islamic character of the state is not compromised and the ideological demands are not sacrificed on the altar of so called "tolerance."[95]

This might be analogized to the modern concept of "bona fide occupational qualification" in employment law which permits discrimination when the job requires it.[96] In a state where religion and government are fully integrated, the justification would apply to official positions as well as to private ones. Moreover, it is important to recognize that on a broad continuum, apostates who were former Muslims were probably treated more harshly than non-Muslims. And the treatment of minorities in general in Islamic lands of the time was comparably more favorable than in other pre-modern cultures such as the Roman or the Persian.

The Closing Door. The eighth and ninth centuries were a fruitful time for Islam. Through the process of *ijtihad*, the exercise of independent juristic reasoning, Islamic jurists were able to interpret unclear passages of the Qur'an and Sunna in dynamic ways and to discern new rules or to apply old ones where the two primary sources of law were silent. When the fresh interpretations achieved a scholarly consensus (*ijma*), they attained a legal status of their own. Moreover, through exposure to cultures as diverse as the Hellenic, Christian, Syrian, Persian, Judaic, Byzantine-Roman, and Zoroastrian in the regions that had been conquered, both Islamic culture and Islamic law were creatively enriched.[97]

Eventually, however, Shari'a evolved to the point where *ijtihad* and further innovation were deemed no longer necessary. It was in the tenth century that the "door of *ijtihad*" was "closed" and "Islamic jurisprudence . . . resigned itself to the inevitable outcome of its self-imposed terms of reference."[98] As further explained by Coulson: "[The] permissive and inclusive function of ijma is in fact limited to the ratification of the status quo at the time of its formation; from this stage onwards it becomes a purely prohibitive and exclusive principle. Once formed, the

---

[95] Siddiqi, *Non-Muslims Under Muslim Rule*, 2. The author also notes that non-Muslims "got more than their due share in government service. In such lucrative occupations as banking, large commercial ventures, linen trade, land ownership, medical profession etc., the Christians and Jews were well represented and firmly established." Ibid., 8-9.

[96] Section 703(3)(1) of Title VII states: "[I]t shall not be an unlawful employment practice for an employer to hire...on the basis of . . . religion, sex, or national origin in those circumstances where religion, sex or national origin is a bona fide occupational qualification reasonably necessary to the normal operation of that particular business or enterprise." 42 U.S.C. 2000e-2(e). For instance, the Christian Science Church could lawfully prefer employees who are Christian Scientists. *Madsen v. Erwin*, 395 Mass. 715 (1985).

[97] See Hamilton A.R. Gibb, *Studies on the Civilization of Islam* (Boston, 1962).

[98] Coulson, *A History of Islamic Law*, 81.

ijma was infallible; to contradict it was heresy."[99] Henceforth, both the method and spirit of *ijtihad* would be replaced by *taqlid*, the imitation of prior doctrine, and by a much more rigid, formalistic, and often literalist theology.

As the above discussion has revealed, early Islam contained within itself at least two streams: a coercive, aggressive one and a more humanistic, libertarian one. The "closing of the door" resulted in an elevation of the former over the latter. Having conquered so many different peoples in such a short period of time, quickly securing the position of a hegemonic occupation force (thereby provoking the risk of rebellion both among its heterodox adherents and its alien adversaries), Islam forced itself into a perpetual defensive posture, perceiving threats to its autonomy at every turn. As noted by Abdulaziz Sachedina: "In the face of the expansion of Islamic political power and hegemony, the deep Qu'ranic impulse toward religious freedom steadily lost ground—in practice and in theory—to the equally strong concern for defending the faith against active persecution and violent assault. The defensive use of force gradually gave way to more aggressive legal and political policies."[100] While this approach may have spurred Islam's survival during the Crusades and other Christian invasions, as well as through Mongol and Ottoman rule, it would prove less than triumphant when confronted with the advent of European imperialism and other forms of Westernization in the nineteenth and twentieth centuries.

Religious Dissent Under Contemporary Islamic Law

Modern Muslim States. Unlike the classical era of Islam, in which sects and schools of jurisprudence formed the major constituent blocs, contemporary Islam cannot be analyzed in isolation from the modern nation-state, which takes a variety of forms and modes of origin. In the Middle East and Muslim Africa, only Turkey (the Ottoman Empire), Saudi Arabia, Iran (Persia), Egypt, Ethiopia, Sudan (Nubia), and Oman (Muscat and Oman) had independent national identities, as such, that pre-existed the modern era.[101] Most states in this region were created and their borders defined by European powers after World War I; many, in-

---

[99] Ibid., 80. See Khadduri, *The Islamic Conception of Justice*, 78-191 on isolated attempts between the tenth and nineteenth centuries to continue *ijtihad*. An-Na'im, *Toward an Islamic Revolution*, 34-68 covers developments in the period from the nineteenth century to the present.

[100] Sachedina, "Freedom of Conscience and Religion," 85.

[101] See the chapters by Said Arjomand, John Pobee, and Makau wa Mutua included in the sequel to this volume, Witte and van der Vyver, eds., *Religious Human Rights in Global Perspective: Legal Perspectives*.

cluding Algeria, Tunisia, Jordan, Kuwait, Sudan, and Libya, did not achieve sovereignty until after World War II. While some began their modern independence as traditional monarchies, socialist-influenced revolutions turned kingdoms into republics in Egypt, Yemen, and Iraq. Iran's monarchy was replaced by an Islamic revolution in 1979. Of the remaining monarchies, parliamentary elections have recently been held in Jordan, Morocco, and Kuwait, while elections have yet to be held in Saudi Arabia, Oman, or Qatar.[102] The Muslim Asian states of Pakistan, Malaysia, and Indonesia are a parliamentary democracy, a constitutional monarchy, and a military-dominated republic, respectively. Afghanistan's government is currently in "post-Communist Islamic transition."

Regional alliances must also be taken into account, given that Islam, or Islamic/Arab culture, often provides their strongest unifying tie. The Organization of the Islamic Conference and the League of Arab States are predominantly political in mission, while the Organization of Arab Petroleum Exporting Countries, the Economic Cooperation Organization and the Gulf Economic Council chiefly perform economic functions.[103] The six former Soviet Central Asian republics, whose current governmental form can, like Afghanistan's, best be described as "transitional post-Communist," have along with Afghanistan recently joined Iran, Turkey, and Pakistan in the Economic Cooperation Organization to become the third biggest trading bloc after NAFTA and the European Union. Twenty-five percent of the world's Muslim population is now combined in this one bloc.[104]

An analysis of the modern-day interpretations and practices of Islam regarding the same three categories of religious dissidents just reviewed requires an introduction to the legal context in which they sit. Accordingly, this part of the chapter will first describe the development of the constitutional provisions in majority Muslim states concerning religion and make a brief mention of statutory reform. It will then touch on these states' positions on the relevant international law.

Constitutional and Statutory Law. Classical Islamic law contained no system of constitutional law in the sense of machinery to control abuses of autocratic state power, to oversee the regulation of governmental acts, or to hold high officials accountable to fundamental principles of justice. These are modern inventions of Western origin, growing out of the Enlightenment period's glorification of the individual and the distrust of the

---

[102] See Iliya Harik, "Pluralism in the Arab World," *Journal of Democracy* 5 (July, 1994): 43, 52. See also Held, *Middle East Patterns*, 173-175.

[103] See brief descriptions in Mayer, "Current Thinking on Human Rights," 175-177; and *Treaties and Alliances of the World*.

[104] "Central Asian Nations Join ECO," *Reuters* (November 27, 1992): 19.

state. With the onset of the Middle East's colonial era in the nineteenth century, however, growing movements of Muslims exposed to Western ideas began to agitate for the introduction of European models of constitutional monarchy, perhaps with the hope that they would help usher in a wave of prosperity and freedom comparable to that enjoyed by the European powers. While the Muslim constitutionalists often fought with conservative clerics, who believed that constitutional organs and constitutional freedoms conflicted with Islamic law, this was not always the case. For instance, the influential grand *mufti* (religious-legal figure) of Egypt, Muhammad 'Abduh, who died in 1905, was an advocate of their compatibility, while in 1909 the Turkish sultan stated publicly that constitutional government was "prescribed" by the Shari'a.[105]

The first Muslim constitution was promulgated in Tunesia in 1861; Turkey and Persia soon followed, with the Persian terms *dustur* and *kanun-i esasi* being adopted by both Arabic and Turkish as equivalents for the Latin-rooted "constitution" or the more literal "fundamental law." (Although the Shari'a offers a variety of words for "law," it has none connoting a human enactment, fundamental or otherwise, as law is believed to derive only from God's revelations.)[106] With the exception of the traditional Islamic monarchies of Saudi Arabia and Oman, all Muslim states promulgated written constitutions. This development reflected a Middle Eastern trend toward secular nationalism replacing religion as a collectivist organizing mechanism. A backlash would form later.

Today, 34 majority Muslim states have written constitutions.[107] Of those, 23 (to which should be added Oman and Saudi Arabia) have offi-

---

[105] Mayer, *Islam and Human Rights*, 50-52, 78; Lewis, *The Political Language of Islam*, 113-114. See generally John J. Donohue and John L Esposito, eds., *Islam in Transition: Muslim Perspectives* (New York, 1982).

[106] Ibid.

[107] The 34 states with 50% or more Muslims (see note 19, above) whose constitutions are published in Albert P. Blaustein and Gilbert H. Flanz *Constitutions of the Countries of the World*, (Dobbs Ferry, 1993), with irregular updates, are: Afghanistan, Albania, Algeria, Bahrain, Bangladesh, Brunei, Comoros, Djibouti, Egypt, Gambia, Guinea, Indonesia, Iran, Iraq, Jordan, Kuwait, Lebanon, Libya, Malaysia, Mali, Mauritania, Morocco, Nigeria, Niger, Pakistan, Qatar, Senegal, Somalia, Sudan, Syria, Tunisia, Turkey, United Arab Emirates, and Yemen. Libya's constitution was abrogated by the Qaddafi regime in 1977 but is included here in the analysis of the 34.

The Blaustein and Flanz compilation does not yet contain the constitutions of the newly independent, majority Muslim states of Azerbaijan, Bosnia-Herzegovina, Kazakhstan, Kirghizistan, Tajikistan, Turkmenistan, and Uzbekistan. See brief descriptions of these in the chapter by Paul Mojzes included in the sequel to this volume, Witte and van der Vyver, eds., *Religious Human Rights in Global Perspective: Legal Perspectives*. Oman and Saudi Arabia do not have constitutions. When these are added together with the 34, the total number of majority Muslim states equals 43. Another new state, Eritrea, has close to 50% Muslims. *The World Almanac and Book of Facts 1994*, 761.

cially proclaimed Islam to be the state religion and/or Shari'a to be the principal source of law.[108] A few, such as those of Turkey, the Gambia, and Senegal, are avowedly secular, while Iran's is explicitly Islamic; all the other constitutions are attempts at fusing the two perspectives, typically by relegating Shari'a and Shari'a court jurisdiction to a limited area such as family law. These and other relevant provisions concerning freedom of religion in the constitutions of Muslim states are described in detail in the sequel to this anthology.[109] For purposes of this chapter, the two constitutions of Iran deserve special mention. The 1906-1907 document arose out of a tumultuous context in which nationalists sought a Western-type constitution to constrain the despotic shahs, while Shi'ite clerics vehemently condemned its advocates as heretics. As promulgated, it contained limitations on the freedom of publications which were heretical or hurtful of Islam, and permitted freedom of association only where religious order was not provoked.[110] Despite these restrictions, the Ayatollah Khomeini was later to denounce its advocates as "agents of British imperialism."[111]

Khomeini's own, self-consciously Islamic constitution, drafted by the cleric-dominated Assembly of Experts at the end of 1979, merges state and religious authority and expressly and completely subordinates hu-

---

[108] Oman and Saudia Arabia have no written constitutions, but their legal systems are based on Shari'a. Oman is an absolute monarchy; the *Ibadi* sect, derived from the Kharijites, form the majority. The main source of Saudi law is the Wanhabi interpretation of the Hanbali school of jurisprudence, which rejects analogy and *ijtihad*. Saudi legislation, which supplements Shari'a, is referred to as "regulations" (*nazam*) rather than "law," which can only come from God. Amin, *Middle East Legal Systems*, 292-294, 312-313. In response to both internal and external pressures for reform, in 1992 Saudi Arabia promulgated a Basic Law which purports to provide a body of human rights but in fact falls short of even the quite deficient Cairo Declaration of Human Rights. King Fahd has denied that it constitutes a step toward Saudi constitutionalism. See Mayer, "Universal Versus Islamic Human Rights," 353, 350-364.

The 11 additional states which do not establish Islam include Albania, whose Communist-era constitution "recognizes no religion whatever;" Mali, which undertakes "to defend the republican and secular form of the state;" Nigeria, which adopts no state religion; and Senegal and Turkey, which are explicitly secular. Indonesia's constitution is "based upon belief in the One, Supreme God," not mentioning any particular religion. Lebanon, whose population is approximately 75% Muslim and 25% Christian, respects "all religions and creeds," and guarantees "the free exercise of all forms of worship—provided that public order is not disturbed."

[109] See the chapters by Johan van der Vyver, David Little, Said Arjomand, Makau wa Mutua, and John S. Pobee in the second volume of this collection, Witte and van der Vyver, eds., *Religious Human Rights in Global Perspective: Legal Perspectives*.

[110] Mayer, *Islam and Human Rights*, 78-79. See also Azar Tabari, "The Role of the Clergy in Modern Iranian Politics," in Nikki R. Keddie, ed., *Religion and Politics in Iran: Shi'ism from Quietism to Revolution* (New Haven, 1983), 58-59; Donohue and Esposito, eds., *Islam in Transition*, 287-296. The Ayatollah Khomeini later praised Nuri on this point. Rose, "*Velayat-e Faqih* and the Recovery of Islamic Identity in the Thought of Ayatollah Khomeini," 182-183.

[111] Ibid., 183.

man rights to Islamic standards and Islamic goals. For instance, in stating that the role of the executive power is to pave the way for the creation of an Islamic society, the Preamble proclaims that "the confinement of the executive power within any kind of complex and inhibiting system that delays or impedes the attainment of this goal is rejected by Islam." In fact, although the parliament is maintained, sovereignty is based not in the people but in God, an unprecedented concept in Islamic law.[112] The Council of Guardians, all of whom are Islamic clerics, has the authority to review and veto any secular legislation that conflicts with Shari'a. This supremacy makes the state a theocracy rather than a republic. (In fact, it was an autocracy, as Khomeini, before his death, often vetoed the Guardians.) Ideology similarly infuses the sections on the Iranian military, "an Islamic army," which is responsible not only for guarding the country's frontiers, "but also for fulfilling the ideological mission of jihad in God's way; that is, extending the sovereignty of God's law throughout the world (in accordance with the Qur'anic verse: 'Prepare against them whatever force you are able to muster, and strings of horses, striking fear into the enemy of God and your enemy, and others besides them' [Qur'an 8:60])."

While the formally Shi'ite Iranian constitution accords full respect to the various Sunni schools of jurisprudence, "Zoroastrian, Jewish and Christian Iranians are the only recognized religious minorities," according to article 13. Baha'is, who have been persecuted in Iran since before the 1979 revolution (see discussion below), are not even mentioned. Other provisions purport to guarantee freedom of the press, assembly, and association—provided that they are not "detrimental to the fundamental principles" of Islam. Similarly, non-Muslims are to be treated "according to the dictates of virtue and Islamic justice," so long as they "do not become involved in conspiracies and activities which are anti-Islamic or are against" Iran. This appears to be a warning that opposition by non-Muslims will meet with harsher punishment than the same activity committed by Muslims.[113]

Given Iran's dismal revolutionary and post-revolutionary track record on human rights and its failure to "lay great store by principles of le-

---

[112] Ann Elizabeth Mayer, "Islam and the State," *Cardozo Law Review* 12 (1991): 1015, 1037.

[113] See Mayer, *Islam and Human Rights*, 155-158. See also ibid., 78-86, 128-132, and 177-182 for Mayer's other comments on human rights in the 1979 Iranian constitution. The book also describes the "Draft Islamic Constitution," a Sunni alternative to the Iranian constitution, prepared in the same year, 1979, at the Islamic Research Academy of Cairo, affiliated with al-Azhar University.

gality, irrespective of whether these were religious or secular,"[114] it can be said that Iran's new constitution has turned the notion of constitutionalism on its head, allowing it to serve as a warrant for, rather than a safeguard against, tyranny. Whether this demonstrates the ultimate incompatibility of liberalism and Islam, or at least Shi'ite Islam, remains to be seen. At least one scholar believes that the condition of human rights in post-revolutionary Iran has broader implications, given developments in the Sudan and Pakistan and the threat of Islamicist take-overs in Algeria and elsewhere, including the Central Asian states of the former U.S.S.R.[115]

While the relevant provisions of statutory law in Muslim majority states are too numerous even to begin to summarize here, mention should be made of the significant reforms undertaken in many such countries. In most cases, these were concomitant with the reception of European law, the French civil and penal codes having particular influence. For instance, as early as 1858, the French-based Penal Code of the Ottoman Empire abolished the traditional *hudud* punishments—with the notable exception of the death penalty for apostasy. In the post-World War II period, numerous other states, ranging from Morocco, Tunesia, and Algeria in the Maghreb, to Iraq, Iran, and Yemen in the Gulf region, to Pakistan further East, all modernized their family law, with relatively positive impact on the legal status of women. Moreover, with the notable exception of Saudi Arabia, Muslim states now permit *dhimmis* to obtain citizenship.[116]

Reforms of this magnitude and kind required significant doctrinal and ideological deliberation. As explained by N.J. Coulson: "If the law is to retain its form as the expression of the divine command, if indeed it is to remain Islamic law, reforms cannot be justified on the ground of social necessity per se; they must find their juristic basis and support in principles which are Islamic in the sense that they are endorsed, expressly or implicitly, by the divine will."[117] Reform advocates invoked the methodology of *ijtihad*, the Shari'a-endorsed mode of reasoned interpretation, in justification. While primarily limited to the easily severable area of family

---

[114] ". . . and that it was even quite prepared to indulge in violations of basic tenets of Islamic law where the latter stood in the way of its political objectives." Mayer, *Islam and Human Rights*, 86.

[115] Mayer, "Current Muslim Thinking on Human Rights," 142.

[116] See Piscatory, "Human Rights in Islamic Political Culture," 149; Weeramantry, *Islamic Jurisprudence*, 43; Arzt, "The Application of International Human Rights Law in Islamic States," 222-224. See generally J.N.D. Anderson, "Modern Trends in Islam: Legal Reform and Modernisation in the Middle East," *International and Comparative Law Quarterly* 20 (1971): 1, 5; Norman Anderson, *Law Reform in the Muslim World* (London, 1976).

[117] Coulson, *A History of Islamic Law*, 6-7.

law, these reforms serve as an important precedent for future efforts involving a wider range of subjects. If modernizations can be legitimized in regard to the rights of women, why not also for non-Muslims, apostates, and other religious dissidents? Moreover, international law requires states to rescind legislation that serves to discriminate on the ground of religion or belief and to enact legislation to give effect to the right of religious freedom.[118]

As will be noted more fully below, not only have most Muslim states failed to extend the reach of *ijtihad* into these additional areas, but since the 1970s, Islamic revivals in states such as Iran, Pakistan, Libya and the Sudan have in fact ushered in a "reislamicization" of their secular statutes.[119]

International Law. Despite the long-term existence of a scholarly body of Islamic international law, known as *siyar*,[120] the modern relationship between Islamic law and international law is a tortuous one. The case of Libya is emblematic in this regard. Even though international terrorism is a subject unmistakenly regulated by international law, Libya's Colonel Qaddafi has repeatedly insisted that he will not hand over the Libyan suspects in the Pan Am 103 bombing case to British or American authorities unless they will be tried by an Islamic court, with an Islamic jury, a Muslim prosecution team, and a court that "opens its session with recitation from the Koran."[121] Calling such an eventuality, if his conditions were ever to be met, an "historical turning point," Qaddafi explains that it would be a "test" that would "expose [the non-Muslims] and confirm their hostility to Islam."[122] Libya had rebuffed a United Nations Security Council request to cooperate in establishing responsibility for the bombing. Yet it was willing to use international law affirmatively in the same matter, when it sued the United States and the United Kingdom in

---

[118] See article 2(2) of the International Covenant on Civil and Political Rights and article 4(2) of the U.N. Declaration on the Elimination of All Forms of Intolerance and Discrimination Based on Religion or Belief.

[119] See Esposito, *The Islamic Threat*, 77-118; Mayer, *Islam and Human Rights*, 30-42.

[120] *Siyar* included the law concerning *dhimmis, jihad*, and *aman*, described above. Rather than being derived from the Qur'an, Islamic international law was developed by the eminent Hanafi jurist al-Shaybani (749-805) to guide Islamic states in their relations with other nations. See Majid Khadduri, *The Islamic Law of Nations: Shayb an a's Siyar* (Baltimore, 1966); Mohammad T. Al-Ghunaimi, *The Muslim Conception of International Law and the Western Approach* (The Hague, 1968); Arzt, "The Application of International Human Rights Law in Islamic States," 210-213.

[121] "Qadhafi Says Lockerbie Suspects Must be Tried by an Islamic Court," *BBC Summary of World Broadcasts* (February 18, 1994) (ME/1925/MED) (translation from Libyan TV, Tripoli).

[122] Ibid. In the same speech, Qaddafi decried American intervention in the crisis in Somalia. "We reject absolutely Christians dealing with Islamic issues." Ibid.

the International Court of Justice over the effect of the Security Council's resolutions and the interpretation and application of the Montreal Aircraft Sabotage Convention, of which all three states are parties.[123]

States cannot choose when they want to be part of the international community and when they do not. All Muslim countries are members of the United Nations, whose Charter states the organization's purposes to include "international cooperation . . . in promoting and encouraging respect for human rights and for fundamental freedoms for all without distinction as to race, sex, language or religion. . . ."[124] These principles are not necessarily in conflict with the fundamental tenets of Islamic law. For instance, international law does not require the separation of church and state, so Muslim governments are not absolutely precluded from enacting Shari'a within the formal structure of their domestic legal systems. Indeed, it could even be argued that the right to self-determination under the United Nations Charter and other international treaties includes the right of Muslims to apply Islamic law in their public as well as in their private lives.[125] In the most telling evidence of modern Muslim support for international law, none of the 23 Muslim states to ratify the International Covenant on Civil and Political Rights has entered any reservations as to Article 18's provisions on religious freedom, including its prohibition on coercion in the choice of religion.[126] Yet numerous Muslim states which have ratified the Convention on the Elimination of All Forms of Discrimination Against Women have entered reservations to the effect that they consider themselves bound to the treaty only to the extent that its provisions are not in conflict with Shari'a.[127] This contrast arguably supports the assent to global norms of religious freedom in the Muslim state parties to the Covenant.

---

[123] See Cases Concerning Questions of Interpretation And Application of the 1971 Montreal Convention Arising From the Aerial Incident at Lockerbie (Libyan Arab Jamahiriya v. United States of America and Libyan Arab Jamahiriya v. United Kingdom), Provisional Measures, Orders of 14 April 1992, I.C.J. Reports 3 and 114, concerning Security Council Resolutions 731 and 748. See also Case Concerning the Territorial Dispute (Libyan Arab Jamahiriya/Chad), Judgment, I.C.J. Reports 6 (1994), another recent resort by Libya to a convenient international forum.

[124] Article 1(3), Charter of the United Nations, 59 Stat. 1031, T.S. No. 993, 3 Bevans 1153 (June 26, 1945).

[125] This position has been suggested by An-Na'im in *Toward an Islamic Reformation*, 9, and in "Islamic Law, International Relations and Human Rights," 318-319.

[126] See note 24 above for the full list of Muslim state parties.

[127] See Rebecca J. Cook, "Reservations to the Convention on the Elimination of All Forms of Discrimination Against Women," *Virginia Journal of International Law* 30 (1990): 643; and Arzt, "The Application of International Human Rights Law in Islamic States," 218-221; Donna J. Sullivan, "Gender Equality and Religious Freedom: Toward a Framework for Conflict Resolution," *New York University Journal of International Law and Politics* 24 (1992): 806.

A conspicuous, but not surprising absentee from much of the international human rights treaty regime is Saudi Arabia. It abstained from the 1948 United Nations General Assembly vote on the Universal Declaration of Human Rights—all other Muslim states which were then United Nations members voted affirmatively—and is not a party to the International Convention on the Elimination of All Forms of Racial Discrimination, the Covenants on Civil and Political Rights and on Economic, Social and Cultural Rights, the Convention on the Elimination of All Forms of Discrimination against Women, the Convention Against Torture, or the Convention on the Rights of the Child. It did, however, play a part in the drafting of the Universal Declaration and of the Covenant on Civil and Political Rights. In both fora, the Saudi representative, al-Barundi, strenuously objected to the instruments' respective articles on religious freedom, arguing that giving international legitimacy to the right to change religions would insult Muslims, invite missionaries into the Arabian peninsula, and "raise doubts in the minds of ordinary people to whom their religion [is] a way of life."[128]

Perhaps Saudi Arabia should be applauded for being more honest in its approach to international law than those states, Muslim and non-Muslim alike, which ratify treaties that conflict with their domestic law with no evident intention of complying with the international standards. Several United Nations bodies have considered the question of whether states which recognize an official state religion are in conflict with the principle of non-discrimination. The Human Rights Committee and a United Nations Special Rapporteur on religious discrimination concluded that nothing can be inferred from the mere fact of such recognition that other religions or their members are not treated equally under the law.[129] Nevertheless, international law does not allow states to invoke religious law, or indeed any domestic law, as an excuse for breaching their treaty obligations. That is why states such as Finland, Sweden, and

---

[128] Ibid., 216-218. Afghanistan, Iraq, and Syria initially joined Saudi Arabia in seeking to delete the Universal Declaration provision on changing religion and criticized Lebanon, whose representative, a Christian, served as a principal drafter of the Declaration and initial advocate of this particular phrase, for "insensitivity to its own Muslim people." However, they later voted in favor of the Declaration. Ibid, 216. See also John Kelsay, "Saudi Arabia, Pakistan, and the Universal Declaration of Human Rights," in Little et al., eds., *Human Rights and the Conflict of Cultures*, 33. Iran under Khomeini voiced a Saudi-like rejection of the Universal Declaration, claiming through its UN representative that it reflected a "secular understanding of the Judaeo-Christian tradition" which could obviously not be implemented by Muslims. Therefore, Iran would "not hesitate to violate its provisions, since it had to choose between violating the divine law of the country and violating secular conventions." U.N. General Assembly, 39th Session, Third Committee, December 7, 1984, U.N. Doc A/C.3/SR.65, p.20.

[129] See Sullivan, "Gender Equality and Religious Freedom," 806.

Mexico have officially objected to the reservations entered by certain Muslim states to the Convention on All Forms of Discrimination Against Women to the effect that Shari'a limits their obligations. International law requires that reservations not be incompatible with the object and purpose of a treaty, which in this case was the elevation of the rights of women over religious rules and customs which treat them unequally.[130]

The true test of the relationship between contemporary Islamic law and international human rights law will only come when—or if—viable implementation measures are adopted by Muslim states. Only seven of the 23 Muslim state parties to the International Covenant on Civil and Political Rights have ratified its Optional Protocol, which subjects states to petitions by individual human rights victims.[131] On the regional level, 15 Muslim states are parties to the African Charter on Human and Peoples' Rights, but the Commission created under that instrument does not operate as a true recourse-mechanism for complainants. There is no formally adopted Asian charter on human rights, and neither the Organization of the Islamic Conference nor the Arab League has made human rights a topic of major concern. While the OIC adopted the oxymoronic "Universal Islamic Declaration of Human Rights," it contains no enforcement procedures. In 1968, the Arab League created a Permanent Arab Regional Commission on Human Rights, but it was not intended to receive individual complaints. It has been said that "[t]he paucity of published information about the activities of the Commission suggests that it has not made a conspicuous contribution. Indeed, many Arab lawyers are unaware of its existence."[132] A number of non-governmental Arab or Islamic human rights organizations do exist, but they should not be taken as an adequate substitute for official state action in implementation of

---

[130] Ibid., 807; Arzt, "The Application of International Human Rights Law in Islamic States," 220-221. See articles 19 and 27, Vienna Convention on the Law of Treaties, U.N. Doc. A/CONF. 39/27 (1969). States may only override a treaty obligation if it manifestly conflicts with an internal law of fundamental importance. Ibid, article 46. One could argue that state adherence to Shari'a fulfills this condition. The constitutions of some Muslim states such as Bahrain, Niger, and Djibouti provide that international law commitments that conflict with their constitutional or other internal law will not take effect unless the constitutional or internal law has been amended.

[131] The seven are Algeria, Gambia, Guinea, Libya, Niger, Senegal, and Somalia. A total of 74 states are parties to the Optional Protocol. *Multilateral Treaties Deposited with the Secretary-General*, 158.

[132] Istvan Pogany, "Arab Attitudes Toward International Human Rights Law," *Connecticut Journal of International Law* 2 (1987): 373. A proposal to amend the Arab League's charter to include express references to human rights has apparently been dropped. Ibid., 372.

international standards. In fact, many of these NGO's have themselves been subject to persecution for advocating on behalf of human rights.[133]

Categories of Religious Dissidents. This section of the chapter will present for each of the three categories of religious dissident used above a non-comprehensive selection of recent cases. Within each category, the cases will be followed by reference to the relevant Shari'a and modern international legal standards, so that conclusions can be drawn as to whether the contemporary Muslim states are in compliance with either or both of these two sets of norms.

Apostates and Blasphemers. While the notorious case of Salman Rushdie is the best known example of punishment for apostasy in contemporary Islam, his is by no means a singular instance. Recent examples can be grouped into three categories: (1) officially state-sanctioned enforcement actions; (2) extra-legal enforcement of apostasy decrees issued by vigilante extremist groups; and (3) mixed cases.

In the first category one should note new legislation in Yemen and the Sudan penalizing apostasy and blasphemy. In Yemen, the 1990 Law on the Press and Publications bans any publication which, inter alia, "prejudices the Islamic faith and its lofty principles or belittles religions or humanitarian creeds . . . [and which] distort[s] the image of the Yemeni, Arab or Islamic heritage."[134] While capital punishment for apostasy was first introduced by coup-leader Nimeiri in 1983, article 126 of the post-Nimeiri 1991 Sudanese Penal Code now authorizes the death penalty for any non-repenting Muslim who "advocates the rejection of Islamic beliefs or announces his own rejection of Islam by word or act." Although recent converts are by law to be treated more leniently, many fear prosecution should they revert to their original religion, as they tend

---

[133] Some indigenous Muslim NGO's working in the human rights field include the Arab Organization for Human Rights, the Gulf National Forum, the Union (sometimes called Federation) of Arab Lawyers, the Cairo-based staff of the periodical *Civil Society*, the Iranian Lawyers Association, the Iranian Committee for the Defense of Human Rights, the Iran-based Freedom Movement, the Association for the Defense of Freedom and the Sovereignty of the Iranian Nation, and the North African Students for Freedom of Action. (This list does not include feminist groups, national secessionist movements nor opposition political parties.) See Virginia N. Sherry, "The Human Rights Movement in the Arab World: An Active and Diverse Community of Human Rights Advocates Exists in Several Countries of the Region," Human Rights Watch, *Special Middle East Watch Issue* (New York, 1990), 6-7, as well as the reports of Amnesty International. On the short-lived Committee for the Defense of Legitimate Rights, the first independent human rights group inside Saudi Arabia, see Mayer, "Universal Versus Islamic Human Rights," 365-368; "Saudi Arabia: Son of Banned Rights Group Spokesman Arrested," *Amnesty Action* (Fall 1994), 2. On the fate of some of the Iranian groups, see Middle East Watch, "Guardians of Thought: Limits on Freedom of Expression in Iran" (New York, August, 1993), 114-116.

[134] Middle East Watch, "Yemen: Steps Toward Civil Society" (New York, November, 1992), 8.

to be Christians and animists as well as Ethiopian refugees who nominally converted to Islam or took Muslim names in order to receive relief, avoid discrimination, or marry Muslims.[135] In a recent case illustrating the potential reach of this law, Sudan's justice minister as well as its government-controlled press attacked a human rights investigator reporting to the United Nations Commission on Human Rights. For his report, which describes Sudan's slave trade and notes that its criminal code authorizes punishments such as amputation and crucifixion, Gaspar Biro, a Hungarian law professor, was called "satanic" and "an enemy of Islam" guilty of "blasphemy."[136]

Other state-sanctioned examples reveal the potential for abuse of state power. In Indonesia, two college students, one Muslim, one Catholic, were convicted in 1992 of blasphemy and publicly defaming Muslims when during a rock concert they engaged in a spontaneous word play involving puns on Qu'ranic verses.[137] In Saudi Arabia, two newspaper editors were sentenced to prison and to hundreds of lashes for printing a comic strip from the syndicated series "B.C." which facetiously questioned the existence of God, while in Iran, a cartoonist and his magazine editor were similarly sentenced for a drawing of a soccer player adjudged to resemble the late Ayatollah Khomeini; both cases drew the attention of American cartoonist Garry Trudeau.[138]

Even more disturbing are the non-official vigilante cases, which often result in brutal assassinations, ordered without trial by Islamic revivalists in countries where they threaten government stability. While militants in Egypt and Algeria have killed government officials, foreigners, religious minorities, and average Muslim civilians in the course of their struggles for power, when they target intellectuals they often rely on the Shari'a as a rationale. For instance, Farag Fouda, one of Egypt's leading secular in-

---

[135] Africa Watch, "Sudan: New Islamic Penal Code Violates Basic Human Rights" (April 9, 1991), 7-8. While the Penal Code only applies in Northern Sudan, many non-Muslim Southern Sudanese now live in the North.

[136] See Ringle, "The Next Rushdie?"; Paul Lewis, "Sudan Calls UN Official a Blasphemer," *The International Herald Tribune* (March 9, 1994).

[137] Asia Watch, "Indonesia: Students Jailed for Puns," (March 16, 1993). One pun altered the traditional Muslim greeting, "Peace be upon you with the mercy and blessing of God" to "Peace be upon you, heavy metal experts." Other puns were sexual in nature. Ibid., 1. See also "Indonesia Calls for Reinforcement of Muslim Identity," *National Public Radio* Transcript #1451-13 (October 10, 1994).

[138] Garry Trudeau, "Drawing, Dangerously," *The New York Times* (July 10, 1994): E19. On the soccer example and others from Iran, including a sewing pattern said to contain a profile of Khomeini in the folds of a dress, see Middle East Watch, *Guardians of Thought*. Apostasy and blasphemy charges are not the only method of government censorship. An Iranian author was arrested on charges of espionage and drug abuse for criticizing the clerical leadership, a move protested by 150 Iranian writers. "Iranian Writers Ask for an End to Censorship," *The New York Times* (November 1, 1994): A10.

tellectuals and a vocal critic of militant Islamists as well as the Egyptian government, was murdered in June 1992, his teenage son also wounded in the attack. A statement by the group al-Gama'a al-Islamiya, which took responsibility, justified the killing because Fouda was an apostate, an advocate of separation of religion and state, and an opponent of the use of Shari'a as Egyptian law.[139] His murderers were defended by a senior theologian, Sheik Ahmad Ghazali, who stated in court that Fouda and "secularists" like him are apostates who should be put to death by the government. If the government failed to carry out that "duty," the Sheik testified, individuals were free to do so.[140]

Other Egyptian writers, such as Nobel Prize winner Naguib Mahfouz, are subject to relentless attacks as "corrupters of youth" and "the filth of the artistic community." Mahfouz, who had publicly denounced the death warrant against Rushdie and supported Anwar Sadat's peace accord with Israel, was "excommunicated" by the *fatwa* of Sheik Omar Abdul Rahman, who demanded that the author denounce his own 1959 novel, *Children of Gebelawi.* The author was recently stabbed in the neck by a militant.[141] In Algeria, the poet and teacher Youssef Sebti was found with his throat cut in his office in an Islamic militant-controlled region in December 1993, while in May of that year, Algerian writer Tahar Djaout was murdered.[142] A university professor was shot after he refused to start his classes with readings from the Qur'an. These are only three of the over 50 Algerian intellectuals murdered since early

---

[139] See Amnesty International, "Egypt: Grave Human Rights Abuses Amid Political Violence" (May, 1993), 11; Farag Foda, "A Murdered Writer's Prophecy," *The New York Times* (November 10, 1993): A27. Sheik Omar Abdul Rahman, the spiritual leader of the militant group that took responsibility for Fouda's killing, is also the lead defendant in the second New York City terror conspiracy case.

[140] Youssef M. Ibrahim, "Fundamentalists Impose Culture on Egypt," *The New York Times* (February 3, 1994): A1, A10. See also Youssef M. Ibrahim, "As Islamic Fundamentalist Abroad Talks Freely on Limits on Freedom," *The New York Times* (January 9, 1994): E7.

[141] Karim Alrawi, "Goodbye to the Enlightenment," *Index on Censorship* 23 (May/June, 1994): 112, 113; "Fires of Hell," *Index on Censorship* 23 (May/June, 1994): 118; Chris Hedges, "Novelist's Unwitting Role: Sword Against Militants," *The New York Times* (November 15, 1994): A4. The Egyptian government has ended its ban on *The Children of Gebelawi,* which will now be reissued there for the first time since 1959, but given the continuing threats against Mahfouz, publication may constitute "a second assassination attempt." Ibid.

[142] "Algerian Poet Slain in Muslim Militant Area," *The New York Times* (December 29, 1993): A5. Egypt and Algeria are not the only sites of such vigilante murders of writers. For instance, the Saudi Arabian poet, Sadiq Melallah, was decapitated. See *For Rushdie: Essays by Arab and Muslim Writers in Defense of Free Speech* (New York, 1994) (unpaginated Publisher's Statement). This book, created by over 100 intellectuals from a dozen countries, was first published in French in 1993 in order to draw attention to the threats and assassinations by Islamic extremists against numerous writers, not only Rushdie. Alan Riding, "Muslim Thinkers Rally for Rushdie," *The New York Times* (November 4, 1994): C17.

1993 because of their secular views.[143] The militants, however, claim the intellectuals are targeted because they collaborate with the military government, which cancelled January 1992 National Assembly elections that Islamists would have won.

The vigilante cases often shade into the "mixed cases," in which official state pronouncements serve to encourage private actions—or vice versa. For instance, after a committee at state-sponsored Cairo University denied full professorship to Nasr Hamid Abuzeid, he became a target of the same group that had killed Fouda. The committee had determined that his scholarship—on eighth century Islamic writing—had contained "discussions resembling atheism."[144] In Pakistan, a 1986 blasphemy law, which mandates fines, life imprisonment, or the death penalty for anyone who "by any imputation, innuendo, or insinuation, directly or indirectly, defiles the sacred name of the Holy Prophet," has given encouragement to militants. In a move reminiscent of Southern lynchings of African-Americans, a frenzied mob, inspired by a Pakistani cleric, stormed a jail and set fire to a man awaiting trial for burning a page of the Qur'an. He had accidentally slipped and fallen onto a stove while holding the holy book.[145] Several hundred people, including Christians as well as Muslims, have been arrested under the Pakistani blasphemy law; at least two have been sentenced to death.[146]

"Mixed cases" can also operate in the other direction, with the government taking action in response to militant outcries. In Bangladesh, prominent author Taslima Nasrin attained the unofficial title, "the female Salman Rushdie," when the Council of Islamic Soldiers accused her of blasphemy for her latest novel, *Lajja*, and formed a 100-person death squad to kill her. Her fifteenth book, which depicts a Hindu family's torment by Muslims in conjunction with the Babri Mosque controversy in India, sold a remarkable 50,000 copies before the government banned it. In earlier works, she had criticized the treatment of women in Islamic

---

[143] Middle East Watch, "Human Rights Abuses in Algeria: No One is Spared"(January, 1994), 59. About 60 foreigners and 4,000 Algerians have been killed in the crossfires of the two-and-a-half-year armed struggle between Islamicists and the military government, which has caused thousands more, including many intellectuals and professionals, to flee to France and other Arab countries. Lynn Terry, "Islamic Fundamentalists Murder Thousands of Algerians," *NPR Morning Edition* Transcript No. 1408-5 (August 10, 1994). See the collection of essays by censored Algerian authors, "Between Two Fires," *Index on Censorship* 23 (September/October, 1994): 135.

[144] Ibrahim, "Fundamentalists Impose Culture on Egypt."

[145] John Ward Anderson, "Islamic Vigilante Justice: Critics Say Pakistani Blasphemy Laws Fuel a Rise in Religious Fanaticism," *International Herald Tribune* (June 18-19, 1994): 1.

[146] "Pakistan: Asia Watch Says Drive to Islamicize Laws Hurts Rights," *Inter Press Service* (September 19, 1993); Human Rights Watch/Asia, "Persecuted Minorities and Writers in Pakistan" (September, 1993).

states. Although Bangladeshi society is relatively secular, crowds as large as 200,000 have supported militant demands for her death for allegedly stating in a newspaper—Indian, not Bangladeshi—that the Qur'an should be thoroughly revised to eliminate passages which discriminate against women. She claims she was misquoted, that it is Shari'a that should be revised, not the Qur'an. Despite this significant distinction, on the same day that militants stormed through the city of Dhaka, a local court issued a warrant for her arrest for "deliberately hurting religious sentiments." After spending two months in hiding from the death squads, Nasrin was offered asylum by the European Union.[147] If her case really parallels Rushdie's, her fears have not ended.

David Lawton, author of a recent book on blasphemy, explains that certain kinds of writing (particularly fiction) are considered blasphemous because "they set out to assert the rights of the new community outside existing law."[148] Religious orthodoxies, of Christian as well as Islamic persuasion, treat such assertions as a dangerous threat. However, "[i]t is not God whom such fictions would affront but the religious community that they seek to transform, and which exercises whatever power it can wield to resist a transformation." Thus, it is a human community, not religion or God as such, that "receives" the blasphemy, or feels the victim of it. And in Lawton's view, it is a community "that by its violent response identifies itself as fundamentalist."[149] Sadiq al-Azm, a Syrian philosopher who has studied the recent history of apostasy and blasphemy in the Middle East, essentially concurs with Lawton's observation: "[E]very one of these affairs had far more to do with the affairs of state than the affairs of faith."[150]

The Lawton and al-Azm thesis is aptly illustrated by the Salman Rushdie case, with the qualification that the community whose "rights" are being "asserted" in his writing is not completely "new" but the merger of an emerging, pluralistic, modernized Muslim culture and an old community, the "Godless West," all the more threatening to orthodox Islam for being a known enemy. It is helpful to recall the highly politi-

---

[147] Eric Weiner, "Bangladeshi Writer Draws Death Threat," *The Christian Science Monitor* (April 1, 1994): 8; "Bangladesh Is Searching for Author," *The New York Times* (June 8, 1994): A6; John F. Burns, "Dhaka Court Grants Bail for Feminist," *The New York Times* (August 4, 1994): A5. Another Muslim advocate of feminism, the Moroccan sociologist Fatima Mernisse, author of *The Veil and the Male Elite* and *Islam and Democracy: Fear of the Modern World*, has also had her books banned in her native country. See Martin Kramer, "Politics and the Prophet," *The New Republic* (March 1, 1993): 39.

[148] Lawton, *Blasphemy*, 141.

[149] Ibid.

[150] Mayer, "Universal versus Islamic Human Rights," 385, quoting Sadiq al-Azm, "The Importance of Being Ernest About Salman Rushdie," *Die Welt des Islams* 31 (1991): 1, 34.

cized context out of which the Ayatollah Khomeini's February, 1989 apostasy *fatwa* against Salman Rushdie originated. Although Khomeini had ambitions to be recognized as the global leader of an Islamic revolution, only months before the *fatwa* he had been forced to accept a humiliating ceasefire in Iran's eight-year war with Iraq. Rushdie's book *The Satanic Verses* was already banned in South Africa and in his native India, where the book was inspiring riots. In England and Pakistan, however, *The Satanic Verses* would conveniently provide Khomeini with a new *cause celebré*, particularly given Rushdie's vigorous denunciations of Khomeini and his regime.[151] That so few other non-Iranian Muslim institutions officially supported the *fatwa* provides further support for its peculiarly political context.[152]

It was not considered necessary for the non-English-speaking Khomeini or, apparently, any of his advisors, to obtain first-hand evidence by reading the 250,000 word book, which in February 1989 had not yet been translated into Farsi or even Arabic.[153] Nor did the self-appointed adjudicator offer Rushdie the benefit of a trial by a properly constituted tribunal. Even Rushdie's expression of repentence—a means for clemency held out by Shari'a—was disregarded, with Khomeini restating the "duty of every Muslim" to kill him, even if Rushdie were to somehow become the most pious Muslim in the world. That the one million dollar reward (subsequently increased to two million) for assassinating Rushdie was also offered to non-Muslims, and that his non-Muslim publishers, translators, and distributors were also threatened with violence (in some cases, carried out) are factors probably unprece-

---

[151] See Appignanesi and Maitland, eds., *The Rushdie File*, xiii; Mayer, "Islam and the State," 1050-1051. As for Khomenini, if he had actually read the book, he could not fail to notice its thinly disguised portrait of himself, "an unflattering and compelling portrait of the Imam, as a murderous modern tyrant masquerading in a guise of religious rectitude." Lawton, *Blasphemy*, 182. This was not Khomeini's first *fatwa*. In 1944, he issued a death sentence against Achmed Kasravi, a critic of Shi'ite Islam, who was eventually assasinated by the Muslim Brotherhood. Ibid.

[152] After Khomeini's death in mid-1989, the new Iranian religious leader, the Iranian President and parliament reaffirmed the *fatwa*. Middle East Watch, *Guardians of Thought*, 89. However, no other Muslim governments—all of which are either Sunni or secular—supported Iran's call for Rushdie's execution. While numerous individual Muslims, such as Egyptian Nobel laureate Naguib Mahfouz, supported banning of the book, only a few, such as the Mufti of Nigeria and Sheik Omar Abdel Rahman, also called for Rushdie's death. See Esposito, *The Islamic Threat* 191. Although the Organization of the Islamic Conference labeled the book blasphemous and Rushdie an apostate, it did not endorse the death sentence, despite Iran's efforts to drum up support. "Forty-Six Muslim Nations Oppose Iran's View on Rushdie's Death," *The New York Times* (March 17, 1989): A6; *Treaties and Alliances of the World*, 565.

[153] Perhaps all that had been translated was the title, which would have been enough for many militants. In Arabic "The Satanic Verses" translates as "The Satanic Qur'an" or "The Qur'an is Satan's Work." See Lawton, *Blasphemy*, 183.

dented in Islamic history.[154] Lest it be thought that the threat of Rushdie's murder is merely idle, the assassination of 59 exiled Iranian dissidents between the revolution of 1979 and the end of 1993, constitute rebuttal testimony.[155]

If the *fatwa*-issuer's motivation had been solely religious and not political, one would expect a closer adherence to the criminal procedure that Islamic law mandates in such cases. Of all the procedural oversights in the Rushdie case,[156] perhaps the most egregious is the extraterritorial application of the accusation and sentence. Shari'a applies only within the Muslim world and can only be administered by Muslim rulers within their own communities. Muslims living outside the *dar al-Islam* are not subject to Islamic law.[157] Rushdie, nevertheless, was born and raised in

---

[154] Ibid. Among other connected deaths and assaults, Rushdie's Japanese translator was stabbed to death, his Norwegian publisher wounded by gun shots, and his Italian translator injured by stabbing. Bookstores selling the book have been bombed. His would-be Turkish translator had the death *fatwa* extended to him, as recently as February, 1993. Iranian writers who signed a declaration of support for Rushdie have had their works banned there. Middle East Watch, *Guardians of Thought*, 89-91.

[155] See Mansour Farhang, "Iran Wants to Assassniate Me. Why?" *The New York Times* (December 8, 1993): A25. Other than nine in Pakistan, six in Iraq, and eight in Turkey, these murders occurred in non-Muslim countries, including France, England, Switzerland, and the Phillipines. One took place in the United States (Ali Akbar Tabatabai, allegedly by an employee of the Iran interest section of the Algerian Embassy in Washington). Ibid.

[156] Although the Qur'an and Sunna offer criminal defendants relatively few procedural rights, within the purview of *ijtihad*, the state authorities are granted the discretion to provide the necessary procedures to achieve justice and truth. Muhammad Salim al-Awwa, "The Basis for Islamic Penal Legislation," in Bassiouni, ed., *The Islamic Criminal Justice System*, 127, 142. These include the right to present a defense before an unbiased tribunal. See Awad M. Awad, "The Rights of the Accused Under Islamic Criminal Procedure," in Bassiouni, ed., *The Islamic Criminal Justice System*, 91, 97.

Under one scholarly Islamic view, a conviction cannot rely solely on the judge's personal or extrajudicial knowledge of the case. But even those scholars who would allow such evidence in regular criminal cases prohibit it in the case of *hudud* offenses such as apostasy, where proof is limited to confession and the testimony of witnesses. This is because in *hudud* offenses which are against God, testimony is God's providence. Ma'amoun M. Salama, "General Principles of Criminal Evidence in Islamic Jurisprudence," in Bassiouni, ed., *The Islamic Criminal Justice System*, 109, 111-113. Finally, as to the apostate's right to repent, Mohamed Talbi points out that only the Hanbali school put apostates to death immediately. Three other schools of jurisprudence would give them three days to retract. Talbi, "Religious Liberty," 183 n.16. Note that none of these discussions of Islamic criminal procedure refers explicitly to Shi'ite doctrines.

[157] See Awad, "The Rights of the Accused," 96; Mayer, "Islam and the State," 1051; al-Turabi, "The Islamic Awakening's Second Wave," 53. This raises a question posed by many of Rushdie's opponents living in the West: why do the blasphemy laws of, for instance, the United Kingdom, protect only Christian sensibilities and not also Muslims? As a Muslim living in Wales noted: "The Muslim community in this case saw itself as fighting a battle of principle: the injustice of the fact that the law of blasphemy applied only to a particular group [the Anglican majority] within the society and not to other groups." Quoted by Esposito, *The Islamic Threat*, 192; see Lawton, *Blasphemy*, 7-9. See also the chapter by Peter Cumper in the sequel to this volume, Witte and van der Vyver, eds., *Religious Human Rights*

India, a secular, non-Muslim majority state, and resided and published in England, another secular, non-Muslim state. From a Sunni family, he had never set foot in Shi'ite Iran. In other words, regardless of whether he should have anticipated that orthodox Muslims—either in his own England or in geographically remote locales—would be offended,[158] Rushdie simply did not write the book for them. He did not ask to be subject to their jurisdiction, to be held accountable under the norms of a community he was not part of. But that very rejection—Rushdie's preference for, and renown within, Western secular culture—may be what is most galling to the offended.

A related factor is what makes the Rushdie case so startling and exceptional: its global reverberations. "Whereas such issues [of freedom of belief and of expression] have always been debated, mediated and resolved in relative privacy within relatively homogeneous settings, they are now cast, and demand resolution, at a global, public and publicised level."[159] The Rushdie case is not merely notorious for its own notoriety, or even because it appears to represent such a stark clash between secular acculturation and religious fundamentalism. It is emblematic, a coalescent microcosm, of so many late twentieth-century phenomena: the global communications revolution, global mobility (not coincidentally, *The Satanic Verses*, like its author's life, involves a case of migration), postcolonialism, and transnational terrorism. It is also an exemplar of the distortion of classic Islamic law for contemporary political ends.

While it is not necessary to engage in an elaborate exegesis of *The Satanic Verses* to determine if it really is blasphemous or whether Rushdie is truly an apostate within the parameters of Islamic law, the question of whether the *fatwa* fulfills the purposes of the Shari'a law of apostasy is worth examining. There is no scholarly consensus on whether apostasy was purely a religious or a quasi-political offense, and whether death

---

in the World Today: Legal Perspectives. By contrast, sections 295A and 298 of the Indian Penal Code, which punish speech maliciously intended to insult or wound the religious feelings of another, have been successfully applied in cases involving Islam, a minority religion in India. See John Mansfield, "Religious Speech Under Indian Law," in Mahendra Singh, ed., *Comparative Constitutional Law*, (Lucknow, India, 1989), 204. Therefore, the Indian ban on *The Satanic Verses*, made in the interest of community relations, seems justifiable, though no less painful to its native son, Rushdie. See Lawton, *Blasphemy*, 185.

[158] This particular question seems to lie at the heart of the Western debate among those who, while claiming to support Rushdie's freedom of expression, criticize him for deliberately or recklessly writing to offend. See Appignanesi and Maitland, eds., *The Rushdie File*. But as Rushdie responds: "I expected that the mullahs wouldn't like it. But I didn't write it for the mullahs. . . . It's very simple in this country [England]. If you don't want to read a book, you don't have to read it." Ibid., 21.

[159] An-Na'im, "What Do We Mean by Universal?" 127.

was its mandated penalty.[160] Even those scholars who contend that execution was used as a punishment for treasonous rebellion against the early Muslim political power and not for apostasy alone would be hard-pressed to find that a solitary book is capable of subverting a political order and threatening its community, whether that community is defined as the 60 million Muslims of the state of Iran or the fastest growing religion in the world today, currently numbering more than 900 million worldwide.

As Rushdie himself has said: "It seems to me that nothing I can do can destroy Islam. . . . How can I unmake Islam? It's not possible. So even if it were my desire, which it isn't, the idea that, somehow, a book should exist which takes a different point of view from that of the imams and be such a dangerous thing, is not convincing to me."[161] Rushdie also claims that he has not rejected Islam, a factor which should be significant in any test for apostasy as a purely religious offense:

> Anybody who reads any of my books knows how powerful the influence of Islam has been. The fact that I would not call myself a religious person doesn't mean that I can reject the importance of Islam in my life. If you come from India or Pakistan, how can you reject religion? Religion is the air everyone breathes. If you're trying to write about that world, you can't make a simple rejection of religion. You have to deal with it because it's the centre of the culture.[162]

Ironically, the fact that Rushdie writes in English, while perhaps absolving him of the charge of deliberately writing to insult and malign Muslims in Iran or in most of the Islamic world, does not necessarily redeem him in the eyes of the Muslims of India, the United Kingdom, or any of its other former colonies who do read English. Moreover, while it may support the technical defense that he had no intention of subjecting himself to the jurisdiction of Islamic law in Muslim majority states, his use of English contributes to the suspicion that he serves as a treasonous agent of the hated, Godless West, a power which could, according to Islamists, be incited by his book to destroy the Islamic political order. And what of the many other alleged apostates writing in Arabic for audiences

---

[160] See Mayer, *Islam and Human Rights*, 170.

[161] Appignanesi and Maitland, eds., *The Rushdie File*, 23. Rushdie has said more recently, "If there is a God, what kind of a God would He be that could be rocked from his perch by someone like me." Interview with Rushdie, "Talking with David Frost," WSKG-TV (PBS) Broadcast, August 4, 1994. See also Mansour Farhang, "Iran's Getting Away with Murder."

[162] Appignanesi and Maitland, eds., *The Rushdie File*, 24.

in Egypt, Algeria, and Pakistan, or drawing pictures for Iranian periodicals? Can they be absolved from the charge of incitement to rebellion?

International law has an answer for this. Both the International Covenant on Civil and Political Rights and the Declaration on the Elimination of All Forms of Intolerance Based on Religion and Belief provide that freedom to manifest one's religion or belief (including nonreligious beliefs) may be subject to limitations prescribed by law which are necessary to protect public safety, order, health, or morals or the fundamental rights and freedoms of others.[163] It would appear that under this formulation, a book ban issued in reasonable response to or legitimate anticipation of widespread riots could be justified as a protection of public safety or order. International law encourages the recognition that freedom of expression can vary according to its cultural and religious context.

On the other hand, nowhere does international law authorize the death penalty for apostasy or blasphemous speech (or, indeed, for any crime[164]). It certainly does not sanction it in the application of a religious law that itself leaves so much unsettled as to the penalty for apostasy.

Heretics and Renegades. While the terms "apostasy" and "heresy" are often used interchangeably in popular discussions of Islam, particularly when the terms themselves are used to stigmatize, in this chapter the former has been applied to Muslims who have rejected Islamic belief while the latter is used to refer to Muslim believers who advocate internal reform or a heterodox interpretation of Islam. As already noted, heterodox has been a common feature of Islam since its origins in the seventh century. However, as Mayer has noted, while "premodern Islamic culture was generally tolerant of diverging views on questions of Islamic theology and law, when contemporary Middle Eastern governments have pressed forward with Islamicization campaigns, they have tended to impose a uniform standard of orthodoxy on their Muslim citizens and to reject the legitimacy of the positions of Muslim groups that do not accept what is being presented as the official norms of Islam."[165] Beginning in the nineteenth century, after 900 years in which the "door of *ijtihad*" was effectively closed, a series of Muslim scholars proposed new interpretations of traditional theology. In a synthesis with modernist po-

---

[163] Articles 18(2) and 1(3), respectively. The language is identical in each document. See also article 20(2) of the Covenant, which prohibits advocacy of national, racial, or religious hatred that constitutes incitement to discrimination, hostility, or violence.

[164] While international human rights law does not absolutely prohibit capital punishment, it attempts to limit and discourage its use. See article 6 of the International Covenant on Civil and Political Rights; William Schabas, *The Abolition of the Death Penalty in International Law* (Cambridge, 1993).

[165] Mayer, *Islam and Human Rights*, 165.

litical and religious thought, they demonstrated that Islam, too, was grounded in libertarian and rationalist values. Responding to challenges posed to Islamic hegemony by Western Christian colonialism, the break-up of Muslim empires, the division into separate nation-states, and the exposure to modern technology and secular consumer culture, reformers such as Muhammad Abduh (b. 1849), Sayyid Ahmad Khan (b. 1817), and Ali Abd al-Raziq (b. 1888) hoped their fresh approaches would help re-vitalize Islamic thought and identity. Posing the question, "whether or not the Law of Islam is capable of evolution," Muhammed Iqbal (b. 1877) argued that "[t]he teaching of the Qur'an that life is a process of progressive creation necessitates that each generation, guided yet unhampered by the work of its predecessor, should be permitted to solve its own problems."[166]

Others such as the Syrian Sadiq al-Azm (b. 1936) and the Iraqi Abd al-Rahman al-Bazzaz (b. 1913) adapted socialism or nationalism to effect more concrete and widespread changes. The jurist Asaf A.A. Fyzee (b. 1899) developed specific rules for a modern reinterpretation of Shari'a. More recently, the sociologist Ali Shariati (b. 1933) called for a rethinking of Islam and a rereading of the Qur'an in contextual rather than in metaphysical terms.[167] Even King Fahd of Saudi Arabia proposed in 1983 that a global theological review of Islamic law be undertaken in the spirit of *ijtihad*, despite formal doctrine in his country which rejects any novel innovations after the eighth century.[168]

Some of these advocates of a kind of "Protestant reformation" of Islam ran afoul of religious authorities and suffered the fate of heretics. Al-Raziq was condemned by a council of clerics and forbidden to hold public office; the Marxist al-Azm was tried (and acquitted) on charges of provoking religious trouble; al-Bazzaz was imprisoned, eventually dying in exile, after the Ba'th coup in 1968; Shariati suffered a similar fate after his arrest in Iran in the mid-1970s.[169]

Better known is the story of Mahmud Muhammad Taha, founder and leader of the Republican Brothers movement in the Sudan, who was summarily tried for various anti-state offenses and publicly hung in

---

[166] Kelsay, "Saudi Arabia, Pakistan, and the Universal Declaration of Human Rights," 47, quoting Muhammad Iqbal, *The Reconstruction of Religious Thought in Islam* (Lahore, 1968), 168.

[167] Translated excerpts from the writings of each of the scholars mentioned in this paragraph are found in Donohue and Esposito, *Islam in Transition*. On Shariati, see also Reeves, *Female Warriors of Allah,* 115-118. On Abduh, Khan, and others, see also Ilan Pappe, "Moderation in Islam: Religion in the Test of Reality," *Palestine-Israel Journal* (Spring, 1994): 11.

[168] See Weeramantry, *Islamic Jurisprudence*, 43-44.

[169] See Donohue and Esposito, *Islam in Transition*.

January, 1985. The Republican Brothers, established in 1945, first worked for the formation of a Sudanese republic independent of Egyptian and British control, which was in fact achieved in 1956. When President Nimeiri declared an "Islamic Revolution" in 1983 which would immediately impose traditional Islamic rules throughout the Sudan, including the one-third that is non-Muslim, Taha and his followers called instead for a liberal, openly-debated, and humanistic revision of Shari'a. Taha's vision was of a socialist, democratic state, in which men and women, Muslims and non-Muslims, would have complete equality. He called his approach the "Second Message of Islam," as it distinguished between the Qu'ranic passages revealed in Medina, which he argued dealt only with circumstances in Arabia at that time, and the Qu'ranic passages revealed in Mecca, which contained an eternal message. This allowed him to justify discarding Shari'a rules which violated modern human rights norms. Spurning violence, Taha and the Republicans used litigation, unsuccessfully, to try to invalidate Nimeiri's Islamization campaign on constitutional grounds.[170]

Although neither apostasy nor heresy were then crimes in the Sudan, Taha's appellate court (rather than the prosecutor) introduced hearsay evidence of the 76-year-old leader's heresy and ordered him executed without the opportunity to repent. This violated Shari'a and multiple articles of Sudan's Constitution, as well as the Code of Penal Procedure's prohibition on execution of persons over 70 years of age.[171] The court also ordered that the "infidel" and "renegade faction" Republican Brothers be banned, their publications seized from libraries and destroyed, and that Taha neither be mourned nor buried in a Muslim cemetery. Nimeiri announced that he supported the execution "on the basis of Shari'ah law to protect the nation from the danger of Mahmud Muhammad Taha and his slander of God and his insolence towards Him and to protect this homeland from heresy."[172] Nimeiri's stance backfired, however, as an international outcry led to his toppling by a popular coalition only three months later.

While cases like Taha's represent the abuse of traditional Islamic law in the employ of contemporary, political power struggles, age-old relig-

---

[170] See Mayer, *Islam and Human Rights*, 182-186 and id., "Islam and the State," 1047-1050. Abdullahi Ahmed An-Na'im, a follower of Taha, has translated Taha's *Second Message of Islam* (Syracuse, 1987). See An-Na'im, *Toward an Islamic Reformation*, passim, for an extensive exploration of Taha's reform methodology.

[171] See An-Na'im, "The Islamic Law of Apostasy and its Modern Applicability: A Case from the Sudan," 207-210. See also Peter Bechtold, "The Sudan Since the Fall of Numayri," in Robert O. Freedman, ed., *The Middle East From the Iran-Contra Affair to the Intifada* (Syracuse, 1990), 371.

[172] Mayer, *Islam and Human Rights*, 185.

ious schisms between various Islamic sects continue into the present. Shi'ites comprise about 10% of the current one billion Muslim population worldwide. While they are found in significant numbers in Pakistan and southern Lebanon, as well as predominating in Iran, Iraq, and Azerbaijan, small communities also exist in Yemen (the Shi'ite subsect *Zaydi*), Syria (the *Druze* and *Alawi* subsects), Saudi Arabia, northern Israel (*Druze*), Bahrain, India, Oman, Afghanistan, the United Arab Emirates, and Somalia (*Ismailis*). Kurds, who live in Iran, Iraq, Turkey, Syria, and Azerbaijan, are usually Sunni, which makes them a religious as well as an ethnic minority in Iran and Iraq.[173] In Iraq, where the Sunni minority controls the government, the Kurds, an Indo-European people, are persecuted because of their movement for national and cultural autonomy. Likewise in Iran, where Kurds are ethnically distinct from the 80% Persian majority, they do not appear to be targeted on the basis of their Sunni beliefs per se.[174]

While victimization of Shi'ites is occasionally reported in states such as Bahrain[175] and the United Arab Emirates,[176] the most persistent cases of their persecution are in Iraq and Saudi Arabia. In Iraq, the publication of Shi'ite books and the broadcast of Shi'ite radio or television programs are banned, as are public meetings on Shi'ite holy days. In response to an uprising in 1991, the Iraqi army reportedly destroyed Shi'ite shrines, mosques, and archives and forcibly relocated or "disappeared" tens of thousands of persons. Civilian residences have also been destroyed and water sources systematically poisoned. An American, French, and British "No Fly Zone" was created in 1992 to prevent the Iraqi military from conducting further indiscriminate bombing and other attacks on Shi'ite communities in the southern marshlands.[177] Because the Sunni-dominated Iraqi regime is Baathist and therefore secular, one can specu-

---

[173] Held, *Middle East Patterns*, 84-85, 95. Although only about 36% of Iraqis are Sunni, they have dominated the political and economic centers of the country for centuries. Only a very small percentage of the Shi'ites of Iraq are of Persian ethnicity. The majority are, like Sunni Iraqis, Arab. Ibid., 281-283.

[174] Human Rights Watch has published a number of reports on Iraqi treatment of its Kurdish population, most recently, Middle East Watch, *Genocide in Iraq: The Anfal Campaign Against the Kurds* (New York, 1993). The condition of other Sunni minorities in Iran appears not to be readily known.

[175] Fourteen Shi'ites were arrested in January, 1994 as they gathered at a mosque to commemorate the recent death of their spiritual leader. "See Bahrain: Arrest of Shi'ites," *Article 19 Bulletin* Issue 20 (June, 1994): 4.

[176] Shi'ites are not permitted to have mosques in the Emirate of Ras al Khaimah. U.S. Department of State, *Country Reports on Human Rights Practices for 1993* (Washington, 1994), 1304.

[177] See ibid., 1184-1189; Human Rights Watch, *World Report 1993* (New York, 1992), 305-308; Human Rights Watch, *World Report 1994*, 295-299.

late that the Shi'ites are suspect for their physical proximity to and religious affinity with arch-enemy Iran, rather than persecuted on religious
grounds per se. (As the majority of Iraqi Shi'ites are Arab and not Persian, ethnic discrimination can be ruled out.)

Saudi persecution of Shi'ites, on the other hand, is a somewhat
harder case to fathom. Comprising at most 10% of the Kingdom's population, Saudi Shi'ites follow one of three Ayatollahs, two from Iraq and
the late Khomeini from Iran. The Kingdom follows the Wahabi interpretation of the Hanbali school of Sunni jurisprudence, which strongly condemns polytheism, defined broadly to include many non-Wahabi beliefs
and rites, including Shi'ism because of its worship of imams. Eighteenth-
century Wahabis once defaced the tomb of Ali's son Hussein. As in Iraq,
Shi'ite publications, broadcasts, and public gatherings are prohibited.
Even more invasively, objects used in Shi'ite prayer are confiscated and
their users beaten, while the Shi'ite call to prayer (which differs from the
Sunni version only by the addition of eight words referring to Ali) is considered "contrary to pure Islam" and punishable "with no leniency."
Public school textbooks and officially sanctioned *fatwas* routinely deni-
grate the Shi'ite faith, while government-sanctioned forced conversions
and numerous cases of arrest and torture have also been reported.[178]
Moreover, almost every year since 1979 during the *haj* or pilgrimage to
Mecca, conflicts, often violent, have broken out between Shi'ites or other
minority sects and the Saudi military. Iranians have frequently been arrested on charges of agitation or deported before completion of their
haj.[179] Because the pilgrims often carried placards with Khomeini's photograph or loudly chanted about extending his Islamic Revolution, it has
been difficult to label the disputes either solely religious or solely political. Clearly, at least, the rise of Khomeini threatened to usurp the place of
the wealthy Wahabis as the most religiously and politically influential
Muslim school of interpretation.

Perhaps the Muslim sect most persecuted today is the one million
member Ahmadi of Pakistan, founded as an Islamic revivalist movement
in India in 1889 by Mirza Ghulam Ahmad, who claimed to be the messiah and whom followers treat as a prophet. That is anathema to orthodox Muslims, who fervently believe that Muhammed was the Final

---

[178] Amnesty International, "Saudi Arabia: Religious Intolerance: The Arrest, Detention
and Torture of Christian Worshippers and Shi'a Muslims" (September 14, 1993), 14-21.

[179] See, e.g., John Kifner, "Twenty Iran Pilgrims at Saudi Shrine Reported Hurt in Clash
with Police," *The New York Times* (September 25, 1981): A3; "Saudi Arabia Expels 69 Visiting
Iranians After Riot in Medina," *The New York Times* (October 9, 1982): 6; Michael Collins,
"Saudis and Iranians Fight a War of Words over Hajj," *The Christian Science Monitor* (August
9, 1983): 4; "Saudis Free 113 Iranians Arrested in Pilgrimage," *The New York Times* (August 29,
1986): A7.

Messenger of God. Opposed to the use of violence, the Ahmadis were the target of a 1953 pogrom incited by Muslim clerics. In 1974, Pakistani Prime Minister Zulfikar Ali Bhutto agreed to amend the constitution to declare the Ahmadis non-Muslims. A 1984 decree made it criminal for Ahmadis to call themselves Muslims and their places of worship mosques, to use Islamic terminology or the Muslim call to prayer, to proselytize their beliefs or merely to say the name of the Prophet Muhammed.[180] The decree was challenged in the Federal Shari'a Court by group members sentenced to three years imprisonment and heavy fines. In a peculiar analogy to trademark law, the Court held that the law was not contrary to the Qur'an or Sunna, nor that it violated the rights to freedom of religion and to equality. Only one judge viewed the decree as violating fundamental human and constitutional rights.[181] Over 100 Ahmadis, including a baby, have also been arrested and subjected to death sentences under the Pakistani blasphemy law, described above. These official acts have inspired harassment by vigilantes such as the "Finality-of-the-Prophet Youth Force," forcing many Ahmadis into exile in the U.S. and Canada.[182]

Muslim history teaches that Islam is simultaneously capable of both sectarian diversity and sectarian intolerance. Sects that slaughtered each other's leaders and followers in the seventh and eighth centuries today use the power of state-sanctioned legislation and judicial decision to accomplish similar purposes: spiritual supremacy and physical domination. While all religions have the right to define their own membership, the difficulty is knowing where to draw the line between differences of opinion and outright heresy. Not so perplexing is knowing what is an appropriate sanction. Although international law, as noted above, is less than forthcoming on the specific subject of internal religious pluralism,[183] it clearly denies the purported right of religious orthodoxy to punish heresy and dissension through criminal sanction or any form of physical or

---

[180] "Anti-Islamic Activities of the Quadiani Group, Lahori Group and Ahmadis (Prohibition and Punishment) Ordinance XX of 1984." Mayer, *Islam and Human Rights*, 159-160.

[181] Ibid., 160; Robert F. Drinan, "Pakistan Falls Short on Religious Freedom," *The Christian Science Monitor* (January 5, 1994): 23. The case is *Mujeeb-ur-Rehman v. Federal Government of Pakistan*, PLD FSC (1984), 136.

[182] "Pakistan: Asia Watch Says Derive to Islamicize Hurts Rights," *Inter Press Service* (September 19, 1993); "Ahmadi Muslims Suffering at Hands of Pakistanis: Reports," *The Montreal Gazette* (February 6, 1993): 17; Rashid Ahmad Chaudhry, "Persecution in Pakistan," *The Economist* (October 24, 1992): 6.

[183] U.N. Special Rapporteur Benito has interpreted the international provisions on religious freedom and non-discrimination to include, inter alia, intolerance *within* religions. Odio Benito, *Elimination of All Forms of Intolerance and Discrimination Based on Religion or Belief*, 39.

psychological coercion.[184] While threats to public order may, in appropriate cases, justify a limitation on the public expression of heretical religious views, a Muslim regime that uses a religious rationale to silence its
political enemies abuses both human rights and its Muslim cultural
heritage.

Non-Muslims and Infidels. Of the three categories of religious dissident, this final one may be the most politically charged today, representing as it does the clash between Islamic and Western value systems,
while undergirding if not fueling the Islamic revivalist movements. For
instance, the word "jihad," which has multiple meanings in traditional
Islamic thought, today carries the exclusive connotation in the Western
mind of "terrorism," the result of both uneducated simplifications by the
media and deliberate appropriation of the term by radical Palestinian
and other militant groups based everywhere from Algeria to Somalia.[185]
Connoting virtually everything from moral self-scrutiny to agricultural
transformation to an analogy to the Protestant ethic[186] to outright genocide, the very ambiguity of "jihad" has been exploited for maximum
propaganda use, most effectively when directed at two or more audiences simultaneously.[187]

Somewhat less politicized today, or at least less notorious, is the term
dhimmi. Only in the formally Islamic states of Saudi Arabia, the Sudan,
Iran, and Oman are non-Muslim minorities afforded an officially unequal

---

[184] At a minimum, tolerance means that it is "not legitimate to exert physical or psychological pressure on persons because of their religion or belief." Ibid., 40.

[185] "Islamic Jihad" is the name of one of the Palestinian groups opposing the Israeli-
P.L.O. accords which has claimed responsibility for violent attacks on Israeli civilians as well
as Palestinians alleged to have collaborated with Israel. See "Under Islam's Banner," *The
Economist* (February 20, 1993): 39; Malik, "Jihad—its Development and Relevance," 29. The
"troops" which carry out violent attacks on behalf of these organizations are called *mujahidin*
("holy warriors"). On use of the term *jihad* as a rallying cry against infidels other than Israelis,
see for example, "Muslim Group Threatens Algerian Schools," *The New York Times* (August 7,
1994): 21; "Somalia: SSNM Interim Chairman Says SNA is Ready for Dialogue to End Conflict
with UNOSOM," *BBC Summary of World Broadcasts* (August 2, 1993); "Al-Qadhdhafi Blames
Christians, Jews for Problems," *Middle East Intelligence Report* (February 16, 1994) (translated
from Arabic from Tripoli Libyan Television Network).

[186] In a creative twist, Sudanese religious leader Hassan al-Turabi refers to transforming
Sudan from near-famine to self-sufficiency in food, "when people are taught that agriculture
is their *jihad*, their holy struggle." al-Turabi, "The Islamic Awakening's Second Wave," 53.
Although to "the rich West that may sound strange," he asks, "[W]hat role did Puritanism
play in carving America out of the wilderness? What role did the Protestant ethic play in the
development of the European economies? Religion is the motor of development." Ibid.

[187] For instance, while in South Africa for Nelson Mandela's inauguration, Yasser Ara-
fat told an audience in a mosque: "Jihad will continue. . . . You must come to fight, to begin
the jihad to liberate Jerusalem." "Documents and Source Material," *Journal of Palestine Studies*
24 (Autumn, 1994): 131-132. See "'Jihad' not Necessarily a Call to Religious War," *NPR All
Things Considered* (May 18, 1994). But see "The Happiest Jihad," *The New Republic* (June 13,
1994): 8.

status under law; distinctions between *dhimmi* and non-*dhimmi* minorities are also lawful in these countries. Such discrimination, of course, is incompatible with the norms of international law[188] and contrary to the modern conception of the pluralistic nation-state. In more secularized Muslim countries, as in most other societies in the post-apartheid era, religious discrimination tends to be *de facto* rather than *de jure*.[189] Non-Muslims are now eligible for citizenship in every Muslim state except Saudi Arabia, although with the exception of the occasional Fariq Aziz of Iraq or Boutros-Ghali of Egypt (both Christians who rose to prominence in their respective foreign ministries), non-Muslims rarely share in political power or social influence. While no less invidious, religious persecution which is not officially sanctioned by state law allows governments to disavow responsibility, blaming such acts on ostensibly eradicable, ancient, culturally-based prejudices.

The classical *dhimma* system had been given reinforcement in the fifteenth century when the Ottoman Empire, under Muhammed II, introduced the *millet* system, which confined Orthodox Christians, Armenian Christians, and Jews in communities more segregated and hermetically sealed than they had been under the Khalifahs. The religious leaders of these non-Muslim groups were held responsible for all acts and activities, both secular and religious, of their members, none of whom were eligible for civilian office on the imperial level. The *millets* were not abolished until 1856, by which time their cultural influence was established in what would become modern-day Turkey, Syria, Lebanon, Israel, Iraq, Iran, Jordan, Egypt, all of North Africa, Greece, and the other Balkan states, and parts of India and Russia.[190] It was at this same time in the mid-19th century that the *jizya* tax, paid by *dhimmis* in lieu of military service, was abolished in Egypt. However, another 1856 Egyptian decree prohibited

---

[188] See articles 2-4 of the Declaration on Elimination of All Forms of Intolerance and Discrimination Based on Religion and Belief. See also the chapter by Natan Lerner included in the sequel to this volume, Witte and van der Vyver, eds., *Religious Human Rights in Global Perspective: Legal Perspectives*.

[189] See, e.g., Robert A. Goldwin, Art Kaufman and William A. Schambra, *Forging Unity Out of Diversity: The Approaches of Eight Nations* (Washington, 1989); Ted Robert Gurr, *Minorities At Risk: A Global View of Ethnopolitical Conflicts* (Washington, 1993). On the unique approaches of Ireland and Israel, see respectively G.W. Hogan, "Law and Religion: Church-State Relations in Ireland from Independence to the Present Day," *American Journal of Comparative Law* 35 (1987): 477 and David Kretzmer, *The Legal Status of the Arabs in Israel* (Boulder, 1990).

[190] See generally Haim Gerber, *State, Society and Law in Islam: Ottoman Law in Comparative Perspective* (Albany, 1994); J.J. Saunders, *The Muslim World on the Eve of Europe's Expansion* (Englewood Cliffs, NJ, 1966).

any building or renovation of Christian churches without presidential permission, which has never been readily granted.[191]

Whether on account of the *dhimma* and *millet* systems, or purely for purposes of political expediency, non-Muslims still serve as scapegoats in parts of the Muslim world, as when Mummar Qaddafi blames "Christians, non-believers and Jews" for a war in Afghanistan in which Muslims killed fellow Muslims during the holy month of Ramadan.[192] Recent reports of persecution of Christians, both official and vigilante-based, come from Iran, Indonesia, Saudi Arabia, and Pakistan,[193] as well as Egypt and the Sudan. Islamists seek to revive the most demeaning of the *dhimma* rules by calling on Muslims to shun Christians and to refuse to shake their hands, wish them well on Christian holidays, or walk on the same sidewalk.[194]

Of the one dozen separate Christian denominations that reside in the Middle East today, the largest and most consistently persecuted are the two Coptic Churches, found in both Catholic and Christian Orthodox forms. Constituting about 10% of the population of Egypt, with smaller communities in Ethiopia and the Sudan, the Copts are extremely endogamous, insisting on a separate existence in order to maintain their pre-Muslim, non-Arab, ancient Egyptian lineage.[195] Before the arrival of Muslims in about the year 640, Egypt was a Christian province of the

---

[191] William Soliman Kilada, "Christian-Muslim Relations in Egypt," in Kail C. Ellis, ed., *The Vatican, Islam and the Middle East* (Syracuse, 1987), 254.

[192] "Al-Qadhdhafi Blames Christians, Jews for Problems."

[193] For instance, Bishop Haik Hovsepian-Mehr, leader of the Assemblies of God Christian community in Iran, was tortured and murdered after protesting the closure of evangelical churches and the Bible Society of Iran, refusing to sign a government-drafted declaration that non-Muslims were not oppressed in Iran, and after working to save from execution a Muslim who had converted to Christianity. Bernard Levin, "Martyred for his Faith," *The London Times* (February 15, 1994). See also Chris Hedges, "Persecution of Christians Mounts in Iran," *The International Herald Tribune* (August 2, 1994). In Indonesia, Christians as well as Buddhists and Hindus, must officially register with the government. Harvey Shepherd, "In the Name of God; Human-Rights Group Reports Religious Persecutions," *The Montreal Gazette* (February 20, 1993): K6.

Non-Muslim worship, both public and private, is completely forbidden in Saudi Arabia. Hundreds of Christians, including women and children as well as men, have been arrested there, mostly without charge or trial, often leading to deportation. See Amnesty International, "Saudi Arabia: Religious Intolerance: The Arrest, Detention and Torture of Christian worshippers and Shi'a Muslims" (September 14, 1993). Christians have also been sentenced under Pakistan's blasphemy law, one man reportedly when he refused to support a Muslim League candidate in local elections. Harvey Shepherd, "In the Name of God." Another Pakistani Christian was murdered after posters appeared at his workplace accusing him of blasphemy. Local police officers reportedly congratulated his killer. "Pakistan: Asia Watch Says Drive to Islamicize Hurts Rights," *Inter Press Service* (September 19, 1993).

[194] Ibrahim, "Fundamentalists Impose Culture on Egypt."

[195] Held, *Middle Eastern Patterns*, 88, 91, 364-365.

Byzantine Empire. Early Muslim-Coptic relations there were mutually respectful. Centuries later, Copts supported Egyptian nationalist movements which sought independence from British and French colonial rule.

But Muslim Egyptians began to resent the Copts for what was perceived as favoritism by the Western imperial powers. In the early eighteenth century, waves of Coptic refugees were forced to flee Egypt for the Sudan. More recently, Egyptian Copts have been the targets of Islamic revivalists and other militants, beginning with the breakdown of pluralistic Egyptian life in the 1950s, under President Nasser and later under President Sadat. In 1957, the Coptic community formally protested against restrictions on the building of churches and discrimination in housing, land distribution, and the holding of public office. In 1972, planned provocations against the Copts were publicly announced by the Egyptian Ministry of Religious Affairs. The lowest blow was delivered in 1981 when Sadat exiled the Coptic pope, censored the Coptic press, and held Coptic bishops and priests under house arrest after they defended their community from violence incited by Islamic militants.[196] In the last few years, Egyptian Islamists have attacked and killed numerous Copts, publicly harassed them and prevented them from performing religious rituals and celebrating social events.[197] Copts have also been harassed and tortured by state security forces for attempting to convert Muslims to Christianity.[198]

In the Sudan, where they live mainly in the north, Copts were, because of their solid economic status, traditionally considered a prestigious minority and treated equally in most respects except in their ability to marry Muslims. Although Sudanese Copts initially welcomed Nimeiri's military government, which temporarily supported their community there, as his and then his successor Bashir's Islamization campaigns progressed, Copts became both targets and critics of Islamization. They

---

[196] See An-Na'im, "Religious Freedom in Egypt: Under the Shadow of the Islamic *Dhimma* System," in Swidler, ed., *Religious Liberty and Human Rights*, 43, 51-52; Kilada, "Christian-Muslim Relations in Egypt"; Nadia Ramsis Farah, *Religious Strife in Egypt: Crisis and Ideological Conflict in the Seventies* (New York, 1986). On the role of European powers as self-appointed protectors of non-Muslim minorities, see Mayer, *Islam and Human Rights*, 143-145.

[197] In 1992, at least 18 Copts were killed by Islamists in Egypt, including a physician murdered in his clinic. Africa Watch, "The Copts: Passive Survivors Under Threat" (February 10, 1993), 2. See also Human Rights Watch: Middle East, "Egypt: Violation of Freedom of Religious Belief and Expression of the Christian Minority" (November 1994).

[198] U.S. Department of State, *Country Reports on Human Rights Practices for 1993*, 1171. Similarly, in Pakistan, Christians may convert non-Muslims, but not Muslims. Joseph Cardinal Cordeiro, "The Christian Minority in an Islamic State: The Case of Pakistan," in Ellis, ed., *The Vatican, Islam and the Middle East*, 279, 282. 99% of Pakistani Christians are Pakistani-born. Ibid., 288.

objected to the imposition on them of Shari'a rules, such as the strict *hudud* penalties, and to being made second-class citizens in their own country. Seen as "fifth columnists," in the late 1980s hundreds of Copts were dismissed from civil service and judicial positions, their churches closed, and their children persecuted in schools for refusing to recite from the Qur'an or to wear Islamic dress. Young Coptic men have been conscripted into the army and forced to fight the government's jihad in the south of the country, which is directed at their fellow Christians (Catholics, Episcopalians, Presbyterians, and others), as well as the non-Muslim African animists who compose the majority of the southern population. After a Coptic airline pilot, Giorgis Yustus, was summarily tried and executed in 1991 on grounds of possessing foreign currency, hundreds of Copts fled the country.[199]

Have Copts and other Christians become the special target of particularized Muslim prejudice, perhaps as symbols of the infidel West—or are they simply being treated in accordance with traditional *dhimma* rules in a time when international norms reject such unequal standards? (*Dhimmis*, it will be recalled, were entitled to protection of their life, honor, and property, including the sanctity of their holy places.) This question may also be asked in reference to the estimated 75,000 Jews still living in Muslim countries.[200] In medieval times, Jews and Muslims mutually enjoyed a culturally-synergetic, economically-prosperous, persecution-free era in the Iberian peninsula that has been called "the Golden Age of Spain."[201] But a historical change in Muslim treatment of Jews occurred, which Bernard Lewis ties to Muslim resentment that the Western colonial powers were favoring non-Muslim minorities. This favoritism allowed indigenous Christians, as well as Jews, to achieve positions of

---

[199] See An-Na'im, "Christian-Muslim Relations in the Sudan: Peaceful Coexistence at Risk," in Ellis, ed., *The Vatican, Islam and the Middle East*, 265; "The Copts: Passive Survivors Under Threat"; Alan Cowell, "Pope, in the Sudan, Assails Religious Persecution," *The New York Times* (February 11, 1993): A3; Khalid Duran, "Religious Liberty and Human Rights in the Sudan," in Swidler, ed., *Religious Liberty and Human Rights*, 61. Since the Sudanese civil war began in 1983, 1.3 million civilians, mostly non-Muslims in Southern Sudan, have been killed or starved to death. Human Rights Watch/Africa, *Civilian Devastation: Abuses by All Parties in the War in Southern Sudan* (New York, 1994).

[200] "World Jewish Population," in Richard Siegel and Carl Rheins, eds., *The Jewish Almanac*, (New York, 1980), 113-114. Between 1948 and 1954, approximately 640,000 Jews emigrated to Israel from ten Muslim countries, including 300,000 from Morocco and 140,000 from Iraq. Michael Wolffsohn, *Israel, Polity, Society and Economy 1882-1986* (Atlantic Highlands, NJ, 1987), 131. See generally Joseph B. Schechtman, *On Wings of Eagles: The Plight, Exodus, and Homecoming of Oriental Jewry* (New York, 1961). An estimated 30,000 Jews live in Iran today, compared to 80,000 Christians, 350,000 Baha'is, and 3.5 million Sunni Muslims, out of a total Iranian population of 62 million. Hedges, "Persecution of Christians Mounts in Iran."

[201] See Solomon Grayzel, *A History of the Jews: From the Babylonian Exile to the Establishment of Israel* (Philadelphia, 1967), 323.

power and wealth that were a subversion of the proper *dhimma* relationship. But in the case of Jews, Lewis believes, the hostility reflected an additional element: "From the late nineteenth century, as a direct result of European influence, movements appear among Muslims of which for the first time one can legitimately use the term anti-Semitic. Hostility to Jews had, of course, roots in the past, but in this era it assumed a new and radically different character."[202]

Muslims picked up from European Christians some of the classic anti-Jewish caricatures of long-nosed money-bags and old canards, such as blood libels and plots to gain world domination. The first Arabic edition of the notorious forgery, *Protocols of the Elders of Zion*, appeared in 1927, followed by translations of classic Nazi works.[203] From exile, the Ayatollah Khomeini harped on these themes, calling Jews "cursed," a "dirty people," and "a disgrace" to work for, even though such employment was legally permissible.[204] Interestingly, once his revolution in Iran was achieved, Khomeini tempered his rhetoric, perhaps because Jewish scapegoats no longer served his political purposes.

Lewis points out that a major element in the development of Muslim anti-semitism was the Palestine question and the establishment of the state of Israel. But in its origin it is a political conflict, not a religious or ethnic one, even though, at times, the traditional imagery of anti-

---

[202] Lewis, *The Jews of Islam*, 184-5.

[203] Ibid., 185, 188. "[T]here are now more translations and editions of *Protocols* in Arabic than in any other language, and the text is still required reading in departments of comparative religion in a number of Arab universities." Ibid., 185. In 1958, Egypt's President Nasser endorsed the *Protocols* as a guide to Jewish designs. Ibid., 186. Commenting on the terrorist massacre of Jews in an Istanbul synagogue in September 1986, the Saudi Arabian paper *al-Jazira* contended that the attack was carried out by Israel: "Those who are familiar with *The Protocols of the Elders of Zion*, that were authored during the First Zionist Congress, know that Israel is the country that created all terrorist conspiracies." Press Release, American Jewish Committee (September 24, 1986). On the history of the *Protocols* in the Arab world, see also Patai, *The Seed of Abraham*, 291-296. See generally Norman Stillman, *The Jews of Arab Lands* (Philadelphia, 1979) and Norman Stillman, *The Jews of Arab Lands in Modern Times* (Philadelphia, 1991).

Given the translation of Nazi works such as *Mein Kampf*, it is perhaps not so surprising that many Muslim countries have banned the Steven Spielberg film about the Holocaust, "Schindler's List." Even in non-Arab Indonesia and Malaysia, it has been denounced as "too sympathetic in its treatment of Jews" and "propaganda with the purpose of asking for sympathy." The official censorship board of Malaysia said the film unfairly depicted Jews as "stout-hearted" and "intelligent" while showing Germans as brutal. Bernard Weinraub, "Islamic Nations Move to Keep Out 'Schindler's List'," *The New York Times* (April 7, 1994): C15.

[204] David Menashri, "Khomeini's Policy Toward Ethnic and Religious Minorities," in Milton J. Esman and Itamar Rabinovich, eds., *Ethnicity, Pluralism and the Middle East* (Ithaca, 1988), 215, 222-228.

semitism has been used in Muslim attacks on Israel.[205] Zionism's role in
the resulting deterioration in Arab state/Jewish minority relations should
therefore not be exaggerated, he believes.[206] In fact, Jews living in Arab
countries in the period before 1948 had usually been anti-Zionist or ag-
nostic on the question, either out of genuine opposition to a Jewish state
or fear for their own security as vulnerable minorities. When they did finally become adherents, it was as much in response to Arab persecution
as for any other reason.[207]

Here, too, as in so many previous examples, religious themes, doctrines, and rationales are intertwined with political slogans, motivations,
and objectives. While most frequently it has been a religious veneer that
has served to camouflage a political core, in the case of Jewish minorities
it may sometimes have been the reverse. A final case, that of the Baha'is
of Iran, is perhaps the most enigmatic of all in this regard.

The Baha'i faith was founded in Persia in 1863 by Baha'u'llah, a follower of the Bab, who two decades earlier had prophecized the coming of
Islam's "Twelfth Imam," who would prepare humanity for the universal
divine Messenger that is anticipated by all the major scriptural religions.
Baha'u'llah, who claimed to be God's messenger, preached that humanity is a single race and a single religion which should be unified into one
global society, organized through a world federal system. His other principles included the elimination of all prejudice, gender equality, elimination of extreme poverty and wealth, universal education, the harmony of
science and religion, and a sustainable balance between nature and technology. The faith would have no clerics or individually powerful leaders;
all decisions would be made by democratically elected, collective assemblies. Baha'is, moreover, would be obedient to civil government but forbidden to engage in partisan political activity.[208]

These teachings were very popular in nineteenth century Persia and
therefore threatening to both the secular and religious authorities, particularly given the direct challenge to Shi'ism over determination of the

---

[205] For instance, in the mid-1980s the Syrian Ministry of Defense published a book
called *The Matza of Zionism* which invoked the ancient libel about Jews using Christian blood
to make the Passover bread. Sidney Liskofsky and Donna Arzt, "Incitement to National, Racial, and Religious Hatred in United Nations Fora," *Israel Yearbook on Human Rights* 17 (1988):
41, 49. For other examples of the slurring of the Jewish/Zionist distinction, see Menashri,
"Khomeini's Policy Toward Ethnic and Religious Minorities," 224.

[206] Lewis, *The Jews of Islam*, 189-190.

[207] Ibid.

[208] Mayer, *Islam and Human Rights*, 157-158; Baha'i International Community, *The Baha'i
Question: Iran's Secret Blueprint for the Destruction of a Religious Community: An Examination of
the Persecution of the Baha'is of Iran 1979-1993* (New York, 1993), 10-12; Baha'i International
Community, *The Baha'is: A Profile of the Baha'i Faith and its Worldwide Community*
(Leicestershire, 1992), 17-23.

Twelfth Imam. Baha'u'llah was accordingly imprisoned and then banished, while the Bab and 20,000 followers were executed as apostates. Baha'is, who today number over five million in more than 232 countries and dependent territories,[209] believe that the Bab and Baha'u'llah are the latest in a series of God's messengers, who have included Abraham and Moses, Krishna, Buddha, Jesus, and Muhammed. To Muslims, this is heretical and blasphemous, as they consider Muhammed to be "the Seal of the Prophets," God's final messenger. Moreover, Baha'i egalitarianism challenges the Shari'a's strict notions of gender differences, not to mention Shi'ite Islam's formal hierarchy of clerical power. However, while acknowledging that the faith originated in Persia among Muslims, Baha'is claim theirs to be an independent religion, not a sect of Islam.[210] This makes their case a kind of mirror image of the persecuted Ahmadi Muslims of Pakistan, whom Islamic authorities treat as an independent religious minority, not a sect. Both Ahmadis and Baha'is follow a prophet who post-dates Muhammed, without, however, denying or denigrating his teachings. Regardless of their own respect for Muhammed, each group risks being treated as apostates from or blasphemers of Islam—despite their claims to heterodox, in the case of the Ahmadis, or to being non-Muslims, in the case of Baha'is.

The 1979 Iranian constitution, as noted, formally recognizes Jews, Christians, and Zorastrians but makes no mention of Baha'is, who constitute Iran's largest religious minority,[211] even though, as a scriptural monotheism, the Baha'i faith should be entitled to *dhimma* status. There is little doubt, however, that Baha'is are the most persecuted minority in Iran. Since 1978, more than 200 Baha'i administrative officials or teachers have been executed (including two teenage girls), sometimes after summary trials in abstentia, or otherwise stoned or burned to death. Hundreds of others have been imprisoned and tens of thousands have been dismissed from civil service jobs and universities and deprived of pensions and businesses. Baha'i administrative structures have been banned

---

[209] Ibid., 5. The faith claims adherents from over 2,100 different ethnic and tribal groups around the world. Ibid. Of the over five million Baha'is, only 350,000 live in Iran, but they constitute that state's largest religious minority. "The Baha'i Question," 6. Although the Baha'is living in Iran are mainly fifth or sixth generation descendants of Muslims and of the same Persia ethnicity as the majority of Iranians, on a global basis few Baha'is of today have such origins. It is among the fastest growing of the world's independent religions. Baha'i International Community, "The Baha'is," 14.

[210] "Today, religious specialists recognize that [referring to the Baha'i faith as a 'sect' of Islam] would be equivalent to calling Christianity a 'sect' of Judaism, or referring to Buddhism as a 'denomination' of Hinduism." Ibid., 10, citing historian Anrold Toynbee in support of the independent status of the faith.

[211] Article 13.

and holy places and cemeteries destroyed, confiscated, or vandalized.[212] In 1993, a secret document surfaced which confirmed that these acts were all officially sanctioned by Iranian President Rafsanjani and the state's religious leader, Ali Khamenei.[213]

Iranian officials have been inconsistent in the justifications employed in their campaign to "block" Baha'i "progress and development," the language used in the secret document. Sometimes overtly religious grounds are used, as when the words "Enemy of Islam" were found written on the leg of a Baha'i executed in 1981, or when the Attorney General said about death penalties carried out that same year: "The Qur'an recognizes only People of the Book as religious communities. Others are pagans. Pagans must be eliminated."[214] Before execution, Baha'is are often pressured to recant as apostates—another indication of the religious basis of their persecution. On the other hand, the Iranian government has also charged Baha'is with supporting the late Shah's regime and collaborating with his secret police; engaging in prostitution, adultery, and immorality; and serving as agents of Zionism. In actuality, Baha'is were also persecuted by SAVAK and the Pahlavi regime; the criminal charges stem from the government's refusal to recognize Baha'i marriages and from the mixed seating at Baha'i gatherings; and from the coincidental location in Haifa, Israel of the Baha'i World Center, established in the nineteenth century at the instructions of the exiled Baha'u'llah.[215]

The Iranian government has gone to great lengths to portray the Baha'i faith as a political movement committing political crimes. It claims to permit freedom of belief by Baha'i individuals while criminalizing their conduct when they associate collectively within Baha'i institutions. However, as noted by Mayer, this conceptual distinction is itself circular under the Iranian constitution, which explicitly defines political crimes in accordance with "law, [which is] based upon Islamic principles."[216] In other words, political crimes are whatever Iran's politico-clerical leaders say they are.

---

[212] See Mayer, *Islam and Human Rights*, 158; Baha'i International Community, "The Baha'is," 59; Odio Benito, *Elimination of All Forms of Intolerance*, 10, citing the UN Special Representative's report; Mark Jolly, "Too Good for Hanging," *The London Times* (June 26, 1993); Baha'i International Community, "The Baha'i Question," 14-23.

[213] Ibid., 36-41.

[214] Ibid., 25, 17.

[215] Ibid., 24-26; Mayer, *Islam and Human Rights*, 169, 178. See "Iran Dismisses U.N. Report of Rights Abuses," *Reuter Library Report* (November 26, 1993), reporting that "Iranian officials say that the Baha'is who were executed were convicted of specific charges, usually spying, and were not killed because of their beliefs."

[216] Mayer, *Islam and Human Rights*, 179, citing article 168 of the Iranian Constitution.

Iranian policy—like all such oppressive policies described in this section—also fails the test of international law. Freedom of religion is protected "either individually or in community with others and in public or private," and includes the right "to manifest [one's] religion or belief in worship, observance, practice and teaching,"[217] all of which are performed in group settings. As in the case of all persecuted non-Muslim religious minorities, discrimination on the basis of religion or between religious groups is expressly prohibited.[218] Moreover, the existence of a state religion does not legitimize any such discrimination.

Conclusion: Revivalism, Liberalism, or Synthesis?

This chapter has examined religious dissidents in Muslim societies and the policies and practices of Muslim authorities, both classical and contemporary, in respect of the right to religious freedom. While acknowledging some conceptual overlap, it has classified religious dissidents according to whether they are former believers ("apostates and blasphemers"), heterodox believers ("heretics and renegades"), or nonbelieving religious minorities ("infidels"). Classical Islam had separate rules of treatment for each of these three categories of people. The following conclusions are drawn from this study.

First, Islam is not, and has never been, a monolithic religious or cultural system. As early as the year 656, only 24 years after Muhammed's death, divisions and heterodox interpretations began to emerge, including some particularly democratic and tolerant ones. The undifferentiated Muslim image may have been created by the intensity with which the orthodox varieties of Islam have struggled to repress dissent—if not due also to Western ignorance about the religion. "The blanket labeling of Islam as a fundamentalist threat is dangerous, because it plays into the purposes of the Islamists themselves. Such stereotypical thinking tacitly accepts the assertion of fundamentalist ideologues that they represent the *real* Islam. It also lends credence to the Islamists' insistence that there is a kind of primal, irreconcilable hostility between Islam and 'the West' that inevitably makes them archenemies."[219]

Second, Islam is capable of internal reform. *Ijtihad*, or creative interpretation, is a classic Muslim methodology for adapting archaic or obsolete doctrines, including those derived from divine revelation. Resistance to such adaptation is not mandated by the original sources of Shari'a themselves but only by later authorities who benefited from the con-

---

[217] Article 18(1), International Covenant on Civil and Political Rights.

[218] See the Covenant, article 27; and the Declaration, articles 2, 3, 4 and 7.

[219] Hottinger, "The Real Perils of Islamism."

tinuation of outmoded doctrines. (An example of a tenet—of question-able authenticity in its own right—which is ripe for reinterpretation is that execution is the punishment for apostasy. Why is capital punishment necessary for the occasional rejectionist when Islam is no longer a tiny, threatened tribal creed but the world's fastest growing religion?) The re-discovery of early, heterodox schools of thought, such as that of the democratic Kharijites, could revitalize Islam and bring it new admirers.

Third, throughout Muslim history, and particularly in the contempo-rary era, much of the persecution of alleged apostates, heretics, and infi-dels has been politically motivated, designed to benefit hegemonic, orthodox groups who have resorted to religious justifications to legiti-mize their abusive power. As stated by the Jordanian journalist Rami Khouri: "The modern tradition of Arab police states and oligarchies is far from traditional Arab culture; it is a distortion engendered largely by the circumstances of mid-20th century history, when Arab individuals, fami-lies and clans were either handed governmental power by the retreating European colonial powers or seized it soon after and maintained their in-cumbency in association with the armed forces. . . ."[220] Therefore, it is im-proper to conclude that Islam is inherently militant, violent, coercive, or intolerant. While it may have some anti-ecumenical tendencies and an unusually fierce commitment to monotheism, it is hardly the only relig-ion that has killed or oppressed in its own name.

Finally, Muslim dissidents and religious minorities in Muslim lands need and deserve more support from international human rights move-ments. The same is true for those within orthodox Muslim circles who are willing—but for their fear of persecution—to criticize abuses of human rights by their governments. Similarly, the international media must avoid giving undue prominence to violent Muslim militants, which in re-ality are small in number, and give proportional attention to liberal Mus-lim groups, albeit fledgling, who oppose violence, favor democratization and seek to promote accommodation and reform.[221]

---

[220] Rami G. Khouri, "Democracy East and West: Culture, Authenticity and Universal Values," unpublished paper presented in Washington, D.C., at a conference sponsored by the Foundation on Democratization and Political Change in the Middle East, May 26-28, 1994, 2. A very similar point can be made about Islam generally, not only the Arab regimes. See Mayer, *Islam and Human Rights*, 21: "The great problems of human rights in Muslim countries are not ones created by the increasingly rare survival of traditional cultures: They are created by governmental policies and laws inimical to rights and democratic freedoms."

[221] Admittedly, the liberal groups are less well-organized than the militants, in part be-cause of their vulnerability to persecution. They also tend to include Western-educated elites who may, for reason of that very association, lack credibility with the Muslim masses. See Timothy D. Sisk, *Islam and Democracy: Religion, Politics and Power in the Middle East* (Washington, 1992), 17-21. See also "The Silence in Arab Culture," *The New Republic* (April 6, 1987): 27. For more on these contemporary, liberal Muslim groups, see Harik, "Pluralism in

Or is support for Islamic liberalism futile? After all, economic, political, and demographic trends seem to augur the worsening of the very conditions that have led to support of Islamic militancy: "[S]tate political brutality, humiliation by Israel and the West, economic disparity . . . the stresses of brisk social transformation and Westernization, ... the burgeoning mass of uneducated, unskilled, displaced, and often unemployed urban slum dwellers, along with the shrinking, increasingly worried and resentful middle class and educated professionals who were unsatisfied with the Westernization of their societies."[222] Put another way, is Muslim democracy possible? Does it require an almost oxymoronic "Islamic secularism," an unprecedented Muslim rejection of the intermingling of mosque and state and acceptance of Western-style individualism, or the creation of a kind of Islamic Protestantism or a Muslim version of the Second Vatican Council?

Whether or not these developments are possible, probable, or even necessary for the protection of religious freedom, it is certain that any new belief system that eventually emerges will have to be authentically Muslim in form and content, developed indigenously rather than externally imposed, to have any chance of taking hold.

---

the Arab World"; Pappe, "Moderation in Islam"; Mayer, "Universal Versus Islamic Human Rights," 364-371; Muhammad Faour, *The Arab World After Desert Storm* (Washington, 1993).

[222] Rami G. Khouri, "Hamas, Islamism and the Last Two Decades: The View from Fourth Circle," unpublished article (November, 1994), 3, 1.

An Apologia For Religious Human Rights

JAMES E. WOOD, JR.
Baylor University

For all too long, religious human rights have been given short shrift in both the debate over and the struggle for human rights throughout the world. It is the purpose of this chapter, therefore, to offer an apologia for religious human rights, for such rights lie at the heart of the struggle for human rights around the world and involve the very sanctity of the human person. An apologia for religious human rights also stands to strengthen the cause of human rights in general.

The term "religious human rights" is used here interchangeably with the term "religious liberty." By religious human rights are meant the inherent right of a person in public or in private to worship or not to worship according to one's own conscience, understanding, or preferences; to profess and to propagate one's faith; to join in association with others of like faith; and to change one's religious identity—all without hindrance, molestation, or discrimination. Religious human rights require the equality of all religions,[1] as well as irreligion, before the law, and that, according to the law, a citizen neither enjoys advantages nor suffers disadvantages because of one's religious faith or identity.

Historically and ideologically, religious rights and political rights are inextricably intertwined, a point which will be advanced later in this chapter. For now, let it be said that the very emergence of the concept of religious human rights, more familiarly referred to as religious liberty, was the inevitable result of a way of thinking about the nature of religion and the nature of the state.

The recognition of religious human rights as a valid principle in law has become one of those axiomatic commitments that is almost universally shared among the family of nations; this recognition is surely one of

---

[1] In the words of Lord Acton, "Religious liberty . . . is possible only where the co-existence of different religions is admitted, with an equal right to govern themselves according to their own equal principles." John Emerich Edward Dalberg-Acton, *The History of Freedom and Other Essays* (New York, 1967), 152.

J. Witte, Jr. and J.D. van der Vyver (eds.), Religious Human Rights in Global Perspective, 455-483.
© 1996 *Kluwer Law International. Printed in the Netherlands.*

the major achievements of this century. While there is overwhelming evidence to indicate that religious human rights or religious liberty are far from being an existential reality in most of today's world, and no-where fully realized, religious liberty has become a normative principle for most of the nations of the world and, conversely, the denial of religious liberty is almost everywhere viewed as morally and legally invalid. Consequently, guarantees of religious rights and religious liberty presently appear in the vast majority of the national constitutions throughout the world today, including (except for Albania which outlawed all religions during the years of 1967-1989) even those governments committed to atheistic communism or irreligion. Although respect for religious rights and religious liberty—namely the absence of discrimination based upon religion or belief and the equality of all religions before the law—can hardly be said to be descriptive of conditions as they exist in most countries of the world today, there is profound significance to be found in the fact that the concept of religious liberty has come to have normative value almost universally.

Despite an almost universal commitment to religious human rights, as witnessed in the United Nations Declaration of Human Rights in 1948 and, even more explicitly, in its Declaration on the Elimination of All Forms of Intolerance and of Discrimination Based on Religion or Belief of 1981, there is no universal consensus as to their intellectual or philosophical basis. While religious human rights or religious liberty in broad principle have come to be widely endorsed in both national constitutions and in international law, there is no universal consensus as to their rational or philosophical basis. To be sure, there are important political and practical reasons for arguing the case for religious rights and religious liberty, which will be noted later in this essay, but even those political or practical reasons need ultimately to be rooted in some philosophical principles and not depend primarily, not to mention solely, on political expediency.

Religious Human Rights and Early Religious Teachings

An apologia for religious human rights may be found, first of all, in the early teachings of the religions themselves. While the emergence of religious human rights or religious liberty, although nowhere completely realized, is a relatively modern phenomenon, the concept of religious liberty has a long, albeit tortuous, history. The notion of religious rights is one to be found in the teachings of the great world religions, even though it has been far less descriptive of the history of the religions themselves. Even tolerance has not been characteristic of the history of religions.

Since religion generally served as the basis of one's identity as a member of the tribe, the community, or the nation, one's religious identity virtually formed the basis of one's differentiation from membership in another tribe, community, or nation and from the world at large. What is more, religion often became the root cause of intergroup conflict between tribes, communities, and nations—for example, Israelites and Canaanites, Christians and Romans, Sikhs and Hindus, Muslims and Jews, Eastern Orthodox and Roman Catholics, and Catholics and Protestants. In this way, religion fostered division and not unity, conflict and not concord, and at the heart of this division or conflict has been each religion's perception of the truth, whether based upon its claims of prophetic revelation, some mystical experience(s), or a rational apprehension of existence. The very historical particularity of religion did not make for tolerance or the recognition of religious human rights outside of one's own religious tradition. Each religion generally claimed, or at least assumed, a uniqueness or superiority of its own even when it maintained a posture of inclusivity and embraced some form of syncretism in its philosophical or theological propositions of truth.

Nonetheless, it is well here to acknowledge that voices against intolerance and respect for religious human rights may be traced back even to the ancient world. In arguing the case for religious human rights today, it should not be overlooked that there are explicit teachings of tolerance and condemnation of religious coercion and disrespect for religious views other than one's own to be found in the major world religions.[2] Furthermore, these teachings from the religions themselves stand to serve as helpful reminders to their adherents today that the sacred writings of their religious traditions' endorsing religious human rights may constitute a basis for interfaith relations based upon mutual respect and good will, even dialogue. In addition, these teachings provide support for constitutional and legal provisions on religious human rights that are being increasingly called for in both national and international law. Obviously, however, these teachings from the major world religions in support of religious human rights need to be lifted above the historical and nationalistic expressions of the religions themselves and to serve as a call

---

[2] Among recent publications that have highlighted this phenomenon, see: Leonard Swidler, ed., *Religious Liberty and Human Rights in Nations and in Religions* (Philadelphia, 1986); David Little, John Kelsay, and Abdulaziz Sachedina, *Human Rights and the Conflicts of Culture: Western and Islamic Perspectives on Religious Liberty* (Columbia, SC, 1988); Arlene Swidler, ed., *Human Rights in Religious Traditions* (New York, 1982); Leroy S. Rouner, *Human Rights and the World's Religions* (Notre Dame, IN, 1988); Robert Traer, *Faith in Human Rights: Support in Religious Traditions for a Global Struggle* (Washington, 1991); Hans Küng and Jürgen Moltmann, eds., *The Ethics of World Religions and Human Rights* (Philadelphia, 1990); David Cohn-Sherbok, ed., *World Religions and Human Liberation* (Maryknoll, NY, 1992).

to their adherents to be true to the ethical norms and teachings of their respective faiths with regard to religious human rights and religious liberty.[3]

In the ancient teachings of Hinduism, for example, intolerance and the very denigration of the religious rights of other faiths are expressly condemned. Basic to the Hindu tradition is the declaration, "Truth is One; sages call it by different names."[4] Or again, from Hindu Sacred Writings, "Ignorant is he who says, 'What I say and know is true; others are wrong.' It is because of this attitude of the ignorant that there have been doubts and misunderstandings about God. It is this attitude that causes dispute among men. But all doubts vanish when one gains self-control and attains tranquility by realizing the heart of Truth. Thereupon dispute, too, is at an end."[5] The ancient Sacred Writings of Hinduism affirm not only that tolerance and respect are to be shown those of other religious traditions, but also these writings reason that tolerance and respect are rooted in the belief that there is good to be found in all religions. "Like the bee, gathering honey from different flowers," Hindu Scriptures declare, "the wise man accepts the essence of different scriptures and sees only good in all religions."[6] In the words of one of Hinduism's most renowned twentieth-century thinkers and apologists, Sarvepalli Radhakrishnan, "The faiths of others all desire to be honoured for one reason or another. By honouring them, one exalts one's own faith and at the same time performs a service to the faith of others. By acting otherwise, one injures one's own faith and also does disservice to that of others. For if a man extols his own faith and disparages another, because of devotion to his own and because he wants to glorify it, he seriously injures his own faith."[7]

Similarly, Buddhism is deeply rooted in the concept of religious freedom and respect for religious human rights. A charitable attitude toward

---

[3] The purpose here in citing the teachings from the sacred writings of the major world religions bearing upon respect for religious human rights is not to suggest that there is an essential oneness among the major world religions in their concepts of ultimate reality or that they share a common world view or way of salvation. Rather, it should be understood that the selections from the sacred writings of the major world religions cited here are made solely because they reflect views of these traditions on religious human rights and the concept of religious liberty. As one Buddhist scholar, Phra Khantipolo, has rightly warned, "To try to steamroller every religion into the concept of basic sameness or 'all-is-one-ness' is to ignore facts in favor of a pre-conceived ideal." For, Kantipolo concludes, "in trying to believe in everything, one does in fact neither believe anything sincerely nor understand anything thoroughly." Phra Khantipolo, *Tolerance: Study from Buddhist Sources* (London, 1964), 35, 37.

[4] Rig Veda Book 1, Hymn 164:46.

[5] Srimad Bhagavatam 11:15.

[6] Ibid., 11:3.

[7] S. Radhakrishnan, *Religion in a Changing World* (London, 1967), 174.

all religious views and their adherents is encouraged. The founder of Buddhism, Siddhartha Gautama, urged that his followers not bear ill-will toward anyone who spoke ill of him. Rather, Gautama declared, "If anyone were to speak ill of me or my doctrine or my Order, do not bear ill-will towards him, do not be upset or perturbed at heart; for if you were to be so, it will only cause *you* harm."[8] Again, to quote from Buddhist Scriptures, "The Buddha says, 'To be attached to a certain view and to look down upon other views as inferior—this the wise men call a fetter [i.e., a wrong].'"[9] In teaching respect for all believers, Gautama declared, "If a man says 'This is my faith,' so far he maintains truth. But by that he cannot proceed to the absolute conclusion: 'This alone is Truth, and everything else is false.'"[10] In the Sacred Writings of one Buddhist sect in Japan, the Omoto Kyo, is to be found the following: "There is not a single place in all the corners of the world where God is absent."[11] The first of the great world religions to become international, Buddhism has demonstrated throughout much of its history a spirit of tolerance and a respect for religious human rights in its encounters with other faiths.

Still other ancient religious traditions call for respect to be shown toward those of other faiths. In the Scriptures of Jainism, founded like Buddhism six centuries before the dawn of Christianity, appears the following: "Those who praise their own doctrines and disparage the doctrines of others do not solve any problem."[12] Jains are admonished in their sacred scriptures to "comprehend one philosophical view through comprehensive study of another one."[13] This regard for other religious traditions is affirmed also in Confucianism. "In the world there are many different roads," Confucius said, "but the destination is the same. There are a hundred deliberations but the result is one."[14]

The tradition of Judaism has long contended for religious human rights. In Judaism, the very covenant which God established with Israel affirmed that God's love is for all people, and purposed that through that covenant, "All the families of the earth are to be blessed."[15] In the Holy Scriptures of Judaism, which are, of course, also viewed as Sacred Scripture by those in the Christian tradition, are these words: "For from the rising of the sun to its setting my name is great among the nations, and in

---

[8] Digha Nikaya 1:3.
[9] Sutta Nipata 798.
[10] Majjhima Nikaya 2:176.
[11] Michi-no-Shiori.
[12] Sutrakritanga 1.1:50.
[13] Acarangasutra 5:113.
[14] I Ching, 2:5.
[15] Genesis 12:3.

every place incense is offered to my name, and a pure offering; for my name is great among the nations, says the Lord of hosts."[16] In the *Tosefta*, Rabbi Joshua is recorded as saying, "There are righteous men among the nations who have a share in the world to come."[17] The ultimate ground for respect for all human rights in Judaism is to be found in its teachings concerning the infinite worth of every person or the sanctity of every individual life. Respect for divergent faiths is clearly and explicitly affirmed in the Talmudic writings of Judaism. In the Mishnah are to be found these words, "Therefore, was a single person [first] created to teach thee that if anyone destroys a single soul. . . . Scripture charges him as though he had destroyed a whole world, and whosoever rescues a single soul. . . . Scripture credits him as though he had saved a whole world. . . . The Holy One has stamped all mankind with the die of the first man and yet not one of them is like to his fellow. Therefore, everyone is bound to say, 'For my sake was the universe created.'"[18] One of Judaism's most beloved and respected scholars in this century, the late Rabbi Abraham Heschel, was fond of saying, "God's voice speaks in many languages"—a view widely shared in Judaism.[19]

In Christianity, religious tolerance and the sanctity of religious rights may be found, as with Judaism, in the affirmation that all of humanity is created in the image of God. Beyond that, Christian Scripture categorically declares that "God has not left himself without witness"[20] and speaks of "the true Light, which lighteth every man that cometh into the world."[21] Religious tolerance and respect for religious rights may be found also in Christian Scripture in the manner of God's dealings with all human beings. Peter, one of the disciples of Jesus who early became a leader of early Christianity, is quoted as saying, "God has shown me that I should not call any one common or unclean." "Truly I perceive that God shows no partiality, but in every nation any one who fears him and does what is right is acceptable to him."[22] Between Jews and Gentiles, Paul also declared, "God shows no partiality."[23] A person's capacity for freedom, the Scripture maintains, is from God. As Paul wrote, "Where the spirit of the Lord is present, there is freedom."[24] The very invitation

---

[16] Malachi 1:11.

[17] Tosefta Sanhedrin, 13.2.

[18] M. Sanhedrin, 4:5.

[19] Abraham Joshua Heschel, *God in Search of Man: A Philosophy of Judaism* (New York, 1955), 142.

[20] Acts 14:17.

[21] John 1:9.

[22] Acts 10:34-35.

[23] Romans 2:11.

[24] 2 Corinthians 3:17.

of Jesus throughout the Gospels is repeatedly conditioned with the words, "whosoever will. . . ." or "if you want to. . . ,"[25] words which by their very nature constitute an invitation born out of respect for the human will in matters of religious belief. God's very approach to all of humankind is perhaps nowhere in Christian Scripture more clearly portrayed than in the last book of the New Testament, *The Revelation*, in which respect for the inviolability of the religious rights of every person is presented dramatically and unequivocally: "Behold I stand at the door and knock; if any person hears my voice and opens the door, I will come into his house and eat with him, and he will eat with me."[26]

In Islam, the Qur'an categorically declares that "there shall be no compulsion in religion."[27] The Qur'an further declares that belief is ultimately a matter of personal choice: "Proclaim, O Prophet, This is the truth from your Lord; then let him who will, believe, and let who will, disbelieve."[28] Tolerance toward other religions is explicitly enjoined on those who follow the Qur'an, as follows: "Revile not those deities whom the unbelievers call upon and worship."[29] Indeed, according to the teachings of the Qur'an, Muslims can respect the believers and the teachings of all religions—even those not mentioned in the Qur'an, such as Hinduism, Buddhism, Jainism, and Confucianism.[30] According to Islam, a person's freedom to choose is prerequisite to faith. Again, in the words of the Qur'an, "If it had been the Lord's will, all the people on the earth would have come to believe, one and all. Are you then going to compel the people to believe except by God's dispensation?"[31]

Similar teachings may be found in Scriptures of Sikhism, whose founder, Nanak, declared, "Search not for the True One afar off; He is in every heart."[32] According to Sikhism, people of God are to be found in all religions. The Scriptures of Sikhism declare, "There are those who read the Vedas and others—Christians, Jews, Muslims—who read the Semitic scriptures. Some wear blue, some white robes. Some call themselves Muslims, others Hindus. Some aspire to *bahishat* [Muslim heaven], some

---

[25] See, e.g., Matthew 19:21-22.

[26] The Revelation 3:20.

[27] Qur'an 2:256.

[28] Ibid., 18:29.

[29] Ibid., 6:108.

[30] Ibid., 35:24; 40:78; and 22:67.

[31] Ibid., 10:99-100; still another translation given ends with these words: "Wilt thou then compel mankind against their will, to believe?"

[32] M.A. MacAuliffe, *The Sikh Religion: Its Gurus, Sacred Writings, and Anthems*, 6 vols. (Oxford, 1909), 1:328.

to *swarga* [Hindu heaven]. Says Nanak, Whoever realizes the will of the Lord, he will find out the Lord's secrets!"[33]

While these citations from the teachings of the religions hold special significance for the formulation of an apologia for religious human rights, at the same time, it must once again also be acknowledged that the spirit of tolerance and respect for religious human rights have not, by any means, been historically characteristic or descriptive of the religions themselves. Alas, none of the world religions has lived up to its own teachings with regard to religious human rights.[34] This is readily observable in the history of Christianity, not only with respect to religious human rights, but also with respect to its original teachings on peace and its repudiation of the use the sword or violence. The disparity between the teachings of the religions and their historical expression is simply undeniable. This disparity between faith and practice has plagued all of the world religions, which, without exception, have all too often been but pale shadows, sometimes even perversions, of their true essence. As alluded to earlier, the historical record of the religions has often been one of contradiction to the teachings cited above. Admittedly, the sanctity of the rights of the individual person and the basic human right to religious self-identity have been flagrantly and repeatedly violated by the religions themselves. In fact, the hallmarks of the history of religion have been intolerance not tolerance, conformity not nonconformity, and assent and not dissent.

It cannot be denied that for more than a thousand years the history of Christianity was marked by intense intolerance and persecution of Jews and all religious dissenters, who were readily branded as "heretics." It is no exaggeration to say that in the broad sweep of history more wars have been fought, more persecutions have been carried out in the name of religion than for any other single cause. As one historian has succinctly expressed it, "Nowhere does the name of God and justice appear more frequently than on the banner and shield of the conqueror."[35] Nevertheless, despite any disparity between the history of the religions and their sacred writings, an apologia for religious human rights needs first to recognize the presence of the concept of religious human rights in the scriptures of the major religions themselves, since these writings provide for each of the religious traditions the authoritative teaching norms of the

---

[33] Adi Granth, Rag Ramkali, 885.

[34] There are those who would readily cite passages in the Scriptures of Judaism, Christianity, and Islam, in particular, that would appear to be contradictory to showing respect or even tolerance toward those of other religious traditions. The point being made here, however, is that there are sacred writings of the world's religions that do affirm a respect for the religious rights of others.

[35] Hubert Muller, *Religion and Freedom in the Modern World* (Chicago, 1963), 52.

faith. Even from this brief sampling, there are clearly valuable resources to be found in the great world religions to show that the concept of religious human rights, far from being an alien concept, is expressly endorsed within the very core of the teachings of the major world religions.

Religious Human Rights and the Nature of Religion

An apologia for religious human rights is not only to be found in the sacred writings of the major religions of the world, but is also directly linked to the nature of religion. For this reason, religious intolerance is antithetical to religion and is, indeed, religion's worst adversary. To believe is a *voluntary* act. To be true to itself, authentic religion must wait upon the voluntary responses of persons who are free of coercion in order for religious faith to be genuine and to be true to itself. Recognition of this was conceded by the early church fathers. Near the close of the second century, Justin Martyr, who argued for the principle of the *logos spermatikos*, namely that the seed of the divine word is also present outside of the Christian tradition, perceptively wrote, "Nothing is more contrary to religion than constraint."[36] In the third century, when Emperor Septimus Severus issued a decree in 202 forbidding conversion to Christianity, Tertullian wrote that freedom of religion is a fundamental right. "It is a matter of both human and natural law," he declared, "that every man can worship as he pleases. . . . It is not in the nature of religion to impose itself by force," but "should be adopted freely."[37] Almost a century later, and with considerable insight into the nature of religion, Athanasius declared, "It is not with the sword and spear, nor with soldiers and armed force that truth is to be propagated, but by counsel and sweet persuasion."[38] Similarly, Lactantius, the tutor of Emperor Constantine's son, argued that "it is only in religion that liberty has chosen to dwell. For nothing is so much a matter of free will as religion, and no one can be required to worship what he does not will to worship. He can perhaps pretend, but he cannot will."[39]

During the Middle Ages, when religious liberty existed nowhere in Europe, Marsilius of Padua, a Catholic lawyer, eloquently argued in the fourteenth century that coercion is completely foreign to the nature of religion and that religious convictions by their very nature cannot be

---

[36] Quoted in M. Searle Bates, *Religious Liberty: An Inquiry* (New York, 1945), 137.

[37] Tertullian, *Ad Scapulam*, 2, in Migne, *Patrologia Latina*, 1:699, quoted in Joseph Lecler, S.J., "Religious Freedom: An Historical Survey," in Neophytos Edelby and Teodoro Jimenez-Urresti, eds., *Religious Freedom* (New York, 1966), 5.

[38] Athanasius, *Divina Instituta*, 54, in Migne, *Patrologia Latina*, 6:1061.

[39] Lactantius, *Divina Instituta*, 1,5c 20, in Migne, *Patrologia Latina*, 6:516.54.

forced. No religious authority has the right to exercise coercion for compliance to religious commandments. "For it would be useless," Marsilius wrote, "for him to coerce anyone to observe them, since the person who observed them under coercion would be helped not at all toward eternal salvation."[40] "For Christ did not ordain that anyone should be coerced to observe in this world the law made by him, and for this reason he did not appoint in this world a judge having coercive power over transgressors of his law."[41] "Even if it were given to the bishop or priest to coerce men in those matters which relate to divine law, it would be useless. For those who were thus coerced would not be helped at all toward eternal salvation by such compulsion."[42] As with earlier voices for religious liberty, Marsilius espoused religious liberty as a matter of principle and viewed religious liberty as an essential feature of authentic religion.

Two centuries later, Desiderius Erasmus, the great Catholic humanist and irenicist, wrote similarly that the use of coercion is contrary to the nature of religion and, therefore, he argued for "the futility of persecution."[43] In a letter to John Carondolet, Erasmus wrote, "When faith is in the mouth rather than in the heart, when the solid knowledge of Sacred Scripture fails us, nevertheless by terrorization we drive men to believe what they do not believe, to love what they do not love, to know what they do not know. That which is forced cannot be sincere, and that which is not voluntary cannot please Christ."[44]

Special tribute must always be given to the Radical Reformers who championed voluntarism in religion and its corollary the separation of church and state, that is, the separation of religious affairs from temporal power and the denial of the use of temporal power in religious matters.[45]

---

[40] Marsilius, *Defensor Pacis*, Alan Gewirth, trans. (New York, 1956), II, ix, 2.

[41] Ibid.

[42] Ibid., II, v, 6.

[43] Quoted in Roland H. Bainton, *Erasmus of Christendom* (New York, 1969), 185.

[44] Ep. 1334, 5 January 1523, in Desiderius Erasmus, *Opus epistolarum*, 5:11.362-81, quoted in Sebastian Castellio, *Concerning Heretics: Whether They Are To Be Persecuted and How They Are To Be Treated: A Collection of the Opinions of Learned Men, Both Ancient and Modern*, Roland H. Bainton, trans. (New York, 1935), 34. Later in 1519, in response to Martin Luther's dramatic public challenge at Wittenberg of the Roman Catholic Church, Erasmus wrote to the Archbishop of Mainz, the following: "If he is innocent, I would not like to see him crushed by evil factions; if he is in error, I would like to see him cured, not lost. Such conduct would agree better with the example of Christ who . . . did not extinguish the smoking flax, nor break the bruised reed." Quoted in Joseph Lecler, S.J., *Toleration and Reformation*, T. L. Westow, trans., 2 vols. (New York, 1960), 1:116.

[45] In his monumental study of the Radical Reformation, George H. Williams concluded that "almost all of the Radicals [i.e., Radical Reformers] insisted on the utter separation of the church from the state and found in the willingness of the Magisterial Reformers [e.g., Martin Luther, Huldreich Zwingli, and John Calvin] to use coercive power of princes, kings, and

The voices of the Radical Reformation for religious liberty were predicated upon the uncoerced response to the gospel. This, they held, was essential for the *esse* of the true church. Thus, the use of coercion in religion was opposed. "A Turk or a heretic," Balthasar Hubmaier wrote, "is not convinced by our act, either by the sword or with fire, but only with patience and prayer; and so we should await with patience the judgment of God."[46]

Writing a century later in England, in a book which boldly set forth for the first time in the English language the right of universal religious liberty, Thomas Helwys argued that the nature of religion removed it from the jurisdiction of the civil ruler.

> Our Lord the King is but an earthly King, and he hath no authority as a King, but in earthly causes, and if the Kings people be obedient & true subjects, obeying all humane lawes made by the King, our Lord the King can require no more: for men's religion to God, is betwixt God and themselves; the King shall not answere for it, neither may the King be jugd betwene God and Man. Let them be heretikes, Turks, Jewes, or whatsoever it apperteynes not to the earthly power to punish them in the least measure.[47]

Similarly, a few years later, Leonard Busher, a member of the first Baptist congregation of England, wrote also in opposition to the use of temporal power in religion: "It is not only unmerciful, but unnatural and abominable, yea, monstrous, for one Christian to vex and destroy another for difference and questions of religion."[48]

The voluntariness of religious faith has come to be increasingly recognized in contemporary thought.[49] Reaffirmation of the voluntary character of religion has been clearly affirmed, for example, in twentieth-century Christian ecumenical thought. The World Council of Churches has on various occasions seen religious liberty as integral to the nature of religion and religious faith. "God's redemptive dealing with men is not

---

town councilors an aberration from apostolic Christianity no less grievous than papal pretensions." George H. Williams, *The Radical Reformation* (Philadelphia, 1962), 860.

[46] Henry C. Vedder, *Balthasar Hubmaier* (New York, 1905), 86; see also Article 16 of "On Heretics and Those Who Burn Them," in *Balthasar Hubmaier: Theologian of Anabaptism*, H. Wayne Pipkin and John H. Yoder, trans. and ed. (Scottdale, PA, 1989), 62.

[47] Thomas Helwys, *A Short Declaration of the Mistery of Iniquity*, facs. repr. ed. (London, 1935), 69.

[48] Leonard Busher, *Religious Peace or a Plea for Liberty of Conscience*, quoted in Anson Phelps Stokes, *Church and State in the United States*, 3 vols. (New York, 1950), 1:113.

[49] See James E. Wood, Jr., "Religious Liberty in Ecumenical and International Perspective," *Journal of Church and State* 10 (1968): 421-36.

coercive. Accordingly, human attempts by legal enactment or by pressure of social custom to coerce or eliminate faith are violations of the fundamental ways of God with men. The freedom which God has given . . . implies a free response to God's love. . . ."[50] In the words of Vatican II, "God calls men to serve him in spirit and in truth; hence they are bound in conscience, but they stand under no compulsion."[51]

The heart of the matter is that for religion to be authentic, it must be a voluntary, personal, and free act, and membership in a faith community is one of voluntary association. Faith is not faith if its voluntary character is abridged by coercion. As Augustin Leonard, a Catholic theologian, wrote, "An imposed faith is a contradiction in terms . . . faith must be free if it is not to destroy itself."[52] Recognition of religious liberty is fundamental to religious human rights and, indeed, to all other human rights. In the words of the late A. F. Carrillo de Albornoz, for some years the Secretary of the Secretariat on Religious Liberty of the World Council of Churches, "No intellectual ingenuity, no organized institution, no kind of compulsion and no power of persuasion can change the fact that God deals with men as free and responsible beings and that he expects from them an uncoerced response."[53] Or, as Albert Hartmann expressed it, "A person's one and only means of learning God's will is the voice of one's conscience."[54] The right to religious identity and to a personal religious faith, including association with others of like faith, requires voluntariness. Religious human rights are thereby undermined and vitiated whenever any form of external coercion is superimposed on the individual.

Religious Human Rights and Human Dignity

A compelling argument for religious human rights is to be found in the sanctity of the human person and respect for the inviolability of the human conscience, for together they constitute the basis of a limited state and a free and democratic society. The Preamble of the United Nations Universal Declaration of Human Rights (1948) rightly speaks of "the inherent dignity . . . of all members of the human family" and "the dignity and worth of the human person." The Preamble common to both the In-

---

[50] "Statement on Religious Liberty," in *The New Delhi Report: The Third Assembly of the World Council of Churches, 1961* (New York, 1962), 159.

[51] "De Libertate Religiosa: A Declaration of Religious Freedom," in *The Documents of Vatican II: All Sixteen Official Texts Promulgated by the Ecumenical Council, 1963-1965,* Walter M. Abbott, S.J., ed. and Joseph Gallagher, trans. (New York, 1966), 690.

[52] Augustin Leonard, "Freedom of Faith and Civil Toleration," in id., *Tolerance and the Catholic* (New York, 1955), 113.

[53] A.F. Carrillo de Albornoz, *The Basis of Religious Liberty* (New York, 1963), 74.

[54] Albert Hartmann, *Toleranz und christlicher Glaube* (Frankurt am Main, 1955), 5.

ternational Covenant on Civil and Political Rights (1966) and the International Covenant on Economic, Social, and Cultural Rights (1966) declares, "These rights derive from the inherent dignity of the human person." While the sacredness of personhood is widely acknowledged as the foundation of all human rights, it has particular meaning in the exercise of one's sense of the sacred, that is, one's religious faith. Søren Kierkegaard wrote with profound insight that "man is himself primarily and genuinely in his free choice."[55]

The intrinsic worth of the human person is simply too sacred to be violated by religious coercion or enforced conformity, which are a denial of the dignity and worth of a person. If religious human rights are to have any real meaning, there must be legal recognition on the part of the state of the inalienable right of a citizen to decide matters of ultimate beliefs and commitment for oneself. As the World Council of Churches affirmed at the time of its founding almost forty years ago, "The nature and destiny of man . . . establish limits beyond which the government cannot with impunity go."[56] And as Vatican II also rightly proclaimed, "The protection and promotion of the inviolable rights of man ranks among the essential duties of government."[57]

Inextricably bound to the sanctity of the human person is the concept of liberty of conscience. Marsilius was perhaps the first to recognize the right of conscience both as a natural and a political right. Although religious liberty in the modern world is deeply rooted in religious thought, it stems from the concept of "liberty of conscience," a phrase of modern origin which came into use after the sixteenth century. Even though the Protestant Reformation, by and large, did not espouse the principle of religious rights or religious liberty, it did represent a revolt against both established religious as well as political authority and, in turn, fostered the emergence of new nation-states and a new national spirit throughout Europe and Great Britain. As is well known, however, the Reformation was, first of all, rooted in a revolt against established religious authority. When his views of Christian Scripture were challenged by the ecclesiastical authorities of his day, Martin Luther proclaimed, "I cannot and will not recant anything, for it is neither safe nor right to go against conscience." For, "I am more afraid of my own heart than the Pope and all

---

[55] Søren Kierkegaard, *Training in Christianity* (1850), quoted in Niels H. Soe, "The Theological Basis of Religious Liberty," *The Ecumenical Review* 11 (January, 1958): 41.

[56] W.A. Visser 't Hooft, ed., *The First Assembly of the World Council of Churches: Held at Amsterdam, August 22-September 4, 1948* (New York, 1949), 93-95 ("Declaration on Religious Liberty").

[57] "De Libertate Religiosa," in *Documents of Vatican II.*

his cardinals."[58] Aided by the humanism of the Renaissance, a bold new spirit of freedom in religion appeared, which inevitably gave rise to the cry, "faith is free." Gradually the principle of religious liberty was forthrightly affirmed, leading finally to an insistence upon "the competency of the individual under God in all matters of religion." Religious liberty was proclaimed as both a natural and a divine right. Furthermore, it was argued, religious liberty demanded civil liberty and civil liberty required liberty of conscience. "Give me the liberty to know, to think, to believe, and to utter freely, according to conscience, above all other liberties," wrote John Milton in his great work *Areopagitica* in 1644.

In their plea for religious liberty, however, the Free Churches contributed greatly to the emergence of liberty of conscience as the basis for religious liberty. In the words of Franklin H. Littell, "The most direct contribution of the Free Churches to the individual citizen, whether church member or not, was in the establishment of liberty of conscience."[59] As generally used then, as now, liberty of conscience claimed the inherent right of each person to follow the dictates of his or her own conscience without interference from civil authority or reference to popular opinion. In his monumental and trenchant work, *History of Freedom*, Lord Acton wrote that liberty of conscience is "the assurance that every man shall be protected in doing what he believes [to be] his duty, and against the influence of authorities and majorities, custom and opinion."[60]

In the Western world, liberty of conscience has been based upon two fundamental principles. First, freedom of conscience is held to be a natural and sacred right of all persons, inalienable, a domain which the true state must protect and into which it must not lightly intrude. Whereas the final aim of religion is truth, the ultimate goal of the state is freedom, or what Baruch (Benedictus) Spinoza called, "the true aim of government."[61] The second axiom is that because conscience is a natural and sacred right, innate and universal, no person is to be above another in the freedom of its exercise. All persons are equal in rights as in duties, which human authority cannot take away in the case of the former, and to which it cannot add in the case of the latter.

---

[58] See Bertram Lee Woolf, ed., *Reformation Writings of Martin Luther*, 2 vols. (London, 1956), 2:155.

[59] Franklin H. Littell, *The Free Church* (Boston, 1957), 48.

[60] Acton, *The History of Freedom*, 3.

[61] See Baruch Spinoza, *Tractatus-Theologica-Politicus* (1670), chap. 16 ("The Basis of the State"). Spinoza vigorously defended the principle of religious toleration and opposed any established form of religion.

Recognition of the religious right of liberty of conscience means the acknowledgment of one's right to believe or not to believe a religious dogma; to worship one God or many or not to worship; to be a member of a religious association or of none; and the "free exercise" of religion, without civil disabilities, so long as such exercise is not deemed to be detrimental to the basic fabric of society and the security of the state.

By its very etymology, conscience refers to moral awareness or moral insight, by which one experiences the impulse to do right and experiences restraint from doing wrong. The very nature of religion requires that it be rooted in conscience, which theologians have termed a "gift" or the "voice" of God. The Westminster Confession of Faith, Section XX, "Of Christian Liberty and Liberty of Conscience" (left unchanged in the American version) affirms the following:

> God alone is Lord of the conscience; and hath left it free from doctrine and commandments of men, which are in any thing contrary to His Word—or beside it, if matters of faith or worship. So that to believe such doctrines or to obey such commandments out of conscience, is to betray liberty of conscience; and the requiring an implicit faith, and an absolute and blind obedience, is to destroy liberty of conscience, and reason also.[62]

More than a half century ago, United States Supreme Court Chief Justice Harlan F. Stone wrote, in the *Gobitis* case, that if the constitutional guarantees of liberty "are to have any meaning they must . . . be deemed to withhold from the state any authority to compel belief or the expression of it where that expression violates religious convictions."[63] For the state to intrude on the inviolability of conscience is for the state to assume a role of transcendency and ultimate power that belong only to the Divine. Religious human rights can never be secure if the state and state institutions, even if supported by the collective will of majorities, are allowed to ignore the rights of conscience. For recognition of liberty of conscience lies at the heart of a free and democratic society and is a check on political absolutism. As Henry David Thoreau wrote more than a century ago, "There will never be a really free and enlightened State until the State comes to recognize the individual as a higher and independent power, from which all its own power and authority are derived, and

---

[62] Henry Bettenson, ed., *Documents of the Christian Church*, 2d ed. (London, 1963), 347.

[63] *Minersville School District v. Gobitis*, 310 U.S. 586 (1940), at 604.

treats him accordingly. I please myself with imagining a State at least which can afford to be just to all men."[64]

Religious Human Rights and the Secular State

An apologia for religious human rights is to be found in the concept of the secular state. There is both an historical and a philosophical connection between religious human rights and the secular state. The secular state is one in which government is limited to the *saeculum* or temporal realm; the state is independent of institutional religion or ecclesiastical control and, in turn, institutional religion is independent of state or political control. It is a state that is without jurisdiction over religious affairs, not because religious affairs are beneath the concerns of the state, but rather because religious concerns are viewed as being too high and too holy to be subject to the prevailing fallible will of civil authorities or to popular sovereignty. In application, the secular state is one which denies the use of political means to accomplish religious ends or the use of religious means for the accomplishment of political ends. Because its power is limited to temporal affairs, the relationship of the state to religion should be one of neutrality, toward both the various faith communities and to irreligion, a state where citizens are neither advantaged nor disadvantaged because of their religion. It is a state where government is denied the right of domination over the institutions of religion and the institutions of religion are denied the right of domination over the state.

Like religious liberty, the emergence of the secular state reaches back through the centuries. Throughout its history, until the modern era, the idea of the secular state has been closely related to the history of Western civilization. Historically, it has meant the repudiation of the Christian or religious state and stands, therefore, in contrast to the concept of national identity based upon a particular religious tradition, whether the Christian, the Hindu, the Buddhist, the Shinto, the Muslim, or the Sikh state. Inherent in the view of the secular state is the clear separation of spiritual and temporal powers— the religious and civil covenants—and the institutions of religion and the state. What is more, the secular state requires that the authority and jurisdiction of the state be limited to the secular or temporal realm. In the case of the secular state, the basis of the state's authority is civil and natural law, not religious decree or any claim of divine authority or divine law. All claims of a particular political authority as being based on a divine right, whether by a monarch or some other

---

[64] See Henry David Thoreau, "Essay on Civil Disobedience," in Owen Thomas, ed., *Henry David Thoreau: Walden and Civil Disobedience: Authoritative Texts, Background Reviews and Esssays in Criticism* (New York, 1966), 243.

political entity, are expressly eschewed. Similarly, all claims of a nation's being a religious state are viewed as incompatible with the concept of the secular state.

One of the major architects of the concept of the secular state was Marsilius of Padua, the renowned Roman Catholic thinker of the fourteenth century. In his great treatise, *Defensor Pacis,* published in 1324, Marsilius vigorously challenged the claims of the supremacy of the church over the state and likewise rejected the notion of the Christian state or *mundus Christianus.* He did so on the basis of a sharp distinction, which, he argued, must be made between divine and human law. He insisted that the state must be founded upon law inherent in nature, and that the church should not have jurisdiction over the state. Clearly ahead of his time, Marsilius held thus:

> Laws derive their authority from the nation, and are invalid without its assent. As the whole is greater than any part, it is wrong that any part should legislate for the whole; and as men are equal, it is wrong that one should be bound by laws made by another. But in obeying laws in which all men have agreed, all men, in reality, govern themselves. . . . He [the monarch] is responsible to the nation, and subject to the law; and the nation that appoints him and assigns him his duties, has to see that he obeys the Constitution, and has to dismiss him if he breaks it.[65]

Marsilius not only upheld the notion of the secular state, he denied the right of the church to have or to exercise temporal power. He maintained that since Christ and the apostles did not claim temporal power, neither must the church. Furthermore, he argued, divine law cannot be enforced or established by temporal power; only God is the judge of divine law. Therefore, no form of temporal coercion may be used to enforce conformity in religion. Because of the nature of the secular state, which is limited to the temporal realm, and the very nature of divine law which cannot be coerced, there can be no coercion in religious matters. "The rights of citizens," Marsilius wrote, "are independent of the faith they profess; and no man be punished for his religion." Of the state, he argued that "the source of law is to be found, not in any divine right or rulers, not in any superior wisdom of any class or society, but in the whole of its citizens."[66] Although the ideas of Marsilius on the secular state and religious liberty were almost entirely ignored for two centuries, "Marsilius's ideas," as one constitutional law scholar wrote, "were destined to have a profound influence not only on those who later were re-

---

[65] Marsilius, *Defensor Pacis,* I, xii, 5.

[66] Ibid.

sponsible for the Reformation, but also on the founders of modern constitutional history."[67]

Two centuries later, out of the Radical Reformation, there arose a reform movement built upon the concept of the voluntary church, the church of the redeemed, *corpus Christi*, comprised of persons voluntarily committed to Christ, rather than the *corpus Christianum*, or Christendom, in which membership in the church and the community or state were virtually made conterminous. This left wing of the Protestant Reformation furthered the notion of the secular state. For, unlike the Magisterial Reformers, the Radical Reformers championed the principle of voluntarism in religion, believer's baptism, and a voluntary or gathered church comprised of those committed to Christ, the corollary of which was nothing less than the institutional separation of the church from the state. The faith they proclaimed and its propagation were predicated upon an uncoerced response to religious witness. This, the radical reformers held, was essential not only for authentic religion, but also for the *esse* of the true church. In an admonition to Jacob Sturm of Strassburg, Caspar Schwenckfeld, many of whose spiritual descendants would later come to America, wrote in 1549 as follows: "Civil authority has no jurisdiction over the Kingdom of God; that government was divinely ordained for the sole purpose of maintaining an orderly life in human society, but has no right either to influence or to interfere with religious convictions; the individual is accountable to Jesus Christ as the head of the Kingdom of God."[68]

The concern of the Radical Reformation was not individual rights as such, which came to be espoused later by John Locke, the Enlightenment, and John Stuart Mill, but in the removal of the power of the state over religion. As church historians Roland H. Bainton, Franklin H. Littell, and George H. Williams, among others, have clearly shown, the "left wing of the Reformation" was dominated by one common characteristic—the espousal of religious liberty and the denial of the state's jurisdiction over religion.[69]

The realization of the secular state—although long advocated by certain political and social philosophers, Anabaptists, and certain other religious groups—did not finally occur until the inauguration of the "livelie experiment" of Rhode Island. Here, for the first time, under the

---

[67] Leo Pfeffer, *Church, State, and Freedom*, rev. ed. (Boston, 1967), 19.

[68] Quoted in Selina Schultz Gerhard, *Caspar Schwenckfeld von Ossig: 1849-1561* (Morristown, PA, 1946), 311-12.

[69] See Roland H. Bainton, *The Reformation of the Sixteenth Century* (Boston, 1952); id., *The Age of Reformation* (Princeton, 1956); Franklin H. Littell, *The Anabaptist View of the Church* (Boston, 1958); id., *The Free Church*; and Williams, *The Radical Reformation*.

dominant influence of Roger Williams, an essentially secular state was established, with full political rights guaranteed to all regardless of their religious beliefs, as Williams said, "for the good of the whole."[70]

The acknowledged architect of the American tradition of the separation of church and state, Williams sought to provide a theological basis for the secular state. The authority of the state, Williams argued, is "not religious, Christian, etc., but natural, human, [and] civil"; and therefore it is "improper" for the state to prescribe or proscribe matters of conscience and religion. "All Civil States with their Officers of justice in their respective constitutions and administrations are proved essentially Civil, and therefore not Judges, Governors or Defenders of the Spiritual or Christian State and Worship." "Therefore," Williams argued, "No civil state or country can be truly called Christian, although true Christians be in it."[71] Thus, Williams denied the right of any state to be Buddhist, Hindu, Jewish, or Muslim. To Williams, church and state must be separate not only for the church to be the church, but for the state to be the state, for God to be God, and for Christians to be Christian. "An inforced uniformity of Religion throughout a Nation or civil state," Williams declared, "confounds the Civil and Religious, [and] denies the principles of Christianity and civility. . . ."[72] Consequently, Williams held that compulsory and tax-supported religion is unchristian, that biblical Israel is not a model state for Christians, and that equality of all persons and groups before the law is a fundamental responsibility of all civil government.

Through John Locke, the view of the secular state was given still fuller expression, not on the Christian theological basis of liberty, but on the basis of natural rights, not upon mere popular or democratic sovereignty, but upon constitutional government. The starting point for Locke's political thought was not the state, but the individual. Every person is born with natural rights to life, liberty, and property. The authority of the state is derived from the consent of the governed, for example through mutual agreement or social contract, and is not subordinate to ecclesiastical power. The truth is that the state was created by individuals for their own conscience—for the protection of private property and the "execution of . . . laws . . . for the public good." All laws, Locke reasoned, are always accountable to the citizens and political absolutism is "inconsistent with civil society." Therefore, the power of all government

---

[70] See Roger Williams, *The Bloody Tenent of Persecution, for Cause of Conscience Discussed* (1644), in Joseph L. Blau, ed., *Cornerstones of Religious Freedom in America: Selected Basic Documents, Court Decisions, and Public Statements*, rev. ed. (New York, 1964), 48.

[71] Ibid., 36; see also James Ernst, *Roger Williams: New England Firebrand* (New York, 1932), 429ff.

[72] See Williams, *Bloody Tenent of Persecution*, in Blau, ed., *Cornerstones of Religious Freedom in America*, 37.

is inevitably limited by the natural rights of a person as an individual.[73] To Locke, the secular state is essentially a limited state, a view still held to be quintessential to the meaning of the secular state.

Although the concept of the secular state exerted considerable influence in England and France during the Age of Enlightenment, the United States became the first nation in history to adopt constitutionally the pattern of the secular state, wherein government is prohibited from jurisdiction over religious matters or from denying "the free exercise of religion," there is to be no religious test for public office, all religious groups are equal before the law and are to be free from discrimination or preferential treatment, and all religious groups are regarded by the state as private and voluntary associations. The secular state is to be neutral toward religion and irreligion and is to recognize its utter incompetence in purely religious matters. It seeks neither to promote nor to inhibit religion, and views religious identity as being irrelevant to the rights of citizenship. More than 120 years ago, in the first real church-state case to come before the United States Supreme Court, the Court declared,

> In this country the full and free right to entertain any religious belief, to practice any religious principle, and to teach any religious doctrine which does not violate the laws of morality and property, and which does not infringe personal rights, is conceded to all. The law knows no heresy, and is committed to the support of no dogma, the establishment of no sect. The right to organize voluntary religious associations to assist in the expression and dissemination of any religious doctrine, and to create tribunals for the decisions of controverted questions of faith within the association, and for the ecclesiastical government of all the individual members, congregations and officers within the general association, is unquestioned.[74]

With regard to the secular state, it should be remembered that the *concept* of the secular state was not born out of hostility toward religion. Rather, hostility toward religion is incompatible with the nature of the secular state, since it is uncommitted in matters of religion or ultimate belief. Rather, the secular state is rooted in the inalienable right of conscience and the principle of voluntarism in religion. That there is tension, even conflict, between church and state—the religious community and the political community—is not only inevitable, but is one to be welcomed. For the person of religious faith should be especially aware that

---

[73] See John Locke, *Two Treatises of Government [1689]* (New York, 1989), bk. 2, chap. 1, sec. 3, lines 4-6 and bk. 2, chap. 7, sec. 90, line 3.

[74] *Watson v. Jones*, 13 Wall. 679 (1872) at 729.

the tensions between the faith to which one is committed necessarily transcend the historical context in which a person lives within any given society or nation-state. This is a conflict that can never be completely resolved because of the very nature of religion which is rooted in religious vision of becoming or change, both for the person and society. At the same time, the concept of the secular state is in harmony with both the freedom of religion and freedom of the state. For these reasons, it is argued, the secular state is best for religion and best for the state, and substantially secures the freedom of both. When viewed in historical perspective, the emergence of the secular state may be seen as of major historical significance to the emergence of religious human rights and religious liberty in the modern world.

Religious Human Rights and Other Human Rights

An apologia for religious human rights is to be found in the special relationship that religious rights have to all other human rights, both individual and social.[75] This arises from the sanctity or intrinsic worth ascribed to the human person (even when personhood is defined in radically different ways as in the various religious traditions), which ultimately form the basis of all human rights. It is the sanctity or intrinsic worth of the person, whether explicitly acknowledged or not, that form the basis of democracy and constitutional government in which some principle of human rights is accepted as inalienable and, therefore, as binding on government. Religious human rights are rooted in the inviolable sacredness of the human conscience. Each human being has juridical rights because he or she possesses certain inalienable moral rights as a person. And basic to all human rights are religious rights, without the guarantee of which, it is argued, all other human rights are in peril.

It is widely conceded that religious liberty is a basic human right. As noted at the beginning of this chapter, religious liberty has become a normative principle for virtually all nations, as expressed in their constitutions. While there is a sense in which all human rights, both individual and social, may be said to be indivisible, there is clearly a special place to be given religious human rights in the widening horizons of understanding of human rights in contemporary society throughout the world.

---

[75] There are those who argue that the very concept of human rights is ineliminably religious. See, e.g., Michael J. Perry, "The Idea of Human Rights: Is the Idea of Human Rights Ineliminably Religious?" in James E. Wood, Jr. and Derek Davis, eds., *Problems and Conflicts Between Law and Morality in a Free Society* (Waco, TX, 1994), 55-116. In the words of Perry, "If the conviction that every human being is sacred is inescapably religious, it follows that the idea of human rights is ineliminably religious, because the conviction is an essential, even foundational, constituent of the idea." Ibid., 79.

This is not in any way intended to diminish the critical role to be played on behalf of economic and social rights, as well as other civil and political rights, in the overall struggle for human rights, for all human rights are ultimately interrelated. Religious human rights are integral to the advancement of all other human rights because of their intimate grounding in the nature and sacredness of the human person. For this reason, as affirmed in American jurisprudence and in much ecumenical thought, religious liberty is made the virtual cornerstone of all other human rights. On numerous occasions since World War II, ecumenical conferences, including those held even outside the West, have affirmed that "the most fundamental freedom is religious freedom."[76]

For many reasons, too numerous to be expanded upon here, religious liberty is widely regarded as the foundation of all other civil liberties and is fundamentally interrelated to all other human rights. In the words of the World Council of Churches, "religious freedom is the condition and guardian of all true freedom."[77] Without religious freedom, it is obvious that freedom of speech, freedom of press, freedom of assembly, and freedom of association are endangered. Without recognition of religious human rights, the very right of dissent is in jeopardy. And, in the words of a former Chief Justice of the United States Supreme Court, Charles Evans Hughes, "When we lose the right to be different, we lose the right to be free."[78]

Respect for religious human rights is profoundly important in the state's regard for other human rights and its view of the worth of its individual citizens. Indeed, by respecting *religious* rights, the state is giving substantive expression to its regard for the dignity and worth of its citizens. Such recognition is not only an acknowledgment of the state's limited political authority, as over against the claims of the totalitarian state, but is quite likely to result in giving far greater recognition to other human rights, both civil and political, economic and social. It is entirely reasonable to argue, in the words of the late A. F. Carrillo de Albornoz, that

> respect for the highest values or loyalties of man (which are the religious ones) will be the final "test" and also the best guarantee of the respect for all other human values. If, for instance, a totalitarian state does not recognize even the most sacred sphere of religion and the most intimate human autonomy, it will most probably not stop before other less important values and less in-

---

[76] Eastern Asia Conference, Bangkok, 1949; see Albornoz, *The Basis of Religious Liberty*, 27-41.

[77] "Statement on Religious Liberty," in *Minutes and Reports, Central Committee of the World Council of Churches* (Chichester, 1949), 15.

[78] Quoted in Stokes, *Church and State in the United States*, 2:462.

timate spheres. In this sense it seems perfectly correct to affirm that, if society does not respect religion and its liberty, one does not have any security that the rest will be respected.[79]

With the adoption by the United Nations of the Declaration on the Elimination of All Forms of Intolerance and of Discrimination Based on Religion or Belief, the United Nations went out of its way to note that such discrimination must be regarded not only as an "affront" to human dignity, but also a "disavowal" of the very principles of the Charter of the United Nations and a violation of the other freedoms guaranteed in the Universal Declaration of Human Rights. As noted earlier, religious human rights are not only individual, but also corporate and social, since they must include the right of religious association and the free exercise of religion within a social context. Recognition of religious rights as the cornerstone of all human rights—civil, economic, and social—augurs well for the emergence of free and pluralistic nation-states in which respect for both individual and social rights may be realized.

Religious Human Rights and the International Community

Finally, an apologia for religious human rights may be found in the recognition accorded religious rights in the norms of international law and by international agreements affirming these rights as an international standard among signatory nation-states, such as The Universal Declaration of Human Rights (1948), The International Covenant on Civil and Political Rights (1966), The Principles of the Helsinki Final Act (1975), and The Declaration on the Elimination of All Forms of Intolerance and of Discrimination Based on Religion or Belief (1981).

Although religious liberty was long advocated by individuals and religious dissenters, who at least sought religious freedom for themselves, full religious liberty was nowhere legally realized until the modern era and, even today, is far from being a reality in most of today's world. As late as World War II, one worldwide study declared, "No writer asserts that there is a generally accepted postulate of international law that every State is under legal obligation to accord religious liberty within its jurisdiction."[80] Today, religious liberty has come to be recognized as an accepted postulate in international law.

It is of profound historical significance that following the organization of the United Nations in 1945, concerted efforts were soon directed

---

[79] Albornoz, *The Basis of Religious Liberty*, 41.

[80] Norman J. Padelford, "International Guarantees of Religious Liberties," quoted in Bates, *Religious Liberty: An Inquiry*, 476.

toward the formulation of the principle of religious liberty as a fundamental right to which all member nations were to subscribe—a recognition of the vital relationship of religious liberty to relations between states. As is well known, one of the basic principles included in the Charter of the United Nations is that of "the dignity and equality inherent in all human beings." Therefore, all members nations "pledged themselves to take joint and separate action in cooperation with the Organization to promote and encourage universal respect for an observance of human rights and fundamental freedoms for all without distinction as to race, sex, language, or religion."

Three years after its founding, the United Nations General Assembly adopted the "Universal Declaration of Human Rights" in which it gave specific attention to a person's right to religion as a basic human right. Article 2 affirmed that everyone is to be entitled to all the rights and freedoms in the Declaration without respect to religion. Article 18 declared, "Everyone has the right to freedom of thought, conscience, and religion; this right includes freedom to change his religion or belief, and freedom, either alone or in community with others and in public or private, to manifest his religion or belief in teaching, practice, worship and observance." In various forms, this portion of the Declaration has been incorporated in the national constitutions of many nations, particularly in the nations emerging since 1948.

After more than four decades of consultation and negotiation, the United Nations Assembly in November 1981 adopted the "Declaration on the Elimination of all Forms of Intolerance and of Discrimination Based on Religion or Belief," in which the religious rights of the "Universal Declaration of Human Rights" were affirmed. In addition, the 1981 Declaration categorically declared that "no one shall be subject to discrimination by any State, institution, group of persons or person on grounds of religion or other beliefs." Such discrimination, the Declaration went out of its way to note, must be regarded as not only an "affront" to human dignity, but also a "disavowal" of the principles of the Charter of the United Nations and violation of the freedoms guaranteed in the "Universal Declaration of Human Rights." Thus, at long last, religious human rights were given explicit recognition in the family of nations as an inviolable and sacred human right.

The growing recognition of religious liberty in international law was accompanied by broad ecumenical endorsements of religious liberty by the churches. With the convening of the First Assembly of the World Council of Churches in Amsterdam in 1948, a clear voice for religious rights and religious liberty was sounded in a document titled, "Declaration on Religious Liberty." The Declaration called on the churches "to support every endeavor to secure within an international bill of rights adequate safeguards for freedom of religion and conscience, including the right of all men to hold and change their faith, to exercise it in worship and practice, to teach and persuade others, and to decide on the religious education of their children." The Declaration further asserted that religious liberty is "an essential element in a good international order . . . . [that] should be secured everywhere. In pleading for this freedom," the Declaration declared, "[Christians] . . . do not ask for any privilege to be granted to Christians that is denied to others."[81] Adopted unanimously, the Amsterdam Declaration remains a landmark in the history of religious liberty and must be credited with having exerted some influence on the final adoption a few months later of the "Universal Declaration of Human Rights" by the United Nations.

Subsequent assemblies of the World Council of Churches have not only reaffirmed the Amsterdam Declaration but have continued to give voice to the Council's commitment to religious rights and religious liberty. Likewise, the endorsement of religious liberty by the Roman Catholic Church in Vatican II remains a significant chapter in the advancement of religious human rights. Affirming both the natural right of corporate religious freedom as well as individual religious freedom, Vatican II declared that "the right to religious freedom has its foundation in the very dignity of the human person" and that a person "should not be coerced to act against his own conscience, nor be impeded to act according to this conscience" and religious communities "have the right not to be hindered from publicly teaching and testifying to their faith both by the written and the spoken word."[82]

Here it should be remembered that historically pleas for religious toleration and religious liberty have come primarily from religious minorities and dissenters, the religiously disenfranchised, and the religiously persecuted. At the same time, let it be noted, that the major advances toward the recognition of religious human rights and religious liberty in the modern world have come not from religious confessions of faith, councils, or synods, but from constitutions, legislative bodies, and courts of law. After the Middle Ages, the emergence of new nation-states and a new national spirit weakened the political power of old religious establishments to a degree from which they generally could not recover. In widely varying degrees, religious liberty became inexorably linked to the modern democratic state. In the twentieth century, among both the communities of faith and nation-states throughout the world, a broad

---

[81] Visser 't Hooft, ed., *The First Assembly of the World Council of Churches*, 93-95.
[82] "A Declaration on Religious Freedom," in *Documents of Vatican II*, 679-682.

consensus gradually evolved toward support of the principle of religious liberty, at least in some form.

Legal recognition of religious liberty has been particularly aided, both in principle and in practice, by international relations that resulted in the ratification of treaties between states. As one major study on religious liberty written almost fifty years ago affirmed, "International law and religious liberty grew in intimate association."[83] The study found that a substantial majority of the writers of general treaties on international law following the time of Hugo Grotius, long recognized for his work as a codifier of international law, specifically referred to religious liberty in their documents. In the nineteenth century, with sovereign states identified with different religious traditions, it became common in the drawing up of treaties to include provisions granting the right of religious expression to the nationals of each contracting party in the territory of the other. Since these foreign nationals were identifiable by both their nationality and their religion, it was inevitable that specific safeguards came to be provided for freedom of conscience, worship, and religious work "upon the same terms as nationals of the state of residence," to use a phrase common to many of these international treaties with provisions of religious liberty.

There are many examples of the role of international agreement in the advance of religious liberty. The Treaty of Berlin of 1878 at the close of the Russo-Turkish War, with its provisions for the equal rights of religious minorities, has been called "the most important single expression of international agreement for religious liberty" prior to the post-World War I era.[84] Similar guarantees of religious liberty were embodied in the General Act relating to African Possessions (signed at Berlin in 1885) and the Minorities Treaties of 1919-23, following World War I. More recently, thirty-five nation-states in 1975 signed the Helsinki Final Act (The Final Act of the Conference on Security and Cooperation in Europe) in which religious rights were made an integral part of a major international agreement between thirty-five nations of Europe, Canada, and the United States. Principle 7 of the document gives special attention to "respect for human rights and fundamental freedoms, including freedom of thought, conscience, religion, or belief." Meanwhile, more and more states throughout the world voluntarily entered into constitutional and treaty commitments to secure religious liberty for their own citizens as well as for foreign residents. With the increasingly wide geographical distribu-

---

[83] Bates, *Religious Liberty*, 476. From this study, Bates observed, "A review of the forty-seven writers of the more important treaties on international law, following the time of Grotius, shows that [a] full thirty refer to religious liberty." Ibid.

[84] Ibid., 478.

tion of adherents of the world's major religions, the religions themselves challenged those national policies' denying the religious rights of their adherents and communities of faith.

Indeed, the principle of religious liberty has increasingly become one of those axiomatic commitments that is almost universally recognized. In at least some modified form, the principle of religious liberty has come to be affirmed by virtually all national governments as a part of national law. Even if highly restrictive, some guarantees of religious liberty now appear in almost all national constitutions throughout the world.

Nonetheless, religious liberty and respect for religious human rights remain far from realized in most of today's world. Ironically, the very century that has witnessed the emergence of religious liberty and religious human rights as norms in international law and virtually universally recognized in principle has been the very century in which religious rights and religious liberty have repeatedly and flagrantly violated on a wholesale scale throughout much of the world. For the first time in human history and for much of this century, governments came into power with a sworn hostility to religion and expressly dedicated to the eradication of all religion.

For the new democracies of both old and new nation-states, religious human rights—religious liberty—are increasingly being recognized as crucial to a free society as seen most recently in the emerging democracies of the New Europe. Throughout the New Europe, for example, constitutional reform commissions have been involved in providing guarantees of religious rights and religious liberty, along with a broad range of other human rights. In some countries, permanent standing committees have been named by parliaments to address on an ongoing basis, questions relating to new laws on religion. While there are many complex and difficult questions yet to be resolved, the subject of religious human rights or religious liberty has become, as never before, a subject that is being addressed as fundamental in the movements of nations toward democracy and freedom. Among the questions inextricably intertwined with religious rights and religious liberty is one of ethnic identity, which in many countries throughout the world is virtually conterminous with the rights of religious minorities.

Conclusion

In this chapter, an apologia for religious human rights has been proposed as a necessary foundation for arguing the case for religious human rights, all the more so since religious human rights are all too often slighted in many of the dialogues and discussions on human rights. An apologia for religious human rights has been presented in this chapter from a variety of perspectives. The concept of religious human rights is one to be found in the teachings of the great world religions, although far less descriptive of their history. Nevertheless, voices against intolerance and for religious human rights may be traced back to the ancient world. The case for religious human rights may also be found in the nature of religion since authentic religion must wait upon the voluntary responses of persons who are free of coercion in order to be true to itself. A compelling argument for religious human rights may be posited in the sanctity of the human person and the inviolability of the human conscience. It has also been argued in this chapter that the emergence of the concept of the secular state—a state uncommitted in matters of religion and ultimate belief in which religion enjoys institutional independence from the state—is one in which government is denied jurisdiction over religion and religious freedom is essentially assured. Attention is also given in this essay to the special relationship that religious rights have to all other human rights, both individual and social. For without guarantees of religious human rights all other human rights are in peril. Finally, it is argued, that an apologia for religious human rights may be found in the recognition accorded these rights in the norms of international law and international agreements.

The issue of religious human rights is one of growing significance in today's world. The growth of religious pluralism is worldwide and constitutes one of the major challenges facing all of the religions of the world today. The increasing presence of multiple faiths in secular societies makes religious isolation impossible and interfaith encounters inevitable. The worldwide distribution of communities of virtually all of the major religious traditions exacerbates the concern of all religions for guarantees of religious liberty and the protection of the religious rights of their own adherents and thereby for religious minorities generally.

To be sure, the call for the recognition of religious human rights in the world community needs to be sounded by the religions themselves as well as by instruments of national and international law. The international dimension of the major world religions holds the promise of effecting important gains not only for the advancement of religious human rights, but also for genuine interfaith dialogue and collaboration on behalf of religious freedom and the building of a world community. Religious liberty, like world peace, is not only a moral imperative worthy of universal support of religions around the world, it also needs to be seen as essential for the creation of a world community and may well prove to be crucial in the survival of the human family.

It is to be fervently hoped that the words of the Charter of Paris for a New Europe, signed by thirty-four member nations of the Helsinki Final Act, in which religious freedom and other fundamental freedoms are made "the birthright of all human beings . . . inalienable, guaranteed by law" may become realized throughout the world.

Religion and Human Rights:
A Theological Apologetic

MAX L. STACKHOUSE
Princeton Theological Seminary
and
STEPHEN E. HEALEY
Boston College

I n our deliberations on the reciprocal relationships of religion and human rights, one key issue is the question of whether there are any common ethical standards, especially in an emerging global society where multiple religions, the sources and sustainers of morality in most cultures, encounter both each other and a variety of doubts about the place of religion in the common life. On the one hand, the concept of human rights stands in the modern world as a set of universalistic ethical norms that state ideals for all human societies. They identify first principles and goals by which the community of nations may legitimate (or delegitimate) various legal systems or cultural practices (including religious ones, where religions are viewed as part of a culture), and limit the use of state power against persons and groups.

On the other hand, the very idea of universalistic norms is viewed by some as nothing more than the imposition of some particular set of religio-cultural values on the other peoples of the world.[1] That is due to the fact that in most of human history and in much of the world still today, ethical norms are rooted in religious orientations that seldom embrace human rights except insofar as they advance the particular religion. The idea of ethical principles standing beyond religions, cultures, and societies, and able to evaluate and alter them, is to many a strange and hostile notion. Such an understanding of ethics requires that we tie thought and faith together in a philosophical theology, which is able to defend itself in

---

[1] For one particularly important critique of several presuppositions that underlie such a view, see Frederick Buell, "Conceptualizations of Contemporary Culture," *Comparative Civilizations Review* 27 (Fall, 1992): 127-142.

J. Witte, Jr. and J.D. van der Vyver (eds.), Religious Human Rights in Global Perspective, 485-516.
© 1996 *Kluwer Law International. Printed in the Netherlands.*

public discourse, critically evaluate the relative adequacy of various religions on key questions, and provide the deep guidance system for complex societies and cultures.

What an irony we face. Modern articulations of human rights were born out of the attempt to constrain the great barbarisms of the twentieth century. In this context, ancient insights, which had been obscured or suppressed, were retrieved and made the basis for what is today called human rights. For the most part, the surge of interest in human rights that occurred after World War II turned to the formulations of human rights and democracy that grew out of the Enlightenment. However, it was only sometimes noted that these developments were themselves rooted in previously established theological assumptions that derive from antiquity—which the Enlightenment had claimed to overcome. While the great thinkers of the Enlightenment were familiar with the ancient sources, their heirs were not. Hence, the interpretations of human rights that have come to triumph in the West are both derived from and opposed to their deeper religious roots. They nearly always ignore the greatest contribution of faith to human rights: namely, that some religious positions in alliance with selected philosophical traditions developed a transcendental view of the world and began to conceive of it as a whole, and thus to recognize that there is a perspective which is beyond the time and space, culture and society, religion and morality which we inhabit when we imagine the unity. If we grasp something of this perspective, or are grasped by it, we think and experience theologically, and see the nature of justice more clearly, for we see it *sub species aeternitatis.*

If the world is a unity, and we can conceive of it as a whole—this, of course, means that we transcend it in some degree and do not simply live within it, trapped by its horizons—then we begin to suspect that it is governed by a unified moral law, even though the customs and habits of many people in the world and their ways of modeling the whole differ. Further, these customs, habits, and models can be altered according to a more ultimate and reliable pattern. The most pertinent developments of modernity, in this view, have to do with the recovery, radicalization, propagation, and relative institutionalization of an ethical vision of this sort. The late twentieth century has been the period in which these principles have become spread throughout the world. Human rights provisions are now built into the constitutions of more peoples than any previous civilization could have imagined, and are among the decisive criteria[2] as to whether a religion, a culture, a regime, or a society should be honored or altered, isolated or revolutionized.

---

[2] Other criteria also are increasingly used: particularly economic and ecological viability. Thus, political, legal, religious, and cultural patterns that do not encourage democracy,

However, this has also been the century in which we have faced dramatic challenges to these ideas. These challenges have taken and continue to take many forms—most notably the quests for the solidarity of a particular community against such universal and transcendental claims. Indeed, the greatest struggles of the twentieth century are of this order—one against the pagan anti-modernism of Hitlerian-Fascist National Socialism, another against the secularist hyper-modernism of Marxist-Leninist Proletarian Socialism. Each manifested itself in massive political-military movements that became the chief threats to human rights and to modernity in this century. Both have, in substantive measure, been defeated, although, like all great terrors, they writhe in their bonds and threaten to reappear from their graves in new forms.

For instance, a direct challenge to human rights from these defeated forces appeared in a new conspiracy of anti-modernists and hyper-modernists who, while having apparently abandoned the Nazism of Hitler's politics and Communism of Stalinist economics, now join the internal entrepreneurs of Asia's "liberalizing" economic policies and the business interests of the West who want access to Asia's cheap labor and vast markets to echo the defeated arguments. In 1993, China led a coalition of nations, including Indonesia, Vietnam, Burma, Syria, and Iran that posed concepts of national sovereignty and state-supported development against democracy and human rights, as stated in the "Bangkok Declaration," which became the basis for their postures in the U.N. conference on human rights in Vienna.[3] The domestic forum for this took place when the United States authorities approved "most-favored nation" status for China, in spite of human rights abuses.[4]

The triumph of these developments in the long run is unlikely, unless the fundamental conception of human rights itself begins to collapse. The immediacy of political or economic gain may be decisive in many matters of indeterminate policy, but the deeper theological and ethical influences shape determinate matters of polity, and over time polity guides, leavens, and sets boundaries for policy. The more profound threat to the idea of

---

promote development, and do these in a way that limits destruction of the environment, are all subject to rapid and radical transformation. These too are a distinctive features of modernization.

[3] See Douglas Payne, Charles Brown, and James Finn, "Human Rights: Showdown in Vienna," *Freedom Review* 24(5) (October, 1993): 5-24; Max L. Stackhouse, "The Future of Human Rights: Multi-Culturalism in Vienna," *Christian Century* (June 30-July 7, 1993): 660-662.

[4] See, e.g., T.L. Friedman, "Profit Motive Gets the Nod: The Favored Status Is Economic Interest," and D. Jehl, "A Policy Reversal: No Wish to Jeopardize Billions in Trade," both under the headline "U.S. Is To Maintain Trade Privileges For China's Goods," *New York Times* (May 27, 1994): A1 and A8.

human rights as a determinate of polity, thus, is an attack from both its detractors and, unwittingly, from many of its defenders.

A number of contemporary philosophers, social theorists, and religious thinkers of note have begun to doubt that there are such things as human rights, or have attempted to defend them in such terms as to make them impossible to sustain. In perhaps the most famous absolutist denial of the validity of human rights, one of the premier philosophers of our day, Alasdair MacIntyre, wrote that the concept has no meaning at all:

> [T]he truth is plain: there are no such rights, and belief in them is one with belief in witches and unicorns. . . . The best reason for asserting so bluntly that there are no such rights is [the same] . . . reason for asserting that there are no witches. . . . [E]very attempt to give good reasons for believing that there *are* such rights has failed . . . . Natural or human rights . . . are fictions.[5]

Although MacIntyre has been discerningly criticized, he is not alone. Leo Strauss, the widely regarded political philosopher who taught at Chicago for many years, has convinced a generation of young minds to become "neo-conservative" on the grounds that the classical ethical notion of natural rights (*physis*) and the proper exercise of virtue especially of "prudence" (*phronesis*) are subverted by this modern ideology of "rights."[6]

On the other side of the ideological spectrum, a major attempt to defend human rights from a "liberal" point of view has been advanced by Rhoda E. Howard and Jack Donnelly. They use sociological and anthropological theory to argue that human rights involve the affirmation of the autonomy and equality of every individual, in contrast to all the tribalisms, feudalisms, socialisms, communisms, and communitarianisms, old and new, that view the individual as a part of a whole. They argue that the idea of rights "is rooted in structural changes that began to emerge in late medieval and early modern Europe, gained particular force in the eighteenth and nineteenth centuries, and today are increasingly the norm throughout the world. The creation of the private individual separate from society is closely linked to the rise of a new, more complex division

---

[5] Alasdair MacIntyre, *After Virtue: A Study in Moral Theory*, 2d ed. (Notre Dame, 1984), 69, 70. See the careful critique of this view by Sander Griffioen, "Entering into a Scheme of Belief: MacIntyre's Account of Moral Traditions," in A. W. Musschenga, B. Voozanger, and A. Soetman, eds., *Morality, Worldview, and Law: The Idea of a Universal Morality and its Critics* (Assen, The Netherlands, 1992). The whole volume is dedicated to the question of whether a universal morality can be defended.

[6] Leo Strauss, *Natural Right and History* (Chicago, 1958).

of labor, the resulting changes in class structure . . . and [thus] a new vision of the individual's relationship to God, society and the state."[7]

Leaving aside historical questions as to whether Abraham, Moses, Sara, Ruth, Jeremiah, Amos, Jesus, and Paul, or for that matter, Cleopatra, Socrates, Plato, Aristotle, Confucius, or the Buddha were in any serious sense individuals, we do not view human rights as an imaginative literary or political fiction on the order of unicorns. Instead, we view ethical norms such as human rights as the cultural by-products of socio-evolutionary processes. Thus, human rights (and the persons and groups to which they apply) are seen to be an historical artifact, pertinent only insofar as social conditions stand at a particular stage of development, and subject to disappearance if those conditions do not obtain or eventually pass away. These philosophical and sociological views would be a great comfort to those in closed societies who use torture as a policy of governance or allow slave labor, for they can claim that they are at a particular stage of development. And neither are these scholars alone. Literally hundreds of social commentators and clergy share this understanding of morality, even if they read the "signs of the times" of societal evolution differently.

What is missing in these philosophical and sociological views is an account of why such matters as human rights, which cannot be derived from the empirical analysis of the world, prudentially or socio-historically, are plausible or why people should be committed to them, since it is empirically obvious that human rights are violated often and not everyone believes in them. Two things are required for a full analysis: (1) a social hermeneutical theory of how such things come into consciousness— a matter that shall take us into questions of religion and social theory; and (2) a way of evaluating which kinds of normative, but non-empirical, matters like human rights might be valid—a matter that requires theology.

This is not to suggest that we can abandon all philosophy and social theory. Some forms of them can be extremely useful when they are stabilized or undergirded by a a theological perspective—a perspective that they can help analyze, but which they can neither generate nor surpass. An historically and cross-culturally comparative view of these questions suggests that ideas of human dignity, human rights, and the great liberties of speech and association derive from certain kinds of religious views, indeed, a distinct set of religious views developed in dialogue with key strands of philosophy and particular theories of social life that are different from, and in fact contended against, positions analogous to

---

[7] Rhoda E. Howard and Jack Donnelly, "Human Dignity, Human Rights and Political Regimes," *American Political Science Review* 80(3) (September, 1986): 801-816, esp. 804.

the ones we have just noted. In fact, it is quite likely that human rights are based on nothing less than decisive theological convictions, distinct from but incorporating and utilizing some of the best insights of philosophy and social theory.

The challenges to human rights today, thus, are more subtle than the threats of Nazism and of Communism, for what we face is not likely to be overcome so quickly as these rose and fell—in a mere century or so. The three great challenges for human rights in the next century are these: (1) the decay of philosophy, and the consequent suspicion of any onto-theological account of how things are; (2) the attempt to establish normative principles for civil society on the basis of social description alone— the sadly unfulfilled promise of the social sciences; and (3) the power of resurgent, ancient religions, particularly Islam and Hinduism, which do have a normative metaphysical-moral vision and which have shown their capacity to organize complex and vast civilizations over long periods of time.

In their present forms, it is doubtful that any one of these three can sustain the idea of human rights in the long run—although it may turn out that Islam and Hinduism, or at least key strands of them, like key strands of Christianity critically refined by theology, will come closer than philosophy and sociology insofar as these try to remain detached from religion and theology. To be sure, all of these are potential companions of the kind of ethic that could sustain human rights, if and when they develop a "public theology" in the sense that they seek to discern, under God, the moral and spiritual architecture whereby just and humane civilizations can be constructed. But it is also the case that if any one of them should become the dominant view without substantial reform, human rights are likely to be subordinated or lost.

As this volume and its sequel testify, the place of religion in human rights discussions is an area of considerable debate. John Witte has rightly argued that the study of this interaction has been underway for a long time, and that the echoes of the older debates continue to shape us in many ways. But a new interest has erupted since World War II, and however much it presumes the older discussions, it rarely explicitly refers to them. Instead, the discussion has focused domestically on "the removal of discrimination based on sex, race, and culture, . . . the enhancement of freedoms of speech, press, and association, . . . [and] the safeguarding of criminal and cultural rights." Similarly, the international debate has centered on the "democratic/socialist" polarity, with each attempting to show that it can best provide for "the eradication of sexual, cultural, and ethnic discrimination" and economic injustice.[8] And, throughout this recent period, the place of religion in human rights has been relatively muted, except that religion became one item on the list of socio-cultural factors to be protected, and the hegemony of any one religion became something to be feared.

The remarkable resurgence of the question of religion in relation to human rights over the past few years, however, has many causes. Perhaps the most profound cause is that societies and souls cannot flourish without a deep substratum of awareness about the moral basis of life, a substratum that generally does not occur without a religious orientation. This is not to say that all religious orientations are good or equal or supportive of human rights. They are not; some religions are quite destructive of all that human rights stands for, and the very intensity and potency of religion makes the destructiveness all the more vicious. It therefore makes a good deal of difference what sort of religion is at hand. But the key point here is that such intensity and potency has at times been supportive and even generative of human rights, and that the commitment to a moral substratum which can guide the common life seems to appear most strongly in those societies informed by certain kinds of religious influence, and to be least vigorous in those societies shaped by other religious traditions or by anti-religion. We have a situation, thus, in which the freedom and vitality of religion at one level appears to depend on human rights, but in which the intensity and viability of human rights in society at another level seems to depend on the extent of certain kinds of religious influence. In the vast literature on religion and human rights, this second aspect is the least discussed and often the most superficially treated.[9]

Although there is considerable evidence that human rights are deeply and fundamentally dependent on religion and specifically on certain kinds of theological issues, it is equally clear that not all are convinced of this rather substantive point. Indeed, it is probable that for human rights to be recognized and sustained in the common life, two things are necessary: a theological understanding of normative reality, and a set of con-

---

[8] John Witte, Jr., "A New Concordance of Discordant Canons: Harold J. Berman on Law and Religion," *Emory Law Journal* 42 (1993): 523, 555-557.

[9] Cf. Alison Dundes Renteln, *International Human Rights* (London, 1990), who purports to give a survey of the major options, but simply presumes that if theology is brought into the discussion it must involve some "leap of faith" that cannot be argued in public discourse, although she quotes *arguments* of a theological sort about what might be "the truest description of the human condition," and whether all peoples seek some degree of freedom, rationality and community with a minimum of violence and does not recognize the normative quasi-theological character of the claims she makes herself in the name of anthropology.

crete institutional channels to actualize these normative visions in society and make them accessible in a civilization.

The Central Issue of Religion and Human Rights

The main contentions of this chapter are (1) that the very idea of human rights is rooted in a theological ethic; and (2) that this ethic needs to be defended from contemporary challenges—philosophical, sociological, and religious—in order that, as an ethical norm, human rights may more fully be actualized in societies, and so that philosophy, social theory, and religion supportive of human rights may flourish among all peoples. The challenges to human rights are based upon doubts about the nature of theology as well as the confusion between confessionalism and theology. Religion is often treated as a strictly personal, cultural, or historical experience, and theology is understood to be its formal, dogmatic articulation. Thus, to root human rights in religion or theology is seen as a form of personal, cultural, or historical imperialism. Further, since we have come to wider awareness of the variety of religions in the world, it is hard for some to imagine that not all the religions contribute equally to moral matters. Although the world religions have been around for centuries, they did not seem to many to be present as living options or necessarily related to human rights.

Yet historically, the evidence is rather clear, as Brian Tierney has already suggested.[10] The deep roots of human rights ideals are rooted nowhere else than in the biblical tradition,[11] for it is here that we find the decisive unveiling of a perspective in which moral first principles demanding the respect for the neighbor are made known to humanity by a reality that is universal and absolute. This reality, which the Western traditions call "God," is neither a figment of human imagination, a projection of our personal needs or tribal consciousness, nor a product of human creativity. Nor is this God morally neutral. This is an ethical God, the source and norm of a kind of justice and righteousness and contends against what we often find as we look around the world. Richard Deats puts it this way:

> The universal implications of this faith in the righteous God, creator of the earth and all living things . . . [permeated] the life of Israel, expanding their faith to widened horizons of inclusiveness and compassion. "Am I my brother's keeper?" and "Who is my neighbor?" are questions that never ceased to stir the

---

[10] See the chapter by Brian Tierney included herein.

[11] See Walter Harrelson, *The Ten Commandments and Human Rights* (Philadelphia, 1979).

> conscience of the people of God. . . . [T]he universality of this
> faith . . . is to be a "light for all the peoples."[12]

This heritage was applied to all the peoples of the world in the prophetic traditions, when the prophets protested the exploitation of the poor and weak, and demanded that the various nations, especially those who claimed to be most loyal to this God, must submit to a moral law not of their own making. Some things simply ought not be done by one human to another, even if they are approved or commanded by an impious political authority.

In this context, Christianity arose and radicalized the prophetic point of view, carried it into the Graeco-Roman world, and linked it to philosophical and jurisprudential theories that, on quite other grounds, also had begun to articulate a notion of a universal normative moral order.[13] This interaction of faith and philosophy created theology and ethics as basic modes of discourse to guide thought and action on the most universalistic bases possible.[14]

These developments remained a minority tradition for centuries, and were often suppressed by pagan tendencies, power interests, and forms of myth and magic that could not be said to be universalistic, moral, faithful, or philosophically sound. But periodically this tradition was retrieved and made central to attempts to reform life, and to establish it on a more universalistic, more humane, and more godly foundation. This we can see in the revolutionary transformations of law and society so central to the history of the West,[15] in the theological theories of "conciliarism" that anticipated and approximated constitutional democracy,[16] and especially in parts of the Reformation that influenced the modern formation of human rights.[17]

However, it was periodically the case that precisely this tradition was distorted by both the ideological use of religion at the hands of political power to legitimate its interests, and the betrayal of the rational and ethical character of theology by religious leaders who made Christianity into

---

[12] Richard Deats, "Human Rights: An Historical and Theological Perspective," *Engage* 38 (1978): 10.

[13] See A. O. Miller, ed., *A Christian Declaration on Human Rights* (Grand Rapids, MI, 1977).

[14] See Max L. Stackhouse, *Creeds, Society, and Human Rights: A Study in Three Cultures* (Grand Rapids, MI, 1984), esp. chaps. 2-3.

[15] See, especially, Harold J. Berman, *Law and Revolution: The Formation of the Western Legal Tradition* (Cambridge, MA, 1983).

[16] See, e.g., J.N. Figgis, *Studies in Political Thought from Gerson to Grotius* (New York, 1960).

[17] Perhaps the first major study documenting the profound connections suggested here was Georg Jellinek, *Die Erklärung der Menschen-und Burgerrechte* (Leipzig, 1904).

a series of arbitrary dogmas to be accepted on blind faith, without intellectual justification, moral rigor, or a sense of what it meant to be "a light for all peoples." When the wars of religion of early modern Europe combined these perversions, the heritage was discredited in the eyes of many. All sorts of post-Christian views of human moral *a priori*, self-evident truths and natural rights were developed to attempt to guide and constrain political authority without religion, and to develop a cosmopolitan ethic that would allow the various obscurantist religions to hold their own dogmas—albeit only as private preferences. Theology, in a public sense, was destroyed in favor of apolitical or pietistic fideism, on one side, and an ontologically free-floating rationality, on the other. The destruction was called Enlightenment. However, the Enlightenment could not carry the full load of what it attempted, and its rational fruits became instruments of oppression, even as it struggled to establish and maintain a sense of universal moral order. Its godless foundations could not bear the weight of all that the Enlightenment philosophers confidently placed upon them. The Enlightenment's initial success depended upon the deeper, but hidden, foundations which had been laid by theology. Apart from them, philosophy began to deconstruct—into romanticism, historicism, existentialism, and now postmodernism.

Our argument is not only that we need to get and keep our history straight, although that would be a very good idea. Our argument is also that it is quite possible for an idea that is generated out of one context to be found valid in another, and to become contextualized in forms of thought and life in ways that enhance possibilities within those adopted forms of thought and life that were only latently central to the new host. This, of course, produces "revisionist" history in the secondary tradition, as happened to Greek philosophy and Roman law when they were wedded to biblical insights to form a theology which surpassed these original sources. Our argument is, in brief, that today human rights can best be seen as a part of the process of the recognition of the validity of decisive ethical concepts that, while offered and made actual by a particular tradition, are recognizably valid for all people and are essentially true for the world. Human rights are a modern way of speaking about cross-cultural ethical concepts that actualize certain valid theological presuppositions and in turn legitimates constraints on what humans or states can do to each other, where theology is understood to be the critically examined and systematically stated interpretation of what humanity is—sinful creatures not driven entirely by nature and nurture, that know we live under a God who establishes moral laws and ends and contexts of life we cannot attain alone.

Theology, in this view, is not merely the rationalized form of a social or cultural view legitimated by a privileged religion. It is also a necessary partner of philosophy and the social sciences, and a critic of religions, in clarifying, and establishing universal and valid ethical norms for an emerging global civilization. Theology tells us whether this or that religion, our own or someone else's, is valid or whether it ought to be challenged on the grounds of its truth or its justice. This hypothesis then bears within it an ironic implication: it suggests the likelihood of religious, philosophical, and social conflict, for not all religions are equally capable of developing or sustaining a theology that can generate a universalistic ethic of jurisprudential importance. Indeed, in its strongest form, this argument suggests that it is doubtful whether human rights can be sustained without a theology that has certain definable characteristics, which we will attempt to indicate.

Yet, as the threats of the anti-modernists on the right and the hypermodernists on the left fade, increasingly frequent attacks are made upon the theological genealogy of human rights and the very possibility of anything being universal, especially anything with normative content. A new surge of pragmatic anti-Enlightenment and anti-theological philosophy has attempted to deconstruct all aspects of culture, including language, with the reductive techniques of the social sciences, and to view the great world religions as evidence against the possibility of developing and sustaining a universalistic theological ethic. These deconstructive arguments suggest that both theology and modernity are to be faulted for trying to supply a basis for human rights, for they rest on strictly untenable universalistic claims.

In what follows, we first consider aspects of these deconstructive philosophical arguments, and then we use a preliminary discussion of postmodern social theory as a segue into a consideration of Islam and Hinduism as interlocutors in the rights dialogue. We argue (1) that the postmodern case against universalistic theological principles is inconsistent and not convincing; (2) that certain postmodern social theories already realize this; and (3) that aspects of classical Hinduism and Islam can be enlisted as allies in the struggle for the global recognition of human rights, even if aspects of them, along with aspects of historical Christianity, also are judged to contain features which could potentially subvert human rights.

Postmodern Philosophy and Human Rights

Philosophers since the Enlightenment have frequently argued that only human reasoning *carried out as philosophy* adequately grounds human rights, for religions are usually enemies of rights, unless they are relegated to optional personal preference. Theology, in this view, is no less passé, for it is but the rationalization of fideist belief. The serious work of establishing ethical and political values is accomplished by philosophy. This view, it is widely acknowledged, is in considerable difficulty today, and it is doubted whether human reasoning carried out as philosophy can justify anything, let alone human rights.

Reason no longer speaks with the booming confidence of Archimedes, nor even in the conversational and receptive tones of Hermes. Both the "clear and distinct" arguments of epistemology and subtler shades of hermeneutics are thought to be maniacal ravings of the pompous predicament of Enlightenment reason. Modern philosophy here is thought to be a kind of pretentious insanity, as was religion and theology.

Two thinkers represent this "postmodern" turn of mind with special clarity: Jean-Francois Lyotard and Richard Rorty. They believe that a theoretical defense or justification of human rights is neither possible nor desirable. Yet they have both recently given lectures in the Oxford Amnesty Lecture Series, the funds of which are used to support Amnesty International and human rights.[18] The ambiguity in Lyotard's and Rorty's arguments is this: they are opposed to all universalistic theory—religious, theological, or epistemological—that attempts to establish first principles.[19] And yet they want a world where the "dignity" of each self, and of each unique locale, story, biography, and group identity is honored.

The substantiality of this view is not at all clear, for human rights are by definition both universalistic, practical, and highly theoretical. Rorty has argued that it is possible to "de-universalize" and "de-theorize" both democracy and human rights, and yet to maintain them as a good way to live. As ways of life, democracy and human rights are prior to philosophy. Enlightenment philosophy's most profound self-deception, he argues, was to believe that its theory of rights was foundational and prior to the form of democratic life.[20] Rorty argues, to the contrary, that En-

---

[18] Richard Rorty, "Human Rights, Rationality, and Sentimentality," in S. Shupe and S. Hurley, eds., *On Human Rights: The Oxford Amnesty Lectures 1993* (New York, 1993), 111-134 and Jean-Francois Lyotard, "The Other's Rights," in ibid., 135-147.

[19] Some of Lyotard's critics, however, have claimed that he is bound to the prescriptivist aspects of the Kantian program. See, e.g., Honi Fern Haber, *Beyond Postmodern Politics: Lyotard, Rorty, and Foucault* (New York, 1994); David Ingram, "The Postmodern Kantianism of Arendt and Lyotard," *The Review of Metaphysics* 42 (September, 1988): 51-77. Haber claims this residual Kantianism seriously undermines Lyotard's "pagan" politics; she commends an "oppositional" feminist postmodern politics.

[20] See Richard Rorty, "The Priority of Democracy to Philosophy," in Merrill Peterson and Robert Vaughn, eds. *The Virginia Statute of Religious Freedom* (Cambridge, 1988), 257-282.

lightenment justifications were always justifications of *this* way of life; and *this* way of life can be "justified," or made sense of, in a number of ways. But, better yet, it needs no justification. In lieu of a theoretical defense of rights and democracy, one has to say merely that these forms of life work well; they have helped us to stop killing one another. That pragmatic justification, if one can call it that, involves certain understandings about what is desirable, but these understandings should be recognized as strictly contingent products of our historical experience.[21]

Rorty is surely correct that the Enlightenment justifications were not prior to democracy and human rights, for in fact it was key theological and ecclesial traditions that established them for at least parts of the human community, long before the Enlightenment.[22] Furthermore, it can easily be argued that democracy and human rights were based upon universalistic theories of right and wrong that were, in fact, resisted by particular local traditions, stories, biographies, and group identities that would have lost the arbitrary power they held over people if rights and democracy were acknowledged. Also, Rorty's theory presupposes a touching vision of a naturally harmonious state of affairs for all life that is not touched by the sin of grand theory. This wonderful polytheistic paradise, with no trees of knowledge since it is "beyond good and evil," is as universalistic and religious a theory as any he rejects, although it is not theological and thus has no grounding beyond arbitrary preference. Finally, he cannot provide a reason why we would stop killing one another, especially if it is to the great advantage of some that the killing continue.

Lyotard also believes, echoing aspects of Heidegger and Neitzsche, that the fundamental error in Western philosophy is that grand narratives storm through history by swallowing up and silencing alternatives and otherness.[23] Grand narratives reign by "terror," even though they are guided by a profound humanism.[24] This humanism is supported by the grand narratives of Marxism and liberalism, which measure all things by

---

[21] Ibid. See also Richard Rorty, *Contingency, Irony, and Solidarity* (Cambridge, 1989), chap. 3.

[22] See James Luther Adams, *On Being Human Religiously* (Boston, 1976), and Stackhouse, *Creeds, Society, and Human Rights*.

[23] Jean Francois Lyotard, *The Postmodern Condition: A Report on Knowledge*, Geoff Bennington and Brian Massumi, trans. (Minneapolis, 1984); see also id., *The Postmodern Explained*, J. Pefanis and M. Thomas, trans. and ed. (Sydney, 1992), chaps. 2-3.

[24] Lyotard, *The Postmodern Explained* (Sidney, 1992), chap. 6; id., *The Different: Phrases in Dispute*, Georges Van Den Abbeele, trans. (Minneapolis, 1988); also see the section in "Oikos," entitled "The Humanism of War," id., *Political Writings*, Bill Readings and Kevin Paul, trans. (Minneapolis, 1993), 96-107.

their ability to produce results for humanity.[25] Marxism promises a catastrophic liberation of humanity; liberalism promises humanity's gradual unfolding and flowering.[26] Yet both liberalism and Marxism agree that human beings stand at the center of history, and that history told rightly tells the story of the ineluctable emancipation of humans from tyranny and need.

Lyotard believes, however, that the ideas of real subjects, general humanity, or the meaning of life or history are pretenses that cannot survive contemporary experience. With Rorty, Lyotard argues that humans are much more "put together" than such an anthropocentric theory of history would indicate.[27] Modern views constitute themselves by denying the constructed character of the self, and thus they invent a mythology of a completely new, unfettered beginning: that it is in this way possible to "set the clock back to zero,"[28] to return to or take one's clues for living from a "state of nature." Postmodernity believes such confident new beginnings merely deny the past and are thus doomed to repeat it.[29] Lyotard's postmodern way forward is much more like psychoanalysis: one can see the pros and cons of one's parents and past but cannot imagine a personal story without them. History is, or rather histories are, like that, too. People are so "put together" that even their new starts are *in medias res*; they are much more ambiguous, gritty, and semi-formal than modernity's Self. Universalistic narratives, public philosophy, or theology conceal and overwrite this "put togetherness."

The idea that some universally conferred dignity stands behind the Enlightenment doctrine of human rights is, in this interpretation, the product of a false consciousness (in a Freudian, psychotherapeutic sense). The recurrence of grand narratives, or bold declarations like claims of natural rights, are a sign that cultural psychotherapy has gone badly awry—that the therapeutic process has mistaken the content of its conversation for an authoritative and normative remembering of "history." Spinning grand narratives, like theoretical defenses of universal human rights, entail a "primal repression" (*Urverdrangung*): all such attempts are tied to a philosophy of consciousness, which is doomed to repeat the horrors of the past.[30] In Western history, the chief example is the Jews:

[25] Lyotard, *The Postmodern Condition*, chaps. 7-8, 11.

[26] Ibid., 11-14.

[27] Ibid., 15: "The self does not amount to very much, but no self is an island; each exists in a fabric of relations."

[28] Lyotard, *The Postmodern Explained*, 76.

[29] Ibid.: "We now suspect that this [Enlightenment idea of] 'rupture' is in fact a way of forgetting or repressing the past, that is, repeating and not surpassing it."

[30] Lyotard, *Political Writings*, 141.

> What is most real about the Jews is that Europe, in any case, does not know what to do with them: Christians demand their conversion; monarchs expel them; republics assimilate them; Nazis exterminate them.[31]

The grand narratives of the Enlightenment, with their promise of equality, did nothing in Lyotard's view to protect the Jews from extermination. Their most benevolent face was to require the abandonment of all of the distinctive features of Judaism.[32] Lyotard wants human rights to be much less than a theoretically comprehensive articulation of the rights and duties of humanity, and so to provide much more of a shield for simply being human. At the core, human rights are about the right to talk with others, and to tell one's own stories.[33] One's stories ensure that one is always "other," not reduced to some alien scheme:

> [T]he strangeness of the other seems to escape any totalization. . . . It is precisely when we think we have reduced the abject or the sacred to transparent meanings that it becomes most opaque. . . . The discontent from which contemporary societies are suffering, the postmodern affliction, is the foreclosure of the Other. It is the reverse of the triumphant identification with the Other which effects modern republics at their birth.[34]

Lyotard is surely correct that the Enlightenment conception of the Self, as autonomous, complete, whole, and unique, is unconvincing. But his view of the socially and narratologically constituted person is equally unconvincing, and it is doubtful that his view can provide the shield from "terror" that he wants. Lyotard recognizes one of the emphases of the biblical and theological tradition, namely, that humans are creatures made from the dust, to which they return after a brief life. The biblical and theological tradition, however, also affirms that humans are created in the image of God. The self does not have an automatic dignity; it has a conferred dignity. The weak, the fragile, the foolish, the faulty also are to be treated with dignity. The biblical view is paradoxical; these creatures from the dust, made in the image of God, may not be violated—in prophetic voice, their heads may not be crushed—at least not without incur-

---

[31] Ibid., 140.

[32] This is an echo of the debate between Marx and the other Left Hegelians. See Karl Marx, "On the Jewish Question," in Robert C. Tucker, ed., *The Marx-Engels Reader*, 2d ed. (New York, 1978), 26-52. For Lyotard, the question is pressing because of the philosophical debt to Heidegger; the remarks were written after the publication of Victor Farías's *Heidegger et la Nazisme in France*.

[33] Lyotard, "The Other's Rights," 143-147.

[34] Ibid., 146.

ring God's wrath. Lyotard cannot provide a convincing reason why we may not manipulate one another's stories and crush each other's heads, even though he desires that we do not.

Just as Rorty falls into an unwitting romantic and presumptively harmonious polytheism, Lyotard falls into a soulless vacuity of chatter. Rorty needs God; Lyotard needs the image of God. Their arguments are insufficient, even though they have helped us see more clearly the insufficiency of key philosophical arguments of the Enlightenment. Nonetheless, if it comes to it, the world would probably be wise to choose the Enlightenment views over their efforts, for in the notions of a universal moral law and a self with inherent dignity, there is a closer approximation to what these two philosophers want to protect than in what they themselves proffer as alternatives.

Several other lines of argument could be marshalled against this vision of Rorty and Lyotard. First, plurality does not take care of itself; in a structural and historical form, plurality without a larger sense of unity is tribalism. Various forms of ethnic exclusiveness and pluralism constitute themselves in terms of "the other" by constant hostility, and it is romantic and historically blind to argue otherwise. Second, the so-called totalistic impulses of the Enlightenment can be criticized, along the lines laid out by Rorty and Lyotard, without denying the importance of inclusivistic narratives. In fact, the lack or denial of comprehensive narratives is historically the source of violence. The problem is that the Enlightenment was not inclusive enough. Its narrative was petty, not grand, for it lacked depth. The Enlightenment conception has only selves, not souls; it has humanism, but neither God nor creation. Rorty and Lyotard are right, then, that the Enlightenment does not deliver on its promise to secure some kinds of particularity and plurality, and thus these are subject to deconstruction, because they have no ground for being honored. Yet that has as much to do with the Enlightenment's denial of the theological foundations of its own presumptions as anything else. The doctrine of the trinity, for example, enables the articulation of ultimate reality, marked by a non-reductive inclusivity, with principles and freedom, otherness and identity. Third, it is possible to see vestiges of the "Enlightenment" all through Rorty's and Lyotard's writings, especially when they are read from a Christian theological point of view. The premature dismissal of theology as a voice in *public* discussion represents the Enlightenment in its most dubious philosophical aspect, and they accept the dismissal at face value. Fourth, it is not at all clear how one can have a non-theoretical practice or form of life, without falling prey to self-referential inconsistencies. It is a noble impulse that should be nurtured, one that has people pause and ask, "Is this practice just, and therefore theoretically justifiable?" Human rights apply to more than one form of practice, because they are highly theoretical. Yet, beyond these issues, there is reason for a deeper critique of Rorty and Lyotard from the perspective we are advancing here.

For all their insights, Rorty and Lyotard undermine the chief source of human rights and obscure the character of the contemporary ethos in which human rights will be advanced or retarded. In short, theology is an indirect, and often a direct, target of their critiques, as it is for enlightened liberals. Moreover, their focus upon the smaller fragments of life leads them to ignore a manifest feature of the ethos of our time, namely that the world's increasingly unified economic, political, ideational, and legal global ethos can support a non-violent plurality. Rorty and Lyotard spool together these features of bad theology and a misunderstood ethos because they believe that the Enlightenment best spoke for its own presuppositions and correctly analyzed the nature and character of religion. But, since they have challenged the Enlightenment on a dozen points, it is not clear why they remain dependent on it for this one. Rorty and Lyotard simply assume that theology is inherently heteronomous and that an irreducible plurality is better than the stifling singularity which theology ostensibly desires. The social hermeneutic of Rorty and Lyotard blinds them to the emerging global ethos, or to view it as some demonic Leviathan, and no more.[35]

The fate of human rights as a sustainable cluster of doctrines is likely to require the apologetical refutation of these sorts of claims. For, on the one hand, if theology cannot enter into first-order dialogue about the nature of humanity, without being destructive or heteronomous, it is hard to see how religious human rights can mean anything. On the other hand, if they show that classical and enlightenment philosophy and all of theology is inherently dehumanizing, it is also hard to see where substantive accounts of "humanity" will come from, since nearly all of the current human rights proclamations depended, directly or indirectly upon the normative anthropological assumptions of biblically influenced philosophical theology.

Rorty's denial of "metanarratives" turns out to be a particular metanarrative that systematically denies the reality of the world. In fact,

---

[35] Lyotard, *Political Writings*, 25-26: "Capitalism is one of the names of modernity. . . . The finality of capitalism is not a technical, social, or political creation built according to rule. . . . [C]apitalist creation does not bend to rules, it invents them. Everything [Walter] Benjamin describes as 'loss of aura,' aesthetic of 'shock,' destruction of taste and experience is the effect of this will that cares little or nothing for rules." The universalistic constructivism of capitalism silences and excludes more than it includes, according to Lyotard. He has a moral response: "Let us wage a war on totality; let us be witnesses to the unpresentable." Lyotard, *The Postmodern Condition*, 82.

both Rorty and Lyotard presume a metaphysical and epistemological but ethically normless polytheism at the level of experience.[36] Their social hermeneutic has decided *a priori* that it will see nothing other than fragments which are threatened by comprehensive unities. That means that the bases for rights which might be used to stave off intrusions on individuality are undermined. To be sure, in the emerging global ethos, there is an intensive plurality that which cannot be denied and that which can often be celebrated, but there is also a quite real unity. There is one ecosystem with multiple climates, one global economy with highly differentiated markets, one emerging cosmopolitan global civilization with many cultures and subcultures, and one need to communicate with many languages.[37] Human rights as a normative concept adds that there is one humanity with a rich variety of individual lives, traditions, communities, and religions that ought not be violated. This is a theological hermeneutic that includes unity and difference. Rorty and Lyotard undermine that dialectic by focussing upon difference; this is quite directly related to their denial of theology as a form of public discourse, since theology joins unity to difference and articulates the real differences found in and under ultimate unity.

From Postmodernism to Social Theory and the Religions

The course travelled by these postmodern philosophers is odd. Rorty and Lyotard tacitly accept several key presumptions of the Enlightenment, turn them on the greatest achievements of modern humanistic thought, and thus destroy the foundations of the very values that they want to affirm. Further, they finally have to rest their case on a sociohistorical reading of how things work in the common life and on *a priori* convictions about what is valuable. Yet they can defend neither, something they disavow at the outset, in any event.

Rorty and Lyotard, however, are not the only contemporary philosophers to address human rights. Terry Nardin and David Maple of the

---

[36] Rorty argues, for example, that a result of his denial of single picture accounts of reality means there is no neutral way of arguing that cruelty is less honorable than benevolence or love. See Rorty, *Contingency, Irony and Solidarity*, Part III. Yet that argument is surely made in the ideational cul de sac formed among the ashes of a collapsed Enlightenment foundationalism and positivism. Rorty, in effect, argues: either all or nothing, either complete ahistorical neutrality or strict ethnocentric prejudice. Such an absolutistic contrast avoids the manifest fact that all the major world religions, and not at all neutrally, have an overlapping consensus that cruelty is less honorable than benevolence. Furthermore, these non-neutral points of view can be translated and compared in some relatively adequate way, even if to the purist and fundamentalist alike, translations are always the works of traitors.

[37] See Roland Robertson, *Globalization: Social Theory and Global Culture* (London, 1992), chaps. 5 and 9.

Thikon Institute, for example, are editing a major volume on *The Constitution of International Society*, in which both classical (conservative) and Enlightenment (liberal) theories of law, in dialogue with certain theological positions, are being retrieved and revised to guide the common life in ways that support and sustain human rights.[38] Similarly, certain self-consciously "conservative"[39] and "liberal"[40] moral philosophers, and some self-consciously liberal[41] and conservative[42] "Christian philosophers," are making very similar arguments against both the reductionism of the Enlightenment and the moral emptiness of many postmodern alternatives.

The Enlightenment thinkers would surely have found it odd that some of the most serious arguments against human rights come not from religion or theology but from philosophy. That may not be enough, were we able to discuss these matters with the Enlightenment thinkers, to turn them to a reconsideration of religion and theology. For a number of social theorists in our day, however, it has been enough, even if the turn these theorists make to religion is not always fully adequate. The work of Jürgen Habermas, for example, represents an attempt to go beyond the narrowness of both Enlightenment philosophy and sociology by commingling their insights in a program of critical theory. He joins Rorty and Lyotard by rejecting a philosophy of consciousness, monological justifications of the social contract, and the foundationalism of Enlightenment philosophy; he also joins them by turning to language and communication theory. Yet here is precisely where Habermas turns away from Rorty and Lyotard, for he attempts to extract a normative justification for rights out of the very nature of communication.[43] At the core, Habermas argues that communication itself is committed to non-coercive modes of interaction. Communication theory is the venue through which

---

[38] Terry Nardin and David Maple, eds., *The Constitution of International Society* (Princeton, forthcoming).

[39] See, e.g., Gertrude Himmelfarb, *On Looking into the Abyss* (New York, 1994).

[40] See, e.g., Seyla Benhabib, *Situating the Self: Gender, Community and Postmodernism in Contemporary Ethics* (New York, 1992).

[41] See, e.g., F.C. Gamwell, *The Divine Good* (Chicago, 1991).

[42] See, e.g., Richard J. Mouw and Sander Griffioen, *Pluralisms and Horizons: An Essay in Christian Public Philosophy* (Grand Rapids, 1993)

[43] See, e.g., Jürgen Habermas, "An Alternative Way out of the Philosophy of the Subject: Communicative versus Subject-Centered Reason," in id., *The Philosophical Discourse of Modernity: Twelve Lectures*, Frederick Lawrence, trans. (Cambridge, MA, 1987), 294-326; see also id., "Discourse Ethics: Notes on a Program of Philosophical Justification," in id., *Moral Consciousness and Communicative Action*, Christian Lenhardt and Sherry Weber Nicholsen, trans. (Cambridge, MA, 1990), 443-115.

Habermas engages the functionalist focus on the "life world"[44] and the themes of rationalization and disenchantment articulated by Max Weber.[45] Habermas remains tied to unnecessarily reductive analyses of religion,[46] and his account of a communication requires the abandonment of theology and teleology in rights discourse. But he comes closer than the postmodernists of our day to providing a sustainable, normative framework for human rights.

Scholars in the sociological tradition of Weber, Emile Durkheim and Talcott Parsons, such as Robert Bellah,[47] are also increasingly, though cautiously, engaging in dialogue with religion. This move is not without controversy. Some writers in this tradition challenge the use of the social sciences as a companion to religion and theology.[48] Others, such as Peter Berger,[49] question whether sociology alone can provide any guidance about human rights as normative claims. To the contrary, other sociologists argue that social sciences are the only disciplines that can provide normative guidance to post-religious civil society.[50] It is not clear whether contemporary sociology, any more than contemporary philosophy, can offer normative guidance about human rights, though both disciplines point to the necessity of dealing with religions as decisive factors in human rights discourse.

It may be that the more urgent approach to human rights is to raise the question of the world religions directly. To do so, however, we need a

---

[44] Jürgen Habermas, *The Theory of Communicative Action, Vol. 2: Lifeworld and System; A Critique of Functionalist Reason*, Thomas McCarthy, trans. (Boston, 1987).

[45] Jürgen Habermas, *The Theory of Communicative Action: Vol. 1: Reason and the Rationalization of Society*, Thomas McCarthy, trans. (Boston, 1984).

[46] See David Tracy, "Theology, Critical Social Theory, and the Public Realm," in Don S. Browning and Francis Schüssler Fiorenza, eds., *Habermas, Modernity, and Public Theology* (New York, 1992), 19-42.

[47] Robert Bellah, et al. *Habits of the Heart* (Berkeley, 1985).

[48] See John Milbank, *Theology and Social Theory: Beyond Secular Reason* (Oxford, 1990).

[49] Berger, from the sociological side, no less than Milbank from a theological perspective, is skeptical about too much identification of the theological and sociological tasks. Berger, however, is willing to acknowledge that one of the tasks of theological ethics is to know the realities of the world which theology addresses, a knowledge that cannot be gained by theology alone. Milbank denies that premise. Thus Berger, unlike Milbank, is willing to contemplate a reciprocal interaction between the social sciences and theology, as is Max Stackhouse. See Max L. Stackhouse, "The Sociology of Religion and the Theology of Society," *Social Compass* 37(3) (September, 1990): 315-330; id., *Public Theology and Political Economy: Christian Stewardship in Modern Society* (Grand Rapids, 1987).

[50] Alan Wolfe, *Whose Keeper? Social Science and Moral Obligation* (Berkeley, 1989), 6-7: "The gap between the need for codes of moral obligation and the reality of societies that are confused about where these codes can be found is filled, however uncomfortably, by the contemporary social sciences. . . . For all their tendency toward jargon and abstraction, the ideas of social scientists remain the most common guideposts for moral obligation in a secular, nonliterary age."

method that both focuses directly on religious realities and joins the study of religion to philosophy and social theory. Such a method is found in theological ethics, or what some traditions call social theology, philosophical theology or natural theology. Theological ethics, along with certain forms of philosophy of religion and jurisprudence which are alert to theological issues,[51] goes to the deepest normative perspective in which human rights can be talked about without sacrificing concrete socio-historical institutions.

Surely, human rights would be on a more secure footing if we could place them on a foundation that has both a sustainable normativity and a concrete, institutional footing.[52] The theological ethical considerations of the world religions bring these concerns together, because all of the axial religions express metaphysical-moral visions that entail normativity, and their civilizational expansiveness verifies their sustainability. The major religions also interact with the chief and indispensable social structures—familial, political, economic, and cultural. Indeed, in many classic societies, religion is identified with one or more of these social structures, so that it is not strange to speak of a tribal, clan, or caste religion, an imperial, political or civic religion, a religion focused around the hunt, the harvest, or the expected "cargo, or a religion of a cultural-linguistic grouping. In some societies, however, where religion is focused upon a culture-transcending, ethical reality, it becomes distinguished from these so that it is not to be identified with any one of them. There, quite often, we find the formation of voluntary associations—centers of bonding and meaning that are intentionally not tied to any of these, even if these associations continue to influence any or all of them. When this begins to happen, we find also the emergence of other independent institutions of society—law, science, medicine, and business—which also segregate particular activities into distinctive institutions and shape the fabric of the whole society.[53]

---

[51] See, especially, Berman, *Law and Revolution*; John Witte, Jr. and Frank S. Alexander, eds., *The Weightier Matters of the Law: Essays on Law and Religion* (Atlanta, 1988). On a less theoretical basis, see Robert F. Drinan, S.J., "Human Rights in the 21st Century and the Role of the Churches," *Theology and Public Policy* 6(1) (Summer, 1994).

[52] Even those branches of Protestantism that have been at the forefront of promoting human rights encounter the difficulty of being undialectically deconstructive and critical. See H. Richard Niebuhr, "The Problem of Constructive Protestantism," in id., *The Kingdom of God in America* (Middletown, CT, 1988; New York, 1937), 17-44. See also Paul Tillich, "The End of the Protestant Era," in id., *The Protestant Era*, abridged ed. (Chicago, 1957), 222-233. Tillich's solution to this problem is to synthesize the Protestant Principle and the Catholic Substance. See Paul Tillich, *Systematic Theology* (Chicago, 1963), 3:245: "[The Protestant principle] alone is not enough; it needs the 'Catholic substance,' the concrete embodiment of the Spiritual Presence; but it is the criterion of the demonization (and profanization) of such embodiment."

[53] In *Creeds, Society and Human Rights*, Stackhouse sets forth an institutional grid of the institutional arenas of social life which all civilizations require because they are rooted in ba-

Historically, it has been in certain kinds of traditions—those which, on ecclesiological grounds, have spawned voluntary associations, and thereby institutional pluralism—nearly always populated by minorities at the outset, that we find the most promising institutional focus for the creedal recognition, affirmation, and nurture of human rights.[54] Such associations are primarily called into existence by proselyting, ethical religions, where these transcend family, governments, special economic or cultural interests and try to influence them to approximate justice.

Voluntary associations are also created in secular forms, once the space is established and rationalized by religious groups, and these associations can transmit the ethical ideas in routine institutions, quite often in forms which are not recognized as religious.[55] Anthony Giddens' thesis may be promising here with some modification, for he argues that globalization is the "radicalization of modernity," the realization of its consequences.[56] Giddens' "discontinuist" account,[57] however, does not sufficiently engage the question of the religious and theological antecedents of modernity.[58] It is likely that the global radicalization of moder-

---

sic human needs. These arenas also develop and transmit basic values, and can under certain conditions embody, enhance, or inhibit and resist human rights. See also id., "Religion, Society, and the Independent Sector: Key Elements of a General Theory," in Conrad Cherry and Roland A. Sherrill, eds., *Religion, The Independent Sector and American Culture* (Atlanta, 1992).

[54] See D.B. Robertson, ed., *Voluntary Associations: A Study of Groups in Free Societies* (Richmond, 1966); J.R. Peacock and J.W. Chapman, *Voluntary Associations* (New York, 1969); James Luther Adams, *Voluntary Associations*, J.R. Engel, ed. (Chicago, 1986).

[55] See Robert Wuthnow and Virginia Hodgkinson, *Faith and Philanthropy in America* (San Francisco, 1990).

[56] See Anthony Giddens, *The Consequences of Modernity* (Stanford, 1990), 51-52, where Giddens argues that we are not yet in post-modernity, but that we are experiencing the consequences of modernity. "We have not moved beyond modernity but are living precisely through a phase of its radicalization. . . . The declining grip of the West over the rest of the world is not a result of the diminishing impact of the institutions which first arose there but, on the contrary, a result of their global spread. . . . We can interpret this process as [one] of globalization . . ." Giddens uses the term "post-modernism" to refer to the "aesthetic reflection upon the nature of modernity," which he treats as distinct from post-modernity. Ibid., 45.

[57] Giddens argues: "By this I mean that modern social institutions are in some respects unique—distinct from all types of traditional order." Ibid. 3. "[W]e have to break away from the traditional sociological perspectives [of Marx, Durkheim, and Weber]. We have to account for the extreme dynamism and globalizing scope of modern institutions and explain the nature of their discontinuities from traditional cultures." Ibid., 16.

[58] Though Giddens does note, in referring to the collapse of foundationalism as "modernity coming to understand itself," "We can interpret this in terms of what I shall label providential outlooks. Enlightenment thought, and Western culture in general, emerged from a religious context which emphasized teleology and the achievement of God's grace. . . . Without these preceding orientations, the Enlightenment would scarcely have been possible in the first place." Ibid., 48. Modernity, Giddens argues, took time to realize the "fuller understanding" of the Enlightenment (that is, that it is self-contradictory to "justify a commitment to reason in the name of reason"). Ibid., 49.

nity is the most recent actuation of the deep fount of modernity, that is, of what Max Weber saw in his treatment of "the city," and more fully in his study of the spirit of capitalism—the "secular" rationalizations of life prompted by religious transformations. But Giddens' thesis holds that we are now experiencing the consequences of that ethic in ways that Weber did not and could not envision. Newly emerging global patterns, reflected in international law, media, and markets, but largely evoked and facilitated by new forms of the multinational corporation, concretely shape the world in which we live and in which human rights are recognized or violated. We should investigate what drives these new patterns, because they harbor the ability to create inclusive institutions and to nurture normative ideas about what is true and just, at least latently.

This raises the question: do global institutions, since they are universal in scope, bear within them an ethic which can be allied to that of human rights?[59] If so, with theological ethical guidance, they may support human rights more securely than either philosophy or sociology alone, that is, of either an uninstitutional normativity or an institutional anomie. Answering that question requires a consideration of the chief fount of voluntary associations, the world religions. It requires a *theological ethical* consideration of them, a consideration that seeks to articulate which religious claims are true, and how one could know their truth. In sum, important as philosophy and sociology are, both finally depend upon religion—the investigation of which finally requires theological analysis, if a universalistic ethic such as human rights is to be sustained by religion.

For our purposes, only some religions are interesting—those that have demonstrated a capacity to shape large scale civilizations. Only these religions can reach toward human rights in the relevant respects; only these make claims to universality. The world's major civilizational religions are, to use postmodernism's contemptuous phrase, totalizing theories. God's covenant with Israel commissions it to be a prophet to the nations. The Christian gospel is to be taken into all the world. The Qur'an is the Arabic words of Allah. The sounds of the Sanskrit words preexist the cosmos itself. These traditions know something about what Christians also say, "In the beginning was the word." Indeed, in what Karl Jaspers called the religions of the axial age (*Achsenzeit*),[60] several tradi-

---

[59] See Alice Evans, Robert Evans, and David Roozen, eds. *The Globalization of Theological Education* (Maryknoll, NY, 1993); Max L. Stackhouse, Charles West, Stephen Healey, et al. *Globalization in Theological Education: An Evaluative Report* (Philadelphia, 1993).

[60] See Karl Jaspers, *The Origin and Goal of History*, Michael Bullock, trans. (New Haven, 1953). John Hick, among others, has utilized Jaspers' term in *An Interpretation of Religion: Human Responses to the Transcendent* (New Haven, 1989), 21-35. Other reference to the "axial age"

tions discovered that the cosmos could be comprehended as a single whole thousands of years before such an idea could begin to make empirical sense, as it does now in what social theorists call globalization, internationalization, or the world system.[61]

Three distinct elements are present in the ethics of each of these religions; these need to be sorted if we are to find out where and how we are similar, and where and how we are different in regard to human rights.[62]

First, the world religions are allies in identifying a fundamental need to transform reality as we now find it, and together they form a cluster of formal deontological claims that categorically address all humans and all human societies. Every religion has something like universal moral laws that condemn murder, rape, lying, stealing, dishonoring religion and proper authority, and commending truth-telling, promise-keeping, and upright living. In broad terms, members of the religions can agree with each other, and often with philosophies that also seek to know the "right order" of things, and can cooperate on these bases about many matters concerning human rights.[63]

Second, however, all the great religious traditions have a way of interpreting and guiding the social context of life. There is considerable tension on this point, although it does not perhaps involve ultimate differences. This second area of ethics has to do with the ways in which

---

predate Jaspers. See, e.g., A.C. Bouquet, *Comparative Religion* (London, 1941); G.F. Moore, *History of Religions* (New York, 1948).

[61] Globalization, international, and the world systems theory are competing theories; the debate about the epiphenomenality or independence of culture vis-à-vis economics and politics continues to rage in these new conceptual forms. However, these theories share the notion that new forms of interrelatedness are emerging in the world, and that these are conceived as such by social participants, though there is sharp disagreement about what the key elements of interrelatedness are. For representative materials on globalization, see Robertson, *Globalization*. For representative materials on world systems theory, see Immanuel Wallerstein, *The Capitalist World Economy* (Cambridge, 1979). Internationalization refers to the economic interdependence of the world; a sole focus upon it leads to world systems theory. Robertson argues: "I have argued . . .that the process of global internationalization (the expansion and consolidation of the international system) has to be set conceptually and empirically alongside processes of global societalization (the global generalization of a particular conception of the modern form of society); global individualization (the global generalization of a conception of a modern person); and global humanization (the global diffusion of a homogenous, but gender-distinguished, humankind)." Roland Robertson and William Garrett, *Religion and Global Order* (New York, 1991), 282-283.

[62] These follow H. Richard Niebuhr's typology in *The Responsible Self* (New York, 1963), 60-68. See also Max L. Stackhouse, "Ethics: Social and Christian," *Andover Newton Quarterly* 13 (January, 1973): 182-186.

[63] See, e.g., David Little, John Kelsay, and A.A. Sachedina, *Human Rights and the Conflict of Cultures: Western and Islamic Perspectives on Religious Liberty* (Columbia, SC, 1988); Arlene Swidler, ed., *Human Rights in Religious Traditions* (New York, 1982); Robert Traer, *Faith in Human Rights: Support in Religious Traditions for a Global Struggle* (Washington, 1991).

commonly held first principles and final aims become embedded in the necessary contexts of life. Frequently, they become attached to a socially and historically conditioned ideal, which determines what the most fitting context of life ought to be, and what kinds of concrete social arrangements best allow the right order of things to be actuated.

If we look briefly at Islam and Hinduism, we can see important elements of this dimension of religious ethics that bear upon human rights. As we already noted, every society has to have a way of dealing with familial, political, economic, and cultural matters; if the societies are complex, they must also have independent institutions for law, science, medicine, and business. Religious institutions and loyalties have been, and presumably always will be, closely allied with these, but how that connection is made from the standpoint of the religion will be decisive for the actual functioning of the first principles of right and wrong, including the ways in which human rights operate.

Islam was led by Mohammed, of blessed memory, who was not only professionally given to commerce, but also a political-military leader who, by being the mediator of the Qur'an and the first judge in legal cases, established a direct and immediate connection between the faith and political and legal rule. It would, indeed, be very strange if religious organizations in that tradition did not draw a close connection between political, military, and legal principles, especially as they dealt with property, trade, and agreements among the heads of households, clans, tribes, and nations. Over the centuries, that has been quite characteristic, from the rise of the Caliphate, to the Iranian Revolution, to the new militancy nearly every Islamic country is now facing. Religion encouraged political and military expansion and thereby the establishment of the Shari'a and of trade. When political and military expansion went well, religion flourished, marked by wider establishment of the sacred law and commercial success. When any one these declined, the others fell into frustration or disrepair.[64]

To be sure, there have been grand moments in the history of Islam, when issues of cultural and philosophical genius, medicine, science, commercial fairness, and generosity to the poor have surpassed most other civilizations, and these "arenas of life" remain highly regarded by many devotees of the tradition. And, of course, Islam, has quite distinctive teachings about family life, presumably born out of the political, military, and legal history of the faith, and quite supportive of an ethic which nourished their common life. In general it might be said that the

---

[64] See W.C. Smith, *Islam in Modern History* (Princeton, 1957).

"brotherhood of Islam" basically supports the "nation of Islam," and that both bring political power, law, and religion into intimate proximity.[65]

In contrast, Hinduism is organized by a priestly caste that is viewed as superior to the military-political-legal custodians of public order, and they, in turn, are superior to those given to commerce and production. The fact that priestly domination triumphed over political and military rule in India is of basic significance; the priests have first-order contact with the first principles of morality, in a way that no other vocational group does. A casted hierarchy, determined by birth, sets the extended familial patterns at the core of religious association in a way that has no real analogy in Islam or Christianity. Thus, dynastic institutions, guided by a marriage-conscious and highly educated literate dynasty tends to dominate life in those areas where Hinduism is predominant.[66]

Both traditions have elements of transcendence, of the dignity of the human soul, and of the necessity of legal protections for life. But neither has developed a general theory of human rights. However, these deeply embedded social orders are not beyond change, any more than the imperial and feudal structures of medieval Christianity were. Further, once the concept of human rights is presented to these traditions, and once the possibilities of a pluralistic and open civil society becomes accessible to them, and people within these faiths begin to adopt patterns of organization that are neither totally given to political-legal militancy or to familiar-dynastic hierarchy, elements in their own traditions can be found that support the notion of human rights. Human rights can be used to catalyze growth in the latent depths of these traditions which are already have profound universalistic dimensions.

In brief, religious traditions can alter and reform themselves in the light of new ideas and circumstances. Gandhi is the great symbol of what that kind of transformation might look like in Hinduism, and present debates in Islam suggest that some changes in a comparable direction are available to Islam.[67] Great traditions change only uneasily, and some traditions get lost or simply become minority themes in other grand traditions—as the history of Hinduism poignantly suggests, but as is also evident in the heterodox sects of Islam. Even more important is how the religions react to cosmopolitan, inter-cultural, and inter-religious contact—a crisis that is currently confronting Islam, Hinduism, and Christi-

---

[65] Hamid Enayat, *Modern Islamic Political Thought* (London, 1982); Robin Wright, *In the Name of God* (New York, 1989).

[66] Louis Dumont's *Homo Hierarchicus* (Chicago, 1970) remains the most compelling statement of this continuing face in Indian life.

[67] See especially Abdullahi Ahmed An-Na'im, , *Toward an Islamic Reformation: Civil Liberties, Human Rights, and International Law* (Syracuse, 1990); id., ed., *Cross-Cultural Perspectives: A Quest for Consensus* (Philadelphia, 1994).

anity.[68] To be sure, the direction of change is not fully predictable, and it is ambiguous whether these will bring about recognition of human rights. Under the impact of the emerging formation of a global civilization, various principles and trends that are revealed to, or discovered in, one tradition refuse to remain within a single societal, cultural, political, economic, or familial framework. They influence and are selectively and voluntarily adopted by other traditions, including other religious traditions.

Third, the world religions offer constructive, forward-looking visions or teleologies, that is, guidance about how to discern good from evil consequences of our actions by considering them in reference to ultimate aims. This third, teleological dimension of ethical discourse is rather decisive in this process of selective adoption. As the traditions now stand, they have deeply formed, rich contexts, and these make the deontological and teleological conceptions concretely available to people. While all the religions deconstruct the world with the absolute specter of religious criticism and the call to transformation, they all also reconstruct it through imagination, doctrine, practice, and ritual so as to redeem or sanctify the world realities. They acknowledge the moral and spiritual legitimacy of the basic institutions of life, although the kind and character of the religion, and specifically its affinities to particular kinds of institutions, will shape the context in quite distinctive ways.

All the world religions also know that without a vision the people perish. Here, however, no hasty synthesis is possible: the Kingdom of God is neither Nirvana nor the Paradise of the Qur'an, and liberation in Latin America means something quite different than the *moksa* and *bhakti*. Thus human rights find possible support in the metaphysical moral visions of the world religions, though these are indigenized in various contexts, sometimes in ways that suppress the deontological insights. But what shall be made of the world (and what shall become of the soul) is not so clear. It may well be the case, as many human rights advocates argue, that a high degree of agreement and clarity exists about the possible cooperation of religious believers on some matters bearing on human rights. Most also agree that contexts should be treated with care, although some appeals to context become contextualist ideologies of identity and pluralism that effectively resist every call to transform society toward greater justice.[69] On the question of teleology, however, there is

---

[68] Peter van der Veer, *Religious Nationalism: Hindus and Muslims in India* (Berkeley, 1994); Mark Juergensmeyer, *The New Cold War: Religious Nationalism Confronts the Secular State* (Berkeley, 1993).

[69] See, e.g., Priscilla Pope-Levinson and John R. Levinson, *Jesus in Global Context* (Louisville, KY, 1992). A way to view liberation theology, and Marxism as well, is that they destroy deontology by focussing exclusively upon teleology. The inviolability of context and

neither agreement nor clarity. Often the role played by teleology in human rights is ignored, and when it is treated, it usually compromises the
deontological character of rights. Undoubtedly this is partly the case because of the conflict between communitarians and universalists.[70] We
have been pressed from both sides to adopt either/or positions. However, one also wonders whether some of the failure to treat the issue is
not a way of avoiding the difficulty it entails. We are delighted that we
can invoke the dharma, the *dhamma*, the Mosaic law, the Qur'an, the Holy
Spirit, and, in times past, the proletariat against the injustices we perceive
in the world. However, that is not enough; for we must also speak about
what we and the various constituencies of the world's religions are for.
And that moves us into an area where many are not comfortable—an
area where one must not only be against the injustices of the world, but
also ready to claim that some teleologies see farther and more than others, an area in which apologetics is a chief form of dialogue.[71]

Conclusions in Light of the Emerging Global Ethos

The unwillingness to engage in discussion and debate at this level
and to raise critical questions about the most decisive levels of human
existence represents a failure of intellectual nerve.[72] It prevents us from
finding an approach to this problem of conflicting teleologies, one which
will only become more intense with the phenomenon of globalization.
What we call "fundamentalism" is one key response to this intellectual
vacuum, because it supplies what theologians too often have avoided—a

---

culture has been a chief tenet of much thinking on the matter of rights, universality, and relativism. In the concern to protect cultures from destruction lies a partial truth, namely, that
universal truths must be taken up and indigenized, and that when they are, they should be
protected, so that a people has an enduring sense of moral guidance. However, this does not
mean that all cultural or religious views or practices incarnate universal truths; falsehoods or
distortions are not inviolable. For an account of the critique of the view that cultures are
"primordially separate, bounded . . . units," and thus are not strictly inviolable, see Buell,
"Conceptualizations of Contemporary Global Culture." Buell summarizes Roseberry thus:
"[T]raditional fears about homogenization in [cultures] . . . are false. They are based on a belief in distinctive primordial cultural units, which is historically inaccurate, and they omit
consideration of important, non-monolithic mechanisms by which local cultures interiorize
and indigenize outside influences, rather than swallow them whole hog." Ibid. 128.

[70] See. e.g., the debate between John Rawls and Michael Sandel. For a recent installment
in this debate, which appears to make some headway, see David Rasmussen, ed. *Universalism
vs. Communitarianism: Contemporary Debates in Ethics* (Cambridge, MA, 1990).

[71] See Max L. Stackhouse, et al., *Apologia: Contextualization, Globalization, and Mission in
Theological Education* (Grand Rapids, 1988). See also Mouw and Griffioen, *Pluralisms and Horizons.*

[72] See Stephen Healey, "Religious Truth Claims, Violence, and the Pluralistic Hypothesis: A Defense of Interreligious Apologetics," *Andover Newton Review* 3(1) (1992): 17-30; Mark
Heim, *Salvations* (forthcoming).

comprehensive assessment of the state of affairs in the world today, including teleology. Fundamentalists may be faulted in many respects, but they cannot be said to lack intellectual courage. They are not wholly wrong-headed in seeking foundations on which we can stand as we build the civilization which will be the *oikos* of the twenty-first century. Fundamentalists are surely right to seek these foundations in religious traditions. They demand that any who speak with authority be forthright about the ultimate foundations for what they say, and if there are none, they suggest that people pay no attention.

Since the world is increasingly interconnected and interdependent, and is known to be such, in its media, its international organizations, its politics, and its economy, we have before us the possibility of a broader and deeper *telos*, which invites us again to ask, as Augustine asked for his age in the fifth century, about the chief end of life. The answer to the question, What is the meaning of it all? in order to be sustainable in the future, has to be correlated in some way to the civilization which is emerging.

Roland Robertson, the sociologist who has thought about this the most, refers to this process as globalization.[73] Robertson and William Garrett say:

> [T]he world is rapidly coming to be apprehended as "one place," that is a totality wherein discrete selves, nation-states, and even civilizational traditions have their respective niches, each interconnected by complex, reticular relations of belligerence and beneficence, competition and compromise, discordance and detente. Yet, whatever the mode of linkage among the sub-sets, the crucial fact remains that each unit is couched within the frame for the whole so that, willy nilly, action must be referenced against the coordinates of "the world."[74]

In this emerging context, focussing in a normative theological way upon the role played by the world religions in the support or denial of human rights is essential. For world religions tie principles, aims, and contexts together in a way that few philosophies and social theories do. Philosophical theories fail to help us address this ethos because they are often strictly abstract. Sociological theories fail because they are usually norm-

---

[73] Robertson does not assign an unambiguous value to globalization; he is to that extent value-neutral. He is a sociologist, not an ethicist or philosopher. See, e.g., Robertson, *Globalization*, 6.

[74] Roland Robertson and William Garrett, "Religion and Globalization: An Introduction," in id., *Religion and Global Order: Religion and the Political Order* (New York, 1991), 4:ix-xxiii.

less.[75] But theological ethics succeeds, for it ties a concrete, institutional focus with normative thinking. As Anthony Giddens has pointed out, the whole consideration of the modernity/post-modernity question, and for our purpose the status of human rights, becomes quite different when the focus is upon institutions and not philosophical epistemology.[76] However, new ground must be broken by considering the relatively neglected role apologetics must play in interreligious dialogue and in discerning the most fitting shape for the world's institutions.[77]

However, we must face another option: perhaps all the world religions will not enter this dialogue. Perhaps some are unlikely to engage in it, or will discourage their members from doing so, because their teleologies do not allow for the possibility that all can be included in the more proximate or even in the final future. All this does privilege certain religions against others—now, as always, only those which are capable of reaching globally should be taken seriously as ways of organizing the greater cosmopolitan life.

All religions and peoples, however, face the fact of modernity—"modernization," as it is usually called by social theorists, with its development of a new world order.[78] The world is increasingly interconnected and interdependent as well as differentiated and pluralistic, and is known to be such, in its media, its international organizations, its politics, its economy, its technology and its awareness of a common ecological destiny.

Awareness of these developments brings with it an anxiousness about the fate of individual cultures, means of expression, and localities.[79] Will they all be destroyed as the world becomes one? Must those

---

[75] But see Alan Wolfe, *Whose Keeper?* (Berkeley, 1989). Wolfe argues that modernity is no longer guided normatively by religion, philosophy, literature, or politics, and thus it falls to the social sciences to provide such guidance. Social sciences, for Wolfe, are essentially three disciplines—economics, political science, and sociology. Ibid. 3-13. Wolfe underestimates the role played by religion in ostensibly secular societies and overestimates the potential of the social sciences to provide such guidance.

[76] See Giddens, *The Consequences of Modernity*, 1-4 and Robertson's critique of Giddens in Roberston, *Globalization*, chap. 9. Contrary to Giddens, Robertson believes globalization cannot be identified simply as the "consequences of modernity."

[77] For an example of what is required, see Paul J. Griffiths, *An Apology for Apologetics: A Study in the Logic of Interreligious Dialogue* (Maryknoll, NY, 1991). For an attempt to establish a "new universalism" while avoiding an apologetical relationship between faiths, see David Krieger, *The New Universalism: Foundations for a Global Theology* (Maryknoll, NY, 1991); Stackhouse, et al., *Apologia*.

[78] S.N. Eisenstadt, *The Protestant Ethic and Modernization* (New York, 1968).

[79] A particularly salient example of what such anxiousness can lead to is found in Paul Kennedy, *The Rise and the Fall of the Great Powers* (New York, 1987). Robertson and Garrett, who cite this study, argue that in the Ming Dynasty the Chinese were quite capable of exploring West Africa and even Europe before the Europeans explored Asia. However, all that

committed to the value of individuals and particular communities fight against globalization? Human rights stand awkwardly in the middle of these concerns. On the one hand, they are avowedly universalistic, and, on the other, they aim to recognize and protect the legitimate claims of individuals and those decisive associations by which human life is sustained at concrete levels. But that may not be so awkward; perhaps postmodernism, like romanticism (and its institutional form, nationalism) are the real enemies of individuals and of pluralism of communities. In either their embrace of chaos, or the unique, lies a promise to protect individuals from totalistic destruction, but an even deeper inability to deliver on that promise, since individuals are only instruments of larger purposes or processes in these notions.[80]

Thus, alongside the development of "globalization as a concept," of the "compression of the world and the intensification of consciousness of the world as a whole"[81] also developing is an increasing propensity to tribalization and radical recommunizations. The "ethnic cleansings" in areas that are nominally Christian, from Bosnia to Burundi, are matched by forms of anti-modern and anti-global militance in parts of Islam and Hinduism.[82] These tragic dramas remind us that it takes well-maintained, civilizationally-held and transmitted ideas, mediated by and routinized in enduring social structures, to create and maintain a humane ethos,[83] in which a pluralistic unity is possible. Human rights, acknowledged in the fabric of civil society, recognized in international covenants and national constitutions, and honored by governments, are a decisive set of ideas and institutions. Human rights are theories that enable, much like the

---

suddenly came to a close when, "the resurgence of neo-Confucianism in the 1430s resulted in an Imperial Edict of 1436 which halted Chinese exploration, prompted the scuttling of Cheng Ho's warships, and urged the Chinese to turn inward in order to protect her cultural heritage against contamination by foreigners." Robertson and Garrett, *Religion and Global Order*, xvii.

[80] The end of the Enlightenment and the beginning of Romanticism, in Hegel's philosophy, shows the tenuous nature of individuals, who might legitimately be swallowed up (*Aufgehoben*) in the development of the final polis. Political theories of right, wittingly or not, draw from this philosophical tradition, whose monism goes back to Jean Jacques Rousseau. Nationalism is its project, and historicism is its methodology. Postmodernism rightly questions totalistic theories that eventuate in the destruction of the individuals, but its own anti-universalistic logic cannot adequately ground uniqueness and differences, which its anti-democratic and anti-rights tendencies illustrate. The social theory of politics developed in Anglo-American political philosophy is an alternative to both romanticism and post modernism; it is this kind of liberalism that conjoins uniquely with Puritan public theology to form the basis for human rights in the liberal-Puritan synthesis.

[81] Roland Robertson, *Globalization*, 8.

[82] See Paul Mojzes, *Lament for Yugoslavia: Ethnoreligious Warfare in the Balkans* (New York, 1994); Jürgensmeyer, *The New Cold War*; van der Veer, *Religious Nationalism: Hindus and Muslims*.

[83] Stackhouse, *Creeds, Society, and Human Rights*.

Ten Commandments, the founding of viable covenants and the formation of a community which extends beyond the boundaries of any given nation-state into the community of nations, the new world order. But human rights are also, like the Ten Commandments, dependent as binding moral commandments on a deeper theological vision. They cannot themselves tell us the purpose of life.

The fate of human rights is not yet decided in our time. Much, much hangs in the balance. The long term recognition of human rights requires the engagement of a social hermeneutic which is philosophically open to universality, socio-historically attuned to the role played by religion in society, and theologically ready to proffer apologetical arguments for and against religious claims in the quest for a true account of human nature under God. All of these arguments are in considerable disrepute today. Yet human rights will best be fulfilled if and when a theological ethic brings these orientations into an integrated focus. If it does so, it will be a "light to all the peoples," a "light which enlightens the whole world."

The articulation of human rights in this way may well enable humanity to approximate more nearly God's truth and justice in our time. That covenantal calling, articulated in an exemplary, if secular and inevitably temporal, way in efforts to state and defend human rights, speaks from the deep unity of creation, Sinai, Calvary, and the New Jerusalem, and it promises to touch and renews also Athens, Benares, and Mecca.

Identity, Difference and Belonging: Religious And Cultural Rights

—————————————— ❧ ☙ ——————————————

CHARLES VILLA-VICENCIO

University of Cape Town

W estern experiments in human coexistence have undergone a radical revolution in the last half century. Martin Marty's recent essay "From the Centripetal to the Centrifugal in Culture and Religion" says it all: The shift is from the "global village," "the spaceship earth," "homogenization" and "planetization" to "particularism" and "difference," if not "'tribal warfare.'"[1]

The South African revolution is different. While many nations are breaking apart, South Africa is seeking unity. It is neither innocent nor unaware of the difficulties involved. The compulsion is for unity without uniformity. The reality is diversity. The fear is disintegration. The theme of President Nelson Mandela's inauguration address was "One Nation: Many Cultures." Not everyone in South Africa believes in non-racism, non-sexism, and the quest for oneness. The search for something new that transcends difference without collapsing the many into the one nevertheless constitutes a message of hope to many people both in South Africa and around the world. South Africa is a microcosm of the global challenge for people of difference to live together. It is this that has persuaded me to comment (as a particular South African) on a particular South African problem, in a volume seeking a measure of universal consensus on *Religious Human Rights in Global Perspective*.

Others, in this volume and elsewhere, have properly lamented the lack of sufficient emphasis on religion in the human rights debate.[2] In this chapter, I shall approach the question of religion in terms of the contri-

---

[1] Martin E. Marty, "From the Centripetal to the Centrifugal in Culture and Religion: The Revolution Within This Half Century," *Theology Today* 51(1) (April, 1994): 5-16.

[2] See, e.g., John Witte, "The State of Religious Human Rights in the World: A Comparative Religious and Legal Study," *Preliminary Documents of Religious Human Rights Project* 1 (1993); Johan van der Vyver, "Report on The World Conference on Human Rights, Vienna, 14-25 June, 1993," *Preliminary Documents of Religious Human Rights Project* 3 (1993), 50.

J. Witte, Jr. and J.D. van der Vyver (eds.), Religious Human Rights in Global Perspective, 517-538.
© 1996 *Kluwer Law International. Printed in the Netherlands.*

bution it can make to cultural renewal, while mindful of the human rights violations to which it has often contributed—in South Africa and beyond.

South African history is marred by exclusion. The political center has notoriously and aggressively denied access to blacks. Seen to be "non-white" from the perspective of the racist regime, blacks have been assigned a place on the lower slopes of the pyramid of humanity. The political center has in various earlier seasons excluded "non-English," "non-Afrikaners," "non-Calvinists," "non-Christians," "non-racists" —and, of course, "non-males," "non-monied," and more. We now pride ourselves as being a "new" South Africa that includes. In reality, however, exclusion continues.

Some suggest that the quickest way out of the spiral is to ensure that we forget difference, and learn to be the same. It is this that makes the minimum consensus of liberal democracy (what Charles Taylor has called "difference-blind" liberalism[3]) an attractive option for those who fear difference in the wake of apartheid-imposed separation. Such an ideal is expressed perhaps nowhere better than in John Rawls' notion of a "thin consensus."[4] It requires all "thick" cultural, ethnic, and religious baggage to be left outside the public square or hidden in dark and private recesses of one's soul.[5] This, it is argued, is the only reasonable way around the quarrel that inevitably ensues from "non-commensurable" notions of the common good.[6] This kind of liberalism is questioned in what follows:

First, I shall argue that the liberal consensus is not thin at all but in fact thick with white, male, Eurocentric particularisms deceptively sold in the name of value-free common sense and universal realism. "It is marvelously easy," suggests Renato Rosaldo, "to confuse 'our local culture' with 'universal human nature'."[7] Only the excluded—those who are "other" in their own home know that it is not. In the United States, African-Africans, Hispanics, and Chicanos feel excluded by a melting pot ideology that is sold as inclusive. In the United Kingdom, West Indians are alienated by the best of British culture, described by Lord Durham as having "a high estimate of [its] own superiority, [taking] no pains to con-

---

[3] Charles Taylor, *Multiculturalism and the Politics of Recognition* (Princeton, 1992), 62.

[4] See, inter alia, John Rawls, *A Theory of Justice* (Cambridge, MA, 1971); Terry Pinkard, *Democratic Liberalism and Social Union* (Philadelphia, 1987).

[5] For a discussion on "thick" and "thin" notions of social identity, see Richard J. Mouw and Sander Griffioen, *Pluralisms and Horizons* (Grand Rapids, 1993).

[6] John Rawls, "Justice as Fairness: Political not Metaphysical," *Philosophical and Public Affairs* 14(3) (1985).

[7] Renato Rosaldo, *Culture and Truth: The Remaking of Social Analysis* (Boston, 1989), 39.

ceal from others [its] contempt and intolerance of usages" that differ.[8] In South Africa, blacks see no reason to tolerate what once passed for "Christian civilization."

Second, I shall argue that in the South African context, where race, ethnicity, culture, and group identity have been used to sustain the apartheid monster, multiculturalism runs the danger of becoming a sophisticated form of neo-apartheid. Difference for the sake of difference can indeed collapse into tribalism of the worst kind.

Third, reaching beyond the options of both classical liberalism and multiculturalism, I shall explore the option of difference as a means of striving towards a common destiny and a common core culture—as yet unknown and undefined. To attain this end the importance of cultural, religious, gender, ethnic, and other differences needs to be protected against all imposed agendas of domination by dominant political chiefs and elitist cultural brokers.

The Failure of Liberalism

The affirmation of individual rights has much to offer a country like South Africa, emerging as it does from decades of human rights violations and apartheid abuse, where human rights have been sacrificed in pursuit of ideological madness.

Although an emphasis on individual rights is not the sole prerogative of liberalism, the liberal tradition has laid claim to these rights in a special way. It has frequently done so at the cost of socio-economic rights, as well as cultural, religious, and group rights. But personal well-being cannot be reduced to freedom of choice; "first generation" rights cannot be fully realized in isolation from "second generation" and "third generation" rights. Culture and religion involve more than *laissez-faire* supermarket-style choice. To the extent that liberalism downplays religious, cultural, and other "thick" sources of belonging such as memory, language, ethnicity, class identity and gender, it ignores an essential dimension of what it means to be fully human. It undermines the participation of those whose identity does not enable them to enter fully into the prevailing ethos of society. Indeed, to argue that human identity *can* exclude issues of religion and culture is itself a cultural position. It is an attempt, in the name of an imposed consensus, to sanitize the public square of cultural, religious, and other differences that violate the dominant ideas of the existing order.

---

[8] Quoted in F.A. Van Jaarsveld, "A Historical Mirror on Blood River," A. König and H. Keane, eds., *The Meaning of History* (Pretoria, 1980), 9.

History shows that the greater the capacity and willingness of the outsider to assimilate the culture of the guardians of the public square, the greater the chances that outsider becoming an insider. Those who cannot and will not submit to assimilation are left with one of two choices: they are side-lined, or they rebel. Missionized nineteenth-century Africans who dressed in Western clothes and lived in square houses soon found themselves in a category above the "red people" who refused to be Westernized. African chiefs who sent their children to Governor Grey's Kaffir College in Cape Town, designed to produce "black Englishmen," were regarded as the "good kaffirs."[9] Colonial authorities were ready to regard them as part of "Christian civilization" in Africa. The white National Party would, in time, shift the goalposts, demanding that white skin be an added ingredient to what makes for civilization. The South African conflict has, however, always involved more than color.[10]

In a word, not all Africans have a desire to become "black Englishmen" or black appendages of some other imposed identity. Steve Biko's words stand as a warning against any notion of assimilation which makes passivity the conduit that leads from rejection to acceptance: "Blacks are tired of standing at the touchlines to witness a game that they should be playing. They want to do things for themselves."[11] Predictably accused of racism in liberal circles, Biko responded:

> If by integration you understand a breakthrough into white society by blacks, an assimilation and acceptance into white society by blacks, an assimilation and acceptance of blacks into an already established set of norms and codes of behaviour set and maintained by whites, then YES I am against it.[12]

The imposition of a ruling hegemony on those most alienated from it is often fertile ground for counter-hegemonic cultures. At the very least it generates what W.E.B. du Bois has called a sense of "double consciousness":

> One ever feels his twoness—an American, a Negro; two souls, two thoughts, two unreconciled strivings; two warring ideas in one dark body, whose dogged strength alone keeps it from being torn asunder.

---

[9] Janet Hodgson, "Zonnebloem College and Cape Town," *Studies in the History of Cape Town: Centre for African Studies, University of Cape Town* 1 (1979):125-52.

[10] See Les Switzer, *Power and Resistance in an African Society: The Ciskei Xhosa and the Making of South Africa* (Pietermaritzburg, 1993), 115.

[11] Steve Biko, *I Write What I Like* (London, 1987), 154.

[12] Ibid., 24.

[The American Negro] would not bleach his Negro soul in a flood of white Americanism, for he knows that Negro blood has a message for the world. He simply wishes to make it possible for a man to be both a Negro and an American, without being cursed and spit upon. . . .[13]

Charles Long has argued that African-Americanism, driven by white American cultural hegemony, has located itself beyond the right to participation for which du Bois asked. It has given expression to "an-other" (a counter-hegemonic) space within American society—over against white hegemony.[14] In a similar vein, other minorities have found a space apart from mainstream America. To this South African observer looking in, the American melting pot option has failed. Sensitivity to issues of color, race, and difference is foremost in the minds of South Africans who are committed to genuine unity. If a rainbow is a unity of different colors, the notion of a rainbow people is not something that South Africans readily recognize in the American experiment.

The South African history of struggle against apartheid has many contours, including those of race, gender, ethnicity, class, and other divisions. It has, at the same time, brought people of difference into unity. This process reminds us that identity never has been something stable and inherently given, but is instead a social construct that emerges in dialogue. Louise du Toit, seeking to unravel the notion of identity, writes: "What we call our 'selves' and our 'world' are effects or products of the particular, historical [cultural] communities in which we find ourselves always already immersed." She argues that according to this theory "identity itself, previously regarded as the innermost essence of any particular person or thing, is seen as itself nothing more or less than a [social] construct. . . . It is not bestowed from above, but rather generated from the sides."[15] The borders of cultural and religious encounter are invariably ambiguous, and it is precisely here—in what Renato Rosaldo calls the "border zones" of identity—that future possibilities of genuine encounter are to be found rather than in the spheres of cultural hegemony that are under the watchful eye of the cultural elite.[16] A political

---

[13] W.E.B. du Bois, *The Souls of Black Folk* (New York, 1982), 45.

[14] Charles Long, *Significations: Signs, Symbols and Images in the Interpretation of Religion* (Philadelphia, 1986), 153.

[15] Louise du Toit, "A Narrative-Communicative Approach to Identity and Ethnicity," unpublished paper delivered at the "Global Change and Social Transformation Conference," Centre of Social Development, November, 1993. The words "cultural" and "social" have been substituted for "linguistic" in du Toit's text. The words are not synonymous, but do not violate her essential argument.

[16] Rosaldo, *Culture and Truth*, 196ff.

model that seeks to limit or exclude the ongoing encounter of cultures
and religions limits the future growth and possibilities of the very culture
it seeks to protect. In generating counter-cultural hegemonies, it contributes to the inevitability of cultural wars.

To the notion of "culture in dialogue and change" as a basis for living
together, we return later in quest of a new culture of openness. The reality is that this dialogue (although happening wherever people meet) is
not promoted as the engine that unites people in classical liberal society.
In most liberal societies different cultures, religions, and other ethnic expressions coexist. They do not obviously enrich one another. There is
certainly no attempt to bring them into structural engagement as a basis
for reaching beyond "what is" to "what is not yet." Most liberals, in fact,
see no reason for something new.

It is this that makes multiculturalism an attractive alternative, although it, too, can be used to defend the structures of the dominant order. Difference can be controlled, manipulated, and censored to ensure
that dissent is kept to a minimum, never being allowed to challenge the
ruling consensus that steers the nose of the ship. This aside, at best multiculturalism knows that there can be salvation outside of "difference-
blind" liberalism.

The Limits of Multiculturalism

> The Zulu is proud to be a Zulu the Xhosa is proud to be a Xhosa
> and the Venda is proud to be a Venda, just as proud as they were
> a hundred years ago. The lesson we have learned from history
> during the past 300 years is that these ethnic groups, the whites
> as well as the Bantu, sought their greatest fulfillment, their great-
> est happiness, and the best mutual relations on the basis of sepa-
> rate and individual development . . . the only basis on which
> peace, happiness, and mutual confidence could be built up.[17]

When multiculturalism is uncritically promoted as an end in itself,
these words, spoken in 1959 by Minister of Bantu Administration and
Development Mr. De Wet Nel, cause South Africans instinctively to experience a sense of *déjà vu*. Apartheid was built on difference. "To each its
own." "Separate but equal." "Autonomy and cooperation." These are the
slogans of South Africa's past. "Group identity," "a federation of independent states," "Boerestaat politics," and Inkatha-style "Zulu national-

---

[17] Quoted in T. Dunbar Moodie, *The Rise of Afrikanerdom: Power, Apartheid and Afrikaner
Civil Religion* (Berkeley, 1980), 266.

ism"—these are notions still employed by those who cling to the old in the midst of the new.

The question is whether the multicultural model, which views ethnicity and culture as the distinguishing categories of individual and social identity, can help heal the South African nation. Given the close link between culture, race, and economic disparity in South Africa, the pertinent question is whether ethnic categories such as "blackness" are in fact critical and radical enough to deal with the underlying divisions in South African society. Neville Alexander's critique of black consciousness in this regard must be taken into account.[18] He argues that "any cultural product that enhances humanity, by weakening the perpetuation of the system which enables men to exploit others, is beautiful. Anything, whether black, blue or red, which does the opposite or tends to do so, is ugly." His concern is, however, that like any other ideology, black consciousness can be co-opted by the very forces it seeks to overthrow. If its leaders are "bought off by the powerful and all-pervasive oligarchy to become satellite 'capitalists' or apologists for these, the Black Consciousness Movement will become another conformist attempt: it will become a consumerist movement providing the ideological basis of firms catering for Afro-styles. It will give the appearance of militant opposition while in reality constituting a necessary and even a vital aspect of the establishment."

Alexander continues: "The Black Consciousness Movement correctly stresses the unity of the oppressed people of South Africa. . . ." His argument, however, is that a critique of apartheid must necessarily go beyond color. It must penetrate the socio-economic roots of the apartheid system—a point belabored by many proponents of black consciousness. "It is not the 'white' man [sic]," he writes, "but the system that oppresses us." He at the same time shares black consciousness' rejection of white liberals, while suggesting it would be a mistake to believe that all liberals are white. "Liberalism," he declares "is a greater danger in the long run to the struggle of the oppressed than Fascism."

While, for the foreseeable future, alienation and exploitation in South Africa is likely to continue to be accurately symbolized by categories such as "black" and "female," an increasing number of black males (at least) are likely to find themselves in privileged and socially unhindered positions in South African society. And, if human nature can be predicted, some will in turn defend the structures that make this possible. In brief,

---

[18] Neville Alexander "Black Consciousness: A Reactionary Tendency" (1974), reprinted, with revisions as "Black Consciousness: A Reactionary Tendency?" in N. Barney Pityana, Mamphela Ramphele, Malusi Mpumlwana, and Lindy Wilson, eds., *Bounds of Possibility: The Legacy of Steve Biko and Black Consciousness* (Cape Town, 1991), 238-52.

there is already every indication that race, color, and ethnicity will become increasingly ambiguous social terms in South Africa. Not all blacks are of a common ilk. Not all white males are quite the same! Further Martin Marty reminds us that "Latino/a America is not a homogeneous group. Rather, it includes wealthy right-wing, Miami-based Cuban exiles, the undocumented workers of the Southwest, Puerto Ricans in Manhattan ghettoes, illegal Haitian immigrants, and Salvadoreans in search of sanctuary."[19]

The question is whether the particularities identified by mainstream multiculturalism are indeed particular. Who decides what constitutes a particular identity? Differently stated, the question is whether multiculturalism takes the dynamic and fragmentary character of cultures seriously. Does it give sufficient consideration to the blurred borders and margins of group formation as being crucial to future cultural development? In other words, does this model of living together not presuppose a chauvinistic rigidity and "God-givenness" to culture that lays at the root of the very conflict that almost thrust South Africa into an apocalyptic demise?

James Moulder offers a sobering and lucid word on culture:

> According to the dictionaries, we call a crop of artificially and experimentally grown bacteria a culture. This fact is worth noting for at least two reasons: Firstly, it reminds us that the word "culture" is derived from the Latin word *cultura*, a word for farming, for a complex process in which we deliberately and intentionally interfere with nature and try to improve its performance. Secondly, it points to the fact that, whatever one's culture is, it is something that has been created, artificially and experimentally; it is not something that is given to us in the way in which the number and the color of our eyes are given to us. What this all boils down to is that when one is talking about one's culture, one is talking about the product of a complex process of socialisation.[20]

Moulder proceeds to make five important points regarding culture: First, everyone's culture has been created by others for him or her; he or she is born into it. Second, everyone's culture is changing. Third, cultural groups are never totally homogeneous. Fourth, no cultural group is totally unique. Fifth, nobody finds it particularly easy to change cultures.[21]

---

[19] Marty, "From Centripetal to Centrifugal," 15.

[20] James Moulder, "Moral Education in a Multicultural Environment," *Acta Academica* 24(2) (1992): 17.

[21] Ibid., 19.

It is, Moulder suggests, naive to suggest that cultures need to be protected in the shape that they find themselves at any particular point in history. Cultural "border zones" simply must be taken seriously in cultural analysis.

It is equally naive to suggest that the process of cultural formation has been devoid of political manipulation. This means that cultural engineering, especially at this crucial point of South African history, is not quite as despotic as the notion might at first appear. Indeed a certain amount of cultural reconceptualization and "gentle nudging" is not only inevitable but probably to be commended as a basis for countering the artificial racist cultures that presently dominate the South African scene. The democratic focus of contemporary South African politics, at the same time, makes it likely that any form of "hard" cultural engineering would meet with an appropriate level of resistance.

Cultural Openness

The promise of openness is inherent to cultural border zones. T.S. Eliot has suggested that the greatest creativity occurs at the friction edge of cultures—where the old meets the new, where cultures fuse, where the growing edges of traditions are most vibrant and fragile.[22] For societies in transition, where people are obliged to face that which is new, there is a disposition to discover options for living together that "stable" societies never know. Empires that have not yet fallen and people who live as happily in the iron cage of intransigence usually regard adventure as unnecessary and stupid. It takes a certain kind of compulsion to embark an Abrahamic and Sarahaic journey into "the unknown not knowing where [we] are going."

Gloria Anzaldua, in *Borderlands/La Frontera*, a story written from the perspective of a Chicano lesbian woman, shows how the struggle for survival on the edges of society contains the potential for new forms of human understanding. "The new *mestiza* [person of mixed ancestry]," she says, "copes by developing a tolerance for contradictions, a tolerance for ambiguity. She learns to juggle cultures. She has a plural personality, she operates in a pluralistic mode—nothing is thrust out, the good the bad and the ugly, nothing rejected, nothing abandoned. Not only does she sustain the contradictions, *she turns the ambivalence into something else.*"[23] Rosaldo comments: "In making herself into a complex persona,

---

[22] Quoted by Jerzy Smolicz in a dialogue with Neville Alexander in "The Quest for a Core Culture," *Bau* 8(3) (September, 1993): 5.

[23] Gloria Anzaldua, *Borderlands/La Frontera: The New Mestiza* (San Francisco, 1987), 79 (quoted in Rosaldo, *Culture and Truth*, 216, italics added).

Anzaldua incorporates Mexican, Indian, and Anglo elements at the same time that she discards the homophobia and patriarchy of Chicano culture. In rejecting the classic 'authenticity' of cultural purity, she seeks out the many-stranded possibilities of the borderlands." She argues that because of their long practiced art of cultural blending, Chicanos have become leaders in developing "new forms of polyglot cultural creativity."[24]

Anzaldua's story is repeated every day in Soweto and in the Cape Flats (a "colored" resettlement area in Cape Town). Sowetan culture is a polyglot. Migrant workers from the Transkei, from Venda, Zululand, and Qwa Qwa encounter urbanized neighbors and unlawful immigrants from Zaire, Nigeria, Ghana, and elsewhere. There are gangsters and thieves, frightened people and an emerging bourgeoisie. They speak English to enter the realm of employment. They speak Afrikaans in order to negotiate the still entrenched apartheid bureaucracy. They speak "tsotsi-taal" in the shebeens, while, in the mine compounds, the lingua-franca is "fanakalo," a dialect which is ultimately non-language. "Soweto 1976" has been followed sixteen years later by a hero's welcome for a Robben Island fugitive who was to become the first president of a democratic South Africa. This is all part of a dynamic Sowetan culture. It is an identity that "is." It is also *en route*. In its openness it reaches into the future.

The Cape Flats is not Soweto. It is Muslim, Christian, Hindu, and atheist. It is Malay. It is colored. It is black. It is communist, workerist, and survivalist. It also provided the reviled (but "new") National Party, that imposed apartheid on a nation for 45 years, with its only provincial victory in the country's first democratic election. It too is a polyglot.

The interim constitution of the emerging South African nation is designed to bring different cultures—those that were, in terms of apartheid ideology, supposedly each sufficient unto themselves, into a unity. South Africa has always been a place of difference. Difference is palpably felt. Now, however, for the first time in a long history of struggle, it is viewed positively. To have spoken of difference in many progressive circles prior to 1990 would have been to provoke anger. Apartheid-insulated difference was necessarily spurned. Today the *kairos* challenge is how difference can be employed to build a united nation.

Will the polyglot of cultures, the numerous subaltern identities, eventually blend in difference and unity as Soweto, the Cape Flats, Kwa Zulu, the former Bantustans, Johannesburg, Potchefstroom, Pretoria, and Cape Town (each with evolving cultures of their own) encounter one another? Alternatively, will Christians, Muslims, Hindus, Jews, and atheists

---

[24] Rosaldo, *Culture and Truth*, 216.

who fought a common struggle against apartheid, having been beaten by the same apartheid police, locked up in the same prisons and having gone together into exile, be able to maintain the unity that forged unity in difference? Will the separate cultures coexist side by side—"separate but equal" (to use a bad phrase)? If so, from where will the social tissue come that binds the nation? Will the center hold? Will everything collapse in disintegration? It is too early to tell. There are, however, some tentative signals hidden in the journey travelled thus far. I offer a few observations:

A Dynamic Culture. Culture is more than a light coat that rests on one's shoulders, to be discarded at will. It is more than a channel through which one has an option to express one's being. Culture *is* being. It is the story, memory, symbol, language, and place within which we live, move and have our being. It is religion and belief. It is life. To quote Franz Fanon, culture is "the action through which [a] people has created itself and keeps itself in existence."[25] Or, in the words of Raymond Williams: "Culture is ordinary."[26] To the extent that a person is alive, responding to new challenges, ready to engage the other in dialogue, culture is dynamic. Culture is *en route* because people are *en route*.

Africans instinctively understand this. A traditional African understanding of *ubuntu* affirms an organic wholeness of humanity—a wholeness realized in and through other people. The notion is enshrined in the Xhosa proverb: *umuntu ngumuntu ngabantu* (a person is a person through persons).[27] This is a belief that recognizes within other people the presence of the divine through which a person attains full humanity. *Ubuntu* constitutes a residual presence in the inevitable mix of African cultures, that is being rediscovered as a binding imperative in South African society. It is built on the realization that, like it or not, we are shaped for good and bad by a host of others with whom we share our lives. Meaningful relationships, whether "by blood," "by marriage," or even "by association," are dearly cherished by traditional African culture.[28] Such relationships constitute an organic identity that the Western world can only with difficulty comprehend. Primarily it involves kinship within one's own clan, but it is also possible with personal strangers"[29]—people within whom I grow humanity, whether through affirmation or conflict. There is

---

[25] Franz Fanon, *Wretched of the Earth* (London, 1983), 188.

[26] Raymond Williams, "Culture is Ordinary," in N. Mackenzie, ed., *Conviction* (London, 1958).

[27] See Gabriel Setiloane, *African Theology: An Introduction* (Johannesburg, 1986), 13-16.

[28] Ibid., 9.

[29] See discussion on culture, ethnicity, and group identity in Gerhard Marè, *Ethnicity and Politics in South Africa* (London, 1993), 12.

ample evidence in South African history of traditional Africans drawing others (whether missionaries or white settlers—some of whom turned against the Africans) into kinship with themselves. In sum, an African sense of community includes and unites,[30] and in so doing it changes. The story of Soweto, with all its cultural assets and liabilities makes the point. It also reminds us that neither African culture, nor any other culture, should be romanticized.[31] Still the insights of traditional and contemporary African culture should not be overlooked in the quest for what is new.

At the heart of Africa, despite its changing character, there is dialogue with one's own and with the other. It is a deep-seated anthropological and religious given. There is recognition that within the other, however different, there is humanity and the promise of an enriched life which makes social bonding possible. A common South African culture does not exist. But given the place of belonging, forging, and uniting in African encounter, it might yet emerge. The celebration of African culture ensures that whatever the nature of future South African culture, at the center of human encounter will be mutual respect.

A Quest for Unity. If South Africa is to be one nation, there must be a nexus where the different cultures meet or at least where common values within these cultures enable some form of organic union.

Welsh neo-Marxist Raymond Williams recognizes the existence of a plurality of working-class cultures, while arguing that a common culture will dawn to unite the diverse strands of struggle in unity. He insists that humanity "needs a common culture, not for the sake of an abstraction, but because we shall not survive without it."[32] Countering any sense of imposed uniformity, he writes: "The distinction of a culture in common is that . . . *selection is freely and commonly made and remade.*"[33] Thus he sees culture as the voluntary outcome of human solidarity grounded in democratic socialism. Neville Alexander, a dedicated South African Marxist, on the other hand, favors differentiation, whether between religions, regions, languages, or other cultural phenomena. He stresses the dialectic relationship which exists between sub-cultures and as an important ingredient of any society—"provided they don't undermine the core culture."[34]

---

[30] For further discussion see, inter alia, Leopold Senghor, *On African Socialism* (London, 1964); Setiloane, *African Theology*; Leo Apostel, *African Philosophy: Myth or Reality* (Ghent, 1982); Augustine Shutte, *Philosophy for Africa* (Cape Town, 1993).

[31] See Archie Mafeje, "African Philosophical Projections and Prospects for the Indigenisation of Political and Intellectual Discourse," *Seminar Paper Series No. 7* (Harare, 1992), 27.

[32] Raymond Williams, *Culture and Society 1780-1950* (Harmonsworth, 1963), 304.

[33] Ibid., 322 (emphasis added).

[34] Alexander, "The Quest for a Core Culture," 5.

The debate over a common culture and/or a core culture continues. Williams' point is, at the same time, well taken. Alexander would agree: A common culture does not yet exist—not in South Africa and not in most liberal democracies around the globe. To suggest that it does is to exclude those from the nation-building exercise whose being is shaped and expressed by alternative cultures. It is to collapse the democratic process into a thin liberal paradigm that excludes difference.

Yasmin Sooka provides a vivid example of the cost involved in such cultural exclusion: South African Indians trace their historical origins to two immigrations. The first is the immigration of indentured laborers who came to the country in 1860 to work on the Natal sugar cane farms. "The Colonial Government [in India] was instructed to send no Brahmins . . . [and] requested medical officers to examine the hands of the immigrants to assess whether they were the hands of people accustomed to work."[35] The second wave of immigration was that of "free passage" Indians, consisting of traders and professionals who paid their own way. They were able to move freely around the country and soon emerged as the leaders of the Indian community, being elected to leadership positions in the South African Indian Congress (SAIC). Some called themselves "Arabs" in order to be differentiated from the "coolies" who worked as laborers on farms. When the colonial governments of India and South Africa entered into the Cape Town Agreement of 1927, the agreement was supported by the SAIC and rejected by spokespersons for the descendants of the indentured laborers. The Agreement allowed for the repatriation to India of those Indians who so chose, while an upliftment scheme was introduced for those who chose to remain in South Africa—provided they *assumed Western standards of living.*[36] Few Indians chose repatriation. Those able and willing to adapt to the demands of Western culture were gradually absorbed into mainstream society, at least to the extent that whites allowed this to happen. Those who clung to Indian culture were increasingly sidelined from mainstream society. In reality, however, they had minimum access to Indian cultural institutions, and their links with "established" Indian culture and customs became increasingly limited. Many adopted the Christian religion. Apartheid segregation and the impact of Christian national education in turn gave rise to an underclass Indian culture that separated the descen-

---

[35] Yasmin Sooka, "Hindu-Muslim Relations in a Reconciliatory South Africa" (unpublished paper).

[36] For the "Cape Town Agreement, 1927," see Government of India, *Papers Relating to the Second Round Table Conference,* 1932, Appendix 1, quoted in Sooka, Sooka, "Hindu-Muslim Relations." See also Surendra Bhana and Bridglal Pachai, eds., *A Documentary History of Indian South Africans* (Cape Town, 1984), 150ff.

dants of indentured laborers from whites as well as from merchant-class Indians. They were also separated from working-class Africans whom the underclass Indians came to regard as their chief rivals for work, housing and other material needs.

It is this kind of exclusionary experience that has persuaded constitutional negotiators in South Africa to adopt a language policy which recognizes all eleven major languages spoken in South Africa as "official." The adoption of English as the sole official language (which has been the case in many other African countries) would exclude large sections of the black community from participation in the affairs of the emerging democracy, while further empowering those proficient in this language. Douglas Young argues that a single-language policy—whether it succeeds or fails—would have detrimental effects on the democratic process. If it were to succeed, the privileges of first-language English speakers would be indefinitely entrenched. If it were to fail, the nation could revert to entrenched socio-political disintegration and ethno-linguistic divisiveness.[37] Concerned to avoid the emergence of a cultural basis that gives rise to a new form of elitism, Neville Alexander insists: "Some of us have arrived at the position that first of all a multilingual nation *is* possible."[38]

Culture, language, and other identity-creating realities such as religion, memory, gender-consciousness, and social location can be neglected only at the cost of excluding people from the democratic process. Democracy is about the proliferation of stories, symbols, languages, and religions. The exclusion of these is tantamount to the exclusion of people whose identity is constituted by them. The challenge is to find that which holds diversity together. Current debate suggests that Gadamer's understanding of a fusion of horizons, overagainst a Hegelian-type synthesis, which implies cultural hegemony, has the most to offer. Such a fusion suggests the possibility of what has been called a polycentric unity.[39] In South Africa, however, the quest is for something to hold the nation together after generations of racial, ethnic, cultural, and religious division.

This quest that something to do with discerning that which transcends what is immediately evident in any particular. It involves recognizing the possibility of such transcendence in every story—the hope for something more, than what is immediately before us.[40] It has something

[37] Douglas Young, "The Role and Status of the First Language in Education in a Multilingual Society" (unpublished paper submitted to the National Education Policy Initiative, 1992).

[38] Alexander, "A Quest for a Core Culture," 5.

[39] See Barney Pityana, "Culture as Evangelism," unpublished address to the South African Council of Churches in July 1994.

[40] Du Toit, "A Narrative-Communicative Approach to Identity and Ethnicity," 9.

to do, moreover, with discerning meaning in one's own story and the stories of others. It is also about discovering something greater than any particular story in the encounter between stories. It involves the glimpse of something radically new, yet grounded in the traditions of the present.

A prerequisite for this quest is openness to something more than that which emerges through unpromoted dialogue and encounter. A commitment to openness involves creating socio-political and cultural structures that facilitate and promote encounter, dialogue, and openness, without making any attempt to determine or prescribe the ultimate shape of the culture. The emerging culture is and will be a polyglot—insofar as all cultures are essentially such. It will probably also contain the co-existence of differentiated sub-cultures—insofar as no one culture is broad enough to include the dynamic of new and renewed cultural alternatives.

Resources for Renewal. Particular religions often assume that they contain all the spiritual resources and moral authority that any future society may need. The religious wars of early modern Europe were a consequence of such thinking. It was this that forced modernity to face the challenge of pluralism, which shifted the primary moral question away from what constituted the absolute "good" to how people of different religious and ethical persuasions could coexist. Harold Berman has argued that it took six great revolutions, the Papal Revolution plus five, to separate secular law from the turmoil of religious conflict.[41] For all the good that secularism has produced, it has also, suggests John Witte, reduced the public role of religion to the level of non-religion.[42] Yet ultimately it is religion, uncleansed of its *elan vital*, despite the negative elements of this package, that contributes most to the art of living together.

The amazing thing about religion is that it has the capacity to renew itself. Just when a particular religion seems to be an established part of a particular oppressive ideology, resources are discovered in that same religion that enable it to be renewed. It is this dynamic that is lost when religion is tamed to fit the liberal paradigm. It is unrestrained black, feminist, and other liberation theologies that challenge the hegemony of

---

[41] Harold J. Berman, "Religious Foundations of Law in the West: An Historical Perspective," *Journal of Law and Religion*, 1(1) (Summer, 1983): 3; id., *Law and Revolution: The Formation of the Western Legal Tradition* (Cambridge, MA, 1983). Berman identifies the five later revolutions as the Protestant Reformation in Germany in the sixteenth century, the English Revolutions between 1640 and 1689, the American and French Revolutions of 1776 and 1789, and the Russian Revolution of October 1917.

[42] John Witte, Jr., "The South African Experiment in Religious Human Rights," *Journal for Juridical Science* 18(1) (July, 1993): 1.

white ruling-class male domination in Christianity.[43] Unchastened feminism rocks the boat of Muslim patriarchy.[44] Some Jewish theologians
challenge right-wing political and religious movements in Israel, the
United States, and elsewhere.[45] The rigors of modernization challenge the
cultural captivity of traditional Buddhist,[46] Hindu[47] and other Eastern religious practices.

Religious dogmatism and exclusivism have taken a heavy toll on
South African society. Adjacent to this exclusivism there has, however,
also been universalism, inclusivism, and openness within these religions.
This openness is being discovered anew in contemporary South Africa, as
witnessed in the publication of *The Declaration on Religious Rights and Responsibilities* and the proposed clause for a bill of rights which emerged at
the World Conference on Religion and Peace consultation held in Pretoria in November 1993. While the grassroots faithful in churches,
mosques, synagogues, temples, and shrines are not always ready to embrace the "religious other," a new-found interest in other religions can be
observed in South Africa, which is commensurate with the quest for a
broader sense of unity in this country.[48]

---

[43] The *Kairos Document*, first published in 1985, together with feminist and black theological critiques of the document, called the dominant white, male character of "church theology" in South Africa into radical question.

[44] In Cape Town, death threats were directed at Abdurrashid Omar, Imam of the
Claremont mosque, by conservative Muslims after African-American Muslim scholar Dr.
Amina Wadud-Muhsin became the first woman to speak immediately prior to a Jumah service in South Africa. The attack of Taslima Nasreen, recipient of Calcutta's Ananda Bazar Pa-
trika literary award, on Islamic antifeminist practices, was of a more radical kind. It resulted
in Nasreen leaving Bangladesh. She presently lives in exile in Sweden.

[45] The New Jewish Agenda, in its 1982 *Statement of Purpose* appeals to the religious concept of *tikkun olam* (the just ordering of society and the world) as a basis for opposing injustices in Israel and elsewhere. The Oz VeShalom movement, established in Israel in 1975,
provides theological resources in support of the exchange of "land for peace." More recently,
Meimad has emerged as a moderate party in Israeli politics, with support from religious
groupings.

[46] The growth of Buddhism in the West has resulted in an adaptation of Eastern cultural
practices that at one time limited the appeal of this religion to Asians and those who chose to
adopt such Eastern practices. The majority of the approximately 3,000 Buddhists in South Africa are of European descent. While silent contemplation associated with Zen does not appeal
readily to Africans, the chanting, movement, and instruments used in Nichiren and Tibetan
Buddhism is more appealing. The Friends of the Western Buddhist Order (FWBO), of which
there is a small group in South Africa, promotes the idea of Buddhism being adaptable to all
cultures.

[47] Child marriage and *sati* (the practice of the widow throwing herself on the funeral
pyre of her husband) was outlawed in India prior to independence, and the 1948 constitution
of the Republic of India has officially outlawed discrimination against untouchables—all
practices attributed to traditional forms of Hinduism.

[48] See, inter alia, Denise Ackermann, "From 'Difference' to Connectedness? A Feminist
View on the Question of Difference" and Ron Nicholson, "Rights, Rorty and Religion," both

I offer only the briefest indications of the quest for openness, for "something more," within the dominant religious traditions. In so doing, I pay tribute to the importance of the observation by the once-maligned Bishop of Woolwich, John A.T. Robinson, that true theological reflection begins on "the other side of the atheist critique."[49]

Some Christians, for example, are emphasizing anew that the incompleteness and unfulfilled dimension of all religions is a preeminent part of Christian belief. The Scriptures recognize that the coming kingdom which promises something new may well result in a *rejection* of much to which Christians cling most firmly in their quest for certainty.[50] "Now we see in a mirror dimly, but then face to face"(1 Corinthians 13:13).

Openness is also found in Islam. Muhammad's status as a prophet was recognized on the basis of *shura* (consultation) and *muhasaba* (accountability). Indeed, an increasing number of Muslim scholars are insisting that hierarchical exclusivism in Islam must be attributed to the emergence of Muslim royal dynasties in the seventh and eighth centuries, which entrenched the interpretation of Muslim law exclusively in the hands of religious leaders.[51] The Qur'an allows for an openness to other religions (e.g., 2:62; 5:84-89; 11:118). In stating that Allah could have made everyone a Muslim, Surah 11:118 suggests there is something to be gained from diversity, inviting Muslims to appreciate the religious traditions of others.

Universalism is an important part of Judaism as well. It is this universalism that partly explains the absence of missionary zeal in Judaism. The God of the Hebrew prophets is never the private God of Israel and Judah (see e.g., Isaiah 7; Amos 1 and 2). Rabbinic theology develops this theme further in recognizing that the divine judgment of Jew and non-Jew alike is executed solely on the basis of godly living. *Whoever lives a godly or moral life is, we are told, like a high priest.*[52] Shubert Spero goes to great lengths to show that Jewish ethics, grounded in the Torah, shares a moral basis with other (non-Jewish) moral traditions.[53] The *Yalkut* commentary on Deuteronomy 6:5 ("Thou shalt love the Lord thy God. . . ."), in turn, introduces an eschatological dimension to the Hebraic understanding of the Torah which is boldly universalistic in teach-

---

unpublished papers delivered at the South African Academy of Religion, Pretoria, January 1994.

[49] John A.T. Robinson, *The New Reformation* (London, 1965), 106.

[50] Wolfgang Pannenberg, "Towards a Theology of Religions," in id., *Basic Questions in Theology* (Philadelphia, 1971), 2:92-96.

[51] Fazlar Rahman, *Islam* (Chicago, 1966).

[52] C.G. Montefiore and H. Loewe, *A Rabbinic Theology* (London, 1938), 559.

[53] Shubert Spero, *Morality, Halakha and the Jewish Tradition* (New York, 1983).

ing that at the end of time "God will sit and expound a new Torah which will . . . be given by the Messiah's hand." "His voice will reach from one end of the universe to the other and all the inhabitants of the universe will respond 'Amen'."[54]

"Hinduism," suggests South African activist and granddaughter of Mohandas Ghandi, "is the most tolerant of all the major religions of the world."[55] She opposes all forms of proselytization and religious exclusivism, defining Hindu belief as the ability to discern, through prayer and ethical living, the presence of the absolute (the Brahman) in all that exists. Her understanding of Hinduism is in continuity with the teaching of the Indian philosopher-statesman Sarvepalli Radhakrishnan, who understood religion to be "not a creed or a code, but an insight into reality." For him, the attainment of steady spiritual insight is the aim of religious endeavour and the means to it is ethical life and the art of meditation."[56] More exclusivist forms of Hinduism have gained a certain amount of currency in recent Indian political developments—not least, in the activities of the Bharatiya Janata Party in India. These developments are, however, less prominent than the exclusivism of most other faiths.

Buddhism's recognition of the Buddha as example rather than savior and the eight-fold pathway precludes any sense of Buddhist exclusivism. Indeed, a small but increasing number of South Africans, most of whom have no East Indian cultural affinity, are finding in Buddhism precisely the kind of religious openness denied them within the religions in which they were raised.

Tolerance and acceptance of others is part of African traditional religion and culture as well. Swahili identity is a blend of African, Persian, Islamic, and Indian influences. The Tanzanian notion of *Ujamaa*, in reaching to the heart of Swahili culture, drew together Christians, Muslims, traditional Africans, and Marxists under Julius Nyerere. Nation-building exercises in Somalia, Kenya, the Sudan, and other African states, on the other hand, that looked elsewhere for social cohesion failed.

Of course the suggestion of religious tolerance can be challenged with the most horrific stories of religious warfare. For many, this makes the very idea of religious epistemological openness absurdly utopian. But then any vision, at its best, is necessarily utopian. If a corporate reach is not beyond the immediate political grasp, then, to appropriate a Pauline phrase, "We are of all people most miserable." And if religious and cul-

---

[54] Ibid., 558.

[55] Quoted in Charles Villa-Vicencio, *The Spirit of Hope: Conversations on Politics, Religion and Values* (Braamfontein, 1993), 101.

[56] Sarvepalli Radhakrishnan, *An Idealist View of Life*, quoted in Sarvepalli Radhakrishnan and Charles A. Moore, eds., *A Sourcebook in Indian Philosophy* (Princeton, 1971), 611, 637.

tural encounter is no more than a power struggle—aptly captured in Sir Hartley Shawcross' axiom (contra Lord Atkin) which suggests that "power is delicious and absolute power absolutely delicious"[57]—then we in South Africa should still be in the trenches bludgeoning one another.

Suffice it to say, within the very plurality that is South Africa, an incentive exists for different cultures and religions to engage one another in quest of something new. Grounded in the particular, it drives the adherents of these groups to reach beyond that which is familiar and safe.

Looking for the New

Everything is not always what it seems to be. Liberalism is invariably culturally thicker than it itself would allow. Multiculturalism is often under the control of an elite who seek to control the character of the multiple cultures. What are projected as universals are often rather parochial. Indeed, particulars to which culturally-specific zealots rigidly cling are often a consequence of cultural hybridization.

Cultural openness, which is always struggling for survival against exclusivist religious fundamentalism, presupposes continuing cultural change. It involves the quest for what Franz Fanon has seen as the infusing of the outer garment with a new "hidden life." Culture is for him the "awakener of the people." It is to "speak to [the] nation, to compose the sentence which expresses the heart of the people and to become the mouthpiece of a new reality in action."[58] Fanon is at the same time aware of how easy it is for culture to become reified and static, providing legitimation to established groups who cling to the past rather than journey into the future.

Cultural openness must involve at least the following. First, it must involve the celebration of the dynamic nature of human existence. This requires the freedom of choice between cultures and religions. Second, cultural openness requires the democratic right of individuals to participate in the shaping and changing of their respective cultures and religions. As Denise Ackermann insists, there can be "no freedom *of* religion without freedom *in* religion."[59] Third, it involves a consideration of the relationship between culture and power. To the extent that group identity is promoted as a basis for empowerment, it invariably undermines

---

[57] Quoted in Judge Richard Goldstone's unpublished address to The South African Conference on Truth and Reconciliation, organised by the Institute for Democracy in South Africa, Cape Town, 29-31 July, 1994.

[58] Fanon, *Wretched of the Earth*, 178.

[59] Denise Ackermann, "Women, Religion and Culture: A Feminist Respective on 'Freedom of Religion'," unpublished paper delivered at the University of Cape Town Summer School, January 1994.

cultural openness. Amilcar Cabral never tired of warning against the dangers of classism within the cultural struggle. "It is vital not to lose sight of the decisive significance of the class character of culture in the . . . liberation struggle, even in the case when a category is or appears to be still embryonic."[60] Fourth, it requires recognition of the place and importance of the flexibility of the borders or margins of religio-cultural movements in the formation of identity.[61] The assumption that the hegemony of the center extends to the peripheral sections of society needs to be challenged. The subaltern, incipient cultures of oppressed people are often more dominant, more dynamic, and more counter-hegemonic than is realized by the cultural, political, and religious elite. Fifth, cultural openness requires a willingness—indeed a sense of compulsion—to grow beyond the village limits or the garden gate. It is often those who are compelled to risk themselves in order to survive that understand openness best. Finally, it requires recognition that as important (and warm) as it is to look inwardly, there is within the particular an incentive to search for more.

Such considerations make Gadamer's notion of the fusion of horizons ultimately more attractive than Hegel's notion of synthesis.[62] The willingness to understand the other involves more than empathy. It is also involves more than seeing the other in terms of our own particularity. Gadamer's words deserve repeating. The fusion of horizons, he says, "always involves the attainment of a higher universality that overcomes, not only our own particularity, but also that of the other. The concept of the horizon suggests itself because it expresses the wide, superior vision that the person who is seeking to understand must have. To acquire a horizon means that one learns to look beyond what is close at hand—not in order to look away from it, but to see it better within a larger whole and in truer proportion."[63]

Gadamer reminds us that the horizons of life are continually being formed and reformed. For him understanding, and by implication human community, consist in the fusion of horizons.[64] This involves more than a clinging to the particular as an end in itself. It involves discerning something transcendent in the particulars and the potentiality of all cultures. In the words of Heidegger, it is "to dwell poetically" in the place

---

[60] Amilcar Cabral, *Unity and Struggle* (London, 1980), 147.

[61] Rosaldo, *Culture and Truth.*

[62] This is recognized in Taylor's *Multiculturalism and the Politics of Recognition.* I am grateful to Mieke Holkeboer, a graduate student, for her work on Hans-Georg Gadamer.

[63] Hans-Georg Gadamer, *Truth and Method* (New York, 1988), 272.

[64] Ibid., 273.

where we reside.[65] It is to recognize the unequivocal right of others to do the same in their respective places and imaginatively to share in the creation of a new level of meaning. In the words of Amilcar Cabral, Guinea-Bissau philosopher and political leader, true openness involves the conservation of positive cultural values of every cultural group. It is "to achieve the confluence of these values into the stream of struggle, giving them [the established cultural values] a new dimension."[66] It fills the future, which is "not yet" and sometimes seen as the abyss, with meaning and hope.

Writing from a particular perspective within Christianity, I cannot but be conscious of the vitally important challenges to religious hegemony that have for so long been located in the hands of historically-privileged autocrats, somewhere amidst the infamous twenty percent of the human race. When the narratives of oppressed peoples and classes and gender-interest groups are heard, the liberating dimensions of religion are often rediscovered which point beyond the self-indulgence with particularisms to that which no one particular can ever fully represent. This requires the study of religion to become what Marty calls a "multiplex, multivocal and multimodel exercise."[67] Such study involves the vulnerability and willingness to forsake all that is symbolized in the Cross. The Gospel speaks of the promise of life in a willingness to die.

To affirm the freedom of religion as a basic human right is innocuous if it means no more than the entrenchment of historic privilege. Here Denise Ackermann's axiom is again crucial: "no freedom *of* religion without freedom *in religion.*" Protecting the right to challenge religious hegemony is, on the other hand, a vital part of the ongoing renewing of culture in the open venture towards ever shifting horizons. In the words

---

[65] Martin Heidegger, *Existence and Being* (Chicago, 1968), 280-90.

[66] Cabral, *Unity and Struggle*, 147.

[67] Marty, "From the Centripetal to the Centrifugal," 15. See also id., "Religion: A Private Affair in Public Affairs," *Religion and American Culture: A Journal of interpretation* 3(2) (Summer, 1993): 122-24. Barney Pityana's essay on "Culture and Evangelism," drawing on the work of Leonardo Boff and Richard Shorter, recognizes the need for a meztizo, polycentric, koinonia church that incorporates the many into the one.

of Dag Hammerskjold, it involves "being *driven* forward into an unknown land. . . ." Hammerskjold continued: "If [our] goal is not determined by [the] most secret pathos [of ourselves and others], even victory
will only make [us] painfully aware of [our] own weakness."[68] The quest
is for what is new, what is different, and what unites.

---

[68] Dag Hammersköld, "Thus It Was," in id., *Markings by Dag Hammerskjöld*, W.H.
Auden and Lief Sjöberg, trans. (London and Boston, 1964), 31-32.

Bibliography of Books
and Articles Cited

Abe, Masao, "A Buddhist Response to Mohamed Talbi," in Leonard W. Swidler, ed., *Religious Liberty and Human Rights in Nations and in Religions* (Philadelphia, 1986), 189

Abelard, Peter, *Peter Abelard's Ethics*, D.E. Luscombe, ed. and trans. (Oxford, 1971)

Acton, Lord, *Lectures on Modern History*, J.N. Figgis and R. V. Laurence, eds. (London, 1906)

Adams, James Luther, *On Being Human Religiously* (Boston, 1976)

————, *Voluntary Associations*, J.R. Engel, ed. (Chicago, 1986)

Africa Watch, "Sudan: New Islamic Penal Code Violates Basic Human Rights" (April 9, 1991)

al-Alfi, Ahmad Abd al-Aziz, "Punishment in Islamic Criminal Law," in M. Cherif Bassiouni, ed., *The Islamic Criminal Justice System*, (London, 1982), 227

al-Azm, Sadiq, "The Importance of Being Ernest About Salman Rushdie," *Die Welt des Islams* 31 (1991): 1

al-Ghunaimi, Mohammad T., *The Muslim Conception of International Law and the Western Approach* (The Hague, 1968)

Alexander, Neville, "Black Consciousness: A Reactionary Tendency?" in N. Barney Pityana, et al., eds., *Bounds of Possibility: The Legacy of Steve Biko and Black Consciousness* (Cape Town, 1991), 238

Alexeyeva, Ludmilla, *Soviet Dissent: Contemporary Movements for National, Religious, and Human Rights* (Middletown, 1985)

Ali, Abdullah Yusuf, *The Holy Qur'an* (Brentwood, 1989)

Ali, Said Amer, *The Spirit of Islam* (London, 1896)

Allen, Prudence, *The Concept of Woman: The Aristotelian Revolution 750 B.C. - A.D. 1250* (Montreal, 1985)

————, "Integral Sex Complementarity and the Theology of Communion," *Communio* 17 (Winter, 1990): 523

————, "Sex and Gender Differentiation in Hildegard of Bingen and Edith Stein," *Communio* 20 (Summer, 1993): 389

Ammerman, Nancy, *Baptist Battles* (New Brunswick, NJ, 1990)

Amnesty International, *Annual Report 1987* (London, 1988)

———, "Algeria: Deteriorating Human Rights Under the State of Emergency" (March, 1993)

———, "Egypt: Grave Human Rights Abuses Amid Political Violence" (May, 1993)

———, "Egypt: Human Rights Abuses Mount in 1993" (October, 1993)

———, "Egypt: Trials of Civilians in Military Courts Violate International Law; Executions Continue, No Appeal of Death Sentences to Higher Court" (July, 1993)

———, "Saudi Arabia: Religious Intolerance: The Arrest, Detention and Torture of Christian Worshippers and Shi'a Muslims" (September, 1993)

———, "Tunisia: Heavy Sentences After Unfair Trials" (October, 1992)

———, "Tunisia: Military Courts that Sentenced Islamist Leaders Violated Basic Fair-Trial Norms" (October, 1992)

An-Na'im, Abdullahi Ahmed, "Christian-Muslim Relations in the Sudan: Peaceful Coexistence at Risk," in Kail C. Ellis, ed., *The Vatican, Islam and the Middle East* (Syracuse, 1987), 265

———, ed., *Human Rights in Cross-Cultural Perspectives* (Philadelphia, 1992)

———, "Islam, Islamic Law and the Dilemma of Cultural Legitimacy for Universal Human Rights," in Claude E. Welch, Jr. and Virginia A. Leary, eds., *Asian Perspectives on Human Rights* (Boulder, 1990), 31

———, "Islamic Law, International Relations and Human Rights: Challenge and Response," *Cornell International Law Journal* 20 (1987): 317

———, "Religious Freedom in Egypt: Under the Shadow of the Islamic Dhimma System," in Leonard W. Swidler, ed., *Religious Liberty and Human Rights in Nations and in Religions* (Philadelphia, 1986), 55

———, "Religious Minorities under Islamic Law and the Limits of Cultural Relativism," *Human Rights Quarterly* 9(1) (1987): 1

———, ed., *Second Message of Islam* (Syracuse, 1987)

———, "The Islamic Law of Apostasy and its Modern Applicability: A Case from the Sudan," *Religion* 16 (1986): 197

———, "Toward an Islamic Hermeneutics for Human Rights," in Abdullahi An-Na'im, et al., eds., *Human Rights and Religious Values: An Uneasy Relationship?* (Grand Rapids, MI, 1995), 229

———, *Toward an Islamic Reformation: Civil Liberties, Human Rights and International Law* (Syracuse, 1990)

———, Ann Elizabeth Mayer, Sumner B. Twiss and William Wipfler, "Universality vs. Relativism in Human Rights," in John Kelsay and Sumner B. Twiss, eds., *Religion and Human Rights* (New York, 1994), 31-60

——— and Francis M. Deng, eds., *Human Rights in Africa: Cross-Cultural Perspectives* (Washington, 1990)

———, et al., eds., *Human Rights and Religious Values: An Uneasy Relationship?* (Grand Rapids, MI, 1995)

Anderson, James Norman D., *Law Reform in the Muslim World* (London, 1970)

———, "Modern Trends in Islam: Legal Reform and Modernisation in the Middle East," *International and Comparative Law Quarterly* 20 (1971): 1

Anderson, Lisa, "Lawless Government and Illegal Opposition: Reflections on the Middle East," *Journal of International Affairs* 40 (1987): 219

Anderson, Norman, *Law Reform in the Muslim World* (London, 1976)

Andrysek, Oldrich, "Non-believers: A New Aspect of Religious Intolerance?" *Conscience and Liberty* 2 (1990): 15

Anzaldua, Gloria, *Borderlands/La Frontera: The New Mestiza* (San Francisco, 1987)

Apostel, Leo, *African Philosophy: Myth or Reality* (Ghent, 1982)

Appignanesi, Lisa and Sara Maitland, eds., *The Rushdie File* (Syracuse, 1990)

Arendt, Hanna, "Es gibt nur eine einziges Menschenrecht," *Die Wandlung* 4 (1954): 754

———, *On Revolution* (New York, 1963)

Arkoun, Mohammed, *Rethinking Islam: Common Questions, Uncommon Answers* (Boulder, 1994)

Arzt, Donna E., "The Application of International Human Rights Law in Islamic States," *Human Rights Quarterly* 12 (May 1990): 202

Asad, Muhammad, *The Message of the Qur'an* (Gibraltar, 1980)

Ash, T.G., "Eastern Europe: Year of Truth," *New York Review of Books* (February 15, 1990): 1

Ashburn, Daniel G., ed., "The State of Religious Human Rights in the World: Preliminary Consultation," *Preliminary Documents of Religious Human Rights Project* 2 (1993)

Asia Watch, "*Indonesia: Students Jailed for Puns,*" (March 16, 1993)

Athenagoras, *Embassy for the Christians: The Resurrection of The Dead*, C.B. Gulick, trans. (Cambridge, MA, 1956)

Auerbach, Jerold S., *Justice Without Law* (Oxford, 1983)

Austin, Granville, *The Indian Constitution: A Cornerstone of the Nation* (London, 1966)

Azevedo, M., "Basic Ecclesial Communities: A Meeting Point of Ecclesiologies," *Theological Studies* 46 (1985): 601

Babylonian Talmud, Isodore Epstein, trans. (London, 1987)

Bachrach, Yair, *Responsa Chavat Yair* (Jerusalem, 1968)

Baha'i International Community, *The Baha'i Question: Iran's Secret Blueprint for the Destruction of a Religious Community: An Examination of the Persecution of the Baha'is of Iran 1979-1993* (New York, 1993)

———, *The Baha'is: A Profile of the Baha'i Faith and its Worldwide Community* (Leicestershire, 1992)

Bainton, Roland H., *The Age of Reformation* (Princeton, 1956)

———, *Erasmus of Christendom* (New York, 1969)

———, "The Parable of the Wheat and the Tares as the Proof Text for Religious Liberty to the End of the 16th Century," *Church History* 1 (1932): 67

———., *The Reformation of the Sixteenth Century* (Boston, 1952)

Baird, Robert D., ed., *Religion and Law in Independent India* (New Delhi, 1993)

Barker, Ernst, *Social and Political Thought in Byzantium from Justinian I to the Last Palaeologus* (Oxford, 1957)

Barth, Karl, *Church Dogmatics*, G.W. Bromiley and T.F. Torrance, eds. (Edinburgh, 1961), 7 vols.

Bassiouni, M. Cherif, ed., *The Islamic Criminal Justice System* (London, 1982)

Bates, M. Searle, *Religious Liberty: An Inquiry* (New York, 1945)

Battin, Margaret P., *Ethics in the Sanctuary: Examining the Practices of Organized Religion* (New Haven, 1990)

Bauer, Jörg, et al. (hrsg.), *Zum Thema Menschenrechte* (Stuttgart, 1977)

Bayle, Pierre, *Philosophical Commentary*, A.G. Tannenbaum, trans. (New York, 1987)

Bear, Robert, *Delivered Unto Satan* (Philadelphia, 1974)

Bechtold, Peter, "The Sudan Since the Fall of Numayri," in Robert O. Freedman, ed., *The Middle East From the Iran-Contra Affair to the Intifada* (Syracuse, 1990), 371

Ben-Menahem, H., *Judicial Deviation in Talmudic Law* (Boston, 1991)

Benhabib, Seyla, *Situating the Self: Gender, Community and Postmodernism in Contemporary Ethics* (New York, 1992)

Benko, Stephen and John J. O'Rourke, eds., *The Catacombs and the Colosseum* (Valley Forge, 1971)

Benson, Robert L., *The Bishop-Elect: A Study in Medieval Ecclesiastical Office* (Princeton, 1968)

Berger, Peter and Richard John Neuhaus, *To Empower People: The Role of Mediating Structures in Public Policy* (Washington, 1977)

Berman, Harold J., *Faith and Order, The Reconciliation of Law and Religion* (Atlanta, 1993)

———, *Law and Revolution: The Formation of the Western Legal Tradition* (Cambridge, MA, 1983)

———, *Recht und Revolution: Die Bildung der westlichen Rechtradition* (Frankfurt am Main, 1991)

———, "Religious Foundations of Law in the West: An Historical Perspective," *Journal of Law and Religion,* 1 (1983): 3

Berman, Saul, "The Status of Women in Halakhic Judaism," in Elizabeth Koltun, ed., *The Jewish Woman: New Perspectives* (New York, 1976), 114

Bermann, George A., "Taking Subsidiarity Seriously: Federalism in the European Community and the United States," *Columbia Law Review* 94 (1994): 331

Berns, Walter, "Walter Berns Comments," *This World* 6 (Fall, 1983): 98.

Berslauer, S. Daniel, *Judaism and Human Rights in Contemporary Thought: A Bibliographical Survey* (Westport, 1993)

Bettenson, Henry, ed., *Documents of the Christian Church,* 2d ed. (London, 1963)

Bhana, Surendra and Bridglal Pachai, eds., *A Documentary History of Indian South Africans* (Cape Town, 1984)

Biale, Rachel, *Women and Jewish Law: An Exploration of Women's Issues in Halakhic Sources* (New York, 1984)

Bihlmeyer, Karl, *Church History*, rev. ed., H. Tuechle, ed., V.E. Mills, trans. (Westminster, 1968)

Biko, Steve, *I Write What I Like* (London, 1987)

Blaisdell, Charles R., ed., *Conservative, Moderate, Liberal: The Biblical Authority Debate* (St. Louis, 1990)

Blankinship, Khalid Yahya, *The End of the Jihad State: The Reign of Hisham Ibn Abd al-Malik and the Collapse of the Umayyads* (Albany, NY, 1994)

Blau, Joseph L., ed., *Cornerstones of Religious Freedom in America: Selected Basic Documents, Court Decisions, and Public Statements*, rev. ed. (New York, 1964)

Blaustein, Albert P., and Gilbert H. Flanz, *Constitutions of the Countries of the World* (Dobbs Ferry, 1993)

Blidstein, Gerald J., "Moral Generalizations and Halakhic Discourse," *S'vara* 2(1) (1991): 8

Bleich, J. David, *Contemporary Halakhic Problems* (New York, 1989), 3 vols.

Bloom, Harold, ed., *The Bible* (New York, 1987)

——, "'Before Moses was, I am': The Original and Belated Testaments," in Harold Bloom, ed., *The Bible* (New York, 1987), 292

Bock, Wolfgang, *Das für all geltende Gesetz und christliche Selbstbestimmung in Dienstrecht* (Ph.D. Diss., Frankfurt am Main, 1992)

Bodin, Jean, *Six Books of the Commonwealth*, M.J. Tooley, trans. (Oxford, 1955)

Boers, Hendrikus, *The Justification of the Gentiles: Paul's Letters to the Romans and Galatians* (Peabody, 1994)

Bouquet, Alan Coates, *Comparative Religion* (London, 1941)

Brecht, Martin, "Divine Right and Human Rights in Luther," in Manfred Hoffmann, ed., *Martin Luther and the Modern Mind: Freedom, Conscience, Toleration, Rights* (New York, 1985), 61

Bassler, Janette, *Divine Impartiality: Paul and a Theological Axiom* (Chico, CA, 1981)

Berlin, Naphtali Tzvi Yehuda, *Meshech Chachma* (Jerusalem, 1949)

Breitowitz, Irving, "The Plight of the Agunah: A Study in Halacha, Contract, and the First Amendment," *Maryland Law Review* 51 (1992): 312

Breuer, Isaac, "The Philosophical Foundations of Jewish and Modern Law," in Jacob S. Levinger, ed., *Concepts of Judaism* (Jerusalem, 1974), 53

Brierley, John E.C., *Major Legal Systems in The World Today* (New York, 1985)

Brohi, A.K., "Islam and Human Rights," in A. Gauher, ed., *The Challenge of Islam* (London, 1980), 179

Brown, Peter, *The Cult of the Saints* (New York, 1993)

Browning, Don S. and Francis Schüssler Fiorenza, eds., *Habermas, Modernity, and Public Theology* (New York, 1992)

Brownlie, Ian, ed., *Basic Documents on Human Rights*, 3d ed. (Oxford, 1992)

Broyde, Michael J., "Child Custody: A Pure Law Analysis," *Jewish Law Association Studies VII: The Paris Conference Volume* (Atlanta, 1994), 1

——, *The Jewish Perspective on Practicing Law* (New York, 1995)

Brundage, James A., *Medieval Canon Law and the Crusader* (Madison, WI, 1969)

Bruna, Isaac, *Terumat Hadeshen* (Jerusalem, 1989)

Buber, Martin, *Kingship of God*, 3d ed., R. Scheimann, trans. (New York and Evanston, IL, 1967)

Buell, Frederick, "Conceptualizations of Contemporary Culture," *Comparative Civilizations Review* 27 (Fall, 1992): 127

Burgsmüller, Alfred (hrsg.), *Kirche als "Gemeinde von Brüdern" (Barmen III)* (Gütersloh, 1980)

Burnet, Gilbert, *History of My Own Times* (Oxford, 1823), 6 vols.

Burton, John, *The Collection of the Qur'an* (Cambridge 1977)

Butterfield, Herbert, *The Whig Interpretation of History* (London, 1931)

Cabral, Amilcar, *Unity and Struggle* (London, 1980)

Canon Law Society of America, *The Code of Canon Law: A Text and Commentary* (Mahwah, NJ, 1985)

Carlyle, A..J., *The Christian Church and Liberty*, repr. ed. (New York, 1968)

Carlyle, Thomas, *Critical and Miscellaneous Essays: Collected and Republished* (London, 1872), 7 vols.

———, *On Heroes, Hero-Worship and the Heroic in History* (New York, 1903)

Castellio, Sebastian, *Concerning Heretics: Whether They Are To Be Persecuted and How They Are To Be Treated: A Collection of the Opinions of Learned Men, Both Ancient and Modern*, Roland H. Bainton, trans. (New York, 1935)

Chafee, Zechariah, "The Internal Affairs of Associations Not For Profit," *Harvard Law Review* 43 (1930): 993

Chaudhry, Rashid Ahmad, "Persecution in Pakistan," *The Economist* (October 24, 1992): 6

Cherry, Conrad, and Roland A. Sherrill, eds., *Religion, The Independent Sector and American Culture* (Atlanta, 1992)

Chillingworth, William, *The Religion of Protestants* (Oxford, 1638)

Cicero, Marcus Tullius "Pro Flacco," in id., *In Catilinum I-IV*, C. McDonald trans., rev. ed. (Cambridge, MA, 1977)

Clark, Donald C., Jr., "Sexual Abuse in the Church: The Law Steps In," *Christian Century* 110 (April 14, 1993): 396

Clement of Alexandria, *The Exhortation to the Greeks*, G.W. Butterworth, trans. (Cambridge, MA, 1919)

Clune, William and John Witte, eds., *Choice and Control in American Education* (Bristol, PA, 1990)

Cochrane, Arthur C., *The Church's Confession Under Hitler* (Philadelphia, 1962)

Cohen, Hermann, *Religion of Reason Out of the Sources of Judaism*, S. Kaplan, trans. (New York, 1972)

Cohn, Haim, *Human Rights in Jewish Law* (New York, 1984)

Cohn-Sherbok, David ed., *World Religions and Human Liberation* (Maryknoll, NY, 1992)

Cole, C. Robert and Michael E. Moody, eds., *The Dissenting Tradition* (Athens, OH, 1975)

Comment, "Religious Torts: Applying the Consent Doctrine as Definitional Balancing," *University of California at Davis Law Review* 19 (1986): 949

Congregation for the Doctrine of the Faith, *Donum Vitae* (Vatican City, 1987)

Cook, Rebecca J., "Reservations to the Convention on the Elimination of All Forms of Discrimination Against Women," *Virginia Journal of International Law* 30 (1990): 643

Coons, John E., "Intellectual Liberty and the Schools," *Notre Dame Journal of Law, Ethics and Public Policy* 1 (1985): 495

————, "Law and the Sovereigns of Childhood," *Kappan* 58 (1976): 19

————, Robert H. Mnookin, and Stephen D. Sugarman, "Puzzling over Children's Rights," *Brigham Young University Law Review* (1991): 307

Coriden, James, "Human Rights in the Church: A Matter of Credibility and Authenticity," in Alois Müller and Norbert Greinacher, eds., *The Church and the Rights of Man* (New York, 1979), 67

————, *We, The People of God* (Huntington, IN, 1969)

————, ed., *The Case for Freedom: Human Rights in the Church* (Washington & Cleveland, 1969)

————, ed., *Sexism and Church Law: Equal Rights and Affirmative Action* (New York, 1977)

Cottrell, J.W., "The Nature of Biblical Authority: A Conservative Perspective," in C.R. Blaisdell, ed., *Conservative, Moderate, Liberal: The Biblical Authority Debate* (St. Louis, 1990), 21

Coulson, Noel, *A History of Islamic Law* (Edinburgh, 1964)

Cover, Robert M., "Nomos and Narrative," *Harvard Law Review* 97 (1983): 4

————, "Obligation: A Jewish Jurisprudence of the Social Order," *Journal of Law and Religion* 5 (1987): 65

Cromwell, Oliver, *The Writings and Speeches of Oliver Cromwell*, Wilbur Cortez Abbott, ed. (Cambridge, MA, 1937-47), 4 vols.

Cross, Frank Moore, *Canaanite Myth and Hebrew Epic: Essays in the History of Israel* (Cambridge, 1973)

Crüsemann, Frank, *Die Tora: Theologie und Sozialgeschichte des alttestamentlichen Gesetzes* (München, 1992)

————, "Tora und christliche Ethik," in R. Rendtorff and E. Stegeman (hrsg.), *Auschwitz, Krise der christlichen Theologie: Eine Vortragsreihe* (München, 1980), 159

Curran, Charles, *New Perspectives in Moral Theology* (Notre Dame, 1974)

Cyprian of Carthage, *On the Unity of the Catholic Church* (Cambridge, MA, 1924)

Dalberg-Acton, John Emerich Edward, *The History of Freedom and Other Essays* (New York, 1967)

Daly, Herman E. and John B. Cobb, Jr., *For the Common Good: Redirecting the Economy Toward Community, the Environment, and a Sustainable Future* (Boston, 1989)

Danzig, Abraham, *Ha'ai Adam* (Jerusalem, 1991)

Daube, David, "The Rabbis and Philo on Human Rights," in David Sidorsky, ed., *Essays on Human Rights: Contemporary Issues and Jewish Perspectives* (New York, 1979), 234

Davis, Richard W., ed., *The Making of Modern Freedom* (Stanford, 1994).

de Albornoz, Aangel Franusco Carrillo *The Basis of Religious Liberty* (New York, 1963)

de Beauvoir, Simone, *The Second Sex* (New York, 1974)

Deats, Richard, "Human Rights: An Historical and Theological Perspective," *Engage* 38 (1978): 10

Dellapergola, Harold and Uziel Schmelz, "Demography and Jewish Education in the Diaspora", in Harold S. Himmelfarb and Sergio DellaPergola, eds., *Jewish Education Worldwide: Cross Cultural Perspectives* (Lanham, MD, 1989), 43

Demedina, Chezkeya, *Sedai Chemed* (New York, 1960)

Department of State, *Country Reports on Human Rights Practices for 1993* (Washington, 1994)

Derrett, J. Duncan M., *The Death of a Marriage Law: Epitaph for the Rishis* (New Delhi, 1978)

Detrick, Sharon, *The United Nations Convention on the Rights of the Child: A Guide to the travaux préparatoroires* (Dordrecht/Boston, 1992)

Devadason, E.D., *Christian Law in India: Law Applicable to Christians in India* (Madras, 1974)

Dinstein, Yoram, *Freedom of Religion and Protection of Religious Minorities* (New York, 1981)

Dio Chrysostom, *Works*, J.W. Cohoon and H. Lamar Crosby, trans. (London/New York, 1932-1951), 5 vols.

Doerries, Herman, *Constantine and Religious Liberty*, Roland H. Bainton, trans. (New Haven, 1960)

Dombois, Hans, *Das Recht der Gnade* (Witten, 1969), 3 vols.

Donohue, John J. and John L. Esposito, eds., *Islam in Transition: Muslim Perspectives* (New York, 1982)

Dorff, Eliot N. and Arthur Rosett, *A Living Tree: The Roots and Growth of Jewish Law* (New York, 1988)

Downing, F.G., "Common Ground with Paganism in Luke and Josephus," *New Testament Studies* 28 (1982): 546

Drinan, Robert F., "Human Rights in the 21st Century and the Role of the Churches," *Theology and Public Policy* 6(1) (Summer, 1994): 1

du Bois, W.E.B. *The Souls of Black Folk* (New York, 1982)

Dulles, Avery, *Models of the Church: A Critical Assessment of the Church in All Its Aspects*, rev. ed. (Garden City, 1987)

Dumont, Louis, *Homo Hierarchicus* (Chicago, 1970)

Dunn, John, *The Political Thought of John Locke* (Cambridge, 1969)

Dworkin, Ronald, *Taking Rights Seriously* (New York, 1977)

Eckhardt, A. Roy, *Jews and Christians: The Contemporary Meeting* (Bloomington, 1986)

Edelby, Neophytos and Teodoro Jimenez-Urresti, eds., *Religious Freedom* (New York, 1966)

Edwards, Thomas, *Antapologia* (London, 1641)

Ehler, Sidney Z. and John B. Morrall, eds., *Church and State Through the Centuries* (Newman, MD, 1954)

Eichstädt, G. Schmidt, *Kirchen als Körperschaften des öffentlichen Rechts* (Köln, 1975)

Eisenstadt, Abraham, *Pitchei Teshuva* (Jerusalem, 1990)

Eisenstadt, S.N., *The Protestant Ethic and Modernization* (New York, 1968)

Elazar, Daniel J., *Covenant and Polity in Biblical Israel* (New Brunswick, NJ, 1995)

Ellis, Kail C., ed., *The Vatican, Islam and the Middle East* (Syracuse, 1987)

Elon, Menachem, *Jewish Law: History Sources and Principles* (Philadelphia, 1994), 4 vols.

Elshtain, Jean Bethke, "Christianity and Patriarchy," *Modern Theology* 9(2) (April, 1993): 110

Elwes, Robert Harvey Monro, ed., *The Chief Works of Benedict de Spinoza* (London, 1883), 2 vols.

Emden, Jacob. *Responsa Shelat* Yavetz (Lemberg, 1881)

———, *Responsa Yavetz* (Lemberg, 1887)

Enayat, Hamid, *Modern Islamic Political Thought* (London, 1982)

Encyclopedia Talmudit, Shlomoh Yosef Zevin, ed. (Jerusalem, 1976)

Engineer, Ali Asghar, ed., *The Shah Bano Controversy* (Bombay, 1987)

Enzensberger, Hans Magnus, *Aussichten auf den Bürgerkrieg* (Frankfurt am Main, 1993)

Ernst, James, *Roger Williams: New England Firebrand* (New York, 1932)

Esbeck, Carl H., ed., *Religious Beliefs, Human Rights and the Moral Foundations of Western Democracy* (Columbia, MS, 1986)

Esman, Milton J. and Itamar Rabinovich, eds., *Ethnicity, Pluralism and the Middle East* (Ithaca, 1988)

Esposito, John L., *The Islamic Threat: Myth or Reality?* (New York, 1992)

European Consortium for Church-State Research, *The Legal Status of Religious Minorities in the Countries of the European Union* (Thessalonica/Milan, 1994)

Evans, Alice, Robert Evans, and David Roozen, eds. *The Globalization of Theological Education* (Maryknoll, NY, 1993)

Everett, William Johnson, "Religion and Constitutional Development in India," *Journal of Church and State* 37(1) (1995): 61

Falconer, A.D., ed., *Understanding Human Rights* (Dublin, 1980)

Falk, Ze'ev W., *Jewish Matrimonial Law in the Middle Ages* (Oxford, 1966)

———, *Law and Religion* (Jerusalem, 1981)

Fanon, Franz, *Wretched of the Earth* (London, 1983)

Faour, Muhammad, *The Arab World After Desert Storm* (Washington, 1993)

Farah, Nadia Ramsis, *Religious Strife in Egypt: Crisis and Ideological Conflict in the Seventies* (New York, 1986)

Fazlur, Rahman, *Islam* (Chicago, 1979)

Federle, Katherine Hunt, "Looking for Rights in all the Wrong Places: Resolving Custody Disputes in Divorce Proceedings," *Cardozo Law Review* 15 (1994): 1523

Feinstein, Moses, *Responsa Iggrot Moshe Yoreh Deah* (New York, 1959)

Feldman, David, *Marital Relations, Birth Control and Abortion in Jewish Law* (New York, 1974)

Figgis, John Neville, *Churches in the Modern State* (London, 1913)

Finkelman, Marilyn, "Self-Defense and Defense of Others in Jewish Law: The Rodef Defense," *Wayne State Law Review* 33 (1987): 1257

For Rushdie: Essays by Arab and Muslim Writers in Defense of Free Speech (New York, 1994)

Fortin, E., "Human Rights and the Common Good," *CCIA Annual: Rights Authority and Community* 13 (Philadelphia, 1994): 1-7

Fortune, Marie M., "How the Church Should Imitate the Navy," *The Christian Century* 109 (August 26/September 2, 1992): 76

Fox, Robin Lane, *Pagans and Christians* (New York, 1989)

Freedman, Robert O., ed., *The Middle East From the Iran-Contra Affair to the Intifada* (Syracuse, 1990)

Friedman, Lawrence M., "The Law and Society Movement," *Stanford Law Review* 38 (1986): 763

Friesenhahn, Ernst, Ulrich Scheuner and Joseph Listl (hrsg.), *Handbuch des Staatskirch-enrechts der Bundesrepublik Deutschland* (Berlin, 1974-1975)

Fyzee, Asaf A.A., *A Modern Approach to Islam* (Lahore, 1978)

Gabriel Setiloane, *African Theology: An Introduction* (Johannesburg, 1986)

Gadamer, Hans-Georg, *Truth and Method* (New York, 1988)

Gaddis, J.L., "Toward the Post-Cold War World," *Foreign Affairs* 70 (1991): 102

Gaertner, Bertil E., *The Areopagus Speech and Natural Revelation* (Lund, 1955)

Gaffney, Edward McGlynn, Jr., Philip C. Sorenson, and Howard R. Griffin, *Ascending Liability in Religious and Other Nonprofit Organizations* (Macon, GA, 1984)

Gager, John G., *The Origins of Anti-Semitism* (New York, 1985)

Gamwell, F.C., *The Divine Good* (Chicago, 1991)

Garraty, John A. and Peter Gay, eds., *The Columbia History of the World* (New York, 1972)

Garrett, Susan R., *The Demise of the Devil: Magic and the Demonic in Luke-Acts* (Minneapolis, 1989)

Gauher A., ed., *The Challenge of Islam* (London, 1980)

Gedicks, Fredrick, "Toward A Constitutional Jurisprudence of Religious Group Rights," *Wisconsin Law Review* (1989): 99

Gerber, Haim, *State, Society and Law in Islam: Ottoman Law in Comparative Perspective* (Albany, 1994)

Gerhard, Selina Schultz, *Caspar Schwenckfeld von Ossig: 1489-1561* (Morristown, PA, 1946)

Gerson, Jean, *Oeuvres complètes*, P. Glorieux, ed. (Paris, 1960-73), 10 vols.

Ghanoonparvar, Mohammed R. and Faridoun Farrokh, eds., *In Transition: Essays on Culture and Identity in Middle Eastern Societies* (Laredo, TX, 1993)

Ghatan, H.E. Yedidiah, *More Precious than Rubies: The Unique Status of Women in Judaism* (New York, 1986)

Gibb, Hamilton A.R., *Studies on the Civilization of Islam* (Boston, 1962)

Giddens, Anthony, *The Consequences of Modernity* (Stanford, 1990)

Ginzberg, Louis, *The Legends of the Jews* (Philadelphia, 1909)

Glendon, Mary Ann, *Rights Talk: The Impoverishment of Political Discourse* (New York, 1991)

—— and Raul F. Yanes, "Structural Free Exercise," *Michigan Law Review 90* (1991): 477

Goitein, S.D., "Human Rights in Jewish Thought and Life in the Middle Ages," in David Sidorsky, ed., *Essays on Human Rights: Contemporary Issues and Jewish Perspectives* (Philadelphia, 1979), 254

Goldwin, Robert A., Art Kaufman and William A. Schambra, *Forging Unity Out of Diversity: The Approaches of Eight Nations* (Washington, 1989)

Gomien, Donna, "Whose Right (and Whose Duty) Is It? An Analysis of the Substance and Implementation of the Convention on the Rights of the Child," *Human Rights* 7 (1989): 161

Gooch, Paul W., *Partial Knowledge: Philosophical Studies in Paul* (Notre Dame, 1987)

Goodenough, Erwin Ramsdell, *An Introduction to Philo Judaeus*, 2d ed. (New York, 1963)

Goodman, Lenn Evan, "Equality and Human Rights: The Lockean and the Judaic Views," *Judaism* 25 (1976): 357

Gotein, S.D., "Human Rights in Jewish Thought and Life in the Middle Ages," in David Sidorsky, ed., *Essays on Human Rights: Contemporary Issues and Jewish Perspectives* (New York, 1979), 247

Gottlieb, Yitzchak, "Understanding the Heter Mechira," *Journal of Halakha and Contemporary Society* 26 (1993): 5

Grayzel, Solomon, *A History of the Jews: From the Babylonian Exile to the Establishment of Israel* (Philadelphia, 1967)

——, *The Church and the Jews in the XIIIth Century* (Philadelphia, 1933)

Greeley, Andrew, *The Denominational Society: A Sociological Approach to Religion in America* (Glenview, IL, 1972)

Green, Thomas J., "Future of Penal Law in the Church," *The Jurist* 35 (1975): 212-275

Greenawalt, Kent, "Religion as a Concept in Constitutional Law," *California Law Review* 72 (1984): 753

Greenberg, Blu, *On Women and Judaism: A View from Tradition* (Philadelphia, 1981)

——, "Woman Today—An Orthodox View," in Steven Katz, ed., *Frontiers of Jewish Thought* (New York, 1992), 76

Gremillion, Joseph, ed., *The Church and Culture Since Vatican II* (Notre Dame, 1985)

Griffioen, Sander, "Entering into a Scheme of Belief: MacIntyre's Account of Moral Traditions," in A.W. Musschenga, Voozanger, B. and A. Soetman, eds., *Morality, Worldview, and Law: The Idea of a Universal Morality and its Critics* (Assen, 1992)

Griffiths, Paul J., *An Apology for Apologetics: A Study in the Logic of Interreligious Dialogue* (Maryknoll, NY, 1991)

Grisez, Germain and Joseph M. Boyle, Jr., *Life and Death with Liberty and Justice: A Contribution to the Euthanasia Debate* (Notre Dame, 1979)

Grohs, Gerhard and Gernot Czell (hrsg.), *Kirche in der Welt: Kirche der Laien?* (Frankfurt am Main, 1990)

Grossman, Naomi, "Women Unbound: Breaking the Chains of Jewish Divorce Law," *Lilith* (Summer, 1993): 8

Guiness, Os and James Davison Hunter, eds., *Articles of Faith, Articles of Peace* (Washington, 1990)

Gurr, Ted Robert, *Minorities At Risk: A Global View of Ethnopolitical Conflicts* (Washington, 1993)

Haber, Honi Fern, *Beyond Postmodern Politics: Lyotard, Rorty, and Foucault* (New York, 1994)

Habermas, Jürgen, *Moral Consciousness and Communicative Action*, Christian Lenhardt and Sherry Weber Nicholsen, trans. (Cambridge, MA, 1990)

———, *The Philosophical Discourse of Modernity: Twelve Lectures*, Frederick Lawrence, trans. (Cambridge, MA, 1987)

———, *The Theory of Communicative Action, Vol. 1: Reason and the Rationalization of Society*, Thomas McCarthy, trans. (Boston, 1984)

———, *The Theory of Communicative Action, Vol. 2: Lifeworld and System; A Critique of Functionalist Reason*, Thomas McCarthy, trans. (Boston, 1987)

Hallaq, Wael B., "Was the Gate of Ijtihad Closed?" *International Journal of Middle Eastern Studies* 16 (1984): 3

Haller, William, *Liberty and Reformation in the Puritan Revolution* (New York, 1955)

———, *Tracts on Liberty in the Puritan Revolution, 1638-1647* (New York, 1934), 3 vols.

——— and Godfrey Davies, eds., *The Leveller Tracts, 1647-1653* (New York, 1944)

Hammerskjöld, Dag, *Markings by Dag Hammerskjöld*, W.H. Auden and Lief Sjöberg, trans. (London and Boston, 1964)

Harakas, Stanley, "Human Rights: An Eastern Orthodox Perspective," *Journal of Ecumenical Studies* 19 (1982): 13

Harik, Iliya, "Pluralism in the Arab World," *Journal of Democracy* 5 (July, 1994): 43

Harrelson, Walter, *The Ten Commandments and Human Rights* (Philadelphia, 1979)

Harrington, James, *The Political Works of James Harrington*, J.G.A. Pocock, ed. (New York, 1977)

Hartmann, Albert, *Toleranz und christlicher Glaube* (Frankurt am Main, 1955)

Hasan, Ahmad, *Early Development of Islamic Jurisprudence* (Islamabad, 1970)

Hastings, Adrian, ed., *Modern Catholicism: Vatican II and After* (New York, 1991)

Hauptman, Judith, "Images of Women in the Talmud," in Rosemary Radford Ruether, ed., *Religion and Sexism* (New York, 1974)

Haut, Irwin, *Divorce in Jewish Law and Life* (New York, 1983)

Haut, Rivka, "The Agunah and Divorce," in Debra Orenstein, ed., *Lifecycles* (Woodstock, 1994), 198

Healey, Stephen B., "Religious Truth Claims, Violence, and the Pluralistic Hypothesis: A Defense of Interreligious Apologetics," *Andover Newton Review* 3(1) (1992): 17

Hehir, J. Bryan, "The United States and Human Rights," in Kenneth A. Oye, Robert J. Lieber and Donald S. Rothchild, eds., *Eagle in a New World: American Grand Strategy in the Post-Cold War Era* (New York, 1992), 233

Heidegger, Martin, *Existence and Being* (Chicago, 1968)

Heidelmeyer, Wolfgang (hrsg.), *Die Menschenrechte: Erklärungen, Verfassungsartikel, Internationale Abkommen* (Paderborn, 1972)

Held, Colbert C., *Middle East Patterns: Places, Peoples and Politics* (Boulder, 1994)

Helmholz, R.H., ed., *Canon Law in Protestant Lands* (Berlin, 1992)

———, *Roman Canon Law in Reformation England* (Cambridge, 1990)

Helsinki Watch, "Human Rights in Uzbekistan" (May, 1993)

Helwys, Thomas, *A Short Declaration of the Mistery of Iniquity*, facs. repr. ed. (London, 1935)

Henkin, Louis, *The Rights of Man Today* (Boulder, CO, 1978)

———, Richard Crawford Pugh, Oscar Schacter and Hans Smit, *International Law: Cases and Materials*, 3d ed. (St. Paul, 1993)

Henry, Carl F.H., "The Judeo-Christian Heritage and Human Rights," in Carl H. Esbeck, ed., *Religious Beliefs, Human Rights and the Moral Foundations of Western Democracy* (Columbia, MS, 1986), 29

Herring, Basil, "Putting an End to the Agunah Problem," *Amit* (September, 1994): 18-19

Heschel, Abraham Joshua, *God in Search of Man: A Philosophy of Judaism* (New York, 1955)

Hesse, Konrad, "Die Entwicklung des Staatskirchenrechts seit 1945," *Jahrbuch des öffentlichen Rechts der Gegenwart, Neue Folge* 10 (1988): 1

Hick, John, *An Interpretation of Religion: Human Responses to the Transcendent* (New Haven, 1989)

Himmelfarb, Gertrude, *On Looking into the Abyss* (New York, 1994)

Himmelfarb, H. and S. DellaPergola, eds., *Jewish Education Worldwide: Cross Cultural Perspectives* (Lanham, MD, 1989)

Hitti, Philip Khuri, *History of the Arabs* (London, 1937)

Hodgson, Janet, "Zonnebloem College and Cape Town," *Studies in the History of Cape Town: Centre for African Studies, University of Cape Town* 1 (1979): 125

Hoerster, Norbert, *Abtreibung im säkularen Staat: Argumente gegen den § 218* (Frankfurt am Main, 1991)

Hoffman, Manfred, ed., *Martin Luther and the Modern Mind: Freedom, Conscience, Toleration, Rights* (New York, 1985)

———, (hrsg.), *Toleranz und Reformation* (Gütersloh, 1979)

Hogan, G.W., "Law and Religion: Church-State Relations in Ireland from Independence to the Present Day," *American Journal of Comparative Law* 35 (1987): 477

Hoibraaten, Helge, "Secular Society: An Attempt at Initiation," in Tore Lindholm and Kari Vogt, eds., *Islamic Law Reform and Human Rights: Challenges and Rejoinders* (Oslo, 1993), 231

Hollenbach, David, *Claims in Conflict: Retrieving and Reviewing the Catholic Human Rights Tradition* (New York, 1979)

———, "Human Rights and Religious Faith in the Middle East: Reflections of a Christian Theologian," *Human Rights Quarterly* 4 (1982): 94

Hooper, J. Leon, ed., *Religious Liberty* (Louisville, 1993)

Horan, Kathleen Conrey, "Postminority Support for College Education—A Legally Enforceable Obligation in Divorce Proceedings?" *Family Law Quarterly* 20 (Winter, 1987): 589

Horowitz, Donald, "The Challenge of Ethnic Conflict: Democracy in Divided Societies," *Journal of Democracy* 4(4) (1993): 18

Howard, Rhoda E. and Jack Donnelly, "Human Dignity, Human Rights and Political Regimes," *American Political Science Review* 80(3) (September, 1986): 801

Huber, Wolfgang, "Christianity and Democracy in Europe," *Emory International Law Review* 6 (1992): 35

————, *Die tägliche Gewalt. Gegen den Ausverkauf der Menschenwürde* (Freiburg im Breisgau, 1993)

————, "Grenzen des medizinischen Fortschritts aus ethischer Sicht," *Zeitschrift für Evangelische Ethik* 38 (1994): 41,

————, "Kirche in der Welt: Zum Verhältnis von Laien und Theologen in der Kirche," in Gerhard Grohs and G. Czell (hrsg.), *Kirche in der Welt: Kirche der Laien?* (Frankfurt am Main, 1990), 11

————, "Rights of Nature or Dignity of Nature?" *The Annual of the Society of Christian Ethics* (1991): 43

———— und Hans-Richard Reuter, *Friedensethik* (Stuttgart, 1990)

———— und Heinz Edward Tödt, *Menschenrechte: Perspektiven einer menschlichen Welt*, 3d. ed. (München, 1988)

Human Rights Watch/Africa, "Civilian Devastation: Abuses by All Parties in the War in Southern Sudan" (New York, 1994)

Hunter, Howard O., ed., *The Integrative Jurisprudence of Harold J. Berman* (Boulder/San Francisco, 1995)

Hunter, James Davison, *Culture Wars* (New York, 1991)

Huntington, Samuel P., "Religion and the Third Wave," *The National Interest* 24 (Summer, 1991): 30

————, "The Clash of Civilizations?" *Foreign Affairs* (Summer, 1993): 22

————, "Transnational Organizations and World Politics," *World Politics* 25 (1973): 333

Hurd, John Coolidge, *The Origin of 1 Corinthians* (London, 1965)

Ingram, David, "The Postmodern Kantianism of Arendt and Lyotard," *The Review of Metaphysics* 42 (September, 1988) 51

International Commission of Jurists, et al., *Human Rights in Islam: Report of a Seminar Held in Kuwait, December, 1990* (Geneva, 1982)

Iqbal, Muhammad, *The Reconstruction of Religious Thought in Islam* (Lahore, 1968)

Isaac Herzog, Yizchak, *Hechal Yitzchak* (Jerusalem, 1961)

Ishaque, K.M., "Islamic Law—Its Ideals and Principles," in A. Gauher, ed., *The Challenge of Islam* (London, 1980), 57

Jacob ben Asher, *Tur* (Jerusalem, 1992).

Jacobs, Louis, "The Relationship Between Religion and Ethics in Jewish Thought," in Gene Outka and John P. Reeder, eds., *Religion and Morality* (New York, 1973)

Janis, Mark W. and Richard S. Kay, *European Human Rights Law* (Hartford, 1990)

Janssens, Louis, *Freedom of Conscience and Religious Freedom*, B. Lorenzo, C.F.X., trans. (Staten Island, 1965)

Jaspers, Karl, *The Origin and Goal of History*, Michael Bullock, trans. (New Haven, 1953)

Jellinek, Georg, *Zur Geschichte der Erklärung der Menschenrecht*, R. Schnur, hrsg. (Darmstadt, 1974)

Jerez, Cesar, *Prophetic Possibilities for the Church in Central America* (London, 1987)

Jerusalem Talmud (Villna, 1907)

Jervell, Jacob, *Imago Dei: Gen. 1:26f in Spätjudentum, in den Gnosis, und in den paulinischen Briefen* (Göttingen, 1960)

Johnson, Elizabeth A., *She Who Is: The Mystery of God in Feminist Theological Discourse* (New York, 1992)

Johnson, Luke Timothy, *Decision-Making in the Church: A Biblical Model* (Philadelphia, 1983)

———, "Romans 3:21-26 and the Faith of Jesus," *Catholic Biblical Quarterly* 44 (1982): 77

———, *The Acts of the Apostles* (Collegeville, 1992)

———, "The Authority of the New Testament in the Church: A Theological Reflection," in C.R. Blaisdell, ed., *Conservative, Moderate, Liberal: The Biblical Theology Debate* (St. Louis, 1990), 87

———, *The Literary Function of Possessions in Luke-Acts* (Missoula, 1977)

———, "The New Testament's Anti-Jewish Slander and the Conventions of Ancient Polemic," *Journal of Biblical Literature* 108 (1989): 419

———, "II Timothy and the Polemic Against False Teachers: A Re-Examination," *Journal of Religious Studies* 6/7 (1978-79): 1

———, *Writings of the New Testament* (Philadelphia, 1986)

Johnson, Paul, *A History of Christianity* (New York, 1979)

Jordan, Wilbur Kitchener, *The Development of Religious Toleration in England* (Cambridge, MA, 1932-40), 4 vols.

Josephus, Flavius, *The Works of Flavius Josephus*, Ralph Marcus et al. trans. (New York/London, 1926-1965)

Juergensmeyer, Mark, *The New Cold War: Religious Nationalism Confronts the Secular State* (Berkeley, 1993)

Jullundhri, R.A., "Human Rights in Islam," in A.D. Falconer, ed., *Understanding Human Rights* (Dublin, 1980)

Justin Martyr, *The First Apology, The Second Apology, Dialogue with Trypho, Exhortation to the Greeks, Discourse to the Greeks, The Monarchy or the Rule of God*, Thomas B. Falls, trans. (New York, 1948)

Kafih, Y., ed., *Commentary on the Mishnah* (Jerusalem, 1976)

Kamel, Taymour, "The Principle of Legality and Its Application in Islamic Criminal Justice," in M. Cherif Bassiouni, ed., *The Islamic Criminal Justice System* (London, 1982), 150

Kamen, Henry, *Inquisition and Society in Spain in the Sixteenth and Seventeenth Centuries* (Bloomington, 1985)

———, *The Rise of Toleration* (New York, 1967)

Kant, Immanuel, *Groundwork of the Metaphysic of Morals*, H.J. Paton, trans. (New York, 1964)

———, *Werke*, W. Weischedel, hrsg. (Wiesbaden, 1956)

Kaplan, Lawrence, ed., *Fundamentalism in Comparative Perspective* (Amherst, MA, 1992)

Karo, Joseph, *Shulchan Aruch* (Vilna, 1896)

Karris, R.J., "Rich and Poor: The Lukan Sitz-im-Leben," in C.H. Talbert, ed., *Perspectives on Luke-Acts* (Danville, 1978), 112

Kasper, Walter, "The Theological Foundations of Human Rights," *The Jurist* 50 (1990): 148

Katz, Jacob, "Orthodoxy in Historical Perspective," *Studies in Contemporary Jewry* 2 (1986): 3

Katz, Steven, ed., *Frontiers of Jewish Thought* (New York, 1992)

Kaufmann, Ludwig, *Ein ungelöster Kirchenkonflikt: Der Fall Pfürtner, Dokumente und zeitgeschichtliche Analysen* (Freiburg, 1987)

Keddie, Nikki R., ed., *Religion and Politics in Iran: Shi'ism from Quietism to Revolution* (New Haven, 1983)

Kelley, Dean, ed., *Government Intervention in Religious Affairs* (New York, 1986)

Kellner, Menachem Marc, ed., *Contemporary Jewish Ethics* (New York, 1978)

Kelsay, John, "Saudi Arabia, Pakistan, and the Universal Declaration of Human Rights," in David Little, John Kelsay and Abdulaziz Sachedina, eds., *Human Rights and the Conflict of Cultures: Western and Islamic Perspectives on Religious Liberty* (Columbia, SC, 1988), 33

―――― and Sumner B. Twiss, eds., *Religion and Human Rights* (New York, 1994)

Kennedy, Paul, *The Rise and the Fall of the Great Powers* (New York, 1987)

Keohane, Robert O. and Joseph S. Nye, *Power and Interdependence* (Boston, 1977)

――――, eds., *Transnational Relations and World Politics* (Cambridge, MA, 1970)

Khadduri, Majid, "Human Rights in Islam," *Annals of the American Academy of Political and Social Science* 243 (1946): 79

――――, "Nature and Sources of Islamic Law," *George Washington Law Review* 22 (1953): 22

――――, *The Islamic Conception of Justice* (Baltimore, 1984)

――――, *The Islamic Law of Nations: Shayb an a's Siyar* (Baltimore, 1966)

――――, *War and Peace in the Law of Islam* (Baltimore, 1955)

Khan, Muhammad Zafrulla, *Islam and Human Rights* (London, 1967), 112

Khodie, Narmada, ed., *Readings in Uniform Civil Code* (Bombay, 1975)

Khory, Kavita R., "The Shah Bano Case: Some Political Implications," in Robert D. Baird, ed., *Religion and Law in Independent India* (New Delhi, 1993), 121

Kierkegaard, Søren, *Training in Christianity* (London, 1850)

Kilada, William Soliman, "Christian-Muslim Relations in Egypt," in Kail C. Ellis, ed., *The Vatican, Islam and the Middle East* (Syracuse, 1987), 254

King, Michael, "Children's Rights as Communication: Reflections on Autopoietic Theory and the United Nations Convention," *Modern Law Review* 57 (1994): 385

Kirschenbaum, Aaron, "Human Rights Revisited," *Israel Yearbook on Human Rights* 6 (1975): 228

――――, "The Good Samaritan: Monetary Aspects," *Journal of Halacha & Contemporary Society* 17 (1989): 83

Kishwar, Madhu and Ruth Vanita, "Inheritance Rights for Women: A Response to Some Commonly Expressed Fears," *Manushi* 57 (March/April, 1990): 3

Klein, Charlotte, *Anti-Judaism in Christian Theology*, E. Quinn, trans. (Philadelphia, 1978)

König A. and H. Keane, eds., *The Meaning of History* (Pretoria, 1980)

Konvitz, Milton, ed., *Judaism and Human Rights* (New York, 1972)

Kook, Avraham Yitzchak, *Responsa Da'at Cohen Yoreh Deah* (Jerusalem, 1983)

Koshy, Ninan, *Religious Freedom in a Changing World* (Geneva, 1992)

Kramer, Martin, "Politics and the Prophet," *The New Republic* (March 1, 1993): 39

Kretzmer, David, *The Legal Status of the Arabs in Israel* (Boulder, 1990)

Krieger, David, *The New Universalism: Foundations for a Global Theology* (Maryknoll, NY, 1991)

Küng, Hans, *Das Projekt Weltethos* (München, 1991)

———, "Eine Welt—eine Menschheit—ein Ethos: Zehn Thesen," *Evangelische Kommentare* 26 (1993): 488

——— and K.J. Kuschel, eds., *A Global Ethic: The Declaration of the Parliament of the World Religions* (London and New York, 1993)

———, and Jürgen Moltmann, eds., *The Ethics of World Religions and Human Rights* (Philadelphia, 1990)

Lactantius, *Divinae institutiones* (München, 1963)

Lamm, Norman, *Torah Umaddah* (Northvale, NJ, 1992)

Landau, Ezekiel, *Responsa Nodah BeYehudah* (New York, 1955)

Lawrence, Bruce, "Woman as Subject/Woman as Symbol: Islamic Fundamentalism and the Status of Women," *Journal of Religious Ethics* 22(1) (Spring, 1994): 163

Lawton, David, *Blasphemy* (Philadelphia, 1993)

Laycock, Douglas, "The Remnants of Free Exercise," *Supreme Court Review* (1990): 45

———, "The Right to Church Autonomy as Part of Free Exercise of Religion," in Dean Kelley, ed., *Government Intervention in Religious Affairs* (New York, 1986), 28

Lea, Henry C., *A History of the Inquisition in Spain* (New York, 1922), 4 vols.

LeCler, Joseph, "Religious Freedom: A Historical Survey," *Concilium* 18 (1966): 3

———, *Toleration and Reformation*, T.L. Westow, trans. (New York, 1960), 2 vols.

——— et Marius-Francois Valkhoff, *Les premiers défenseurs de la liberté religieuse* (Paris, 1969), 2 vols.

Leimans, Sid Z., "Critique of Louis Jacobs" in Menachem Marc Kellner, ed., *Contemporary Jewish Ethics* (Brooklyn, 1978), 58

Lerner, Natan, *Group Rights and Discrimination in International Law* (Dordrecht/Boston/London, 1991)

Levenson, Jon D., *Creation and the Persistance of Evil* (San Francisco, 1988)

Levesque, Roger, "International Human Rights Grow Up: Implications for America Jurisprudence and Domestic Policy," *California Western International Law Journal* 24 (1994): 193

Levin, H., "The Theory of Choice Applied to Education," in W. Clune and J. Witte, eds., *Choice and Control in American Education* (Bristol, PA, 1990), 1:247.

Levinas, Emmanuel, *Totality and Infinity*, A. Lingis, trans. (Pittsburgh, 1969)

Levine, Aaron, *Free Enterprise and Jewish Law* (New York, 1980)

Levine, Daniel, ed., *Churches and Politics in Latin America* (Beverly Hills, 1979)

Levinger, Jacob S., ed., *Concepts of Judaism* (Jerusalem, 1974)

Levini, D.H., "From Church and State to Religion and Politics," *World Affairs* 150 (1987): 93

Levy, Leonard W., *Blasphemy: Verbal Offense Against the Sacred, From Moses to Salman Rushdie* (New York, 1993)

Lewis, Bernard, *The Jews of Islam* (Princeton, 1984)

———, *The Political Language of Islam* (Chicago, 1988)

———, *Race and Slavery in the Middle East* (New York, 1990)

Libanius, *Selected Works of Libanius*, A.F. Norman trans. (Cambridge, MA, 1969)

Liebesny, Herbert, *The Law of the Near and Middle East* (Albany, 1975)

Lindholm, Tore, and Kari Vogt, eds., *Islamic Law Reform and Human Rights: Challenges and Rejoinders* (Oslo, 1993)

Liskofsky, Sidney and Donna Arzt, "Incitement to National, Racial, and Religious Hatred in United Nations Fora," *Israel Yearbook on Human Rights* 17 (1988): 41

Listl, Joseph (hrsg.), *Grundriss des nachkonziliaren Kirchenrechts* (Regensburg, 1980)

Littell, Franklin H., *The Anabaptist View of the Church* (Boston, 1958)

———, *The Free Church* (Boston, 1957)

Little, David, John Kelsay and Abdulaziz Sachedina, eds., *Human Rights and the Conflict of Cultures: Western and Islamic Perspectives on Religious Liberty* (Columbia, SC, 1988)

Locke, John, *A Letter Concerning Toleration*, M. Montuori, ed. (The Hague, 1963)

———, *Two Treatises of Government* [1689], Peter Laslett, ed. (Cambridge, 1960)

Long, Charles, *Significations: Signs, Symbols and Images in the Interpretation of Religion* (Philadelphia, 1986)

Lopez, P.G., "La Democracia como regimen politico Christiano, III," *Razon y Fe 134* (1946): 166

Lorenz, Eckehart, ed., *How Christian are Human Rights?* (Geneva, 1981)

Luther, Martin, *Ausgewählte Schriften*, K. Bornkamm und G. Ebeling, hrsg. (Frankfurt am Main, 1983)

———, *Reformation Writings of Martin Luther*, Bertram Lee Woolf, ed. (London, 1956), 2 vols.

Lutz, Heinrich (hrsg.), *Zur Geschichte der Toleranz und Religionsfreiheit* (Darmstadt, 1977)

Lyotard, Jean Francois, *Political Writings*, Bill Readings and Kevin Paul, trans. (Minneapolis, 1993)

———, *The Different: Phrases in Dispute*, (Minneapolis, 1988)

———, "The Other's Rights," in Stephen Shupe and Susan Hurley, eds., *On Human Rights: The Oxford Amnesty Lectures 1993* (New York, 1993), 135

———, *The Postmodern Condition: A Report on Knowledge*, Geoff Bennington and Brian Massumi, trans. (Minneapolis, 1984)

———, *The Postmodern Explained*, J. Pefanis and M. Thomas, trans. and ed. (Sydney, 1992)

MacAuliffe, M.A., *The Sikh Religion: Its Gurus, Sacred Writings, and Anthems* (Oxford, 1909), 6 vols.

MacIntyre, Alasdair, *After Virtue: A Study in Moral Theory*, 2d ed. (Notre Dame, 1984)

Mackenzie, N., ed., *Conviction* (London, 1958)

MacMullen, Ramsay, *Christianizing the Roman Empire, A.D. 100-400* (New Haven, 1984)

Madina, Maan Z., "The Disruption and Decline of the Arab Empire," in John A. Garraty and Peter Gay, eds., *The Columbia History of the World* (New York, 1972), 271

Mafeje, Archie, "African Philosophical Projections and Prospects for the Indigenisation of Political and Intellectual Discourse," *Seminar Paper Series No. 7* (Harare, 1992), 27

Maharam M'Lublin (Jerusalem, 1960)

Maimonides, Moses, *Commentary on the Mishnah* (Jerusalem, 1976)

——, *Guide of the Perplexed*, S. Pines, trans. (Chicago, 1963)

——, *Mishneh Torah*, Isodore Twersky, trans. (New Haven, 1976)

Makdisi, George, "The Juridical Theology of Shafi'i: Origins and Significance of Usul Al-Fiqh," *Studia Islamica* 59 (1984): 5-47

Makiya, Kanan, *Cruelty and Silence: War, Tyranny, Uprising and the Arab World* (New York, 1993)

Malik, Ibrahim, "Jihad—Its Development and Relevance," *Palestine-Israel Journal* 2 (Spring, 1994): 26

Manoach, Narbonne, *Shevitat Haessor* (Lemberg, 1881)

Mansfield, John H., "Religious Speech Under Indian Law," in Mahendra Singh, ed., *Comparative Constitutional Law* (Lucknow, India, 1989), 204

——, "The Personal Laws or a Uniform Civil Code?" in Robert D. Baird, ed., *Religion and Law in Independent India* (New Delhi, 1993), 139

Mansour, Aly Aly, "Hudud Crimes," in M. Cherif Bassiouni, ed., *The Islamic Criminal Justice System* (London, 1982), 195

Marcus, Jacob Rader, *The Jew in the Medieval World: A Source Book: 315-1791* (New York, 1969)

Marè, Gerhard, *Ethnicity and Politics in South Africa* (London, 1993)

Maritain, Jacques "Introduction," in UNESCO, *Human Rights: Comments and Interpretations* (New York, 1949), 1

——, *Man and the State* (Chicago, 1954)

——, *The Rights of Man and Natural Law* (New York, 1943)

Marsilius of Padua, *Defensor Pacis*, Alan Gewirth, trans. (New York, 1956)

Martin, Karl, (hrsg.), *Frieden Statt Sicherheit: Von der Militärseelsorge zum Dienst der Kirche unter den Soldaten* (Gütersloh, 1989)

Marty, Martin E., "From the Centripetal to the Centrifugal in Culture and Religion: The Revolution Within This Half Century," *Theology Today* 51(1) (April, 1994): 5

——, "Religion: A Private Affair in Public Affairs," *Religion and American Culture: A Journal of Interpretation* 3(2) (Summer, 1993): 122

——, "The Virginia Statute Two Hundred Years Later," in Merrill D. Peterson and Robert C. Vaughn, eds., *The Virginia for Religious Freedom* (Cambridge, 1988), 1

—— and R. Scott Appelby, eds., *Fundamentalisms and the State* (Chicago, 1993)

————, eds., *Fundamentalisms Comprehended* (Chicago, 1995)

Marx, Karl, *On Society and Social Change*, N.J. Smelser, ed. (Chicago, 1973)

————, *The Essential Writings*, F.L. Bender. ed. (New York, 1972)

Mathew, Babu, et al., *Cases and Materials on Family Law I* (Bangalore, 1990)

Matzner-Bekerman, Shoshana, *The Jewish Child: Halakhic Perspectives* (Hobokin, 1984)

Maududi, Abdul A'la, *Human Rights in Islam* (Lahore, 1977)

————, *Rights of Non-Muslims in Islamic States* (Lahore, 1961)

May, William W., ed., *Vatican Authority and American Catholic Dissent* (New York, 1987)

Mayer, Ann Elizabeth, "Current Muslim Thinking on Human Rights," in Abdullahi Ahmed An-Na'im and Francis Deng, eds., *Human Rights in Africa* (Philadelphia, 1992), 113

————, *Islam and Human Rights: Tradition and Politics* (Boulder, 1991)

————, "Islam and the State," *Cardozo Law Review* 12 (1991): 1015

————, "Universal Versus Islamic Human Rights: A Clash of Cultures or a Clash with a Construct?" *Michigan Journal of International Law* 15 (Winter, 1994): 307

McCann, Dennis, *New Experiment in Democracy: The Challenge for American Catholicism* (Kansas City, 1987)

McConnell, Michael W., "The Origins and Historical Understanding of the Free Exercise of Religion," *Harvard Law Review* 103 (1990): 1410

McGovern A.F. and T.L. Shubeck, "Updating Liberation Theology," *America* (July 16, 1988): 32

McGrath, Marcos N., "The Impact of *Gaudium et Spes*: Medellin, Puebla and Pastoral Creativity," in J. Gremillion, ed., *The Church and Culture Since Vatican II* (Notre Dame, 1985), 99

Medvedev, Roy, *On Soviet Dissent: Interviews with Piero Ostellino*, George Sanders, ed. (New York, 1980)

Meeks, Wayne A., "The Man from Heaven in Johannine Sectarianism," *Journal of Biblical Literature* 91 (1972): 1

Meeks, Willem Adolph, *The First Urban Christians: The Social World of the Apostle Paul* (New Haven, 1983)

Mehrzad Boroujerdi, "Can Islam be Secularized?" in M.R. Ghanoonparvar and Faridoun Farrokh, eds., *In Transition: Essays on Culture and Identity in Middle Eastern Societies* (Laredo, TX, 1993), 57

Meiselman, Moshe, *Jewish Women in Jewish Law* (New York, 1978)

Mekhilta (Jerusalem, 1960).

Menashri, David, "Khomeini's Policy Toward Ethnic and Religious Minorities," in Milton J. Esman and Itamar Rabinovich, eds., *Ethnicity, Pluralism and the Middle East* (Ithaca, 1988), 215

Mernissi, Fatima, *Beyond the Veil* (Cambridge, 1975)

Middle East Watch, "Genocide in Iraq: The Anfal Campaign Against the Kurds" (1993)

————, "Guardians of Thought: Limits on Freedom of Expression in Iran" (August, 1993)

————, "Human Rights Abuses in Algeria: No One is Spared" (January, 1994)

————, "Yemen: Steps Toward Civil Society" (November, 1992)

Milbank, John, *Theology and Social Theory: Beyond Secular Reason* (Oxford, 1990)

Miller, Allen O., ed., *A Christian Declaration on Human Rights* (Grand Rapids, 1977)

Miller, Judith, "Faces of Fundamentalism: Hassan al-Turabi and Muhammed Fadlallah," *Foreign Affairs* (November/December, 1994): 123

Milton, John, *Complete Prose Works of John Milton*, rev. ed. (New Haven, 1980)

Mitchell, Margaret Mary, *Paul and the Rhetoric of Reconciliation* (Louisville, 1991)

Mittlemen, Alan, "From Private Rights to Public Good: The Communitarian Critique of Liberalism in Judaic Perspective," *Jewish Political Studies Review* 5 (1993): 79.

Mnookin, Robert H. and D. Weisberg, *Child, Family and State*, 2d ed. (Boston, 1989), 455

Moellin, Jacob, *Minhagai Maharil* (Jerusalem, 1991).

Mojzes, Paul, *Lament for Yugoslavia: Ethnoreligious Warfare in the Balkans* (New York, 1994)

Montefiore C.G. and H. Loewe, *A Rabbinic Theology* (London, 1938)

Moodie, T. Dunbar, *The Rise of Afrikanerdom: Power, Apartheid and Afrikaner Civil Religion* (Berkeley, 1980)

Moore, George Foote, *History of Religions* (New York, 1948)

Morrell, Samuel, "An Equal or a Ward: How Independent is a Married Woman According to Rabbinic Law?" *Jewish Social Studies* (Summer/Fall, 1982): 190

Moulder, James, "Moral Education in a Multicultural Environment," *Acta Academica* 24(2) (1992): 17

Mouw, Richard J. and Sander Griffioen, *Pluralisms and Horizons: An Essay in Christian Public Philosophy* (Grand Rapids, 1993)

Moxnes, Halvor, *Theology in Conflict: Studies of Paul's Understanding of God in Romans* (Leiden, 1980)

Mueller, Lori Leff, "Religious Rights of Children: A Gallery of Judicial Visions," *Review of Law and Social Change* 14 (1986): 323

Muller, Hubert, *Religion and Freedom in the Modern World* (Chicago, 1963)

Müller Alois and Norbert Greinacher, eds., *The Church and the Rights of Man* (New York, 1979)

Murray, John Courtney, "Arguments for the Human Right to Religious Freedom," in J.L. Hooper, ed., *Religious Liberty* (Louisville, 1993), 229

————, "Current Theology: Religious Freedom," *Theological Studies* 6 (1945): 85

————, "Current Theology on Religious Freedom," *Theological Studies* 10 (1949): 409

————, ed., *Freedom and Man* (New York, 1965)

————, "Freedom of Religion I: The Ethical Problem," *Theological Studies* 6 (1945): 229

————, "Leo XIII: Two Concepts of Government," *Theological Studies* 14 (1953): 551

————, "Religious Freedom," in John Courtney Murray, ed., *Freedom and Man* (New York, 1965), 131

————, "The Problem of Religious Freedom," *Theological Studies* 25 (1964): 503

————, *We Hold These Truths: Catholic Reflections on the American Proposition* (New York, 1960)

Musschenga, A.W., B. Voozanger, and A. Soetman, eds., *Morality, Worldview, and Law: The Idea of a Universal Morality and its Critics* (Assen, The Netherlands, 1992)

Nachmanides, Moses, *Commentary of Nachmanides [on the Bible]*, Charles Chavel, trans. (New York, 1971)

Nardin, Terry and David Maple, eds., *The Constitution of International Society* (Princeton, 1995)

Natapoff, Alexandra, "1993: The Year of Living Dangerously: State Courts Expand the Right to Education," *Education Law Reporter* 92 (1994): 755

Neuhaus, Richard John, *The Naked Public Square* (Grand Rapids, 1984)

Newman, J., *On Religious Freedom* (Ottawa, 1991)

Nicholson, Reynold Alleyne, *The Secrets of the Self [Translation of Asrar-e-Khudi (Farsi)]* (Lahore, 1964)

Niebuhr, H. Richard, *Christ and Culture* (New York, 1956)

————, *The Kingdom of God in America* (Middletown, CT, 1988)

————, *The Responsible Self* (New York, 1963)

Note, "Defining Religion in the First Amendment: A Functional Approach," *Cornell Law Review* 74 (1989): 754

Noonan, John T., Jr., "Principled or Pragmatic Foundations for the Freedom of Conscience," *Journal of Law and Religion* 5 (1987): 205

Novak, David, *Halakhah in a Theological Dimension* (Chico, CA, 1985)

————, "Is There A Concept of Individual Rights in Jewish Law?" *Jewish Law Association Studies* (Atlanta, 1994), 129

————, *Jewish Social Ethics* (New York, 1992)

————, *Jewish-Christian Dialogue: A Jewish Justification* (New York, 1989)

————, *Law and Theology in Judaism* (New York, 1976)

————, *Suicide and Morality* (New York, 1975)

————, *The Theology of Nahmanides Systematically Presented* (Atlanta, GA, 1992)

O'Brien, David J. and Thomas A. Shannon, eds., *Catholic Social Thought: The Documentary Heritage* (Maryknoll, 1992)

O'Brien, Sharon, *American Indian Tribal Governments* (Norman and London, 1989)

Offler, Hilary Seton, "The Three Modes of Natural Law in Ockham: A Revision of the Text," *Franciscan Studies* 37 (1977): 207

Or Zaruah, Chaim, *Or Zaruah* (Jerusalem, 1963)

Orenstein, Debra, ed., *Lifecycles* (Woodstock, 1994)

Origen, *Contra Celsum*, Henry Chadwick, trans. (Cambridge, 1980)

Orme, N., "Children and the Church in Medieval England," *Journal of Eccclesistical History* 45 (1994): 563

Otto, E., "Sozial- und rechtshistorische Aspekte in der Ausdifferenzierung eines altisraelischen Ethos aus dem Recht," *Osnabrücker Hochschulschriften, Schriftenreihe des FB 3/9* (Osnabrück, 1987): 135

Oye, K., R. Lieber and D. Rothchild, eds., *Eagle in a New World: American Grand Strategy in the Post-Cold War Era* (New York, 1992)

Pannenberg, Wolfgang, *Basic Questions in Theology* (Philadelphia, 1971), 2 vols.

Panikkar, Raimundo, "Is the Notion of Human Rights a Western Concept?" *Breakthrough* 31 (Spring, 1989)

Parkes, James, *The Jew in the Medieval Community: A Study of His Political and Economic Situation*, 2d ed. (New York, 1976)

Parker, T.M., *Christianity and the State in the Light of History* (New York, 1955)

Parwez, G.A., *Islam: A Challenge to Religion* (Lahore, 1968)

————, *Tabweeb-ul-Qur'an* (Lahore, 1977)

Patai, Raphael, *The Seed of Abraham: Jews and Arabs in Contact and Conflict* (New York, 1986)

Pavan, P., "The Right to Religious Freedom in the Conciliar Declaration," *Concilium* 18 (1966): 37

Payne, Douglas, Charles Brown, and James Finn, "Human Rights: Showdown in Vienna," *Freedom Review* 24(5) (October, 1993): 5

Peacock, J.R. and J.W. Chapman, *Voluntary Associations* (New York, 1969)

Pelikan, Jaroslav, *The Excellent Empire: The Fall of Rome and the Triumph of the Church* (San Francisco, 1987)

Perry, Michael J., "The Idea of Human Rights: Is the Idea of Human Rights Ineliminably Religious?" in James E. Wood, Jr. and Derek Davis, eds., *Problems and Conflicts Between Law and Morality in a Free Society* (Waco, TX, 1994), 55

Peter, Nichols, *The Pope's Divisions: The Roman Catholic Church Today* (New York, 1981)

Peterson, Merrill D. and Robert Vaughn, eds. *The Virginia Statute of Religious Freedom* (Cambridge, 1988)

Pfeffer, Leo, *Church, State, and Freedom*, rev. ed. (Boston, 1967)

Pickthall, Marmaduke, *The Glorious Koran: A Bi-Lingual Edition with English* (London, 1976)

Pinkard, Terry, *Democratic Liberalism and Social Union* (Philadelphia, 1987)

Pinto, William E., *Law of Marriage and Matrimonial Reliefs for Christians in India* (Bangalore, 1991)

Pipkin, H. Wayne and John H. Yoder, ed. and trans. *Balthasar Hubmaier: Theologian of Anabaptism* (Scottdale, PA, 1989)

Piscatory, James P., "Human Rights in Islamic Political Culture," in Kenneth Thompson, ed., *The Moral Imperatives of Human Rights: A World Survey* (Washington, 1980), 153

Pityana, N. Barney, Mamphela Ramphele, Malusi Mpumlwana, and Lindy Wilson, eds., *Bounds of Possibility: The Legacy of Steve Biko and Black Consciousness* (Cape Town, 1991)

Pliny the Elder, *Natural History*, H. Rackham, trans. (Cambridge, MA, 1938-1963), 10 vols.

Pobee, John S., "An African Christian in Search of Democracy," in John Witte, Jr., ed., *Christianity and Democracy in Global Context* (Boulder/San Francisco, 1993), 267

Pogany, Istvan, "Arab Attitudes Toward International Human Rights Law," *Connecticut Journal of International Law* 2 (1987): 373

Pollis, Adamantia, "Eastern Orthodoxy and Human Rights," *Human Rights Quarterly* 15 (1993): 339

Pope Gregory IX, *Decretales Gregorii Papae IX cum glossis* (Lyons, 1624)

Pope Innocent IV, *Commentaria Innocentii . . . super quinque libros decretalium* (Frankfurt, 1570)

Pope John Paul II, *Address to the United Nations* (1979)

——, *Apostolic Letter on the Dignity and Vocation of Women* (Boston, 1988)

——, *Centesimus Annus* (1991)

———, *Original Unity of Man and Woman: Catechesis on the Book of Genesis* (Boston, 1981)

——, *Redemptor Hominis* (Washington, 1979)

——, *Veritatis Splendor* (Vatican City, 1993)

——, "Women: Teachers of Peace," *Origins* 24(28) (December 22, 1994): 465

Pope-Levinson, Priscilla and John R. Levinson, *Jesus in Global Context* (Louisville, KY, 1992)

Porras, Ileana M., "On Terrorism: Reflections on Violence and the Outlaw," *Utah Law Review* (1994): 119

Preus, J. Samuel, *Explaining Religion: Criticism and Theory from Bodin to Freud* (New Haven, 1987)

Provost, James H., "Excommunication," in *Encyclopedia of Religion*, Mircea Eliade, ed. (New York, 1987), 5:218

—— and Knut Walf, eds., *Canon Law Church Reality* (Edinburgh, 1986)

——, eds., *The Tabu of Democracy Within the Church Concilium* (London, 1992)

Purdy, Laura Martha, *In their Best Interest? The Case Against Equal Rights for Children* (Ithaca, 1992)

Quaritsch, Helmut und Hermann Weber (hrsg.), *Staat und Kirchen in der Bundesrepublik. Staatskirchliche Aufsätze* (Bad Homburg, 1967)

Radhakrishnan, Sarvepalli, *Religion in a Changing World* (London, 1967)

—— and Charles A. Moore, eds., *A Sourcebook in Indian Philosophy* (Princeton, 1971)

Rahman, Fazlar, *Islam* (Chicago, 1966)

Rahner, Karl, *Theological Investigations*, K.H. and B. Kruger, trans. (New York, 1974), 6 vols.

Rashi, *Commentary on the Torah*, M. Rosenbaum and A.M. Silvermann, trans. (London, 1946)

Rasmussen, David, ed., *Universalism vs. Communitarianism: Contemporary Debates in Ethics* (Cambridge, MA, 1990)

Rawls, John, *A Theory of Justice* (Cambridge, MA, 1971)

——, "Justice as Fairness: Political not Metaphysical," *Philosophical and Public Affairs* 14(3) (1985)

Reeves, Mina, *Female Warriors of Allah* (New York, 1989), 133

Reid, Charles J., *Rights in Thirteenth Century Canon Law: An Historical Investigation* (Ph.D. Diss. Cornell, 1994)

Reisher, Jacob, *Chak Yaakov* (New York, 1961)

Reformed Ecumenical Synod, *RES Testimony on Human Rights* (Grand Rapids, 1983)

Renegger, N.J., *Treaties and Alliances of the World* (Essex, 1990)

Reteln, Alison Dundes, *International Human Rights* (London, 1990)

Reuther, Rosemary Radford, *Faith and Fratricide: The Theological Roots of Anti-Semitism* (New York, 1974)

———, ed., *Religion and Sexism* (New York, 1974)

Reynolds, Noel B. and W. Cole Durham, Jr., eds., *Religious Liberty in Western Thought* (Atlanta, 1995)

Ringeling, Hermann, "Der Fall Stephan Pfürtner," *Zeitschrift für Evangelische Ethik* 32(4) (1988): 292

Risala, Shafi'i's, *Islamic Jurisprudence*, Majid Khadduri, trans. (Baltimore, 1961)

Riskin, Shlomo, *Women and Jewish Divorces, the Rebellious Wife, The Agunah and the Right of Democracy to Initiate the Divorce in Jewish Law, A Halakhic Solution* (Hoboken, 1989)

Robertson, D.B., ed., *Voluntary Associations: A Study of Groups in Free Societies* (Richmond, 1966)

Robertson, Roland, *Globalization: Social Theory and Global Culture* (London, 1992)

——— and William Garrett, *Religion and Global Order* (New York, 1991)

Robinson, John A.T., *The New Reformation* (London, 1965)

Rorty, Richard, *Contingency, Irony, and Solidarity* (Cambridge, 1989)

———, "Human Rights, Rationality, and Sentimentality," in S. Shupe and S. Hurley, eds., *On Human Rights: The Oxford Amnesty Lectures 1993* (New York, 1993), 111

———, "The Priority of Democracy to Philosophy," in Merrill D. Peterson and Robert Vaughn, eds. *The Virginia Statute of Religious Freedom* (Cambridge, 1988), 257

Rosaldo, Renato, *Culture and Truth: The Remaking of Social Analysis* (Boston, 1989)

Rosannes, Judah, *Mishnah Lemelech* (Jerusalem, 1992)

Rose, Gregory, "Velayat-e Faqih and the Recovery of Islamic Identity in the Thought of Ayatollah Khomeini," in Nikki R. Keddie, ed., *Religion and Politics in Iran: Sh'ism from Quietism to Revolution* (New Haven, 1983), 168

Rosenzweig, Franz, *The Star of Redemption*, W.W. Hallo, trans. (New York, 1970)

Rouner, Leroy S., *Human Rights and the World's Religions* (Notre Dame, 1988)

Rudge, Peter, *Ministry and Management* (London, 1968)

Runciman, Stephen, *A History of the Crusades*, (Cambridge, 1951-1954), 3 vols.

———, *The Orthodox Churches and the Secular State* (Auckland/Oxford, 1971)

Rusk, Richard C., "Educational Obligations for Children of Dissolved Marriages," *Res Gestae* 36 (October, 1992): 156

Sachedina, Abdulaziz A., "Al-Bukhari's Hadith on `Killing Those Who Refuse to Fulfill the Duties Enjoined by God and Considering them Apostates'," in David Little, John Kelsay and Abdulaziz Sachedina, eds., *Human Rights and the Conflict of Cultures: Western and Islamic Perspectives on Religious Liberty*, (Columbia, SC, 1988), 97

———, "Context for the Ayatollah's Decree: The Religious and Political in Islam," in Lisa Appignanesi and Sara Maitland, eds., *The Rushdie File* (Syracuse, 1990), 121

Saddiqi, Amir Hasan, *Non-Muslims Under Muslim Rule and Muslims Under Non-Muslim Rule* (Karachi, 1969)

Salama, Ma'amoun M., "General Principles of Criminal Evidence in Islamic Jurisprudence," in M. Cherif Bassiouni, ed., *The Islamic Criminal Justice System*, (London, 1982), 109

Samet, Moshe S., "The Beginnings of Orthodoxy," *Modern Judaism* 8 (1988): 249

Samuel, G., "Epistemology, Propaganda and Roman Law: Some Reflections on the History of the Subjective Right," *The Journal of Legal History* 10 (1989): 161

Sandel, Michael, "Freedom of Conscience or Freedom of Choice?" in Os Guiness and James Davison Hunter, eds., *Articles of Faith, Articles of Peace* (Washington, 1990), 72

Sanders, Thomas G., *Protestant Concepts of Church and State* (New York, 1964)

Saunders, J.J., *The Muslim World on the Eve of Europe's Expansion* (Englewood Cliffs, NJ, 1966)

Schabas, William, *The Abolition of the Death Penalty in International Law* (Cambridge, 1993)

Schacht, Joseph, *An Introduction to Islamic Law* (Oxford, 1964)

———, *The Origins of Muhammadan Jurisprudence* (Oxford, 1959)

Schacter, Hershel, "Synagogue Membership and School Admission," *Journal of Halacha and Contemporary Society* 12(50) (1986): 64

Schechtman, Joseph B., *On Wings of Eagles: The Plight, Exodus, and Homecoming of Oriental Jewry* (New York, 1961)

Scheler, Max, *Formalism in Ethics*, M.S. Frings and R.L. Funk, trans. (Evanston, IL, 1973)

Scholem, Gershom G., *On the Kabbalah and its Symbolism*, R. Manheim, trans. (New York, 1969)

Schroeder, Henry Joseph, ed. and trans., *The Disciplinary Decrees of the General Councils* (St. Louis, 1937), 242.

Scott, Elizabeth, "Judgment and Reasoning in Adolescent Decision Making," *Villanova Law Review* 37 (1992): 1607

Senghor, Leopold, *On African Socialism* (London, 1964)

Sforno, Ovadiah, *Commentary of Sforno [on the Bible]* (Jerusalem, 1981)

Shochetman, Eliav, *Civil Procedure in Jewish Law* (Jerusalem, 1994)

Shupack, Martin, "The Churches and Human Rights: Catholic and Protestant Human Rights Views and Reflected in Church Statements," *Harvard Human Rights Journal* 6 (1993): 127

Shupe S. and S. Hurley, eds., *On Human Rights: The Oxford Amnesty Lectures 1993* (New York, 1993)

Shutte, Augustine, *Philosophy for Africa* (Cape Town, 1993)

Sidorsky, David, ed., *Essays on Human Rights: Contemporary Issues and Jewish Perspectives* (Philadelphia, 1979)

Sifre, L. Finkelstein, ed. (New York, 1969)

Silber, Michael K., "The Emergence of Ultra-Orthodoxy: The Invention of a Tradition," in Jack Wertheimer, ed., *The Uses of Tradition: Jewish Continuity in the Modern Era* (New York, 1992), 23

Simon, Jules, *La liberté de conscience*, 2d ed. (Paris, 1857)

Singh, Mahendra, ed., *Comparative Constitutional Law* (Lucknow, India, 1989)

Sisk, Timothy D., *Islam and Democracy: Religion, Politics and Power in the Middle East* (Washington, 1992)

Skillen, James W. and Rockne M. McCarthy, eds., *Political Order and the Plural Structure of Society* (Atlanta, 1991)

Smallwood, E. Mary, *The Jews under Roman Rule from Pompey to Diocletian* (Leiden, 1976)

Smith, B.H., "Churches and Human Rights in Latin America—Recent Tends on the Subcontinent," in Daniel Levine, ed., *Churches and Politics in Latin America* (Beverly Hills, 1979), 155

Smith, Mark S., *The Early History of God: Yahweh and the Other Deities in Ancient Israel* (San Francisco, 1990)

Smith, Stephen D., *Foreordained Failure: The Quest for a Constitutional Principle of Religious Freedom* (Oxford, 1994)

Smith, W.C., *Islam in Modern History* (Princeton, 1957)

Soe, Niels H., "The Theological Basis of Religious Liberty," *The Ecumenical Review* 11 (January, 1958): 41

Sonn, Tamara, "Secularism and National Stability in Islam," *Arab Studies Quarterly* 9 (Summer, 1987): 302.

Spero, Shubert, *Morality, Halakha and the Jewish Tradition* (New York, 1983)

Spinoza, Baruch, *Tractatus Theologico-Politicus* (Leiden, 1670)

Southern, Richard William, *Western Views of Islam and the Middle Ages* (Cambridge, MA, 1962)

Stackhouse, Max L., et al., *Apologia: Contextualization, Globalization, and Mission in Theological Education* (Grand Rapids, 1988)

———, *Creeds, Societies and Human Rights* (Grand Rapids, 1986)

———, "Ethics: Social and Christian," *Andover Newton Quarterly* 13 (January, 1973): 182

———, *Public Theology and Political Economy: Christian Stewardship in Modern Society* (Grand Rapids, 1987)

———, "Religion, Society, and the Independent Sector: Key Elements of a General Theory," in Conrad Cherry and Roland A. Sherrill, eds., *Religion, The Independent Sector and American Culture* (Atlanta, 1992), 11

———, "The Future of Human Rights: Multi-Culturalism in Vienna," *Christian Century* (June 30-July 7, 1993): 660

———, "The Sociology of Religion and the Theology of Society," *Social Compass* 37(3) (September, 1990): 315-330

———, Charles West, Stephen Healey, et al. *Globalization in Theological Education: An Evaluative Report* (Philadelphia, 1993)

"Statement on Religious Liberty," in *The New Delhi Report: The Third Assembly of the World Council of Churches, 1961* (New York, 1962), 159

Stehle, Hansjakob, *Eastern Politics of the Vatican 1917-1979* (Athens, OH, 1981)

Stillman, Norman, *The Jews of Arab Lands* (Philadelphia, 1979)

————, *The Jews of Arab Lands in Modern Times* (Philadelphia, 1991)

Stoddard, William, *Sufism* (Wellingborough, 1982)

Stokes, Anson Phelps, *Church and State in the United States* (New York, 1950), 3 vols.

Stone, Suzanne Last, "In Pursuit of the Counter-text: The Turn to the Jewish Legal Model in Contemporary American Legal Theory," *Harvard Law Review* 106 (1993): 813, 894.

Strabo, The *Geography of Strabo*, Horace L. Jones, trans. (Cambridge, MA, 1917-1919), 8 vols.

Strauss, Leo, *Natural Right and History* (Chicago, 1950)

Sullivan, Donna J., "Advancing the Freedom of Religion or Belef Through the UN Declaration on the Elimination of Religious Intolerance and Discrimination," *American Journal of International Law* 82 (1988): 487

————, "Gender Equality and Religious Freedom: Toward a Framework for Conflict Resolution," *New York University Journal of International Law and Politics* 24 (1992): 806

Swidler, Arlene, ed., *Human Rights in Religious Traditions* (New York, 1982)

Swidler, Leonard W., ed., *Biblical Affirmations of Woman* (Philadelphia, 1979)

————, "Demokratia, The Rule of the People of God, or Consensus Fidelium," in Leonard W. Swidler and Piet F. Fransen, eds., *Authority in the Church and the Schillebeeckx Case* (New York, 1982), 226

————, ed., *Küng in Conflict* (Garden City, 1981)

————, ed., *Religious Liberty and Human Rights in Nations and Religions* (Philadelphia, 1986)

———— and Piet F. Fransen, eds., *Authority in the Church and the Schillebeeckx Case* (New York, 1982)

Switzer, Les, *Power and Resistance in an African Society: The Ciskei Xhosa and the Making of South Africa* (Pietermaritzburg, 1993)

"Symposium on Religious Law," *Loyola of Los Angeles International & Comparative Law Journal* 16 (1994): 9

Tabari, Azar, "The Role of the Clergy in Modern Iranian Politics," in Nikki R. Keddie, ed., *Religion and Politics in Iran: Shi'ism from Quietism to Revolution* (New Haven, 1983), 58

Tal Doar, *Tal Amarti* (Jerusalem, 1992)

Talbi, Mohammed, "Religious Liberty: A Muslim Perspective," in Leonard W. Swidler, ed., *Religious Liberty and Human Rights in Nations and in Religions* (Philadelphia, 1986), 182

Tatiani oratio ad Graecos (Leipzig, 1888)

Taylor, Charles, *Multiculturalism and the Politics of Recognition* (Princeton, 1992)

Tcherikover, Avigdor, *Hellenistic Civilization and the Jews*, S. Appelbaum, trans. (New York, 1970)

Tertullian, *Apology: De Spectaculus*, T.R. Glover trans. (Cambridge, MA, 1931)

Theissen, Gerd, *The Social Setting of Pauline Christianity: Essays on Corinth*, J.H. Schuetz, trans. and ed. (Philadelphia, 1982)

Thomas Aquinas, *Summa theologica*, Fathers of the English Dominican Province, trans. (London, 1922)

Thomas, Owen, ed., *Henry David Thoreau: Walden and Civil Disobedience: Authoritative Texts, Background Reviews and Esssays in Criticism* (New York, 1966)

Thompson, Kenneth, ed., *The Moral Imperatives of Human Rights: A World Survey* (Washington, 1980)

Thornberry, Patrick, *International Law and the Rights of Minorities* (Oxford, 1991)

Tierney, Brian, "Aristotle and the American Indians—Again," *Cristianesimo nella storia* 12 (1991): 295

———, "Conciliarism, Corporatism, and Individualism: The Doctrine of Individual Rights in Gerson," *Cristianesimo nella storia* 9 (1988): 81

———, "Origins of Natural Rights Language: Texts and Contexts, 1150-1250," *History of Political Thought* 10 (1989): 615

———, *Origins of Papal Infallibility*, 2d ed. (Leiden, 1988)

———, *Religion, Law, and the Growth of Constitutional Thought, 1150-1650* (Cambridge, 1982)

———, *The Crisis of Church and State, 1050-1300* (New York, 1964)

———, "Villey, Ockham and the Origin of Individual Rights," in John Witte, Jr. and Frank S. Alexander, eds., *The Weightier Matters of the Law: Essays on Law and Religion* (Atlanta, 1988), 1

Tillich, Paul, *Systematic Theology* (Chicago, 1963), 3 vols.

———, *The Protestant Era*, abr. ed. (Chicago, 1957)

Tosefta Sotah (New York, 1957).

Tracy, David, "Theology, Critical Social Theory, and the Public Realm," in Don S. Browning and Francis Schüssler Fiorenza, eds., *Habermas, Modernity, and Public Theology* (New York, 1992), 19

Traer, Ronald, *Faith in Human Rights: Support in Religious Traditions for a Global Struggle* (Washington, 1991)

Tribe, Laurence, *American Constitutional Law*, 2d ed. (St. Paul, MN, 1988)

Trible, Phyllis, *Texts of Terror: Literary-Feminist Readings of Biblical Narratives* (Philadelphia, 1984)

Troeltsch, Ernst, *The Social Teachings of the Christian Churches*, Olive Wyon, trans. (New York, 1960)

Tuck, Richard, *Philosophy and Government, 1572-1651* (Cambridge, 1993)

Tucker, Robert C., ed., *The Marx-Engels Reader*, 2d ed. (New York, 1978)

Turchin, Valentine, *The Inertia of Fear and the Scientific Worldview* (New York, 1981)

Twenty-Four Human Rights Documents (Center for the Study of Human Rights, Columbia University, New York, 1992)

Twersky, Isadore, "Shulhan 'Aruk: Enduring Code of Jewish Law," *Judaism* 16 (1967): 141

———, *Studies in Jewish Law and Philosophy* (New York, 1982)

Underhill, Edward Bean, ed., *Tracts on Liberty of Conscience and Persecution (1614-1661)* (London, 1846)

UNESCO, *Human Rights: Comments and Interpretations* (New York, 1949)

United States Catholic Conference, *The Küng Dialogue: Facts and Documents* (Washington, 1980)

Vallier, Ivan, "The Roman Catholic Church: A Transnational Actor," in R.O. Keohane and J.S. Nye, eds., *Transnational Relations and World Politics* (Cambridge, MA, 1970), 129

van der Meer, F., *Augustine the Bishop* (London, 1961)

van der Veer, Peter, *Religious Nationalism: Hindus and Muslims in India* (Berkeley, 1994)

van der Vyver, Johan, "Report on The World Conference on Human Rights, Vienna, 14-25 June, 1993," *Preliminary Documents of Religious Human Rights Project* 3 (1993)

——, *The Juridical Functions of State and Church* (Durban, 1972)

—— and John Witte, Jr., eds., *Religious Human Rights in Global Perspective: Legal Perspectives* (The Hague/Boston, 1995)

van Jaarsveld, F.A., "A Historical Mirror on Blood River," in A. König and H. Keane, eds., *The Meaning of History* (Pretoria, 1980), 9

Vane, Henry, *A Healing Question Propounded* (London, 1656)

Vatican II, *The Documents of Vatican II*, Walter M. Abbot, trans. (New York, 1966)

Vedder, Henry C., *Balthasar Hubmaier* (New York, 1905)

Villa-Vicencio, Charles, *A Theology of Reconstruction: Nation-Building and Human Rights* (Cambridge, 1992)

——, *The Spirit of Hope: Conversations on Politics, Religion and Values* (Braamfontein, 1993)

Villey, Michael, *La formation de la pensée juridique moderne*, 4th ed. (Paris, 1975)

——, "Les origines de la notion de droit subjectif," *Revue historique de droit francais et etranger ser.* 4, 24 (1946): 201

Vincent, R.J., *Human Rights and International Relations* (Cambridge, MA, 1986)

Vischer, L., "Religious Freedom and the World Council of Churches," *Concilium* 18 (1966): 53

Visser 't Hooft, W.A., ed., *The First Assembly of the World Council of Churches: Held at Amsterdam, August 22-September 4, 1948* (New York, 1949)

Waldenberg, Eliezer, *Responsa Tzitz Eliezer* (Jerusalem, 1989

Wallerstein, Immanuel, *The Capitalist World Economy* (Cambridge, 1979)

Walzer, Michael, *Just and Unjust Wars: A Moral Argument with Historical Illustrations* (New York, 1977)

——, *Spheres of Justice: An Argument for Pluralism and Equality* (New York, 1983)

Weeramantry, C.G., *Islamic Jurisprudence: An International Perspective* (New York, 1988)

Wegner, Judith Romney, *Chattel or Person? The Status of Women in the Mishnah* (New York, 1988)

Weiss, Isaac, *Responsa Minchat Yitzchak* (New York, 1992)

Welch, Claude E., Jr. and Virginia A. Leary, eds., *Asian Perspectives on Human Rights* (Boulder, 1990)

Wertheimer, Jack, ed., *The Uses of Tradition: Jewish Continuity in the Modern Era* (New York, 1992)

Wilken, R.L., "Collegia, Philosophical Schools, and Theology," in S. Benko and J. O'Rourke, eds., *The Catacombs and the Colosseum* (Valley Forge, 1971), 268

William of Ockham, *Guillelmi de Ockham opera politica* Hilary Seton Offler, ed. (Manchester, 1956-74), 3 vols.

Williams, George H., *The Radical Reformation* (Philadelphia, 1962)

Williams, Raymond, "Culture is Ordinary," in N. Mackenzie, ed., *Conviction* (London, 1958)

———, *Culture and Society 1780-1950* (Harmonsworth, 1963)

Williams, Roger, *The Complete Writings of Roger Williams* (New York, 1963), 7 vols.

Wills, Gary, *Inventing America* (Garden City, 1979)

Wilson, J., *The Moral Sense* (New York, 1993)

Witte, John, Jr., "A New Concordance of Discordant Canons: Harold J. Berman on Law and Religion," *Emory Law Journal* 42 (1993): 523

———, ed., *Christianity and Democracy in Global Context* (Boulder/San Francisco, 1993)

———, "Christianity and Democracy: Past Contributions and Future Challenges," *Emory International Law Review* 6 (1992): 55

———, "The Reformation of Marriage Law in Martin Luther's Germany, Its Significance Then and Now," *Journal of Law and Religion* 4 (1986): 293

———, "The Theology and Politics of the First Amendment Religion Clauses: A Bicentennial Essay," *Emory Law Journal* 40 (1991): 489

———, "The South African Experiment in Religious Human Rights," *Journal for Juridical Science* 18(1) (July, 1993): 1

———, "Whether Piety or Charity: Classification Issues in the Exemption of Churches and Charities From Property Taxation," in Conrad Cherry and Rowland A. Sherill, eds., *Religion, The Independent Sector and American Culture* (Atlanta, 1992), 135

——— and Frank S. Alexander, eds., *The Weightier Matters of the Law: Essays on Law and Religion* (Atlanta, 1988)

Wittgenstein, Ludwig, *Philosophical Investigations*, 2d ed., G.E.M. Anscombe, trans. (New York, 1958)

Wolfe, Alan, *Whose Keeper? Social Science and Moral Obligation* (Berkeley, 1989)

Wolffsohn, Michael, *Israel, Polity, Society and Economy 1882-1986* (Atlantic Highlands, NJ, 1987)

Wood, James E., Jr., "Editorial: Religion and Religious Liberty," *Journal of Church and State* 33 (1991): 226.

———, "Religious Liberty in Ecumenical and International Perspective," *Journal of Church and State* 10 (1968): 421

——— and Derek Davis, eds., *Problems and Conflicts Between Law and Morality in a Free Society* (Waco, TX, 1994)

Woodhouse, Arthur Sutherland Piggott, ed., *Puritanism and Liberty: Being the Army Debates (1647-9) from the Clarke Manuscripts* (Chicago, 1951)

Wright, Robin, *In the Name of God* (New York, 1989)

Writings on the Donatist Controversy: Library of the Nicene and Post-Nicene Fathers, J.R. King, trans. (New York, 1887)

Wuthnow, Robert and Virginia Hodgkinson, *Faith and Philanthropy in America* (San Francisco, 1990)

Yecheil, Asher ben, *Responsa of Asher (Rosh)* (New York, 1957)
Yehuda, ben Asher, *Zikhron Yehuda* (New York, 1957)
Yosef, Ovadia, *Responsa Yachave Daat* (Jerusalem, 1989)

Biographical Sketches of Contributors

Abdullahi Ahmed An-Na'im, LL.B. (Khartoum), LL.M. (Cambridge), Ph.D. (Edinburgh), is Professor of Law and Fellow in Law and Religion at Emory University and former Executive Director of Human Rights Watch/Africa. Dr. An-Na'im is a widely acclaimed authority on human rights, Islam, and African politics, and has participated in conferences and panels around the world. He has taught human rights and comparative law in universities in Europe, North America and Africa, including in his native Sudan, and has received several prestigious fellowships and grants to support his work. Dr. An-Na'im's numerous publications include *Human Rights in Cross-Cultural Perspectives*, *Toward an Islamic Reformation: Civil Liberties, Human Rights and International Law*, and *Human Rights and Religious Values: An Uneasy Relationship?*.

Donna E. Arzt, J.D. (Harvard), LL.M. (Columbia), is Professor of Law at the Syracuse University College of Law and Project Director for the Council on Foreign Relations project on "The Shape of the Palestinian/Israeli Settlement: Demographic & Humanitarian Issues." Professor Arzt is an expert in comparative constitutional law and jurisprudence and from 1979-1989 served as Director and General Counsel for the Soviet Jewry Legal Advocacy Center. She has been active in human rights advocacy in the former Soviet Union and the Middle East, and has published a number of articles on international law and religious minorities.

Michael S. Berger, Ph.D. (Columbia), is Assistant Professor of Religious Authority and Ethics in Judaism at Emory University. He has received a number of distinguished awards and fellowships at Columbia, Princeton, and the Hebrew University, including the Memorial Foundation for Jewish Culture Award. He has published a number of articles and book chapters on the Jewish legal and moral tradition, and has a book forthcoming on *The Authority of the Babylonian Talmud*.

Michael Jay Broyde, J.D. (New York University), is Visiting Assistant Professor of Law and Fellow in Law and Religion at Emory University.

He serves on the Executive Board of the Jewish Law Association and ed-
its its journal. Professor Broyde received his Advanced Ordination at the
Rabbi Isaac Elchanan Theological Seminary of Yeshiva University, and is
a widely recognized authority in Jewish law. He has published some 50
articles in both English and Hebrew on comparative law and contemporary Halachic approaches to technology, ethics, and public policy issues
and is the author of a new volume *The Jewish Perspective on Practicing Law.*

John E. Coons, J.D. (Northwestern), is Bridges Professor of Law at
the University of California at Berkeley. Professor Coons co-chairs the
Lawyers' Committee for Equal Rights in Education, and has served as a
consultant to various organizations and associations committed to education, social justice, and the protection of children. He has received several distinguished fellowships for his work, and written some 70
professional articles and book chapters and seven books, including *Private Wealth and Public Education, Education by Choice, Scholarships for Children*, and a forthcoming title *Created Equal.*

Irwin Cotler, LL.D. (York University), is Professor of Law and Member of the Institute of Comparative Law at McGill University in Montreal
and a regular visiting professor at Harvard Law School and the Hebrew
University of Jerusalem. Professor Cotler is a distinguished authority and
advocate of international human rights and constitutional protections,
and has led a number of celebrated campaigns to free prisoners of conscience in the former Soviet bloc, including Natan Sharansky and Andrei
Sakharov. He has lectured frequently and testified in human rights cases
in North America, Latin America, Europe, Russia, and the Middle East.
His recent publications include *The Sharansky Case, International Human
Rights Law: Theory and Practice*, and *Nuremburg, Forty-Five Years Later.*

Jean Bethke Elshtain, Ph.D. (Brandeis), is the Laura Spelman Rocke-
feller Professor of Social and Political Ethics at the University of Chicago
and has been a Fellow at the Institute for Advanced Study, Princeton
University and Scholar-in-Residence at the Bellagio Conference and
Study Center, Bellagio, Italy. An eminent authority on politics, ethics,
and feminist thought, she has published *Public Man, Private Woman:
Women in Social and Political Thought, Meditations on Modern Political
Thought, Women and War, The Family in Political Thought*, and *Democracy on
Trial*, and has contributed more than 120 other essays to scholarly jour-
nals and journals of civic opinion.

William Johnson Everett, Ph.D. (Harvard), is Professor of Christian
Ethics at Andover Newton Theological School, Director of the OIKOS
Project on Work, Family, and Faith, and an editor of the *Journal of Pastoral
Care*. A specialist on covenant theology, comparative politics, and Chris-

tian ecclesiology, Professor Everett has lectured and taught throughout America, Western Europe, and India. He is the author of numerous scholarly articles and eight books, including *God's Federal Republic: Reconstructing our Governing Symbol, Gottesbund und Menschliche Oeffentlichkeit,* and *Blessed be the Bond: Christian Perspective on Marriage and the Family.*

M. Christian Green, J.D. (Emory), Ph.D. Candidate (Chicago) is a specialist in law, religion, and ethics, with a focus on issues of feminism and abortion as well as on Russian politics and international human rights. She has published several articles on these topics in American and South African law journals, and has prepared comprehensive annotated bibliographies and source collections on "Law, Religion, and Violence," "Religious Human Rights," "The Protestant Reformation and Law."

Riffat Hassan, Ph.D. (St. Mary's, Durham), is Professor of Religious Studies at the University of Louisville, Member of the International Advisory Board of *The Journal of Feminist Studies in Religion,* and served as Consultant to the International Council of Christians and Jews regarding Jewish-Christian-Muslim Trialogue. She has lectured and written on the rights of women in Islam, Islam and interreligious dialogue, and the concept of peace and justice in Islam. Her numerous books and articles include *Men's and Women's Liberation: Testimonies of Spirit, The Sword and the Sceptre,* and *An Iqbal Primer.*

Stephen E. Healey, Ph.D. Candidate (Boston College), is a Teaching Fellow at Boston College and consultant to the Pew Study of Globalization in Theological Education. He has written a number of articles and reviews on topics in theological ethics and sociology of religion and has volumes forthcoming on *Theological Foundations of Law* and *Public Theology and Postmodernism.*

J. Bryan Hehir, Th.D. (Harvard), is Professor of the Practice in Religion and Society at Harvard Divinity School, Faculty Associate of the Harvard Center for International Affairs, Pastor of St. Paul Parish, and Senior Chaplain of the Harvard-Radcliffe Catholic Student Center. He has also served as Counselor for Social Policy to the U.S. Catholic Conference, and is a former Director of the Office of International Justice and Peace and of the Bernardin Committee. Dr. Hehir has offered refined Roman Catholic reflections on questions of war, society, rights, and politics in numerous lectures and publications, including *The Church and Politics, Transnational Allegiances in a World of Nation States, The Church and the Arms Race.* He has received more than 20 honorary degrees, and won the Albert Koob Award and Letelier-Moffitt Human Rights Award.

Wolfgang Huber, Th.D. (Tübingen), is Lutheran Bishop of Berlin-Brandenburg and formerly Professor of Systematic Theology (Social Ethics) at the University of Heidelberg and Director of the Protestant Institute for Interdisciplinary Research in Heidelberg. Dr. Huber is an eminent Lutheran ethicist and Barth scholar and has served as President of the Deutschen Evangelischen Kirchentag and co-editor of the authoritative edition of Barth's collected works. He has written and lectured at length on ecclesiology, historical theology, and political and social ethics. His 250 articles and 20 books include *Konflict und Konsensus, Friedensethik, Protestantismus und Protest*, and *Auf Gottes Erde Leben*.

Luke Timothy Johnson, Ph.D. (Yale), is Robert W. Woodruff Professor of New Testament and Christian Origins at the Candler School of Theology of Emory University. Professor Johnson has served as associate editor of the *Journal of Biblical Literature* and the *Catholic Biblical Quarterly*, and has received a number of prestigious fellowships and honors for his teaching and scholarship. He is the author of more than 100 professional articles and reviews, and a dozen books, including *The Writings of the New Testament, Faith's Freedom: A Classic Spirituality for Contemporary Christians, A Commentary on the Gospel of Luke* and *A Commentary on the Acts of the Apostles*.

Deborah E. Lipstadt, Ph.D. (Brandeis), is Dorot Associate Professor of Modern Jewish History and Holocaust Studies at Emory University, Director of Research at the Skirball Institute on American Values, and Consultant on America and the Holocaust at the United States Holocaust Memorial Museum in Washington, D.C. Dr. Lipstadt is also a Member of the Board of Directors of the Association for Jewish Studies and Senior Contributing Editor of the *Jewish Spectator*. She is a widely-respected authority on Holocaust studies and American Jewish History and has received numerous grants and awards for her work. Her publications include *Beyond Belief: The American Press and the Coming of the Holocaust, 1933-1945*, and *Denying the Holocaust: The Growing Assault on Truth and Memory*.

Martin E. Marty, Ph.D. (Chicago), is the Fairfax M. Cone Distinguished Service Professor at the University of Chicago, founding President and George B. Caldwell Senior Scholar-in-Residence at the Park Ridge Center for the Study of Health, Faith, and Ethics, and Senior Editor of *Christian Century*. He is Director of "The Fundamentalism Project" for the American Academy of Arts and Sciences. Dr. Marty is a world-renowned authority in the field of American religious history and Christian ethics, and serves on numerous public policy advisory boards, including The Carter Center at Emory University and St. Olaf College. He has served as President of the American Academy of Religion, the American Catholic Historical Association, has been elected to membership in the Society of American Historians and the American Antiquarian Society, and holds forty-nine honorary degrees. He has authored more than forty books, including the prize-winning *Righteous Empire* and the multi-volume work, *Modern American Religion*.

David Novak, Ph.D. (Georgetown), is the Edgar M. Bronfman Professor of Modern Judaic Studies at the University of Virginia, Vice-President of the Institute on Religion and Public Life, and founder and Vice President of the Union for Traditional Judaism. Dr. Novak is an internationally acclaimed scholar in the field of Jewish law, ethics, and theology and has lectured throughout the world. Among his books are *Jewish Social Ethics, The Theology of Nahmanides, Jewish-Christian Dialogue*, and *The Image of the Non-Jew in Judaism*.

Max L. Stackhouse, Ph.D. (Harvard), is Stephen Colwell Professor of Christian Ethics at Princeton Theological Seminary. He is also President of the Berkshire Institute for Theology & the Arts, and serves on the editorial board of a number of journals, including the *Journal of Religious Ethics* and *Religion in Eastern Europe*. A world recognized Christian ethicist and theologian, Dr. Stackhouse has lectured extensively in the Americas, Europe, and Asia, and has published 150 professional articles and a dozen books, including *Ethics and the Urban Ethos, Creeds, Society and Human Rights, On Moral Business*, and *Public Theology and Political Economy: Christian Stewardship in Modern Society*.

Brian Tierney, Ph.D. (Pembroke College, Cambridge), is the Bryce and Edith M. Bowmar Professor in Humanistic Studies at Cornell University. Dr. Tierney is a world authority on medieval history and canon law, and serves on the editorial and advisory boards of several journals, including *Studies in Christian Thought, History of Political Thought*, and *Archivum Historiae Conciliorum*. He has published some 300 articles and a dozen books, including *Religion, Law, and the Growth of Constitutional Thought, 1150-1650, The Crisis of Church and State, 1050-1300, Medieval Poor Law, Great Issues in Western Civilization*, and *A History of the Middle Ages*. Dr. Tierney has held a number of distinguished fellowships and received honorary degrees from the University of Uppsala and Catholic University of America.

Desmond M. Tutu, D.D. (King's College, London), is the Anglican Archbishop of Cape Town, South Africa, Chancellor of the University of Western Cape, and President of the All Africa Conference of Churches. The Archbishop has been a formidable foe of apartheid in South Africa, and an eloquent advocate of human rights protection and democratic reform in South Africa and throughout the world. Today, he continues to play a critical role as a mediator and a moral voice in post-apartheid South Africa. The Archbishop has been awarded the Nobel Peace Prize, the Athena Prize, and the Albert Schweitzer Humanitarian Award, and holds honorary degrees and distinguished fellowships from King's College, Harvard, Columbia, Aberdeen, Ruhr, and Kent, among others. His publications include *Crying in the Wilderness, Hope and Suffering, The Words of Desmond Tutu,* and *The Rainbow People of God.*

Johan David van der Vyver, LL.D. (Pretoria), is I.T. Cohen Professor of International Law and Human Rights at Emory Law School, Fellow in the Human Rights Program at the Carter Center, and formerly Professor of Law at the University of Witwatersrand in Johannesburg, and Professor of Law and Dean of Pochefstroom University. Dr. van der Vyver is a widely-known authority on international human rights and comparative constitutionalism, and was one of the leading scholarly proponents for constitutional and human rights reform in his native South Africa. He is the author of more than 200 articles and eight books, including *Seven Lectures on Human Rights, Reformed Christians and Social Justice, The Juridical Function of Church and State,* and *The Republic of South Africa Constitution Act.*

Charles Villa-Vicencio, Ph.D. (Drew), is Professor of Religion and Society at the University of Cape Town, Executive Member of the South African Theological Society, and Associate Editor of *Journal of Theology for South Africa.* He is a widely recognized Christian ethicist and anti-apartheid activist, who writes from a strong historical and liberationist perspective. He has published nearly 100 professional articles, and a dozen book titles, including *Civil Disobedience and Beyond, Trapped in Apartheid, A Theology of Reconstruction: Nation-Building and Human Rights,* and *The Spirit of Hope: Conversations on Politics, Religion and Values.*

John Witte, Jr., J.D. (Harvard), is the Jonas Robitscher Professor of Law and Director of the Law and Religion Program at Emory University, and member of the Project on Religion, Culture and the Family at the University of Chicago and the Law, Religion. A specialist in legal history, church-state relations, and law and religion, he has published 50 professional articles and book chapters, edited *Christianity and Democracy in Global Context, A Christian Theory of Social Institutions* and *The Weightier Matters of the Law: Essays on Law and Religion,* and is author of three forthcoming volumes, *From Sacrament to Contract: Law, Religion, and Family in the West, The Law and the Protestants: The Lutheran Reformation,* and *The American Experiment in Religious Rights and Liberties.*

James E. Wood, Jr., Ph.D. (Southern Baptist), LL.D. (Seinan Gakuin, Japan), is Simon and Ethel Bunn University Professor of Church-State Studies and former Director of the J.M. Dawson Institute of Church-State Studies at Baylor University. Dr. Wood also serves as President of the International Academy for Freedom of Religion and Belief, and is active on the boards and advisory committees of numerous organizations, such as the Baptist World Alliance Commission on Human Rights, the Society for the Study of Religion Under Communism, Americans for Religious Liberty, and the National Council of Churches Committee on Religious Liberty. For more than three decades, he served as Executive Editor of the *Journal of Church and State* and is a member of the Board of Advisors for the *Religious Freedom Reporter*. Dr. Wood has written over 200 articles and authored and edited fifteen books on religious liberty questions, including *The First Freedom: Religion and the Bill of Rights, Ecumenical Perspectives on Church and State: Protestant, Catholic and Jewish,* and *Nationhood and the Kingdom.*

Index